DUE PROCESS OF LAW

THE CANADIAN SYSTEM OF CRIMINAL JUSTICE

by

STANLEY A. COHEN

B.A., LL.B., LL.M. (Tor.)
of the Manitoba bar
Lecturer in Criminal Law,
University of Manitoba

THE CARSWELL COMPANY LIMITED
Toronto, Canada
1977

© The Carswell Company Limited 1977

ISBN 0 459 31730 X

To my family

FOREWORD

This book provides us, for the first time, with a comprehensive analysis of certain aspects of our criminal justice system viewed in the light of what has come to be called due process. Few of us know what that is, and even fewer of us can define it and yet society's sense of fair play has permeated the entire development of the common law for at least seven hundred years.

When one talks of civil rights on the one hand and the interests of the community on the other, one perpetuates a picture of the individual in a state of constant tension with the larger community of which he is part. But the interests of the individual and the interests of the community cannot conflict in this manner. The individual has no absolute rights upon which society cannot impinge. The community has values and must make value judgments, which may vary according to time and place, and it is in the community's interest to foster and enforce those values. By very definition, the rights of the individual are merely one aspect of the interests of the community.

In any situation of dispute or potential dispute there are competing values. Efficiency is one; certainty is another. To convict the guilty and acquit the innocent are desirable objectives only if they can be achieved without sometimes convicting the innocent. To achieve the best possible system may necessitate acquitting the guilty, not because they have the right to be acquitted but because society prefers to see them acquitted rather than run the risk of convicting the innocent. Often, of course, only the accused, and maybe not even he, knows whether he is guilty or innocent. When we talk of the accused's right to be presumed innocent until proven guilty, we merely mean that it is in society's interest to ensure, as far as possible, that the value it puts upon fair play, due process or strict proof is maintained.

Much of the criminal justice system is discretionary. That is to say, there are many instances where the relevant person—policeman, prosecutor or judge—may or may not act, or may or may not act in a particular way. How he exercises this discretion will depend upon his values, and these in turn will be, or should be, a reflection of the values of the community.

Due process must, therefore, be determined in the light of the value judgments of all of us, and the courts must interpret what these value judgments are. The Bill of Rights has forced upon Canadian courts a role to which they, as common-law courts, were unaccustomed. Social, economic, ethical and moral factors must all be weighed in the scales of justice and precedent and black letter law be discounted. What offends our sense of due process today may not have done so yesterday and may not do so tomorrow.

The author examines how well our courts have performed the role assigned to them. As things legal go, this aspect of law is in its infancy, but his book will point the way to its healthy development.

ALAN W. MEWETT

v

PREFACE

In the mind of the public, "criminal law" is the law that is reserved for dealing with criminals. "Protection of the rights of the individual" when addressed in the context of a criminal proceeding is something of an engima to the lay observer. To many the phenomenon is comprehended simply as excessive tenderness towards accused persons at the expense of the value of "protection of the public". The trite response that the law that protects the accused person protects us all is an adequate retort to such contentions, although it is an oversimple one. More fundamental and complex jurisprudential concepts blanket the entire field of citizen/state interplay. A civilized reliance upon the principle of legality and a constant, expressed concern for the observance of due process of law pervades and permeates our legal institutions.

How effective these concepts have been in restraining excessive, authoritarian developments in the prosecutorial practices and mechanisms of the Canadian state is open to serious question. The drift of the reported judgments in criminal law-related matters emanating from Canadian courts for at least the last quarter century confirms a variance between the espoused standards and actual practical procedures.

This study examines many Canadian criminal procedures and evidentiary issues with an eye directed towards their congruence with the notion of due process of law. It is hoped that due to the intrinsic nature of the subject matter it will be of interest and use to both the practitioner and academic. Certainly there has been an attempt made to evaluate current practices against theoretical limitations (an exercise which has practical importance for the practitioner seeking to question the propriety of certain practices, as well as possessing intellectual properties which should be of interest to the academic or serious student of law).

This book can scarcely be said to be the result of my endeavours alone. Others have made invaluable contributions which should be recognized. At the risk of omitting recognition of some whose contribution should be recognized, and also, at the risk of appearing "unprofessional", I nevertheless owe, and here express, deeply felt gratitude to the following persons and organizations:

The Carswell Co. Ltd. — Gary Rodrigues, Robert Stonehouse and Alan Turnbull, for making this opportunity available to me.

The Canadian Institute for the Administration of Justice — and specifically Allen Linden its Executive Director for support and assistance (both monetary and spiritual) in a major portion of my research. My debt to Dr. Linden extends beyond his role with the Institute.

The University of Toronto Faculty of Law — Dean M. L. Friedland, Derek Mendes Da Costa, Richard Fox, Edward Greenspan; all of whom played a role in the development of this project. Special thanks must go to Alan Mewett and Desmond Morton whose helpful criticisms, keen insights and positive encouragement were indispensable.

Fellow practitioners, friends and advisers — Bryan Klein, Butch Nepon, Marion Cohen, Vincent Del Buono, Manly Israel, Julian Glowacki, Robert Tapper, Ivan Padjen, Richard Israels, Jeffrey Gindin and Stanley Nozick. Each has in some positive fashion contributed to my thinking on these matters whether in the heat of argument, the light of experience, or, yes, even in the glow of rational dialogue.

Also, several members of the Manitoba Judiciary were good enough to offer irreplaceable personal insights, and made room amidst busy schedules for my pedantic intrusions.

Carole Swan has remained a bright, perceptive and smiling presence throughout; even through my darkest hours when the books were piled high and the completion of my stated goal seemed an impossibility.

Of course, my largest debt is to my parents and family, who have made unfailing help, constancy of support and affection quite simply a condition of my existence.

While my debt to all of these people and others is clear, the responsibility for what is propounded in the pages which follow is obviously my own. This is not to minimize the contribution and fundamental groundwork which has been provided by serious Canadian scholars: A. E. Popple, L. J. Ryan, W. Tarnopolsky, P. K. McWilliams, and R. E. Salhany are but the most notable of these.

Stanley A. Cohen

Winnipeg, Canada
December, 1976

CONTENTS

TABLE OF CASES

In order to avoid unduly long footnotes throughout the book, only one citation has been used for each case. However, complete citations are listed in the following Table. Whenever the Crown was one of the parties, the case is listed under the name of the accused.

1

INTRODUCTION: DUE PROCESS OF LAW—WHAT DOES IT MEAN?

1. INTRODUCTION

"Crime" is that conduct which society has prohibited by law. For the control of crime, certain "criminal law processes" have been created and refined.[1] Determinations have been made as to who, how and what to criminalize.

The "criminal justice system" is the sum of these criminal law processes. Within its confines the guilty are found out, convicted and punished. The entire accusatory mechanism of the state feeds into this system. The police, prosecutors, lawyers and judges — the *dramatis personae* of this human endeavour — are the technicians who service the system.

Since the endeavour is, in essence, a "human" one, it is no accident that throughout the play of this system efficiency concepts are constantly being balanced or juxtaposed against considerations of fairness and justice. If efficiency alone were allowed to prevail state control over the lives of its citizenry would be absolute. But pure efficiency in a system such as this leads to the brutalization of the state and to the denial of popular consensus.

The presumption of innocence, and the right of an accused person to remain silent in the face of his accuser are not efficiency concepts. Neither is the requirement that proof of guilt in a criminal trial be demonstrated beyond all reasonable doubt.

A police force not answerable to the law in the discharge of its duties would undoubtedly prove efficient. Unrestrained force and brutality, pervasive and unchecked wiretapping and surveillance, trickery, fraud and deceit would all be invaluable aids to efficient police work.

The prosecution of a criminal charge would be a simple matter if the nature of the charge and the evidence supporting it were secreted from the accused until the moment of trial. If all evidence however unreliable and prejudicial were admissible against the accused at his trial, without restraint or the need for verification few prosecutions would fail.

If judicial decision-making were not referable to ascertainable standards, to enunciated rules and procedures, and if judges were not required to rationalize their decisions in a permanent and open fashion,

---

1. J. D. Morton, *The Function of the Criminal Law in 1962* (1962) at p. 45.

swift but mysterious (or arbitrary) adjudication would occur. That too, would be efficient.

The prevalence of efficiency would work its cost in human wreckage — a cost which civilized societies eschew.

Consequently processes predicated ultimately upon just and fair methods have evolved and been rationalized. These have been gathered under the protective umbrella of the Rule of Law. These processes which control and regulate the inner workings of the criminal justice system are institutional, procedural, and evidential in nature. In theory they adhere to standards of predictability of result, consistency, and impartiality. But they also embrace the sometimes contradictory demands of the need for openness, individualization, fairness and compassion.

Processes which are blind to these latter concerns could mechanically prescribe results. But, such legal processes would be of a different kind from those which we include under the phrase "due process of law".

The Plan of This Study

"Due process of law" is an expression which is familiar to lawyers and laymen alike. Nevertheless its meaning is imperfectly understood. Modern developments have added confusion rather than clarification to our understanding of the subject.

This work represents an effort to assay "due process" in a systematic manner with the hope of better understanding its meaning.

Since due process may be said to infuse and permeate the entire fabric of the criminal justice system of Canada this effort of analysis will survey many of the essential processes of the system in order to assess the role and importance of the due process factor in those processes.

Obviously, the subject matter to be canvassed will of necessity be vast. In consequence, although more would be desirable, at this juncture we will have to content ourselves with a broad and sweeping perspective. To be sure, many areas will come in for detailed analysis and consideration, but there can be no pretense possible with regard to labelling this effort as a "comprehensive undertaking".

Large areas have been left untouched. For example, the sentencing process, post-trial correctional processes, and the specific processes for dealing with juvenile offenders, and the mentally disordered, have been by-passed. Hopefully, these matters may form part of the subject matter of a larger and more detailed work.

Also, since due process cuts across the orthodox and hitherto discrete classifications of law the reader may be somewhat dismayed to find himself moving about among diverse and otherwise divergent topics in criminal procedure, evidence, and civil liberties. But all of these matters fall within the proper province of "due process of law".

In a certain sense the development of this theme shall take place along chronological lines; chronological, that is, in terms of the processes as they are confronted by an individual being transported through the criminal justice system. In this regard from the moment of suspicion and interrogation, this individual's progress — from arrest through trial — may be plotted through the chronology of this book.

Viewed another way, thematic development is attempted through an analysis of the roles and jurisdictional competence of the leading players in the system: the police, the prosecutors, and the judges. (The role of defence counsel is essayed as well, but in a different fashion since his involvement is super-imposed upon that of his client, the accused.)

But most importantly, it is the processes themselves which are being observed. If one begins with even the most elemental definition of "due process" imaginable the task of understanding what is meant by due process remains gargantuan. Ritchie J. in *Curr v. R.* offered one such definition:

> "due process of law" . . . is to be construed as meaning "according to the legal processes recognized by Parliament and the courts in Canada".[2]

This is a definition which itself invites definition. It invites us to take those "legal processes recognized by Parliament and the courts in Canada" and lay them end to end in order finally to see the cumulative picture of "due process" in this country, and thus to understand its content. This too, has been attempted in the work which follows.

But "due process" one suspects, possesses elusive qualities: qualities which are not capable of simple encapsulation or formulaic reduction. These qualities originate in metaphysical realms of "justice" and "morality", and are inextricably bound up in due process, although they do not readily show on the exterior surfaces of legal institutions and procedures.

These are the qualities which are reflected in our finest customs and traditions, and in our most revered precedents. They find expression in the preamble to the *Canadian Bill of Rights,* an instrument to which all federal legislation is said to be referable. These are some of the assertions to be found there:

> The Parliament of Canada, [affirms] that the Canadian Nation is founded upon principles that acknowledge the supremacy of God, the dignity and worth of the human person and the position of the family in a society of free men and free institutions;
>
> [It affirms] also that men and institutions remain free only when freedom is founded upon respect for moral and spiritual values and the rule of law.[3]

---

2. (1972) 18 C.R.N.S. 281 at p. 284 (Can.).
3. R.S.C. 1970, Appendix III.

Against this backdrop the *Bill* proclaims "the right of the individual to life, liberty, security of the person and enjoyment of property, and the right not to be deprived thereof except by due process of law".[4]

Thus due process of law must be contemplated not only as an ascertainable reality, but also as an ideal to strive for.

Due process must be the quality which imbues our processes, but it is also the standard against which our processes must be measured.

Poverty, alcoholism, drug abuse, racial discrimination, and mental disease lie at the root of "crime". These are basically massive social problems with which Canadian society has been unable to come to grips. The "criminal law" has been called in aid, and is said to be a major tool in our efforts to control and eradicate "crime". In reality our combined efforts are a less than adequate dressing over large and festering wounds.

The decisions as to who, how, and what to criminalize, and the creation of processes to accomplish these aims are among the most important that a society makes. As has been mentioned the sum of these decisions and processes is the "criminal justice system". It is undeniable that beneath the great brooding exterior of the criminal justice system lies much of the tragedy and suffering of Canadian society.

If we are unequal to the utopian task of ridding our society of its most grievous ills we do not ask too much by insisting upon general standards of fundamental fairness, impartiality, and integrity, of "due process of law", in order that the "good will" and "humanity" of our endeavours be clearly visible.

The examination which follows adheres to this general format:

(1) Due Process of Law: What Does it Mean?
(2) The Police: When Does the Process Begin?
(3) The Prosecutor: Selected Pre-Trial and Trial Processes
(4) The Judge: Controlling and Conducting the Trial Process
(5) Abuse of Process: Protecting the Process from Abuse

This is no idealized portrait. The pock-marks and scars of the system are clearly evident.

We do not in fact have, or exhibit, due process merely because we have proclaimed its use. Rhetoric and substance must be distinguished. If "the lady doth protest too much" the lie must be put to her outraged virtue.

2. DUE PROCESS OF LAW: WHAT DOES IT MEAN? WHERE DOES IT COME FROM?

[I]n my opinion, the phrase "due process of law" . . . is to be construed as meaning "according to the legal processes recognized by Parliament and the courts in Canada.[5]

---

4. *Ibid.,* s. 1(*a*).
5. *Curr v. R.* (1972) 18 C.R.N.S. 281 at p. 284 (Can.) *per* Ritchie J.

The *Canadian Bill of Rights*[6] by section 1(*a*) exhorts that in Canada there has existed, and shall continue to exist, the right of the individual to life, liberty, security of the person and enjoyment of property, and the right not to be deprived thereof *except by due process of law.*

Undoubtedly this is true. But what is the content of the phrase "except by due process of law"?

The definition offered by Ritchie J. in *Curr v. R.* was a minority view. (Fauteux C.J.C. agreed with Ritchie J.; Martland J. with Judson J. concurring, would "not adopt, as final any specific definition of the phrase 'due process of law', as used in s. 1(*a*) of the Canadian Bill of Rights, 1960 (Can.), c. 44".[7]) Laskin J. (as he then was) on behalf of the majority put forward a more complex and perplexing view of the subject premised, in part, upon the original English meaning of the phrase being "overlaid by American constitutional imperatives".[8] Further, the Supreme Court of Canada was constituted far differently in 1972 than it is today.[9] Accepting either the complex view adopted by Laskin J., or the "simpler approach"[10] utilized by Ritchie J. does not greatly alleviate the difficulty in ascertaining the precise meaning of the due process clause.

In sum, at present we in Canada possess an undeveloped and relatively undefined notion of "due process". The answers of 1972 were not really answers at all although those solutions do lend a certain "tracing" to the outline or shape of our present confusion.

The temptation is to accept, blindly, Ritchie J.'s proposal in *Curr.* in the hope that its surface simplicity will yield simple configurations when the actual content of due process is to be explored. This is perhaps possible if one is allowed to assume that the learned justice implied some sort of happy juxtaposition or equation of the concepts of "law" and "justice" in his definition. To do so is not to strain the words there employed beyond their ordinary or natural limits.

The preamble of the *Canadian Bill of Rights* affirms "that men and institutions remain free only when freedom is founded upon respect

---

6. R.S.C. 1970 Appendix III.
7. *Supra* footnote 2 at p. 283.
8. *Ibid.* at p. 292. Note that in connection with these remarks Laskin J. draws a distinction not mentioned in the minority opinions; namely, the distinction between "procedural" and "substantive" due process. The quotation more fully set out in context reads as follows: "The very large words of s. 1(*a*), tempered by a phrase ("except by due process of law") whose original English meaning has been overlaid by American constitutional imperatives, signal extreme caution to me when asked to apply in negation of substantive legislation validly enacted by a Parliament in which the major role is played by elected representatives of the people".
9. Fauteux C.J.C., Abbott and Hall JJ. have since retired. Laskin J. was elevated to the post of Chief Justice and Beetz, de Grandpre and Dickson JJ. have joined the Court in the interim.
10. The characterization is that of Fauteux C.J.C. in *Curr supra* footnote 2 at p. 283.

for moral and spiritual values *and* the rule of law". This sentiment accords with the common law evolution of the criminal law of evidence and procedure. Lord Devlin in *Connelly v. D.P.P.* asserted "that nearly the whole of the English criminal law of procedure and evidence has been made by the exercise of the judges of their power to see that what was fair and just was done between prosecutors and accused".[11]

Thus it is, in conceptual terms, difficult to speak of "due process of law" without at the same time invoking notions of "fundamental justice" and "fairness".

But does the rhetoric of the common law necessarily coincide with the application of law in practice? No modern commentator has been naive enough to answer this question in the affirmative. Obviously imbalances exist, and the particular texture of much of the fabric of the law in action does not measure up to the generally espoused standard. It is said that it is for this reason that we have created and continue to fund the various Canadian law reform bodies whose mandate it is to "bring law into line with prevailing concepts of justice".[12] It has also been said (at an earlier point in our history before the *Bill of Rights* had been denied the promised potency implicit in the *Drybones* decision)[13] that Parliament in passing the *Canadian Bill of Rights* had "recognized that on occasion legislation does not always restrain its action within the limits of due process", and that therefore, by its own declaration Parliament had placed a duty on the courts to restrain its legislative processes but "only in that degree in which they are unnecessary".[14]

> What are to be struck down are the gross excrescences which are foreign to age-old traditions of the reasonable measures which within a substantial span of time prove their acceptability.[15]

These "gross excrescences" falling outside the realm of due process would also by the same token offend against accepted ideas of justice and fairness.

Although a reasonably precise and lucid definition of due process is difficult to ascertain and enunciate, an understanding in general terms of the scope of the subject matter falling within its ambit (in the field of criminal law) is more readily attainable. In Canada the *Bill of Rights* exists as an authoritative declaration and enumeration of many of these matters.

Section 1(*a*) of the *Bill,* it has been mentioned, affirms an indi-

---

11. [1964] 2 All E.R. 401 at p. 438 (H.L.).
12. J. D. Morton, "Injustice: Through the Eye of a Lawyer" in M. J. Lerner and M. Ross (ed.), *The Quest for Justice: Myth, Reality, Ideal* (1972) p. 53 at p. 61.
13. *R. v. Drybones* [1970] S.C.R. 282.
14. I. C. Rand, "Except by Due Process of Law" (1961) 2 O.H.L.J. 171 at p. 190.
15. *Ibid.* at p. 190.

vidual's rights to life, liberty, security of the person and enjoyment of property and his further right not to be deprived of these things without due process of law. Section 1 further declares that all fundamental rights and freedoms have existed and shall continue to exist "without discrimination by reason of race, national origin, colour, religion or sex". Freedom of speech, of assembly and association, of religion, and of the press are also there affirmed. The right of the individual to equality before the law and the protection of the law is also recognized by section 1. These particular matters unquestionably possess content and substance in their own right, but they exist as well as corollary propositions relevant to the total conception of due process.

Section 1 of the *Canadian Bill of Rights* is "given its controlling force over federal law by its referential incorporation into s. 2".[16] Section 2 particularizes what section 1 sets out in general terms (without restricting the generality of that section) by enumerating specific rights and protections which may not be abridged, abrogated and infringed by the operation, construction or application of any law of the Federal Parliament of Canada. The section provides against: the "arbitrary detention, imprisonment, or exile of any person"; the "imposition of cruel and unusual treatment or punishment"; the deprivation of an arrested or detained person's "right to be informed promptly of the reason for his arrest or detention", or his "right to retain and instruct counsel without delay", or of that person's "remedy by way of *habeas corpus* for the determination of the validity of his detention and for his release if the detention is not lawful". Further, the section protects against authorizing a court, tribunal, commission board or other authority to compel a person to give evidence if that person is denied counsel, protection against self crimination or other constitutional safeguards. No person may be deprived of the right to a fair hearing (which, it is said must accord with "the principles of fundamental justice"). Neither may an accused person be stripped of his right to be presumed innocent until proven guilty according to law. His trial must be before an impartial tribunal and the hearing itself must be fair and public. He may not be denied reasonable bail without just cause. Whether or not the individual is a party or merely a witness if he does not understand the language in which the legal proceedings are conducted he may not be deprived of the assistance of an interpreter.

All of these matters (which exhaust the provisions of section 2) may be said to add flesh to the bones of the due process clause. But each in its turn may also be said to require greater elucidation. What are the "principles of fundamental justice"? What is "cruel and unusual" punishment? And so on. A question, or questions, for each heading. But all of these matters taken together do not set the limits of due process. Section 2 merely provides specific manifestations of

---

16. *Per* Laskin J. *supra* footnote 2 at p. 288.

possible infringements against life, liberty, security of the person and enjoyment of property. Remove these specific provisions and "due process" is not drained of all content.

It must be remembered that when we speak of "due process" in effect we are talking about the totality of "*the* process".[17]

It also should be borne in mind that the due process clause of the *Canadian Bill of Rights,* although useful as a modern guide to determining the status of that concept in present day Canada, can hardly be said to represent the *origin* of the concept in Canadian legal history.[18]

If there can truly be said to be a source for the due process clause contained in the *Canadian Bill of Rights* it seems to be correct to identify *Magna Carta* as that source, while it is probably also accurate to say that the legislative draftsmen preparing the *Bill* for introduction in the late 1950's borrowed their phraseology in part from the American constitution (which in turns owes a debt to *Magna Carta* as well).[19] Professor Albert Abel in his examination of "The Bill of Rights in the United States: What Has It Accomplished?"[20] by explaining the American reliance upon *Magna Carta* also sheds some light on the Canadian situation since our legal history (to even a greater extent than the American) has been tied to developments in England:

> The substantial portion of the [U.S.] Bill of Rights which was a "restatement of the law" rested on venerable, indeed as to some of it on very ancient English precedent. It is this which makes the grand documents of English constitutional history to American lawyers no less a part of their legal tradition than of England's. That Fifth Amendment due process of law was a direct descendant of the *lex terrae* of Magna Carta was clearly established. Other provisions, such as the "speedy . . . trial" provisions of the Sixth Amendment, and the jury trial provisions of that and the Seventh Amendment are also foreshadowed by phrases in Magna Carta. It may be that Magna Carta has been over romanticized and was at its inception a cruder piece of class legislation than later ages have supposed but in any event it was, and indeed still continues to be, for Americans a main strand in their constitutional fabric. The classic documents which issued from the constitutional struggles of the seventeenth century — the Petition of Rights, the

---

17. Restricting "due process" to matters purely procedural in nature is not a view which is here endorsed. It shall be argued *infra* that the concept applies to substantive as well as procedural law a point which Laskin J. develops in *Curr.* (These matters will be discussed more fully in connection with a more detailed analysis of *Curr v. R. infra.*)
18. Nor should the short and unhappy history of the *Bill of Rights* be thought to be indicative of an atrophication of the concept.
19. For an instructive discussion of *Magna Carta* in a related context see C. H. McIlwain, "Due Process of Law in Magna Carta" (1914) 14 Col. Law Rev. 26.
20. (1959) 37 Can.Bar.Rev. 147.

Habeas Corpus Act, the Bill of Rights — were also reflected in the American constitutional provisions. While they have not been elevated — or reduced — to the status of a charm, as the more ancient instrument has, they were familiar to and cherished by the generation which drafted the American Bill of Rights. Besides the habeas corpus guarantee itself, the provisions respecting excessive fines and bail, cruel and unusual punishment, quartering of troops, and the right to petition are among those having clear antecedents in these documents. All these were rights of identifiable provenance.[21]

Chapter 39 of Magna Carta, identified as the well spring of the due process clause, reads as follows:

> No free man shall be captured or imprisoned or disseised or outlawed or exiled or in any way destroyed, nor will we go against him or send against him *except by the lawful judgment of his peers or by the law of the land.*[22]

The Fifth, and Fourteenth Amendments to the American Constitution both contain due process provisions almost identical to that employed in s. 1(*a*) in the *Canadian Bill of Rights.*[23] In both the American constitution and in the *Canadian Bill of Rights* the due process clause does not stand in isolation.

> As in the first eight amendments (which may be compendiously referred to as the American Bill of Rights) so in the Canadian Bill of Rights, the due process clause does not stand alone, but is part of a scheme which includes among the protected "human rights and fundamental freedoms" (1) the political liberties, (2) the right to counsel, (3) the right to reasonable bail, (4) protection against self-crimination and (5) protection against cruel and unusual punishment. In addition to these common features, the American Bill of Rights is express on protection against unreasonable searches and seizures, double jeopardy, and the taking of private property for public use without just compensation.[24]

Although the due process clause of the *Bill* has received very little attention in Canadian courts in the last sixteen years, and the phrase "due process" has similarly kept a low profile for an even longer period of time in this country, it is clear "that the subjects dealt with in the 1st, 5th, and 14th amendments bear on topics which within the last

---

21. *Ibid.* at pp. 154-155.
22. Laskin J. *supra* footnote 2 at p. 289 sees chapter 39 of *Magna Carta* as backing up 1354 (Imp.), c. 3: "No man of what estate or condition that he shall be put out of land or tenement, nor taken nor imprisoned, nor disinherited, nor put to death, *without being brought in answer by due process of law*". See also W. S. Tarnopolsky *The Canadian Bill of Rights* (2nd ed. 1975) at pp. 222-223.
23. The Fifth Amendment contains the phrase: ". . . nor be deprived of life, liberty, or property, without due process of law". The Eighth Amendment states: ". . . nor shall any State deprive any person of life, liberty or property, without due process of law".
24. *Per* Laskin J. in *Curr v. The Queen supra* footnote 2 at p. 291.

20 years have become matters of concern to Canada, [and, in 1960 culminated] in the passage of the Bill of Rights".[25] Evan prior to the passage of the *Bill* into law in 1960 it could fairly be said that the Canadian legal and political tradition had evolved to the point where the country's courts were seen "as wielders of protective authority against an invasion of the liberty of the individual by government or its agencies".[26] The enactment of the *Canadian Bill of Rights* as a federal measure, has served to reinforce that vision and has fed the public expectation that over time the Supreme Court of Canada will more boldly speak out on these matters:

> It is well to recall that judges of the Supreme Court spoke strongly on aspects of individual liberty in the *Alberta Press* case, the *Switzman* case, the *Roncarelli* case, and in other cases too, without the back-up or the direction of the Canadian Bill of Rights, which became effective only in 1960. It was able to do so because the avenues for recognizing individual rights, or civil liberties had not been closed by competent legislation, nor did any relevant legislation as interpreted by the judges of the Supreme Court preclude them. Legislation may however appear to be preclusive in some areas of civil liberties, and if interpreted with that result the judicial duty of fidelity to legislation as superior law must be acknowledged whatever be the consequences, although the acknowledgement may be accompanied by an expression of regret or even of remonstrance that the legislation went so far. . . .
>
> The Canadian Bill of Rights has now provided a legislative measure and standard of protection of civil liberties but, in the generality of some of its language, it adds to the dilemmas of interpretation which are so often evident in civil liberties cases.[27]

Against this back-drop "due process", past and present, must be considered. It is a phrase which during the past seventy or eighty years has engaged, "more than any other, the attention and application of the Supreme Court of the United States as well as many state courts".[28] For Canada, whose legal history in this regard must be regarded as "undeveloped", the lessons, culled by analogy to the American experience,[29] are too close, and too apt, to be profitably ignored.

---

25. I. C. Rand *supra* footnote 14 at p. 177.
26. B. Laskin, "The Role and Function of Final Appellate Courts: The Supreme Court of Canada" (1975) 53 Can.Bar.Rev. 469 at p. 480. See also B. Laskin "The Judge and Due Process" (1972-73) 5 Man.L.J. 235.
27. *Ibid.* at pp. 480-481. In this regard see also W. F. Bowker, "Basic Rights and Freedoms: What are They?" (1959) 37 Can.Bar.Rev. 43.
28. I. C. Rand, *supra* footnote 14 at p. 174. See also W. J. Brockelbank, "The Role of Due Process in American Constitutional Law" (1954) 39 Cornell L.Q. 561. Brockelbank notes (p. 565): "Probably more cases, more articles and more books have been written concerning due process than any other single statutory phrase in American law. There are about 2,000 cases in this century, and over 2,000 articles and case notes since 1926." (Reproduced in Tarnopolsky, *supra* footnote 22 at p. 223.)
29. See Rand, *supra* footnote 14 at p. 174 where the "analogy" to American

It is however, not proposed that the American accomplishments and/or shortcomings in the field of due process be assayed or greatly pursued in the course of this work. Others have lent a tracing to this endeavour,[30] and Laskin J. puts forward a short, but competent survey of the subject in *Curr v. R.*[31] Nevertheless, American developments do bear in some degree upon a consideration of the question of whether or not the phrase "due process of law" is restricted to matters purely procedural in nature or whether due process might also provide a standard against which to monitor substantive legislation. As has been mentioned the point was developed (although not fully) by Laskin J. in the course of delivering judgment in *Curr*.

It will be recalled that the accused *Curr* was charged under s. 223(2) (now s. 235(2)) of the *Criminal Code* with refusing without reasonable excuse to supply a sample of breath on demand. Although the Provincial Judge before whom the charge was tried concluded that the Crown had proved the case beyond a reasonable doubt, he nevertheless dismissed the charge on the basis that s. 223 of the *Code* was inoperative by virtue of the provisions of the *Canadian Bill of Rights*. The matter ultimately found its way before the Supreme Court of Canada with the accused Curr occupying the status of appellant. Curr contended that ss. 223 (now s. 235) and 224A (now s. 237) offended against s. 1(*a*), (*b*) and s. 2(*d*), (*e*), (*f*) of the *Bill of Rights*. The appeal in the result was unanimously dismissed, and none of the sitting justices found a conflict to exist between the relevant *Code* provisions and any of the provisions of the *Bill of Rights*.

In regard to the application of s. 1(*a*) of the *Bill* (the due process clause) Laskin J. remarked:[32]

> Assuming that "except by due process of law" provides a means of controlling substantive federal legislation — a point that did not directly arise *Regina v. Drybones* [[1970] S.C.R. 282] — compelling reasons ought to be advanced to justify the Court in this case to employ a statutory (as contrasted with a constitutional) jurisdiction[33] to deny

---

experience is said to be an exact one in view of "its appearance in the setting of American constitutionalism, both federal and state". Rand cautions that "it would be unwise, in the interpretation of the qualification of our own declared rights and freedoms, to ignore the process of reaching a sufficient degree of definiteness if not of precision for use as a standard through which [the due process clause] has passed in that country".

30. See Rand, *supra* footnote 14 at pp. 180-188; Abel, *supra* footnote 20 at pp. 166 *et seq.;* Brockelbank, *supra* footnote 28; and for a more detailed and concentrated endeavour see V. Wood, *Due Process of Law 1932-1949; The Supreme Court's Use of a Constitutional Tool* (1951). See also Tarnopolsky, *supra* footnote 22 pp. 223-226.

31. *Supra* footnote 2, at pp. 290-293.

32. *Supra* footnote 2 at pp. 290-291.

33. The characterization by Laskin J. of the *Bill of Rights'* area of operation as a "statutory jurisdiction" yields in *Hogan v. R.* (1974) 18 C.C.C. (2d) 65

operative effect to a substantive measure duly enacted by a Parliament constitutionally competent to do so, and exercising its powers in accordance with the tenets of responsible government, which underlie the discharge of legislative authority under the B.N.A. Act, 1867. Those reasons must relate to objective and manageable standards by which a court should be guided if scope is to be found in s. 1(a) due process to silence otherwise competent federal legislation. Neither reasons nor underlying standards were offered here. For myself I am not prepared in this case to surmise what they might be.

The learned Justice does indeed decline to surmise upon the precise nature of standards which would be appropriate to the task of monitoring and, where necessary, overriding competent *substantive* federal legislation. He does outline the leading American decisions which have poured content into the due process provisions of the U.S. Constitution in *procedural* matters.[34] Also he comments on one ill-considered American venture in the realm of substantive due process — namely, economic due process. The reason for the retreat of the U.S. Supreme Court in *West Coast Hotel Co. v. Parrish*[35] was thought to be a "realization that a court enters a bog of legislative policy-making in assuming to enshrine any particular theory, as for example, untrammelled liberty of contract, which has not been plainly expressed in the Constitution."[36]

Laskin J. indicates that the "very large words of s. 1(a), tempered by a phrase 'except by due process of law' . . . signal extreme caution to me when asked to apply them in negation of substantive legislation", *but he does not say that he would not, where a proper case has been demonstrated, so negate otherwise valid substantive legislation.* In fact, the inference is quite clear that he would. Presumably, the other justices who concurred in the reasons given for his majority judgment would likewise do the same.[37]

(Can.) to a description (by Laskin J.) of the *Bill of Rights* as a "quasi-constitutional" instrument.

34. See *Curr supra* footnote 2 at pp. 291-292. Reference is made by Laskin J. to the following American decisions: *Mapp v. Ohio* (1961) 81 S. Ct. 1684; *Benton v. Maryland* (1969) 89 S. Ct. 2056; *Chicago, Burlington Ry. v. Chicago* (1897) 17 S. Ct. 581; *Gideon v. Wainright* (1963) 83 S. Ct. 792; *Betts v. Brady* (1942) 62 S. Ct. 1252; *Twining v. New Jersey* (1908) 29 S. Ct. 14; *Malloy v. Hogan* (1964) 84 S. Ct. 1489.
35. (1936) 57 S. Ct. 578.
36. *Per* Laskin J. *supra* footnote 2 at p. 292.
37. *Stare decisis* supports this assertion, but there is reason for scepticism. Abbott and Hall JJ. are no longer on the court. Pigeon J.'s concurrence with these reasons is almost inexplicable given his position on litigated issues touching on the *Bill of Rights* to date. Laskin C.J.C. dissenting in *Morgentaler v. R.* (1975) 20 C.C.C. (2d) 449 (Can.) tentatively affirms the view that he would be prepared to extend s. 1(a) due process beyond procedural matters. At p. 462 he says: "I am not, however, prepared to say, in this early period of the elaboration of the impact of the *Canadian Bill of Rights* upon federal legislation, that the prescriptions of s. 1(a) must be rigidly

The analysis offered by the majority judgment in *Curr* assumes a difficult proposition; namely, that there exists a clear and easily ascertainable distinction between matters of "substance" and matters of "procedure". The distinction exists of course, but it is not readily comprehended by many. And certainly, there is a large grey area where, even when armed with an adequate definition, it is difficult to separate that which is substantive from that which is procedural. The words of Schroeder J.A. in *Sutt v. Sutt* are of some help in drawing these distinctions and attention should therefore be paid to them:

> It is vitally important to keep in mind the essential distinction between substantive and procedural law. *Substantive law creates rights and obligations and is concerned with the ends which the administration of justice seeks to attain, whereas procedural law is the vehicle providing the means and instruments by which those ends are attained.* It regulates the conduct of Courts and litigants in respect of the litigation itself whereas substantive law determines their conduct and relations in respect of the matters litigated.[38]

The distinction between procedural and substantive law may be of some import in the search for acceptable and manageable standards to regulate the Court's monitoring function. (Laskin J. seems to indicate in *Curr* that "greater caution" is necessary with regard to overseeing the propriety of substantive legislation). However, this distinction should not be drawn in such a way as to effectively block any meaningful supervision of substantive legislation by the Court. Limiting section 1(*a*) of the *Bill of Rights* purely to matters of procedure would be to do violence to the language of that enactment.

> Procedure, obviously, may be of high importance, the progress of centuries has to some degree crystallized essential features of modes of ascertaining issues or of the processes of adjudication; and complaints are not against those modes primarily but their abuse in administration. Obviously those vital interests in procedure, due process must be taken to protect. But to confine its application to them would be to reduce radically the scope envisaged by the language used. What the prohibition against abridgement of freedom of speech certainly appears to be directed against, preserving the most meticulous procedure, is substantive law encroaching upon it; otherwise substantive encroachment could destroy that liberty. To be given any effect whatever interpretation is essential even in procedure, to be worked out by means of principle or

---

confined to procedural matters. There is often an interaction of means and ends, and it may be that there can be a proper invocation of due process of law in respect of federal legislation as improperly abridging a person's right to life, liberty, security and enjoyment of property. Such a reservation is not, however, called for in the present case". However, at p. 461 it is also pointed out: "This Court indicated in the *Curr* case how foreign to our constitutional traditions, to our constitutional law and to our conceptions of judicial review was any interference by a Court with the substantive content of legislation".

38. *Sutt v. Sutt* [1969] 1 O.R. 169 at p. 175 (emphasis added).

standard or balance or reconciliation. That this is so can be seen from the specific matters of section 2 which prescribe and limit procedure. In fact, withdrawing these matters from the general head of due process in section 1 leaves a minimal residue of procedure to which it could apply.[39]

3. THE CANADIAN BILL OF RIGHTS' DUE PROCESS SAFEGUARDS AND THE SUPREME COURT OF CANADA[40]

The previous discussion of *Curr v. R.* and of the *Canadian Bill of Rights'* due process clause would have to be regarded as academic and somewhat irrelevant if one accepts the prevailing cynicism and pessimism about the status of our *Bill of Rights.* An examination of the treatment of the *Bill* in our court of last resort can hardly be expected to engender optimism.

When answering the question "how civil libertarian[41] has the Supreme Court of Canada been in interpreting the *Canadian Bill of Rights?*" Professor Tarnopolsky replies: "With few exceptions, hardly at all".[42]

Fortunately, a study of what has actually been said and decided by the Supreme Court reveals that it is premature to relegate the Bill of Rights to the status of an "ineffectual instrument". Professor Tarnopolsky agrees.[43]

Much of the difficulty which has been encountered concerning the *Bill of Rights* seems to arise from the fact that the *Bill* as drafted was not explicit enough in commanding the courts to declare as invalid or inoperative legislative enactments which are at variance with its terms.[44] Had Parliament paid sufficient attention to critics of the *Bill* at the time of its introduction this difficulty could easily have been

---

39. I. C. Rand, *supra* footnote 14 at p. 179.
40. Decisional law on the *Bill of Rights* emanating from courts other than the Supreme Court of Canada are to be discussed from time to time throughout the body of this work. Readers are referred to Professor Tarnopolsky's excellent and comprehensive work on the subject: *The Canadian Bill of Rights* (2nd ed. 1975); and also to Prof. Tarnopolsky's most recent contribution to the literature: "The Supreme Court and the Canadian Bill of Rights" (1975) 53 Can.Bar.Rev. 649.
41. In "The Supreme Court and the Canadian Bill of Rights" *ibid.* Tarnopolsky at p. 650 defines "civil libertarian" to mean "to what extent, within the limits of precedent has the Supreme Court tended to promote human rights and protect fundamental freedoms?" This process has taken place both under the Bill of Rights and in its absence. See Tarnopolsky's discussion of "Judicial Interpretation Protective of Civil Liberties in the Absence of a Written Bill of Rights" in his article on "The Supreme Court and Civil Liberties" (1976) 14 Alta.L.R. 58 at p. 60. (The article appears to have been prepared in conjunction with the article in 53 Can.Bar.Rev. 649 *supra* footnote 40.)
42. *Ibid.* at p. 671.
43. *Ibid.* at p. 671. See also at p. 652.
44. *Ibid.* at p. 653.

avoided. One such critic was L. P. Pigeon (now Pigeon J. of the Supreme Court of Canada) who in 1959 wrote this self-fulfilling prophecy:

> The proposed Bill would not bring about any constitutional restriction of legislative power in Canada, it would merely involve an assumption by the federal Parliament of the power of defining the fundamental principles which all legislation, federal or provincial, would have to obey.
>
> Even this is not strictly accurate because the Bill itself shows that Parliament reserves to itself the power of deciding that it may derogate from those principles so that, in the federal field, they become principles of construction rather than overriding fundamental principles.[45]

Thus the first ten years of the *Bill's* life were characterized by extreme caution and restraint, and until the landmark decision in *R. v. Drybones*[46] it was felt by many that the future course of the *Bill of Rights* in Canada had been charted by Davey J.A. in *R. v. Gonzales* when he said:

> In so far as existing legislation does not offend against any of the matters specifically mentioned in clauses (*a*) to (*g*) of s. 2, but is said to otherwise infringe upon some of the human rights and fundamental freedoms declared in s. 1, in my opinion the section does not repeal such legislation either expressly or by implication. On the contrary, it expressly recognizes the continued existence of such legislation, but provides that it shall be construed and applied so as not to derogate from those rights and freedoms. *By that it seems merely to provide a canon or rule of interpretation for such legislation.* The very language of s. 2, "be so construed and applied as not to abrogate" assumes that the prior Act may be sensibly construed and applied in a way that will avoid derogating from the rights and freedoms declared in s. 1. If the prior legislation cannot be so construed and applied sensibly, then the effect of s. 2 is exhausted, and the prior legislation must prevail according to its plain meaning.[47]

In *Drybones,* the accused (an "Indian" as that term is defined by the Indian Act) was deemed to be denied equality before the law under s. 1(*b*) of the *Canadian Bill of Rights* where it was made a punishable offence for him, on account of his race, to do something which his fellow Canadians were free to do without being liable to punishment for that offence. In larger terms, the case decided that the *Canadian Bill of Rights* was more than a mere interpretation statute whose

---

45. L. Pigeon, "The Bill of Rights and the British North America Act" (1959) 37 Can.Bar.Rev. 66 at p. 70.
46. (1970) 10 C.R.N.S. 334 (Can.). For an examination of the *Bill's* history up to *Drybones* see W. Tarnopolsky, "The Canadian Bill of Rights from Diefenbaker to Drybones" (1971) 17 McGillL.J. 437. As to later developments (up to 1970) see P. Cavaluzzo "Judicial Review and the Bill of Rights: Drybones and Its Aftermath" (1971) 9 O.H.L.J. 511.
47. (1962) 132 C.C.C. 237 (B.C. C.A.) at p. 239 (emphasis added).

terms would yield to a contrary intention. By that case it was for the first time authoritatively asserted that the *Bill of Rights* had a paramount force where a federal enactment conflicted with its terms. (In the event of such a conflict it was the incompatible federal enactment which had to give way.)

Drybones appears to put to rest the preliminary debate over the meaning in effect to be given to the *Bill of Rights* as a controlling enactment. It fetters the notion of Parliamentary supremacy, but in view of the provision of the *non obstante* clause (s. 2, "unless it is expressly declared by an Act of the Parliament of Canada that it shall operate notwithstanding the Canadian Bill of Rights . . ."), the fetter is not absolute, and it can hardly be said to restrict a Parliament bent upon circumventing the provisions of the *Bill of Rights.*

The expression "appears to put to rest the preliminary debate" is about the best that one can do in view of the decision rendered in *A.G. Can. v. Lavell; Isaac et al. v. Bedard.*[48]

The *Lavell* case is difficult to distinguish from *Drybones.* Both cases involved the *Indian Act.* In *Drybones* the alleged discrimination was "on account of race" while in *Lavell* it was "on account of sex". (By s. 12(1)(b) of the *Indian Act* women who marry white men are not entitled to be registered, and consequently they lose their status and benefits under the *Act.* Indian men who marry white women do not suffer similar disqualification under the *Act.*) While s. 94 of the *Indian Act* was rendered inoperative by the decision in *Drybones,* s. 12(1)(b) was held not to contravene the *Bill of Rights* in *Lavell.*

The distinctions between the two cases urged by Ritchie J. (who wrote for the majority in both instances) are difficult, if not impossible, to comprehend. It is arguable that in all but the result the case is inconclusive and of little authority. (Pigeon J. joined in the *result* but did not concur with the *reasons* of the majority. The court was split 5:4.) That result however is, rather a serious one insofar as Indian women are concerned. Laskin J. (as he then was) described their plight as one of "statutory excommunication".[49]

Assuming then, that the *Canadian Bill of Rights* does possess a controlling effect over federal legislation, albeit a somewhat undeveloped one, it is proposed to pass on to an examination of the treatment of various alleged infringements of specific *Bill of Rights* due process safeguards. The matters to be dealt with here are matters which have come before the Supreme Court of Canada for adjudication since the decision in *Drybones.*[50]

---

48. (1973) 23 C.R.N.S. 197 (Can.). In this regard see the "case comment" on *Lavell* by S. A. Cohen in (1974) 39 Man.B.N. 197.

49. *Lavell, ibid.* at p. 225.

50. The subject matter to be discussed will be restricted to matters arising in a criminal law context.

(a) *Due Process of Law* (s. 1(*a*))

Curr v. R.[51] is the only case in which the Supreme Court of Canada has directly addressed itself to the nature of the due process clause and attempted a definition.[52] As has been mentioned no precise definition has come forward as a result of that case.

There is some question as to whether Ritchie J.'s definition ("according to the legal processes recognized by Parliament and the courts in Canada") actually precludes Laskin J.'s conception of the clause (. . . "whose original English meaning has been overlaid by American constitutional imperatives").

In *Hogan v. R.*[53] a case indirectly dealing with s. 1(*a*) of the *Bill* Ritchie J. (writing for the majority) appears to reject the possible use or influence of "American constitutional imperatives" upon Canadian development of the concept:

> These American cases, however, turn on the interpretation of a Constitution basically different from our own and particularly on the effect to be given to the "due process of law" provision of the 14th Amendment of that Constitution for which I am unable to find any counterpart in the *British North America Act, 1867* which is the source of the legislative authority of the Parliament of Canada and is characterized in the *British North America (No. 2) Act,* 1949 (U.K.), c. 81, as "the Constitution of Canada".[54]

About all that presently may meaningfully be said about s. 1(*a*) of the *Bill of Rights* is that "objective and manageable standards by which a court should be guided if scope is to be found in s. 1(*a*) due process to silence otherwise competent federal legislation"[55] have yet to be formulated in this country.

(b) *The Right to Counsel* (s. 2(*c*)(ii))[56]

Brownridge v. R.[57] marks the highwater mark for the *Bill of Rights*

---

51. (1972) 18 C.R.N.S. 281 (Can.).
52. Tarnopolsky *supra* footnote 40, (53 Can.Bar.Rev.) indicates (p. 653) two cases which arose within a year of the enactment of the *Canadian Bill of Rights* in which the Supreme Court had an opportunity to define the due process clause but declined to do so: *Louie Yuet Sun v. A.G. Can.* [1961] S.C.R. 70; *Rebrin v. Bird* [1961] S.C.R. 376. Both involved deportation orders made under the *Immigration Act* R.S.C., 1952, c. 325, now R.S.C. 1970, c. I-2 as am., and in both there was found to be no deprivation of liberty "except by due process of law". *Morgentaler v. R.* (1975) 20 C.C.C. (2d) 449 (Can.) involved s. 1(*a*) due process and the *Bill of Rights* but only one of the three judgments written (the dissent of Laskin C.J.C.) discussed the issue.
53. (1974) 18 C.C.C. (2d) 65 (Can.). The primary discussion centred around s. 2(c)(ii) and the common law rule of admissibility formulated in *R. v. Wray* [1971] S.C.R. 272.
54. *Ibid* at pp. 71-72.
55. *Curr v. R. supra* footnote 51 at p. 291 *per* Laskin J.
56. The right to counsel generally is discussed in connection with police powers of arrest and detention in the Chapter on "The Police" *infra*.
57. (1972) 7 C.C.C. (2d) 417 (Can.).

in the Supreme Court of Canada after the decision in *Drybones*. The case involves a denial of the right to counsel to the accused Brownridge. Brownridge had requested the opportunity of first consulting with his lawyer before submitting to a breathalyzer test. When he was denied access to legal advice Brownridge refused to perform the test. The Supreme Court of Canada in considering Brownridge's appeal from his conviction for refusal of the breathalyzer (*Code* s. 235(2)) held (6:3) that the conviction must be quashed and an acquittal entered because of the violation of Brownridge's basic rights under the *Canadian Bill of Rights*. The majority of the court was sub-divided into two camps as to how this result was to be achieved.

Ritchie J. (Fauteux C.J.C., Martland and Spence JJ. concurring) held that the denial of the right to counsel under s. 2(*c*)(ii) of the *Bill* constituted a reasonable excuse for a refusal to provide a breath sample. Laskin J., with Hall J. concurring, held that above and beyond the "reasonable excuse" provision of s. 235(2) of the *Code,* the infringement of a provision of the *Canadian Bill of Rights* vitiated the conviction. According to his view the words "without reasonable excuse" added a defence or a bar to successful prosecution which would not be there without those words, but did not encompass defences or bars existing without them. In consequence, the denial of counsel did not constitute a reasonable excuse since that right existed independent of those words. In other words, the right to counsel with respect to s. 235 (then s. 223) would not be vitiated by repeal of the words "without reasonable excuse".

Hogan v. R.[58] was a case which flowed naturally from *Brownridge*. It was inevitable that there would one day be an accused person who, after being denied his right to counsel, would nevertheless, upon further prompting from the authorities, agree to submit to the test.

Once again Laskin J. and Ritchie J. were of different views and this time they were unable even to agree as to the result of the case. Ritchie J. wrote for the majority and the Court divided 7:2 on the issue. (Spence J. concurred with Laskin J.)

The differences which divided Laskin J. and Ritchie J. in *Brownridge* were to prove material in *Hogan*. According to Laskin J. the denial of a right accorded under the *Bill of Rights* will, in a breathalyzer situation vitiate the conviction.[59] Ritchie J., while finding that the denial of the right to counsel provides a reasonable excuse for *refusing* the breathalyzer is unable to find a "causal connection" between being denied counsel and *submitting* to the breathalyzer.

Ritchie J. did not view the results of Hogan's test as having been

---

58. *Supra* footnote 53.
59. Laskin J. in *Hogan* does not speak in terms of "vitiating the conviction" but achieves the same result by seeking to bar the admissibility of the results of the test. See *ibid.* pp. 80-82.

obtained illegally. (Presumably this would clearly be the case if the test were coerced from Hogan by the threat of, or application of physical force.) He goes on to say that "even if this evidence had been improperly or illegally obtained, there were therefore no grounds for excluding it at common law",[60] and although Laskin J. was prepared to adopt an absolute exclusionary rule for Canada for violations of provisions of the *Canadian Bill of Rights* (along the lines pursued in the U.S. in such case as *Mapp v. Ohio*)[61] Ritchie J. was unwilling to qualify the narrow and restrictive rule of admissibility established in *R. v. Wray*.[62]

Phrasing the dispute between Ritchie J. and Laskin J. in another manner, Laskin J. favours the elevation of the *Bill* to the status of a constitutional instrument[63] while Ritchie J. would not go so far (although he re-affirms the position with respect to the *Bill* which was adopted in *Drybones*.)[64] The reluctance of the Supreme Court to ascribe a constitutional status to the *Bill of Rights* is both vexing and perplexing. As Professor Tarnopolsky points out "any country which has a written *Bill of Rights* considers it to be a part of its constitution".[65] He then goes on to make the case for the constitutionalism of the *Bill* well:

> An instrument does not have to be entrenched to be considered constitutional. Much of the British North America Act is in no way entrenched as against amendment by simple Act of the provincial legislatures or of Parliament. Thus, for example, section 63 of the British North America Act has in effect been rendered inoperative by "simple" statutes of the Legislature of Ontario, this is, the Executive Council Act, and of Quebec, that is, the Executive Power Act. . . . Are any of these "simple" statutes" of the Legislatures of Ontario or Quebec any the less constitutional than were the original provisions of the British North America Act, whose effect was changed? It appears mistaken to argue that inclusion in, or exclusion from, the British North America Act is a test of constitutionality.[66]

The decision in Hogan although not directly addressed to s. 1(*a*) due process (Laskin J. does not refer to the section or to the phrase)[67]

---

60. *Hogan v. R., supra* footnote 53 at p. 71 *per* Ritchie J.
61. (1961) 367 U.S. 643.
62. [1971] S.C.R. 272. See the discussions of illegally obtained evidence in chapters 2 and 6, *infra*. For a discussion of a rule of *qualified exclusion* see L. Taman, "The Adversary Process on Trial: Full Answer and Defence and the Right to Counsel" (1975) 13 O.H.L.J. 251 at pp. 274-277.
63. Although Laskin J. employs the term "quasi-constitutional instrument" he dearly attaches constitutional significance to the role which he envisions the *Bill of Rights* as playing.
64. See *Hogan v. R. supra* footnote 53 at p. 72.
65. Tarnopolsky *supra* footnote 40 at p. 672.
66. *Ibid* at p. 672.
67. His proposals respecting an absolute exclusionary rule however are clearly designed to furnish *meaningful* due process safeguards. The American due

must be seen as at least partially destructive of the wider view of the concept discussed *supra* in relation to the decision in *Curr*. If what Ritchie J. intends by the phrase "according to the legal processes recognized by Parliament and the courts in Canada" is that "all relevant evidence is admissible *even if obtained in deliberate and knowing violations of the accused's right to counsel*"[68] then the portents for the future of the *Bill of Rights* are sad indeed. At present the vindication of an accused whose rights have been violated in a breathalyzer situation appear to depend only upon the fortitude or resoluteness of the accused so as to give rise to a *Brownridge* situation. In other words, he who is denied counsel and refuses the breathalyzer shall be acquitted, whereas he who succumbs to pressure, intimidation or coercion and takes the test is lost.

In *Brownridge v. R.* Laskin J. observed that "the right to retain and instruct counsel without delay can only have meaning to an arrested or detained person if it is taken as raising a correlative obligation upon the police authorities to facilitate contact with counsel".[69] This "obligation" was said to involve at least allowing the accused to use the telephone for the purpose of contacting counsel if a telephone was in fact available. The case was not concerned with how many calls must be permitted since Brownridge was denied the opportunity of making even one. Laskin J. did however go so far as to opine that s. 2(c) (ii) does not entitle an accused person to insist on the personal attendance of his counsel if he can reach him by telephone.[70]

The "obligation upon the police authorities to facilitate contact with counsel" fell to be determined in subsequent cases. That process is not yet complete, but a measure of definition has been introduced into the area by subsequent litigation of the aspect of privacy in the context of retaining and instructing counsel without delay.

It is undoubtedly correct to say that the right to retain and instruct counsel carries with it the essential element of privacy.[71] But is this right to privacy in retaining and instructing counsel something which must be *requested by the accused,* or, is it sufficient for the accused merely to invoke his right to counsel[72] and thenceforward to have his

---

process provisions are raised in connection with the evolution of rules of absolute exclusion in that jurisdiction. See *Hogan supra* footnote 53 at p. 80.

68. L. Taman, *supra* footnote 62 at p. 276.

69. *Brownridge v. R. supra* footnote 57 at p. 436.

70. *Ibid*. This view seems largely to have been confirmed by subsequent litigation in various lower courts: See *R. v. Doherty* (1974) 16 C.C.C. (2d) 494 (N.S. C.A.); *R. v. Bond* (1974) 14 C.C.C. (2d) 497 (N.S. C.A.); *R. v. Stasiuk* (1974) 25 C.R.N.S. 309 (Sask.); *R. v. Anderson* (1974) 19 C.C.C. (2d) 301 (Sask. C.A.) although the latter two cases indicate that the rule is not absolute.

71. See *R. v. Penner* (1973) 22 C.R.N.S. 35 (Man. C.A.) especially at p. 469; *R. v. Balkan* (1973) 13 C.C.C. (2d) 482 (Alta. C.A.).

72. That the accused must in fact *request* counsel seems to have been decided in *Brownridge*. In speaking of the obligation on the police to "facilitate con-

contact with counsel facilitated by the authorities' providing him with a condition of privacy without further request? This issue came before the Supreme Court of Canada recently in the case of *Jumaga v. R.*[73]

The case (one of refusing the breathalyzer) originated in Manitoba. An earlier decision of the Manitoba Court of Appeal[74] had asserted the proposition that "the failure to *provide* privacy to the accused . . . while he consulted with his lawyer, *even in the absence of a request for same,* constituted an abridgment of the positive injunction against being deprived of the right to retain and instruct counsel without delay contained in s. 2(*c*)(ii) of the Bill of Rights [R.S.C. 1970, App. III]."[75] *Jumaga,* in terms of this issue[76] seemed only to involve a departure by a county court judge from the Appeal Court's previous ruling — a breach of the doctrine of *stare decisis.* In *Jumaga* the Manitoba Court of Appeal therefore re-asserted its position on privacy and the right to counsel. The case was appealed to the Supreme Court of Canada.

The reasons for judgment in *Jumaga* reveal a sharply divided court (5:4). The majority was of the view that if privacy is desired it must be requested; this notwithstanding a previous invocation of the right to counsel. Pigeon J. could not see how Jumaga could say that he was " 'deprived' of that which he did not ask for".[77] The implication of these remarks is that "privacy" is in fact *not* an essential element carried with, or inherent in, the right to retain and instruct counsel. The policy behind this majority position is revealed by the following remarks:

> It would be very detrimental to the proper administration of the breathalyzer legislation, to allow a motorist suspected of impairment to accept without objection the facilities offered to him for seeking legal advice and later to complain of the adequacy of those facilities in order to justify his refusal.[78]

With great respect, there is more involved in this issue than the "proper administration of breathalyzer legislation". Privacy and the right to counsel are involved in any circumstance where an accused person confronts the accusatory apparatus of the state. It is of greatest

---

tact with counsel" Laskin J. stated that "this means allowing him *upon his request* to use the telephone for that purpose if one is available" (*supra* footnote 57 at p. 436). This rule stands in contrast to the American position which requires the authorities to advise an arrested person of his right to counsel. No first request from the accused is necessary. See, *Escobedo v. Illinois* (1964) 378 U.S. 478; and *Miranda v. Arizona* (1966) 384 U.S. 436.
73. 34 C.R.N.S. 172 (Can.).
74. *R. v. Makismchuk* [1974] 2 W.W.R. 668 (Man. C.A.).
75. *Ibid.* at p. 669, *per* Freedman C.J.M. quoting Kopstein Prov. J. with approval (emphasis added).
76. Also involved was an issue of so-called "first refusal".
77. *Supra* footnote 73 at p. 176 of Pigeon J.'s reasons for judgment.
78. *Ibid.* at p. 176 *per* Pigeon J.

import at the interrogation stage of criminal proceedings. Furthermore, it is not all circumstances short of a condition of complete privacy which need result in the vitiation of a charge in a breathalyzer situation.[79] And, as to the fear that an accused might abuse the system by an open manipulation of it (*e.g.* where he has no desire to consult counsel or obtain advice, privately or otherwise, and is merely attempting to delay or thwart the process), the function of the trial court remains to assess the *bona fides* of the accused and to determine his true purpose. A vigilant court could certainly adequately safeguard the administration of justice against such abuse. That is the role which the court is called upon to play under the law as pronounced in *Brownridge*:

> Having regard to the provisions of the *Bill of Rights*, s. 223 is required to be construed and applied [so that a denial of the right to counsel constitutes a reasonable excuse for refusal], so that, unless it is apparent that an accused person is not asserting his right to counsel *bona fide*, but is asserting such right for the purpose of delay or for some other improper reason, the denial of that right affords a "reasonable excuse" for failing to provide a sample of his breath as required by the section.[80]

Laskin C.J.C. in *Jumaga* once again was the author of the dissenting judgment. The force of his remarks is captured in the following passage:

> I do not think that it can reasonably be made a condition that an accused be shown to have asked for [privacy] before consideration is given to providing it. Once an accused has requested that he be permitted to consult counsel, that should carry with it, to the knowledge of the police, a right to have the consultation in private, so far as circumstances permit. *The right to counsel is diluted if it can be secured only by adding request to request.* I would not put the police in an adversary position on this question; they are better placed than the ordinary person (who has been detained or arrested and is in police custody) to recognize what the right to counsel imports, and they should be alert to protect that right as an important element in the administration of justice through law, for which they are as much accountable as any others involved in the judicial process.[81]

The decision in *Jumaga* can hardly be said to end the process of defining s. 2(*c*)(ii) right to counsel. Other important issues bearing on that section of the *Bill of Rights* have yet to come before our highest Court. For example, the right of an indigent who has been

---

79. See *R. v. Irwin* [1974] 5 W.W.R. 744 (Man. C.A.) where a waiver of the right to counsel bars subsequent reliance on s. 2(c)(ii). See also *R. v. Walkington* (1974) 17 C.C.C. (2d) 553 (Sask. C.A.) where a private consultation is said to mean one out of the hearing of third parties, not out of sight.
80. *Supra* footnote 57 at p. 421 *per* Ritchie J.
81. *Supra* footnote 73 at p. 8 of Laskin J.'s dissenting judgment (emphasis added).

denied legal aid to be represented by counsel at his trial is at present uncertain.[82] The right of a witness being compelled to give evidence to have counsel appointed by the Court is also vague.[83] Privacy and the right to counsel in the context of police interrogation requires elucidation in view of the decision in *Jumaga*.[84]

Thus this area like others in the *Bill of Rights* must be seen to be evolving and in flux, rather than settled. While the rights themselves, vague as they are, are old and hard-won, the modern statement of them must be cast against the framework of the *Bill of Rights*.[85] This fact alone must give rise to some uneasiness in view of the judicial reluctance to accord constitutional status to this "simple statute". The danger here is that basic rights and fundamental freedoms are being skewered on the lance of statutory construction and interpretation.

(c) *Self-crimination, Fair Hearing and the Presumption of Innocence (s. 2(d), (e) and (f))*

Despite the provisions of s. 2(d) of the *Canadian Bill of Rights* offering protection against self-crimination it is to be doubted whether the right is presently of any real significance in this country.

> It is difficult to say that there exists in Canada today, a general right against self-incrimination in any functional sense. We do have a number of specific rules such as the voluntariness rule with respect to confessions, the non-compellability rule with respect to the accused and the rule embodied in section 5(2) of the *Canada Evidence Act*. But the courts have treated these as specific rules rather than as reflections of a more vigorous principle. Indeed, the courts seem to have bent over backwards in some situations to allow encroachments upon the rules.[86]

---

82. See *Ewing v. R.* [1974] 5 W.W.R. 232 (B.C. C.A.) where it was held (3:2) that indigent accused have no right to have counsel appointed for them at trial (in this case a summary conviction narcotics offence). The case was sought to be appealed to the Supreme Court of Canada but was later abandoned. See generally W. W. Black, "The Right to Counsel at Trial" (1975) 53 Can.Bar.Rev. 56.
83. See *R. v. Hawke* (1974) 3 O.R. 210.
84. Contrast the decision in *Jumaga* to that rendered in *R. v. Ballegeer* [1969] 3 C.C.C. 353 (Man. C.A.), a case involving the denial of counsel's access to his client at the interrogation stage.
85. A decision involving the right to counsel was handed down recently in the Supreme Court of Canada without reference to s. 2(c)(ii), despite the obvious applicability of its terms: *R. v. Barrette* (1976) 33 C.R.N.S. 377 (Can.). The Court held (6:3) that the decision by a trial judge refusing an adjournment to an accused who had been abandoned at trial by his counsel was in error and ordered a new trial. While the decision to grant an adjournment was with the trial judge it is a discretion which must be exercised judicially, especially in a case where the accused is deprived of his right to counsel (Pigeon J. for the majority, dissenting reasons by de Grandpre J.).
86. E. Ratushny, "Is there a Right Against Self-Incrimination in Canada?" (1973) 19 McGill L.J. 1 at p. 76. For earlier examinations of the subject

When Canadians speak of "pleading the fifth" they are speaking, as so often happens, of a practice which prevails in the United States but has no counterpart here. Once testifying, a witness in this country may not stand mute or refuse to answer questions on the ground that they may tend to incriminate him.[87] However, section 5(2) of the *Evidence Act* will operate so as to prevent the answers elicited being used against the accused in a subsequent criminal trial or proceeding brought as a prosecution for perjury resulting from the giving of such evidence. This statutory protection must be invoked at the time of giving testimony, and the failure to do so may result in the testimony being utilized at the subsequent trial. Such is the case notwithstanding that at the time of giving testimony the accused did not know his rights under the *Evidence Act.*[88]

This much may be said with certainty of the protection against self-crimination: ". . . it includes, first, the privilege of an ordinary witness not to have his testimony used against him at a future proceeding; and, secondly, the privilege of a person, whose guilt is being considered at a particular proceeding, not to be required to testify at that proceeding".[89] It does not extend to the extraction of incriminating substances from the body (such as blood and breath samples).[90] At present, in view of the Supreme Court of Canada's position in *Begin,* and more recently in *Curr* and in *Hogan,* it appears to be settled that once a sample has been obtained it is immaterial whether or not the accused consented to its being taken. The mere fact that a statute provides that an individual must reveal an incriminatory condition of his body is said not to infringe any rights against self-crimination. "There is no compellability of an accused to self-crimination by reason only of the statutory prescriptions for presumptive proof of facts in issue."[91]

---

generally see two articles by G. A. Martin: "Self-Incrimination in Canada" (1960-61) 3 Cr.L.Q. 431; "The Privilege Against Self-Incrimination Endangered" (1962) 5 C.B.J. 6.

87. See the *Canada Evidence Act* R.S.C. 1970, c. E-10, s. 5(1).
88. *Tass v. R.* (1946) 87 C.C.C. 97 (Can.).
89. E. Ratushny, *supra* footnote 86 at p. 72. See also *R. v. D'Aoust* (1902) 5 C.C.C. 407 (Ont. C.A.). Even the accused's privilege of remaining silent and uncompellable is not absolutely sacrosanct. In prosecutions for provincial offences the defendant is compellable by virtue of the provisions of Provincial evidence acts. (E.g. see, the *Ontario Evidence Act,* R.S.O. 1970 c. 151, s. 8(1). Similar provisions exist in the Evidence Acts of Prince Edward Island and Manitoba.) The practice regarding these Acts is such that prosecutors rarely resort to calling the accused as provided for under the Act see, Martin *supra* footnote 86 at p. 8 C.B.J., and Ratushny *supra* footnote 86 at p. 45.
90. See *A.G. Quebec v. Begin* [1955] S.C.R. 593.
91. *Reference Re Proclamation of s. 16 of the Criminal Law Amendment Act, 1968-69* [1970] 3 C.C.C. 320 at p. 340 (Can.) *per Laskin J.* These remarks must be read in conjunction with Laskin J.'s dissent in *Hogan* which indi-

No case to date indicates that s. 2(*d*) has in any way altered or modified the *Canada Evidence Act* or the pre-existing common law position on self-crimination.

The *Curr* case (only discussed thus far with reference to s. 1(*a*) of the *Bill of Rights*) dealt with the effect of a statutory pre-trial compulsion of suspected persons to submit to tests which could yield incriminating results. It was submitted that such statutory enactments infringed s. 2(*d*) of the *Canadian Bill of Rights*. No such infringement was found to exist.

Ritchie J. indicated in his minority opinion in *Curr* that he preferred to base his interpretation of the meaning of the words "protection against self-crimination" as they occur in s. 2(*d*) on the cases decided in the Supreme Court, especially the *Begin* case, and also *Reference Re s. 92(4) of the Vehicles Act 1957 (Sask.).*[92]

> I think, therefore, that the words "protection against self-crimination" as they occur in s. 2(*d*) of the Bill of Rights are to be taken as meaning protection against "self-incriminating statements" and not as embracing "incriminating conditions of the body" such as the alcoholic content of the breath or blood.[93]

Laskin J. reads section 2(*d*) as relating to the protection against self-crimination in the giving of evidence before a "court" or "tribunal".

> . . . I cannot read s. 2(*d*) as going any farther than to render inoperative any statutory or non-statutory rule of federal law that would compel a person to criminate himself before a court or like tribunal through the giving of evidence, without concurrently protecting him against its use against him.[94]

A.G. Que. v. Begin was discounted by Laskin J. as being at the base of his statement of the law *supra,* since there was no question of illegally obtained evidence being involved in *Curr.*[95]

Laskin J.'s assertion that the provisions of the *Criminal Code* requiring suspected persons to submit samples of their breath for analysis are not tantamount to a statutory compulsion to criminate oneself has come under attack by at least one observer:

> It is hardly possible to believe, however, that a contention based on the "self-crimination" clause and directed towards attacking the validity of the new s. 223 [now s. 235] . . . could be disposed of quite so blandly. Indeed, if a legal duty to provide a sample, which can be later used against one in criminal proceedings, backed by the threat of a fine of up

---

cates that where a violation of the terms of the *Bill of Rights* is also involved a rule of exclusion should operate notwithstanding that the evidence thus obtained is otherwise unobjectionable.
92. [1958] S.C.R. 608.
93. *Curr v. R. supra* footnote 51 at p. 285 *per* Ritchie J.
94. *Curr v. R. supra* footnote 51 at p. 300 *per* Laskin J.
95. *Ibid.* at p. 296.

to one thousand dollars or imprisonment for up to six months, or both, for failure or refusal to provide such sample, does not amount to compellability, it is difficult to see what could![96]

A similar problem arises where an accused person has been obliged to supply information by statutory command, and subsequently that information is adduced against him in a criminal trial. Such a situation occurs often as a result of the operation of provincial *Highway Traffic Acts* which require individuals to report to police and to supply information upon request in the event of a motor vehicle accident. The compelling legislation is provincial (and hence its terms are outside of the scope and operation of the *Bill of Rights*), however, the subsequent proceedings and charges may well be under federal domain. Can the *Bill of Rights* be effective to abridge the common law rule of admissibility on this subject? ("It has long been settled that statements made under compulsion of a statute are not by reason of that fact alone rendered inadmissible in criminal proceedings against the person making them."[97]) If so, such a use of the provisions of the *Bill* would, in effect, control the scope and operation of a provincial statute. (Presently almost the reverse is true. The provincial statute is affecting the subsequent proceedings against an accused person commenced under Federal law.) Given the prevailing disposition of the Court towards the *Bill* such a result appears unlikely indeed. But it should be borne in mind that in *Hogan v. R.* Laskin J. (although in the minority) sought to alter another common law rule of admissibility by reference to the terms of the *Bill of Rights.*

Section 2(*e*) affirms the right of an accused person to a "fair hearing in accordance with the principles of fundamental justice for the determination of his rights and obligations". For a time it was thought that this provision might not be referable to criminal proceedings; it being concerned only with hearings to establish civil rights and liabilities.[98] The Supreme Court of Canada in *Lowry v. R.*[99] and *Duke v. R.*[100] laid that notion to rest.

> The various paragraphs in s. 2 particularize aspects of those human rights and fundamental freedoms defined in s. 1. Paragraph (*a*) of s. 1 refers to the right to life, liberty and security of the person, as well as to enjoyment of property and the right not to be deprived thereof except by due process of law. The right to a fair hearing in accordance with the principles of fundamental justice for the determination of rights

---

96. P. C. Stenning, "The Breathalyzer Reference" (1970) 12 Cr.L.Q. 394 at p. 4. Also, for discussions of Self-Crimination, The Bill of Rights and the Breathalyzer see J. B. McIntosh, "Self-Incrimination and the Breathalyzer" (1972) 36 Sask.L.R. 22; D. A. Ball, "The Breathalyzer and the Canadian Bill of Rights" (1976) 40 Sask.L.R. 147.

97. *Marshall v. R.* (1960) 34 C.R. 216 at p. 221 (Can.) *per* Cartwright J.

98. Such was the view of Jessup J.A. in *Duke v. R.* [1972] 1 O.R. 61.

99. (1972) 19 C.R.N.S. 315 (Can.).

100. (1972) 7 C.C.C. (2d) 474 (Can.).

and obligations, provided for in s. 2(*e*), relates back to those rights guaranteed by s. 1. In my opinion it includes the right to a fair hearing in criminal proceedings.[101]

Lowry was a case involving two accused whose acquittals (on charges of assaulting a peace officer in the execution of his duty) were overturned on appeal by the Manitoba Court of Appeal. Sentences of six months each were imposed by the Court of Appeal. The two accused were not present in court at the time of the appeal, and the appeal court did not hear representations as to sentence by counsel on their behalf. On appeal to the Supreme Court of Canada the appellants contended that the Manitoba Court of Appeal was not entitled to impose sentence upon them *in absentia* and certainly not without their first having the opportunity to make submissions in respect of sentence.

In the light of the history of the relevant provisions of the *Criminal Code* Martland J. held that the appellants' right to a fair hearing was not infringed by the fact of their absence. "Where it is intended by the Code that the accused must be present, it specifically so provides".[102] Thus by s. 577 "an accused other than a corporation must be present in court during the whole of his trial", but s. 613(4)(*b*)(i), according to the reasoning of Martland J. does not require that the accused be present when sentence is passed by a Court of Appeal.

Section 613(4) of the *Code* is nevertheless a federal enactment which must be referable to the provisions of the *Canadian Bill of Rights,* and the substantive rights set out therein:

> When s. 613(4) of the Code is to be construed, it must be done in a manner which does not abridge or infringe those rights. In my opinion a fair hearing of a criminal trial includes the matter of sentence, and, accordingly, the power to pass sentence is a power which can only be exercised after a fair hearing on that issue. The appellants had the right to be heard on that issue before sentence was passed.[103]

In *Reference Re Proclamation of s. 16 of the Criminal Law Amendment Act, 1968-69*[104] the Supreme Court of Canada expressed the opinion that, although provisions in the breathalyzer legislation providing for the accused to be provided by the authorities with a sample of his breath had not been proclaimed in force, the remaining provisions had nevertheless been validly proclaimed in force.

In *Duke v. R.* the accused, through his counsel, requested a sample of his breath for analysis. When the authorities failed to provide such a sample to him it was argued that his right to a fair hearing had been compromised. Section 2(*f*) of the *Bill of Rights* was said also to be involved in this argument and at both the Court of Appeal and Su-

---

101. *Lowry v. R. supra* footnote 99 at p. 319 *per* Martland J.
102. *Ibid.* at p. 318.
103. *Ibid* at p. 320.
104. *Supra* footnote 91.

preme Court levels the two sections of the *Bill* are used almost inter-changeably.

The case is authority for the proposition that pre-trial occurrences may well affect the fairness of a hearing and consequently the section should not narrowly be confined to matters arising at trial. Fauteux C.J.C. does not elaborate upon this however. He states that the question of how far pre-trial occurrences may be taken to have prevented a fair hearing "must be decided as the cases arise".[105] One *obiter* comment made by the then Chief Justice does reveal however a rather rigid conception of the controlling force of the section:

> In my opinion, the failure of the Crown to provide evidence to an accused person does not deprive the accused of a fair trial unless, by law, it is required to do so.[106]

This sweeping statement is rather inconsistent with the entire judgment which seeks to limit itself at almost every turn to its particular factual situation. Most of the obligations under which the Crown labours respecting the pre-trial disclosure of information reside in the realm of discretion, not statutory prescription.[107] Where the Crown acts unfairly, or, out of some oblique motive the opportunity for a fair hearing may be greatly impaired. Undoubtedly it was for this reason that Laskin J. (as he then was) reserved his opinion on that proposition although agreeing in the *result* achieved in the case.[108]

That result re-affirmed the position adopted by the Court in the *Breathalyzer Reference* as to the validity of the legislation.

A "fair hearing in accordance with the principles of fundamental justice" was defined in this fashion:

> Without attempting to formulate any final definition of those words, I would take them to mean, generally, that the tribunal which adjudicates upon his rights must act fairly, in good faith, without bias and in a judicial temper, and must give to him the opportunity adequately to state his case.[109]

Section 2(*e*) and (*f*) were also involved in the determination in *Curr v. R.* In that case compulsory breath tests were held not to contravene those provisions of the *Bill of Rights* as the legislation did not operate so as to preclude the accused from making his full answer and defence at trial.

In some instances delay in the bringing of a prosecution may very well be said to affect the likelihood of the accused's receiving a fair

---

105. *Duke v. R. supra* footnote 100 at p. 479.
106. *Ibid.* at p. 479.
107. See the discussion on Prosecutorial Discretion and Disclosure in Chapter 4 *infra.*
108. *Duke v. R. supra* footnote 100 at p. 480. (Spence J. concurred with Laskin J.)
109. *Ibid.* at p. 479 *per* Fauteux C.J.C.

trial. (This is another example of a pre-trial occurrence affecting the fairness of a hearing as hinted at by Fauteux C.J.C.) These and other "abuse of process"[110] considerations are matters which in the future could occupy the attention of the Supreme Court of Canada with reference to s. 2(e) and (f) of the *Bill of Rights*.[111] Also, notwithstanding the *obiter* comments in *Duke* as to the Crown's failure to provide evidence not affecting s. 2(e) unless the obligation exists by law, some lower courts have utilized s. 2(e) in order to compel the production of inconsistent statements made by witnesses for use in cross-examinations at a preliminary hearing.[112]

Clearly the role of the Supreme Court in defining and clarifying the meaning of section 2(e) and (f) is only just beginning.

The presumption of innocence referred to in s. 2(f) of the *Bill of Rights,* most will agree, does no more than re-state the common law on the subject. To this extent Nemetz J.A. was correct in *R. v. Silk*[113] when he stated:

> There is no doubt in my mind, that the *Canadian Bill of Rights* in s. 2(f) gives express statutory approval to Lord Sankey's memorable words in *Woolmington v. Directors of Public Prosecutions,* [1935] A.C. 462, . . . The golden thread, as he described it, which runs through the web of English criminal law, was clearly identified by Martin, J.A. in the *Lee Fong Shee* case [[1933] 3 W.W.R. 204] and by Davey, C.J.B.C. in *Reg. v. Hartley and McCallum* (1968) 63 W.W.R. 174 . . . . In my respectful view, sec. 2(f) does nothing more than restate the common law by providing that the primordial burden of proving the guilt of an accused beyond a reasonable doubt is always on the crown.

The *Silk* case involved an allegation under the *Food and Drugs Act*.[114] By section 35 of that Act an onus is placed on an accused where "the court finds that the accused was in possession of a controlled drug". In such a circumstance it is provided that the accused "shall be given an opportunity of *establishing* that he was not in possession of the controlled drug for the purpose of trafficking".

The Silk case asserted that the statutory presumption created in s. 35 could be discharged by evidence which did nothing more than raise a reasonable doubt. It was argued by the Crown in that case that the onus might only be discharged by adducing proof on a balance of probabilities that the accused had no intention to traffic. Relying on s. 2(f) of the *Bill of Rights* Tysoe J.A. made this rejoinder:

> When interpreting a provision such as sec. 33, the fundamental right of an accused as expressed by Lord Sankey, L.C. in *Woolmington v.*

---

110. See the Chapter *infra* entitled "Abuse of Process".
111. S. 2(e) of the *Bill* in a situation involving delay was considered by the Ontario Courts in *R. v. Chapman* (1970) 2 C.C.C. (2d) 237. (Ont.).
112. See *R. v. Littlejohn* [1972] 3 W.W.R. 475 (Man.).
113. (1970) 71 W.W.R. 481 at p. 513 (B.C. C.A.).
114. R.S.C. 1970, c. F-27.

Director of Public Prosecutions, [1935] A.C. 462, 25 Cr. App. R. 72, must be kept in mind and an interpretation which destroys that fundamental right should not be adopted unless the words used permit of no other interpretation. Any doubt as to the meaning should be resolved in favour of an accused.[115]

What Lord Sankey actually said in *Woolmington* was as follows:

Throughout the web of the English Criminal Law one golden thread is always to be seen, that it is the duty of the prosecution to prove the prisoner's guilt subject to what I have already said as to the defence of insanity and *subject also to any statutory exception.*[116]

Silk did not come before the Supreme Court of Canada. But the decision in *Silk* was considered and rejected by the Supreme Court in a later case which placed the same point in issue. This was the decision in *R. v. Appleby.*[117]

At issue in *Appleby* was the question of whether the accused (on a charge of care and control of a motor vehicle while impaired) could rebut the statutory presumption created by s. 224A(1)(a) of the *Code* (now s. 237(1)(a)) by raising a reasonable doubt as to his intention on entering the vehicle. The Crown in *Appleby* contended that once it was established that Appleby occupied the seat ordinarily occupied by the driver of the vehicle it was then incumbent upon him to establish, *on a balance of probabilities,* that he did not enter or mount the vehicle for purposes of setting it in motion. Ritchie J. in upholding the Crown's contentions spoke as follows.

In my view, . . . when Lord Sankey used the words "subject also to any statutory exception" in relation to the burden of proof in criminal cases, he must be taken to have been referring to those statutory exceptions which reverse the ordinary onus of proof with respect to facts forming one or more ingredients of a criminal offence . . . It seems to me, therefore, that if the *Woolmington* case is to be accepted, the words "presumed innocent until proven guilty according to law", as they appear in s. 2(f) of the Bill of Rights, must be taken to envisage a law which recognizes the existence of statutory exceptions reversing the onus of proof with respect to one or more ingredients of an offence in cases where certain specific facts have been proved by the Crown in relation to such ingredients.[118]

By a lengthy examination of the history of the word "establishes" in relation to proof in criminal matters Ritchie J. somewhat convincingly demonstrates that the contemplated usage of the word remains proof "on a balance of probabilities".[119] With this contention Laskin J., who wrote separate reasons, agrees.

---

115. *Supra* footnote 113 at p. 489.
116. *Woolmington v. D.P.P.* [1935] A.C. 462 at p. 481 (emphasis added).
117. (1972) 16 C.R.N.S. 35 (Can.).
118. *Ibid.* at pp. 44-45.
119. *Ibid.* at p. 45. See also pp. 38-39. This analysis rests on the contention that

Ritchie J. although he finds the reverse onus provision of s. 224A (1)(a) of the *Code* inoffensive to s. 2(f) of the *Bill of Rights* even though it imposes a burden upon the accused (where certain facts are first proven) to rebut an inference (which would be conclusive if unanswered) by adducing proof on a balance of probabilities, does not elaborate on whether the burden so placed would amount to the placing of an *ultimate* burden of proof upon the accused. By the view of Laskin J. "it would be offensive to s. 2(f) for a federal criminal enactment to place upon the accused the ultimate burden of establishing his innocence with respect to any element of the offence charged".[120] Part of his elaboration of this view follows:

> In a . . . refined sense, the presumption of innocence gives an accused the initial benefit (after the Crown's evidence is in and, as well, any tendered on behalf of the accused) of any reasonable doubt: see *Coffin v. United States* (1895), 156 U.S. 432 at 452 . . . .[121]
>
> In my opinion, the test for the invocation of s. 2(f) is whether the enactment against which it is measured calls for a finding of guilt of the accused when, at the conclusion of the case, and upon the evidence, if any, adduced by Crown and by accused, who have also satisfied any intermediate burden of adducing evidence, there is a reasonable doubt of culpability.[122]

It may be a matter of some significance that Laskin J., although expressing the opinion that s. 16(4) of the *Criminal Code* dealing with the insanity defence does not infringe his conception of the role of s. 2(f) of the *Bill of Rights*, does not express an opinion as to the propriety of the possession for trafficking trial procedures found in the *Food and Drugs Act* and in the *Narcotic Control Act*.[123] The decision in *Silk* is not considered or commented upon in Laskin J.'s reasons for judgment, and that portion of Ritchie J.'s judgment disapproving of *Silk* is not there endorsed.

Presumably, then, the question raised by *R. v. Silk* may still be regarded as an open one. The argument, if tenable by the terms of the judgment rendered by Laskin J. in *Appleby*, would be framed with a

---

the word "establishes" is indistinguishable from the word "proves" which occurs in other statutory reverse onus clauses. Criticism of the approach adopted by Ritchie J. is to be found in a comment on *Appleby* by G. A. Smith, "Reverse Onus Clauses — Burden of Proof — Bill of Rights s. 2(f)" (1972) 37 Sask.L.R. 117. However, it is submitted that although certain valid points are struck this comment contains evidence of a serious misreading of the judgments of both Laskin J. and Ritchie J., as well as confusion regarding evidential and persuasive burdens of proof. For a better treatment of these matters see M. Mandel, "The Presumption of Innocence and the Canadian Bill of Rights: R. v. Appleby" (1972) 10 O.H.L.J. 450.

120. *Ibid.* at p. 46 *per* Laskin J.
121. *Ibid.* at p. 46.
122. *Ibid.* at p. 47.
123. R.S.C. 1970, Chap. N-1, s. 8.

view to regarding the possession for trafficking trial procedures referred to *supra* as creating procedurally unique, two-tiered, or bifurcated offences. The special nature of those offences is revealed by the special procedure for trying them.

According to that procedure, in effect, two trials take place for one offence. The first, concerns itself with ordinary possession of the prohibited substance. If the accused is not found to be in possession of that substance he must be acquitted. If, however, the jury upon deliberation, makes a finding of possession then the second tier, or state, is entered. The question which is then to be considered is whether or not such possession was to facilitate a purpose of trafficking.

> Procedurally, then, the accused must lead evidence in the second constituent trial before the Crown, as well as bear the evidentiary onus. This complete reversal of the traditional procedure and evidentiary onus, in combination, in these cases is quite unparalleled in the criminal law of the common law world.[124]

The question raised then is whether this special statutory provision, which is different from ordinary reverse onus provisions (at least in the procedure it imparts and employs), offends against s. 2(*f*) of the *Canadian Bill of Rights* since, in the second stage of the prosecution, a trial commences which places the ultimate burden of proof upon the accused.

There is also in the judgment of Laskin J. a hint of the fear that his brothers on the bench might one day, in confronting a statute which squarely alters the ultimate burden of proof ("beyond a reasonable doubt") which the Crown must bear in any criminal trial, find it to be without conflict with the terms of s. 2(*f*). That section speaks only of the "right to be presumed innocent until proved guilty *according to law*". It does not speak of the right to be presumed innocent *until the guilt of the accused is established beyond a reasonable doubt*. Therefore, although s. 1(*a*) due process of the *Bill* was not raised in argument before the Court it merits passing reference in the judgment of Laskin J.[125] "According to law" by implication means "according to due process of law".

In this regard it is useful to remember the words of Lord Sankey, not quoted by Ritchie J. which follow his reference of "subject to any statutory exception" in *Woolmington*:

> If, at the end of and on the whole of the case, there is a reasonable doubt, created by the evidence given by either the prosecution or the prisoner, as to whether the prisoner killed the deceased with malicious

---

124. A. Whealey, "Drugs and the Criminal Law" (1969-70) 12 Cr.L.Q. 254 at p. 267.
125. See *R. v. Appleby, supra* footnote 117 at p. 46. In this regard see M. Mandel, "The Presumption of Innocence and the Canadian Bill of Rights: R. v. Appleby" (1972) 10 O.H.L.J. 450 at p. 474 *et seq.* (*supra* footnote 119).

intention, the prosecution has not made out the case and the prisoner is entitled to an acquittal. No matter what the charge or where the trial, the principle that the prosecution must prove the guilt of the prisoner is part of the common law of England and *no attempt to whittle it down can be entertained*.[126]

(d) *Equality Before the Law* (s. 1(b))

It has been observed that it is "unfortunate" that in three important cases which the Supreme Court had occasion to consider s. 1(b), equality before the law, the *Indian Act* was involved.[127] Since s. 91(24) of the *British North America Act* is racially based, being addressed as it is to "Indians and Lands reserved for Indians", it appeared that any legislation specifically addressed to Indians or differentiating them from other Canadians could be challenged under s. 1(b) of the *Bill of Rights* "particularly if it is interpreted in the light of the non-discrimination clause in the opening paragraph of section 1".[128] As Professor Tarnopolsky goes to elaborate there are really two difficult questions that must be answered:

(1) In assessing equality or inequality before the law in a federal system, who does one compare with whom?

(2) Does the clause prohibit all cases of inequality, or must one sensibly recognize that in some instances what would appear to be unequal treatment is rationally justified and even, when applied to people who are not equal to all other Canadians, more equal than an equally-applied law?[129]

Drybones established at least the base line for interpreting the meaning of s. 1(b) equality before the laws

. . . without attempting any exhaustive definition of "equality before the law" I think that s. 1(b) means at least that no individual or group of individuals is to be treated more harshly than another under that law, and I am therefore of the opinion that an individual is denied equality before the law if it is made an offence punishable at law, on account of his race, for him to do something which his fellow Canadians are free to do without having committed any offence or having been made subject to any penalty.[130]

This definition by its very terms was said not to be exhaustive. As has been mentioned much of what *Drybones* appeared to stand for was recanted in *Lavell*. Ritchie J. in the latter case argues for a narrow standard; one considerably reduced from the bare but broad indi-

---

126. *Supra* footnote 116 at p. 482 (emphasis added).
127. W. Tarnopolsky, (1975) 53 Can.Bar.Rev. 649 at p. 664. The three cases were *R. v. Drybones supra* footnote 46; *A.G. Can. v. Lavell supra* footnote 48; and *A.G. Can. v. Canard* [1975] 3 W.W.R. 1 (Can.).
128. *Ibid.* at p. 665.
129. *Ibid.* at p. 665.
130. *R. v. Drybones* (1970) 10 C.R.N.S. 334 pp. 346-347 (Can.) *per* Ritchie J.

cation of the scope of the right which he sketched in *Drybones*.[131]
Fortunately, in view of the sharp division of the Court, and in Pigeon
J.'s "go it alone" attitude, the case must be regarded as inconclusive
and of little authority.

The power of Attorney-General of Canada to elect whether a person charged with a breach of s. 132 of the *Income Tax Act*[132] should
be tried summarily or upon indictment was challenged as being offensive to s. 1(*b*) of the *Bill of Rights* in *R. v. Smythe*.[133] That case shall
be dealt with in some detail *infra*.[134] Fauteux C.J.C. wrote the unanimous judgment of the court, but failed to offer any substantial insight
into the operation of the section. Since the legislation did not discriminate on its face but merely provided for alternative modes of
procedure to be adopted in the discretion of the Attorney-General
there was said to be no denial of equality before the law.

Curr v. R. also involved s. 1(*b*) of the *Bill*. In that case there was
found to be no merit in the appellant's submission that the new breathalyzer legislation deprived the accused of the equal protection of the
law since this submission amounted, in effect, to a contention that the
pre-existing state of the law which was more favourable to the accused,
could not be changed to his disadvantage without offending the provision.

The decision in *A.G. Can. v. Canard*[135] did not concern a penal
statute or the federal criminal law power. The case involved the right
of an Indian woman to administer the estate of her deceased husband.
The *Indian Act* by section 43 allows for the Minister of Indian Affairs
and Northern Development to appoint an administrator to administer
the property of Indians who die intestate. Mrs. Canard's claim to
administer her husband's estate and her so doing concluded that s. 43
of the Indian Act was inoperative because of incompatibility with
s. 1(*b*) of the *Canadian Bill of Rights*. The Supreme Court of Canada
(5:2) overturned the Appeal Court decision and through no less than
three majority opinions asserted that the provisions of the *Canadian
Bill of Rights* did not render s. 43 of the *Indian Act* inoperative.

Undoubtedly of concern to the court was a scruple that a construction of a provision of a "simple statute" (in this case s. 1(*b*) of the
Bill of Rights) might in effect operate so as to ultimately obliterate
an entire head of conferred jurisdiction under the *British North
America Act* (s. 91(24) *Indians and Indian Lands*). This had been

131. "s. 1(*b*) of the Bill of Rights is to be treated as meaning equality in the
administration or application of the law by the law enforcement authorities
and the ordinary courts of the land". (*A. G. Can. v. Lavell, supra* footnote
48 at p. 212 *per* Ritchie J.). See also Tarnopolsky *supra* footnote 40,
(Can.Bar.Rev.) at pp. 666-667.
132. R.S.C. 1970, c. I-5.
133. (1971) 3 C.C.C. (2d) 366 (Can.).
134. See chapter 3, *infra*.
135. *A.G. Can. v. Canard* [1975] 3 W.W.R. 1 (Can.).

Pigeon J.'s major anxiety throughout, beginning with his dissent in *Drybones,* continuing through *Lavell,* and down to *Canard.* It was a concern which earmarked the retreat of Ritchie J. in *Lavell,* and caused him to state in *Canard*:

> If the provisions of the Indian Act and the Regulations made there-under are to be declared inoperative as offending against the guarantee provided by s. 1(*b*) of the Bill of Rights wherever they have the effect of treating Indians differently from other Canadians, then it seems to me to follow that eventually all such differences will be eradicated and Indians will in all respects be treated in the same way as their fellow citizens under the law. I cannot believe that the special Indian status so clearly recognized in the B.N.A. Act is to be whittled away without express legislation being passed by the Parliament of Canada to that effect.[136]

This aspect is what renders the evolution of s. 1(*b*) "unfortunate" by Professor Tarnopolsky's view. "Equality before the law", complex enough by its own terms, has had its complexity compounded by the fact that the *B.N.A. Act* provides a classification of jurisdictional competence which is racially based.

As the dissenting reasons of Laskin C.J.C. in *Lavell* and *Canard* indicate, the problem of Indian legislation need not be approached in this manner. (In *Canard* Laskin C.J.C. would not have rendered the impugned sections inoperative but would merely have required them to be applied consistently with the *Bill of Rights.*) The *Bill of Rights* need not be accorded any higher constitutional status than that which was explicit in *Drybones* and s. 91(24) of the *B.N.A. Act* need not be regarded as destroyed by s. 1(*b*) of the *Bill of Rights* if the only function of the *Bill* is to monitor the construction and application of legislation validly enacted under that head of jurisdiction to insure its compliance with fundamental values.

The *Canard* case is of interest for yet another reason. It raises the question of to what extent is provincial legislation applicable to the operation of the *Canadian Bill of Rights.* Laskin C.J.C. saw the point as obstructing "an irrelevant factor into the matter at issue".

> . . . I see no reason to refer to provincial legislation to test the opera-bility of federal legislation under the Canadian Bill of Rights. The question whether any of the prescriptions of the Canadian Bill of Rights are offended by federal legislation depends on what that legislation pro-vides and on the reach of the Canadian Bill of Rights itself.[137]

This view is not far different from that expressed by Ritchie J. on the same point:

> It appears to me that in the present context there can only be a conflict between the Bill of Rights and the Indian Act if the Indian Act, standing

---

136. *Ibid.* at p. 16.
137. *Ibid.* at p. 6.

alone or read in conjunction with other federal legislation, can be said to result in a denial to Indians of the equality before the law guaranteed by s. 1(b) of the Bill.[138]

Undoubtedly more will be said on this issue in a future case.

R. v. Burnshine,[139] a case decided prior to Canard, also considered s. 1(b) equality before the law, this time in relation to the imposition of indeterminate sentences on young offenders as provided for by s. 150 of the *Prisons and Reformatories Act*.[140]

Section 150 allowed the courts in British Columbia to sentence anyone who is under 22 years of age and is convicted of an offence under Canadian law which carries a punishment of 3 months or more, to a term of not less than three months and to an indeterminate period of incarceration thereafter not to exceed two years less one day. The accused, aged seventeen years, was acquitted at his trial of first instance. On appeal by trial *de novo* (the offence was summary conviction) the Crown appeal was allowed, and upon being thus convicted Burnshine was sentenced to three months definite and two years less one day indeterminate. On appeal to the British Columbia Court of Appeal the Court by a majority (Branch and Nemetz JJ.A.; MacLean J.A. dissenting) held that s. 150 offended against s. 1(b) of the *Canadian Bill of Rights,* and was consequently inoperative. (The sentence imposed was subsequently varied by striking out the indeterminate portion.) The decision of the British Columbia Court of Appeal was reversed on appeal by the Supreme Court of Canada.

Martland J. in delivering the majority opinion sought to expand upon Laskin J.'s remarks in *Curr* to the effect that "compelling reasons ought to be advanced to justify the Court . . . to employ a statutory (as contrasted with a constitutional) jurisdiction to deny operative effect to substantive measure duly enacted by a Parliament constitutionally competent to do so . . .". By "compelling reasons" Martland J. understands that the Court must be satisfied that the disputed legislation was passed by a Parliament "not seeking to achieve a valid federal objective."[141]

Exactly how legislation passed by a Parliament "constitutionally competent to do so"[142] can be said not to be in aid of a "valid federal objective" is a rather large mystery; one upon which Martland J. chooses not to elaborate. If legislation which offends against equality before the law or against any of the other fundamental rights and freedoms contained in the *Bill of Rights* is legislation which does not seek to achieve a valid federal objective then the proposition asserted

---

138. *Ibid.* at p. 16.
139. (1974) 25 C.R.N.S. 270 (Can.).
140. R.S.C. 1970, Chap. P-21, s. 150.
141. *R. v. Burnshine supra* footnote 139 at p. 281.
142. It is assumed that this phrase entails the exercise by Parliament of legislative powers which are *intra vires*.

is little more than a tautology, obfuscating a truth which is already clearly evident by the very terms of the *Bill of Rights*. In fairness to Martland J., this does not appear to be the only meaning which he intends.

By the phrase "valid federal objective" the learned Justice appears to invite the judicial examination of "legislative purpose". In his examination of the legislative purpose of s. 150 of the *Prisons and Reformatories Act* Martland J. finds no incompatibility with the "equality before the law" provisions of the *Bill*:

> The legislative purpose of s. 150 was not to impose harsher punishment upon offenders in British Columbia in a particular age group than upon others. The purpose of the indeterminate sentence was to seek to reform and benefit persons within that younger age group. It was made applicable in British Columbia because that province was equipped with the necessary institutions and staff for that purpose.[143]

Laskin C.J.C. who penned the dissent in *Burnshine* does not disagree with this formulation of the legislative purpose of s. 150. He would not render s. 150 inoperative. However Burnshine was convicted of a summary conviction offence. The maximum sentence ordinarily possible in such a circumstance is six months.[144] Laskin C.J.C. therefore would seek to circumscribe to operation of s. 150 to conform with the maxima provided under the *Code* in those instances where the sentencing range permissible is less than two years:

> It seems to me to be very much more consonant with the suggested purpose [of s. 150], considered in the light of the Canadian Bill of Rights, that the combined fixed and indeterminate sentences be limited in their totality by the maximum term of imprisonment prescribed by the Criminal Code or other federal enactment creating an offence and prescribing its punishment. In this way, there is an umbrella of equality of permitted length of punishment and within that limit a scope for relaxing its stringency to accommodate a rehabilitative and correctional purpose. On this view, which commends itself to me, the age factor under s. 150 does not amount to a punitive element in that provision but rather redounds to the advantage of an accused who is within the age group.[145]

The opinion of the Chief Justice is appealing in that it embraces both of the claims of inequality which arose in *Burnshine* at one time. Section 150 does not contravene s. 1(*b*) equality as it results in a group of individuals being treated beneficially rather than (as it was contended) being treated more harshly than others under the law. By insisting that the construction and application of the section conform to the provisions of the *Bill* the claim of discrimination (yielding in

143. *R. v. Burnshine supra* footnote 139 at p. 280.
144. The maximum length of incarceration Burnshine was liable to by s. 150 was two years less one day.
145. *R. v. Burnshine supra* footnote 139 at pp. 288-289.

equality) based on age and locality likewise disappears. Martland J. deals with this latter issue by claiming firstly, that s. 1(*b*) does not evoke egalitarian concepts such as those "exemplified by the 14th Amendment of the U.S. Constitution as interpreted by the Courts of that country",[146] and secondly, that the concept of 'equality before the law' "did not and could not include the right of each individual to insist that no statute could be enacted which did not have application to everyone and in all areas of Canada."[147]

Some Concluding Words on the Canadian Bill of Rights

It would be wrong to contend that the path of the *Bill of Rights* has become fixed and its future course charted. Sixteen years is a very short time span in terms of the life of a statute, especially one as important and fundamental as the *Bill of Rights*. Caution, indeed even excessive caution, and restraint, is not unexpected given the constitutional realities involved in the resort to the use of such a statute. Even the United States courts were slow to rise to the challenge provided by their constitutionally encrusted *Bill of Rights*.

> We should not forget that the Bill of Rights is not yet fifteen years old. After all, in the United States it was not until some ten years after the passing of the Amendments which created the United States Bill of Rights that judicial review was asserted by Chief Justice Marshall in the case of *Marbury v. Madison,* and it was probably not until some one hundred years later, and some would say almost a century and a half later, that the American Supreme Court started to apply the Bill of Rights in accordance with what would appear to be the intentions of the framers.[148]

It should be remembered as well that the judicial reluctance to give wide-ranging effect to the *Canadian Bill of Rights* on the one hand may be regarded as judicial "timidity", but on the other, peculiarly enough, it may be seen as a demonstration of unimpeachable integrity. Judges have denied to no other but *themselves* the awesome power of a greatly expanded version of judicial review than that they presently possess. Perhaps, in the absence of the *very clearest* legislative statement of such a grant of power, the march toward such an end ought indeed to be marked by caution and restraint. It is to be hoped, however, that the out-pouring of commentary by legal scholars, the lower court judgments evident at virtually every other judicial level, and the clear indications contained in the Parliamentary debates preceding the passage of the *Bill* into law, have all received due notice from the nine wise men in Ottawa, and that the day draws near when the cloak of judicial reticence will finally be shed.

On the horizon loom important issues concerning the *Bill of Rights*.

---

146. *Ibid.* at p. 278.
147. *Ibid.* at p. 279.
148. W. S. Tarnopolsky, (1976) Alta.L.R. 58 at p. 81.

Cruel and unusual punishment (s. 2(b) in the context of the death penalty, and mandatory terms of imprisonment is presently before the Court).[149] The whole process of prisoner's rights is beginning to find its way before the Supreme Court of Canada for consideration in the context of the provisions of the *Bill of Rights*.[150] It is possible that the doctrine of abuse of process, as yet treated as separate and independent from s. 1(a) due process, may be allied to that concept in some future case coming before the Supreme Court.[151]

Clearly Abbott J. was correct in his surmise in *Lavell*:

> Of one thing I am certain, the Bill will continue to supply ample grist to the judicial mills for some time to come.[152]

---

149. See *Miller v. R.* 24 C.C.C. (2d) 401, affirmed [1976] 5 W.W.R. 711 (Can.); *R. v. Shand* (1976) 33 C.R.N.S. 82, reversed 35 C.R.N.S. 202 (Ont. C.A.).
150. See, *Mitchell v. R.* (1976) 24 C.C.C. (2d) 241 (Can.), and see *Howarth v. Nat. Parole Bd.* (1975) 18 C.C.C. (2d) 385 (Can.).
151. See the Chapter on "Abuse of Process" *infra*.
152. *A.G. Can. v. Lavell* (1973) 23 C.R.N.S. 197 at p. 229 (Can.).

2

WHEN DOES THE PROCESS BEGIN?: THE POLICE

1. THE CONSTABLE: HIS STATUS AND DUTIES

It has been said that the Police are necessarily in close relation to the state; that they stand, in fact, between the Crown and the people, maintaining law and order.[1] It was this aspect of "necessary closeness" which was primarily responsible for hampering the creation and development of statutory police forces throughout the common law world. The last 100 years have been witness to such development, but it occurred only in the face of the fears and trepidations of many who were reluctant to improve the effectiveness of the police for fear of creating an instrument capable of serving the ends of tyranny.[2]

The results of the creation of modern police forces have demonstrated to the satisfaction of many "that the apprehension quite generally felt that the new force(s) might be used for political purposes was unjustified".[3] Others have not felt quite so sanguine:

> Since their establishment, there has been sedulously built up around the police an image of general perfection. Politicians, government committees and commissions, the magistracy and the judiciary, most of the press, television and radio, and many educational establishments, constantly foster the belief that police serve the common good and that any bad behaviour on their part is exceptional, not a reflection of either the nature of policemen or the role they perform. In fact however, the entire history of the police shows that first and foremost, they were designed to protect property, and therefore the wealth and privilege of the minority who in Britain control the major part of industry, trade, finance and land. This minority is to be protected not only from robbers and other criminal individuals but from popular movements that might threaten their position and power. Thus when there is a strike the police act on behalf of the employers; when there is opposition to war preparations, they act on behalf of those who gain from preparing for war. When the police spy, they spy on those whose views and activities are considered subversive of the Establishment.[4]

---

1. See H. Coatsworth "Police Efficiency" (1929) 7 Can.BarRev. 169 at p. 171.
2. See Great Britain, *Royal Commission on the Police* (Final Report) (1962) at p. 13.
3. R. A. Smith "Police Control" (1928) 6 Can.BarRev. 521 at p. 522.
4. S. Bowes, *Civil Liberties and the Police* (1966) at pp. 18-19.

From the above passages it is clear that unanimity is lacking if one attempts to speak of the creation of the modern police force as a triumph in social engineering. But, if one examines the past it is equally clear that present developments can be described as "progressive". Great Britain indisputably has been the leader in the development of modern police organization.

In its final report in 1962 the English *Royal Commission on the Police* observed that the "creation in the last century of statutory police forces throughout Great Britain marked a major break with the past. For hundreds of years constables had been unorganized, generally inefficient, not infrequently corrupt. Until the middle of the eighteenth century these rudimentary arrangements made for the protection of the public were no doubt generally adequate for the needs of a predominantly rural community but they were quite unable to cope with the consequences of the industrial revolution, the rapid expansion of the population and the growth of towns".[5]

It is generally acknowledged that the Police Reforms of Sir Robert Peel (particularly the establishment of London's Metropolitan Police Force in 1829) signalled the era of modern police organization and modern policing. One office, ancient in origin, survived the transition and remained central to the workings of the modern force—the office of the constable.

The powers of the constable, like the office itself, are ancient in origin and are rooted in the common law. These powers were examined in England (in 1929) by a Royal Commission which commented as follows:

> The police of this country have never been recognized either in law or by tradition, as a force distinct from the general body of citizens. Despite the imposition of many extraneous duties on the police by legislation or administrative action, the principle remains that a policeman, in the view of the common law, is only "a person paid to perform, as a matter of duty, acts which if he were so minded he might have done voluntarily".
>
> Indeed a policeman possesses few powers not enjoyed by the ordinary citizen, and public opinion, expressed in Parliament and elsewhere, have shown great jealously of any attempts to give increased authority to the police. This attitude is due, we believe, not to any distrust of the police as a body, but to an instictive feeling that, as a matter of principle, they should have as few powers as possible which are not possessed by the ordinary citizen, and that their authority should rest on the broad basis of the consent and active co-operation of all law-abiding people. At the same time it must be realized that there are certain duties of a special nature which if they are to be entrusted to the police and adequately performed by them, require the grant of special powers.

---

5. *Supra* footnote 2 at p. 13.

It follows that the police, in exercising their functions are, to a peculiar degree, dependent upon the goodwill of the general public and that the utmost discretion must be exercised by them to avoid over-stepping the limited powers which they possess. A proper and mutual understanding between the police and public is essential for the maintenance of law and order.[6]

Thus, in England (and presumably also in Canada), the principle appears to exist that police powers are for the most part grounded in the common law and differ little from those of ordinary citizens. Also, it has been asserted that the police can be fully effective only if they enjoy the support of public opinion.

Logically, public opinion would only support police activity if it is seen to be fair and impartial. Once the constable is seen only to be doing the bidding of a given master his credibility (and consequently his ability to perform his appointed duties) will be destroyed. The police, at least in theory, must be seen to serve society as a whole, not merely one particular section of it—this, no matter how powerful or influential that particular section might be. In consequence from earliest times the "necessity" has existed for the constable to present himself as an independent entity free from influence or favor. This "necessity" is reflected in the constitutional derivation and implications of the constable's authority.

The powers of the constable are described as "original, not delegated",[7] and since they are original he enjoys a degree of independence in the exercise of these powers. Further conveying the sense of the constable's independence is the fact that upon appointment he swears an oath of allegiance to the Crown,[8] a fact which has been said to possess "far-reaching implications of constitutional significance",[9] Also, there is other evidence of the independent character of the constable's office.

The evidence placed before us includes a wealth of judicial pronouncements, the effect of which has been to deny any relationship of master and servant as between the police authority and the constable or as between the Crown and the constable, and in thus denying that

---

6. Great Britain, *Royal Commission on Police Powers and Procedures* (1929).
7. See "The Legal Status of a Policeman", (1955) 19 J. Crim. Law 264.
8. See H. Silving "The Oath". Note also the form of the oath. In Ontario, the *Police Act* R.S.O. 1970, chap. 351 s. 64 sets out the oath: "I, ————, do swear that I will well and truly serve Her Majesty the Queen in the office of constable for the ———— of ———— without favour or affection, malice or ill-will; and that, to the best of my power, I will cause the peace to be preserved, and prevent all offences against the persons or properties of Her Majesty's subjects and that, while I continue to hold the said office, I will, to the best of my skill and knowledge, discharge all the duties thereof faithfully according to the law. So help me God."
9. *Royal Commission on the Police* (1962) *supra* footnote 2 at p. 11.

he is a servant of either, a local or a central authority, the courts have been led to assert the independent character of his office.[10]

The above judgments have led on occasion to the assertion that there was immunity in all ranks of the police service from interference or control by a police authority (or by anyone else) in the discharge of police duties.

Such an assertion if honestly pressed is naive and does not truly square with the historical and present reality of the office of the constable.

It appears that in early Tudor times, and certainly at least by the end of the fourteenth century "constables in the matter of keeping the peace were beginning to lose their initiative and becoming the mere subordinates of local ministers of the Crown"[11] or justices of the peace.

The Reforms of Sir Robert Peel in the nineteenth century in Britain introduced change into this historical system, but the subordinate position of the constable was nevertheless preserved, albeit in altered form:

> The 19th Century statutes which created modern police forces in England and Wales preserved the traditional obligation laid upon a constable to obey the legal orders of a justice of the peace, thus providing a form of control over the police which combined the virtue of ancient usage and political acceptability. This form of control, although unrepealed by Parliament has now fallen into virtual disuse and is today little more than a historical survival. As a result, a situation has gradually come about, unregulated and probably unrecognized by Parliament, in which chief constables, able and intelligent men, growing in professional stature and public esteem, have assumed authority and powers which their predecessors would formerly have sought from justices, now praying in aid their tenure of the independent office of the constable, which as we have seen they cherish to this day as a bulwark against interference or control by the police authorities which appointed them.[12]

What these extracts illustrate is that although the constable operates under a broad and powerful mandate to enforce the law, from very early times he has been subject to control and discipline from superiors. When he was beholden to the justices of the peace the constable was in effect to do the bidding of "officers under the Crown". This led the 1962 English Royal Commission on the Police to declare that "from about the end of the fourteenth to the second quarter of

---

10. *Ibid.* at p. 22. See also "The Legal Status of a Policeman" *supra* footnote 7. Also see *Fisher v. Oldham Corpn.* [1930] 2 K.B. 364; *Simpson v. Magistrates of Dundee* 1928 S.N. 30; *Enever v. R.* [1906] 3 Commonwealth L.R. 969; *A. G. New South Wales v. Perpetual Trustee Co.* [1955] A.C. 457.
11. *Supra* footnote 2 at p. 11.
12. *Ibid.* at p. 29.

the nineteenth century the justice of the peace was the superior, the constable the inferior, conservator of the peace."[13] Such an arrangement in the eyes of the commission was seen to be both curious and confusing inasmuch as the office of the constable was regarded as local in nature (not national, and hence requiring guidance from sovereign officers) and independent in character (before the statutory reforms of Peel the authority of the office was seen to be derived exclusively from the common law, and thus theoretically it was immune to external control or manipulation). In an effort to come to grips with the contradictory nature of the phenomenon of the office of constable legal theorists and constitutional historians have taken to describing the constable, in relatively recent times, as a "ministerial officer of the Crown", "a description which appears to effect a reconciliation between the independent nature and common law origins, and powers of the office and its subordination to the justice".[14]

As has been mentioned the constable's subordination to the justice in modern times has yielded to subordination to the "chief constable".[15]

While historically and currently, the constable has occupied the status of a "subordinate", he is, nevertheless, a subordinate who is not wholly subordinate.

> It is true that as a member of a disciplined body the constable is subject to the orders of his superior officers; but for the way in which he executes these orders he has a dual responsibility: he is answerable to his superiors for any disciplinary lapse and to the courts for any misuse or abuse of authority. Thus either when acting alone on his own initiative or when acting under orders he is himself answerable for any error of judgment.[16]

A good example of the dual nature of the constable's loyalties is to be found in the following passage extracted from the judgment of McCardie, J. in *Fisher v. Oldham Corpn.*:[17]

> Suppose that a police officer arrested a man for a serious felony? Suppose, too, that the watch committee of the borough at once passed a resolution directing that the felon should be released? Of what value would such a resolution be? Not only would it be the plain duty of the police officer to disregard the resolution, but it would also be the duty of the chief constable to consider whether an information should not at once be laid against the members of the watch committee for a conspiracy to obstruct the course of criminal justice.

---

13. *Ibid.* at p. 12.
14. *Ibid.* at p. 12.
15. This title — chief constable — is synonymous with police chief, police commissioner, etc., terms which are employed in various common law jurisdictions.
16. Great Britain, *Royal Commission on the Police* (Interim Report) (1960) at p. 12.
17. *Supra* footnote 10 at pp. 372-373.

Judging from these comments it seems that the constable in many instances will have a "higher duty" than merely to follow the instructions of his superiors. The reality of attempting to adhere to this "higher duty", however, in the face of disciplinary procedures and other pressures may well be subsumed under a "good soldier" doctrine of conduct.

The removal of the chain of command in police work from the office of the justice of the peace to the office of the chief constable did not effect a removal of the elements of government oversight and control from the domain of police enterprise. The chief constable like the justice of the peace before him retains a connection to governmental superiors. For example, in London the Commissioner of Police acts under the general authority of the Home Secretary and he is accountable to the Home Secretary for the way in which he uses his force.[18] Also, in both England and Canada the institution and conduct of proceedings in the case of certain grave offence is statutorily reserved for the Director of Public Prosecutions (England) or the Attorney-General (Canada).[19] There is also in both countries undoubted liaison between the offices of the chief constable and their governmental superiors.

In Canada one need only cite the very recent examples offered by the newly appointed Attorney-General for Ontario who has issued "directives" concerning prosecutions for hockey violence and for impaired driving proceedings to his local agents and, purportedly, to the police themselves.

In England control over the police has been, in large measure, overtly centralized.

> It was plain that it was the intention of the legislature to put the police force under the authority of the Secretary of State and to hold him fully responsible, not for every detail of the management of the force, but in regard to the general policy of the police in the discharge of their duty . . .[20]

Canada has modelled its police forces to some extent upon the English example:

> In Canadian urban centres the system adopted is the English plan less the centralized control: it is of course true that any provincial officers may function within the corporate limits of a city or town either with or without the co-operation of the local authorities: and that the Provincial Government may require the appointment by municipalities of constables: but beyond that the province has no supervision

---

18. *Supra* footnote 2 at p. 31.
19. *Ibid.* at p. 30. See also, the Criminal Code, R.S.C. 1970, Chap. C-34 ss. 2, 496, 505, 507.
20. *Royal Commission on the Police* (1962) *supra,* footnote 2 at p. 37 *per* Mr. Henry Matthews.

over the way in which the local authority discharges its duty. . . . So far as police systems are concerned neither Canada as a whole nor any of its provinces has any direct control over the urban police, if provincial forces charged primarily with the duty of law enforcement in rural districts are excepted . . .[21]

The expressions above are somewhat dated and inaccurate (they were written in 1928). It is true that in many provinces provision is made under the *Provincial Police Act* specifically preserving the decentralized situation described above. For example, in Ontario section 2(1) of the *Police Act* reads:

> 2(1) Every city and town is responsible for the policing of and maintenance of law and order in the municipality and for providing and maintaining an adequate police force in accordance with the police needs of the municipality.[22]

This section appears to place policing and the maintenance of law and order solely within the jurisdiction of local authorities. However, section 8 of the *Ontario Police Act* provides for every municipality with a population of more than 15,000 to have a board consisting of the head of the municipal counsel, a judge of *any* county or district court designated by the Lieutenant Governor in Council, and *any* other person whom the Lieutenant Governor in Council designates. By various other sections of the *Act* the board so constituted is given powers to appoint members of the police force, establish rates of remuneration, provide for and pay for the accommodation, arms, equipment and other things for the use and maintenance of the force.[23] Supervision over boards and mediation of disputes involving boards and municipal councils is the responsibility of a Police Commission.[24]

Thus a supervisory and regulatory bureaucracy—one not necessarily local in nature—surrounds the police force and controls (at least in theory) even the activities of individual constables. Section 17 of the *Police Act* makes this arrangement abundantly clear:

> 17(1) Notwithstanding section 2, the board is responsible for the policing and maintenance of law and order in the municipality and *the members of the police force are subject to the government of the board and shall obey its lawful directions* (emphasis added).

In 1928 it was observed that the lack of direct control by the provinces over their various police forces and the lack of uniform procedures, standards and practices was dysfunctional, inefficient,

---

21. *Supra* footnote 3 at p. 523.
22. R.S.O. 1970, c. 351, s. 2(1).
23. See *The Police Act* R.S.O. 1970, c. 351, ss. 14-16. Note also that s. 16 of the *Act* gives the board power to make regulations "for the government of the police force, for preventing neglect or abuse, and for rendering it efficient in the discharge of its duties."
24. See *The Police Act*, s. 441 (Ont.).

and deleterious to public respect for the administration of justice. The need for at least some form of central control was seen as necessary, and the suggested proposals for reform did not necessarily entail great expense:

> That control might be given to a small commission appointed by the province; the object of the supervision would be to secure uniformity equipment, organization and discipline and to secure that the activities of the police shall be properly directed and shall not be subject to political interference of any kind: the supervision would be achieved by regular inspection of every force in the province; by investigating any complaints by the public as to police methods and by any person whether a member of the force affected or not as to any matter affecting the internal discipline of the force; any enquiries would be made in public and full reports made covering every force would be annually presented to the legislature. If the commission found a state of affairs which required remedial measures it would be their duty to recommend to the local authority the steps which should be taken: and if these recommendations should be ignored, the government should have the power to disband the force, and provide any necessary police facilities at the cost of the local authority.[25]

Almost all of this (and more) is to be found within the present powers of the Ontario Police Commission as set out under Part III of the *Police Act*.[26]

In the result the constable in Canada must be viewed as a subordinate; one stationed well down on the ladder of authority. It is, however, simplistic to assert that there exists a clear chain of command running from the Police Commission to the board, to the chief constable and finally down through the ranks to the constable. The constable is rather, "unique among subordinates"; this being so as a result of the nature and degree of personal responsibility that he is required to exercise. He remains, in Canada, as in England, the holder of twin loyalties—to his superiors firstly, but above this, to the law. In addition to his statutory responsibilities the constable in Canada still retains his common law duties and responsibilities. Section 55 of the *Police Act* of Ontario expressly preserves this situation:

> 55. The members of police forces . . . are charged with the duty of preserving the peace, preventing robberies and other crimes and offences, including offences against the by-laws of the municipality, and apprehending offenders, and laying informations before the proper tribunal, and prosecuting and aiding in the prosecuting of offenders, *and have generally all the powers and privileges and are liable to all the duties and responsibilities that belong to constables* (emphasis added).

The 1962 English *Royal Commission on the Police* summarised

---

25. R. A. Smith, *supra* footnote 3 at pp. 523-524.
26. Note especially s. 41 which sets out the functions of the Commission.

the main functions of the police in present-day England[27] in terms that are equally applicable to Canadian police:

(1) The police have a duty to maintain law and order and to protect persons and property.
(2) The police have a duty to prevent crime.
(3) The police are responsible for the detection of criminals and in the course of interrogating suspected persons, they have a part to play in the early stages of the judicial process, acting under judicial restraint.
(4) The police have the responsibility of deciding whether or not to prosecute persons suspected of criminal offences.
(5) The police themselves (in some but not all jurisdictions) conduct many prosecutions for the less serious offences.
(6) The police have the duty of controlling road traffic and advising local authorities on traffic questions.
(7) The police carry out certain duties on behalf of government departments.
(8) The police have by long tradition a duty to befriend anyone who needs their help, and they may at any time be called upon to cope with minor or major emergencies.

These duties bespeak by implication the necessary ingredient of individual initiative. At first glance such initiative seems incompatible with the undoubted bureaucratic subordination of the constable to the orders and supervision of his superiors. However, the very nature of police work—the lonely patrol of the beat, the spontaneous exigencies of emergency situations, the element of violence and the necessity for the resort to the use of force—requires a high degree of personal responsibility. Intrinsic to the constable's ordinary duties lie a myriad of situations calling for personal, often instantaneous discretionary decisions. This feature, inherent in the constable's office, lies outside the ordinary realm of bureaucratic control. Directives, guidelines, regulations and disciplinary proceedings may well surround the constable, but in his normal, day-to-day world, he is very much on his own.

Nevertheless it is useful to remember that the net of authority which surrounds the constabulary is not merely bureaucratic in nature; it is political as well. The mandate of the various boards and commissions in existence stems from political appointment and statutory enactment.

In addition, the office of the Attorney General maintains close liaison with the police through the agency of local Crown Attorneys. (It scarcely bears repeating that the Attorney General himself is an elected politician and is a member of the Cabinet only by virtue of his allegiance to the party maintaining control over the legislature.) The local Crown Attorney performs both supervisory and advisory func-

---

27. *Supra* footnote 2 at p. 22.

tions with respect to police activity. In certain instances prosecutions cannot be commenced without the written consent of the Attorney General either of Canada,[28] or of the province having jurisdiction over the offence.[29] The Attorney General and his agents, the Crown Attorneys, always possess the power to intervene in the conduct of a prosecution,[30] and at discretion, to stay, or terminate any prosecution.[31] In this sense the constable has yet another master to serve. But there is much which occurs long before the laying of an information to commence an action — in fact most police work occurs in that preceding time frame. According to the Commissioners of the Ontario Law Reform Commission, however, even at relatively early stages the Crown Attorney may well be influencing the course of police activity:

> Crown attorneys perform an important function in advising members of the public and the police concerning proposed prosecutions or prosecutions that have been instituted. *They advise the police not only on cases immediately coming before the courts, but also on general procedural matters, investigations and the preparation of cases not immediately before the courts.* In the smaller centres, the Ontario Provincial Police and the municipal police seek the advice of Crown attorneys concerning what charges if any should be laid in respect of particular fact situations. In nothern Ontario, the police are especially dependent upon Crown attorneys.
>
> In Metropolitan Toronto, and to a lesser degree in the larger centres, the police in most cases determine in the first instance what charges should be laid, but advice as to the propriety of the charges as the cases develop is the responsibility of the Crown attorney.
>
> *Although there is no statutory obligation to advise the police, it is assumed that this is the proper function of the office.* Much reliance is placed on the advice and assistance of Crown counsel at the Police College in Toronto and the Ontario Police College at Aylmer. A member of the Crown Attorney's Association is an official representative to the latter.[32]

The picture of the constable which emerges from all of this is something of a paradox. On the one hand he is a captive on the bottom rung of a ladder of authority. On the other hand he is a unique individual set loose with a tremendous arsenal of weaponry, and the decisions involving the use or non-use of that store of power are by and large his, and his alone.

Although there are many who would eschew any analogy between

---

28. See the *Criminal Code* R.S.C. 1970, Chap. C-34, ss. 54, 82, 108, 243, and 433(2).
29. *Ibid.* ss. 124, 162(3), 168, 170, 343(2), 434(3).
30. See the *Crown Attorneys Act* R.S.O. 1970, c. 101, s. 12(d).
31. See the *Criminal Code*, ss. 508, 732.
32. Ontario Law Reform Commission, *Report on the Administration of Ontario Courts* (Part II) (1973) at p. 87.

the policeman on the beat and the soldier in the field the two phenomena nevertheless provide suitable features of comparison.

The panorama of events which conceivably could compel the intervention of the constable is immense. In the real world which he confronts the constable formulates policy, mediates disputes, and makes decisions. He does so notwithstanding the pervasive web of authority which surrounds him. Directives, guidelines, regulations and statutory restrictions may or may not be relevant to the exigencies of the particular situation which confronts the constable. The issues are complex and do not afford simple solutions. For example the constable must somehow resolve whether to refrain from arresting a violator because:

(a) the police believe the legislative body does not desire enforcement;

(b) the police believe the community wants no reinforcement or lax enforcement;

(c) a policeman believes another immediate duty is more urgent;

(d) a policeman interprets a broad term (such as "vagrancy") in his own unique fashion;

(e) a policeman is lenient with one who did not intend the violation;

(f) the offender promises not to commit the act again;

(g) the statute has long been without enforcement but is unrepealed;

(h) lack of adequate police manpower is believed to require non-enforcement;

(i) the policeman believes a warning or a lecture preferable to an arrest;

(j) the policeman is inclined to be lenient to those he likes;

(k) the policeman sympathizes with the violator;

(l) the crime is common within the subcultural group;

(m) the victim does not request the arrest or requests that it not be made;

(n) the victim is more likely to get restitution without the arrest;

(o) the only witness says he will refuse to testify;

(p) the victim is at fault in inciting the crime;

(q) the victim and the offender are relatives, perhaps husband and wife;

(r) making the arrest is undesirable from the policeman's personal standpoint because of such reasons as the extra effort required, he goes off duty in ten minutes, the record keeping necessary when an arrest is made is onerous, or he wants to avoid the expenditure of time for testifying in court;

(s) the police trade non-enforcement for information or for other favors;

(t) the police make other kinds of deals with offenders;

(u) the police believe the probable penalty to be too severe;

(v) the arrest would harm a psychiatric condition;

(w) the arrest would unduly harm the offender's status.[33]

His decision may merely be a reflection of his own social attitudes and those of other policemen. Yet by his conduct, the policeman acts not only as a policeman, but as a prosecutor, jury, judge and parole board.

This distinct exercise of discretion by police officers determines the kind of persons who enter our criminal justice system. This grey area of decision-making is unknown to the public who, for the most part, continued to believe that law is enforced as it is written — that any deviation by the police from full enforcement is unlawful.[34]

2. POLICE DISCRETION NOT TO INVOKE THE CRIMINAL PROCESS

(1) The ideal of full enforcement

Sanford Kadish in an article on "Legal Norm and Discretion in the Sentencing Process"[35] makes the point that insofar as police function is concerned "the official assumption of the system seems to be that there is no place for expert administrative discretion; police are supposed to enforce all laws against all offenders in all circumstances."[36]

Presumably, this "official assumption" rests on the belief that full enforcement of the law is an ideal worth pursuing. Bound up in the belief in this ideal is the fear that without uniform and complete enforcement of the law the administration inevitably becomes impugned; tainted by the spectre of unequal treatment under law. "Fairness and the non-discriminatory application of the criminal law requires that similar cases be treated, so far as possible, in the same way."[37]

The ideal is no mere sentiment unaccompanied by official sanction or favor. As Professor Kadish indicates:

The need of full enforcement by the police is preserved officially in formal law as well as in popular conception. Statutes, mostly nineteenth century vintage, tend to speak in terms of the duty of the police diligently and faithfully to enforce all the penal laws. Decisions of appellate courts dealing with the legality of arrest commonly assert that the officer had not only the right but the duty to arrest or face charges of recreancy to that duty.[38]

Anyone at all familiar with the actual workings of the police and the administration of justice realizes that in terms of the viability of

---

33. This formulation of policy problems encountered by police constables at the time of arrest is that of K. C. Davis and is to be found in *Discretionary Justice: A Preliminary Inquiry* (1969) at pp. 82-83.
34. B. A. Grosman, *Police Command: Decisions and Discretion* (1975) at p. 81.
35. (1961-62) 75 Harv. L. Rev. 904.
36. *Ibid.* at p. 906.
37. Canada, *Report of the Canadian Committee on Corrections* (1969) at p. 44 (Ouimet Report).
38. S. Kadish, *supra* footnote 35 at pp. 906-907.

the ideal of full enforcement "the practice reduces this ideal to myth".[39] Indeed it appears that none of the recent commentaries, either in the journals[40] or in the decisions of the courts[41] bearing on this subject, go so far as to say that the police do not have a discretion in enforcing the law. The only actual dispute appears to centre around the desired breadth of this discretion and the possible means of controlling its exercise. The complex nature of these issues is partially revealed in these passages taken from the *Report of the Canadian Committee on Corrections*:

> The Committee is, however, of the view that the element of the exercise of police discretion cannot be separated from law enforcement and that its complete elimination would not advance the ends of justice. We think that a decision not to prosecute and merely to give a warning may best advance the ends of justice in some circumstances. Where the offence is minor or marginal, especially where the offender is young and unsophisticated, or undergoing mental treatment, a warning may be more appropriate than invoking the massive machinery of the criminal law.[42]

(2) Factors tending to demonstrate the undesirability of full enforcement

R. M. Jackson in his text on *Enforcing the Law* notes that "a chief constable who decided to prosecute every ascertainable breach of the law would exhaust his force, overload offices and courts, and be an appalling nuisance."[43] But the problems in this area go beyond mere mechanics and nuisance. Involved as well is the lack of legislative response to obsolescent legislation, the present unpopularity of certain laws, the secret agreements struck with undercover agents and informants, and the appropriateness of the probable penalty which would

---

39. *Supra* footnote 35 at p. 907.

40. See in addition to Kadish, *supra* footnote 35: B. Barker, "Police Discretion and the Principle of Legality" (1965-66) 8 Cr.L.Q. 400; G. Williams, "The Police and Law Enforcement" [1968] Crim.L.R. 351; W. Lafave, "The Police and Non-Enforcement of the Law" (Parts I and II) (1962) Wis.L.Rev. 104 and 179; J. Goldstein, "Police Discretion Not to Invoke the Criminal Process: Low Visibility Decisions in the Administration of Justice" (1959-60) 69 Yale L.J. 543; N. Osborough, Police Prosecutorial Discretion and the Police Image: Reflections on the Problem in England" (1965-66) 5 West.L.R. 62.

41. See especially *R. v. Commr. of Police of the Metropolis; Ex parte Blackburn* [1968] 1 All E.R. 763; and *R. v. Metropolitan Police Commr., ex parte Blackburn (No. 3)* [1973] 1 All E.R. 324.

42. Ouimet Report, *supra* footnote 3, at pp. 45-46. See also *R. v. Zwicker* 69 C.C.C. 301 at p. 305 *per* Roberts C.C.J.: "In this country a policeman is a peace officer and his duty is not only to the public generally but to every individual citizen, and to protect that citizen, and to protect him as far as possible, even against his own weakness, and not to hail him before the Magistrate for every foolish thing he does".

43. R. M. Jackson, *Enforcing the Law* (1967) at p. 50.

be imposed upon due enforcement, in relation to the harm initially occasioned.

The presence of discretion is one means by which a level of responsiveness is introduced into an otherwise rigid system. By the same token the presence of uncontrolled or "unbridled" discretion is an invitation to the influence of corruption and the forces of special interest.

The Ouimet Committee have asserted that the police cannot refuse to enforce an unpopular law,[44] and in support it cites the English Court of Appeal in *Blackburn (No. 1)*.[45] But what is to be the proper response of our law enforcement authorities to out-dated and out-moded Blue laws? Do the police have the right to refrain to enforce sanctions against overt breaches of the terms of an unrepealed statute?

An offender who has "gone straight" after a checkered criminal career may through inadvertence or momentary weakness become "involved with the law" in a trivial or technical way. Prosecution of such an individual may well result in a lengthy jail term due to his criminal record, or in the compulsory service of the unexpired portion of a jail term which had previously been excused under Parole provisions of the *Parole Act*. Must the police initiate prosecution or will a warning suffice?

Are the police required to prosecute all offenders irrespective of whether they (a) are actually in the employ of the police as undercover agents, or, (b) are paid informers operating under a grant of authority?

What response is required of the police where the victim of crime for reasons other than fear or extortion does not wish to press a complaint against the offender?

To what extent should the police be concerned with the mental condition of the accused? Or, with the humiliation which has been experienced by the accused or his family?

If all offences are to be uniformly enforced and prosecuted to what extent can the police be excused for inefficiency and lack of effectiveness due to lack of money and manpower resources?

Obviously, the police discretion not to invoke the criminal process involves a host of perplexing questions. By and large these questions reveal the factors which militate against a policy of full enforcement: (a) the human values of compassion, understanding and charity, (b) the practical considerations of allocation of resources, and (c) the efficiency concerns, involving the necessity to penetrate the underworld, to commit small crimes in order to uncover larger ones.

---

44. *Supra* footnote 37 at p. 45.
45. *Supra* footnote 41.

(3) Controlling police discretion: Non-enforcement through administrative policy vs. discretionary non-enforcement on an individual level

In its task force report on the Police the President's Commission on Law Enforcement and the Administration of Justice makes out a strong case for the existence of an ascertainable and sound basis for the exercise of police discretion. The informal exercises of discretion by police officers when unaccompanied by the controlling feature of administrative and legislative policy guidelines is too fraught with uncertainty, too liable to appear, or to be, "discriminatory" (in the worst sense of that word), and is too often plainly inconsistent. The need for sound, rational criteria upon which to base the propriety of a given discretionary response is patent:

> Proper and consistent exercise of discretion in a large organization, like a police department, will not result from the individual judgment of individual police officers in individual cases. Whatever the need for the exercise of judgment by an individual officer may be, certainly the development of overall law enforcement policies must be made at the departmental level and communicated to individual officers. This is necessary if the issues are to be adequately defined and adequately researched and if discretion is to be exercised consistently throughout the department.[46]

The Canadian Committee on Corrections was similarly minded but did not address the problem in precisely the same terms. As most Canadian observers are aware the recommendations contained in the Ouimet Report formed the basis of the *Bail Reform Act*. That *Act* sought to confine and structure the discretion of the individual police officer at the time of arrest. Statutory provisions indicate the considerations which should determine whether the police officer should issue, or cause to be issued a summons rather than make an arrest. In addition the Committee's Report contained these recommendations:

> The Committee is of the opinion that police departments should develop systems for recording the exercise of police discretion where a caution has been administered to a possible offender as an alternative to a prosecution. Moreover, guidelines with respect to the exercise of police discretion should be enunciated by senior officials in the police forces with a view to developing uniform practices. We are further of the view that the subject of police discretion is deserving not only of emphasis in police training programmes, but that further research on this subject is desirable.[47]

The modern perspective on the police officer's discretion has moved away from the hypocritical double standard which previously prevailed. This hypocrisy provoked one scholar to protest that "most departments

---

46. United States, *Task Force Report*: The Police (1967) at p. 19.
47. Ouimet Report, *supra* footnote 37 at p. 46.

attempt to maintain the existing stereotype of the police as ministerial officers who enforce all the laws, while they actually engage in a broad range of discretionary enforcement."[48] Of late the approach has been to acknowledge the existence of this discretion and hopefully then to structure and confine it in a meaningful way.

Where structuring and confining is attempted through the imposition of policy guidelines which are administrative rather than legislative in origin other concerns arise. Who controls these *new* exercises of administrative discretion? How broad is the power to establish a policy of non-enforcement? The questions lay at the heart of the problem considered by the English Court of Appeal in the *Blackburn* cases. Further, the Court was asked to consider whether or not it had a role to play in monitoring the performance of chief police officers in the performance of their policy making duties.

> Although the chief officers of police are answerable to the law, there are many fields in which they have a discretion with which the law will not interfere. For instance, it is for the Commissioner of Police, or the chief constable, as the case may be, to decide in any particular case whether enquiries should be pursued, or whether an arrest should be made, or a prosecution brought. It must be for him to decide on the disposition of his force and the concentration of his resources in any particular crime or area. No court can or should give him direction on such a matter. He can also make policy decisions and give effect to them, as, for instance, was often done when prosecutions were not brought for attempted suicide; but there are some policy decisions which, I think, the courts in a case can, if necessary, interfere. Suppose a chief constable were to issue a directive to his men that no person should be prosecuted for stealing any goods less than 100 pounds in value. I should have thought that the Court could countermand it. He would be failing in his duty to enforce the law.[49]

In 1973 the English Court of Appeal again had the opportunity to consider an application for mandamus brought by Mr. Blackburn. (The 1968 case involved alleged non-enforcement of gambling laws; in 1973 his concern was for the non-enforcement of the law in regard to obscene publications.) In summing up the position of the English courts on the general issue of non-enforcement Lord Denning remarked that "we made it clear that, in the carrying out of their duty of enforcing the law, the police have a discretion with which the courts will not interfere. There might, however, be extreme cases in which he was not carrying out his duty. And then we would."[50]

The *Blackburn* cases are useful insofar as they go. They do leave

---

48. W. Lafave, *Arrest* at p. 493.
49. *R. v. Commr. of Police of the Metropolis, ex Parte Blackburn (No. 2)* [1968] 1 All E.R. 763 at p. 769 *per* Lord Denning M.R.
50. *R. v. Metropolitan Police Commr., ex parte Blackburn (No. 3)* [1973] 1 All E.R. 324 at p. 331.

unanswered some questions which require answering: Will the courts interfere with a policy of non-enforcement of obsolete, or generally unpopular laws? Blackburn's cases seem to indicate that the police cannot refuse to enforce such laws, and where a policy of non-enforcement is articulated the courts may intervene to compel enforcement.[51] What will the court's response be to non-enforcement of laws against the illegal activities of informers who have been granted immunity in return for information?[52] The answer to this query at present is by no means certain.

K. C. Davis in his book *Discretionary Justice: A Preliminary Inquiry* suggests that a police chief "be permitted discretion in deciding that since certain laws are obsolete, they . . . remain unenforced. Yet he decries informal discretionary decision-making based on low-visibility and unknown criteria".[53]

> The seven instruments that are most useful in the structuring of discretionary power are: open plans, open policy statements, open rules, open findings, open reasons, open precedents, and fair informal procedure. The reason for repeating the word "open" is a powerful one: openness is the natural enemy of arbitrariness and a natural ally in the fight against injustice.[54]

By Davis' view open rules represent a great gain for justice. What follows is *his* formulation of policy guidelines concerning the use of informants in narcotics prosecutions:

> Whereas, various statutes make distribution of narcotics a crime; whereas, the federal and state constitutions guarantee equal protection of the laws; and whereas, the Police Department of the City of X finds that law enforcement with resources at its disposal is inadequate when the statutes and constitutions are complied with; now therefore, the Police Department of the City of X, pursuant to power which it necessarily assumes but which no statute or ordinance has granted to it, does hereby promulgate the following rules, which shall supersede all constitutional provisions, statutes, and ordinances to the contrary:
>
> 1. The arresting officer may release a violator of a narcotic statute, no matter how clear the evidence against him, upon making a finding that he may become an informer.
>
> 2. Upon releasing such a violator, no officer shall interfere with his

---

51. See the Ouimet Report *supra* footnote 37 at p. 45 in support of this view.
52. See *Evans v. Pesce* (1969) 8 C.R.N.S. 201 (Alta.) where mandamus was sought to compel a justice of the peace to receive an information against an undercover agent involved in a narcotics prosecution. The case is discussed in the section of this work entitled "The Police Officer as Witness and as an Accused or Defendant".
53. As interpreted by B. Grosman in *Police Command: Decisions and Discretion* (1975) at p. 99.
54. K. C. Davis *Discretionary Justice: A Preliminary Inquiry* (1969) at p. 98 (cited in Grosman, *supra* footnote 53 at p. 99.)

further purchase or sale of narcotics, so long as a finding is made that he is supplying information to the police or may be about to do so.

3. All transactions by which an officer trades nonenforcement for information shall be kept secret, so that the absolute discretion of the officer will be immune to check or review by any other governmental authority and immune to criticism by the public.

4. When two violators of the narcotics laws have committed the same offense in the same circumstances, no principle concerning equal justice under law or equal protection of the laws shall control when an officer chooses to trade nonenforcement for information; all provisions of constitutions, statutes, and ordinances to the contrary are hereby superseded.

5. Whenever an informer becomes recognized as such by the underworld, the officer who has made promises of immunity from arrest shall request another officer to arrest and prosecute the informer, and the second officer shall falsely pretend to have no knowledge of such promises of immunity; as soon as an informer's effectiveness has been spent, considerations of decency and fairness about keeping promises shall be given no weight.[55]

If nothing else is accomplished by such rule-making procedure the "dirty little secret"[56] no longer remains a secret, and the choice between conflicting values can thus more truly be described as a "choice".

3. THE IMPORTANCE OF THE ILLEGALLY OBTAINED EVIDENCE RULE TO THE ROLE OF THE POLICE

Throughout the common law world it appears that few countries have evolved quite so rigid and authoritarian a formulation of the judicial response to illegally obtained evidence as that which presently prevails in Canada.[57] The rule, such as it is, was expressed definitively by Martland J. in *R. v. Wray*:[58]

the exercise of a discretion by the trial judge arises only if the admission of the evidence would operate unfairly. The allowance of admissible evidence relevant to the issue before the Court and of substantial probative value may operate unfortunately for the accused, but not unfairly. It is only the allowance of evidence gravely prejudicial to the accused, the admissibility of which is tenuous, and whose probative force in relation to the main issue before the Court is trifling, which can be said to operate unfairly.[59]

---

55. K. C. Davis, *ibid.* at p. 96.

56. See G. E. Parker, "Copping a Plea" (1972) 20 Ch.L.J. 310 where the phrase occurs in connection with the larger question of plea bargaining.

57. See "Developments in the Law: Confessions" (1966) 79 Harv. L.Rev. 935. See also Canada, *Report of the Canadian Committee on Corrections* (1969) (Ouimet Report) at pp. 70-75.

58. [1970] 4 C.C.C. 1.

59. *Ibid.* at p. 17.

This, of course, is little more than a re-formulation in more elegant terms of this sentiment:

> It matters not how you get it; if you steal it even, it would be admissible.[60]

Laskin J. (as he then was) had occasion to comment on the rule in the relatively recent decision of the Supreme Court of Canada in *R. v. Hogan*:[61]

> Short of legislative direction, it might have been expected that the common law would seek to balance the competing interests by weighing the social interest in the particular case against the gravity or character of the invasion, leaving it to the discretion of the trial Judge whether the balance should be struck in favor of reception or exclusion of particular evidence.[62]

These remarks are basically a statement of the English position on the subject as distilled from the decisions of the English Superior Courts in *Noor Mohammed v. R.*,[63] *Kuruma v. R.*,[64] *King v. R.*,[65] *Callis v. Gunn*,[66] and *R. v. Payne*.[67]

The matter was forcefully put by Lord Denning in *Ghani v. Jones*[68]

> The common law does not permit police officers, or anyone else, to ransack anyone's house or to search for papers or articles therein, or to search his person, simply to see if he may have committed some crime or other. If police officers should do so, they would be guilty of a trespass. Even if they should find something incriminating against him, I should have thought that the court would not allow it to be used in evidence against him, if the conduct of the police officers was so oppressive that it would not be right to allow the Crown to rely upon it.[69]

---

60. *Per* Crompton J. in *R. v. Leatham* (1861) 8 Cox C.C. 498 at p. 501.
61. (1974) 18 C.C.C. (2d) 65.
62. *Ibid.* at p. 80.
63. [1949] A.C. 182 (P.C.).
64. [1955] A.C. 197 (P.C.).
65. [1969] 1 A.C. 304 (P.C.).
66. [1964] 1 Q.B. 495.
67. [1963] 1 All E.R. 848.
68. [1969] 3 All E.R. 1700.
69. *Ibid.* at p. 1703. Note that this position contradicts the assessment of the English situation by Laskin J. in *R. v. Hogan* (*supra* footnote 61) where he indicates *supra* footnote 61 at p. 80, "It appears that only in a line of Scottish and Irish cases has there been any consideration of striking a balance between the competing interests involved where there is a challenge to admissibility because of illegality or impropriety." For further review of primarily the Commonwealth position on illegally obtained evidence see G. Williams, "Evidence Obtained by Illegal Means" [1955] Crim. L.R. 339; Heydon, "Illegally Obtained Evidence" (1) and (2), [1973] Crim. L.R. 603 and 690; Coplan, "The Judicial Discretion to Disallow Admissible Evidence" (1970) 114 Sol.J. 945.

The English position on illegally obtained evidence is markedly different from the American approach to the subject. In the United States evidence which has been obtained by illegal search and seizure is inadmissible in both federal and state criminal prosecutions.[70]

> The American exclusionary rule, in enforcement of constitutional guarantees, is as much a judicial creation as was the common law of admissibility. It is not dictated by the Constitution, but its rationale appears to be that the constitutional guarantees cannot be adequately served if their vindication is left to civil actions in tort or criminal prosecutions, and that a check rein on illegal police activity which invades constitutional rights can best be held by excluding evidence obtained through such invasions.[71]

In Canada, prior to the Supreme Court of Canada's decision in *R. v. Wray* the Canadian Committee on Corrections had occasion to make a comparative study of the various approaches to evidence secured as a result of illegal or unlawful police conduct.[72] The report of the Committee was issued in 1969, and contained the following recommendations for the enactment of legislation on the subject:

(1) The court may in its discretion reject evidence which has been illegally obtained.

(2) The court in exercising its discretion to either reject or admit evidence which has been illegally obtained should take into consideration the following factors:

   (i) Whether the violation of rights was wilful or whether it occurred as a result of inadvertence, mistake, ignorance or error in judgment.

   (ii) Whether there existed a situation of urgency in order to prevent the destruction or loss of evidence, or other circumstances which in the particular case justified the action taken.

   (iii) Whether the admission of the evidence in question would be unfair to the accused.

(3) The legislation should provide that the discretion to reject evidence illegally obtained provided for by such legislation does not affect the discretion which a court now has to disallow evidence if the strict rules of evidence would operate unfairly against an accused.[73]

---

70. See *Weeks v. U.S.* (1914) 232 U.S. 383; *Mapp v. Ohio* (1961) 367 U.S. 643.
71. *Per* Laskin J. in *R. v. Hogan supra* footnote 61 at pp. 80-81. In this regard see *infra*, Part 5 in this Chapter. See Scowle, C.R. (3d) "The Exclusionary Rule Regarding Illegally Seized Evidence; The Exclusionary Rule in the American Law of Search and Seizure". *Police Power and Individual Freedom* (Part II); cited in the Ouimet Report, *supra* footnote 57 at p. 72.
72. See Ouimet Report *supra* footnote 57 at pp. 70-75.
73. *Ibid.* at pp. 74-75. (Note that the Committee's point #3 was overturned by the decision in *Wray*.)

No legislative initiatives in keeping with the above proposals have been forthcoming. In fact if one examines the recent history of legislative enactments in the field of criminal law and civil liberties quite a different picture emerges to the one suggested in general terms by the Ouimet Report. The tendency in this country has been to place ever-greater and more all-encompassing powers under the control of police and police-like agencies.

> In comparison with many other jurisdictions governed by the British legal system, Canada has been very susceptible to demands for placing broad and sweeping powers in the hands of police and other enforcement officers. The expediency of maintaining law and order has been the justification for the official acquiescence in such requests.[74]

As a threshold observation it might be noted that the tendency to expand police powers has not in general been accompanied (in the legislation) by the provision of adequate safeguards against possible excesses in the unbridled exercise of those powers.[75]

In practical terms what this means is that in Canada evidence may be secured by illegal search or seizure; by trespass or by force; or, through the use of falsehoods, fraud trickery or deception; or, in open violation of a fundamental right (such as a denial of the right to counsel). Such evidence is always admissible — no matter how wilful or objectionable the conduct of the police — subject only to a concern for probative value and relevancy.

This is not a truth which is only discovered surreptitiously during the trial of an issue and is then forgotten. The police are aware of it.

> It may be said that the exclusion of relevant evidence is no way to control illegal police practices and that such exclusion merely allows a wrongdoer to escape conviction. Yet where constitutional guarantees are concerned, the more pertinent consideration is whether those guarantees, as fundamentals of the particular society, should be at the mercy of law enforcement officers and a blind eye turned to their invasion because it is more important to secure a conviction. The contention that it is the duty of the Courts to get at the truth has in it too much of the philosophy of the end justifying the means . . .[76]

It is possible to assert that in Canada there exists a "discretion" (albeit a non-legal discretion) in police officers to act illegally in order to secure evidence for use in a criminal prosecution. This is not a spurious contention. The instances of openly illegal (or, at least, questionably legal) police actions are numerous and well documented.[77]

---

74. G. E. Parker, "The Extraordinary Power to Search and Seize and the Writ of Assistance" (1959-63) 1 U.B.C.L.R. 688.

75. For an example of this see the discussion of the legislative history of the police powers to wiretap *infra* Part 4, in this Chapter.

76. *Per* Laskin J. in *R. v. Hogan, supra* footnote 61 at p. 81.

77. See P. K. McWilliams, *Canadian Criminal Evidence* (1974) Chap. 3 (5) "Evidence Illegally Obtained" at pp. 24-25 for a lengthy list of proceedings involving cases of evidence impugned by reason of alleged illegal police conduct.

There appears to be a hesitancy among those aggrieved to seek redress by way of civil or criminal proceedings against offending officers. There are real, practical, difficulties to be overcome before successful resolution of such a proceeding can be achieved. It is questionable whether civil liability operates as any kind of effective deterrent to unlawful police conduct. This is especially the case since the trend of most recent legislation "has been to make the doctrine of *respondeat superior* applicable to actions in tort against police officers, with the result that the municipality is liable for damages recovered against the police officer."[78]

The actual possibilities for success in any action against the police, be the cause civil or criminal in nature, are highly circumscribed. The reasons for this are manifold and shall be dealt with *infra* in Part 5 of this Chapter.

The foregoing analysis points up a disturbing feature of the "illegally obtained evidence rule" in Canada. In practical terms this rule of evidence may actually serve as an *incentive* to illegal conduct where the fruits of ordinary lawful investigation have not been forthcoming, or (even worse) it may serve as an easy substitute for lawful effective police work.[79]

4. POLICE POWERS

Up until relatively recent times the accepted conception of the powers of the police rested on the principle that a policeman, in the view of the common law, is only "a person paid to perform, as a matter of duty, acts which if he were so minded he might have done voluntarily."[80]

The English Royal Commission on the Police writing in 1962 endorsed this view of police powers which was expressed by an earlier Royal Commission:

> Indeed a policeman possesses few powers not enjoyed by the ordinary citizen, and public opinion, expressed in Parliament and elsewhere has shown great jealousy of any attempts to give increased authority to the police. This attitude is due, we believe, not to any distrust of the

---

78. Ouimet Report *supra* footnote 57 at p. 74. The writer tends to doubt the assertion which follows immediately (p. 74) that "those who are required to pay the bills incurred as a result of the violation of the citizens' rights are likely to exercise stricter control over the actions of the individual police officer". Rather, save for the most exceptional of cases, it is suspected that such payments euphemistically become part of the general municipal budget with respect to police expenditures, and convey to the individual officer the impression that his illegality is being "subsidized" by the municipality.

79. See Ellwyn R. Stoddard's excellent sociological analysis of "Blue Coat Crime" in Johnston, Savitz, and Wolfgang (ed.) *The Sociology of Punishment and Correction* (2nd ed.) (1962) at p. 66.

80. Great Britain, *Royal Commission on the Police* (1962) at p. 10.

police as a body but to an instinctive feeling that, as a matter of principle, they should have as few powers as possible which are not possessed by the ordinary citizen, and that their authority should rest on the broad basis of the consent and active co-operation of all law-abiding people. At the same time it must be realised that there are certain duties of a special nature which if they are to be entrusted to the police and adequately performed by them, require the grant of special powers.[81]

As an expression of sentiment the Commissioners comments probably lie close to the heart of today's average Canadian citizen. However the Canadian condition is not identical to that which prevailed in Britain in 1929, or for that matter, in 1962, although there are many similarities.

It is undeniable that for at least the last decade we in Canada have been experiencing the rising public concern over issues involving "crime in the streets", "law and order", or, to use an expression of more recent vintage, "peace and security". Our laws reflect this concern, and legislative initiatives (with the sole exceptions of the passage of the *Canadian Bill of Rights* in 1960 and the *Bail Reform Act* in 1969) continue to mirror our penchant for elevating the value of efficient law enforcement to a higher station than the competing value of civil liberty. This dilemma posed by competing values is one which faces all free societies. As John Honsberger observed in his 1963 Special Lecture before the Law Society of Upper Canada:

> The protection of the individual from oppression and abuse is a major interest in a free society; but so is the effective prosecution of crime, an interest which at times seems forgotten. As against the rights of the individual must be set the interests of society but as Lord Simonds found in *Christie et al v. Leachinsky* it is not easy so to state the law as not on the one hand to impinge upon the liberty of the subject or on the other hand to make more difficult the duty of every subject of the King to preserve the King's peace.[82]

While the resolution of the problem of the balance to be struck between competing interests is not an easy task it appears that historically the Canadian courts and the Canadian legislatures have tended to approach the problem *largely* from a fixed anti-civil libertarian perspective. This is not to downplay the importance of the great constitutional/civil liberties decisions of the 1950's — *Roncarelli*,[83] *Samur*[84], and *Switzman*,[85] or the 1938 decision of the Supreme Court of Canada in the *Alberta Press*[86] case.

---

81. *Ibid.* at pp. 10-11.
82. J. Honsberger, "The Power of Arrest and the Duties and Rights of Citizens and Police (1963) *L.S.U.C. Special Lectures* 1 at p. 5.
83. *Roncarelli v. Duplessis* [1959] S.C.R. 121.
84. *Saumur v. Quebec (City)* [1953] S.C.R. 299.
85. *Switzman v. Elbing* [1957] S.C.R. 285.
86. *Reference Re Alberta Legislation* [1938] S.C.R. 100.

Simply put, in Canada we tend, on balance, to favor the value of the efficient prosecution of crime over the value of the protection of the individual from oppression. This is not as crass a determination as it might first appear since both values may be said *ultimately* to redound to the benefit of the individual. What causes difficulty is that in certain instances we go so far as to sanction unlawful behavior by our prosecuting agencies and in terms of comparison with other common law countries the content of our legislation and jurisprudence is found to be more repressive.

Of unlawful official behavior in the detection and prosecution of criminal offences the following has been said:

> The choice of policy here is to favour the social interest in the repression of crime despite the unlawful invasion of individual interests and despite the fact that the invasion is by public officers charged with law enforcement. Short of legislative direction, it might have been expected that the common law would seek to balance the competing interests by weighing the social interest in the particular case against the gravity or character of the invasion, leaving it to the discretion of the trial judge whether the balance should be struck in favour of reception or exclusion of particular evidence. I have already indicated that the discretion has been narrowed, and, I would add, to an extent that underlines a wide preference for admissibility.[87]

Canadian law respecting the admissibility of confessions when contrasted to prevalent standards in Britain and the United States merited this terse commentary (in 1966):

> On the whole, there is probably little question that the police in Canada are less restricted than in many other common law countries.[88]

By favoring efficient policing (or the "social interest in the repression of crime") we have by slow degrees moved away from the situation where our police were clothed merely with those powers enjoyed by all the citizenry. More and more, by the same incremental process, we have chosen to enlarge that grant of special powers which our police employ.

Although, in the modern era police duties have become more varied, crime more rampant, and more organized, "much less time is spent on crime detection and the apprehension of offenders than on other phases of police work."[89] But police powers have grown as well — presumably in the name of the goddess Efficiency.

The police enjoy a plethora of specific, procedural powers. But in the main police powers can be described by three main adjectives

---

87. *Per* Laskin J. (as he then was) in *R. v. Hogan* (1974) 18 C.C.C. (2d) 65 at p. 80.
88. "Developments in the Law: Confessions" (1966) 79 Harv.L.Rev. 935 at p. 1106.
89. Canada, *Report of the Canadian Committee on Corrections* (1969) at p. 40 (Ouimet Report).

which identify the function of a particular power. Police powers are either "preventive" and "investigatory" or "remedial" (perhaps "curative" would be an equally apt expression.)

In general terms that part of police work which is aimed at the prevention and detection of crime, the apprehension of offenders, and the maintenance of order in the community involves resort to, and use of, the following substantive powers:

(1) surveillance (preventive and investigatory)
(2) interrogation (preventive and investigatory)
(3) Identification procedures (investigatory)
(4) Search and seizure (preventive and investigatory)
(5) Arrest and detention (remedial or curative).

Ancillary to numbers (4) and (5) *supra* may be the use of force. Augmenting the power to employ surveillance techniques is the use of wiretaps and electronic listening devices. Incidental to police powers of arrest and detention are limited police powers of release (bail — non-judicial).

A more detailed analysis of the breadth and general nature of these four substantive police powers follows:

(1) Surveillance

Physical surveillance by locating a person suspected of to be engaging in criminal activity; following him, observing his activities, and over-hearing his conversations with others, has been an important aspect of police investigation as long as there has been police forces.[90]

Since no one can seriously doubt that it is a valid police function to *prevent* crime and to detect *incipient* crime there presently is, and probably always has been, unquestioned acceptance of the rights of police to watch and beset suspected criminals and even (within reasonable limits) to commit minor and sometimes major, trespasses without fear of reprisal in the pursuit of this general duty. In fact it has always been the historical duty of the citizen to assist the constabulary in the enforcement of the criminal law.[91] And this historical duty in present-day Canada has been transposed into a statutory duty the breach of which may result in punishment by indictment.[92]

---

90. *Ibid.* at p. 80.
91. See J. Honsberger, *supra* footnote 82 at p. 1.
92. See the *Criminal Code,* R.S.C. 1970, chap. C-34, s. 118 especially subsection (*b*) which reads:
    118. Everyone who
        (*b*) omits, without reasonable excuse to assist a public officer in the execution of his duty in arresting a person or in preserving the peace, after having reasonable notice that he is required to do so, . . .
    is guilty of
        (*d*) an indictable offence and is liable to imprisonment for two years, or
        (*e*) an offence punishable on summary conviction.

An overt role played by the police — patent stake-outs, marked cruiser cars, uniformed officers — may be as equally important to the prevention of crime as the secret undercover activity. A clear and unmistakable police presence is an effective short term deterrent to criminal activity.

However there is a line to be drawn between effective policing and unwarranted harrassment. Police activity can be regarded as hostile and threatening to the entire community if it is too overt and too ubiquitous.

> It follows that the police, in exercising their functions, are, to a peculiar degree, dependent upon the goodwill of the general public and that the utmost discretion must be exercised by them to avoid over-stepping the limited powers which they possess. A proper and mutual understanding between the police and the public is essential for the maintenance of law and order.[93]

Undercover activity does not challenge public sentiment as directly as overt police activity. And to a certain extent it may be said that the more discreet police operations become, the less public antipathy towards the police they generate. This is nevertheless consistent with the general sentiment which holds to the non-legal belief in the "right to be let alone."

Balancing this consideration (the right to be let alone) is the equally important desire in the public for reassurance, the desire for an indicator of safety from the perils of crime.

Thus police work has two faces — one public and the other private; or, symbolically, in the form of the uniformed man in the boldly emblazoned cruiser, and the nondescript attire of the "plainclothesman" in the unmarked car.

But privacy and secrecy among those charged with public duties constitutes something of a paradox to a democratic society and it is in this area that the fear of "creating an instrument capable of serving the ends of tyranny" once again surfaces.

The growth and evolution of modern science and technology has placed in the institutional hands of our police, surveillance devices far beyond anything that could have been imagined by the 19th century architects of that institution.

> It seems not impossible that in the future it will be possible to keep a person under complete surveillance — visual as well as auditory — for an indefinte period.[94]

See also J. Honsberger, *supra* footnote 82 at pp. 31-32 re. the *moral* duty of the citizen to assist peace officers in the execution of their duties.

93. *Royal Commission on the Police* (1962) *supra* footnote 80 at p. 11.

94. Ouimet Report, *supra* footnote 89 at p. 80 citing in support A. F. Westwin, "Science, Privacy and Freedom; Issues and Proposals for the 1970's" (1966) 66 Col. L. Rev. 1003.

In 1969 in Canada the situation was such that the Ouimet Committee on Canadian Corrections felt constrained to note that "there is no adequate Canadian legislation at the present time to deal with the threat to privacy involved in wiretapping and electronic eavesdropping".[95]

By 1975 the situation had changed so dramatically (via the avenue of legislative intervention) that one commentator examining the statutory innovations which had occurred characterized the new legislation in the following terms: "The Protection of Privacy Act (or is it the Invasion of Privacy Act?)".[96]

Presently in 1976 new legislation is before the House of Commons which is designed to enhance and extend the "privacy" law as promulgated in June, 1974.[97]

The use by police of electronic surveillance techniques (particularly wiretaps) has been, and still remains, the recipient of a high degree of public cynicism. Legal or not it has long been assumed that the police have been doing it. Official voices have affirmed as much.

> The Committee is of the view that wiretapping and electronic eavesdropping for law enforcement purposes, under conditions of strict control, should be authorized by legislation. *We point out that it is in fact taking place and that at the present time it is not subject to any effective control.*[98]

N. M. Chorney in a 1965 article on wiretapping and electronic eavesdropping surveyed the powers of police at that time to use wiretapping devices in Canada in the course of criminal investigations:

> Until the power of the police forces to use wiretapping devices in the course of criminal investigations is expressly defined and controlled by legislation, as it appears to have been in England and some American states, it is possible that any member of a police force who is acting under this general statutory duty of criminal investigation may give an employee of a telephone or telegraph company the required lawful authority or direction to disclose communications. *There is no provincial or Dominion legislation to prevent a police officer from using wiretapping equipment to assist him to perform this duty of preventing crime or apprehending criminals.*[99]

Thus the situation confronting the legislators at the time of the framing of Bill C-176 *(The Protection of Privacy Act)* was something of a "fait accompli". Domestic spying by local police forces was well

---

95. *Ibid.* at p. 82.
96. G. Kileen, "Recent Developments in the Law of Evidence" (1975) 18 Cr.L.Q. 103 at p. 104.
97. The *Protection of Privacy Act,* 1973-74 c. 50 proclaimed in force June 30, 1974.
98. Ouimet Report *supra,* footnote 89 at p. 85 (emphasis added).
99. N. M. Chorney, "Wiretapping and Electronic Eavesdropping" (1964-65) 7 Cr.L.Q. 434 at pp. 449-450 (emphasis added).

under way. Nevertheless there were still several alternative courses open to the law makers of the land:

(1) They could prohibit electronic surveillance of any type absolutely.

(2) They could permit the authorities an unlimited unreviewable discretion in the use of such techniques.

(3) They could impose controls over the use of devices, the time period in which such devices would remain in use, the prospective targets of such surveillance, and over the admissibility of evidence gathered as a result (direct or indirect) of the unlawful use of such devices.

An absolute prohibition on all electronic surveillance was never seriously considered by the Parliamentarians. However the following exchange which took place before the Justice and Legal Affairs Committee is illustrative of the civil libertarian perspective on this issue. Ramsay Clark the former U.S. Attorney-General was at that time being questioned by Mr. Wagner of the Committee;

> Mr. Wagner: Do you not believe that since the underworld is using wiretapping against honest people that it might be a good idea to have electronic surveillance under certain conditions in certain cases? Or do you believe that all these weapons may be used by people who live outside the law, but as far as honest people are concerned they should simply sit back and say: "We are sorry, this would not be right. Really we should not use these weapons".
>
> Mr. Clark: The last place I would look for my standard of conduct would be the criminal community. They murder. I do not think police should murder. They steal. I do not think police should steal. If they wiretap, police should wiretap — who needs it?[100]

By the same token the legislators were unwilling to give "carte blanche" to police officers in the field of electronic surveillance. Therefore it was proposed

(1) That no interception of communication would be possible without Court authorization.[101]

(2) That interception of communications would only be possible in relation to a limited list of specified crimes.[102]

(3) That direct evidence secured by unlawful interception in general would be inadmissible.[103]

---

100. Extracted from R. J. Delisle, "Evidentiary Implications of Bill C-176" (1973-74) 16 Cr.L.Q. 260 at pp. 266-267. For the opposite view see the position enunciated in the Birkett Committee Report on Interception of Communications (1957 Cmnd. 283) quoted in Chorney, *supra* footnote 99 at p. 450.

101. The Criminal Code, s. 178.12.

102. *Ibid.* s. 178.1.

103. *Ibid.* s. 178.16.

(4) That derivative evidence secured by reason of unlawful interception would be similarly inadmissible.[104]

(5) That court authorization for electronic surveillance would only be available for thirty days.[105]

(6) That any person under electronic surveillance be notified of the fact of his surveillance within 90 days of the date when surveillance was lawfully terminated.[106]

(7) That evidence secured by lawful interception in general would be inadmissible for use in the prosecution of an offence other than one for which the initial authorization was obtained.[107]

Placing control over initial authorization of police conducted electronic surveillance under judicial auspices does not necessarily build a safeguard into the system as the following passage reveals:

> In the light of American experience under the Omnibus Crime Control and Safe Streets Act of 1968, Title III, Wiretapping and Electronic Surveillance, which has been substantially plagiarized in our own legislation, one is constrained to be pessimistic: Samuel Dash, counsel to the Senate Watergate Committee, and a recognized expert in this field, said in an address to members of the Ontario Bar, on March 23, 1974, that he was not aware of a single wiretap application which had been refused under Title III. It seems obvious, therefore, that members of the Canadian judiciary must pre-arm themselves with some evidentiary guidelines to be applied on such applications.[108]

What Judge Kileen is indicating in the foregoing quotation is that if procedures evolve to the state that the judicial imprimatur for a wiretap becomes little more than a rubber stamp then the legislative safeguards will have become a mockery, and "de facto" there will exist a situation of police carte blanche.

But other safeguards are built into the present procedures in order to shore up the inherent weaknesses of an "ex parte" procedure initiated at the behest of the police.

Firstly, it should be noted that the authorization for a wiretap must be renewed under the legislation on a fairly short periodic basis (30 days). Presumably on each such instance the presiding justice could require fresh proof substantiating the necessity for the authorization in keeping with the strictures of s. 178.13, namely that such an authorization would be in the interests of justice and

(a) other investigative procedures have been tried and have failed;

(b) other investigative procedures are unlikely to succeed; or

(c) the urgency of the matter is such that it would be impractical to

---

104. *Ibid.* s. 178.16.
105. *Ibid.* s. 178.13(2)(*e*).
106. *Ibid.* s. 178.23.
107. *Ibid.* s. 178.16.
108. G. Kileen, *supra* footnote 96 at p. 105.

carry out the investigation of the offence using only other investigative procedures.[109]

Secondly, by restricting the types of crimes which could validly be the subject of electronic surveillance and by altering the common law position with respect to unlawful behavior by the police (specifically *vis-a-vis* illegally obtained evidence) a substantial degree of "purposive guidance" has been built into the legislation.

Finally, the notification provision offered a public safeguard and removed some of the clandestine and incestuous aspects (the "appearance" of a too close connection between the police and the courts) from the area. An aggrieved party would first of all be aware of the invasion of his privacy and would have available the options of "going public" with his complaint or of seeking redress — both more than nominal deterrents against unfounded or frivolous harrassment.

This is not to say that the legislation is defect-free. Already in the short two year span since its inception a novel form of electronic entrapment has arisen to partially undermine the admissibility provisions of the *Act*. G. Kileen refers to this phenomenon as "the consenting agent provocateur" loophole, and sees the provisions as encouraging the police to use such agents "under a tacit grant of immunity from prosecution".[110] In support of his contention he cites two recent Ontario examples *R. v. Demeter*[111] and *R. v. Elliot.*[112]

Nevertheless, existing defects aside, the present situation seems preferable to that which prevailed prior to the passage of the legislation — some control being preferable to no control at all. Prior to the enactment of the *Protection of Privacy Act* the characteristic response of the courts to challenged interception practices carried on by the police was that in the face of Parliamentary lethargy and disinterest the courts were powerless. Grant J. of the Supreme Court of Ontario in dismissing an application for an order of mandamus requiring the Chief of the Metropolitan Toronto Police Department to desist from wiretap operations in contravention of s. 112 of the *Telephone Act* put the matter in this manner:

> If they [the police] are to be restrained in the use of electronic surveillance of persons suspected of crime, it is Parliament that should prescribe such limitations. The role of the Court is to rule on the

---

109. See also, the *Criminal Code* s. 178.13(3).
110. *Supra* footnote 96 at p. 108 and see s. 178.11(2) which expressly excepts and exempts from the offence of wilful interception anyone who "has the consent to intercept, express or implied, of the originator of the private communication or of the person intended by the originator himself to receive it.
111. (1975) 19 C.C.C. (2d) 321 (Ont.).
112. Unreported, but notorious case sometimes referred to as the "Hamilton Harbour-gate Scandal".

admissibility of evidence so obtained when it is offered during the course of a particular trial.[113]

Before we go too far in congratulating ourselves for even the modest successes which have been achieved in this area it is important to look at the great violence which the Minister of Justice is presently proposing to visit upon the legislation.

What follows is taken from the Minister of Justice's brochure entitled *The Highlights of the Peace and Security Program*:

> After almost two years of experience with the Protection of Privacy Act, some aspects of that law are seriously impairing the effectiveness of the police, particularly in combatting organized crime.
>
> The legislation introduces several changes designed to increase the effectiveness of police use of electronic surveillance, while at the same time maintaining the fundamental protection of the individual's rights to privacy adopted by Parliament in 1974, including the criminal and civil sanctions for the violations of these rights.[114]

Included in the six principal amendments proposed are five substantive measures designed to effectively remove most of the safeguards which had been built into the original legislation:

(1) The courts will be empowered to grant authorization to intercept communications in relation to all indictable offences instead of the limited list of crimes now specified. In addition, any offence, indictable or otherwise, may justify an authorization where it forms part of a pattern of criminal activity of an organized nature;

(2) Evidence derived directly or indirectly from an unlawful interception may be admitted by the court. This restores the common law rule (with respect to illegally obtained evidence) but the unauthorized intercepted communication itself remains inadmissible and the act of 'interception' punishable as a criminal offence. (This is a dubious deterrent in view of the discretionary powers possessed by Crown Attorneys and justices of the peace with respect to the initiation, commencement and termination of proceedings.)

(3) Court authorization for electronic surveillance will be extended from thirty to sixty days.

(4) The requirement to notify the person under surveillance, of this fact will be repealed.

(5) Evidence of an offence other than the one for which the authorization was obtained will be made admissible in prosecuting that other offence.

With respect, the present proposals are patently ridiculous. Furthermore, they demean the judicial process inasmuch as they retain a

---

113. *Re Copeland and Adamson* (1972) 7 C.C.C. (2d) 393 at p. 406 (Ont.).
114. Canada, Department of Justice, *Highlights of the Peace and Security Program* (1976) at p. 5.

system of judicial authorization for electronic surveillance while at the same time removing any possibility of *effective* judicial sanction for unlawful police conduct. They provide an incentive for the police to utilize lawful process where it suits them and to cavalierly disregard it where it does not. Sham procedures to obtain an authorization are likewise encouraged. Fishing expeditions might thus be surrounded by the appearance of legality, and any evidence (no matter how unrelated to the original purpose of the authorization) thus secured might be admissible in subsequent prosecutions of offences allegedly disclosed.

The situation which prevailed prior to the passage of the *Protection of Privacy Act* now, with the benefit of hindsight, seems preferable to that which is presently evolving. Prior to 1974 the police were at least somewhat in doubt as to the legality (or the legal effectiveness) of their ability to spy. Now, or at least in the near future, they will be positively encouraged to do so.

(2) Interrogation

Without the ability to conduct inquiries, to ask questions and to expect a high degree of citizen-cooperation in this aspect of their endeavours, the police would unquestionably be hamstrung in their efforts to conduct a thorough investigation of a complaint.[115] The duty on a citizen to anwer questions, save in certain very limited circumstances, is not a legal duty; it is a moral one. Wells J. of the Ontario High Court is of the opinion that it should remain so:

> Citizens are under a moral obligation, although not a legal duty, to answer questions politely put to them by police officers. However the law should not be changed so that the moral obligation would become a legal duty.[116]

The general public, it is to be assumed, is not aware of this distinction. Ignorance of rights in this regard probably cuts in both directions — some citzens feel that they are under no obligation whatsover, legal or otherwise, to answer police questions, while others undoubtedly feel that they are legally bound to answer a police officer's questions.

It has been said that police questioning is employed in order to achieve two purposes:

(1) To obtain knowledge of facts which may be independently estab-

---

115. See *R. v. Fitton* (1956) 116 C.C.C. 1 at p. 30 (Can.): ". . . it would be quite impossible to discover the facts of a crime without asking questions of persons from whom it was thought that useful information might be obtained."

116. *Report of the Royal Commission of Inquiry Respecting the Arrest and Detention of Rabbi Leiner by the Metropolitan Toronto Police* at p. 69 cited in Honsberger *supra* footnote 82 at p. 31. Note that Wells J. speaks of the moral obligation to answer questions that are *politely* put. Apparently "rudeness and bad language may create a different situation" such that even the moral obligation might disappear. (Report p. 72 and Honsberger at p. 32.)

lished by further investigation and thus may subsequently lead to the arrest of an offender, and may form a part of the proof of guilt offered at trial.

(2) To obtain incriminating statements from the offender himself which may also be offered as proof of his guilt at trial.[117]

It is therefore possible to say that interrogation (especially when coupled with arrest, or the threatened arrest of a suspect) is among the most potent of police powers.

> In the investigation of the commission or alleged commission of an offence, a police officer is entitled to question any person, whether or not the person is suspected, in an endeavour to obtain information with respect to the offence. While the police officer may question, he has no power to compel answers. There is no doubt, however, that a police officer by reason of his position and his right to arrest in certain circumstances, has a power (factual but not legal) to exert very great psychological pressure to obtain answers.[118]

> The citizen, be he suspected or not, when interrogated by the police with a view of obtaining information, is protected from violence or the threatened application of violence or illegal detention only by the general laws which protect every citizen from illegal assaults, unlawful threats and false imprisonment. In legal theory these are the only limitations upon police questioning. A police officer is in breach of no rule of law who uses trickery, fraud, promises or even an aggressive or intimidating manner in the conduct of interrogation to obtain information — provided his conduct does not constitute an assault or unlawful threat — and provided that he does not deprive the citizen of his liberty.[119]

The Ouimet Committee (to whom the above comments are attributable) goes on to state that it "does not doubt . . . that there are considerations other than legal restraints which tend to keep such interrogation within acceptable limits". In support of this contention it puts forward the contention that "abusive or unacceptable practices would lead to loss of confidence in the police and result in loss of community support". Undoubtedly this is a countervailing factor tending to curb some police excesses. However, other factors such as are discussed *infra* in Part 5 of this chapter, work toward the opposite effect.

Since interrogation serves the dual purpose of gathering facts and securing incriminating statements there will routinely be instances when investigating officers will be questioning a person suspected of the crime and not yet charged, or a person who upon initial inquiry does not present himself as a suspect but later attracts suspicion.

---

117. Ouimet Report *supra* footnote 89 at p. 49.

118. *Ibid.* at p. 49.

119. *Ibid.* p. 50.

Channell J. in *R. v. Thayre*[120] described the responsibility of the peace officers in such cases in the following terms:

> I think it is clear that a police officer, or anyone whose duty it is to inquire into alleged offences may question persons likely to be able to give him information, and that, whether he suspects him or not, provided that he has not already made up his mind to take him into custody. *When he has taken anyone into custody, and also before doing so when he has already decided to make the charge, he ought not to question the prisoner.* A magistrate or judge cannot do it, and a police officer certainly has no more right to do so.[121]

These comments gave rise (quite naturally) to the impression that once a police officer had determined to arrest or charge a person that he should desist in questioning that person. This "rule", if it can be so described, was relaxed in time by the addition of the proviso that the police officer might continue his questioning if he first *cautioned* the suspect as to his possible jeopardy.[122] Thus in 1927 Anglin C.J.C. was able to say that "questioning of the accused by the police, if properly conducted and after warning duly given will not *per se* render his statement inadmissible".[123]

In Canada the admissibility of all confessions, inculpatory as well as exculpatory,[124] turns upon the application of this rule pronounced by Lord Sumner in *Ibrahim v. R.*:

> It has long been established as a positive rule of English criminal law, that no statement by an accused is admissible in evidence against him unless it is shewn by the prosecution to have been a voluntary statement, in the sense that it has not been obtained from him either by fear of prejudice or hope of advantage exercised or held by a person in authority.[125]

This rule was adopted in Canada by the Supreme Court of Canada in 1932 in the case of *Prosko v. R.*[126]

"Voluntariness" and its subsidiary considerations of "fear of prejudice" and "hope of advantage" proved in the Canadian jurisprudence

---

120. (1905) 20 Cox C.C. 711.
121. *Ibid*. (emphasis added).
122. In this regard J. Honsberger *supra* footnote 82 at p. 8 refers us to Rule 2 of the English Judge's Rules (1964) (a reproduction of the rules may be found in F. Kaufman, *The Admissibility of Confessions in Criminal Matters* (2nd ed.) (1974), Appendix pp. 269-276.) Rules of the Judges' Rules reads "Whenever a police officer has made up his mind to charge a person with a crime, he should first caution such person before asking him questions, or any further questions as the case may be."
123. *Sankey v. R.* (1927) 48 C.C.C. 97 at p. 101; see also *Posko v. R.* 37 C.C.C. 199 (Can.).
124. See *Piche v. R.* [1971] S.C.R. 23; see also *R. v. Sweezey* (1974) 27 C.R.N.S. 163 (Ont. C.A.).
125. [1914] A.C. 599 at p. 609.
126. *Supra* footnote 123.

to be of far greater import than the mere presence of a warning to a suspect. Numerous examples exist of confessions which have been held to be admissible despite the absence of a caution.[127] As Lawrence J. said in *R. v. Voisin*[128] the caution, or its absence, is but "one of the circumstances which must be taken into consideration" in determining voluntariness and consequent admissibility.

Rand J. in *Boudreau v. R* said:

> It would be a serious error to place the ordinary modes of investigation of crime in a strait jacket of artificial rules; and the true protection against improper interrogation or any kind of pressure or inducement is to leave the broad question to the Court. *Rigid formulas can be both meaningless to the weakling and absurd to the sophisticated or hardened criminal*; and to introduce a new rite as an inflexible preliminary condition would serve no genuine interest of the accused and but add an unreal formalism to that vital branch of the administration of justice.[129]

The fear that the "sophisticated or hardened criminal" might manipulate the circumstances of a possible arrest by refusing the volunteer information if cautioned is an unreal fear. The sophisticated criminal will refuse to volunteer information in *any* circumstance. Left unprotected by the dicta in *Boudreau* are the unsophisticated, the naive, and the ignorant. Procedural fairness is left to reside only with those defendants who have sufficient knowledge of their rights to assert them. A leading American decision dealing with the right to counsel makes this point well:

> The defendant who does not realize his rights under the law and who therefore does not request counsel is the very defendant who most needs counsel. We should not penalize the defendant who, not understanding his legal rights does not make the formal request and by such failure demonstrates his helplessness.[130]

The most widely propounded view of the rationale for the exclusion of confessions which have been held to be involuntary is "that they have the smell of untrustworthiness about them".[131] Wigmore was of

---

127. See *R. v. Fitton* (1956) 116 C.C.C. 1 (Can.); *Prosko v. R.* (1922) 37 C.C.C. 199 (Can); *R. v. Voisin* (1918) 13 C.A.R. 89; *R. v. Theriault* (1953) 17 C.R. 269 (Que. C.A.); *Mitchell v. R.* (1956) 116 C.C.C. 392 (Can.); *R. v. Beddoes* (1952) 103 C.C.C. 131 (Sask. C.A.); *R. v. Johnston* (1948) 91 C.C.C. 59 (Ont. C.A.) and see especially, *Boudreau v. R.* (1949) 7 C.R. 427 (Can.) overruling *Gach v. R.* (1943) 79 C.C.C. 221 at p. 225 (Can.) where Taschereau J. had declared that "there is no doubt that when a person has been arrested all confessions made to a person in authority, as a result of questioning, are inadmissible in evidence, unless proper caution has been given."
128. (1918) 13 Cr.App.Rep. 89.
129. (1949) 7 C.R. 427 at pp. 435-436 (Can.) (emphasis added).
130. *People v. Dorado* 398 P. 2d 361 (1965).
131. S. Bushnell, "The Confession Rule: Its Rationale (A Survey)" (1973) 12 West.L.R. 47 at p. 53.

the opinion that the "ground of distrust of confessions made in certain situation is, in a rough and indefinite way, judicial experience":[132]

> Under certain stresses a person, especially one of defective mentality or peculiar temperament, may falsely acknowledge guilt. This possibility arises whenever the innocent person is placed in such a situation that the *untrue* acknowledgement of guilt is at the time the more promising of two alternatives between which he is obliged to choose: that is, he chooses any risk that may be in *falsely* acknowledging guilt in preference to some worse alternative associated with silence.[133]

Lord Sumner in *Ibrahim* preferred not to say that the law "presumed" involuntary statements to be "untrue" but that the "dangers" inherent in receiving such statements had rendered it preferable, in the interests of the "due administration of justice", to exclude them.[134]

"Untrustworthiness" and a concern for the "due administration of justice" are both cogent reasons for insisting upon procedural fairness at even the earliest stages of police investigation.

Fundamental fairness would seem to require that an individual in possible conflict with the law would, at an early stage, be informed of his basic rights in order that the appearance of justice be maintained. Rights which disappear in the absence of invocation, or which are hidden behind a veil of secrecy cannot be regarded as rights at all.

In England the Judges' Rules, and in America the *Miranda*[135] and *Escobedo*[136] rules, insist upon a modicum of police propriety in this regard. The accused must be advised that he has a right to remain silent in the face of police questioning, and that he has a right to the assistance of counsel without delay.[137]

The English rule-making approach in practice is quite different from the American "constitutional" approach.

The Judges' Rules in England do not have the force of law. Their significance was expressed by A. T. Lawrence J. in the course of giving judgment in *R. Voisin*:[138]

> These rules have not the force of law; they are administrative directions the observance of which the police authorities should enforce upon

---

132. Wigmore, *Evidence* (3rd ed.) (1940) s. 822, p. 246 cited in Bushnell, *supra* at p. 53.
133. *Ibid.*
134. *Supra* footnote 125 at p. 611.
135. *Miranda v. Arizona* (1966) 384 U.S. 436.
136. *Escobedo v. Illinois* (1964) 378 U.S. 478.
137. For comparisons of the Canada/U.S./England experiences with protecting the right to counsel see: "Developments in the Law Confessions" (1966) 79 Harv. L. Rev. 935 B.A. Grossman, "The Right to Counsel in Canada" (1967) 10 C.B.J. 189; Waldbilling, "Symposium on Legal Aid" 30 Sask. B.R. 85; B. Donnelly, "Right to Counsel" (1968-69) 11 Cr.L.Q. 18; *Ouimet Report, supra* footnote 89 at pp. 49-54 and pp. 140-155; *J. Marshall,* 'Denial of Counsel at Police Investigation" (1965) 23 U.T.F.L.R. 117.
138. *Supra* footnote 128.

their subordinates as tending to the fair administration of justice. It is important that they should do so, for statements obtained from prisoners contrary to the spirit of these rules, *may be rejected* as evidence by the judge presiding at the trial.[139]

The American approach as expressed by the decisions in *Miranda* and *Escobedo* does not allow the ultimate decision respecting admissibility to remain in the realm of judicial discretion. Derogation from the court's strictures as enunciated in those two leading decisions *mandatorily* results in the exclusion of the evidence thus secured.

The Canadian attitude differs markedly in contrast to both the English and the American orientations. In Canada "the broad question as to whether a statement has been made voluntarily must be decided by the court unfettered by a set of predetermined rules".[140]

Consquently it has been stated, probably accurately that "on the whole, there is probably little question that the police in Canada are less restricted than in many other common law countries."[141] One Canadian commentator summed up this country's present circumstance thusly:

> Canadian courts have, in general, not discouraged questioning by the police: "It would be a lamentable thing, if the police were not allowed to make inquiries, and if statements made by prisoners were excluded because of a shadowy notion that if the prisoners were left to themselves they would not have made them." Chief Justice Campbell of Prince Edward Island had this to say: "[*During the investigation phase*] *the police are allowed a considerable degree of latitude*. Third degree methods, of course, are never encouraged in British police work but *the police may examine and cross-examine, and within proper limits threaten and hold out inducements* — one restriction on such legitimate methods of enquiry being unless information elicited is in the nature of a voluntary statement by the person giving it, then it is not admissible in evidence as a confession. In other words, a witness (other than the accused person) from whom information is elicited by express or implied threats, express or implied inducements, may be called as a witness in a criminal trial to substantiate the information which he has given to the police. [After a person has been charged, then] if any prospective statement is sought to be used against the person making the statement, it must be borne in mind that the onus will be on the prosecution which tenders the statement to establish its voluntary character to the satisfaction of the presiding judge.
>
> *Few will take issue with the proposition that the police should ask questions while in the process of investigating a crime, but where the line is drawn by many is when the person is in custody because of*

---

139. *Ibid.* at p. 96 (emphasis added). For a discussion of the history and significance of the Rules see, Kaufman, *supra* footnote 122 at pp. 97-101.
140. Ouimet Report, *supra* footnote 89 at p. 51.
141. "Developments in the Law: Confessions" (1966) Harv. L. Rev. 935 at p. 1106.

suspicion of committing a crime, or the person actually charged with the crime in issue is questioned. There was probably a great deal of truth in Pound's statement that questioning is associated with torture in the minds of many people. One remembers Stephens' statement: "It is pleasanter to sit comfortably in the shade rubbing pepper into a poor devil's eyes than to go about in the sun hunting up evidence."[142]

The concluding remarks above indicate that the simplest road to securing a conviction is the presence of an admission of guilt from the accused himself. The remarks point out an inherent danger in the Canadian approach to the admissibility of confessions: namely, the danger that police efforts might, in view of our comparatively relaxed standard, be directed towards "extracting" a confession (the use of the coercive verb is deliberate) rather than towards the carrying out of solid investigative work—it being easier to pursue the former tack "than to go about in the sun hunting up evidence".

Lest this tableau of the Canadian judicial approach to the scrutiny of police-obtained confessions appear distorted attention should also focus upon the fact that many controverted confessions are rejected due to shortcomings in police conduct; shortcomings which relate to the right to be made aware of one's potential jeopardy, the right to counsel, or the right to remain silent.

The law is not uniform as to whether or not the explicit denial of the right to counsel by police authorities will render inadmissible a confession otherwise properly obtained. The *Canadian Bill of Rights* specifically declares that no law of Canada shall be construed or applied so as to "deprive a person who has been arrested or detained . . . of the right to retain and instruct counsel without delay".[143] However, in *R. v. Steeves*[144] it was held that the operation of the *Bill of Rights* does not render a confession inadmissible where an accused was not permitted to have his solicitor present during his interrogation. Authority for the contrary point of view is to be found in the strongly worded judgment of Freedman J.A. of the Manitoba Court of Appeal in *R. v. Ballegeer.*[145] As the learned Justice of Appeal noted "the facts surrounding this aspect of the case [the denial of the right to counsel] are disturbing to anyone who prizes the rights of individual liberty in a free society":[146]

> The sorry episode which occurred here, in denial of the civil rights of the accused, may now be described:
>
> Shortly after 9:00 p.m. on Friday, June 21st, two constables of the

---

142. S. Bushnell, *supra* footnote 131 at p. 56 (emphasis added).
143. R.S.C. 1970, Appendix III s. 2(c)(ii).
144. [1964] C.C.C. 266 (N.S. C.A.). See also *O'Connor v. R.* [1966] 4 C.C.C. 342 (Can.) and see *R. v. Emele* [1940] 3 D.L.R. 758 (Sask. C.A.).
145. (1969) 1 D.L.R. (3d) 74 (Man. C.A.); see also *Richard v. R.* (1957) 126 C.C.C. 255 (N.B. C.A.).
146. *R. v. Ballegeer, ibid.* at p. 76.

R.C.M.P. came to the Remote Weather Observation Site of the Department of Transport at the City of Winnipeg where the accused was employed as a meteorological technician. They informed the accused that he was being charged with break, enter, and theft. He asked to be allowed to make a telephone call to his lawyer. It may be noted that there was a telephone in the adjoining room. His request was refused. Here unquestionably was a patent and deliberate denial to the accused of a legal right . . . [Subsequently, while] the constables were talking with [another] employee the accused went into the adjoining office and, without the knowledge of the constables, placed a call to his lawyer.[147]

While this telephone conversation was in progress one of the constables came into the room and demanded the telephone. Ballegeer complied with the constable's request. His lawyer's affidavit, filed with the Court of Appeal, sets out the ensuing events:

I discussed bail with Constable Taylor and then asked to again speak to Ballegeer. Constable Taylor refused saying he wanted to get a statement first and get the tires back. I told Constable Taylor that I wanted to advise Ballegeer not to make a statement until I could talk to him but Taylor refused. I asked Taylor to relay my advice to Ballegeer but he said he would not do so.[148]

The incident met with a strong rebuke in the Manitoba Court of Appeal:

Here is a spectacle of a police officer wilfully, and alas successfully, *frustrating the due process of law*. What the constable did was wrong and unjustifiable, and his conduct cannot receive the sanction of the Court.[149]

Ballegeer appears to stand for the proposition that violations of the rights accorded under the *Bill of Rights* and "enshrined in English common law" will not be sustained by resort to the ordinary controlling tests of *Ibrahim* and *Boudreau*.[150] However, since the case was decided in 1969 the validity of the proposition has not been tested in other courts.

This is possibly due to the fact that many lawyers have yet to

---

147. *Ibid.* at p. 76.
148. *Ibid.* at p. 77.
149. *Ibid* at p. 77 (emphasis added).
150. *Ibid* at p. 76: "Among these is assuredly the right, on being arrested or detained, to retain and instruct counsel without delay. This is a right enshrined in English common law, vindicated by many judicial decisions of high authority, and unmistakably affirmed in the *Canadian Bill of Rights* 1960 (Can.) c. 44, s. 2(c)(ii)."
     See also, Kaufman, *supra* footnote 122 at pp. 107-110 especially p. 107 where *Brownridge v. R.* (1972) 18 C.R.N.S. 308 (Can.) is discussed: "At present, refusal to permit an accused to consult counsel is 'cogent' proof on the voir dire, but no more. *Brownridge* may possibly change that".

realize that the police have no right to bar them access to an accused or suspect "until the investigation is complete". This remains the case irrespective of whether the lawyer is first retained by the accused himself or, (more likely) by a friend or relative calling at the behest of an accused who has been swept away by the police before being accorded an opportunity to engage counsel.[151] The police are not justified in barring counsel from the interview room *even* if they fear that the only advice counsel will give to his client is to tell him to invoke the right to remain silent, and to say nothing.

Very few affidavits of the type filed by the lawyer, Brock, in *Ballegeer* find their way before the courts although, there is reason to believe that the situation which prevailed in *Ballegeer* is not unique.

It can be stated without reservation that the accused has a right to be informed of the charge which he is likely to be facing in order that he might be able to reasonably assess the full extent of his present jeopardy. This will not spare him from the consequences of a confession or admission volunteered before questioning or arrest,[152] or of one made upon arrest.[153] The general consideration still governs: the presence, or absence, of a caution is only one of the circumstances to be considered in determining whether a confession is to be deemed voluntary, and thus, admissible.

A confession volunteered when being questioned on extraneous or unrelated matters has been held to be admissible.[154] But some of the cases indicate that where a caution has been given with respect to possible jeopardy on a relatively minor charge and this is done as a ruse to gain inculpatory admissions to form the basis of a greater charge then the confession thus obtained must be rejected.[155]

---

151. In 1955, the Toronto Police Department acting on the advice of counsel actually took the position at an inquiry before Mr. Justice Roach "In the Matter of an Investigation into the Arrest and Detention of Robert Wright and Michael Griffin" that the police were entitled to refuse counsel access to his client until the police investigation was complete" provided that it is completed in a reasonable time". The Department explained its position by stating that its fear was that counsel might obstruct justice by telling his client not to say anything to the police. Roach J.A. disabused the Department of these in strong terms: "The suggestion that any detective or other police officer is justified in preventing or attempting to prevent a prisoner from conferring with his counsel is a shocking one. The suggestion that counsel, if he is permitted to confer with his client who is in custody, might thereby obstruct the police in the discharge of their duties is even more shocking. The prisoner is not obliged to say anything and the lawyer is entitled to advise him of that right." Excerpts of this report are to be found in Honsberger, *supra* footnote 82 at pp. 55-57.

152. See *Dupuis v. R.* (1952) 104 C.C.C. 290 (Can.).

153. *R. v. Davis* (1959) 123 C.C.C. 242 (Ont. C.A.).

154. *R. v. Wolbaum* [1965] 3 C.C.C. 191 (Sask. C.A.).

155. *R. v. Dick* (1947) 87 C.C.C. 101 (Ont. C.A.). See also *R. v. Deagle* (1947) 88 C.C.C. 247 (Alta. C.A.); and *R. v. Bird* [1967] 1 C.C.C. 33 (Sask.).

Most studies of the law respecting confessions tend to concentrate their analyses in the area of which kinds of police activity will be sufficient to render a confession involuntary and inadmissible.[156] It is however at least equally important to bear in mind the very wide latitude which has been accorded to the police in this area.

In point of fact at present an accused need not be informed that he has a right to counsel and to remain silent when being questioned by the police. *Within limits,* the accused, who may well be unaware of those basic rights, may be examined and cross-examined by police officers, he may be tricked or induced into making a statement; he may be interrogated while drunk; he may be questioned several times and make several statements; he may be held incommunicado. The "limits" upon such police conduct are not precise, and do not, in the light of the reported decisions, appear to be evolving with precision. The police are not aided, in their task by a set of administrative directions such as the English Judges' Rules. Neither are they under the mandatory aegis of the kind of strictures which exist in the United States. Instead, the entire matter rests rather delicately on the thin edge of a judicial discretion which, of necessity, may only be directed to a consideration of evidence emanating from the highly controlled and secretive environment of the squad car and the station house.

(3) Identification procedures

A citizen need not identify himself to the police.[157] However, in so acting an individual may invite his own arrest. Mere suspicion is not a sufficient basis for use of the arrest power, but where other reasonable and probable grounds exist the police will be justified in their use of the arrest power. As Lord Devlin once observed:

---

156. The subject of "confessions" has been much discussed in the literature. In the Cr.L.Q. see A. Cooper, "The Admissibility of Confessions" (Vol. 1, p. 46); N. Borins, "Confessions" (Vol. 1, p. 140); S. Ryan, "Involuntary Confessions" (Vol. 2, p. 389); H. W. McInnes, "Statements to Police by Accused Persons (Vol. 5, p. 14); G. A. Martin, "The Admissibility of Confessions and Statements" (Vol. 5, p. 35); C. C. Savage, "Admissions in Criminal Cases" (Vol. 5, p. 49); L. K. Graburn, "Truth as the Criterion of the Admissibility of Confessions" (Vol. 5, p. 415); Wittfox, "Confessions by Juveniles (Vol. 5, p. 459); C. O. D. Branson, "When is a Confession Not a Confession?" (Vol. 12, p. 133); E. J. Ratushny, "Statements of an Accused: Some Loose Strands" I and II (Vol. 14, pp. 306 and 425). See also Bushnell, *supra* footnote 131; D. W. Roberts, "The Legacy of *Regina v. Wray* (1972) 50 Can.Bar.Rev. 19; The standard work remains, F. Kaufman, *The Admissibility of Confessions in Criminal Matters* (2nd ed.) (1974) with a useful recent supplement provided by P. K. McWilliams in *Canadian Criminal Evidence* (1974) Chapter 14 "Confessions".

157. *Koechlin v. Waugh* (1957) 118 C.C.C. 24 (Ont. C.A.); *R. v. Carroll* (1960) 126 C.C.C. 19 (Ont. C.A.). See also the discussion of the arrest power *infra*.

> Anyone who is innocent must recognize a strong moral duty to assist the police by giving all the information in his power, and anyone who is guilty must appear to accept the same duty if he wishes to be thought innocent.[158]

A suspect will either assist the police voluntarily or his cooperation will be enlisted through the use of the arrest power.

Determining whether one who is suspected is *actually* the man responsible for a crime is often not an easy task. While often there are eye-witnesses to a given offence the opinion expressed by such a witness that a particular suspect "is the man" ultimately is only an *opinion.*

> A positive statement "that is the man" when rationalized, is found to be an opinion and not a statement of single fact. All a witness can say is, that because of this or that he remembers about a person, he is of the opinion that person is "the man". A witness recognizes a person because of a certain personality that person has acquired in the eyes of the witness. That personality is reflected by characteristics of the person, which, when associated with something in the mind of the witness, causes the latter to remember that person in a way the witness does not remember any other person.[159]

Eye-witness testimony unsupported and alone "amounts to little more than speculative opinion or unsubstantial conjecture, and at its strongest is a most insecure basis upon which to found that abiding and moral assurance of guilt necessary to eliminate reasonable doubt."[160]

The dangers inherent in founding a case primarily upon eye-witness identification evidence has been a source of continuing concern to Canadian courts, particularly in jury trials. Accordingly the Ontario Court of Appeal in a series of cases in 1970[161] evolved the principle that in cases "where identification is a substantial issue, the jury's attention . . . 'should be called in general terms to the fact that in a number of instances such identification has proved erroneous, to the possibilities of mistake in the case before them, and to the necessity of caution'."[162]

---

158. The quotation is extracted from J. Honsberger *supra* footnote 82 at p. 33.
159. *R. v. Browne* (1951) 99 C.C.C. 141 at p. 147 *per O'Halloran* J.A. (B.C. C.A.). See also *R. v. Harrison* [1951] 100 C.C.C. 143 (B.C. C.A.); *R. v. Yates* (1946) 85 C.C.C. 334 (B.C. C.A.).
160. *R. v. Smith* [1952] O.R. 432 at p. 436 *per* MacKay J.A. (Ont. C.A.).
161. *R. v. Sutton* (1970) 9 C.R.N.S. 45 (Ont. C.A.); *R. v. Spatola* (1970) 10 C.R.N.S. 143 (Ont. C.A.); *R. v. Howarth* (1970) 13 C.R.N.S. 329 (Ont. C.A.).
162. *R. v. Howarth* 13 C.R.N.S. 329 at p. 331 *per* Jessusp J.A. Note that the principle which evolved was not so strict as to require the Judge in every case to charge the jury in specific and unvarying words. This matter was clarified by the Ontario Court of Appeal in *R. v. Olbey* (1971) 13 C.R.N.S. 316 at p. 327 *per* McKay J.A., "Without derogating in any way from the principle and in identification cases the trial judge should carefully charge the jury on those matters which, *in the circumstances of the particular case,* should receive their anxious consideration in deciding whether

P. K. McWilliams, in his text on *Canadian Criminal Evidence* (1974) sets out the following as "fundamental factors" affecting the weight of eye-witness evidence:[163]

(1) Opportunity to observe, *i.e.,* the duration of the observation, light conditions, the distance from the witness to the object or person observed, the eyesight of the witness, color perception.

(2) Lapse of time since the observation.

(3) Previous acquaintance by eye-witness with accused.

(4) Presence or absence of distinctive features or appearance of the accused.

Naturally, given the inherent frailty of identification evidence the police will be anxious to procure a positive identification of the accused as "the man" at a reasonably early date; one as close as possible to the date of the actual event. Identification by a witness of the accused long after the event carries little weight. Similarly, identification of the accused by the witness for the first time when the accused is in the prisoner's dock is also treated as insubstantial.[164]

Therefore, where eye-witnesses are available and a suspect has been arrested the police will usually at the first practical opportunity attempt to determine whether the eye-witness agrees that the right man has in fact been apprehended. To accomplish this purpose either an identification parade (or line-up) will be held; or, a photograph of the accused will be shown to the witness. Certain basic standards of fairness are said to regulate these procedures.

There is no statutory or other authority to compel a person who is suspected, or even one who has been charged, to participate in a police line-up. However, it has recently been held that evidence of a refusal to participate in a line-up is admissible as a circumstance that the jury is entitled to take into consideration. The significance of such a refusal is a matter to be decided by the jury on the totality of evidence.[165] The Ontario Court of Appeal with only three members presiding on this important issue, was divided in its opinion. Brooke J.A. dissented strongly. His reasons for so dissenting were directed primarily at the danger of diluting the privilege against self-crimination. The learned Justice of Appeal noted that evidence that an accused refused to perform sobriety tests has been held to be inadmissible in impaired driving

they will accept the identification evidence, the weight of authority is against the necessity of a particular form of words, general or specific, failure to use which form will result in a new trial."

See also *R. v. McCallum* (1971) 4 C.C.C. (2d) 116 (B.C. C.A.).

163. P. K. McWilliams, *Canadian Criminal Evidence* (1974) at p. 294.

164. See *R. v. Louie* (1960) 129 C.C.C. 336 (B.C. C.A.) and *R. v. Browne supra* footnote 159.

165. *R. v. Marcoux* (No 2) (1974) 13 C.C.C. (2d) 309 (Ont. C.A.), affirmed on appeal by (1976) 24 C.C.C. (2d) 1 (Can.).

prosecutions for this reason.[166] Similarly, it is misdirection for a trial Judge to direct a jury to draw whatever inference it might from the accused's silence in the face of a warning that he need not say anything.[167] In particular, the learned judge buttressed his arguments with these remarks of Walsh J. in *R. v. Whittaker*:

> There has long been and still is a rule that an accused person is not bound to criminate himself. There are authorities for instance which hold that he cannot be compelled in Court or out of it to submit his foot for comparison with a footprint, or to expose to the Court his hand or other portion of his body as evidence of its condition for the purpose of identification or to write his name. This privilege extends to him however as an accused person and not as a witness.[168]

Marcoux v. R. was appealed to the Supreme Court of Canada and the decision below was affirmed in a unanimous decision of the full bench. *Marcoux v. R.*[169] deals a fairly stunning blow to the rights of an accused during the early investigative stages of criminal proceedings. "Normal" police identification procedure is described (apart from identification with the aid of photographs) to be one of two types:

(1) the show-up—of a single suspect[170]

(2) the line-up—presentation of the suspect as part of a group.

Marcoux had refused a line-up. A show-up (presumably also without his consent) followed. There is nothing in any of the judgments to indicate that Marcoux was *advised* that if he refused to participate in a line-up then he would merely be "shown" to the witness (who would then be asked whether Marcoux was the man).

As Professor Glanville Williams has observed in his essay on "Identification Parades—I":[171]

> If the suspect objects the police will merely have him "identified" by showing him to the witness and asking the witness whether he is the man. Since this is obviously far more dangerous to the accused than taking part in a parade, the choice of a parade is almost always accepted.[172]

---

166. *R. v. Shaw* (1964), 43 C.R. 388 (B.C. C.A.). See also *R. v. Brager* (1965) 47 C.R. 264 (B.C. C.A.).

167. *R. v. Cripps* (1968) 3 C.R.N.S. 367 (B.C. C.A.); *R. v. Ryan* (1964) 50 Cr.App.Rep. 44.

168. (1924) 42 C.C.C. 162 at p. 168.

169. (1976) 24 C.C.C. (2d) 1 (Can.).

170. A variant on this identification procedure is the phenomenon of "dock identification": R. Carter, "Identificaton Evidence" in Salhany and Carter, *Studies in Canadian Criminal Evidence* (1972) p. 247 at p. 252 "Occasionally a witness identifies an accused for the first time when the accused is standing in the prisoner's dock or when he is brought to the witness for the purpose of ascertaining whether or not the witness can recognize the accused. Either procedure is completely wrong and any purported identification rendered valueless."

171. [1963] Crim.L.R. 479.

172. *Ibid.* at pp. 480-481.

Marcoux v. R. is yet another example of the judicial reluctance in Canada to formulate fair and workable standards and guidelines for police to regulate their early investigative encounters with suspected persons. (Others which come to mind are the failure to place an onus upon the police to advise a suspect of his right to remain silent and of his right to retain and instruct counsel without delay.) There is only the vaguest suggestion in the case that an accused "might" be advised of the consequences of non-participation in a line-up. As has been mentioned in the case itself it appears that Marcoux was *not* so advised.

(Dickson J. even goes so far as to suggest in *obiter* that the police might, with the court's consent, go so far as to *"force"* the accused to take part in a line-up.)[173]

Although the decision in *Marcoux* fails to promulgate standards for police identification procedures it does appear to stand as authority for the following propositions:

(1) A line-up and a show-up are both acceptable police identification procedures.
(2) A line-up is to be preferred to a show-up and the police may be justified in the use of "reasonable force".
(3) The privilege against self-crimination is not violated by a police line-up. That privilege extends to the accused "qua" witness, not "qua" accused, and is concerned with testimonial compulsion specifically, and not with compulsion generally.
(4) Evidence of the offer and refusal of a line-up will *not* be relevant and admissible in every case. Normally, such evidence should not be tendered; the danger being that it may impinge upon the presumption of innocence (the jury may gain the impression that there is a duty upon the accused to prove that he is innocent). In this case the evidence was admissible by virtue of an "intemperate and, in the circumstances, unwarranted attack upon police procedures" by defence counsel.

It is respectfully submitted that a "show-up" should never be regarded as an acceptable police identification procedure. A witness surely must be compromised when led to a room containing only a single detained occupant. The deduction that "this is the man that the police suspect" is an obvious and irresistible one.[174] Subsequent identi-

---

173. "The extent of the right of the police to force a subject to take part in a line-up against his will does not, of course, squarely arise in this case, as the police accepted Marcoux' refusal, and indeed the question will usually be of very little practical importance, as the introduction of a struggling suspect into a line-up might make a farce of any line-up procedure" (*Marcoux, supra,* footnote 169 at p. 8 *per* Dickson J.).

174. See *R. v. Smierciak* (1947) 87 C.C.C. 175 at p. 177 (Ont. C.A.): "Submitting a prisoner alone for scrutiny after arrest is unfair and unjust". See also *R. v. Goldhar* (1941) 76 C.C.C. 270 (Ont. C.A.) and *R. v. Armstrong* (1959) 125 C.C.C. 56 (B.C. C.A.).

fication (such as is necessary at trial) can only leave the impression that the witness has identified the accused from a recollection of events at the station house rather than from an accurate remembrance of the event itself.

The "show-up" offends against fundamental fairness and is destructive of the notion of due process. *Stovall v. Denno*[175] a leading American decision states a standard which is meaningful in this context although the comments are directed towards unregulated or unfairly regulated line-ups.

> The [pretrial] confrontation conducted in this case was so unnecessarily suggestive and conductive to irreparable mistaken identification that [defendant] was denied due process of law.[176]

A test which seeks to examine identification procedures to see whether or not they are "unnecessarily suggestive and conducive to irreparable mistaken identification" seems desirable for Canada. Given the present prevailing practices with respect to police line-ups in many jurisdictions of this country a citizen might be well-advised to decline an offer to participate in a line-up. The English Royal Commission on Police Parades[177] outlined a practice for identification line-ups which at least two respected commentators[178] have thought would be salutary for the Canadian practice. C. Dubin, one of these commentators, interlaced his outline of the suggested British practice with observations on the Canadian practice in 1955. For the most part those observations remain valid today:

> I think the best statement of what should be done in the line-up is to be found by the report of the Royal Commission on Police Parades which is found in *Wigmore on Evidence* in Volume III. In 1929 a Commission was appointed and one of the matters that they reported on was the present practice in England of the identification line-ups. I will just read briefly from that practice:
>
> > "In arranging for a personal identification, every precaution should be taken (a) to exclude any suspicion of unfairness or risk of erroneous identification through the witness' attention being directed to the suspected person in particular instead of indifferently to all the persons paraded, and (b) to make sure that the witness' ability to recognize the accused has been fairly and adequately tested."
>
> These are the important factors which unfortunately are not adhered to in our practice:
>
> > "(i) The arrangements for an 'identification parade' should be made by an officer other than the officers in charge of the case against the

---

175. 388 U.S. 293 (1967).
176. *Ibid.* at pp. 301-302. See also *People v. Ballott* (1967) 20 N.Y. (2d) 600.
177. Found in *Wigmore on Evidence* Volume III.
178. See C. Dubin, "Identification Procedures and Police Line-ups" (1955) L.S.U.C. Special Lectures 329; and N. Borins, "Police Investigation and the Rights of the Accused" (1963) L.S.U.C. Special Lectures 59.

prisoner. There is no objection, however, to the officer in charge of the case being present."

With respect, that is not the practice which generally prevails in this province. Most of the time the officer who arranges the line-up is the officer in the case.

"(ii) The witnesses should be prevented from seeing the prisoner before he is paraded with other persons and have no assistance from photographs or descriptions.

(iii) The accused should be placed among persons who are as far as possible of the same age, height, general appearance and position in life."

Of course, you can't find anybody who looks just like the accused but most of the time you can pick him out without knowing what the matter is about because he looks often so different from the others in the line-up. Frequently the others are police rookeys or of a smart appearance.

"(iv) The accused should be allowed to select his own position in the line, and should be expressly asked if he has any objection to the persons present with him or arrangements made. If he desires to have his solicitor or a friend present at the identification, this should be allowed.

(v) The witnesses should be introduced one by one and on leaving should not be allowed to communicate with witnesses still waiting to see the persons paraded, and the accused should be allowed, if he so desires, on being informed of his right, to change his position after each witness has left.

(vi) All unauthorized persons should be strictly excluded from the place where the 'identification parade' is held.

(vii) Every circumstance connected with the identification should be correctly recorded by the officer conducting it, whether the accused or any other person is identified or not."

.   .   .

The Commission recommended that the officer in charge of the case should not be present at all of the police line-ups, and secondly, that the fact that a witness who attends an identification parade has previously picked out a picture of the accused, should be stated in evidence of the police in court. You can see the rigid control that it was endeavoured to bring in by that procedure and that type of practice. I think that is essential before you can safely say that a police line-up has some greater weight than other identification procedures that I have already mentioned.[179]

Where the accused refuses to participate in a police line-up it is suggested that the desirable practice is to establish identification through the use of photographs. This avenue will be readily available in most instances by virtue of the provisions of the *Identification of*

---

179. C. Dubin, *ibid.* at pp. 334-336. See also R. J. Carter, "Identification Evidence" in Salhany and Carter *Studies in Canadian Criminal Evidence* p. 247 at p. 255.

Criminals Act,[180] which allow for the photographing and fingerprinting of accused persons.[181]

Showing a witness a single photograph is equally objectionable as showing him a single suspect under a show-up procedure.[182] The danger to be avoided in both instances is that the witness will be influenced by the memory of the single photograph or the single accused when called upon to testify as to identification at the subsequent trial.

> Where identity is an issue great care must be taken to ensure that a witness who is called to identify the criminal does so without assistance or suggestion from the police or anyone else and that his conclusion is independent. This applies equally to the identification by means of a series of photographs or an album or by means of a line-up.[183]

The use of photographs is an indispensable investigatory tool. Consequently the courts have acknowledged the use of photographs as essential to the discovery of the identity of criminals. At the same time vigilance over the *proper* use of photographs is recognized as being necessary in order to insure fairness to the accused. One black man's picture placed within a series of photographs of white men is patently absurd, and if undetected, undoubtedly prejudicial, yet actual examples of such dubious techniques do exist both with respect to the use of photographs as well as in line-up procedures.[184]

The courts have established that it is permissible for a police officer who is in doubt upon the question as to who shall be arrested for a particular offence "to show a photograph to another person in order to obtain information or a clue upon that matter".[185] However it is *not* permissible for a police officer to show beforehand, to persons who are afterwards called as identifying witnesses, photographs of the persons whom they are about to be asked to identify in a line-up.[186]

---

180. R.S.C. (1970) Chap. I-1.
181. Note that the statute itself does not authorize photography. However Orders-in-Council have perfected the scheme of the Act and thus allow for the photographing of an accused. See N. Borins, *supra* footnote 178 at p. 72.
182. See *R. v. Smierciak* (1947) 87 C.C.C. 175 (Ont. C.A.) and the cases cited therein: *R. v. Dwyer* (1924) 18 Cr.App.Rep. 145; *R. v. Melany* (1924) 18 Cr.App.Rep. 2; *R. v. Watson* (1944) 81 C.C.C. 212 (Ont. C.A.); *R. v. Bagley* [1926] 2 W.W.R. 513 (B.C. C.A.); *R. v. Goldhar* (1941) 76 C.C.C. 270 (Ont. C.A.); see also *R. v. Babb* (1972) 17 C.R.N.S. 366 (B.C. C.A.).
183. P. K. McWilliams, *supra* footnote 163 at p. 296.
184. See Wall, *Eye Witness Identification in Criminal Cases* at p. 53. "In a Canadian case . . . the defendant had been picked out of a line up of six men, of which he was the only Oriental' (quoted in *Wigmore* (Chadbourn Revision) Volume III at p. 207.). See also *R. v. Armstrong* (1959) 125 C.C.C. 56 (B.C. C.A.); and *R. v. Opalchuk* (1958) 122 C.C.C. 85 (Ont.) for similar abuses of *line-up* procedure.
185. *R. v. Dwyer, supra* footnote 182 at p. 147 *per* Lord Hewart C.J.
186. See *R. v. Dwyer, supra* footnote 182; also *R. v. Hayduk* (1935) 64 C.C.C. 194 (Man. C.A.); *R. v. Haslam* (1925) 19 Cr.App.Rep. 59; *R. v. Goldhar supra* footnote 182; *Sutton v. R.* (1970) 9 C.R.N.S. 45 (Ont. C.A.); see

Roberston J.A. condemned the practice of using photographs before conducting a line-up in *R. v. Goldhar:*

> While no doubt it is often necessary to assist police in their search that photographs should be exhibited to someone who may be able to pick out a photograph of the person to be sought for, there is always risk that thereafter the person who has seen the photograph will have stamped upon his memory the face he has seen in the photograph, rather than the face he saw on the occasion of the crime. The usefulness of such a person as a witness may thereafter be seriously impaired, as was pointed out by the Court of Criminal Appeal in England in *R. v. Dwyer,* [1925] 2 K.B. 799. It is important that trial Judges, as well as police, should have this in mind.[187]

Where there are several eye-witnesses to be consulted on the issue of identification it has been held to be improper for the police to show a series of photographs to these witnesses together. This is to avoid the danger of an opinion expressed by one of the witnesses affecting the deliberations of the other witnesses.[188]

One problem that is frequently encountered in the taking of, and in the subsequent use of photographs is that the "mug shot" format or the manner of mounting may at trial convey to the jury the impression that the accused has a criminal record.[189] (He may not. Under the *Identification of Criminals Act* the suspect may be photographed once *charged.* There is no provision for the destruction of such a photographic record upon conviction.) That such an impression will be conveyed in many cases would appear to be unavoidable. However, the impact of such presentation of evidence can be minimized if the courts choose to play a supervisory role by insisting upon the editing or "cropping" of the photographs if the format selected by the police presenting the evidence too overtly suggests the existence of a criminal record.[190]

Robertson C.J.O. affirmed in *R. v. Watson* that "within proper limits, the use of photographs is not only helpful to the administration of justice but is often indispensable". But, the Chief Justice did not allow these remarks to stand unqualified:

---

also, *Nepton v. R.* (1971) 15 C.R.N.S. 145 at p. 146 (Que. C.A.) and note the useful suggestion of Hyde J.A.: "I offer the suggestion that the police should adopt the practice which I have noted in some instances of photographing so that there could be no dispute as to its composition."

187. *R. v. Goldhar, supra* footnote 182 at p. 271.
188. See *R. v. Armstrong* (1959) 125 C.C.C. 56 (B.C. C.A.).
189. See *R. v. Dean* (1942) 77 C.C.C. 13 (Ont. C.A.); *R. v. McLaren* (1935) 63 C.C.C. 257 (Alta. C.A.).
190. The courts perform similar editing functions with respect to statements containing extraneous or prejudicial irrelevancies. (See *Beatty v. R.* (1944) 81 C.C.C. 1 (Can.); *R. v. Mazerall* (No. 1) (1946) 2 C.R. 1 (Ont.); and *R. v. Kanester* [1966] 4 C.C.C. 231). See also, the dissent of Lebel J.A. in *R. v. Simpson* (1959) 124 C.C.C. 129 (Ont. C.A.).

It requires constant watchfulness on the part of trial Judges and Magistrates, and of Crown counsel as well, to see that nothing unfair to an accused person is done, or is stated in evidence, in connection with the use of photographs for purposes of identification.[191]

The police are not entitled to photograph a suspect without his consent before he has been arrested.[192] Presumably the police may not even photograph an accused *after* his arrest if the charge involved is merely a summary conviction offence.[193] However, the unlawful photographing of a suspect is not likely to incur judicial wrath. Nor is it likely to result in the inadmissibility of evidence gathered through the subsequent use of the photographs.[194] The rule respecting such evidence remains as stated by the Supreme Court of Canada in *R. v. Wray,*[195] and if relevant it will be admitted.

As is evident, the powers of the police to employ identification procedures such as line-ups and the use of photographs is relatively unfettered. The decision of the Supreme Court in *Marcoux v. R.* appears to have enlarged the scope of what was already, in practice, an exceedingly broad mandate. In consequence certain of those safeguards which did exist, and which tended to ensure a modicum of procedural fairness to the accused have been substantially eroded.[196]

(4) Search and seizure

It has been established at common law and under the *Canadian Bill of Rights* that it is the fundamental right of every citizen of Canada to the security of his person and to the enjoyment of his property. Each citizen has a right not to be deprived of these things except by "due process of law".[197] Accordingly one assumes that there exists in Canada the right of the individual to be secure against unreasonable and arbitrary searches by the police and against the unlawful seizure of his property for use as evidence. But for the existence of the rule

---

191. *R. v. Watson, supra* footnote 182 at p. 215.
192. See the *Identification of Criminals Act, supra* footnote 180, s. 12.
193. *Ibid.* s. 2. Note, that it has been held that where the offence charged is "dual" or "hybrid" in nature and the Crown has not yet indicated its election, the election is deemed to be indictable for the purposes of the *Identification of Criminals Act* and photographs may therefore be taken: *R. v. Toor* (1973) 11 C.C.C. (2d) 312 (B.C.).
194. See *A. G. Quebec v. Begin* (1955) 112 C.C.C. 209 (Can.) and see the comments of Dickson J. re unlawful line-ups in *Marcoux v. R.* (1976) 24 C.C.C. (2d) 1 at pp. 7-8 (Can.).
195. [1971] S.C.R. 272.
196. For a discussion of the viability of other deterrents to unlawful police activity (other than an exclusionary rule) see the discussion *infra,* Part 4., of this chapter.
197. *The Canadian Bill of Rights* R.S.C. 1970 Appendix III. See especially s. 1(a).

respecting illegally obtained evidence (if relevant, the evidence is admissible, with few exceptions) this proposition would be correct.[198]

The protection of the citizen (such as it is) is *not* to be free of *all* searches and seizures, but rather it is his right to be free of all searches and seizures that are *unreasonable* and *arbitrary*. Where he is violated by police actions which are unreasonable and arbitrary the citizen may seek redress in civil or criminal proceedings, or he may take the more immediate (and infinitely riskier) manoeuvre of resisting the incursions of the police.[199]

The peace officer does in fact possess a lawful right of search. This is a common law right[200] which is "limited to that search which is incidental to the making of an arrest or the continued detention of the prisoner in safe custody."[201] In addition the peace officer wields statutory powers of search which need not be an incident to arrest.

In certain instances a peace officer will be lawfully justified in conducting a search of the premises, or of the person, of a suspect without the necessity of first obtaining a warrant.

After making an arrest a police officer has a right to search his prisoner in order to discover anything which may be helpful as evidence of the crime for which the prisoner has been arrested. Another purpose of such a search is to discover and to remove any weapons which might be utilized by the prisoner to effect his escape.[202]

---

198. See *R. v. Wray, supra* footnote 195; and *R. v. Hogan* (1974) 26 C.R.N.S. 207 (Can.); and re actual illegality concerning search warrants see *R. v. Kostachuk* (1930) 54 C.C.C. 189 (Sask. C.A.); and *R. v. Lee Hai* (1935) 64 C.C.C. 49 (Man. C.A.); *Paris v. R.* (1957) 118 C.C.C. 405 (Que. C.A.).

199. See *R. v. Larlham* [1971] 4 W.W.R. 304 (B.C. C.A.) where one defendant successfully appealed against a conviction for a common assault occasioned in self-defence when illegally searched by peace officers. But see, *Eccles v. Bourque* [1973] 5 W.W.R. 434 (B.C. C.A.) where a civil suit against the police for trespass failed on appeal because it was established that the trespass committeed was permissible provided that the police were operating upon reasonable and probable grounds that such entry was necessary in order to apprehend a fugitive. This decision was appealed to the Supreme Court of Canada in (1974), 19 C.C.C. (2d) 129 where four members of the court (the other five members declining to express any view) held that the *Code* s. 25 does not authorize a forcible trespass on private property to effect a lawful arrest under s. 450(1) of the *Criminal Code,* since that subsection authorizes a peace officer to make an arrest, not to commit a trespass. The full Court held however that a forcible trespass is lawful at common law provided that there are reasonable and probable grounds for the belief that the person sought is within the premises and that a proper announcement is made prior to entry.

200. *Leigh v. Cole* (1853) 6 Cox C.C. 329; *Bessell v. Wilson* (1853) 20 L.T.O.S. 233; and *R. v. Brezack* (1949) 96 C.C.C. 97 (C.A.).

201. *Re Laporte and R.* (1972) 8 C.C.C. (2d) 343 at p. 350 (Que.) *per* Hugessen J.

202. See the Ouimet Report, *Report of the Canadian Committee on Corrections* (1969) at p. 61.

Such force as is reasonably necessary in order to *effectively* conduct the search may be employed. An "effective" search may at times entail an intimate examination of the suspect's body. In *R. v. Brezack*[203] an assault conviction was registered against the accused Brezack. Brezack had bitten the hand of a police officer who was attempting to search the inside of Brezack's mouth for narcotic capsules which were thought to be hidden there. Robertson C.J.O. delivered the judgment in the case on behalf of the Ontario Court of Appeal:

> the attempt to search the inside of the appellant's mouth was a justifiable incident of that arrest. That the appellant was liable to arrest without warrant is, I think, beyond question, and the evidence — and particularly the evidence afforded by the capsules containing a narcotic, found in the appellant's motor car a few minutes later — strongly supports the reasonableness of the constable's belief in the information he had received, that the prohibited drug would be found concealed in the appellant's mouth.
>
> It is important to observe that the search that was made is justifiable as an incident of the arrest. The constable who makes an arrest has important duties, such as to see that the prisoner does not escape by reason of being armed, and to see if any evidence of the offence for which he was arrested is to be found upon him. A constable may not always find his suspicions to be justified by the result of a search. It is sufficient if the circumstances are such as to justify the search as a reasonable precaution.[204]

In general, the power to search the *person* derives from the common law and is preserved in criminal matters by virtue of s. 7 of the *Criminal Code*.[205] It is, in such matters *only* available as an incident to arrest. Specific statutory exceptions such as exist under the *Narcotics Control Act* derogate from the general rule.

An example of derogation from the general rule enunciated above is s. 103 of the *Criminal Code* which allows a peace officer acting on reasonable and probable grounds to search without warrant "a *person* or vehicle, or premises other than a dwelling house" in order to seize anything which evidences the commission or, the intended commission of an offence concerning prohibited or restricted weapons.

Section 10(1) of the *Narcotic Control Act*[206] confers equally broad powers of entry, search and seizure (without warrants) concerning offences in contravention of that Act.[207]

Many other rights of search may be carried out under the authority of a search warrant issued by a justice of the peace for a specified

203. (1949) 96 C.C.C. 97 (Ont. C.A.).
204. *Ibid.* at p. 101.
205. R.S.C. 1970 Chap. C-34.
206. R.S.C. 1970 Chap. N-1.
207. The provision in fact is even broader than s. 103 of the Code discussed *supra* in that it authorizes entry of a dwelling house under a writ of assistance. (Such writs shall be discussed *infra*.)

purpose.[208] The general power to issue a search warrant is conferred upon the justice of the peace by s. 443 of the *Criminal Code*. Before a search warrant may be issued, an information on oath (in compliance with Form I of the *Criminal Code*) must first be sworn before the justice. Strict compliance with the provisions of the statute is essential before the warrant may be issued.[209]

The Justice of the Peace is under a specific duty to satisfy himself as to the reasonableness of the grounds underlying the application for a warrant. If he is not so satisfied he is justified in refusing to issue a search warrant.

> An honest belief on the part of the informant is not sufficient for the Justice to issue a warrant to search. *It is the Justice not the informant who must be satisfied that there is a reasonable ground for believing the facts required to be established before issuing a warrant.*[210]

Once the warrant issues the right of search this conferred is restricted to a person named in the warrant, or to a peace officer. "No other person has the right to compulsory access to the private premises to be searched and to an unrestricted access to private records and documents in the absence of a warrant directed to him."[211]

Broad as the powers of search and seizure undoubtedly are, they do not extend so far as to authorize the surgical removal of substances from the human body. In *Re Laporte and R.*[212] an order for *certiorari* was granted in order to block one such intended manoeuvre. A search warrant had in fact issued in *Laporte*. It purported to authorize the surgical removal of an object corresponding in size and shape to a 38 calibre slug from the body of a suspect. (The object had been revealed in x-rays.) The warrant which had issued was quashed on the basis

---

208. The description (set out in the search warrant) of the evidence to be searched for should be so specific that the officer or other person authorized to search can identify the thing to be seized.
209. See *Re Purdy and R.* (1972) 8 C.C.C. (2d) 52 (N.B. C.A.); and *Shumiatcher v. A. G. Sask.* (1960) 129 C.C.C. 267 (Sask.).
210. *Re Purdy and R., ibid.* at p. 60 *per* Limerick J.A. (emphasis added). See also *Wiens v. R.* (1973) 24 C.R.N.S. 341 (Man.). And see *R. v. P.P.F., Loc. 170* [1972] 5 W.W.R. 641 (B.C.).
211. *Re Purdy and R., ibid.* at p. 60 *per* Limerick J.A.
212. (1972) 8 C.C.C. (2d) 343 (Que.). See also, the Ouimet Report, *supra* footnote 202 at p. 62 where it is said ". . . . the right to search the person and clothing of a person under arrest to obtain evidence of the offence does not authorize the withdrawal of blood, the use of stomach pumps or other quasi-surgical measures to obtain evidence". Contrast this with *Reynen v. Antonenko* (1975) 20 C.C.C. (2d) 342 (Alta.) where a civil action for damages for assault and battery arising out of a rectal examination of the plaintiff (a suspected drug trafficker) by the defendant medical doctor (acting at the instance of the police/co-defendants) was dismissed on the grounds that the officers acted in a reasonable and proper manner without any unreasonable or improper force or threats to the health or well-being of the plaintiff.

that the human body was neither a "receptacle" nor a "place" as contemplated by s. 443(1) of the *Criminal Code*.

In addition to the powers of search discussed *supra* there exists further extraordinary powers of search which are authorized under a document designated as a "writ of assistance". The writ, and the authority which it imports, ranks among the broadest and most sweeping of the powers which are placed in the hands of our law enforcement officers. Its use in Canada has been traced to at least the middle of the nineteenth century.[213] Despite its long usage in this country serious doubts as to its overall efficacy in a democratic society have been raised:

> The extent of the power conferred upon a person to whom a writ of assistance has been granted raises serious questions as to whether such powers should be conferred upon any person in a democratic country.[214]

The actual manner of use, and control over the exercises carried out under the authority of the writ, have also been questioned:

> One would gather that the writs tend to be used in a clandestine manner by the R.C.M.P. and other officers. For enforcement purposes this is one of the virtues of the authority which is furnished by the writ. At the same time it is a frightening fact of its existence that the powers which are exercised under it and the manner in which they are carried out are so veiled in mystery. . . .
>
> Few of the safeguards which have been provided against the wrongful use (or even issue) of the search warrant are available to a person who claims that an officer has wrongfully searched his property under the authority of a writ of assistance.[215]

Despite the dangerous potential of the writs of assistance and the "veil of mystery" generally surrounding them, the Ouimet Committee in 1969 indicated that it does not appear "that the broad powers conferred by the granting of these writs has been abused in Canada."[216]

---

213. See G. E. Parker, "The Extraordinary Power to Search and Seize and the Writ of Assistance" (1959-63), 1 U.B.C.L.R. 688 at pp. 709-711.
214. Ouimet Report *supra* footnote 202 at p. 66.
215. G. E. Parker *supra* footnote 213 at p. 708.
216. Ouimet Report *supra* footnote 202 at p. 67. The report goes on to observe that "a system for recording their use has been developed so that any abuse thereof is more visible, and hence subject to parliamentary scrutiny. Moreover, the writ is granted to a particular person and is not transferable. The number of members of the Royal Canadian Mounted Police to whom the writ is granted is restricted". These views are also shared by P.G.C. Ketchum in his article on "Writs of Assistance" (1971) 2 C.B.J. 26 at p. 27. On the subject of writs of asistance generally, see also Skinner, "Writs of Assistance" (1963) U.T.F.L.R. 26, and J. Faulkner, "Writs of Assistance in Canada" (1971) 9 Alta.L.R. 386. (Faulkner cautions that 'we should not be comforted too much by reassurances that the writ of assistance is not used 'excessively'. Whether it is or not, the potential for abuse in anything which places unrestricted powers in the

The writ of assistance is only available in Canada under four federal statutes—the *Narcotic Control Act*; the *Food and Drugs Act*;[217] the *Customs Act*;[218] and the *Excise Act*.[219] The writ operates in the same manner as a search warrant with respect to crimes suspected of being committed under those statutes. They are, however, different from ordinary search warrants in several important respects as E. W. Trasewick details in the following passage:

> In Canada, writs of assistance are best illustrated as circumventing "futile" rules of court by the fact that they are carried on the person and, once granted, they are valid so long as the person to whom they are granted holds his office. Thus the writ avoids any subsequent application to a justice as is required when seeking a search warrant, and unlike the search warrant once granted can be used over and over again.[220]

Thus the writs have been described as "general warrants not limited to any particular place or time".[221] The only practical limitation upon their use is that reasonable grounds justifying the exercise of authority under the writ must exist.

Application for a writ of assistance is now properly made to a judge of the Federal Court of Canada. The application is that of the Attorney-General of Canada, and where it is properly brought there appears to be no discretion to refuse the application.[222]

In theory the writ of assistance is granted to an "officer" which "means a person employed in the administration of [one of the four applicable] Acts . . . In practice writs of assistance under these Acts are granted to members of the Royal Canadian Mounted Police force."[223]

Regardless of the manner, or of the authority under which a search is conducted, the normal incident of a search is the seizure of evidence. Seizure of goods as a procedure naturally carries with it the threat of forfeiture.

---

hands of a man and then calls upon him to be the sole regulator of those powers, is simply too great" (p. 396).

217. R.S.C. 1970 Chap. F-27, s. 37.
218. R.S.C. 1970 Chap. C-40, s. 145.
219. R.S.C. 1970 Chap. E-12, s. 78.
220. E. W. Trasewick, "Search Warrants and Writs of Assistance" (1962-63) 5 Cr.L.Q. 341 at pp. 345-346.
221. Ouimet Report, *supra* footnote 202 at p. 66.
222. At one time it was thought that by virtue of the wording of s. 145 of the *Customs Act* (which declared that a judge of the Exchequer Court "*may* grant a writ of assistance to an officer") there did exist a discretion to refuse an application for a writ, but the decision in *In Re Writs of Assistance*, [1965] 2 Ex. C.R. 645 reduced this "discretion" to meaningless proportions. In the other 3 applicable statutes the granting of writs of assistance is *mandatory* upon application being made.
223. Ouimet Report, *supra* footnote 202 at pp. 65-66.

Often forfeiture of goods can itself be a more extreme penalty than the offence may merit. The Ontario Royal Commission *Inquiry Into Civil Rights* conducted in 1969 contains a description of one such example under the provisions of the *Ontario Game and Fish Act*:

> If an officer searching an automobile finds that certain fish are being transported in it, and he suspects that they may be over the weight prescribed by the regulations he may seize the automobile. If the alleged offender has exceeded his quota and is convicted of an offence no matter how trivial, the automobile must be forfeited to the Crown. The Court is given no discretion. In such case the Minister has power to grant relief against the forfeiture, in whole or in part, and order the return of the property on such terms and conditions as he deems proper, but the Minister's power is discretionary and is not reviewable by the Court. Thus an arbitrary power to impose a punishment is vested in the Minister, which may be much greater than that vested in the Court, but the Minister's power is controlled by the discretion vested in the officer in the first instance as to whether or not he will seize the automobile.[224]

Similar powers to those described above exist under the *Narcotic Control Act*. The totality of the forfeiture powers under the *Narcotic Control Act* are not as severe, or as arbitrary as those which existed in 1969 *vis-a-vis* the *Ontario Game and Fish Act*. The *Narcotic Control Act* provides a procedure by which a person claiming interest may apply *to a judge* for an order of restoration *after* forfeiture.[225] Also, there is provision for such an application after seizure and *before* conviction and forfeiture.[226]

It appears that where goods have been seized illegally there is an inherent power in the Court to order their return.[227] This proposition is subject to the caveat that the police, though they have obtained goods by illegal means, can hold on to them if they are required as evidence in a prosecution.[228]

In general, the detention and subsequent disposition of things which have been seized pursuant to search is governed by the provisions of s. 446 of the *Criminal Code*. That section exists to insure the safe-keeping, and expeditious return, of seized goods to their lawful owners.[229] Where the goods themselves are contraband they may be ordered forfeit or otherwise dealt with in accordance with law.[230]

---

224. Ontario *Royal Commission Inquiry into Civil Rights* (1969), Report No. 1, Vol. 2 at p. 735 (McRuer Report).
225. *Narcotic Control Act supra* footnote 206, s. 11.
226. *Ibid.*, ss. 5 and 6.
227. *Re Black and R.* (1973) 13 C.C.C. (2d) 446 (B.C.).
228. *Ghani v. Jones* [1969] 3 All E.R. 1700; *Re Purdy and R. supra* footnote 209; *Re MacKenzie and R.* (1973) 10 C.C.C. (2d) 193 (B.C.), (all cited in *Re Black and R. ibid.*).
229. *Code*, s. 446(3)(*a*) and (3)(*b*)(i) (If the owner is not known the goods may be forfeited or otherwise dealt with in accordance with law.)
230. *Code*, s. 446(3)(*b*)(ii). Note that not all seized items fall under the general ambit of s. 446. See *e.g.* ss. 446.1 and 447 which deal with the seizure and possible forfeiture of weapons and explosives.

As this brief survey indicates, the law of search and seizure in Canada permits substantial invasions against both persons and property to occur. Although lip service is paid to the notion of "reasonable and probable grounds" as the basis upon which such invasions are said to be justified, in practice such subjective determinations are extremely difficult to oversee. What is involved in this area is at least the partial destruction of what was once a sacrosanct notion:

> The poorest man may in his cottage bid defiance to all the forces of the Crown. It may be frail — its roof may shake — the wind may blow through it — the storm may enter — but the King of England cannot enter — all his forces dare not cross the threshold of the ruined tenement.[231]

(5) Arrest and detention

(a) *What is an arrest? And why?*

The McRuer Commission's *Inquiry Into Civil Rights* in Ontario defined an arrest in simple and undistorted terms: "Any actual restraint imposed on a person's liberty against his will constitutes an arrest. The restraint may be imposed by the application of force, or by circumstances that imply a threat of force".[232] Mere words will not constitute an arrest unless accompanied by a submission to restraint, or unless the officer is in a position to impose restraint upon the accused if necessary. The matter was accurately put in an 1845 English decision:

> So, if a person should direct a constable to take another in custody, and that person should be told by the constable to go with him, and the orders are obeyed, and they walk together in the direction pointed out by the constable, that is, constructively, an *imprisonment,* though no actual violence be used. In such cases, however, though little may be said, much is meant and perfectly understood.[233]

Arrest then, is a restraint upon liberty. It is therefore also an imprisonment.

> Arrest and imprisonment are in law the same thing. Any form of physical restraint is an arrest and imprisonment is only a continuing arrest.[234]

The purposes of arrest may be said to include the following:

(1) to detain an individual until it is assured that he may be properly dealt with by a court of law;

(2) to establish the identity of a suspect

(3) to prevent the continuation or repetition of an offence;

---

231. The sentiment was expressed by the Earl of Chatham and is reproduced in J. Faulkner, "Writs of Assistance in Canada" (1971) 9 Alta.L.R. 386.
232. McRuer Report, *supra* footnote 224 at pp. 725-726.
233. *Bird v. Jones* (1845) 7 Q.B. 742 at p. 748 quoted in the McRuer Report *supra* footnote 224 at p. 726.
234 Devlin, *The Criminal Prosecution in England* (1958) at p. 82.

(4) to create a legal basis for search and thereby avoid the destruction of evidence;

(5) to prevent interference with legal processes or the discharge of duties by public servants;

(6) to prevent and restrain an accused from harming himself or others.[235]

The sources of the police officer's present powers of arrest are the *Criminal Code* of Canada and the various provincial enactments creating provincial offences. Speaking generally about the creation of a power of arrest the McRuer Commission made the following observations:

> Before the legislature confers a power peremptorily to deprive an individual of his liberty, two questions should always be answered:
>
> (1) Is the power necessary?
> (2) Will the exercise of the power impose a punishment out of all proportion to the penalty that might be imposed by a judicial officer if the person is found guilty of the alleged offence?[236]

The second question is of particular importance to the area of summary conviction offences which, by nature are purportedly "minor" offences. It is in these "minor" areas that the ordinarily law-abiding citizen will most often run afoul of the law. Will his experience with the machinery of justice be a nightmare, or will it be proportionate to his misconduct?[237] The answer to this question resides in good measure with the attitude which individual police officers adopt in relation to the very broad statutory mandate which has been bestowed upon them.

(b) *The arrest power generally*

Depending upon the circumstance a police officer has the power to arrest a suspect either with or without the accompanying authority of a warrant. He is entitled to resort to reasonable force in order to effect his purpose, and once having arrested his suspect the officer, within limits, possesses a discretionary power to detain or release the alleged offender.

(i) *Arrest without a warrant*[238] — In certain instances *anyone* may

---

235. See the Ouimet Report, *supra* footnote 202 at p. 91; and the McRuer Report, *supra* footnote 224 at p. 725.

236. McRuer Report, *supra* footnote 224 at p. 727.

237. At the time of the McRuer Report the situation with respect to arrest without warrant under provincial statutes was deplorable and worthy of condemnation: "Under this Act [the Highway Traffic Act] and under certain other statutes . . . powers of arrest without a warrant have been conferred with abandoned liberality, without regard for historic principles, necessity or elementary safeguards of civil rights or human dignity" (at p. 729).

238. See G. A. Martin, "Police Detention and Arrest Privileges in Canada" (1961-62) 4 Cr.L.Q. 54.

make an arrest without a warrant.[239] The police officer's powers to arrest without a warrant go beyond those possessed by the ordinary person.[240] Section 450(1) of the *Criminal Code* states that a peace officer may arrest without warrant:

> (a) a person who has committed an indictable offence or who, on reasonable and probable grounds, he believes has committed or is about to commit an indictable offence
>
> (b) a person whom he finds committing a criminal offence, or
>
> (c) a person for whose arrest he has reasonable and probable grounds to believe that a warrant is in force within the territorial jurisdiction in which the person is found.

In addition to these enumerated powers the police officer, like any other person, may arrest any person he *finds committing* an indictable offence.

The power to arrest without warrant is presently limited by s. 450(2) of the *Criminal Code.* This subsection indicates that the "peace officer *shall not arrest* a person without a warrant" in certain enumerated situations. The terms "shall not arrest" are somewhat misleading. Since an arrest is "any actual restraint imposed on a person's liberty against his will" what the subsection actually does is empower a police officer to "arrest" a person without warrant, *but,* in these specially designated circumstances he must not unnecessarily detain the accused. Rather, the peace officer making the arrest may compel future appearances by the accused either by issuing to him an appearance notice,[241] or a summons.[242] This procedure is applicable in the following specially designated (or enumerated) circumstances:

(1) The offence is an indictable offence mentioned in s. 483.

(2) The offence is one for which the person may be prosecuted by indictment or which is punishable on summary conviction.

---

239. S. 449 of the *Criminal Code* covers the situation of the "citizen arrest":
    449.(1) Anyone may arrest without warrant
    (*a*) a person whom he finds committing an indictable offence, or
    (*b*) a person who, on reasonable or probable grounds, he believes
       (i) has committed a criminal offence, and
       (ii) is escaping from and freshly pursued by persons who have lawful authority to arrest that person.
    By Subs. (2) the owner or lawful possessor of property (or someone authorized by them) may also arrest without warrant a person found committing a criminal offence on or in relation to that property. In either of the above circumstances any person so arrested must be delivered over to a peace officer "forthwith".

240. The normal statutory sources of the power to arrest without warrant are the *Criminal Code* and certain federal (*e.g. Narcotic Control Act*) and provincial (*e.g.* the *Highway Traffic Act* (Ont.)) enactments.

241. The *Criminal Code* s. 451 and s. 452(1)(*c*).

242. *Code* s. 452(1)(*d*).

(3) The offence is one punishable on summary conviction.[243]

Notwithstanding these provisions the peace officer is justified in detaining the accused where he feels on reasonable and probable grounds that it is in the public interest to do so. The "public interest" under the legislation is ascertainable by having regard to (a) the need to establish the identity of the person, (b) the need to secure or preserve evidence of or relating to the offence, (c) the necessity to prevent the continuation or repetition of the offence, or the commission of another offence. A fear (based on reasonable and probable grounds) that if released, the person in custody would fail to attend in court in order to be dealt with according to law would also justify the continued detention of such an individual by the arresting officer.[244] The same considerations as guide the arresting officer are applicable to the officer in charge into whose custody the suspect is delivered.[245] The public interest, and the concern that the accused will attend as required by the authorities, remain the guiding considerations.[246]

Where the accused is not released by either the arresting officer or the officer in charge he must be taken before a justice in order to be considered for release "without unreasonable delay and in any event within twenty-four hours". Where a Justice is unavailable within twenty-four hours this procedure must be accomplished "as soon as possible".[247]

Basically, then, it is not the power of the peace officer to arrest without warrant which has been limited by the passage of *Bail Reform* provisions, but rather it is the capacity of the officer to *detain* an individual, *once arrested,* that has been restricted.[248] In essence, applying the broad definition of arrest referred to *supra,* the peace officer may arrest an individual without a warrant, whenever he finds an indictable offence about to be committed, or any offence, in the process of its

---

243. See the *Criminal Code* section 450(2)(*a*) to (*c*); and see ss. 451, 452, and 453.
244. See *Code* s. 452(1)(*f*) and (*g*).
245. The officer in charge (by s. 453(1) of the *Code*) is empowered to release the accused as soon as practicable either by compelling his appearance by summons; having him give a written promise to appear; having the accused enter into a recognizance without sureties in an amount not exceeding five hundred dollars (and without actual deposit of money or valuable security; or, if the person is a non-resident (*i.e.* does not live within 100 miles of the place of custody)) by having the accused enter into a recognizance not in excess of five hundred dollars without sureties, and, in the discretion of the officer in charge by a money or valuable security deposit being posted to a value not in excess of five hundred dollars.
246. See *Code* s. 453(1)(*i*) and (*j*).
247. *Code* s. 454(1).
248. Of course, the release of an offender is not a decision which resides solely with the police. Indeed the largest role in this area is played by the judiciary. In this regard see D. Watt, "Judicial Interim Release" (1973-74) 16 Cr.L.Q. 27.

commission. Also, he may arrest a person without a warrant where there exists reasonable and probable grounds for believing that a warrant is in existence, and in force, within the territorial jurisdiction in which the person is found.

The power to arrest without warrant in circumstances where an indictable offence is *about* to be committed is a broader power than the police formerly possessed. G. A. Martin (now Martin J.A. of the Ontario Court of Appeal) examined the power in his consideration of "Police Detention and Arrest Privileges in Canada":[249]

> Section 435 [now s. 450] in its present form gives the police officer much wider powers than were enjoyed by him at common law. The power to arrest one whom he on reasonable and probable grounds believes to be about to commit an indictable offence obviously enables the officer to intervene at a stage prior to the commission of an attempt. The attempt to commit an indictable offence is itself an indictable offence and an attempt to commit an offence punishable on summary conviction only is a summary conviction offence. Since by s. 435 a peace officer has the power to arrest any person whom he finds committing a criminal offence, it is clear he could justify arresting a person attempting to commit any criminal offence by the power there conferred, and the power to arrest a person whom be believes "is about to commit an indictable offence" would be unnecessary if the power were limited to situations where an attempt to commit an offence has already begun. *It follows that a police officer may arrest under s. 435 where he believes the person arrested is about to commit an indictable offence although he has no basis for charging him with the commission of any offence.*
>
>   .   .   .
>
> The wide powers conferred by s. 435 may be justified as a form of preventive justice, and no doubt the taking into custody of a person whom the police believe is about to commit a crime has some therapeutic value. A recent case decided by the Ontario Court of Appeal [*Koechlin v. Waugh* (1957) 118 C.C.C. 24] makes it clear, however, that in order to justify himself under this section the officer must have some objective grounds for believing that the person arrested was about to commit an indictable offence.[250]

---

249. *Supra* footnote 238.
250. *Ibid.* at pp. 56-57 (emphasis added). These remarks should not be taken too literally. W. E. Horkins, "False Arrest Today" (1973) L.S.U.C. Special Lectures 241 at p. 248 makes this comment: "I should think that a peace officer would be on very dangerous ground arresting a person on the assumption that the person was about to commit an offence unless the person had committed an overt act."
See also the Ouimet Report *supra* footnote 202 at pp. 56-57. But see *Kennedy v. Tomlinson* (1959) 126 C.C.C. 175 at p. 211 where Schroeder J.A. seems in part to indicate that a police officer may be justified in arresting a person for the purposes of investigation. The case however, cannot be regarded as persuasive authority on any footing, due to the fact that the Supreme Court of Canada in refusing leave to appeal in-

Martin expands upon this thesis by furnishing the useful example of *R. v. Beaudette*.[251] In *Beaudette* it became evident to the police that the accused intended to drive his car while in a heavily intoxicated condition. Beaudette was arrested before entering his vehicle. The arrest of the accused by the police was held to be justified even though the person arrested had not yet committed any indictable offence.

The police power to arrest without warrant is tempered (in theory, at least) by these ideals expressed by Scott L.J. in *Dumbell v. Roberts*:

> The duty of the police when they arrest without warrant is, no doubt, to be quick to see the possibility of crime, but equally they ought to be anxious to avoid mistaking the innocent for the guilty. The British principle of personal freedom, that every man should be presumed innocent until he is proved guilty, applies also to the police function of arrest — in a very modified degree, it is true, but at least to the extent of requiring them to be observant, receptive and open-minded and to notice any relevant circumstance which points either way, either to innocence or to guilt.[252]

Scott L.J. also had occasion to examine the power of a constable to arrest without warrant in the case of *Christie v. Leachinsky*,[253] a case which was subsequently considered by the English House of Lords.[254] His conclusions, which are still appropriate today were as follows:[255]

---

dicated that although leave was denied they had nevertheless not agreed with all of the reasons for judgment delivered in the case. (See (1959) 126 C.C.C. 175 at p. 230 for the remarks of Kerwin C.J.C., Cartwright and Judson JJ.).

251. (1957) 118 C.C.C. 295 (Ont. C.A.).
252. [1944] 1 All E.R. 326 at p. 329.
253. [1945] 2 All E.R. 395.
254. [1947] 1 All E.R. 567.
255. Reproduced in J. Honsberger "The Power of Arrest and the Duties and Rights of Citizens and Police" (1963) *L.S.U.C. Special Lectures*, P. 1 at p. 23 (or see, [1945] 2 All E.R. 395 at p. 403). A spectre has been raised concerning the applicability of this decision (especially the House of Lords decision) in Canada by virtue of the reasons for judgment rendered in *Gamracy v. R.* (1973) 22 C.R.N.S. 224 a decision of the Supreme Court of Canada. The case stands for the proposition that when a police officer is arresting on a warrant which he does not have with him, it is no part of his duty to obtain the warrant or to ascertain its contents. (All that the accused was told was that there was some kind of warrant "out for him".) Ritchie J. in considering *Christie v. Leachinsky supra*, footnote 253 at p. 227 on behalf of the majority stated: "Although the case is no doubt an interesting one in the English context and naturally entitled to the greatest respect, I think it should be said that such cases afford no assistance in determining the true meaning and effect to be given to ss. 450(1) and 29 of the Criminal Code and I do not think that any further comment is necessary."

(i) Arrest on a criminal charge always was and still is a mere step on the procedural road towards committal, trial, verdict, judgment and punishment — or acquittal as may result;

(ii) the powers of arrest conferred by law is limited to the purpose of the particular proceeding, so, the specific charge formulated;

(iii) the arrest must be made on that charge only; and the person arrested must be told by the constable at the time of arrest what the charge is. The constable cannot lawfully keep an open mind and remain still undecided at the moment of arrest; he must make up his mind and formulate the charge on which he decides, and then arrest on that charge;[256]

(iv) if, having told the accused, before arresting, what the charge is, he then either changes his mind or becomes undecided, he has no no longer any power to arrest on that charge; and if he does so arrest, he acts illegally and is guilty of the tort of false imprisonment;

(v) if he arrests on a specific charge, but before he has brought the prisoner before the appropriate judicial authority he changes his mind and decides to keep him on another charge, his power to detain automatically ceases and it becomes his immediate legal duty then to relase the prisoner and make a new arrest on the new charge.

Irrespective of whether the arrest is with or without a warrant the suspect must be informed of the reason for his arrest at the first reasonable opportunity.[257] If the reason for the arrest is patent (as when the accused is caught in the act) or where the accused by his conduct makes the communication of such information impossible then the requirement of notification may be dispensed with.[258]

(ii) *Arrest with a warrant*[259] — There are seven instances in which

---

256. From this point, and number (v) Honsberger deduces that the law does not allow an arrest *in vacuo,* or without reason assigned "and that the reason assigned must be that the arrest is for the selfsame charge as is the justification of arrest". In support he cites the case of *R. v. Dick* (1947) 87 C.C.C. 101 (Ont. C.A.). (See Honsberger, *supra* footnote 255 at p. 24).

257. See *Code* s. 29(2)(b). See also *Koechlin v. Waugh* (1957) 118 C.C.C. 24 at p. 27; *Garthus v. Van Caeseele* (1959) 122 C.C.C. 369 (B.C.); *Christie v. Leachinsky supra* footnote 253; *Reid v. DeGroot* [1963] 2 C.C.C. 327 (N.S.); *R. v. Acker* [1970] 4 C.C.C. 269 (N.S. C.A.); *R. v. Long* [1970] 1 C.C.C. 313 (B.C. C.A.).

258. Re: accused caught in the act — see *R. v. Bain* (1955) 111 C.C.C. 281 (Man. C.A.); *R. v. George* (1934) 67 C.C.C. 33 (Can.); *Garthus v. Van Caeseele, supra*; *R. v. Hurlen* [1959] 17 D.L.R. (2d) 603 (Ont. C.A.). Re accused's conduct vitiating the need for notice — See *Christie v. Leachinsky supra*; and *Gelberg v. Miller* [1961] 1 All E.R. 291.

259. S. 456(1)of the *Criminal Code* sets out the contents of a warrant:
   (a) name or describe the accused;
   (b) set out briefly the offence in respect of which the accused is charged;

the issuance of a warrant for the arrest of a named person will be authorized:

(1) After the receiving of an information a justice, where he considers that a case for doing so has been made out, may issue a warrant for the arrest of the accused to compel the accused to attend before him to answer to a charge of an offence.[260]

(2) Where new evidence or information demonstrates a necessity to issue a warrant in the public interest a summons, an appearance notice, or promise to appear will be cancelled and the warrant may issue notwithstanding the prior release of the accused.

(3) Where new evidence or information demonstrates a necessity to issue a warrant in the public interest, and the accused had previously been released with the intention of compelling his appearance by way of summons, the warrant may issue notwithstanding the prior release of the accused.

(4) Where an accused fails to attend court in accord with the terms of a summons, appearance notice, promise to appear, or recognizance, a justice may issue a warrant for the arrest of the accused.

(5) Where it appears that a summons cannot be served because the accused is evading service, a warrant for the arrest of the accused may issue.[261]

(6) Where a justice is satisfied that there are reasonable and probable grounds to believe that an accused has violated or is about to violate the promise to appear, undertaking, or recognizance upon which he has been released, he may issue a warrant for the arrest of the accused.[262]

(7) Where a justice is satisfied that there are reasonable and probable grounds to believe that an accused has after his release from custody on a promise to appear undertaking or recognizance, committed an indictable offence, he may issue a warrant for the arrest of the accused.[263]

By s. 29 of the *Criminal Code* "it is the duty of everyone who executes a process or warrant to have it with him, where it is feasible to

---

(c) order that the accused be forthwith arrested and brought before the justice who issued the warrant or before some other justice having jurisdiction in the same territorial division, to be dealt with according to law.

260. *Code* s. 455.3(1)(*b*).
261. *Code* s. 456.1.
262. *Code* s. 458 and s. 455.6 (violation re appearance under *Identification of Criminal Act*).
263. *Ibid.*, note that s. 458 "makes no provision for the issue of a warrant where the accused was given an appearance notice, whether that notice was given in lieu of an arrest or after an arrest" (C. Powell *Arrest and Bail in Canada* (1972) at p. 28.).

do so and to produce it when requested to do so." More importantly, there is a positive duty on everyone who arrests a person with a warrant to give notice (to the person being arrested) of the process or warrant under which the arrest is being made.[264]

Since the warrant is, in point of fact, a written order from a justice of the peace or magistrate to the police in a specified territorial division bidding them to arrest the accused and bring him before either the issuing justice or some other official having jurisdiction, the police usually do not have a role to play in the deliberations concerning the possible subsequent release of the accused. If, however, the offence in question is an indictable offence mentioned in s. 483; a dual or optional offence; an offence punishable on summary conviction; or, any offence that is punishable by imprisonment for five years or less; *and* the warrant has been specially endorsed by the justice[265] *then* the officer in charge may order the release of the accused on similar terms to those he employs when dealing with accused persons arrested without warrant.[266]

Any discussion of the police power to arrest with (and more particularly, without) a warrant would be deficient if it failed to recognize a very prevalent abuse which occurs under a cloak of ostensible legality. This is the use of the blanket powers of search and seizure provided by Provincial legislation as a means to justify otherwise quite illegal search activity. Such searches are conducted in the hope of securing evidence of serious wrong doing which would contravene federal criminal law, and yet they are carried out in the name of enforcing minor provincial law. An example would be stopping a car "to inspect the brakes, or other equipment" when in fact the true purpose might be to conduct a search for stolen property in the absence of reasonable and probable grounds that the operator of the vehicle, or his passengers, were in any way connected with the crime under investigation.

Provincial powers of search and seizure may also provide a handy means of quite simply "harrassing" individuals who are out of favor with the authorities.

(c) *The use of force as an incident to arrest*

By s. 25 of the *Criminal Code* the peace officer is authorized by law to use as much force as is necessary to effect his lawful purpose. By s. 26 of the *Code* he is criminally responsible for the use of excessive force:

> 26. Everyone who is authorized by law to use force is criminally responsible for any excess thereof according to the nature and quality of the act that constitutes the excess.

---

264. *Code* s. 29(2)(a).
265. See *Code* s. 455.3(6).
266. See *Code* s. 453.1.

No person, including a police officer, is justified in using force that is likely to cause death or grievous bodily harm "unless he believes on reasonable and probable grounds that it is necessary for the purpose of preserving himself or anyone under his protection from death or grievous bodily harm".[267] This limitation is subject to the qualification that the peace officer (or anyone lawfully assisting him) who is proceeding to arrest an offender may, with justification, use as much force as is necessary to prevent the escape of an offender who has taken flight. Such force as is necessary may in the circumstances prove to be life-threatening to the offender, or may result in grievous bodily harm to him. Only if the escape may be prevented in a less violent manner is the police officer enjoined from the use of these extreme powers.[268]

As much force as is reasonably necessary may be used to prevent the commission of an offence for which an arrest would have been justified (without warrant) were it committed. The same is true in circumstances where the commission of an offence would be likely to cause immediate and serious injury to the person or property of anyone.[269] So long as the officer (or other person) maintains that his actions were based upon reasonable and probable grounds his use of force is justifiable irrespective of whether the ultimate truth of his belief is borne out.[270] By the same token where the peace officer (or other authorized person) executes a warrant to arrest in good faith, and on reasonable and probable grounds, believing the person whom he is arresting is the person named in the warrant, and he proves to be in error, that peace officer is protected from criminal responsibility by the provisions of s. 28 of the *Criminal Code*.[271]

(d) *The right to resist and obstruct police in cases of unlawful police activity and the right to repel excessive force*

If an arrest is unlawful then any detention will amount to false imprisonment, and any application of force, will amount to an assault.[272]

Section 34 of the *Criminal Code* provides:

34. (1) Everyone who is unlawfully assaulted without having provoked

---

267. *Code* s. 25(3).
268. *Code* s. 25(4); See also *Priestman v. Colangelo* [1959] S.C.R. 615 re justifiable use of force and whether the peace officer acted reasonably in the circumstances.
269. See *Code* s. 27(a)(i) and (ii). The police are also justified in resorting to the use of force in order to suppress a riot.
270. See *Code* s. 27(b).
271. W. E. Horkins draws our attention to the fact that the protection afforded by the section is only from "criminal responsibility". He does not think it protects from civil liabilities and cites the following cases in support of his contention: *Fletcher v. Collins* (1968) 70 D.L.R. 183 (Ont.); *Crowe v. Noon* [1971] 1 O.R. 530; and *Parks v. Frid* (unreported). See Horkins *supra* footnote 250.
272. See *Code* s. 244.

the assault is justified in repelling force by force if the force he uses is not intended to cause death or grievous bodily harm and is no more than is necessary to enable him to defend himself.

(2) Everyone who is unlawfully assaulted and who causes death or grievous bodily harm in repelling the assault is justified if

(*a*) he causes it under reasonable apprehension of death or grievous bodily harm from the violence with which the assault was originally made or with which the assailant pursues his purposes, and

(*b*) he believes, on reasonable and probable grounds, that he cannot otherwise preserve himself from death or grievous bodily harm.

The line between lawful or unlawful conduct is not always clear. Consider the case of two plain-clothes police detectives acting *bona fide* and attempting to arrest the wrong man due to mistaken identity. Assume that the procedures taken by the police to identify themselves are on the borderline between sufficiency and insufficiency, and that the suspect *bona fide* does not, due to the suspicious nature of the circumstances, believe that his interrogators are police officers. He resists and they persist. Force is used by both sides — perhaps even excessive force.

The court is left to sort out the rights and liabilities which accrue during this not unlikely scenario. Under the *Criminal Code* ss. 118 and 246 become relevant.

Section 118 reads in part:

118. Everyone who

(*a*) resists or wilfully obstructs a public officer or a peace officer in the execution of his duty or any person lawfully acting in aid of such an officer, . . .

is guilty of

(*d*) an indictable offence and is liable to imprisonment for two years, or

(*e*) an offence punishable on summary conviction.

The relevant portions of s. 246 of the *Code* are:

246. (2) Everyone who

(*a*) assaults a public officer or peace officer engaged in the execution of his duty, or a person acting in aid of such an officer;

(*b*) assaults a person with intent to resist or prevent the lawful arrest or detention of himself or another person; . . .

is guilty of

(*d*) an indictable offence and is liable to imprisonment for five years, or

(*e*) an offence punishable on summary conviction.

It should be noted that an essential averment in both of the sections of the *Criminal Code* referred to *supra* is that in order to properly found liability (and also, partly to establish lawful conduct) the peace officer must be "engaged in the execution of his duty".

Thus in order for an obstruction to be unlawful a police officer must be acting lawfully *and* in the execution of his duty.[273] Where a peace officer is acting illegally he cannot be said to be "engaged in the execution of his duty."[274]

The essential difference between the two sections is that under s. 118(*a*) obstructing a peace officer does not involve assaulting him. It is sufficient under that section to put in the way of the officer's performance of his duty, any obstacle.[275] It is not necessary for the obstruction to be physical in nature, and it matters not whether it is "actually effective" in obstructing the officer.[276]

There is often a fine line to be drawn between activity which is lawful and activity which amounts to obstruction of an officer lawfully engaged in the execution of his duty. Honsberger suggests that "anything is obstructing an officer in the execution of his duty the natural effect of which would or might be to prevent him from obtaining evidence concerning an offence, real or supposed, against the law, which it is his duty to investigate, or concerning which it is his duty to see or obtain evidence."[277]

There is some truth in this. But the proposition is too sweeping to be accepted without qualification. General safeguards concerning the right to silence and the right not to criminate oneself are the major qualifications. It has been held, however, to amount to obstruction where one urges *others* not to disclose information (*e.g.* their names) to police officers lawfully conducting an investigation.[278] On the other hand, it has been held *not* to be an obstruction merely to *keep* doors locked and to delay opening them.[279] Actually *closing* doors in the face of the police will amount to obstruction.

---

273 See *R. v. Sutherland* [1944] 1 W.W.R. 529 (B.C. C.A.); and *Johanson v. R.*; *Daniluk v. R.* (1947) 3 C.R. 508 (Can.). See also *R. v. Golden* (1936), 67 C.C.C. 292 (B.C. C.A.) and *R. v. Allen* (1971) 4 C.C.C. (2d) 194 (Ont. C.A.).

274. See *R. v. Richardson* (1924) 42 C.C.C. 95 (Sask.); *R. v. Bouchard* (1941) 76 C.C.C. 392 (C.A.); and *R. v. Diamond* (1924) 42 C.C.C. 90 (Alta. C.A.)..

275. *Pelletier v. Riviere-du-Loup* [1947] Que. S.C. 344.

276. *R. v. L.* (1922) 51 O.L.R. 575 and see *Hincliffe v. Sheldon*, [1955] 3 All E.R. 406 (both cited in Honsberger *supra* footnote 255 at p. 29); see also *R. v. Long* (1969-70) 8 C.R.N.S. 298 (B.C. C.A.) where all the accused did was to protest the unnecessary use of force employed by the police when arresting his friend. Accused was charged with obstruction and convicted. His conviction was reversed on appeal.

277. *Supra* footnote 255 at p. 29.

278. *R. v. D'Entremont* (1931) 57 C.C.C. 174 (N.S. C.A.); *R. v. L., supra* footnote 276; *R. v. Snider* (1953) 106 C.C.C. 175 (Ont.).

279. *R. v. Munn* [1938] 4 D.L.R. 504 (P.E.I.), (*R. v. Semeniuk* (1955) 111 C.C.C. 370 (Alta.); *R. v. Jung Lee* (1913) 22 C.C.C. 63 (Ont.). But see

If the obstruction occasioned is accidental or inadvertent no liability is resultant. The obstruction must be "wilful".[280] Since the obstruction must possess this quality it has been said that it is necessary for the accused to know that the person he in fact is obstructing is a police officer:

> This is important in the case of plainclothesmen. Even though the officer is in the execution of his duty, if the accused merely considers him to be an officious bystander or, for example, an intermeddler seeking to break up a fight, then there is no liability under s. 110 or s. 232 [now ss. 118 and 246]. It is not enough, therefore, that the complainant is in fact a police officer in the execution of his duty; the accused must also appreciate that the person he obstructs is a police officer: *R. v. McLeod* (1954), 111 C.C.C. 106.[281]

If the line between lawful activity and obstruction is fine, and none too precise, the line between lawful resistance and the culpable resistance of arrest is similarly vague and imprecise.

It is trite to assert that a person being unlawfully arrested without a warrant is entitled to resist such unlawful arrest.[282] The difficulty lies in determining exactly when an arrest is unlawful. The power of arrest is extremely broad, and, provided the rationale advanced by police for arresting a suspect are sufficiently sophisticated, most instances of arrest will at least bear the appearance of justification.

One case where the rationale advanced proved to be ultimately insufficient (and the resistance of the suspect, therefore justified) was the case of *Koechlin v. Waugh*.[283] Koechlin was a youth. His case, not unlike many others, probably would have died a slow death of attrition were it not for the resolute desire of his father to vindicate his son's good name. The case ultimately resulted in an award of damages against police officers for their false arrest and imprisonment of the youth. It did not reach that end however until Koechlin had first been exonerated of charges of assaulting a police officer.

Ewaschuk v. R. (1955) 111 C.C.C. 377 (Man. C.A.) and *Hinchcliffe v. Sheldon, supra* footnote 276.

280. *R. v. Taillefer* [1954] R.L. 562 (Que.); The word "wilfully" does not necessarily imply an intention to obstruct but rather implies a state of circumstances where the accused knows what he is doing and intends to do it and is a free agent: *R. v. Goodman* (1951) 2 W.W.R. 127 (B.C. C.A.) (Crankshaw's *Criminal Code of Canada* (3rd ed., 1959) at p. 135).

281. R. S. MacKay, "Obstructing a Police Officer in the Execution of his Duty" (1962-63) 5 Cr.L.Q. 294 at pp. 300-301. For a different view see *R. v. Forbes* 10 Cox C.C. 362; *R. v. Maxwell* 73 J.P. 176 and *R. v. McDonald* (1911) 18 C.C.C. 251 (B.C.).

282. *R. v. Hastings* [1947] 4 D.L.R. 748 (N.B. C.A.); *Christie v. Leachinsky* [1947] 1 All E.R. 567 *per* Lord Simonds: ". . . a person is, *prima facie,* entitled to his freedom and is only required to submit to restraint on his freedom if he knows in substance the reason why it is claimed that this restraint should be imposed."

283. (1957) 118 C.C.C. 24 (Ont. C.A.).

The facts of the case are relatively simple. The police attempted to arrest Koechlin because his dress — running shoes and a windbreaker (hardly exceptional) — evoked a suspicion in them that he might have been involved in a spate of recent neighbourhood break-ins. Koechlin was in fact walking home with a friend from a movie, and was entirely innocent of any wrong doing. The officers, Waugh and Hamilton were in plain clothes when they first accosted Koechlin and his friend. Upon being asked to identify himself Koechlin refused wishing the officers first to properly identify themselves. Subsequently, when Koechlin persisted in his refusal, a scuffle ensued. Koechlin was subdued by force, placed in a cruiser car and taken to the police station. At no time was he told of the reason for his arrest. At the station he was informed that he would be charged with assault of a police officer. Although his father attended at the station house at 2:00 a.m. Koechlin was not released until 9 or 10 o'clock the following evening.

The Ontario Court of Appeal was satisfied that the police officers had no reasonable or probable grounds for believing that Koechlin had committed or was about to commit an indictable offence. Consequently his arrest and subsequent imprisonment was unlawful. This being the case, Koechlin was justified in resisting the arrest. It was added by Laidlaw J.A. in his judgment:

> We do not criticize the police officers in any way for asking the infant plaintiff and his companion to identify themselves, but we are satisfied that when the infant plaintiff, who was entirely innocent of any wrongdoing, refused to do so, the police officer has no right to compel him to identify himself. It would have been wise, and indeed, a duty as a good citizen, for the infant plaintiff to have identified himself when asked to do so by the police officers. It is altogether likely that if the infant plaintiff had been courteous and cooperative, the incident giving rise to this action would not have occurred, but that does not in law excuse the defendants for acting as they did in the particular circumstances.
>
> We direct attention to an important fact. The infant plaintiff was not told by either of the police officers any reason for his arrest. The infant plaintiff was entitled to know on what charge or on suspicion of what crime he was seized. He was not required in law to submit to restraint on his freedom unless he knew the reason why that restraint should be imposed.[284]

The Koechlin case quite probably is *the* single most notorious case in Canada dealing with the right of a citizen to resist illegal police behavior. There are others — notably two in Ontario, *R. v. Carroll*[285] and *R. v. Hurlen*,[286] which followed closely on the heels of *Koechlin* —

---

284. *Ibid.* at p. 27.
285. (1959) 126 C.C.C. 19 (Ont. C.A.).
286. (1959) 123 C.C.C. 54 (Ont. C.A.).

where illegal police arrest tactics vitiated counts of obstruction and resisting arrest, but *Koechlin* rests in a more rarefied atmosphere due to the fact that subsequent action taken against the offending police atmosphere actually proved successful.

The fact that the Ontario Court of Appeal in the late 1950's was receptive to the citizen complaints voiced against illegal police arrest practices in *Koechlin, Carroll* and *Hurlen* was distressing to at least one commentator. R. S. Mackay gave vent to these feelings in the course of an address delivered at a seminar of Ontario and Quebec police officers in London, Ontario in 1962:

> The Ontario Court of Appeals appears to be the strictest and most technical of the Canadian provincial courts in upholding the right of a citizen as against the importance of efficient law enforcement and the protection of public interests, and it seems to uphold this right of the citizen even though he displays a flagrant disregard for the law and for those whose duty it is to enforce the law. In British Columbia, for example, in cases very similar to the situations in *Carroll* and *Hurlen* cases, the court had no trouble in finding that the accused's conduct and his insolent resistance to police requests constituted grounds for arrest and amounted to obstruction of or an assault against the arresting officer in the execution of his duty contrary to s. 110 and s. 232 respectively (see *R. v. Shore* (1960) 129 C.C.C. 70 and *R. v. Eye* (1959) 122 C.C.C. 399).[287]

This is gross over-reaction. The assumption that three cases—based upon (at least) arguably justifiable circumstances — which had served to rein in *particular* police excesses, could generally effect a diminution of the over-all effectiveness of police arrest practices is both naïve and unrealistic.

The reality is quite the opposite. In encounters between the citizen and the police we do not attempt to approximate a balance. The controlling factor is the vastness of the power of the state as symbolized in the person of the police officer. The citizen's few and precious rights must jealously be guarded in those moments when the process surfaces for public scrutiny.

The use of excessive force in circumstances where the right of arrest itself is justified is another vexing area which is inextricably bound up in any consideration of the arrest power.[288]

Excessive force may merely be the application of brute physical force. It may, however, also arise through the application of a "uniquely drastic and dangerous type of force" — namely, force resultant from the use of firearms.

At the risk of repetition and tedium it should be reiterated that the

---

287. R. S. MacKay, *supra* footnote 281 at pp. 314-315.
288. For a more detailed and comprehensive treatment of this theme see B.C. McDonald, "Use of Force by Police to Effect Lawful Arrest" (1966-67) 9 Cr.L.Q. 435.

peace officer's rights to use force to effect lawful arrest are substantially greater than those of the ordinary citizen:

> It will be noticed that while a private person may use force to effect an arrest which he is entitled to make that force may only be deadly or likely to cause grievous bodily harm *if* it is reasonably necessary to preserve the arrestor or someone under his protection from death or grievous bodily harm. A peace officer, on the other hand, may use all necessary force to prevent escape by flight from lawful arrest by him. No test of threatened physical harm to anyone conditions this latter authorization.[289]

In determining whether excessive force has been resorted to by arresting officers the court will embark upon an inquiry which seeks, in part, to examine the objective factors which operated upon the minds of the officers. The right to use force must in each case depend upon the surrounding circumstances, which must be considered to determine how they might be expected to act upon the mind and judgment of the officer, and to determine whether he was justified in using the force resorted to.[290]

Except for the basic requirement of "reasonableness" neither the *Criminal Code* nor the decided cases are of much assistance in determining exactly where the line is to be drawn between a reasonable resort to the use of force and the excessive application of force. Presumably a case by case approach is necessary. But even accepting this, one encounters the difficulty that similar factual situations achieve differing results. This is particularly the case in situations involving the police use of firearms.

In *Priestman v. Colangelo*[291] a police chase and shooting episode resulted in the death of innocent by-standers when a misdirected bullet struck the escaping driver causing him to lose control of his car. The Supreme Court of Canada (3:2) absolved the police officer who fired the shot of civil responsibility. Locke J. observed in part:

> In *Rex v. Smith*, Perdue J.A., in charging a jury at the trial of a police officer for manslaughter, is reported to have said that shooting is the very last resort and that only in the last extremity should a police officer resort to the use of a revolver in order to prevent the escape of an accused person who is attempting to escape by flight. With all the great respect that I have for any statement of the law expressed by the late Chief Justice of Manitoba, in my opinion this is too broadly stated and cannot be applied under all circumstances.[292]

> In my opinion, the action of the appellant in the present matter was reasonably necessary in the circumstances and no more than was reasonably necessary, both to prevent the escape and to protect those

---

289. B.C. McDonald, *ibid.* at p. 439.
290. *R. v. Purvis* (1929) 51 C.C.C. 273 at p. 284 (Ont.).
291. [1959] S.C.R. 615.
292. *Ibid.* at p. 624.

persons whose safety might have been endangered if the escaping car reached the intersection with Pape Avenue. So far as Priestman was concerned, the fact that the bullet struck Smythson was, in my opinion, simply an accident. As to the loss occasioned by this lamentable occurrence, I consider that no cause of action is disclosed as against the appellant.[293]

In *Beim v. Goyer*[294] the chase which occurred took place on foot. The police officer chasing a fourteen year old boy stumbled and his gun discharged striking the youth in the back and resulting in permanent partial paralysis. The ensuing action found its way into the civil trial courts with the officer, Goyer, initially being held 40 per cent responsible in negligence. On appeal the Quebec Courts applied the decision in *Priestman* and the judgment was overturned. The Supreme Court of Canada allowed the subsequent appeal and restored the trial judgment.

Factually, the two cases, *Priestman* and *Beim,* are difficult to distinguish. Reconciling the disparity in the results is equally challenging. One commentator goes so far as to claim that "if anything *Priestman* was the stronger case for liability of the officer in negligence."[295]

Ritchie J. attempted to distinguish and reconcile the two cases in the following fashion:

> the case of *Priestman v. Colangelo* . . . is, in my view, distinguishable on the ground that in finding that under the circumstances there disclosed it was reasonably necessary for the policeman to fire at the tire of a fleeing car . . .
>
> In the present case, the fact that Goyer had already fallen twice in running over rough ground in pursuit of the appellant in my opinion created a situation in which he "ought reasonably to have foreseen that his arm might be jolted at the instant he fired . . ." if he should fall again as he was likely to do, and that if he did so while firing a shot he might hit Ralph Beim.[296]

With all due respect it is submitted that it was equally foreseeable for the officer, Priestman, to realize that a car speeding along at 60 miles per hour in a residential area might swerve suddenly, or hit a pot-hole (as it did), and "that his arm might be jolted at the instant he fired".

The guiding considerations, in formulating a standard for assessing the reasonableness of the resort to the use of potentially deadly force, it is suggested ought to accord with these views expressed by Cartwright J. (as he then was) in his dissent in *Priestman*:

---

293. *Ibid.* at p. 627.
294. [1965] S.C.R. 638.
295. B.C. McDonald, *supra* footnote 210 at p. 445.
296. *Beim v. Goyer, supra* footnote 294 at p. 652. For a case similar on its facts (and in its results) to *Beim v. Goyer* see *Woodward v. Begbie* (1961) 132 C.C.C. 145 (Ont.).

The officer should, I think consider the gravity of the offence of which the fugitive is believed to be guilty and the likelihood of danger to other citizens if he remains at liberty; the reasons in favor of firing would obviously be far greater in the case of an armed robber who has already killed to facilitate his flight than in the case of an unarmed youth who has stolen a suitcase which he has abandoned in the course of running away. In the former case it might well be the duty of the officer to fire if it seemed probable that this would bring down the murderer even though the firing were attended by risks to other persons on the street. In the latter case he ought not, in my opinion, to fire if to do so would be attended by any foreseeable risk of injury to innocent persons.[297]

No one seriously disputes that the use of force is often essential to the police functions of prevention and investigation of crime together with the apprehension and detention of suspected offenders. For this reason we lend statutory substance to their right to use force. The only condition which society imposes upon the peace officer is that his resort to force be reasonable, and in any event, not more than is necessary in the circumstances. This is done at a price — with the risk of injury to innocent persons, and occasionally, of disproportionate harm being visited upon guilty ones. The danger in all of this is that the controls be lost, that violence become commonplace, and that the police might lose the general support of the public. Such a loss of support is anathema to a democratic society. Where it does occur a vicious circle, or pattern, occurs, and police activity actually can serve to exacerbate general lawlessness.

There is unanimity of opinion that the police cannot *effectively* carry out their duties with respect to law enforcement unless they have the support and confidence of the public. Not only is the co-operation of the citizen necessary for effective law enforcement, but disrespect for the police creates a climate which is conducive to crime.[298]

5. THE POLICE OFFICER AS A WITNESS AND AS AN ACCUSED OR DEFENDANT

When the voluntariness of a statement is seriously in issue the veracity and credibility of the officer(s) responsible for the arrest of the accused, and the subsequent transcription of his statement, will be subject to close examination by defence counsel during the course of a voir dire. If the circumstances of an arrest or search and seizure are thought to be unlawful the police officers involved may become embroiled in legal processes ultimately leading to criminal law sanctions or civil liability.

In the ordinary trial of a criminal charge the officers concerned

---

297. *Priestman v. Colangelo, supra* footnote 291 at p. 635. This accords with the view of the Ouimet Committee (*supra* footnote 202 at pp. 59-61.)

298. Ouimet Report, *supra* footnote 202 at p. 41.

with the investigation of that charge will be required to testify as to their involvement in the matter before the court.

Innocent parties may suffer injury as the result of police investigatory or arrest activities. High speed police chases and the use of firearms make such occurrences, to a certain extent, inevitable.

Whether at the trial of an apprehended offender, a coroner's inquest or at a civil or criminal proceeding in which he is the accused/defendant, the police officer will many times find himself in the witness box. How he is received and the weight that is attached to his testimony will ultimately result in the success or failure of any prosecution. Naturally, supporting evidence is also important, but the value and importance of police testimony should not be underestimated.

For those wishing to pursue charges or claims against the police there are a number of rather profound institutional impediments to such a course of action:

(1) The investigative apparatus of the state is in the hands of the police

In the ordinary course of events the police are called upon to investigate and handle complaints against *other* members of society. The difficulty which arises when the allegation involves the excessive conduct (in a professional capacity) of one of their own members is patent. At least on the surface, wherever one group is called upon to investigate itself a conflict of interest may be said to exist.

Nevertheless, the police are called upon to investigate complaints involving their own members.[299] In this regard one hears the question raised as to "who shall watch the watchman?"[300]

This is a serious query. Even where the police undertake to investigate a complaint (whether they actually do so or not is a matter of administrative discretion) questions may legitimately be raised as to what allocation of manpower and resources is appropriate to the investigation, or what should be the length of time or breadth of scope of the investigation, and what measure of zeal has earmarked its "actual" conduct.

In short, an investigation of a complaint against the police may have form, but lack substance.

On the other side of the coin, where the possibilities of police investigations of complaints are "stonewalled" and the citizen is left to his own resources, the investigatory apparatus of the state may be utilized for the aid and assistance of the allegedly offending officer.

---

299. The police are hardly alone in this respect. Consider the disciplinary proceedings of most professional bodies — doctors, lawyers, etc. The essential distinction is that, where applicable, an external independent investigation conducted by the police with reference to possible criminal misconduct may be undertaken *in addition to* any internal disciplinary investigations and proceedings.

300. See P. Weiler, "Who Shall Watch the Watchman" Reflections on Some Recent Literature About the Police" (1968-69) 11 Cr.L.Q. 420.

An intimate connection with the information-gathering resources of the state is an invaluable aid to any litigant. Access to criminal records; access to wiretap and other electronic surveillance techniques; and the sheer advantage of increased manpower facilities, are but a few of the available tools.

At least part of the answer to this problem is contained in these remarks of the United States' *Task Force Report: The Police* (1967):

> Formal machinery within every police department for the investigation of complaints against police activity or employees and for the determination of whether departmental policy is being carried out *is an absolute necessity*. Most large police departments now have procedures of some kind for dealing with charges of misconduct by their members, whether those charges originate inside or outside of the department. *When such machinery is fully and fairly used, in concert with internal investigation and inspection programs, it succeeds both in disciplining misbehaving officers and deterring others from misbehaving.*
>
> The job of ensuring fairness and good community relations requires continuous monitoring and creates a need at all times for information as to how well departmental directives are being carried out and what new problems are developing.[301]

In assessing the American situation the President's Commission goes on to remark in its report that "although some departments have recognized the vital role that a good complaint procedure can play in police administration, too few forces today have adequate procedures for dealing with complaints.[302] One survey conducted by Michigan State University in fact concluded that through a variety of techniques (such as laying charges against those who were doing the complaining) "there was a tendency to discourage complaints against police officers.[303]

In Canada, some disquieting statistics have been gathered as a result of the Canadian Civil Liberties Association's efforts in this area:

> We have found that the overwhelming number of people who complain about police attacks resolutely refuse to take any action for the redress of their grievances.
>
> In our 1970 survey, of 59 grievors whom we were able to interview about this, only 7 or 12% proposed to do anything by way of retaliation. In our 1972 survey, of 41 arrested persons who alleged that the police had assaulted them, only 3 or 7% said that they intended to take retaliatory action. In our 1973 survey, only 3 or 12% of the 25 complainants indicated that they would be seeking redress.
>
> In all cases, we questioned the reluctant complainants as to why they

---

301. United States, *Task Force Report: The Police* (1967) at p. 194.
302. *Ibid.* at p. 194.
303. *Ibid.* at p. 195.

refused to take action. On all three occasions, the overwhelming number insisted that it would do no good.[304]

In the opinion of the Canadian Civil Liberties Association there appears to be "some basis for the skepticism expressed by these complainants." The actual reasons behind these feelings of skepticism may be nothing more than basic intuition but an objective appraisal of the remaining "impediments" to such proposed remedial action bear witness to the truth of those feelings.

(2) The supporting institutional apparatus may appear to be resistant to the criminal prosecution of a police officer

Basically in addition to the police department there are three "institutional apparatuses" which, depending upon how they function, and upon how receptive they are to a given complaint, may either impede or facilitate the aggrieved citizen's desire for redress. These are the offices of the justice of the peace, the Crown prosecutor, and the police commission.

In Metropolitan Toronto in 1975 citizen complaints against the police were processed in the following manner:

> a citizen who alleges that he has been the subject of police abuse can proceed to swear a private information before a Justice of the Peace charging the offending officer with a criminal offence. By far the greatest majority of charges laid against the police are for common assault and assault occasioning bodily harm although in rare instances charges will be laid for indecent assault, threatening, wilful damage or public mischief. In Metropolitan Toronto at the present time the swearing of a private information means that the allegation is investigated by the Complaint Bureau which then turns the file over to a special prosecutor appointed by the Ministry of the Attorney General who will then conduct the prosecution.[305]

---

304. Canadian Civil Liberties Association, *Submissions to the Task Force on Policing in Ontario* (1973). But see A. Maloney, *Report to the Metropolitan Toronto Review of Citizen-Police Complaint Procedure* (1975) especially at pp. 21-34, where important distinctions are drawn between various types of complaints *e.g.* casual complaints, chronic complaints, serious complaints, etc. Note also in Maloney Report at p. 22 that it is noted ". . . it may be judged that the citizen has no desire to press the complaint with vigour. In such cases, the Bureau opens what is called a "miscellaneous file for the record, and *relatively little investigation is carried out*". *Cf.* to pp. 26-27.

305. A. Maloney, *ibid.* pp. 35-36. Maloney reports that in 1973 in Toronto "a total of 86 criminal charges were laid by citizens against 91 officers as opposed to a total of 358 "serious" complaints registered in the same year with the Complaint Bureau. Fifty-nine of these charges were for common assault, 26 were for assault causing bodily harm and one charge was laid charging an officer with indecent assault. Sixty-four of these charges were dismissed and twenty-one withdrawn. A single conviction was registered for common assault which remains under appeal."

The *Criminal Code* is specific in declaring that a justice of the peace *shall* receive an information (complaint) sworn under oath upon reasonable and probable grounds (and which meets the jurisdictional requirements of the law).[306] However it has been argued that the phrase "on reasonable and probable grounds" introduces an element of discretion into what at first appears to be a mandatory procedure — *i.e.* mandatory at the instance of the complainant.[307]

That many Justices of the Peace regard their power to receive informations as a discretionary power is undeniable. Apparently the courts concur in this opinion and will not interfere in the judicial exercise of this discretion "save in such exceptional circumstances as prejudice, bias, personal interest, dishonesty, or the like".[308] The law in this respect is much the same as it was when pronounced by Meredith J. in 1899:

> It was the duty of the police magistrate, upon receiving the information, to hear and consider the allegations of the informant, and if of the opinion that cause for issuing a warrant or summons was not made out, to refuse it. And having so acted, this Court has no jurisdiction over him.
>
> It is his judgment, not mine nor that of any other Judge or Court, which is to be exercised under s. 599 of the Criminal Code.[309]

In *Evans v. Pesce*[310] an individual entrapped into selling marihuana to an undercover police constable sought to have the constable prosecuted for his participation in the criminal offence. The magistrate/justice of the peace "did not refuse to embark upon a hearing, but allowed counsel the widest scope in presenting his position, at the conclusion of which the magistrate reached a decision".[311] The decision was *not* to issue a summons or warrant pursuant to *Code* s. 440 (now s. 455.3) requiring the constable to attend before him. The accused Evans thereafter sought an order of mandamus to compel the magistrate to allow proceedings to be initiated against Constable Pesce. The application was dismissed primarily on the grounds that Riley J. of the Alberta Supreme Court felt that Constable Pesce had "done nothing that has not been recognized as a *legitimate* detection effort in the area of drug traffic"[312] — a debatable proposition. However, the decision

---

306. See the *Criminal Code* R.S.C. 1970 Chap. c-34, ss. 455 and 723.
307. See also s. 455.3 which places a judicial duty on the justice to hear and consider *ex parte* the allegations of the informant and, where necessary or desirable, the evidence of witnesses.
308. *Evans v. Pesce* (1969-70) 8 C.R.N.S. 201 at p. 214 (Alta.) *per* Riley J.
309. *Re Parke* (1899) 30 O.R. 498 at pp. 501-502 cited in *Evans v. Pesce, supra* at p. 214. See also the other cases cited in this regard by Riley J. in *Evans* at p. 214-219.
310. *Supra* footnote 308.
311. *Ibid.* at p. 214.
312. *Ibid.* at p. 207.

of the learned Judge taken as a whole was unimpeachable since it was indicated that the discretion exercised by the magistrate below was exercised judicially and therefore was not subject to review.

The *Evans* case (however debateable it is on the merits) is one instance of an individual who was denied access to the courts when what was sought was to question the legality of official police activity.

While statistical studies have been conducted with respect to numerous other aspects of citizen-police complaint procedures, the discretionary activities of justices of the peace *vis-a-vis* citizen complaints have not been so scrutinized.

Thus while the practice of blocking the initiation of proceedings at this stage is known to exist, it is not known how widespread the practice has become, or how responsibly this discretionary power is being utilized.

Justices of the Peace and Crown Prosecutors both necessarily, as a result the inherent nature of their duties, have an extensive and entirely proper liaison with the police. The justice of the peace will have occasion to be consulted by the police with respect to matters of bail and the swearing of informations. Crown Attorneys depend upon the police for the bulk of the investigatory assistance necessary for the successful prosecution of a charge. Police officers are often the most important witnesses called in the presentation of the prosecution's case.

However, in situations where a police officer becomes an accused the closeness of these liaisons with the police becomes a compromising circumstance.

> Criminal prosecutions in court are handled by the same Crown Attorney who is in daily co-operation and association with the police. Because of this many complainants will fear that prosecutions *of* police will not be as vigorously pursued as prosecutions *by* police."[313]

By and large this is a feature of the criminal justice system which is not quantifiable. The problem in *actual* terms may not be great. That is, the level of bias and the disinclination to prosecute offending officers may be minimal or (hopefully) even non-existent. Nevertheless to the extent that the public believes such bias to exist the problem remains important and essentially unamenable to easy resolution. The appointment of special prosecutors from the criminal defence bar might serve to allay some of the public doubt and suspicion on the matter.

Depending upon the jurisdiction in Canada, citizen complaints against the police may be handled through normal channels of command, or under the auspices of boards of police commissioners (or by Bureaus of Complaints appointed by those boards).

The "normal channels of command" have been dealt with *supra.* The Canadian Civil Liberties Association has expressed these reser-

---

313. Canadian Civil Liberties Association, *supra* footnote 304 at p. 15.

vations about the performance of boards of police commissioners in this area:

> While the boards of police commissioners may process complaints more expeditiously, the concern is that they will handle them less impartially. Police commissions are responsible for the daily administration of police departments. They are, therefore, concerned with the public image, efficiency, morale and legal liability of the police force. As a result, there is an inevitable conflict of interest. They must reconcile the need to vindicate the rights of citizens with the need to protect the interests of the police. Thus, no matter how fairly police commissions perform in particular cases, they will not be *perceived* as impartial.[314]

There have been a host of suggestions for improving the entire field of citizen-police complaint procedures.[315] Naturally the ideal features of impartiality, independence, fairness, accessibility, expedition and reduced cost are the central concerns of any such scheme.

(3) Shortcomings inherent in private prosecutions

Presumably the public prosecution of an offence (*i.e.* prosecution of the offence by the Attorney General and his appointed agents) has the following general advantages over the private prosecution of an offence by an aggrieved individual:

(1) the costs are borne by the state;

(2) the investigation occurs through an established channel of liaison between the police and the Crown Attorney.

(3) the prosecutor's presence is a physical and symbolic indicator of the *bona fides* of complaint — the matter being of sufficient import to merit his intervention.

(4) the matter is dealt with in the ordinary court rather than by its being delegated to the docket of "private" matters which contain a certain number of "nuisance disputes" (*e.g.* matrimonial disputes, neighbourly disputes).

(5) the prosecutor's control over his docket is a safeguard against delay and dismissals for want of prosecution.

(6) a certain minimum standard of competence of representation is assured. (It is not uncommon for one or both of the parties in a private prosecution to be unrepresented.)

Given these factors it is not difficult to envision the practical difficulties which will be encountered by any individual choosing to privately prosecute a complaint against a police officer.

If he is fortunate enough to be able to afford counsel the costs

---

314. *Ibid.* at p. 16.
315. See A. Maloney, *supra* footnote 304 especially at pp. 96-179 and Part IX of the Report.

sustained by the private prosecutor will nevertheless be unrecoverable even in the event of successful prosecution.

Investigation without police assistance can be difficult, costly, and on occasion, well nigh impossible.

The appearance of the assent of the state to the bringing of the prosecution will patently be lacking.

Technical difficulties (such as inability to be present at all docket or remand appearances) may well result in a dismissal without a trial on the merits.

If cost is a factor the quality of representation may suffer (especially if the complainant goes shopping for a bargain.)

(4) Tort law provides an inadequate means of redress

The complainant who foregoes his cause of action in the criminal courts embarks on a radically different tack when he chooses to seek redress in the civil courts. In this regard it should be noted that "civil litigation is expensive, time consuming and emotionally taxing . . . [and] very few people have the resources to investigate the facts, engage counsel, withstand pressure by the police, and handle the many expenses which are inevitably involved."[316]

The civil claim is restricted in similar fashion to the criminal process in that manifestations of police misconduct are not actionable. (Examples are verbal abuse and discrimination.)[317] The risk factor, as evidenced by the penalty of costs, looms larger in the civil courts than in courts of criminal jurisdiction.

Actual civil actions commenced against the police usually meet with a minimal level of success and are neither very lucrative for, nor popular with, the citizen complainant.[318]

Above and beyond these considerations Paul Weiler in considering the problem of the control of police arrest practices[319] makes the following cogent observations concerning the efficacy of tort law as a regulatory device:

> the real burden of deterrence [to unlawful police activity] appears to be thrown on the law of torts. Now tort law, ordinarily appears to be institutionally unsuited for its so-called "admonitory" function. Imposition of sanctions depends upon the fact of somebody being hurt, not just a breach of the rules, on the person hurt making the unilateral de-

---

316. Canadian Civil Liberties Association, *supra* footnote 304 at p. 15. And see A. Maloney, *supra* footnote 304 at pp. 40-41.

317. *A. Maloney, supra* footnote 304 at p. 40.

318. See Maloney *supra* footnote 304 at pp. 40 and 42 for a statistical study of actions commenced and rates of success in the period between 1969 and 1973.

319. P. Weiler, "Control of Police Arrest Practices: Reflections of a Tort Lawyer" in A. Linden (ed.) *Studies in Canadian Tort Law* (1968) at p. 416. See also W.E. Horkins, "False Arrest Today" (1973) L.S.U.C. Special Lectures 241 (New Developments in the Law of Torts.)

cision to seek legal redress, and on the effectiveness of his resources alone to establish the breach. The sanction itself is not rationally related to the enormity of the defendant's conduct but rather to the seriousness of the plaintiff's loss.

Weiler's reflections are admittedly (by his title) those of a tort lawyer, and when contrasting whether the more meaningful sanction to unlawful police activity is to be found under criminal law processes or within the domain of tort law he tentatively concludes that "the least deficient of all solutions may well be *punitive* tort law".[320] However, he adds that we must consider that since tort law had deficiencies in both remedy and sanction it may not significantly aid in the judicial control of the police (which, above and beyond the individual instance of abuse, is truly the primary concern of the process). In this regard a serious re-thinking of the Canadian approach to the exclusionary rule seems desirable.[321]

> However, it must be recognized that there are substantial institutional difficulties in using tort law as a means for achieving the ends for which we strive. These stem primarily from the fact that tort law operates after the fact of the breach to award a monetary amount to the plaintiff, in some way related to his loss. This is quite an adequate process when the harm for which the award is made is in some way economic (either out of pocket expenses, loss of profits, loss of earning capacity, *etc.*), and can rationally be reduced into pecuniary terms, but these conditions rarely exist here.[322]

(5) The cost of litigation (civil or criminal) may deter the bringing or pressing of claims by those aggrieved

The preceding analysis makes this point quite adequately. Litigation, save when subsidized by the state, can be a costly process. Often those aggrieved my be least able to bear this burden. Legal aid may or may not be available depending upon the scheme in operation and the nature of eligibility requirements. Loss of a civil suit in addition to failing to compensate for alleged damages, may result in the penalty of costs.

(6) The litigation process (civil or criminal) is productive of delay

Both the civil and criminal processes of the courts have been the subject of strong and pointed criticism on this feature of their operation. Delay works to the disadvantage of the plaintiff/prosecutor. Evidence disappears, witnesses move or die, memory fades, and resolve to see a matter through to its conclusion diminishes.

---

320. P. Weiler, *ibid.* at p. 445 and see W. Horkins, *ibid.* at pp. 255-258.
321. See Weiler, *ibid.* at p. 457 *et seq.* And also see the consideration of "The Importance of the Illegally Obtained Evidence Rule to the Role of the Police" discussed *supra.*
322. *Ibid.* at p. 445.

Although the criminal justice system has been the recipient of the brunt of the attack it is probably true to say that the civil procedures of the courts are more productive of delay than are the criminal law processes. The complexities of civil procedure (irrespective of the cause of action) to a certain extent dictate a degree of delay. "Negotiations for settlement, examinations for discovery, innumerable motions, trials, and appeals could take years to produce results".[323]

As to delay in the criminal justice system the following has recently been written:

> Then, however, by a process which the layman invariably finds difficult to comprehend, this person who is procedurally probably guilty, suddenly becomes, evidentially, presumed to be not guilty, and becomes entitled to all the evidential and procedural protections that the law can afford him. He is entitled to counsel, he is entitled to seek adjournments, he may be entitled to elect various means of trial. In short, he is entitled to put as many obstacles in the way of his being proved guilty as the ingenuity of his lawyer, the tolerance of his judge and the law itself will allow.[324]

(7) To deter the laying of charges by citizens against police or to undermine such charges once laid, anticipatory charges are sometimes lodged against a citizen/complainant by the police

One American study of police brutality demonstrates this fact of unlawful police activity in action:

> The right to protect himself often leads the policeman to argue self-defence whenever he uses force. We found that many policemen, whether or not the facts justify it, regularly follow their use of force with the charge that the citizen was assaulting a policeman or resisting arrest. Our observers also found that some policemen even carry pistols and knives that they have confiscated while searching citizens; they carry them so they may be placed at a scene should it be necessary to establish a case of self-defence.[325]

It is not here suggested that the same level of institutional paranoia presents itself in Canada. Nevertheless, it would be naive to suggest that practice of anticipatory charging does not exist in Canada. Some individuals who are acquitted of charges of resisting arrest or assaulting a peace officer may escape liability on technical grounds, or upon insufficiency of evidence, but clearly others may do so by making out a case of self-defence or justification.

---

323. Canadian Civil Liberties Association *supra* footnote 304 at p. 15.
324. A. W. Mewett, "Editorial: Efficiency in the Court-Room" (1975) 18 Cr.L.Q. (Pt. 1) 1 at p. 2. See also B. Grosman, "Testing Witness Reliability" (1962-63) 4 Cr.L.Q. 318 for a consideration of the importance of delay to the reliability of a witness' recollection of events.
325. A. Reiss Jr., "Police Brutality" in Johnston, Savitz and Wolfgang (ed.) *The Sociology of Punishment and Correction* (2nd ed.) (1962).

(It is well to remember that the youth Koechlin[326] commenced his civil action for damages for false arrest and imprisonment only after being exonerated of a groundless charge laid against him of assaulting a police officer.)

In psychological terms it is easy to see that this instrument—anticipatory charging—carries with it great coercive weight. In simple terms it is pure intimidation. It might be added that it is highly effective intimidation.

In summary it has been contended that these several factors serve as institutional impediments to the bringing or pursuing of charges or claims against the police:

(1) the investigatory apparatus of the state is in the hands of the police;
(2) the supporting institutional apparati (justices of the peace, crown prosecutors, police commissions) may appear to be resistant to the criminal prosecution of a police officer;
(3) there are shortcomings inherent in private prosecutions;
(4) tort law provides an inadequate means of redress;
(5) the cost of litigation is a deterrent;
(6) the litigation process is productive of delay;
(7) anticipatory charges may be lodged against the citizen/complainant as a deterrent.

In addition to the institutional impediments which exist, a facet of human nature, or, better put, a psychological factor has pronounced effect upon the total picture of the status of the police officer as a witness and as an accused/defendant. That factor is *credibility*.

To bring the matter in to sharper focus the role played by credibility, or, the weight attached by judge or jury to the testimony of witnesses, is absolutely crucial to the trial process. In this area, at least, science must yield to intuition. And the rule of law must shed its cloak of rationality and emerge as a "human" institution with all of the frailty that that adjective implies.

In Canada it is presumed that all men stand equal before the law, and that in a court of law each man called to give testimony is entitled to have his story judged or accredited in an atmosphere of impartiality and disinterest. The factual underpinnings of any case are to be discovered (as nearly as possible) without resort by the trier of fact to bias, prejudice, or personal inclination.

The ideal however must accommodate reality.

For a time in the first half of this century it was contended that process of assessing credibility was susceptible of formulaic reduction and somewhat automatic application. This situation arose out of certain comments made by Beck J. in *R. v. Covert*:[327]

---

326. *Koechlin v. Waugh* (1957) 118 C.C.C. 24 (Ont. C.A.) discussed earlier in Part 4 of this Chapter.
327. (1916) 28 C.C.C. 25 (Alta. C.A.).

We are bound to presume the accused was innocent, until proved guilty; he gave all the available evidence and that evidence, if true, explained away the inference or presumption against him.

It will be objected, of course that the magistrate may have disbelieved entirely the evidence on behalf of the accused, and that it was open to him to do so; but in my opinion it cannot be said without limitation that a Judge can refuse to accept evidence. I think he cannot if the following conditions are fulfilled:

(1) that the statements of the witness are not in themselves improbable or unreasonable;

(2) that there is no contradiction of them;

(3) that the credibility of the witness has not been attacked by evidence against his character;

(4) that nothing appears in the course of his evidence or of the evidence of any other witness tending to throw discredit upon him; and

(5) that there is nothing in his demeanour while in Court during the trial to suggest untruthfulness.[328]

These are credible guides which are of use to the trier of fact when seeking to assess the credibility of any witness. In the years following *R. v. Covert* great weight was attached to these pronouncements[329] with some courts even indicating that a Judge cannot refuse to accept evidence and act upon it, if the five conditions laid down in *R. v. Covert supra* are present.[330]

In 1947 the Supreme Court of Canada had occasion to consider the comments made by Beck J. in *Covert*. Estey J. expressed these opinions on the subject:

The issue of credibility is one of fact and cannot be determined by following a set of rules that is suggested to have the force of law, and in so far as the language of Mr. Justice Beck [in *R. v. Covert supra*] may be so construed, it cannot be supported upon the authorities . . .

Eminent Judges have from time to time indicated certain guides that have been of the greatest assistance but so far as I have been able to find there has never been an effort to indicate all the possible factors that might enter into the determination. It is a matter in which so many human characteristics, both the strong and the weak, must be taken into consideration. The general integrity and intelligence of the witness, his power to observe, his capacity to remember and his accuracy in statement are important. It is also important to determine whether he is honestly endeavouring to tell the truth, whether he is sincere and frank or whether he is biased, reticent and evasive. All these questions and others may be answered from the observation of

---

328. *Ibid.* at p. 30.

329. See *R. v. Morin* (1917) 28 C.C.C. 414 (Alta. C.A.). See also *R. v. Barb* (1917) 28 C.C.C. 93 (Alta.).

330. See *R. v. Ciccanti* (1941) 47 R.L.N.S. 283.

the witness' general conduct and demeanour in determining a question of credibility.[331]

It should be noted that Estey J. is not disagreeing with the usefulness of the "guides" which Beck J. proposes but merely with the elevation of these guides to a status of rules of law. He also indicates that the list of factors proposed by Beck J. to assist the triers of fact is not an exhaustive one.

The question of which side is telling the truth in a criminal trial is not a matter to be "solved" by the triers of fact.[332] Rather, where a jury is involved they must be instructed that in arriving at a conclusion they should consider the credibility of all of the witnesses. If the jury has any reasonable doubt of the truth of the story told by the witnesses for the Crown, or, if they thought that the evidence given by the accused might reasonably be true they should return a verdict of "not guilty".

A Judge sitting alone also "must deal with each case as it arises accordingly as the matter of credibility affects his mind".[333] As A. E. Popple notes this judicial function is rarely interfered with on appeal:

> Where there is conflicting evidence and the trial judge accepts the version of one witness for example in preference to that of three others and there is evidence to support the conviction a Court of Appeal will not usually substitute its own opinion as to the guilt of the accused for that of the trial judge who has the advantage of seeing and hearing the witnesses: *Rex v. Bercovitch and Somberg* (1946), 1 C.R. 200.[334]

Credibility is a matter going to the "weight" of evidence (in contrast to "admissibility"). It cannot therefore "be determined by arbitrary rules since it depends mainly on common sense, logic and experience."[335] Since it is such an imprecise area to avoid the appearance of arbitrariness the trial judge should not reject uncontradicted evidence without stating reasons.[336]

---

331. *White v. R.* (1947) 89 C.C.C. 148 at p. 151 (Can.) *per* Estey J.
332. See *R. v. Nykiforuk* (1946-7) 2 C.R. 41 (Sask. C.A.) and see the useful annotation by A.E. Popple which follows at p. 47 of the same Report entitled "Conflict Between Two Sets of Witnesses".
333. *Watt v. Watt* (1909) 10 W.L.R. 699 *per* Wetmore C.J. See also *Yuill v. Yuill* [1945] 1 All E.R. 183; *Roche v. Marston* [1951] 3 D.L.R. 433 (Can.); and *R. v. Bolt* (1958) 121 C.C.C. 210 (Alta. C.A.) which establish that although the appeal court does not have the same opportunity to observe the demeanour and appearance of a witness, it nevertheless has a duty to consider whether the trial judge had in mind the whole of the evidence and the proved circumstances in accepting the evidence of one witness over that of another (as cited in P.K. McWilliams *Canadian Criminal Evidence* (1974) at pp. 653-654).
334. A. E. Popple, *supra* footnote 332 at p. 52.
335. *Ibid.* at p. 54.
336. See *R. v. Gun Ying* (1930) 53 C.C.C. 378 (Ont. C.A.); *R. v. Tonelli* (1951), 99 C.C.C. 345 (B.C. C.A.).

O'Halloran J.A. in the widely known judgment of *R. v. Pressley* set forth these oft-quoted remarks on the subject of credibility:

> The most satisfactory judicial test of truth lies in its [the evidence's] harmony or lack of harmony with the preponderance of probabilities disclosed by the facts and circumstances in the conditions of the particular case. . . . In "General View of the Criminal Law" (1890), Mr. Justice Stephen said at p. 191: ". . . the utmost result that can in any case be produced by judicial evidence is a very *high degree of probability. . . .*" But probability of this kind is not the product of arbitrary decision. It is founded upon a rational review of the evidence step by step, wherein the balance is reached under conditions which push suspicion, preconceived notions, conjecture and guessing into the background.[337]

As Popple notes, the general instruction to juries by trial judges in the ordinary course of events, "is a practical one—pay attention to every witness; gauge as well as you can his or her honesty and capacity; give such effect as you think it deserves; weigh *all* the evidence you believe; and come to the best conclusion you can from the admitted and proven facts."[338]

Presumably these thoughts apply as much to *self-direction* by a judge sitting alone as they do to instructions by a judge to a jury.

The foregoing examination of the legal significance of "credibility" and credibility findings suitably sets the stage for a consideration of the question of why the police officer as witness or accused enjoys the attributed quality of elevated credibility in comparison to the ordinary witness or accused person.

Arthur Maloney Q.C., in his report to the Metropolitan Toronto Board of Commissioners of Police on "Citizen-Police Complaint Procedure" indicated four areas of concern expressed by those who complain about the inadequacy of the criminal law response to alleged police misconduct:

(1) usually the only witnesses to an incident are the victim and the police officer or officers involved;[339]

(2) these charges are almost invariably proceeded with in the Provincial Courts, the same courts in which police officers testify on a regular basis on behalf of the Crown and by virtue of this fact, in addition to acquiring considerable expertise in the art of giving evidence police officers may in a sense be considered as much an integral part of the criminal justice system as the Crown Attorney, the Provincial Court Judges and the Court attendants;

(3) it is difficult in the extreme and unreasonable for us to expect that

---

337. *R. v. Pressley* (1949) 7 C.R. 342 (B.C. C.A.).
338. A. E. Popple, *supra* footnote 332 at p. 55.
339. See W. Westley, "Secrecy and the Police" in Johnston, Savitz, and Wolfgang (ed.) *The Sociology of Punishment and Correction* (2nd ed.) (1962) at p. 80.

the same Provincial Court Judge who may have had an officer appear on behalf of the prosecution in his Court on countless previous occasions, but who is now under charges himself can disabuse himself of a bias favouring the officer, especially in a case where there are numerous fellow officers to testify in support of the version of the incident given by the officer charged; and

(4) in the majority of cases complainants are poor, probably unemployed, and often have criminal records.[340]

The trial of an issue (either respecting an officer's guilt, or *vis-a-vis* the voluntariness of a confession which the officer has secured) begins with these basic pro-police inclinations.

The police officer (often uniformed, but otherwise dressed in suit and tie) presents himself as a professional, experienced witness. He is articulate (at least by comparison to his accuser) and familiar to the Court. Presumably he, himself, has an unblemished record. His accuser may not be so endowed—a fact which will, however irrelevant to the facts in issue, find its way before the Court.[341]

On a voir dire concerning the admissibility of a statement the police officer conveys the appearance of disinterest in the case (in contrast to the accused who is, naturally, a vitally interested party). The police in such circumstances are often described by the courts as "disinterested parties". Such a description is a trifle misleading—the "interest" of the police residing as it does in the securing of a conviction. In celebrated cases where there is an element of public alarm (such as, where a series of violent rapes have gone unsolved for a considerable period of time with resulting detriment to the police public image) this level of "interest" becomes even more pronounced.

Also, it must be remembered that the danger in the police officer's job quite naturally casts him in a sympathetic light.

Since our system of criminal justice is, after all, ultimately only human these are factors which count for much. On balance it is difficult to think of why they should not be so weighted. But that perspective does not of itself alleviate the full burden of the appearance of compromised impartiality which unfortunately arises when the tables turn and the finger of guilt is pointed at the policeman.

It is open to question as to whether or not the criminal justice system is adequate for the task of supervising police misconduct. The same may be said of the ability of the civil courts to deal with citizen-complaints against police misconduct.

The police officer, like any person who becomes an accused or defendant, is entitled to the same protections, benefits, and presump-

---

340. A. Maloney, *supra* footnote 304 at p. 39.
341. See *Canada Evidence Act* R.S.C. 1970 chap. E-10, s. 12. And see *Koufis v. R.* [1941] S.C.R. 481. Also C.A. Wright, "Case and Comment" (1940) 18 Can.Bar.Rev. 808.

tions that our law affords to any individual occupying that status. No special exceptions to the ordinary rules and safeguards appear justified.

Some new mechanical, procedural safeguards might be built into the system (such as the supervised questioning proposal put forward by the Law Reform Commission of Canada). But these safeguards, while possibly proving salutary in a limited way, cannot possibly do away with many of the impediments discussed earlier.

To close off analysis of the problem at this point would not be a particularly satisfactory or satisfying terminus. It is not acceptable simply to address the problems, identify them, and then merely to toss off the response that they are insoluble. Certainly if they are insoluble problems their worst aspects can be greatly mollified.

Basic to any *substantial* change in this area must be a cognizance of the fact that basic, normative police behavior must be modified. But like all "Revolutions of Consciousness" this perhaps the most nebulous, and least likely area for possible immediate, or at least, short term, change to be effected.

One place where an initial assault upon this forboding obstacle may be commenced is in the area of police training and recruitment techniques.[342] One cannot seriously quarrel with the notion that improvement in these initial phases of policing will serve to upgrade the level of public service offered by the police generally.

More difficult to assess is what impact improved recruitment and training techniques will have on the general sociology of internal police relations. Will the appearance of a new breed of "rookie cop" serve to break down the normative patterns of behavior which earmarks the police bureaucracy, or will the entrenched behavioral patterns eradicate the gains produced by improved recruitment and training? What will the effect be on the long-standing code of police secrecy?

> The chief threat to the code of secrecy is the initiate, for he is yet largely a member of the outer world, with no involvement with the group. Therefore, in the beginning care must be taken that he is not given premature access to secrets, and full acceptance occurs only when he is told secrets. Among the police the "rookie" is carefully observed and assessed, at the same time that he is constantly told about the need for secrecy. In fact, there is no area of police work where the code of secrecy is more evident.
>
> Fifty percent of the "rookies" (men in training) were asked what the experienced men had told them. *All* reported that *every* experienced man with whom they had been in contact emphasized the need for secrecy in statements like "Keep your mouth shut—never squeal on a fellow officer". They had dinned into their ears by man after man, as they went the rounds of training, and the admonition was related to every conceivable kind of situation. They were all told to beware of

---

342. See A. Grant "Some Reflections on Police Education and Training in Canada" (1976) 18 Cr.L.Q. 218.

stool pigeons who were regularly characterized in disparaging terms. This is what finally drove the lesson home. The rookies became aware of stool pigeons and learned to fear them. They became suspicious . . . The experienced men, in turn, evaluated the rookies chiefly in terms of their discretion. Forty experienced officers (representing approximately thirty-five per cent of the patrolmen) were asked what they considered the most desirable characteristic in the rookie. Forty-seven percent said that "he should keep his mouth shut" and another thirteen percent said that "he shouldn't be a stool pigeon".

Thus, the role was so important that it was made explicit to every new man by every experienced man; and the ability to keep secrets was considered essential to acceptance and a successful career.[343]

Suggestions that the police be supervised at important stages of investigation (as in the case of the proposal that the only statements admissible against an accused be those obtained under a system of supervised questioning)[344] really operate, by implication, under the assumption that police behavior is extremely secretive and difficult to modify. Accordingly the proposal is put that some public scrutiny should be injected into the process in an attempt to insure "that while in police custody accused persons are treated in a manner which corresponds with our conceptions of human dignity".[345]

Although it is admitted in the supervised questioning proposal of the Law Reform Commission that "the proposal will not guarantee the elimination of all improper police conduct"[346] there is nevertheless no attempt made to expand upon the area of proposed public scrutiny of police conduct in an effort further to deter improper police conduct. If "watching eyes and listening ears" truly do deter such conduct then one wonders why the proposal has yet to be put that recording cameras (such as those which are used in banks and supermarkets) be placed in police station houses, lock-ups, and interview rooms; and why tape recorded logs should not be mandatory in police cruiser and patrol cars. Surely such suggestions must carry at least equal weight to those which are periodically advanced to the effect that the accused's right to remain silent should be further fettered.

Less extreme suggestions for dealing with improper police conduct and citizen complaint procedures centre around the need for greater independence in the complaint gathering and investigatory mechanism

---

343. W. A. Westley, "Secrecy and the Police" in Johnston, Wolfgang and Savitz (ed.) *The Sociology of Punishment and Correction* (2nd ed. 1962) 80 at p. 83.
344. See Law Reform Commission of Canada, *Evidence: 5. Compellability of the Accused and the Admissibility of his Statements* (Study Paper, January 1973) at pp. 12-22 and see the *Manitoba Law Reform Commission's* comments on this paper *per F.C. Muldoon in* (1974) 37 Man.B.N. 172.
345. *Ibid*. Study Paper at p. 16.
346. *Ibid* at p. 17.

provided by the state. Clearly improvements on the existing modes are possible and a plethora of remedial suggestions have been put forward.[347]

Finally, if these matters are regarded as partially concerning themselves with police public relations and the police image then police "concern" over lawlessness "within the ranks" could be evidenced by the application of a standard of proof *less* than what prevails in a criminal trial for alleged infractions with consequences short of disbarment for *internal* disciplinary hearings.[348] In addition, once culpability has been found to be proved, *meaningful* disciplinary measures are essential if the process is to be viewed as credible, and if it is to have some influence in shaping the norms of police conduct.[349]

These proposals barely scratch the surface of the problems involved in citizen-police complaint procedures. A greatly expanded and more ambitious look at reforming the process is to be found in the Maloney Report on citizen-police complaint procedures in Metropolitan Toronto.[350] While impressive in the range and depth of its survey that report should not be viewed as a panacea—especially since its concern resides largely in the area of structural and procedural change when the major difficulties to be confronted fall largely within the realms of sociology and psychology. Structural/procedural changes can effect the system but the question remains: "How much?".

---

347. See A. Maloney, *Report on Citizen-Police Complaint Procedure supra* footnote 304.

348. "Internal" as opposes to "external" complaint procedures — *i.e.* criminal prosecution. See *contra* Maloney, *supra* footnote 304 at p. 243.

349. See A. Maloney, *supra* footnote 304 at pp. 59-63. Also note p. 61 where the observation is made that "one cannot help but be struck by the relatively few instances in which meaningful disciplinary action resulted from a finding of culpability on the part of an officer complained against."

350. *Supra* footnote 304.

3

SELECTED PRE-TRIAL AND TRIAL PROCESSES: THE PROSECUTOR

1. INTRODUCTION

In Canada anyone who has reasonable and probable grounds to believe that a person has committed an indictable offence may initiate criminal proceedings by laying an information before an appropriate justice of the peace.[1] With relatively few exceptions,[2] the right to institute, and subsequently to prosecute, criminal charges may rest solely in the hands of a private prosecutor. In actual practice, in most jurisdictions in Canada the prosecution of criminal offence lies in the hands of public prosecutors—Crown Attorneys, their assistants, and agents. These public prosecutors are the agents of the provincial Attorney General or of the Attorney General of Canada, and they act in the name of the Crown. The office of the Crown Attorney is defined by statute.[3]

Among the statutory functions and duties of a Crown Attorney is the responsibility to

> watch over cases conducted by private prosecutors and without unnecessarily interfering with private individuals who wish in such cases to prosecute, assume wholly the conduct of the case where justice towards the accused seems to demand his interposition.[4]

In consequence of this general duty to oversee and monitor all private prosecutions (and in a proper case to intervene therein), it is clear that in vast measure the "discretion to prosecute" lies with the Crown Attorney as agent for the Crown.[5]

Provision is made in the *Criminal Code* under s. 737(1) for the informant to conduct his case personally, but it has been held that

---

1. The Criminal Code R.S.C. 1970 c. C-34, s. 455
2. Note that *Code* ss. 54, 82, 108, 243, and 433(2) require the consent of the Attorney General of Canada before proceedings may be instituted. Ss. 124, 162(3), 168, 170, 343(2), and 434(3) require the consent of the Provincial Attorney General before prosecutions may be initiated.
3. *E.g.* in Ontario the governing statute is *The Crown Attorneys Act,* R.S.O. 1970, c. 101 (as amended). See also, *R. v. Pelletier* (1975) 28 C.R.N.S. 129 (Ont. C.A.) for discussion of the constitutional aspects of the office.
4. *Ibid.* s. 12(d) as amended by 1972 (Ont.), c. 1, s. 1.
5. See *R. v. Leonard* (1962) 38 C.R. 209 (Alta. C.A.) as an example of how complete and total this discretion to prosecute (in the Attorney General) actually is. In that case the Crown intervened in order to stay proceedings on a private prosecution; much to the chagrin of the private prosecutor who had no intention of abandoning his cause.

while a private person may prosecute at the summary trial of an indictable offence and a preliminary inquiry, he cannot conduct further proceedings following a committal for trial without the subsequent assistance of the Attorney-General. Where the accused has elected for a trial by a judge without a jury the private prosecutor may not appear as prosecutor without the written consent of the Attorney General. Where the accused has elected trial by judge and jury the private prosecutor requires leave of either the Court or of the Attorney General.[6]

Quite clearly in Canada when one speaks of the *power* to prosecute, or of the *discretion* to withhold prosecution, or of the larger, more all-embracing term "prosecutorial discretion", one contemplates those powers which are wielded by Crown Prosecutors under the aegis of the Attorney General.

Great Britain despite "the general compatibility of the substantive and procedural criminal law with that of Canada" does not have an equivalent system of public prosecutors.[7] Nevertheless the historical antecedents to the Canadian system are rooted in British legal history, and of course the initial nexus of the office of the Attorney General itself with its British counterpart was intimate.[8] Wells C.J.H.C. had occasion to consider the history of the office of the Attorney General in *Smythe v. R.*[9] The learned justice was quick to point out that his primary debt was to a single comprehensive source which has been the leading reference since its publication in 1964—Edwards, *The Law Officer of the Crown*. ("An excellent review of the history and development of this ancient office can be found in J. Li. J. Edwards, *The Law Officer of the Crown* (1964).") The following passages extracted from the judgment in *Smythe* adequately describe the growth and development of the office of the Attorney General in Canada and serve to explain the origins of his discretionary power:

---

6. *R. v. Schwerdt* (1957) 119 C.C.C. 81 (B.C.) — The private prosecutor can of course seek to have the Attorney-General intervene on his behalf following the committal stage. See also *R. v. Pelletier supra* footnote 3.

7. Report of the Ontario Law Reform Commission *On the Administration of Ontario Courts,* Part II, Appendix I, p. 130 (1973).

8. Many of the commentators have had occasion to consider comparative modes of criminal prosecution as they exist and have developed in various countries. See the *Report on the Administration of Ontario Courts,* Part II (1973) *supra* for discussion and reference pertaining to Scotland, the Continent, the United States, and England at pp. 129-131; See also Grosman, *The Prosecutor, An Inquiry into the Exercise of Discretion* (1969) Chapter II — an historical perspective on English, American, French and Canadian prosecuting practices. Also K. C. Davis, *Discretionary Justice, A Preliminary Inquiry* (1969) at p. 191 contains an analysis of the prosecuting system in West Germany.

9. (1971) 3 C.C.C. (2d) 97 (Ont. C.A.), affirmed by (1971) 3 C.C.C. (2d) 366 (Can.).

The criminal law of England was declared to extend in Canada in March, 1777, and Courts of Criminal Jurisdiction were set up by an ordinance of Sir Guy Carleton. English criminal law had actually been imposed under the military government prior to the *British North America (Quebec) Act* 1774 (U.K.), c. 83. This action, it is said, met with favour because the English criminal law did not allow torture and in some respects was less severe than the comparable French criminal law which had been enforced in Canada prior to the cession of Canada to Great Britain. And as early as 1769, some six years after the treaty ceding Canada to the British Crown, there was an Attorney-General functioning in Canada, in Quebec, and apparently carrying on the administration of criminal law, or pleas of the Crown as they were sometimes called during that period. That early Attorney-General was Francis Maseres.

The office of the Attorney-General is a very ancient one and goes back in common law history to the 13th century. He became in time the principal law officer of the Crown. The Attorney-General of Canada is the principal law officer of the Crown in Canada. Since the criminal law of England came into effect, its enforcement has been in the hands of an Attorney-General. It was so under the *British North America (Quebec) Act* and under the Constitutional Act ["An Act to re-unite the Provinces of *Upper* and *Lower Canada,* and for the Government of *Canada",* 1840 (U.K.), c. 35 (*B.N.A. Act, 1840*)]. After the Constitutional Act the whole apparatus of British government, including a legislative assembly and council, was set up in Upper Canada. Despite the ordinances of Sir Guy Carleton, the Legislature of Upper Canada in the early years of the 19th century for greater certainty declared that the criminal law of England was vested in the Courts of the Province, at that time the Court of King's Bench. There is no suggestion that the decision of an Attorney-General as to how to prosecute was at any time looked on as an act of discrimination. Instead, it was his duty to perform such an act in a judicial manner without any suggestion of fear or favour for anyone. One cannot deal with the judicial process of even the earliest time without realizing that before the law all men were regarded as being equal and as having the protection of the law. The same systems were followed after the Act of union in 1840 and were enjoyed in the Maritime Provinces which came into Canada, Nova Scotia and New Brunswick in particular, at the time of Confederation. Confederation made no change in this system . . . The result is that our constitution is the same in principle as that which existed in the United Kingdom in 1867. It had been the same so far as the criminal law is concerned since shortly after the middle of the 18th century. The Attorney-General's discretion springs from the Royal Prerogative of the Justice and its enforcement in maintaining the King's Peace.[10]

These last sentiments to the effect that "the Attorney General's discretion springs from the Royal Prerogative of the Justice and its enforcement in maintaining the King's Peace" express the very *funda-*

---

10. *Ibid.* at pp. 103-105 (Ont. C.A.).

mental character—in a constitutional sense—of the Attorney General's office. Magna Charta may have stripped some of the "divinity" from the sovereign's right to rule, but the Attorney General's office, established as it was in the right of the Crown, was ensconced in very lofty realms indeed. According to Wells C.J.H.C. "it was the King's constitutional right to prosecute all crimes and it was on his behalf that the Attorney General instituted the prosecutions."[11]

Since the Attorney General acted on behalf of the King the fiction was propagated that his office was free from influence and abuse. The corollary of this fiction was that one possessing a status so lofty and unsullied was immune from the purview of the Courts.

> It cannot be contended for one moment that there can have been any abuse exercised by one whose functions are of so highly a responsible character; but if there had been — and I only put it hypothetically — the remedy is not by an application to this court to interfere by the exercise of its undoubted power and prerogative, but to hold him responsible before the High Court of Parliament.[12]

Around these core concepts of the "Royal Prerogative" and "immunity from judicial supervision" evolved an ethic as to the manner in which the Attorney General and his appointed agents were to carry out their designated duties and obligations. Primacy was placed upon "fairness" and the "advancement of the cause of justice". Crown counsel were to be fair in comment, unconcerned with the actual end result of prosecution, free from influence or favor, even handed, dignified, and restrained. A relatively recent description of his role is to be found in the case of *R. v. Boucher* where Rand J. stated:

> It cannot be over-emphasized that the purpose of a criminal prosecution is not to obtain a conviction; it is to lay before a jury what the Crown considers to be credible evidence relevant to what is alleged to be a crime. Counsel have a duty to see that all available legal proof of the facts is presented: it should be done firmly and pressed to its legitimate strength, but it must also be done fairly. The role of prosecutor excludes any notion of winning or losing; his function is a matter

---

11. *Ibid.* p. 107. Wells C.J.H.C. relies for this formulation upon *Wilkes v. R.* (1768) Wilm. 322 at pp. 326-8: "As indictments and informations, granted by the Kings Bench, are the King's suits, and under his controul; informations, filed by his Attorney General, are most emphatically his suits, because they are the immediate emanations of his will and pleasure. They are no more the suits of the Attorney General than indictments are the suits of the grand jury . . . The Attorney General is entrusted by the King, and not by the constitution; it is the King who is entrusted by the constitution" (*per* Wilmot L.C.J.).

12. *R. v. Allen* (1862) 9 Cox C.C. 120 at p. 122 *per* Cockburn C.J. See also *Ex parte Newton* (1855) 4 E. & B. 869 at p. 871: ". . . when he has heard and considered, and refused, we cannot interfere. The Attorney General may be made responsible in Parliament. If he has made an improper decision the Crown may and, if properly advised, will dismiss him; but we cannot review his decision."

of public duty than which in civil life there can be none charged with greater personal responsibility. It is to be efficiently performed with an ingrained sense of the dignity, the seriousness, and the justness of judicial proceedings.[13]

With such high qualities ascribed to him, it is not surprising to find that the Crown Counsel has been accorded an enormous grant of discretionary power incidental to his functions as a prosecutor. This historically has been the case notwithstanding the Attorney General's apparent immunity to judicial review or oversight.

Taken at its widest, the foremost power wielded by the Attorney General by virtue of the Royal Prerogative, lies in exercise of the discretion to launch or to withhold prosecution. As has been mentioned it was the sovereign's "constitutional right to prosecute all crimes". The right to prosecute carries with it by necessary implication the right to refrain from prosecution.

> In this country, where private individuals are allowed to prefer indictments in the name of the Crown, it is very desirable that there should be some tribunal having authority to say whether it is proper to proceed further in a prosecution. That power is vested by the constitution in the Attorney General and not in this court.[14]

Once the Attorney General has in fact embarked upon a prosecution the full panorama of discretionary powers available to him becomes visible. The mere listing of these powers does not reveal adequately either their complexity or their importance. Such a listing is useful however, if only to give a vague tracing to the silhouette of this giant.

The Attorney General and his appointed agents routinely have resort to the following areas of discretion:

(1) discretion in the pre-trial disclosure of information to the defence;

(2) discretion in the type and number of charges upon which to proceed;

(3) discretion to seek a more severe penalty for subsequent offences where provided for by statute;

(4) discretion to proceed jointly or separately against two or more accused persons involved in a single allegation;

(5) discretion as to whether or not to reveal the Crown's case upon a preliminary hearing in more than just a prima facie fashion;

(6) discretion in the use of previous convictions of an accused person to impeach his credibility;

(7) discretion in the use of similar fact evidence;

(8) discretion to impede or expedite the speed in which a matter is brought on for trial;

---

13. *R. v. Boucher* [1955] S.C.R. 16 at p. 23.
14. *R. v. Allen supra* footnote 12 *per* Crompton J.

(9) discretion in the use of evidentiary material at trial;

(10) discretion in discharging the advocacy function (in addressing juries, or speaking to sentence);

(11) discretion in the matter of plea negotiation;

(12) discretion to proceed summarily or by indictment;

(13) discretion to stay proceedings or to withdraw charges;

(14) discretion to re-lay information, prefer indictments after discharge, withdrawal, or dismissal.

The above listing does not purport to be complete. Even within the categories enumerated sub-classification would greatly expand the suggested proportions of this phenomenon.[15]

As has been pointed out, these large areas of discretion which reside with the prosecutor are subsidiary to his general discretion to institute or withhold prosecution of a matter. By and large this exercise of authority has historically been free from effective challenge. These words, employed by Montgomery J.A. in the case of *R. v. Court of Sessions of the Peace; Ex parte Lafleur,*[16] expose, as well as any others, the rationale behind this historical approach:

> I cannot conceive of a system of enforcing the law where someone in authority is not called upon to decide whether or not a person should be prosecuted for an alleged offence. Inevitably there will be cases where one man is prosecuted while another man perhaps equally guilty, goes free. A single act, or series of acts, may render a person liable to prosecution on more than one charge, and someone must decide what charges are to be laid. If an authority such as the Attorney-General can have the right to decide whether or not a person shall be prosecuted, surely he may, if authorized by statute, have the right to decide what form the prosecution shall take.

With great respect, the central issue surrounding the grant of the prosecuting power lies *not* in the fact that it has been conferred at all, but rather it involves a consideration of the effective measures which may be taken in order to insure the just and fair application of that power. Consider in this regard the compelling force of these counter-arguments.

> But I wonder: Why should a prosecutor — say, a county prosecutor — have discretionary power to decide not to prosecute even when the evidence of guilt is clear, perhaps partly on the basis of political influence, without ever having to state to anyone what evidence was

---

15. It is open to question whether these 14 categories of prosecutorial discretion are completely discrete or mutually exclusive. *E.g.* number 11 may be regarded as a re-statement of 1-3 and 12-14. Others, *e.g.* 7-10 are not discretions peculiar to the Attorney General but may be viewed as expressions of the advocate's function generally. For elaboration on "discretion in the pre-trial disclosure of information to the defence" see the discussion of "Disclosure" *infra* in Chapter Four: "The Judge".

16. [1967] 3 C.C.C. 244 at p. 248 (C.A.).

brought to light by his investigation and without having to explain to anyone why he interprets a statute as he does or why he chooses a particular position on a difficult question of policy? Why should the discretionary power be so unconfined that, of half a dozen potential defendants he can prove guilty, he can select any one for prosecution and let the other five go, making his decision, if he chooses, on the basis of considerations extraneous to justice? If he finds that A and B are equally guilty of felony and equally deserving of prosecution, why should he be permitted to prosecute B for felony but to let A off with a plea of guilty to a misdemeanor, unless he has a rational and legal basis for his choice, stated on an open record? Why should the vital decisions he makes be immune to review by other officials and immune to review by the courts, even though our legal and governmental system elsewhere generally assumes the need for checking human frailties? Why should he have a complete power to decide that one statute duly enacted by the people's representatives shall not be enforced at all, that another statute will be fully enforced, and that a third will be enforced only if, as, and when he thinks that it should be enforced in a particular case? Even if we assume that a prosecutor has to have a power of selective enforcement, why do we not require him to state publicly his general policies and require him to follow those policies in individual cases in order to protect evenhanded justice? Why not subject prosecutors' decisions to a simple and general requirement of open findings, open reasons, and open precedents, except when special reasons for confidentiality exists? Why not strive to protect prosecutors' decisions from political or other ulterior influence in the same way we strive to protect judges' decisions?[17]

2. DISCRETION

Discretion, if it is not to be regarded as totally arbitrary, whimsical, and *beyond the reach* of the dictates of logic and consistency must be referable to guidelines which "confine", "structure", "check" and otherwise control the use of power. In the ensuing discussion consideration will be given to a variety of modes which exist for "questioning" (at least), if not for confining, structuring, and checking, *some* of the various modes of prosecutorial discretion. These, it will be seen, may be either formal or informal. Their weight may be in purely moral, rather than legal, terms. Consequently, while it may subsequently appear that many of the prosecutor's decision-making powers are exercised in the absence of *effective* guidelines, certain strictures, prohibitions and restraints upon his conduct do, in fact, exist.

The most original recent thinking which has been done on the question "what is discretion?" (in the context of the kinds of discretion exercised by public officials, in the furtherance of their duties) is to be found in K. C. Davis' *Discretionary Justices: A Preliminary Inquiry* (1969).

---

17. K. C. Davis, *Discretionary Justice: A Preliminary Inquiry* (1969) at pp. 189-190.

A public officer has discretion whenever the effective limits on his power leave him free to make a choice among possible courses of action or inaction.[18]

This definition, elegant in its simplicity, shall be operative in this discussion of prosecutorial discretion.

Davis points out that "especially important is the proposition that discretion is not limited to what is authorized or what is legal but includes all that is within 'the effective limits' on the officer's power".[19] He finds this particular wording to be essential because much of the discretion which fell to his examination was found to be either illegal or of questionable legality.

The emphasis in Davis' view of discretion (which revolves around the "effective limits" of an officer's power) is similar to the perspective adopted by B. A. Grosman in his study of *The Prosecutor*.[20]

According to Grosman "criticism of prosecuting practices is founded, in part, on the incompatibility of the exercise of wide powers of discretion with the rule of law."[21] It is to be doubted that K. C. Davis would have any serious disagreement with this proposition. However, what should be noted here is that the essential thrust of this assertion resides in its concern with a basic philosophical incompatibility between the resort to discretionary measures and the rule of law, rather than with the fact that much of what is tolerated as valid discretionary exercise is at least questionably illegal or illegal *per se*.

Hence, Grosman is able to assert,

> Modification of procedural protections and the rule of law standards by police, prosecution, and the defence gives rise to the suspicion that discretion may be used arbitrarily for purposes that are irrelevant to the accused and the charges against him. Conformity to the rule of law requires precise standards for authoritative interference with individual rights and firm procedural safeguards to limit official power. Abasement of the rule of law by the informal exercise of discretion may engender public disrespect and distrust of legal institutions which too often seem subject to administrative manipulation.[22]

Neither Grosman nor Davis would dispute the fact that a discretion may be used arbitrarily and in informal circumstances. Grosman's criticism falls short simply in its failure to recognize that "administrative manipulation" carried on in an atmosphere of accepted legality may well and often be illegal. Many basic human rights possess only a "literary" quality in that a trespass against the right cannot be met by "effective" sanction. Thus Davis finds it necessary to point out that

---

18. *Ibid.* at p. 4.
19. *Ibid.*
20. B. A. Grosman, *The Prosecutor: An Inquiry into the Exercise of Discretion* (1969).
21. *Ibid.* at p. 100.
22. *Ibid.* at p. 101.

his definition of discretion is not limited merely to what is authorized or what is legal but rather includes all that is within the "effective" scope of the power of a public officer.

At times, it should be noted, Grosman appears almost to come to grips with this distinction. For example, in dealing with pre-trial disclosure of information the following observation is made:

> The combination of open, yet informal, negotiation with the observance of due process standards may be started by reducing the prosecutors' exclusive control of information and mechanisms which sustain their present private preserves of power. For example, pre-trial disclosure, which can seriously impair the liberty of the accused and the preparation of his defence, should no longer depend upon the quality of the reciprocal relationship between defence and prosecution.[23]

Again, what is stated *supra* constitutes fair comment. However it leaves untouched the fact that many aspects of pre-trial disclosure concern items of information to which the accused will often have an arguable, valid, and legal claim of entitlement — this notwithstanding that custom, practice, and lack of effective sanctions have left these matters to "depend upon the quality of the reciprocal relationship between defence and prosecution."[24]

The Davis "effective limits" criterion goes beyond the simpler (and less complete) perspective opted for by Grosman. Grosman's view seems to end with "legal limits".

Is the granting of a discretion truly anathema to the rule of law? The point appears to be highly debatable. In fairness to Mr. Grosman, his criticism of prosecuting practices is not phrased in quite so broad a fashion. His assertion is that criticism of prosecution practices is based "*in part,* on the incompatibility of the exercise of *wide* powers of discretion with the rule of law". These are important qualifications. Still, his contention must be examined in terms of its more *general* import.

The contrary proposition is that the granting of a discretion is indispensable to the application of the rule of law.

Legal decision-making, it is trite to say, requires the existence of a decision-maker possessed of the requisite mandate to insure his right to make decisions. As Breitel points out and Grosman acknowledges "(it) is obviously an impossible and undesirable goal to carry out all

---

23. *Ibid.*
24. In this regard see P. Galligan, "Advising an Arrested Client" (1963) Law Society of Upper Canada Special Lectures p. 35 at p. 47 under the title "Information which the Accused is Entitled to Receive from the Crown". See also G. A. Martin on the "Conduct of Preliminary Hearings" (1955) Law Society of Upper Canada Special Lectures pp. 3 *et seq.* Also see *R. v. Littlejohn* [1972] 3 W.W.R. 475 for an interesting and relatively recent development of this area of the law.

laws without discretionary interpretation in applying them".[25] It is precisely this "impossibility" which establishes that the existence of discretion is essential, indeed inherent, within the framework of the rule of law.

The problem of discretion therefore, lies not in its incompatibility with the rule of law, but rather resides in the difficulties inherent in its control. As K. C. Davis points out,

> Discretionary power can be either too broad or too narrow. When it is too broad, justice may suffer from arbitrariness or inequality, when it is too narrow, justice may suffer from insufficient individualizing.[26]

Canadians, like Americans, "unquestionably err much more often by making discretion too broad than by making it too narrow, but we must nevertheless recognize that we do sometimes err by too much confinement of discretionary power".[27] In the area of prosecutorial discretion our error (we shall argue) has clearly been in allowing the prosecutor's discretion to become too broad and far-ranging. Since the problem in Canada is that of excessive discretionary power in the prosecutor rather than that of inadequate discretionary power our needs are two-fold:

> the two principal needs are the elimination of unnecessary discretionary power and better control of necessary discretionary power. The principal ways of controlling are structuring and checking . . . Our present concern is with eliminating and limiting discretionary power, that is, confining discretion. By confining is meant fixing the boundaries and keeping discretion within them. The ideal, of course, is to put all unnecessary such power outside the boundaries, and to draw clean lines.[28]

3. THE DISCRETION TO PROCEED SUMMARILY OR BY INDICTMENT

(1) Number and form of dual offence provisions

In an amazing number of instances the Federal Parliament has ostensibly seen fit to confer upon the proscutor the discretion to elect to proceed against an alleged offender by way of summary conviction or by way of indictment. The best estimates of the size of this grant of power indicate that some thirty sections in the *Criminal Code* and provisions in at least forty other Canadian statutes are involved.[29]

These provisions typically do not specify the prosecutor as possessing the power to elect.[30] They are phrased in a more general fashion.

---

25. Breitel, "Controls in Criminal Law Enforcement", 27 U. of Chi. L. Rev. 427 (1960) cited in Grosman, *supra* footnote 20 at p. 101.
26. K. C. Davis, *Discretionary Justice* (1969) *supra* footnote 17 at p. 52.
27. *Ibid.* at p. 52.
28. *Ibid.* at p. 55.
29. *Smythe v. R.* (1971) 3 C.C.C. (2d) 366 at p. 371 (Can.).
30. S. 132(2) of the *Income Tax Act* R.S.C. 1952, c. 148 which was employed in *Smythe supra* contains specific wording. This reads as follows: "(2)

For example, the offence of criminal negligence in the operation of a motor vehicle[31] is set out in the *Criminal Code* as follows:

233(1) Everyone who is criminally negligent in the operation of a motor vehicle is guilty of

(a) an indictable offence and is liable to imprisonment for five years

(b) an offence punishable on summary conviction

The decided cases concern themselves with the propriety of selective enforcement, and the inherent discriminatory operation of such a power when wielded by the Attorney-General.[32] They do not question whether the actual statutory authority for such an election is unequivocally visited in every instance upon the Attorney General.

Incontestably, the prosecutor has complete hegemony over this area in actual practice — but should he? *Post facto* the Supreme Court of Canada has held (in *Smythe v. R.*)[33] that the accused does not possess the power to determine the mode of procedure which shall be employed against him in these "hybrid" or "dual" offence situations. A welter of decisions have been handed down on the issue as to what result obtains when the Crown fails to elect "its" mode of procedure.[34]

(2) English practice

This aspect of prosecutorial discretion has not grown up out of English legal practices.[35]

Every person who is charged with an offence described by subsection (1) may, *at the election of the Attorney General of Canada,* be prosecuted upon indictment and, if convicted, is, in addition to any penalty otherwise provided, liable to imprisonment for a term not exceeding 5 years and not less than 2 months" [emphasis added]. This wording reinforces, rather than diminishes, the validity of the argument which is to be advanced in this discussion that the Attorney General's presently unencumbered discretion to select the mode of procedure to be employed against an accused is of doubtful validity where the statutory enactment stipulating optional or dual modes of procedure does not use words specifying that the procedure is to be "at the election of the Attorney General."

31. R.S.C. 1970 c. C-34 s. 233(1).

32. *E.g.* see *Smythe v. R. supra* footnote 29 and *R. v. Court of Sessions of the Peace; Ex parte Lafleur,* [1967] 3 C.C.C. 249 (Que. C.A.).

33. *Supra* footnote 29.

34. The "failure to elect" shall be considered within the ambit of this discussion of summary versus indictable proceedings.

35. In the Ontario High Court where *Smythe v. R.* was considered prior to subsequent appeals to the Ontario Court of Appeal and from there to the Supreme Court of Canada (see (1971) 3 C.C.C. (2d) 97 containing the judgments of both Wells C.J.H.C. at p. 98 and Gale C.J.O. at p. 122) Wells C.J.H.C. reasoned that before 1960 the Attorney General had acted with a complete discretion, and this discretion was based upon the English practice. P. G. Barton in examining "The Power of the Crown to Proceed by Indictment or Summary Conviction" (1971-72), 14 Cr. L.Q. 86 at p. 95, was "unable to find any examples in English practice where an Attorney-General or equivalent person had a choice to proceed by felony or by misdemeanour for the same substantive offence." He concludes, as I have, that this type of

Presently in England, where there is an aspect of choice over the mode of procedure to be employed, the prosecutor is only able to act with the concurrence of the Court.

Section 19(2) of the *Magistrates' Courts Act* 1952 was considered in England by the Court of Appeal (Criminal Division) in the case of *R. v. Coe.*[36] That subsection, germane to this discussion, reads as follows:

> 19(2) if at any time during the inquiry into the offence it appears to the court, having regard to any representations made in the presence of the accused by the prosecutor or made by the accused, and to the nature of the case, that the punishment that the court has power to inflict under this section would be adequate and that the circumstances do not make the offence one of serious character and do not for other reasons require trial on indictment, the court may proceed with a view to summary trial.

In *Coe* a number of charges "of a most serious character" were disposed of by summary trial. Parker L.C.J. after reviewing the surrounding facts begins the substantive portion of his judgment with the following remarks:

> This Court is quite unable to understand how it came about that the prosecution *invited* the magistrates, as they did, to deal summarily with the indictable offences . . . No doubt it is convenient in the interests of expedition, and possibly in order to obtain a plea of guilty, for the prosecution to invite magistrates to deal with indictable offences summarily, but there is something more involved than convenience and expedition. Above all, there is the proper administration of criminal justice to be considered, questions such as the protection of society and the stamping out of this sort of criminal enterprise, if it is possible. This Court would like to say with all the emphasis at its command that the prosecution in a serious case such as this is not acting in the best interests of society by inviting summary trial.[37]

These comments are of interest for two reasons. Firstly, they indicate the different thrust of the British practice from that which prevails in Canada. The prosecutor "invites" and the court acting within the confines of statute has the discretion to accept or refuse. Secondly, they are a good example of the supervisory function which courts may perform with respect to an exercise of *qualified* prosecutorial discretion.

---

decision "may not have been part of the discretion exercised in England". Barton omits to note that in England the distinction between a felony and a misdemeanour had been eliminated in recent years. The decision of the English Court of Appeal (Criminal Division) in *R. v. Coe* (1968) 53 Cr.App.R. 66, discussed *infra* sheds some light on current English practices which are decidedly different from those in Canada.

36. (1968) 53 Cr.App.R. 66.
37. *Ibid.* at p. 68.

(3) R. v. Smythe and equality before the law (s. 1(b))

An example of similar legislation extant in Canada is to be found in s. 727 of the *Criminal Code*. The section reads

> 727. Where a defendant is charged with common assault and, before the defendant enters upon his defence, the summary conviction court is, from the evidence, of the opinion
>
> (a) that the assault complained of was accompanied by an attempt to commit an indictable offence other than common assault or was committed in the course of the commission of an indictable offence other than common assault, or
>
> (b) that the defendant should, for any reason, be prosecuted by indictment
>
> The summary conviction court shall not adjudicate thereon, but the proceedings shall be continued as for an indictable offence and the defendant shall be informed accordingly.

Section 727 is an anomaly in the Code. It is strange that similar procedures allowing for greater judicial control over this area of prosecutorial discretion are not elsewhere authorized. Amendments of the thirty odd "dual" offence provisions along the lines of the British practice appears to be desirable.

There are several compelling reasons as to why an unrestricted prosecutorial discretion to proceed either summarily or upon indictment is objectionable.

There is no mechanism evident in the legislation, or in the practical application of this discretionary exercise, which calls for the prosecutor to *justify* his choice of the mode of procedure to be adopted against a given accused. Since no explanation is required the "impartiality" of the office of the Attorney General is likely to become maligned. The word "prosecution" is considered all too close to the word "persecution" in certain enclaves of society.

This area of discretion while being the subject of investigations into its validity (in terms of its infringement of fundamental rights and freedoms, as in *Smythe* and *Lafleur*)[38] has been consistently held to be immune to judicial control.[39] Consequently no objective standards exist to circumscribe its ethical use.

In allowing the prosecutor to select the mode of procedure (summary conviction or indictment proceedings) an important function of the judiciary is effectively usurped — *i.e.* control over the choice of penalty. This is particularly the case when the offence itself carries a mandatory minimum jail term for proceeding by indictment.[40] True, in the final analysis it is the judge who imposes and selects the appropriate sentence but the mode of procedure itself may deprive him of

---

38. *Smythe v. R. supra* footnotes 29 and 35; *R. v. Court of the Sessions of the Peace; ex p. Lafleur, supra* footnote 32.

39. See *Re McClary's Prohibition Application* [1971] 1 W.W.R. 741 (Alta.).

40. Such was the case in *Smythe v. R. supra.*

resort to dispositions which are more appropriate to the particular factual circumstances of a given offence. For example, where a minimum penalty is provided for an offence triable upon indictment (irrespective of whether that minimum penalty involves incarceration or not) the *Criminal Code* provisions concerning absolute and conditional discharges[41] are not available, no matter how desirable.

By its ruling in *Smythe* the Supreme Court of Canada has declared that the right of the Attorney General to *elect* to prosecute either by indictment or by summary conviction proceedings does not violate s. 1(*b*) of *Canadian Bill of Rights*,[42] that is, "the right of the individual to equality before the law and the protection of the law".

That is the legal effect of the ruling. It does not appear to be open to dispute however that the discretion to proceed by one mode as opposed to the other might be used in a discriminatory or morally reprehensible manner. Fanteux C.J.C. writing on behalf of the entire court in *Smythe* dealt with this objection as follows:

> Appellant's argument also fail to recognize that the manner in which a Minister of the Crown exercises a statutory discretionary power conferred upon him for the proper administration of a statute is irrelevant in the consideration of the question whether the statute, in itself, offends the principle of equality before the law. Obviously, the manner in which the Attorney General of the day exercises his statutory discretion may be questioned or censured by the legislative body to which he is answerable, but that again is foreign to the determination of the question now under consideration.[43]

With great respect, the argument of the Chief Justice, binding though it be, is nevertheless fallacious. It is difficult to understand how the "manner" in which a statutory discretionary power is exercised can be "irrelevant" to the consideration of whether a susbtantive provision of the *Bill of Rights* has been infringed. It is clear that in these instances of so-called "prosecutorial discretion" the "manner" of the exercise of the discretion is equivalent to the "construction" or "application" of law as those terms are comprehended in s. 2 of the *Bill of Rights*.[44]

If the Crown Attorney were heard to declare in open court "This is an offence over which the Crown has a right of election. Since the accused is a woman, and since it is the policy of the Attorney General not to proceed against women by indictment, the Crown elects to

---

41. R.S.C. 1970, Chap. c-34, s. 662.1
42. *Canadian Bill of Rights*, 8-9 Elizabeth II, *c*. 44 (Canada) (R.S.C. 1970, Appendix III), amended 1970-71-72, c. 38, s. 29 proclaimed in force January 1, 1972.
43. *Smythe v. R. supra* footnote 29 at p. 370, by s. 2 of the *Bill of Rights* "Every law of Canada shall . . . be so construed and applied as not to abrogate, abridge or infringe . . . any of the rights or freedoms herein recognized and declared . . ."
44. *Supra* footnote 42.

proceed summarily" a clear case of discrimination on the basis of sex would be made out. Should the courts be powerless to put end to such discriminatory practices?

The *Smythe* case was unfortunate in that the suggestion was put that the only response available to the court was to render the impugned legislation inoperative. The consequences of such an action were unthinkable to the Court.

> Indeed, if appellant's fundamental submission was acceded to, some thirty sections of the Criminal Code and others in some forty Canadian statutes where, as in s. 132(2), the power to elect to proceed by way of summary conviction or by way of indictment is conferred, would be rendered inoperative.[45]

It is questionable whether the issue posed for the Court for consideration in *Smythe* need to have presented "so blunt a face". Obviously rendering inoperative the section of the statute would have been the optimum result that Mr. Robinette could have achieved for his client. However, had he aimed for less he might have accomplished more.

One of the principal underpinnings to the arguments advanced by counsel was that the Attorney-General's discretion was uncontrolled and lacking standards.

> He drew my attention to the fact that there is no . . . indication at all of any standard, or guide or control and the Attorney General may, in his unbridled discretion — that is, his word — treat similar cases differently.[46]

Since the concern of counsel lay in the absence of standards — standards being necessary in order to insure against the discriminatory application of law — an acceptable result could have been achieved through the judicial imposition of standards upon the prosecutor. It is arguable that this result is possible by virtue of the intended operation of the *Bill of Rights*.

(4) Use of the Bill of Rights to impose standards upon the prosecutor's discretion

In *Brownridge v. R.* Laskin J. (as he then was) had occasion to consider the various means by which the *Bill of Rights* may operate to control the construction and application of federal statutes.

> This is not a case where the infringement of the Bill of Rights renders a federal enactment inoperative. *Regina v. Drybones, supra* was a case where the particular federal enactment could have no operation at all in the face of the Bill of Rights. The present case does not present such a blunt face; its facts show that s. 223 can operate with due obedience to the Bill of Rights. Hence, all that is required is that in the invocation of or exercise of the powers under s. 223, allowance be made for

---

45. *Smythe v. R. Supra* footnote 29 at p. 371.
46. *Smythe v. R.* (1970) 12 C.R.N.S. 48 (Ont.) at p. 50 *per* Kelly Co. Ct. J.

the exercise of the over-riding right given by s. 2(*c*)(ii) of the Bill of Rights.[47]

The instant problem involves neither the substantive offence of refusing to supply a breath specimen for analysis, nor a violation of the right to retain and instruct counsel without delay. What it has in common with the *Brownridge* case is (1) an ostensible infringement of the Bill of Rights, and (2) the possibility of resolution of the problem without the necessity to render inoperative federal legislation.

The existence of a discretion to choose between available forms of action is not discriminatory *per se*. Fauteux C.J.C. partially struck upon this point in *Smythe*:

> In my opinion, the appellant's views fail to recognize that the provisions of s. 132(2) do not, by themselves, place any particular person or class of persons in a condition of being distinguished from any other member of the community and that, applicable without distinction to everyone, as indeed they are, those provisions simply confer upon the Attorney General of Canada the power of deciding, according to his own judgment, and in all cases, the mode of prosecution for offences described in s. 132(1).[47a]

On its face, legislation conferring optional or dual jurisdiction upon the prosecutor is neutral. In application it may discriminate in a manner violative of fundamental rights and freedoms.

Two possible responses would compel conformity to the provisions of the *Bill of Rights* by a prosecutor exercising his discretion:

(1) Where the exercise of the discretion is challenged an onus might be placed upon the prosecutor to explain or justify the resort to a particular mode of procedure.

(2) Where the exercise of the discretion is challenged, a preliminary onus might be placed upon the "challenger" (the term is used deliberately in order to include either a challenge from the accused or from the court) to establish, on at least a *prima facie* basis, a violation of the *Bill of Rights*. Once established the onus would then shift to the prosecutor to demonstrate *bona fides* and impartiality.

Is it truly within the powers of our courts to compel compliance with the terms of the *Bill of Rights* in this fashion? It is submitted that it is. The *Interpretation Act*[48] as an aid to interpreting the *Bill of Rights* is instructive in this regard.

The *Interpretation Act* has reference to the *Canadian Bill of Rights* by virtue of s. 3 (in the *Interpretation Act*) which asserts the applicability of its provisions to "every enactment, whether enacted before

---

47. *Brownridge v. R.* (1972) 18 C.R.N.S. 308 at p. 329. (Can.)
47a *Smythe v. R. supra* footnote 29 at p. 370.
48. R.S.C. 1970 c. I-23 s. 1.

or after the commencement of this Act".[49] The *Bill of Rights* therefore comes within its ambit.

Section 11 of the *Interpretation Act* prescribes that every enactment shall be given "such fair, large and liberal construction and interpretation *as best ensures the attainment of its objects*". The *Act* indicates that in order to assist in explaining the purport and object of a given Act "the preamble shall be read as a part thereof".[50]

The preamble to the *Bill of Rights* affirms that "men and institutions remain free only when freedom is founded upon respect for moral and spiritual values and the rule of law", and expresses the intention that the Bill should ensure the protection of human rights and fundamental freedoms in Canada.

An "unbridled discretion" exercised arbitrarily and without reference to known standards or within discernible guidelines is anathema to the rule of law. Further, such a discretion possesses the potential to offend against human rights and fundamental freedoms in Canada.

Hence, the *Bill of Rights* (assisted by the provisions of the *Interpretation Act*) compels the exercise of the prosecutorial discretion to proceed summarily or by way of indictment to be conducted in a manner compatible with its terms. The instrument to compel the necessary adherence must be the presiding officer of the court in which the Prosecutor announces his election. The power to adopt the type of procedure suggested on page 00 is ancillary to the general supervisory jurisdiction accorded to all judicial officers in order to supervise and regulate the conduct of proceedings before them.[51] Section 26(2) of the *Interpretation Act* provides:

> (2) Where power is given to a person, officer or functionary, to do or enforce the doing of any act or thing, all such powers shall be deemed to be also given as are necessary to enable the person, officer or functionary to do or enforce the doing of the act or thing.

It is suggested that the adoption of the above approach would have salutory effects for the administration of justice. It would not render inoperative the thirty odd sections of the *Criminal Code* or the miscellaneous provisions of some forty federal statutes, but rather it would serve to inject an aspect of responsibility into an area of "unbridled discretion". Surely it would do much to restore to the office of the prosecutor the attribute of impartiality which had been its historical hallmark.

---

49. Being a federal enactment the *Interpretation Act* only has applicability to other federal statutes. It has no application if a "contrary intention" appears. The *Bill of Rights* is a federal enactment and contains no provisions manifesting an intention contrary to the *Interpretation Act*.
50. The *Interpretation Act*, s. 1.
51. See *Re Sproule* (1886) 12 S.C.R. 140 in support of the proposition that all Superior Courts possess, inherent in their jurisdiction, the power to supervise the regularity and use of their processes.

It would be appropriate at this point to inject a note of realism. The foregoing analysis, it is to be hoped, has logic and a sense of justice to recommend it. It does, however, represent a substantial departure from the decided position of the highest court in the land. One might argue that *Smythe* was decided in the way it was because that was the manner in which the Court was invited to consider the question posed. Thus viewed, judicial interposition into this area of prosecutorial discretion may yet in future prove to be acceptable. In larger terms, when the problem is viewed against the backdrop of the treatment accorded the Bill of Rights by the Supreme Court since the *Drybones*[52] decision such a result appears unlikely indeed.

(5) Effect of the failure to elect

One final issue bearing on this particular exercise of discretion commends analysis: What result obtains when there is a failure to exercise the discretion at all? That is, what happens when the Crown fails to elect its mode of procedure? Do the matters at issue then become summary conviction proceedings or indictable offence proceedings? The answer is not without complexity.

A number of cases in the first half of the century held that, where the Crown fails to elect, the matters at issue are deemed to proceed on summary conviction basis.[53]

In 1973 the Ontario Court of Appeal approved this line of decisions in the case of *R. v. Robert*.[54] In *Robert* the issue was raised as to whether an accused charged with obstructing police, contrary to s. 118(*a*) of the *Criminal Code* was to appeal his conviction to the County Court (a trial de novo appeal of a summary conviction proceeding) or should rather have appealed to the Ontario Court of Appeal (as would have been required upon completion of the summary trial of an indictable offence). Speaking for the Court, Gale C.J.O. said:

> . . . where the Crown fails to elect as to the mode of procedure in the case of an offence punishable on indictment or on summary conviction and the case proceeds in a summary conviction Court, the Crown is deemed to have elected to proceed on a summary conviction basis. That is exactly the situation here, so that this accused had the right to a trial *de novo*.[55]

52. *R. v. Drybones* (1970) 10 C.R.N.S. 334 (Can.) See particularly *A. G. Can. v. Lavell* (1973) 23 C.R.N.S. 197 (Can.), and see *R. v. Hogan* (1974) 26 C.R.N.S. 207 (Can.)
53. See *R. v. Belmont* (1914) 23 C.C.C. 89 (Que. C.A.); *R. v. Barron* (1923) 40 C.C.C. 309 (Alta.); *R. v. Stevens* [1947] 2 D.L.R. 78 (Alta. C.A.); *R. v. Belzberg* (1951) 101 C.C.C. 210 (Alta.); *R. v. Mitzell* (1951) 101 C.C.C. 361 (B.C.); *R. v. Miller* (1953) 105 C.C.C. 366 (Sask. C.A.); *R. v. Hagblom* (1953) 105 C.C.C. 295 (Sask.); *Re Nisgard* (1956) 114 C.C.C. 113. (Alta. C.A.)
54. (1973) 13 C.C.C. (2d) 43 (Ont. C.A.).
55. *Ibid.* at p. 44.

Two other provincial superior courts have recently shown that rule enunciated in *Robert* is not absolute. The case of *R. v. Toor*,[56] a decision of the British Columbia Supreme Court, and *R. v. Monkman*,[57] a Manitoba Court of Appeal decision introduce substantial qualifications.

The *Toor* case seeks to establish that the incipient charge at the pre-trial stage and before election is to be treated as an indictable offence for the purposes of the *Identification of Criminals Act*.[58] Thus an accused may be validly required to appear at a time and place specified in an appearance notice issued for the purposes of the *Act* "where the accused is alleged to have committed an indictable offence".

In *Monkman* a Magistrate in furtherance of his jurisdiction to commit an accused to stand trial on a related offence, discharged the accused on the charge which originally brought him before the Court, and committed him to stand trial on a charge of criminal negligence in the operation of a motor vehicle — a dual or optional offence. The Crown had made no election with respect to this charge, and the originating charges were not of a dual or optional character.

While holding that the decision in *Robert* was "eminently fair", and not purporting to disagree with that case, the Manitoba Court of Appeal chose to follow the decision in *Toor*. Writing on behalf of the Court, Freedman C.J.M. expresses the position as follows:

> Clearly the same situation [as in *Toor*] exists here. The offence of criminal negligence in the operation of a motor vehicle is one that "may" be prosecuted by indictment. It therefore falls within the scope of s. 27(1)(a) of the Interpretation Act and is an indictable offence. That is its nature. We must keep in mind the distinction between the nature of an offence and the nature of the proceedings to enforce an offence. The offence of criminal negligence in the operation of a motor vehicle may indeed be prosecuted by way of summary conviction. But until the Crown should elect to proceed by that alternative route . . . there is no ground for even thinking of the offence . . . as other than indictable.[59]

It would appear that even where the Crown fails through oversight or omission to elect the manner of proceeding he will nevertheless in certain circumstances be accorded substantial procedural advantages which may affect the rights and liberty of an individual.

It would not have been unreasonable to insist, in a situation such as *Toor,* that before the *Identification of Criminals Act* and all that it entails may be utilized the Crown must first indicate its choice of procedure. As matters presently stand a minor violation of an offence possessed of dual characteristics may subject a citizen to the rigors of

---

56. (1973) 11 C.C.C. (2d) 312 (B.C.).
57. (1975) 30 C.R.N.S. 338 (Man. C.A.).
58. R.S.C. 1970, c. I-23, s. 27(1)(a), (c).
59. *R. v. Monkman supra* footnote 57 at p. 343.

fingerprinting and photographing and may result in the production of a record which might survive an eventual acquittal.

In *Monkman* it was open to the Court to have held that it was beyond the jurisdiction of the Magistrate to select an optional offence upon which to commit. This would not have stripped the prosecutor of his rights of action against the accused. A new charge might have been laid in keeping with the recommendation of the Magistrate,[60] or alternatively, an indictment might have been preferred directly.

The line of cases culminating in *Robert* may be regarded as conflicting authority to *Toor* and *Monkman*. Conceptually all the situations ask the same question: Where there is a failure by the Crown to elect, what result will flow?

4. THE DISCRETION TO STAY PROCEEDINGS OR WITHDRAW CHARGES

(1) Statutory basis of the stay

The machinery of justice once set in motion will grind inexorably, though clumsily, on to resolution, disposition, and conclusion. Very little can be done to dissuade it from this course once the Attorney-General has interposed himself in the prosecution and assumed conduct of it. A private prosecutor may decide not to press on with his complaint, and where he has retained conduct over the case, matters will be allowed to die a slow procedural death.[61] But where the Crown has assumed conduct of a matter the desire of the complainant/informant to terminate the issue without proceeding through to trial will not necessarily lead to that result. If the Attorney-General, or the Crown attorney having actual carriage of a matter of complaint, decides that the prosecution of an offence is required, in the public interest, or for some other reason, then he has at his disposal the necessary tools[62] to compel the trial of the issue — this notwithstanding the personal desires of the complainant.

The prosecutor does, however, possess the power to stay proceedings in circumstances which he deems to be appropriate. This is so irrespective of whether the proceedinsg are punishable upon indictment or by summary conviction. The statutory basis of the Attorney-General's stay of proceedings over federal criminal law offences is to be found in the *Criminal Code* of Canada.[63]

---

60. This would have left open to the prosecutor the opportunity to proceed by way of summary conviction proceedings.
61. *E.g.* s. 734 of the *Criminal Code* allows for dismissals for want of prosecution where the prosecutor fails to appear for trial.
62. The "tools" referred to are the power of the summons, the compellability of the complainant, the "adverse witness" sections of the *Canada Evidence Act,* and the supporting appartus of the local police department.
63. R.S.C. 1970, c. C-34, s. 508 [am. 1972, c. 13, s. 43(1)] and s. 732.1 [am. 1972, c. 13, s. 62].

Section 508 of the *Code* makes provision as follows for indictable offences:

508. (1) The Attorney General or counsel instructed by him for the purpose may, at any time after an indictment has been found and before judgment, direct the clerk of the court to make an entry on the record that the proceedings are stayed by his direction, and when the entry is made all proceedings on the indictment shall be stayed accordingly and any recognizance relating to the proceedings is vacated.

(2) Proceedings stayed in accordance with subsection (1) may be recommenced, without laying a new charge or preferring a new indictment, as the case may be, by the Attorney General or counsel instructed by him for the purpose giving notice of the recommencement to the clerk of the court in which the stay of proceedings was entered, but where no such notice is given within one year after the entry of the stay of proceedings, the proceedings shall be deemed never to have been commenced.

Section 732.1 of the *Code* governing summary conviction offences reads:

732.1 (1) The Attorney General or counsel instructed by him for the purpose may, at any time after proceedings are commenced and before judgment, direct the clerk of the court to make an entry on the record that the proceedings are stayed by his direction and when the entry is made the proceedings shall be stayed accordingly and any recognizance relating to the proceedings is vacated.

(2) Proceedings stayed in accordance with subsection (1) may be recommended, without laying a new information, by the Attorney General or counsel instructed by him for the purpose giving notice of the recommencement to the clerk of the court in which the stay of proceedings was entered, but where no such notice is given within one year after the entry of the stay of proceedings or before the expiration of the time within which proceedings could have been instituted, whichever is the earlier, the proceedings shall be deemed never to have been commenced.

(2) When may a stay be entered?

Both sections contain clear wording to the effect that proceedings may be stayed by the Attorney General *any time before judgment has been pronounced.*[64] This is the "terminal parameter" on the Attorney

---

64. At least one of the commentators, C. Sun ("The Discretionary Power to Stay Proceedings" (1973-74) 1 Dal. L.J. 482 at p. 492) interprets "before judgment" to mean "before judgment is *entered*". The date of pronouncement of an order can and, often does, differ markedly from the date of its entry. The subtlety of this distinction is important and leads this writer to the conclusion that the Sun interpretation is untenable as it may lead to absurd consequences. Even by the remarkably relaxed standards of *R. v. Beaudry* (1967) 50 C.R. 1 (B.C. C.A.) there is no hint that the Attorney General might be able to direct a stay after the jury has returned *and* the judge has pronounced judgment.

General's jurisdiction. The "initial parameter" has been the subject of divided opinion as to when it becomes operational.

Section 732.1 confers jurisdiction upon the Attorney General or his instructed counsel to direct a stay of proceedings *at any time after proceedings are commenced.* Presumably this means that proceedings may be stayed at any time after an information has been laid.

Section 508, on the other hand, speaks only of the ability to enter a stay *after an indictment has been found.*

To date the difference in wording between the two sections has been of little *practical* consequence.

Connie Sun in her discussion of "The Discretionary Power to Stay Criminal Proceedings"[65] asserts that difference in wording between the two sections is substantive. The prevailing practice unearthed by Sun[66] of staying indictable proceedings before an indictment is "found" is an example, she contends, of K. C. Davis' doctrine that much discretionary power is of questionable legality or is illegal *per se.*

> It is probable that the correct interpretation of this phrase "at any time after an indictment has been found" is that a stay is legally possible only after an indictment has been preferred by the Crown i.e. after a committal for trial following a preliminary hearing, a presentment by a Grand Jury, or a direct indictment preferred by the Attorney General.[67]

Sun's argument in this regard is appealing, and in Davis' terms, it most certainly renders the exercise of prosecutorial discretion in this area "questionable". It does not, however, adequately come to grips with the " 'indictment' means 'information' " approach that has on occasion been adopted.[68] By this approach the word "indictment" found in s. 508 (previously s. 490) was defined by reference to s. 2 of the *Criminal Code* which includes within the meaning of the word "indictment":

(a) *information,* presentment and a count therein,

(b) a plea, replication or other pleading, and

(c) any record[69] [Emphasis added]

Sun argues that the above reasoning is deficient in that it ignores the "definitive characteristics" of an indictment to be found in the

65. *Ibid.* at pp. 495-498.
66. Sun has been able to ascertain the "prevailing practice" via an exchange of frank correspondence with the various departments of the Attorney General across the nation.
67. Sun, *supra* footnote 64 at p. 497.
68. See *R. v. Leonard* (1962) 38 C.R. 209 (Alta. C.A.).
69. Prior to 1972, s. 508(2) and all of s. 732.1 did not exist. On the face of the legislation it appeared that there was no statutory authority to stay proceedings on summary conviction offences. It is equally clear that the stay of proceedings was widely employed to discontinue such proceedings. See *R. v. Dickson,* cited in "Case Notes" (1969) 27 Advocate 285 and discussed in Sun, *supra* footnotes 64 at p. 494.

Code Part XVII (Procedure by Indictment). "Finding an indictment" may only be accomplished by reference to s. 503 of the *Code* which stipulates that "finding an indictment includes (a) preferring an indictment, and (b) presentment of an indictment by a grand jury". The weakness of this argument lies in its attribution of characteristics of exclusivity to the word "includes".

Maxwell's *On the Interpretation of Statutes* (12th Ed.) indicates the proper rule of construction.

> Sometimes it is provided that a word shall "mean" what the definition section says it shall mean: in this case, the word is restricted to the scope indicated in the definition section. Sometimes, however, the word "include" is used "in order to enlarge the meaning of words or phrases occurring in the body of the statute; and when it is so used these words or phrases must be construed as comprehending, not only such things as they signify according to their natural import, but also those things which the interpretation clause declares that they shall include." In other words, the word in respect of which "includes" is used bears both its extended statutory meaning and "its ordinary, popular, and natural sense whenever that would be properly applicable".[70]

Also undermining the validity of Sun's position on this point are the provisions of the *Interpretation Act*[71] which, by virtue of s. 3(1), has application to every federal enactment (including the *Criminal Code*) "unless a contrary intention appears".

Section 11 of the *Interpretation Act* provides that

> 11. Every enactment shall be deemed remedial, and shall be given such fair, large and liberal construction and interpretation as best ensures the attainment of its objects.

The *fair* and *large* interpretation of s. 503 (although in philosophical terms, not necessarily the *liberal* interpretation) would appear to rest on the supposition that Parliament in enacting these sections (s. 508 and s. 732.1) was conferring upon the Crown the power to stop criminal proceedings almost at will. That abuses may flow from such a large grant of power appears indisputable, and historically this claim has been borne out. The answer to the control of such abuses, however, does not reside in the placing interpretations upon statutory enactments which they are not fairly capable of bearing. The evil consequences for the future interpretation of other statutes would far outweigh the short term benefits accruing from such misapplication of law.

(3) The nolle prosequi

Much of the distress of the modern commentators stems from the fact that evolution of the stay of proceedings in Canada has been con-

---

70. Maxwell, *On the Interpretation of Statutes*, (12th Edition — P. St. J. Langan) (1969) at p. 270.
71. R.S.C. 1970, c. I-23, s. 1.

trary to the history of its common law progenitor, the *nolle prosequi,* in England.

In England a *nolle prosequi* may be entered only by the Attorney General or by some person acting with his *specific* authority in a particular case. The *nolle prosequi* is strictly confined in its operation, and may not be entered until *after* a bill of indictment has been signed.[72] Strict compliance with procedure is requisite for utilization of the power, and the courts in England have consistently blocked any attempts to enlarge the scope of operation of the *nolle prosequi.*[73]

In England, proceedings in a court of summary jurisdiction cannot be terminated by entering a *nolle prosequi.*[74] With respect to indictable offences the use of the *nolle* in actual practice has been extremely limited; the Attorney General usually employing it in circumstances where the fitness of an accused ever to stand trial was deemed to be unlikely. Other circumstances justifying resort to its use in England involved control over frivolous, vexatious and oppressive proceedings instituted by private prosecutors.[75]

Thus the English experience with the *nolle prosequi* presents a striking contrast to the Canadian implementation of the Attorney General's power to stay proceedings.

> In contrast to England, where the use of stays of proceedings has diminished to insignificance, statistics indicate that the annual incidence of stays in Canada has been, and continues to be increasing. Particularly alarming are the figures for the provinces of Manitoba and British Columbia, which have maintained an inordinately high incidence of stays whether considered numerically or as percentages of charges laid.[76]

---

72. See Edwards, *The Law Officers of the Crown* (1964) p. 227 *et seq.;* also the note on *nolle prosequi,* [1958] Crim. L. Rev. 573; further see "Nina Ponomareva" [1956] Crim. L. Rev. 725; and see also Sun, *supra* footnote 64 at p. 483.

73. In *R. v. Wylie, Howe & McGuire* (1919) 83 J.P. 295 a *nolle prosequi* entered during a preliminary inquiry was deemed to be a nullity. See also *Poole v. R.* [1960] 3 All E.R. 398 at p. 404 *per* Lord Tucker; *R. v. London Quarter Sessions Chairman, Ex parte Downes* [1954] 1 Q.B. 1 at p. 6; Halbury, X, 398 as cited in Friedland, *Double Jeopardy* (1969) at p. 30.

74. "Nina Ponomareva", [1956] Crim. L. Rev. 725 at p. 726. This historical restriction of the *nolle* to indictable offences coupled with a too-close analogy of the common law *nolle prosequi* to the statutorily conferred stay of proceedings in Canada led to the faulty first premise in the argument advanced by Sun in her article. Prior to 1972 in Canada there appears to have been no authority for the entry of a stay in summary conviction matters, and Sun's point is well taken but of present academic interest only due to the enactment of s. 732.1 on this issue. The existence of s. 490 (now s. 508) statutorily prescribing the power to stay proceedings in indictable offences appears to obviate the need for resort to examine the common law *nolle prosequi* save for comparative purposes only.

75. Sun, *supra* footnote 64 at p. 485.

76. *Ibid.* at p. 486 basing these remarks on figures released in the D.B.S. Annual Reports, Stats. of Crim. and other offences.

(4) Shortcomings of the stay of proceedings

In this connecion the question arises as to whether the concern over the Attorney-General's power to stay proceedings is real or artificial. Is there anything necessarily improper about frequent resort to the exercise of this discretion?

If the concern of the Attorney-General or his properly instructed agent were merely in correcting "a decision to proscute which has in the light of later factors turned out to be ill-conceived"[77], and this concern were solely addressed to issues of fundamental justice and fairness, there is little likelihood that the exercise of the discretion would come under attack. Unfortunately, in actual practice the employment of the discretion is often carried on far from those pristine realms.

The major shortcomings and abuses of the prosecutorial discretion to stay proceedings may be summarized as follows:

(1) *The prosecutor's decision is not reviewable* — The Criminal Code provisions conferring jurisdiction on the Attorney General or "counsel instructed by him for the purpose" to stay proceedings provide no statutory limits or guidelines restricting the exercise of this discretion. The Courts have repeatedly held that the Crown "has a statutory right to enter a stay of proceedings, a right in the exercise of which the Court has no part".[78]

(2) *The prosecutor can sidestep the consequences of a weak case by resort to his discretion* — the prosecutor at any time up to judgment is able to assess his ability to "win" the case, and may even go so far as to take the contemptuous step of staying proceedings after the trial judge has given the jury instructions to bring in a directed verdict of acquittal (as was sanctioned in the notorious case of *R. v. Beaudry*).[79] This has subsidiary consequences which are herein separately enumerated.

(3) *The prosecutor by recommencing his stayed proceedings has an unjustified power of harrassment over an accused* — This manoeuvre often employed in our courts as a means for coercing pleas, or for shoring up weak or unsubstantial charges flies in the face of basic Anglo-Canadian principles of fair play. The powers of arrest, detention, the restricted liberty of bail are all attendant upon the commencement and re-commencement of proceedings.[80]

---

77. *R. v. Dick* (1968) 4 C.R.N.S. 102 (Ont.).
78. *R. v. Judge of the Provincial Court; Ex parte McLeod* [1970] 5 C.C.C. 128 at p. 130 (B.C.) *per* Kirke Smith J. citing *R. v. Cooke; R. v. Cooke, Dingman and Whitton* (1948) 91 C.C.C. 310 (Alta.) in support of the proposition. See also the discussion *supra* at p.   re the general status of the prosecutor and judicial supervision of his discretionary activities.
79. (1967) 50 C.R. 1 (B.C. C.A.).
80. The recommencement of proceedings shall be dealt with at greater length *infra*. See generally *R. v. Spence* (1919) 31 C.C.C. 365 (Ont. C.A.) and *R. v. Takagishi* (1932) 60 C.C.C. 34 (B.C.).

(4) *The procedure precludes adequate public inspection* — Since the prosecutor need not àpply to the court for permission to stay proceedings, and since he need only "direct" the clerk of the court to enter a stay (virtually at "anytime"), the whole process can be carried on behind closed doors and away from the public eye. Where the weak have been oppressed (*e.g.* an indigent unable to raise bail has his charges stayed after a period of pre-trial incarceration) or where the powerful profit (*e.g.* an alleged Mafia leader has proceedings dropped against him) the public has a right to an explanation.

(5) *The procedure does not provide for aspects of deterrence to prosecutorial misconduct* — Since the prosecutor may exercise his discretion on a sub-stratum level of the administrative process, he need suffer no embarrassment for ill-conceived proscutions guided by "oblique considerations", nor is he required to offer any explanations to the court or the accused. Consequently there is no built-in psychological deterrent to dubious activity.

(6) *The procedure may be employed to avoid adverse rulings and decisions* — *R. v. Beaudry* demonstrates only the most flamboyant aspect of how the stay of proceedings may be utilized to avoid the worst consequences of a judicial ruling. Denials of adjournments on dates set for trial may be met by a stay of proceedings.[81] Where these occurrences take place in open court they cannot help but encourage disrespect for the administration of justice.

(7) *The prosecutor often has the appearance of not truly representing the Attorney General* — In a given situation (one such as prevailed in the *Beaudry* case) the prosecutor may announce his stay of proceedings in a completely spontaneous circumstance; even in the midst of the trial of the proceeding itself. In such a situation it is difficult to envision how a given Crown Attorney can meaningfully contend that he has been "instructed" by the Attorney General for the purpose of staying the particular proceeding. Some provinces treat the authority to enter stays as implicit in the appointment of Crown prosecutors; others interpret ss. 508 and 732.1 as permitting a general delegation of the discretion to enter stays to all Crown Attorneys and they remain so entrusted at all times. These approaches violate the maxim *delegatus non potest delegare.*

The power to stay proceedings is delegated to the Attorney General as part of his function as chief law enforcement officer of the Crown and it is not open to him to sub-delegate.

---

81. See *R. v. Antonin Zetek* (1971) unreported (B.C.) where a Crown attempt to use the stay to defeat an order denying an adjournment was effectively countered by a Provincial Judge. The case is discussed by Sun, *supra* footnote 64 at pp. 507-508.

Parliament, naturally, may authorize sub-delegation and where that express power is found in the legislation no question will arise, except perhaps as to its scope. Sections 508 and 732.1, however cannot be taken as authorizing sub-delegation in view of the use of the word "instructed" . . . in preference to more general terms such as "authorized", "delegated", etc. . . .[82]

Basically these criticisms of the prosecutor's discretion to stay proceedings involve the same kind of profound malaise which was central to the recent American experience with the Watergate affair. When a politically responsible law officer, the attorney general, possesses the power to effectively "suppress the judicial process and override the independence of the judiciary" grave consequences and grave injustice may result.

The "stay of proceedings" stands alongside a similar but more overtly "just" procedure — the "withdrawal of charges". There has been a tendency in some of the cases to use the terms interchangeably as though they were synonymous, but they are not.

The withdrawal, unlike the stay of proceedings, has no *statutory* basis in Canadian law, but is derived from the English common law and has been preserved in force in Canada by virtue of s. 7(2) of the Criminal Code. This provision retains in force in a province "the Criminal law of England that was in force in a province immediately before the first day of April 1955 . . . except as altered, varied, modified or effected" by the Criminal Code or any other federal enactment. "Although there is no provision in the *Criminal Code* allowing for the withdrawal of an information, the procedure has been recognized and adopted by our courts."[83]

The withdrawal of charges procedure[84] is different from the stay of proceedings procedure in two important respects:

82. Sun, *supra* footnote 64 at p. 500. For a more detailed examination of this theme see pp. 498-503. The recent decision of the Supreme Court in *R. v. Harrison* [1976] 3 W.W.R. 536 (Can.) appears to undercut the validity of this point. Although dealing with a different situation (s. 605(1) re appeals by the A. G. to the court of appeal) the point is made that there is implied authority in the Attorney General to delegate even the *power to instruct*. Further, if there is a challenge to counsel's authority normally a letter signed by the Attorney General or an officer in his department will suffice.

83. *Blasko v. R.* [1976] 33 C.R.N.S. 227 (Ont.); see also *R. v. Garcia* [1970] 1 O.R. 821; *R. v. Hatherley* [1971] 3 O.R. 430; and *R. v. Osborne* (1976) 33 C.R.N.S. 211 (N.B. C.A.). See also K. Chasse, "The Crown's Power to Withdraw Charges" (1976) 33 C.R.N.S. 218.

84. M. L. Friedland, in *Double Jeopardy* (1969) p. 31, notes that "English cases which refer to the withdrawal of a prosecution should not be confused with the cases . . . on the withdrawal of a charge. The former term is normally used in cases where, usually because of a weak case, no evidence is offered and the jury bring in a verdict of acquittal". He cites *Abbott v. Refuge Assur. Co.* [1961] 3 All E.R. 1074 at p. 1084-5 as an example of a withdrawal of a prosecution.

(1) In a withdrawal the attorney general or his agent must apply to the Court for permission to withdraw the charge.[85] There is no such necessity in a stay of proceedings. (In certain cases the following procedure has been recommended and utilized: "Prior to the preferring of an indictment or the entering of a plea and the tendering of evidence, an information may be withdrawn without leave of the court. Where a Crown attorney has tendered evidence after the taking of a plea, the trial judge is seized with jurisdiction and the information cannot be withdrawn without the consent of the trial judge.")[86]

(2) A new charge is necessary in order to recommence proceedings after a charge has been withdrawn, whereas when proceedings have been stayed proceedings may be recommenced within one year (with appropriate notice being given) without the laying of a new information or charge; or without the preferring of a new indictment, as the case may be.[87]

A recent Ontario Provincial Court decision[88] asserts that the 1972 amendments to the *Criminal Code* (specifically the enactment of s. 732.1) has removed the right of the Crown to apply to withdraw charges and confines the Crown solely to the stay of proceedings remedies set out in the *Code*. The case, fortunately, cannot be regarded as strong authority for the proposition. The irony of the decision lies in the fact that Clendenning Prov. Ct. J. arrived at his conclusion by applying the so-called "mischief rule" to the interpretation of legislative enactments (the mischief he was seeking to avoid was the acquisition of a criminal record containing "withdrawn" items). By avoiding one "mischief" he inadvertently perpetuated another — namely, he increased the scope of the prosecutor's discretion by removing any obligation upon him in certain circumstances to apply to Court to withdraw charges rather than merely to stay proceedings.[89]

In practice, use of the withdrawal as opposed to the stay of proceedings varies widely according to the jurisdiction. Dean Friedland surmises that "[although] no statistical records of the extent of the use

---

85. *Abbott v. Refuge Assur. Co. ibid.* at p. 1084: "It is a long established practice that, if counsel in charge of a prosecution at any stage is convinced that there is no evidence against the defendant, or so little evidence that it would not be safe to leave the case to the jury, it is then the duty of counsel to acquaint the court with his views and to ask for leave to withdraw the prosecution. I certainly have never known such an application to be refused."

86. *Blasko v. R. supra* footnote 83 at p. 228 *per* Parker J. But see *R. v. Hatherley supra* footnote 83 where Aylesworth J.A. indicates that the Court is seized *after the taking of plea* (there being no requirement that evidence be adduced before the Court is clothed in jurisdiction).

87. See *Criminal Code* ss. 508(2) and 732.1(2); *R. v. Leonard* (1962) 133 C.C.C. 230 at p. 233 (Alta. C.A.) and *R. v. Dick* (1968) 4 C.R.N.S. 102 at p. 107 (Ont.).

88. *R. v. Taylor* (1974) 19 C.C.C. (2d) 79 (Ont.).

89. See *R. v. Dick supra* footnote 87 at p. 110.

of the withdrawal procedure are kept in Canada, it would seem if the Toronto practice is an indication, that more persons in Canada have their cases completely disposed of by a withdrawal of all aspects of the charge than by an acquittal".[90]

Since 1972 the stay of proceedings has also possessed the ability to completely remove "all aspects of the charge", although there is still a one year period of pendancy before the proceedings are "deemed never to have been commenced".

(5) The withdrawal—advantages over the stay

Reference to the discussion *supra* of the major shortcomings and abuses of prosecutorial discretion to stay proceedings will reveal that the withdrawal procedure is to be preferred to the stay of proceedings for a variety of reasons:

(1) *It subjects the discretion of the prosecutor to court scrutiny.* In such a setting the prosecutor is less likely to attempt to sidestep the consequences of a weak case by resort to his discretion.

(2) *The procedure allows for public inspection of the rationale behind the resort to the discretion.* As such, a measure of "deterrence" is injected into the system in the form of public embarrassment and surveillance by the press.

(3) *The court rather than the prosecutor is the final arbiter of the issue.*

Where the matter of mode of procedure (stay vs. withdrawal) to be adopted is, in itself, discretionary (as it presently is) the gains are illusory. To save an occasion backed by a noble motive for open court while hiding instances guided by oblique motives in the back room is only to compound the potential for abuse.

Presently the withdrawal serves the function of a vain-glorious redundancy in the law.

(6) Criteria guiding the discretion to stay

Connie Sun in examining the discretionary power to stay criminal proceedings lists six criteria which most provincial attorney generals claimed guided their determinations as to whether or not to stay criminal proceedings:[91]

(1) when, in the case of a misdemeanour, a civil action is pending for the same cause;

(2) when there has been an attempt to oppress the defendants as by repeatedly preferring defective indictments for the same offence;

(3) when the accused is unable to stand trial or is unable to do so due to some mental infirmity;

(4) when a similar case is on appeal to a higher court;

(5) when a witness is missing or has been intimidated;

---

90. *Double Jeopardy supra* footnote 84 at p. 32.
91. Sun, *supra* footnote 64 at pp. 488-489.

(6) when there is insufficient evidence but a good chance of new evidence coming to light within a short period.

Basically these criteria are not objectionable *per se* although some are rather curious.

For example, it is curious that a prosecutor would have an impetus to resort to criterion (2) since his office has been the one responsible for the "oppression" in the form of the repeated preferring of defective indictments.

Most (probably, all) commentators are not opposed to the fact that the Attorney General possesses the discretionary power to stay proceedings. The criticisms are aimed at what Friedland describes as the "carte blanche" nature of the discretion, and at the abuses which are inevitably part of such a condition. A discretion exercised in the absence of effective controls, in the last analysis, can only be described as "arbitrary". The criteria for the use of the stay enumerated by Sun are of no effective controlling significance in that they are merely expressions of sentiment, or at best, internal guidelines possessed of no imperative qualities. It is not idle to speculate that other less salutary criteria from time to time motivate the entry of a stay. Manitoba and British Columbia were candid enough to admit to two such criteria. Stay of proceedings might be entered

(7) where there was insufficient evidence but not necessarily any likelihood of a change in circumstances so as to allow for recommencement of proceedings;

(8) in "plea bargaining" situations.[92]

The ethics surrounding allowing an accused to remain in jeopardy in the manner described in criterion (7) are highly dubious. The shopworn analogy to the sword of Damocles is appropriate. That the practice has been confirmed in writing by a provincial attorney general is quite remarkable. As the matter is one of demonstrable practice rather than merely being confined to rumor, it exists as a powerful testament to the desirability of diminishing and controlling this private preserve of power.

Plea bargaining ethics shall be discussed *infra* in Part 6 of this Chapter, and need not be examined here.

5. THE DISCRETION TO RE-LAY INFORMATION AND/OR PREFER INDICTMENTS

During the course of the prosecution of a criminal offence a variety of situations may occur which reasonably give rise to an expectation in the mind of an accused that he has escaped the jeopardy which befell him when he was originally changed. Some of these situations occur when

---

92. Sun, *ibid.* pp. 488-9. (The numbering employed is *in seriatim* with the six previously listed criteria.)

(1) the Crown enters a stay of proceeding on the charge;
(2) the Crown withdraws the charge;
(3) the accused makes a motion for want of prosecution and the charges are dismissed;
(4) at the conclusion of the preliminary hearing the Crown's motion for committal is rejected and the accused is discharged;
(5) on the date set for trial the Crown submits no evidence and the accused is acquitted.

Counsel would be remiss in his duty to his client if he did not advise that in any of the above circumstances there remained the possibility of further proceedings. The discretion of whether or not to institute further proceedings belongs to the prosecutor. There have been instances in Canadian legal history where the course of action adopted by a prosecutor has been manifestly unfair, even contemptuous of the court and the jury, and yet fresh proceedings have been allowed.[93] As M. L. Friedland has noted in *Double Jeopardy,* "not all dismissals will bar subsequent proceeding".[94]

(1) Adjudication on the merits

Before proceeding to investigate the various modes by which the prosecutor may re-institute proceedings against an accused it would be useful first, to analyze what is contemplated by the expression "an adjudication on the merits". The courts have on occasion, in determining whether a second proceeding is to be permitted, applied the test of "adjudication on the merits".[95]

Lush J. in *Haynes v. Davis* attempted to explain the phrase in the following manner:[96]

> I quite agree that "acquittal on the merits" does not necessarily mean that the jury or the magistrate must find as a matter of fact that the person charged was innocent; it is just as much an acquittal upon the merits if the judge or the magistrate were to rule upon the construction of an Act of Parliament that the accused was in law entitled to be acquitted as in law he was not guilty, and to that extent the expression "acquittal on the merits" must be qualified, but in my view the expression is used by way of antithesis to a dismissal of the charge upon some technical ground which had been a bar to the adjudicating upon it. That is why this expression is important, however one may qualify it, and I think the antithesis is between an adjudication of not guilty

---

93. See *R. v. Beaudry* [1967] 1 C.C.C. 272 (B.C. C.A.).
94. M. L. Friedland, *Double Jeopardy* (1969) at p. 53.
95. See *R. v. Trainor* (1945) 85 C.C.C. 36 at p. 43 (Alta. D.C.) "While perhaps useful on occasion, it may quite possibly prove a trap for the unwary. No one appears to have defined its meaning, scope or limitatoins, and no clear principle appears to be established by the authorities" (*per* McBride, D.C.J. at p. 43 and cited in Friedland, *supra* at p. 53). See also Davidson "Autrefois Acquit — The Same Offence — Adjudication Upon the Merits" (1958-59) 1 Cr.L.Q. 283.
96. [1915] 1 K.B. 332 at pp. 338-339.

upon some matter of fact or law and a discharge of the person charged on the ground that there are reasons why the Court cannot proceed to find if he is guilty.

According the view expressed above where the "adjudication" concerns a ruling upon a defence to which there is no answer, as opposed to the raising of a technical ground which if successful bars adjudication upon the charge, then there has been an adjudication "on the merits" which will operate as a bar to subsequent proceedings.[97]

Dean Friedland subscribes to the view that although many of the cases have turned on the construction given to the phrase "on the merits" it is a "trap for the unwary". He asserts that basically the cases are understandable in terms of the circumstance which gave rise to the adjudication.[98] Consequently he addresses the question "when will dismissal be a bar?" by examining five substantive areas: (1) offering no evidence; (2) dismissal for failure of the prosecutor to appear; (3) accidental acquittals; (4) dismissal on a procedural matter; and (5) defects in the indictment. This approach has much to recommend it.

Since the primary concern in *this* discussion is with prosecutorial discretion the conceptual approach adopted here will be different. Emphasis will focus on factors motivating the prosecutor to re-institute proceedings; the existence or non-existence of controls over the exercise of this prosecutorial discretion; and trends in judicial thinking on the nature of the discretion. An examination of the legality of re-commencing proceedings (after stay, withdrawal, dismissal for want of proscution, discharge at the preliminary inquiry, and acquittals after the submission of no evidence) is necessary in order to flesh out and comprehend the real world in which these discretionary exercises are carried on.

(2) Re-commencing stayed proceedings

As has been mentioned previously in our discussion of the stay of proceedings, the statutory basis for re-commencing stayed proceedings is to be found in ss. 508(2) and 732.1(2). Under both sections a new charge or new preferred indictment (as the case may be) is unnecessary in order to re-commence proceedings so long as the proceedings are taken, and appropriate notice given, within one year of entry of the stay of proceedings.

In *R. v. Beaudry*[99] proceedings were stayed in order to avoid the consequences of a directed verdict of acquittal. In *R. v. Rosser*[100] pro-

97. This in substance was the dissenting view held by Cartwright J. (as he then was) in *R. v. Karpinski* (1957) 117 C.C.C. 241 (Can.) at p. 247. See also *Re Bond* (1936) 66 C.C.C. 271 (N.S. C.A.).
98. See generally *Double Jeopardy* (1969) Chapter 3, pp. 53-75.
99. *Supra* footnote 93.
100. (1971) 16 C.R.N.S. 321 (Y.T.).

ceedings were stayed against a co-accused in order to call her as a Crown Witness. After the hearing proceedings were re-commenced in order that no evidence be submitted against her so as to result in her acquittal. Both of these procedures were upheld upon appeal.

(3) Withdrawal and subsequent proceedings

The withdrawal of charges procedure also discussed earlier is not derived from the operation of statute. Its origins have been traced to the common law. One lower court decision[101] goes so far as to question whether the withdrawal procedure can validly exist today given the 1972 amendments to the *Criminal Code* with respect to stays. Nevertheless it appears to be the procedure of choice in Ontario. It requires an application to court by the prosecutor in order to be implemented. Subsequent proceedings are commenced by the laying of a new charge or the preferring of a new indictment. No application to court need be made at this stage of the proceeding.

In *R. v. Karpinski*[102] the presiding Magistrate allowed the prosecutor to withdraw an information charging leaving the scene of an accident under what was then s. 221(2) (now s. 233(2)) of the *Criminal Code*. The offence was one that was dual in nature in that it could be dealt with summarily or on indictment. The information on its face showed that more than six months had elapsed since the date of the accident. On arraignment, after the Crown had elected to proceed summarily, the accused moved for dismissal. The Crown sought leave to withdraw the information in order to proceed subsequently by indictment. The accused argued unsuccessfully before the Supreme Court of Canada that the withdrawal in these circumstances was an adjudication on the merits and was tantamount to an acquittal. The Supreme Court, with Cartwright J. dissenting, held that the procedure adopted was valid and the prosecutor was thus entitled to re-commence by indictment. In the result the accused lost the protection of the six month limitation period under the then s. 693(2) (now s. 721(2)) of the *Code*.

There are a great many cases in addition to *Karpinski* which have held that the withdrawal of an information does not bar subsequent proceedings. Further, it matters not at what point in the initial proceeding that the prosecutor successfully sought to have the charges withdrawn; be it before plea, after plea, or, at the conclusion of or during the prosecutor's case.[103]

---

101. See *R. v. Taylor* (1974) 19 C.C.C. (2d) 79 (Ont.) and see the discussion of this case in the section of this paper dealing with the prosecutor's discretion to stay proceedings or withdraw charges.
102. *Supra* footnotes 97 at p. 241.
103. See *R. v. Somers* [1929] 3 D.L.R. 772 (B.C. C.A.); *Re Henderson* (1929) 52 C.C.C. 95 (Can.); *Blanchard v. Jenkins* (1930) 55 C.C.C. 77 (Man.); *R. v. Gallant* [1964] 1 C.C.C. 296 (P.E.I.) (examples of withdrawals before plea). See *Ex parte Mitchell* (1909) 16 C.C.C. 205 (N.B. C.A.);

The following quotation extracted from the decision of Martin J.A. in *R. v. Somers* aptly sums up the general law on this point:

> The main principle to be gathered from all the many cases, not always consistent or exact, and based in varying circumstances, that we have considered is that, unless it can be said on the facts of the particular case that there has been an adjudication and acquittal upon the merits, the permission of the Court to withdraw a charge is not equivalent to a dismissal which can be pleaded in bar of subsequent proceedings.[104]

The general proposition that a withdrawal is not a bar to subsequent proceedings is tempered by the existence of a number of Canadian authorities which hold that in certain circumstances withdrawal may be tantamount to an acquittal. In such circumstances subsequent proceedings have indeed been barred.

In *Que. Liquor Comm. v. Menard*,[105] a case involving the unlawful sale of alcohol, when both parties appeared on the date set for trial prepared to proceed, and the informant sought permission to withdraw the charges (with the defendant's consent), the plea of "autrefois acquit" was successfully invoked as a bar to a subsequent trial. In that case the Court remarked

> If, in order to withdraw her complaint, the complainant had invoked reasons of form, jurisdiction, or irregularities so important that judgment could not have been given on the merits of the case, the question would be different, but no such thing has been alleged, the plea of *'autrefois acquit'* appears to me to be well founded, and the case is dismissed with costs.[106]

The Court in *Menard* viewed matters as having been decided "practically on the merits". The implied rationale of the decision seems to lie in the fact that *no justification whatsoever was evident to explain the failure to prosecute the offence on the duly appointed date.*

In 1916 *Ethier v. Minister of Inland Revenue*[107] held on its facts[108] that the accused Ethier had not been placed in jeopardy so as to bar

---

Ex parte Wyman (1899) 5 C.C.C. 58 (N.B. C.A.); *R. v. Scott* (1939) 73 C.C.C. 254 (Sask.); *In Re McKenzie* (1953) 16 C.R. 104 (Alta.) (examples of withdrawals during the course of, or at the close of the case for the prosecution). (All of these examples are to be found cited in Friedland, *Double Jeopardy* (1969) at p. 33). See also *R. v. Dunn* (1945) 84 C.C.C. 268 (B.C. C.A.).

104. *R. v. Somers supra* footnote 103 at pp. 777-778. This case contains a thorough review of English and Canadian precedents up to 1929 which, as Martin J.A. has pointed out, were "not always consistent or exact".

105. (1921) 36 C.C.C. 385 (Que.).

106. *Menard ibid.* at p. 386.

107. (1916) 27 C.C.C. 12 (Que.).

108. The statute under which *Ethier* was being prosecuted (The War Revenue Act) provided that prosecution for certain offences could only be brought in the name of the Attorney General of Canada or the Minister of Inland Revenue. The first prosecution was brought in the name of an improper informant, therefore the charges were withdrawn and new proceedings were instituted.

a subsequent prosecution, but supported the proposition that, generally speaking, a withdrawal is tantamount to an acquittal.[109]

> It is true that the withdrawal of a summons in general amounts to a discharge of the accused from the complaint, but that consequence does not follow when the trial would be a nullity because of there having been some illegality or irregularity which would have made a conviction void if the trial had gone on. I consider that the appellant was not in jeopardy under the first summons, and that he was subject to be tried on the second one. [110]

Since the decision *R. v. Somers* in 1929 the law has continued to be inconsistent and inexact. What the legal effect of a withdrawal will be in a given case is by no means certain. The *Karpinski* decision by no means resolved matters. Kerwin C.J.C. and Taschereau J. both held on the facts of that case that the withdrawal of the information did not amount to an acquittal giving rise to a plea of "autrefois acquit". (Kerwin C.J.C. stated further tha "the first trial must have been concluded by an adjudication or what amounts thereto").

Fauteux J. and Abbott J. while concurring in the result of that appeal did not feel it necessary to comment on the law in such ultimate terms.

> The submission of respondent, rejected by the trial Judge but accepted in the Court of Appeal, is that the Crown having no right to change its election and withdraw the information after the plea of not guilty, such withdrawal was therefore tantamount to a dismissal giving rise to a plea of *autrefois acquit.*
>
> *In my respectful view, it is unnecessary to deal with the merits of the conclusion of this proposition, for the premises upon which it rests are not established.* In the circumstances of this case, there were no rights for the Crown to elect to proceed by way of summary conviction and no jurisdiction for the Magistrate to accept and act upon the election by receiving a plea. On the face of the information itself, it was manifest that more than 6 months had elapsed from the date when the subject-matter of the proceedings had arisen; and of its nature, the offence charged was not capable of being one having a continuing character. Non-compliance with the statutory requirement of s. 693(2) was fatal to the validity of the election and plea, both of which were void (emphasis added).[111]

Cartwright J., dissenting in *Karpinski* expressed the view that "in the circumstances of the case at bar, the withdrawal of the charge before the learned Magistrate was tantamount to an acquittal".

---

109. See also *Kempston v. Desgagnis* [1921] 1 W.W.R. 244 (Sask.) where "after a full trial on the merits when the accused was undoubtedly in jeopardy" a withdrawal before actual adjudication was held to be a bar to subsequent proceedings.

110. *Ethier v. Minister of Inland Revenue, supra* footnote 107 at p. 13 (*per* Cross J.).

111. *R. v. Karpinski supra* footnote 97 at p. 249 *per Fauteux J.*

Hence, *Karpinski* was in effect an inconclusive ruling. What at first blush appears to be a strong 4:1 decision of our highest court upon closer analysis cannot (in view of the 2:2:1 split in the court) be viewed as having great persuasive weight. In terms of resolving the previous uncertainty of the law in this area it is a less than satisfactory precedent.

(4) Preferring indictments after preliminary inquiries

The preferred indictment is often the means by which the prosecutor will institute subsequent proceedings (as opposed to the re-laid charge in the case of most withdrawals or re-commencement of the original information or indictment in the ordinary case of the stay of proceedings). The preferred indictment will often be employed subsequent to a preliminary hearing, although it may also be used in the case of stayed proceedings in which a year has elapsed since the date of the stay, or, in preference to re-laying a charge after a withdrawal.

Where a person has, following a preliminary hearing, been committed for trial a prosecutor may in his discretion, prefer a bill of indictment in respect of any charge founded on the facts disclosed at the preliminary inquiry. He is not restricted merely to the charge upon which the magistrate has seen fit to commit the accused.[112]

Section 507 of the *Criminal Code* provides for the preferring of a bill of indictment in every jurisdiction of Canada (except Nova Scotia) without resort to the inspection of a Grand Jury, or the judge of a court constituted with a Grand Jury. An indictment may be preferred by the Attorney General or his agent, or by any person with the written consent of a judge of a superior court or of the Attorney General or by order of the court.

Up until 1969 the law was unsettled as to whether or not the prosecutor was entitled to prefer an indictment before the completion of a preliminary hearing. It was further in dispute as to whether or not it was open to the prosecutor to directly indict an accused who had been discharged at a preliminary inquiry.

A not unusual example involved the case of *R. v. Pilot*,[113] a 1964 decision of the Nova Scotia Supreme Court. In *Pilot* the accused, having been charged with non-capital murder was discharged at the conclusion of his preliminary inquiry. The Crown preferred an indictment directly against the accused. The issue raised by the accused in answer to this new indictment was that where the Attorney General had "elected" to proceed initially by information and preliminary inquiry

---

112. See *Criminal Code* s. 504. Note further, that by *Code* s. 507 it is not necessary in certain provinces to prefer a bill of indictment before a grand jury "but it is sufficient if the trial of an accused is commenced by an indictment in writing setting forth the offence with which he is charged".
113. [1964] 1 C.C.C. 375 (N.S.).

he cannot then by-pass the consequences of that hearing by preferring an indictment directly. The Court rejected this so-called "doctrine of election" and held that the power of the Attorney General to prefer an indictment under what was then s. 487(1) (a) of the *Code* was unrestricted.

In its decision the Nova Scotia Court rejected a line of Quebec cases[114] which affirmed the doctrine of election and which indicated that where the attorney general "elects" he is foreclosed from preferring an indictment based on the same facts. The Court preferred instead the contrary position as enunciated in *Re Ecclestone and Dalton*,[115] and *R. v. Summervill and Kaylich*.[116]

R. v. Pilot therefore is a good source for exploring the two competing perspectives which prevailed concerning the right of the attorney general to proceed by preferred indictment. These two perspectives (or "trends" as they were discerned in *R. v. Viau*[117]) may be summarized as follows:

(1) *The right of the attorney general to proceed by preferred indictment is absolute*[118]

(2) *The right of the Attorney General is far from absolute. It is limited by the spirit of law, by the mode of procedure adopted, by the constitutional principle of separation of executive and judiciary powers, and by the spirit which has governed the development of our criminal law.*[119]

Consent of Court or Attorney General

A measure of confusion was ended in 1968-69 by the enactment of s. 507(3) of the *Code* which was added to provide that

(3) Not withstanding anything in this section, where

    (a) a preliminary inquiry has not been held, or

---

114. *R. v. Viau* (1961) 37 C.R. 41 (Que.); and *R. v. Biernacki* (1962) 37 C.R. 226 (Que.); see also *R. v. Russell* [1920] 1 W.W.R. 164 (Man. C.A.).

115. (1952) 102 C.C.C. 305 (Ont..)

116. [1963] 2 C.C.C. 178 (Sask.). See also *Re Schofield and Toronto* (1913) 22 C.C.C. 93 (Ont.); *R. v. Maynard* (1959) 32 C.R. 49 (B.C. C.A.); and *R. v. Mooney* [1960] O.W.N. 401 (C.A.).

117. *R. v. Viau supra* footnote 114.

118. See *R. v. Court* (1947) 4 C.R. 183 (P.E.I.); *R. v. McGavin Bakeries Ltd.* (1950) 10 C.R. 251 (Alta.); *Re Criminal Code* (1910) 16 C.C.C. 459 (Can.) in addition to the cases cited *supra* at footnote 116.

119. Paraphrase of comments of Prevost J. in *R. v. Viau supra*. See *Welch v. R.* (1950) 97 C.C.C. 177 at p. 191 (Can.) *per* Fauteux J. "These considerations suffice to indicate that, general and unrestricted as they may appear, the powers . . . are not absolute and cannot obtain in all circumstances. Like many others in the Code, *they remain subject to qualifications and restrictions implicitly and necessarily flowing from other provisions in the same Act*" (emphasis added). Also see the authorities cited supra at footnote 114.

(*b*) a preliminary inquiry has been held and the accused has been
discharged,

an indictment under subsection (1) shall not be preferred except
with written consent of a judge of the court, or by the Attorney
General.[120]

What is not covered by the above amendment is what result ensues
when an accused who has been discharged at the preliminary inquiry
is sought by the Crown to be indicted by the direct preferring of an
indictment on an included or related offence. Are the requisite consents still necessary? Further, what result ensues when the accused is
discharged at the preliminary inquiry of the offence charged but is
committed to stand trial on a lesser and included offence? May the
Crown prefer an indictment for the greater offence without the consent
of either the trial judge or the Attorney General?

In answer to the first question it is submitted that since is is open
to the magistrate conducting the preliminary hearing to commit the
accused to stand trial on any charge revealed by the evidence,[121] included or otherwise, *the decision not to commit the accused to stand
trial on any charge whatsoever must amount to a discharge on all included and related matters.* By this reasoning, before the agent of the
attorney general may prefer a direct indictment against the accused
on an included or related matter he must first acquire the consent of
the Attorney General himself or of the trial judge of a properly constituted court.

R. v. Miller[122] raised the issue, in 1970, of whether the Crown
might, in the absence of consents, prefer an indictment for a greater
offence when the accused had been committed to stand trial only on
a lesser and included offence. Fraser J. held it to be improper for the
Crown to pursue such a course of action and quashed the indictments
preferred because they were lacking the necessary consents. The enactment of provisions for the preferring of indictments, he reasoned, were
not for the purpose of overriding or reversing the decisions of the Provincial Judge conducting the preliminary inquiry.

The 1968-69 amendments to the *Code* did not contradict the view
"that it was open to the Crown to use a preferred indictment regardless of the outcome of any previous proceedings by way of information

---

120. See s. 505 of the *Criminal Code* for the practice in provinces not employing
the grand jury system.
121. See *R. v. Ostrove* (1967) 1 C.R.N.S. 376 (Man.) for a good consideration
of the decisions on the power to commit. Note these comments of Wilson J.
at p. 378 (citing *R. v. Edwards* (1938) 69 C.C.C. 305 with approval):
". . . it necessarily follows that, if the evidence taken before the justice
reveals an indictable offence as having been committed by the party summoned or apprehended though it may not be the same as the one charged
in the information or complaint, he is bound to adjudicate upon the evidence and to discharge, bind over, or commit the accused . . .".
122. (1970) 3 C.C.C. 89 (Ont.).

and preliminary hearing, and also, regardless of whether or not there had been any preliminary hearing".[123] What these amendments did accomplish was to insist that either the Attorney General himself consented to the procedure, or a judge of a superior court concurred in the exercise of the discretion.

To the extent that a judge is involved in the determination of whether or not a consent is to be given to prefer an indictment this may be regarded as a safeguard. To the further extent that *only* the Attorney General (and not the Deputy Attorney General or the various agents of the Attorney General) may specify his consent, this too may be regarded as a safeguard, although a lesser one. The consent of the judge, unlike the consent of the Attorney General, involves the exercise of a discretion that is reviewable.

Lord Halsbury has made the following statement as to the real significance of what is to be understood by the exercise of discretion:[124]

"An extensive power is confided to the justices in their capacity as justices to be exercised judicially; and 'discretion' means when it is said that something is to be done within the discretion of the authorities that that something is to be done according to the rules of reason and justice, not according to private opinion; . . . according to law, and not humour. It is to be, not arbitrary, vague and fanciful, but legal and regular. And it must be exercised within the limit, to which an honest man competent to the discharge of his office ought to confine himself."[125]

Of the Attorney-General it has been said that "the remedy is not by an application to . . . Court . . . but to hold him responsible before the High Court of Parliament".[126] These are noble sentiments but they bespeak the application of pressures which are ordinarily beyond the reach of ordinary litigants in the criminal process.

R. v. Higham[127], supports the proposition that where there is reason to believe that the Attorney General by reason of his knowledge of the available evidence (other than what was offered at the preliminary inquiry) is in a better position than the judge to give or withhold his consent, the court should refuse an application brought pursuant to s. 505(4). (Section 505(4) refers to preferring indictments in provinces which retain the grand jury system. At the time *Higham* was decided Ontario, Prince Edward Island and Newfoundland had such a system along with Nova Scotia — the only province presently still maintaining the grand jury system. The general principles whether under s. 505(4) or s. 507(3) concerning court approval of the preferred indictment remain the same.) Other courts have gone further in attempting to

---

123. *Ibid.* at p. 93.
124. *Sharp v. Wakefield* [1891] A.C. 173.
125. *Ibid.* cited in *King v. R.* (1925) 43 C.C.C. 20 at p. 23 (N.S. C.A.).
126. *R. v. Allen* (1862) 9 Cox C.C. 120 at p. 122 *per* Cockburn C.J.
127. (1970) 1 C.C.C. (2d) 185 (Sask.).

limit the involvement of the Court in the preferring of indictments whether under s. 505(4) or s. 507(3).[128]

The reluctance of the Courts to accept a measure of control over an area of prosecutorial discretion which was so "unbridled" as to necessitate the passage of affirmative legislation is truly amazing. The information or evidence available to the Attorney General "at highest" can only be regarded as of *prima facie* value. To insist that in the bulk of the instances where the Crown seeks to prefer fresh indictments that the Attorney General should be the primary controlling officer is to sweep the discretionary exercise once again into the sub-sanctum realms of secrecy, with all that that entails. On the other hand, it seems likely that the Courts, armed with the transcripts of the preliminary inquiry[129] and such other information as they may require,[130] would be perfectly suited to the task of scrutinizing ostensible reversals and overrulings of duly considered decisions of provincial judges.

While important as controls over prosecutorial discretion, ss. 507(3) and 505(4) (particularly the "consent of a judge" aspect of those provisions) should not be over-valued. The prosecutor still possesses an enormous degree of freedom from adversarial controls. In this regard it has been held that neither notice to, nor the presence of the accused is required when the Crown seeks the consent of a judge to prefer an indictment.[131]

(5) No case/want of prosecution dismissals and preferred indictments.

Occasionally the prosecutor, for a variety of reasons, may submit no evidence at the hearing of a matter and the accused will be acquitted. In other cases the prosecutor may fail to appear at all and the accused will win a dismissal for want of prosecution.

In summary conviction proceedings when the prosecutor fails to appear, ss. 734 and 738(4) of the *Criminal Code* empower the court to dismiss the information in its discretion. A certificate of dismissal under s. 743 of the *Code* may issue to the accused upon request and by s. 743(2) the certificate is "without further proof a bar to any

---

128. In *R. v. Arthur* (1971) 2 C.C.C. (2d) 589 at p. 592 (Ont.), Costello Co.Ct.J. even went so far as to say (without supporting authority): "If the powers of the Attorney-General are so severely limited by the amendment, it must follow that Judges are only to use the power left to them in any subsection where possibly national security is involved, or instances where the Attorney-General is absent, or ill, or the office of Attorney-General is temporily vacant and no acting Attorney-General has been named."

129. That the Courts might examine the transcripts of the preliminary inquiry was decided in *R. v. Brooks* (1971) 6 C.C.C. (2d) 87 (Ont.) and *R. v. Higham supra* footnote 127.

130. See *Re Athavale and R.* (1973) 11 C.C.C. (2d) 404 (Ont.) where the judge heard the testimony which was inadvertently omitted by a principal Crown witness at the original hearing.

131. *R. v. Higdon* (1973) 21 C.R.N.S. 342 (Ont. C.A.). See also *R. v. Mooney* [1960] O.W.N. 401 (C.A.).

subsequent proceedings against the defendant in respect to the same cause". The wording of the sub-section is misleading. *R. v. Rothman*[132] held that the certificate issued under the section is only a bar to a subsequent summary conviction proceeding and not to proceedings by way of indictment.

Two Ontario cases decided 1955, *R. v. Commodore Hotel (Windsor) Ltd.,*[133] and *Burns v. Gan*[134] held that a certificate of dismissal was ineffective to bar future proceedings unless there was initially a disposition of the issue "on the merits".

Dean Friedland who, it will be recalled, warned that the phrase "on the merits" would be a "trap for the unwary", feels that the *Commoder Hotel* case and *Burns v. Gan* were wrongly decided. Earlier authorities such as *Ex parte Phillips,*[134a] *Tunnicliffe v. Tedd* [134b] and *Vaughton v. Bradshaw*[134c] he contends "are preferable".[135]

The problem of the failure of the prosecutor to appear is one generally confined to private prosecutions. It does on occasion occur where the prosecutor is a Crown Attorney but such instances are comparatively rare. Even less likely is the occasion when the prosecutor fails to appear at the trial of an indictable offence. In practice it would seem that, having regard to the seriousness of the matters alleged, the court would in all likelihood exercise its discretion in favor of the prosecutor and adjourn the hearing to a subsequent occasion.

What follows has been written with respect to the result stemming from a Court's refusal to adjourn an indictable matter in circumstances such as have been described above:

> If a court exercises its discretion not to adjourn . . . the resulting dismissal or acquittal should bar further proceedings. A dismissal in such circumstances should not differ from a dismissal brought about by the prosecutor deliberately offering no evidence.[136]

A more prevalent problem than that of the failure of the prosecutor to appear is that of his failure to proceed and subsequent non-

---

132. (1966) 48 C.R. (Ont.). Also see *R. v. Miles* (1890) 24 Q.B.D. 423 (Ct. for Crown cases reserved) and *R. v. Hilton* (1895) 59 J.P. Jo. 778; both in opposition to the result in *Rothman* and in support of the rule that once acquitted or convicted an accused "shall not be charged again on the same facts in a more aggravated form", Friedland, *Double Jeopardy* (1969) at p. 56.
133. (1955) 111 C.C.C. 165 (Ont.).
134. (1955) 112 C.C.C. 395 (Ont.).
134a. (1884) 24 N.B.R. 119 (C.A.).
134b. (1848) 5 C.B. 553.
134c. (1860) 142 E.R. 40.
135. Friedland, *Double Jeopardy* (1969) at pp. 55-56. See also *R. v. Stokes* (1917) 29 C.C.C. 144 (Man.) and *Davis v. Feinstein* (1915) 24 C.C.C. 160 (Man.); which held that the certificate of conviction was a bar to further proceedings without restriction.
136. Freidland, *Double Jeopardy* (1969) at p. 54.

submission of evidence. Such circumstances often occur after the Crown has sought unsuccessfully to win an adjournment.

Such an occurrence is to be found in *R. v. Cooper*.[137] In *Cooper* the Crown (presumably in anticipation of projected future proceedings) was successful in having quashed a certificate of dismissal issued on the basis of an acquittal registered after no evidence was submitted. The Alberta Court of Appeal (McDermid J.A. dissenting) held that a certificate of dismissal might only issue where there has been a trial on the merits as contemplated by s. 711 (now s. 739) of the *Criminal Code*.

The "upon the merits" basis of the decision in *Cooper* by no means injects a note of predictability into this area of our discussion. A line of old English cases cited in *R. v. Somers*[138] held it to be a bar to further action by the prosecutor because the actions or representations of the complainant amounted to a complete abandonment of the action sufficient to justify a plea of *autrefois acquit*. These cases in their turn, turning as they did upon matters which were quasi-criminal (some would say "civil") in nature may be regarded as "inapplicable to the administration of criminal law".[139]

Kenneth Chasse, the prolific annotator of the Criminal Reports (New Series) has run afoul of the dangerous shoals of the re-laid information. In an annotation contained in volume 10 of the C.R.N.S. dealing with "Abuse of process as a control of prosecutorial discretion"[140] he strikes the position that *autrefois acquit* has absolutely no applicability to the situation of the withdrawn charge or the "dismissal" based upon no evidence.

> When a Crown witness is absent the charge may be withdrawn in order that it may be re-laid. Or it may be dismissed without the hearing of evidence. *Autrefois acquit* would not apply, for there has been no trial on the merits. *And it is best that the plea of autrefois not be extended to any "dismissal", whether there has been evidence heard or not . . .* To extend the plea of autrefois acquit to cover a "dismissal" where no evidence is heard would be saying that nothing can justify the absence of a witness and the resulting re-laying of the charge. [Emphasis added]

Mr. Chasse is a strong advocate for the preservation of, and non-interference with, prosecutorial rights and discretions. In volume 13 of the same report series he takes a closer look at the subject of "The

---

137. (1971) 14 C.R.N.S. 389 (Alta. C.A.); see *contra Ex parte Phillips* (1884) 24 N.B.R. 119 (C.A.).

138. *R. v. Somers supra* footnote 103; citing *R. v. Stamper* (1841) 1 Q.B. 119; *Vaughton v. Bradshaw* (1860), 9 C.B.N.S. 103; *Tunnicliffe v. Tedd* (1848) 5 C.B. 553; *Pickavance v. Pickavance* [1901] P. 60.

139. *Per* Palles C.B. in *R. v. Tyrone JJ.* [1912] 2 I.R. 44 at p. 48.

140. (1970) 10 C.R.N.S. 392 at 401.

re-laid charge and autrefois acquit"[141] and is forced in the light of the inconsistent and inexact state of the law to soften his approach and acknowledge some of the subtleties of the issue. Speaking of the matter of a denied adjournment and resultant "dismissal" he writes:

> The argument would be that the actions of the Crown amounted to a refusal to enter upon its case after the Magistrate or provincial judge had exercised his discretion to refuse a withdrawal such that the "dismissal" that followed amounted to a "trial upon the merits."[141a]

These comments reveal a more dialectical approach adopted by Mr. Chasse in this discussion, although clearly he ultimately adopts an advocate's role in the support of the prosecutor's position on the issue.

> In most cases where a withdrawal is requested because of the absence of witnesses, the charge is not re-laid because of these considerations. If the Court is going to force the case to a "dismissal" in such situations, it can only be on the basis that it knows more about the seriousness of the offence and the need for prosecution than the Crown does. In actual fact, in determining whether a particular prosecution should continue there are a number of factors which should be taken into consideration but which only lie within the knowledge of the Crown attorney. For this reason, it is suggested that the Crown's power to secure a withdrawal should be left relatively unfettered. A wrongful exercise of any Crown prosecutor's discretion leaves him responsible to the Attorney General who is in turn responsible to the Legislature. The fact that these safeguards seem rather remote from the average prosecution has encouraged some Judges to try to assume more control over the traditionally accepted functions of the Crown attorney. However, the dismissals without trials accompanied by unwarranted extensions of the doctrine of autrefois acquit will merely take from the courts the benefit of a quasi-judicially exercised discretion to determine the course of any prosecution exercised by a trusted officer of the court.[142]

To bolster his argument Chasse resurrects the statement or Kerwin C.J.C. in *Karpinski* that "the Crown had the right to change its election before the Magistrate and the right to withdraw the information". He then queries

> If the Crown has a *right* to withdraw, how can the court have a discretion to refuse?

On the very best footing Kerwin C.J.C.'s remarks in *Karpinski* were merely those of a single judge.[143] And in all likelihood Chasse's observations on those remarks suffer from the defect of too-literal interpretation.

---

141. (1970) 13 C.R.N.S. 196 and see also the decision of *R. v. Chambers* (1970) 13 C.R.N.S. 185 (N.S. C.A.).
141a. *Ibid.* at p. 214.
142. *Ibid.* at p. 217.
143. See the discussion of this decision *supra* at p. —.

The argument advanced that the right to withdraw is unrestricted and absolute is partially inconsistent with another interesting argument which Chasse develops; namely, that a withdrawal or dismissal will only operate as a bar to future proceedings when there is clear evidence of abandonment. (If the Crown's rights are absolute what matter if the dismissal possessed qualities of abandonment?). To be perfectly consistent the knowledge of facts peculiarly within the control of the Attorney General should solely guide the consideration of whether proceeding should be re-instituted.

Further, if the courts are possessed of a discretion to refuse withdrawals and compel no evidence submissions should the Attorney General or his agent be allowed in a completely unrestricted fashion to override such an exercise of judicial discretion?[144] Chasse appears quite clearly to be arguing for just such a result.[145]

Two questions arise out of Chasse's argument which merit consideration:

(1) What are these "factors which should be taken into consideration in determining whether to re-commence proceedings but which only lie within the knowledge of the Crown Attorney"?

(2) Does the Crown Attorney in Canada still occupy the status of an impartial functionary, unconcerned with winning or losing but guided solely by the cause of advancing the interests of justice; or is he more nearly approaching the status of a true adversary in the process of criminal litigation?

With respect to the first question posed, what Chasse appears to be saying is an "adjudication upon the merits" should be the sole determinant of whether the prosecutor may re-institute proceedings against an accused. He reasons that a "dismissal" when the Crown is unable to proceed or fails to appear cannot be regarded as a determination "on the merits". If "adjudication" is taken to mean procedures such as are referred to in s. 739 of the *Code* (Re: Summary conviction proceedings) then Chasse's view is logically complete. Section 739 provides that

> 739. When the summary conviction court has heard the prosecutor, defendant and witnesses it shall, after considering the matter, convict the defendant or make an order against him or dismiss the information, as the case may be.

That, however, is only one view of an "adjudication on the merits".

---

144. It is important to distinguish here been dismissals based upon the failure of the prosecutor to proceed and dismissals based upon a technical defect going to jurisdiction (e.g. an improperly sworn or unsworn information). In the latter instance no jeopardy could attach so as to bar future proceedings since a defect going to jurisdiction would render even a conviction a nullity. See *e.g. Re Chambers* (1970) 13 C.R.N.S. 185 (N.S. C.A.).

145. K. Chasse's latest editorial foray into this area is entitled "The Crown's Power to Withdraw Charges" (1976) 33 C.R.N.S. 218.

When an accused has stood in jeopardy—often for many months, with or without the benefit of bail, with the stigma of the charge adhering to him—it is not unreasonable to insist that on the date duly set for trial the prosecution should present its case (weak or strong as it may be) or suffer the consequence of the release of the prisoner. The procedures of withdrawals and adjournments both provide the court with a discretion either to hold the accused in jeopardy by adjourning the matter to a subsequent date, or to release him. The Ontario Court of Appeal in *R. v. Hatherley* was of the opinion "once a plea has been entered, [the accused] was in jeopardy and that if the Crown elected not then to call any evidence, the disposition by acquittal was a disposition on the merits of the case".[146] It is only logical to require cogent justifications to be brought forward by the Crown when it seeks to withdraw charges or adjourn a case at that late hour.

It is at this point, when the prosecutor is seeking an adjournment, that the "special factors" to which Chasse alludes should be revealed to the Court. They should not be saved for informal consideration by the prosecutor at the point in time when he is determining whether or not to *re-lay* the charge. Otherwise, what is there to justify a court in not adhering to this viewpoint espoused by Maule J. in *Tunnicliffe v. Tedd*:[147]

> In an ordinary court of oyer and terminer, if the defendant appears and pleads, he has an undoubted right to have the matter determined. When the complaint is ripe for hearing, and the defendant is ready to take his trial, if the prosecutor alleges nothing against him, or merely something that is unsubstantial, then the magistrates are bound to find the charge not proved and to give a certificate accordingly.

What are "special factors" referred to by Chasse? Chasse does purport to list the considerations which should guide a prosecutor in determining whether or not to re-lay a charge.[148] They are as follows:

(1) Extent of loss—loss of life, property, injury, damage.
(2) Danger to the public—the accused's background and known propensities—possibility of a repetition of the offence.
(3) Strength of the Crown's case.
(4) Expense to the accused in bringing him back to Court.
(5) Were public rights or interest involved or merely private interests?
(6) Civil remedies available to injured parties.
(7) Punishment or loss already undergone by the accused.
(8) Fairness in the handling of the prosecution from the beginning.

---

146. [1971] 3 O.R. 430 at p. 431 *per* Aylesworth J.A., but see *contra Osborne v. R.* (1975) 33 C.R.N.S. 211 (N.B. C.A.).
147. (1848) 5 C.B. 553 at p. 561.
148. See *supra* footnote 140 at p. 402. It should be noted that these listed factors cover the entire spectrum of re-instituted proceedings and are not merely restricted to proceedings which have been initiated after the Crown Attorney has failed to appear or has been unable to proceed.

(9) Accused's inability to withstand a 2nd trial—illness, etc.

(10) Length of time that has passed since the alleged occurrence and since the withdrawal or dismissal of the first charge.

(11) Reasons why the Crown was unable to proceed on the first trial date set on the 1st information.

(12) At the time of the withdrawal or "dismissal" did the Crown give any indication that it was abandoning the prosecution?

(13) The views of the complainant.

Close inspection fails to reveal any particular "magic" in this formulation. Certainly there is nothing in all of this to preclude Court inspection of the process. There is clearly no unique quality in any of these factors such as would compel the information to reside solely within the knowledge of the Crown. There is nothing here to prevent the special nature of the circumstances from being transmitted to the Court "on the advice of counsel".

As to the second question posed, Chasse's position that "as the powers of discretion are taken from the prosecutor there is more justification for his assuming the position of a completely competitive adversary in the adversary system"[149] seems to be more a pronouncement upon things as they are rather than what they might become.

The spectacle of a prosecutor performing in the manner described in *Beaudry*[150] is completely destructive of the notion of the prosecutor as a "quasi-judicial officer", "a silver thread", or as a "thirteenth juryman". This does not mean that the prosecutor should be allowed to assume a completely competitive position in the adversary process. The machinery of justice affords too great an advantage to the prosecutor to allow that to happen. The import of this observation is merely to point up the dangers which exist in allowing ourselves to indulge in the myth of prosecutorial impartiality.

The plea of *autrefois acquit* while important has not been a sufficient safeguard. At best the development of the law in this area has been piecemeal. Certainly there is no evidence of a coherent evolving doctrine allowing the Courts the unqualified right to interfere in the exercise of the prosecutorial discretion to re-commence proceedings by the re-laying of informations or the preferring of indictments.

What follows represents isolated examples of where and how instances of abuse have been blocked. The caveat to be borne in mind is that the examples are "isolated" and hence predictability is a near impossibility:

(1) Where it can be established that there has been an "adjudication on the merits" established to the satisfaction of the court the subsequent proceeding will be barred on the basis of *autrefois acquit*.

---

149. *Ibid.* at p. 408.
150. *R. v. Beaudry supra* footnote 93.

(2) Where the prosecutor seeks to indict directly under circumstances falling within s. 507(3) of the *Criminal Code,* the consent of the Attorney General himself or of the court is necessary or proceedings will be barred.[151]

(3) Where there is clear and unambiguous evidence of "abandonment", subsequent proceedings will be barred.[152]

(4) Where following a preliminary hearing the Crown seeks to prefer additional charges it is limited to included offences.[153]

(5) Where the trial of a matter results in an acquittal or a conviction, subsequent proceedings on a greater offence based on the same facts are barred on the principle that "a man shall not be charged again on the same facts in a more aggravated form".[154]

(6) Where the trial of a principal offence containing included offences which are cognate in the principal offence as a matter of law results in the dismissal of the principal offence, a plea of "autrefois acquit" would be an answer to a new indictment being laid on one of the included offences.[155]

These instances really should not be viewed as more than chips in the façade. Taken to their farthest limit they do not cumulatively represent a substantial inroad on the prosecutorial discretion to revive or re-commence proceedings. While demonstrating that prosecutorial discretion in this area is not absolute they do not go so far as to confirm these words of Prevost J. in *R. v. Viau*:[156]

> I feel that I must fall in line with those whose opinion it is that the powers of the Attorney-General in the matter of "Preferred Indictment" are not absolute but are restricted by the spirit which has pervaded our legislation in criminal matters, by the principle that the executive power cannot interfere with the judicial power, and that the right cannot be exercised by the Attorney-General in an arbitrary fashion.

Further, it should be noted that where the cases do appear to restrict prosecutorial discretion they do not do so by the judicial imposition of "standards" or guidelines of compelling moral force. The limits, such as they are, appear to be purely procedural in nature, although it appears that often the courts in their rigor were acting in response to the morally dubious conduct of a prosecution.

---

151. See *R. v. Miller supra* footnote 122.
152. See dissent of Cartwright J. in *R. v. Karpinski supra* footnote 96; and *R. v. Somers supra* footnote 103 and the cases cited therein.
153. See *Re R. and Ferstel* (1972) 8 C.C.C. (2d) 217 (B.C.) but see *contra R. v. G. & P. Internat. News Ltd.* (1973) 23 C.R.N.S. 369 (B.C. C.A.).
154. See *R. v. Miles* and *R. v. Hilton,* both *supra* footnote 132.
155. See *R. v. Rinnie* (1970) 9 C.R.N.S. 81 at p. 84 (Alta. C.A.).
156. *R. v. Viau supra* footnote 114 at p. 55.

6. THE DISCRETION TO NEGOTIATE A PLEA

The spectacle of high public officials "selling" testimony and "buying" immunity from prosecution in the sorry fiasco of Watergate has recently brought the entire institution of plea negotiation or "plea bargaining" (as it is more commonly called), into public disrepute. Not surprisingly, now that this "dirty little secret"[157] is out a substantial body of opinion is advocating its outright abolition. On the other hand, the elevation of plea bargaining from its previously *sub rosa* position has been met with a number of arguments addressed to the *realities* of the administration of criminal justice.

By these arguments "half a loaf is better than no loaf at all" or, put another way, the public interest is not advanced by the complete exoneration of suspected criminals in situations where the available evidence provides an insufficient basis upon which to prove guilt. Accommodation and compromise in such a circumstance are essential in order to demonstrate at least a measure of efficacy to our prosecutorial procedures.

Also it is argued that without the institution of plea bargaining or plea negotiation the administration of justice would "grind to a halt"[158] and "collapse under its own weight". In this connection, reference is characteristically made to the prosecutor's overcrowded dockets and to our overburdened courts. The accuracy of the information about the seriousness of the congestion has been questioned. One study conducted detailed the situation as follows:

> The [Provincial] courts sat for an average of only 2 hours and 20 minutes per day, and adjourned on an average as early as 1:25 p.m. each day. The Provincial Court Judges rarely have lengthy documents to read before their hearings and they rarely write judgments after their hearings. Clearly then, our over-crowded Provincial Courts are not making the most efficient use of the available time.[159]

It has been suggested that if abolition of plea bargaining is seriously contemplated it could be expeditiously accomplished in one of three possible ways:[160]

(1) Declare the practice unethical and subject it to disciplinary proceedings.

(2) By a judicial pronouncement indicate that any plea of guilty which

---

157. The phrase is Graham Parker's. See "Copping a Plea" (1972) 20 Ch.L.J. 310.
158. See G. A. Ferguson and D. W. Roberts, "Plea Bargaining: Directions for Canadian Reform" (1974) 52 Can.Bar.Rev. 497 at pp. 520-525.
159. Extract from a study conducted by the Canadian Civil Liberties Education Trust cited in E. J. Ratushny, "Plea-Bargaining and The Public" (1972) 20 Ch.L.J. 238 at p. 239.
160. See G. A. Ferguson and D. W. Roberts, "Plea Bargaining: Directions for Canadian Reform" *supra* footnote 158 at p. 573.

was induced by a prosecutorial bargain is involuntary and therefore invalid.

(3) By a legislative pronouncement proclaim that plea bargaining in any form is illegal, and that any guilty plea so procured is a nullity.

Abolition of the practice in Canada seems unlikely in light of the recent incorporation of standards governing the conduct of plea negotiation into the Canadian Bar Association's *Code of Professional Conduct*.[161]

(1) Plea bargaining defined

Most definitions of the expression "plea bargaining" or "plea negotiation" are phrased in terms of the result which ensues if the accused pleads guilty in a given circumstance.[162] It is suggested that a simpler, more comprehensive definition would be as follows:

A "plea bargain" or a "plea negotiation" means that situation which occurs when an accused person agrees to plead guilty, or gives testimony or material information in return for some perceived advantage which is accorded to him by the prosecutor acting within the scope of his ostensible authority.

Types of bargain struck

The variations on the type of bargaining which may be struck are in essence limited only by the imagination of counsel. The extreme parameters are the provisions of the Criminal Code dealing with the bribery of judicial officers[163] and obstruction of justice.[164]

Ferguson and Roberts in their comprehensive study of plea bargaining detail the range of benefits generally available in a plea bargaining situation.[165] These are:

(1) a reduction in the charge to a lesser or included offence;
(2) a withdrawal of other charges or a promise not to proceed on other possible charges;
(3) a recommendation or a promise as to the type of sentence that can be expected (fine, probation, imprisonment, and so on);
(4) a recommendation or a promise as to the severity of the sentence (amount of fine or length of imprisonment).

Other possible benefits mentioned less often are:

(5) the use of summary conviction procedure rather than indictable procedure in offences where the Crown has a choice;

---

161. (1974) Chapter VIII at pp. 30-31 nos. 10 and 11.
162. See *e.g.* A. D. Klein, "Plea Bargaining" (1971-72) 14 Cr.L.Q. 289. ("The expression 'plea bargaining' usually connotes a course of discussions between Crown counsel and defence counsel as to what the result would be if the accused pleaded guilty . . . etc.").
163. See the *Criminal Code* ss. 108 and 109.
164. See s. 127 of the *Criminal Code*.
165. Ferguson and Roberts *supra* footnote 158 at pp. 513-514.

(6) a promise not to apply for a sentence of proventive detention;

(7) a promise not to apply for a harsher penalty in accordance with ss. 592 and 740 of the *Criminal Code* where the accused has a previous conviction for the same offence;

(8) a promise not to force trial by jury under s. 498 of the *Code* where the accused wishes to avoid that mode of trial;

(9) a promise not to charge friends or family of the accused;

(10) a promise not to mention at the time of sentencing any aggravating circumstances of the offence, or not to mention a previous criminal record, or not to make public any embarrassing circumstances of the offence;

(11) a promise or a recommendation as to the place of imprisonment, the type of treatment, or the time of parole;

(12) a promise to arrange for sentencing before a particular judge, who is generally lenient, or a threat to have the accused sentenced by a certain judge who is considered very harsh;

(13) a promise not to oppose release on bail or release after conviction but before sentence.

What emerges from the list suggested above is a feeling for the enormity of the arsenal which is available to the prosecutor in dealing with a prospective charge.

(2) Common law and ethical guidelines

Plea bargaining is not often analysed from the perspective of prosecutorial discretion. Most analyses are concerned with ethical standards for defence counsel and the propriety of conferring advantages on accused persons where convenience or expedience are the only operative considerations.

Consider, for example, the guidelines laid down in what is generally regarded as the leading modern authority on plea bargaining, the English case of *R. v. Turner*.[166] In *Turner* counsel in "strong terms" advised his client to plead guilty to a charge in mid-trial before evidence of his previous convictions was adduced. The early plea, counsel advised, would lessen the likelihood of the imposition of a jail term. The appeal was dealt with by treating the plea that was made as a nullity, with the result that the trial that had taken place was declared to be a mistrial, and an order was made for a *venire de novo*. The appeal succeeded on the basis that the Court felt that the accused

---

166. (1970) 54 Cr. App. R. 352 (C.A.). See also the following articles which discuss the implications of the *Turner* case with particular attention given to the suggestion that a plea of guilty might be a factor to be considered in mitigation of sentence, and the nature of the role to be played by the trial judge in plea negotiation: P. Thomas, "Plea Bargaining in the Turner Case" [1970] Crim.L.R. 559; A. Davis, "Sentences for Sale: A New Look at Plea Bargaining in England and America" [1971] Crim.L.R. 218 (part II of this article is to be found at p. 252 of the same volume).

might have felt that the disposition discussed emanated from the trial Judge and was not merely the expressed view of counsel. The Court indicated the following as guidelines for counsel and judges in any plea bargaining situation:

(1) Counsel must be completely free to do what is his duty, namely, to give the accused the best advice he can, and if need be, advice in strong terms.

(2) The accused, having considered counsel's advice, must have complete freedom of choice whether to plead guilty or not guilty.

(3) There must be freedom of access between counsel and the Judge.

(4) The Judge, subject to one exception, should never indicate the sentence which he is minded to impose. The only exception to this rules is that it should be permissible for a Judge to say, if it be the case, that whatever happens, whether the accused pleads guilty or not guilty, the sentence will or will not take a particular form *e.g.* a probation order or a fine, or a custodial sentence.

The Canadian Bar Association laid down standards for professional conduct in plea bargaining situations based largely upon the guidelines set out in *Turner*. The Code of Professional Conduct provides:

10. Where, following investigation,

(a) a defence lawyer bona fide concludes and advises his accused client that an acquittal of the offence charged is uncertain or unlikely,

(b) the client is prepared to admit the necessary factual and mental elements,

(c) the lawyer fully advises his client of the implications and possible consequences, and particularly of the detachment of the court, and

(d) the client so instructs him it is proper for the lawyer to discuss with the prosecutor and for them tentatively to agree on the entry of a plea of "guilty" to the offence charged or to a lesser or included offence appropriate to the admissions, and also on a disposition or sentence to be proposed to the court. *The public interest must not be or appear to be sacrificed in the pursuit of an apparently expedient means of disposing of doubtful cases,* and all pertinent circumstances surrounding any tentative agreements, if proceeded with must be fully and fairly disclosed in open court. The judge must not be involved in any such discussions or tentative agreements save to be informed thereof.[167] [Emphasis added].

To return again to the point under consideration—the non-emphasis on the role of prosecutor in plea bargaining analyses—the *Turner* guidelines juxtaposed against the C.B.A. standards demonstrate the point in action. *Turner* is totally deficient in this respect, while the C.B.A.

---

167. Can. Bar Assn., *Code of Professional Conduct supra* footnote 161 at p. 30.

standards contain only a bare indication (see the italicized portion, *supra*) that the prosecutor must not give off the impression of being moved by expedient rather than just considerations.

(3) Over-charging

In point of fact prosecutorial discretion in the area of plea bargaining is subject to considerably greater abuses than what has been hinted at thus far. Untouched by either the *Turner* case or the C.B.A. standards is the wide spread practice of "overcharging".

> There is a tendency towards the habitual laying of charges in a manner intentionally designed to put the prosecutor in the position to offer an apparent concession in the reduction of either the number or seriousness of charges. Overcharging, charging a more serious offence than would appear justified on the facts, and charging offences with a fixed minimum penalty, all fall into this category.[168]

Overcharging which fails to induce a plea bargain may lead to over-criminalizing. Many offences possess the quality of divisibility. One prosecutor might instruct the laying of a charge "that A did commit an offence, to wit . . . between the months of April and July, 1975". Another prosecutor might authorize the laying of multiple informations. The results, in terms of sentence (where a conviction(s) ensues) might well be markedly different. Where the sentence that results is cumulatively the same the criminal record which thus accrues will nevertheless appear substantially dissimilar. To a certain degree this situation has been altered by virtue of the decision of the Supreme Court of Canada in *R. v. Kienapple.*[169]

In *Kienapple* an accused charged with rape and with unlawful carnal knowledge was convicted by a jury of both offences although both charges involved "the same delict, and the same girl". The Supreme Court of Canada extended the meaning of *res judicata* in order to avoid the absurdity of multiple convictions. The appeal of *Kienapple* was allowed, and the conviction for unlawful carnal knowledge under s. 146(1) of the *Code* was quashed along with the concurrent sentence of ten years which had been imposed by the trial court. The import of the decision for the future of plea bargaining, while not great, is of substance.

What *Kienapple* should have the effect of doing is to do away with many "sham concessions" made in the course of plea negotiation. Prior to *Kienapple* many inexperienced counsel were duped into advising in favor of pleas due to such concessions, while other experienced

---

168. Ontario Law Reform Commission, *Report on the Administration of Ontario Courts* (1973) Part II at p. 120.

169. (1974) 26 C.R.N.S. 1 (Can.), and see also Annotations subsequent thereto on "A New Meaning For Res Judicata and Its Potential Effect On Plea Bargaining" Part I, p. 20; Part II, p. 48; and Part III, p. 64.

counsel led their clients into believing that a plea was justified in return for such concessions. Hopefully much of this has been curtailed.

(4) Weak case/no case ethics

As abusive as the practice of over-charging undoubtedly is, it is sometimes closely allied to yet another dubious practice—the practice of seeking to negotiate a plea when it is known or strongly suspected that the prosecution's case would completely fail if matters were allowed to proceed to trial.

The *Turner* case does not concern itself with "weak case/no case" ethical considerations. The C.B.A. Code of Professional Conduct contains the following commentary:

> When engaged as a prosecutor the lawyer's prime duty is not to seek to convict, but to see that justice is done through a fair trial upon the merits. The prosecutor exercises a public function involving much discretion and power, and must act fairly and dispassionately. . . . (H)e should make timely disclosure to the accused or his counsel (or to the court if the accused is not represented) of all the relevant facts and witnesses known to him, whether tending towards guilt or innocence.[170]

These sentiments, while laudable, certainly do not *on their face* appear to go so far as to brand the "weak case/no case" bluff conducted by a prosecutor as unethical. For example, is the fact that a vital witness will not be available for trial a "fact" such as is contemplated above? Some of the commentators think not.[171]

In this connection it is important to remember that the prosecutor's control over the pre-trial disclosure of information is not regulated by statute. As commendable as is the formulation of comprehensive canons of professional ethics, one should not forget that generally they are unaccompanied by effective sanctions.[172] Where there is no adequate control over the pre-trial disclosure of information—particularly in a plea bargaining situation—manipulation of the accused and/or his counsel is an inevitable result. To retort that the *Code of Professional Conduct* is our protection is not to do more than pay "lip service to grandiose concepts."[173]

---

170. *Supra* footnote 161 at p. 29.
171. See A. Hooper "Discovery in Criminal Cases", (1972) 50 Can.Bar.Rev. 445 at p. 471. See also W. White, "A Proposal for Reform of the Plea Bargaining Process", (1971) 119 U.Pa.L.Rev. 439 at p. 459.
172. It is submitted that the internal disciplinary proceedings of Law Societies constitute an ineffective sanction in the area of plea bargaining: a) because lawyers are loathe to report prosecutors (or, indeed generally, other lawyers) to a Law Society save for the gravest of misconduct. A great deal of a criminal lawyer's day to day effectiveness depends upon his working relationships with individual prosecutors, b) because the act of disciplining a particular prosecutor does not redress the wrong done to the particular accused of whom the advantage was taken.
173. The words are Professor A. K. Pye's and are cited in Hooper *supra* footnote 169 at p. 469.

The Ontario Law Reform Commission has suggested more comprehensive guidelines with respect to the conduct of prosecutors engaged in plea negotiation than are to be found in any other source.[174] Yet the view of the Commission remained (in 1973) that "legislation is not necessary". If the Attorney-General is indeed only "responsible before the High Court of Parliament"[175] what better way to curb excessive or unethical activity than by express statutory command?

If "the purpose of a criminal prosecution is not to obtain a conviction but . . . is to lay before the jury what the Crown considers to be credible evidence relevant to what is alleged to be a crime",[176] and the prosecutor is aware that the available credible evidence, which is at his disposal will not establish the guilt of the accused, can the prosecutor be said to be acting in "good faith" in bluffing the accused into a negotiated plea? Does such activity not offend against the "dignity, the seriousness, and the justness of judicial proceedings?"[177]

The problem posed is not hypothetical. The "weak case/no case" factor operates to the detriment of at least some accused persons in practice. "(T)here seems little doubt that it is done . . .".[178] Consider the following comments:

> If I don't like a certain defence lawyer I can hold his case up by keeping it at the end of the list for two or three days. Or I can decide not to disclose anything to him. It depends on what I think of the defence, how much I will disclose to him. If I trust him, so he won't use the evidence to bring perjured evidence against the prosecution, I will disclose to him.[179]

Where ill-will can motivate non-disclosure it equally can lead to the abuse of the bluffed plea bargain.

(5) The "buddy system"

The remarks quoted *supra* also call into focus another aspect of prosecutorial abuse within the plea bargaining milieu. This abuse is the "buddy system" facet of plea negotiation. Defence counsel who engage in this practice are equally culpable with their prosecutorial counterparts although the temptation to "play the game" may be said to originate with the prosecution.

What the "buddy system" entails is a reciprocal relationship between defence counsel and the prosecution before meaningful plea negotiations may be entered into. "(T)he very achievement of a bargain, as well as its nature and extent, may depend largely on the

---

174. *Supra* footnote 168 at pp. 122-123.
175. *R. v. Allen* (1862) Cox C.C. 120 at p. 122 *per* Cockburn C.J.
176. *Boucher v. R.* [1955] S.C.R. 16 at pp. 23-24 *per* Rand J.
177. *Ibid.*
178. See Hooper *supra* footnote 171 at p. 470.
179. Grosman, interview with a Crown attorney quoted in *The Prosecutor: An Inquiry into the Exercise of Discretion* (1969) at p. 78.

relationship between the prosecutor and the defence lawyer."[180] The whole notion of such a system is antithetical to the achievement of the ends of justice as based upon the "merits" of a given case.

> . . . (T)he offering of bargains, or better bargains, only to those few defence lawyers whom the prosecutor feels are trustworthy has serious consequences. It leads to unequal bargaining positions because most accused persons are dependant upon the lawyers that they retain or receive and do not have the sophistication to shop around for those lawyers most favored by the prosecution. It also creates a serious ethical problem for defence lawyers since a useful reciprocal relationship with a prosecutor may depend upon the defence lawyer entering a proportionately high number of guilty pleas . . . Lawyers who do not supply their "quota" of guilty pleas and contest every case are subjected to the bare bones of the legal system. Therefore defence lawyers must guard against influencing an accused to plead guilty simply to maintain a bargaining relationship with the prosecutor.[181]

The influence of "personalities" upon any human system is extremely difficult to measure. That "personality" should be a factor at all in plea negotiation is undesirable. It remains however, an aspect of the system which, short of the complete abolition of plea bargaining, is almost impossible to control. The statutory compulsion of complete disclosure of information would restrict the field of operation of this human variable, but it would not result in its eradication.

It is difficult to disagree with the views expressed by the Council of the Law Society in England that "(the) current practice under which a defending advocate must depend not upon the rights of the accused, but upon the goodwill and benignity of the prosecuting advocate is an inadequate basis for procedures designed to determine a citizen's rights to remain at liberty".[182] On the other hand resolution of this conundrum seems to reside outside the bounds of objective, legal, strictures.

(6) Repudiation of plea bargains

Any of the abuses discussed thus far—over-charging, weak case/no case ethics, the buddy system—are capable of further exacerbation where the prosecutor repudiates his bargain. As revealed by the cases prosecutors may repudiate regularly struck plea bargains in one of two ways:

(1) *Repudiation at the time of disposition*—usually takes the form of the prosecutor pressing for a result in excess of what was agreed upon. The accused usually attempts to deal with such a repudiation by applying to withdraw his plea prior to disposition, or by appealing against the disposition.

---

180. Ferguson and Roberts *supra* footnote 158 at p. 538.
181. *Ibid.* at pp. 538-539.
182. See Council of the Law Society of England, Memorandum, December 1965, cited in Grosman *supra* footnote 179 at p. 102.

(2) *Repudiation subsequent to disposition*—this form of action is commenced by the prosecutor's launching an appeal to set aside or alter a regularly agreed upon disposition.

It should be pointed out that "repudiation" is by no means the exclusive preserve of the prosecutor. The accused may attempt it as well. Indeed, the *Turner* case appears to involve such a situation. (In *Turner* the accused, ruminating upon the bad features of the disposition which he had agreed to, hired a new counsel to argue (successfully) on his behalf that his initial plea was coerced and that he should be allowed to withdraw his plea). The focus of the treatment offered here, however, is upon "prosecutorial" discretion and hence discussion shall be restricted to alleged prosecutorial abuses.

The Courts have dealt with the repudiation of a plea bargain by the prosecutor in a variety of ways. There has been a noticeable lack of uniformity in the judicial decisions, not only as to the situation from province to province, but also within a given province. Basically it may be said that the courts have either preserved the bargain, allowed the bargain to be broken and altered the disposition, or in allowing the bargain to be broken the court also allow for the withdrawal of the plea.

Perhaps the greatest inconsistency on the subject of "broken" plea bargains is to be found in the reported decisions emanating from Quebec.

The Quebec Court of Appeal on two fairly recent (1971-72) reported occasions in *R. v. Kirkpatrick*[183] and *R. v. Mouffe*[184] allowed Crown counsel not to be bound by his original undertakings and increased the imposed sentences on both appeals. The same court in *R. v. Fleury*[185] refused to allow the prosecution to override its earlier representations to the sentencing tribunal and dismissed the Crown's appeal against sentence. Montgomery J.A. who had earlier dissented in both the *Kirkpatrick* and *Mouffe* cases phrased his judgment in particularly strong terms:

> I feel it my duty to draw emphatically to the attention of the learned Judges of the Court of Appeal the confusion which has arisen as a result of this appeal by the Crown. Either the Crown is a single responsible entity or it is not. If a trial judge listens attentively to the representations made by counsel for the Crown concerning sentence, and subsequently adopts the suggestions put forward by the Attorney General's representatives, then, in my view, it is illogical and almost unthinkable that an appeal should be taken against the resulting sentence.[186]

---

183. [1971] Que. C.A. 337.
184. (1972) 16 C.R.N.S. 257 (Que. C.A.).
185. (1973) 23 C.R.N.S. 164 (Que. C.A.).
186. *Ibid.* at p. 175.

In *A.G. Can. v. Roy*,[187] a decision of the Quebec Court of Queen's Bench, Huggessen J. refused to tamper with an original disposition and thus rejected an attempt by the prosecution to repudiate its original bargain.

In Ontario the situation has been similarly confused. Two recent Court of Appeal decisions, *R. v. Brown*[188] and *R. v. Agozzino*[189] stand for the proposition that the prosecutor will be bound by his original undertaking. In *R. v. Thomas*[190] the same Court, differently constituted allowed the original bargain to be repudiated and substantially increased the sentence.

Two conflicting tendencies are evidence in these cases. On the one hand the appellate courts are concerned with carrying out their historic supervisory function in overseeing the propriety or appropriateness of sentences imposed by courts of first instance. On the other hand the courts must be concerned that basic features of justice and fair play are not overridden in an area (plea bargaining) which has been recognized as essential to the smooth and efficient administration of justice.

Overriding the original bargain but allowing for the withdrawal of the original plea is a compromise procedure which has occasionally been adopted by the courts.[191] It is submitted that while appealing as an alternative to outright repudiation, this approach does not adequately come to grips with the problem raised by this ethical standard promulgated by the Canadian Bar Association:

> An undertaking given by the lawyer to the Court or to another lawyer in the course of litigation must be strictly and scrupulously carried out. Unless clearly qualified, the lawyer's undertaking is his personal promise and responsibility.[192]

As matters presently stand, the position of the Courts (as evidenced by *R. v. Turner*) and the Canadian Bar Association is that plea negotiation as an institution is necessary and must be retained (putting matters in their very worst light) as an "accommodation to reality". Not everyone, notably the Ontario Law Reform Commission, subscribes to this view. ("We agree that the very fibre of the system of criminal justice is jeopardized if reliance is placed on a concept of plea bargaining as a means of dispatching the disposition of criminal cases.")[193] The writer tends to doubt whether these "concessions", or

---

187. (1972) 18 C.R.N.S. 89 (Que.).
188. (1972) 8 C.C.C. (2d) 227 (Ont. C.A.).
189. (1969) 6 C.R.N.S. 147 (Ont. C.A.).
190. [1968] 2 C.C.C. 84 (Ont. C.A.).
191. See *R. v. Stone* (1932) 58 C.C.C. 262 (N.S.), and *R. v. Ah Tom* (1928) 49 C.C.C. 204 (N.S. C.A.).
192. Can. Bar Assn., *Code of Professional Conduct supra* footnote 161 at p. 31.
193. See also *Report of the National Advisory Commission for Criminal Justice Standards and Goals* (also referred to as *Report of National Conference on Criminal Justice*), (1973), Ct. 42, and excerpts of that report as quoted in the Ontario Law Reform Commission Report, *supra* footnote 168 at

accommodations to reality can be avoided save by the most massive infusion of money and resources into the criminal justice system. Given, then, the present reality, it is submitted that the least damage is done to our fundamental concepts of justice and fair treatment by insisting that the parties engaged in plea negotiation conduct themselves as honorable men and be bound by their undertakings.

7. SOME REMARKS IN CONCLUSION

(1) Six checks on prosecutorial discretion

The observation has been made that there are at least six potential checks on the exercise of any prosecutorial discretion: (a) ministerial accountability, (b) a vigilant press, (c) judicial challenge to the prosecutor's authority, (d) use of the prerogative writs, (e) resort to the *Bill of Rights,* (f) invocation of the doctrine of abuse of process.

Taken singly or together it is impossible to say that these controls place "effective" limits on the prosecutor's discretion.

(a) Ministerial accountability

Ministerial accountability is a rare spectacle and one rarely witnessed in relation to the general day-to-day conduct of criminal prosecutions. In the unitary state there may be some validity to viewing ministerial accountability as a viable check, but in a divided jurisdiction such as exists in Canada the arguments are considerably less compelling.

> The protection of ministerial accountability has worked well in England where only one parliament both enacts and is concerned with the administration of justice. However, the structural safeguard is immensely weakened in Canada because of provincial autonomy over federally enacted criminal law and procedure. While it is theoretically possible that questions in a legislature about particular cases might tend to moderate occasional prosecutorial excesses (if they happened to be complained about), the effectiveness of such means is as variable as the comprehension, initiative, and special interest of individual members of parliament and provincial legislators.[194]

(b) A vigilant press

The vigilance of the press is, at best, a "sometimes thing". Coverage of the proceedings in our courts, it may fairly be said, has been restricted in great measure to flamboyant murder or rape cases, bare reportage of routine docket dispositions, and the odd "human interest" story. The fault does not entirely reside with the press. Much prosecutorial discretion is exercised in impenetrable secrecy behind closed doors and in the deep inner sanctums of administrative offices. The

---

pp. 124-125, and in Ferguson and Roberts, *supra* footnote 158 at pp. 570-571.

194. C. Sun, "The Discretionary Power to Stay Criminal Proceedings" (1973-74) 1 Da. L.J. 482 at p. 509.

informality of the stay of proceedings will often serve to evade even the watchful eye of the press. The "legalese" of the stay and the withdrawal may leave the impression with an accused, or with the press, that proceedings have been completely dropped when in fact the accused may linger in jeopardy.

(c) Judicial challenge to prosecutor's authority

The question of "who is the prosecutor, and by what authority does he act?" is rarely posed in actual practice. Notwithstanding that the Courts have held that where a statute clearly requires the consent of the Attorney General *himself,* the word or representations of his agents will not suffice,[195] it appears doubtful that other less explicit situations will require the same proof of authority before the prosecutor's discretion may be exercisable. While practices vary widely from province to province they are not inconsistent *per se* but rather evidence only the practical variations that different provincial departments of the attorney general employ in conducting their daily affairs. Simply because it is desirable in a great many circumstances that the Attorney General himself should signify his concurrence in a particular course of action adopted by one of his prosecutors, it nevertheless remains unlikely that he will generally be required to do so merely by invoking the maxim *delegatus non potest delegare.* A narrow interpretation of the word "instructed" seems unlikely to find much favor with our judiciary in view of the historical position of the Attorney General, and of the fair, large and liberal interpretation section of the Interpretation Act. Consequently, it is submitted that, if pressed for consideration, our appellate courts would find the Minister capable of delegating discretionary power to his subordinates save in those circumstances where the statute expressly requires his personal initiatives.

The writer accepts the position of the Ontario Law Reform Commission in this regard that "(e)very Crown Attorney is the agent of the Attorney General for the purposes of the Criminal Code".[196] Since it appears desirable to curb the ability of individual prosecutors to exercise large areas of discretion, the solution appears to reside in statutory amendments compelling the Attorney General to play a greater, or even, the "sole" personal, role in the exercise of these discretions. Judicial interpretation does not hold the answer.

Also it should be remembered that the mere fact that the Attorney General himself signifies his agreement with a particular course of action will not necessarily negate an inference that the decision has been made arbitrarily, or in the absence of ascertainable standards.

---

195. See *e.g. R. v. Miller* (1970) 8 C.R.N.S. 336 (Ont.), and *Ferstel v. R.* (1972) 8 C.C.C. (2d) 217 (B.C.).

196. Ontario Law Reform Commission, *Report on the Administration of Ontario Courts,* (1973) Part II at p. 99.

(d) Prerogative writs

It has been suggested that many of the discretionary activities of the prosecutor are creatures of statute and thus are subject to judicial oversight through resort to the use of the prerogative writs.[197] S. A. DeSmith in considering whether or not there are unreviewable discretionary powers addresses the issue in this manner:

> If it is claimed that the authority for the exercise of discretion derives from the royal prerogative, the courts appear to be limited to questions of "vires" in the narrowest sense of the term. They can determine whether the prerogative power exists, what is its extent, whether it has been exercised in the appropriate form and how far it has been superseded by statute; they cannot, it seems, examine the appropriateness or adequacy of the grounds for exercising the power, and they will not allow bad faith to be attributed to the Crown.[198]

This statement appears to express the state of the law in Canada at this time. The four aspects of prosecutorial discretion discussed in this paper—the prosecutor's discretion to (1) proceed summarily or by indictment (2) stay or withdraw charges (3) prefer indictments or re-lay charges and (4) negotiate a plea—while in many instances buttressed by statutory provisions, derive in the final analysis from the Royal Prerogative to prosecute an offence.[199]

In *R. v. Smythe*[200] the issue of whether the prerogative writs might be invoked against the Crown was avoided by concentrating on the Court's powers as guided by the provisions of the Canadian Bill of Rights. The prerogative writs although employed were directed not at the Crown, but at the Court. Kelly Co. Ct. J. remarked upon this approach when matters first arose in the County Court:

> Now, this motion was made after arraignment but prior to the pleading by the accused on any of the counts in the indictment. As I understand it, counsel have agreed that this case is not to proceed in any event today or soon, so that if Mr. Robinette is unsuccessful in his motion he would seek to move by way of prohibition, that is to say, to prohibit me from trying the case; and if Mr. Robinette is successful, then Mr. Sedgwick will seek an order of mandamus to compel me to try the case, and *whether or not prohibition is or could be ordered by*

---

197. See C. Sun, *supra* footnote 194 at p. 514. "Since the power to stay proceedings has been made part of Canadian statute law it can no longer be viewed as an exercise of the Crown's prerogative immune from judicial challenge".
198. S. A. DeSmith, *Judicial Review of Administrative Action,* (1972) at pp. 253-254.
199. See *R. v. Court of Sessions of the Peace; Ex parte Lafleur* [1967] 3 C.C.C. 244 (Que. C.A.) particularly the judgment of Montgomery J.A. (at p. 248) If an authority such as the Attorney General can have the right to decide whether or not a person shall be prosecuted, surely he may, if authorized by statute, have the right to decide what form the prosecution shall take."
200. (1971) 3 C.C.C. (2d) 366 (Can.).

a superior court to restrain me in criminal proceedings is something which I question but, nevertheless, that is what counsel has indicated he intends to do if unsuccessful.[201] [Emphasis added].

Since Kelly Co. Ct. J. decided matters at first instance in favor of Mr. Robinette and his client the issue of the use of the prerogative writs did not arise in the subsequent appeals.

The large issue of the general answerability of the Crown prosecutor is not likely to be resolved in the context of attacking the supporting statutory authority which enables the prosecutor to better implement his discretionary acts. This appears to be a weak and somewhat limited approach to making the Crown answerable by way of the prerogative writs. A more far-reaching and potentially effective solution lies in a general re-evaluation of the role of the Attorney-General. While the Courts in Canada have not demonstrated an inclination to embark upon this path the English Courts have not been so reluctant.

The general position of the Attorney General in England remains as laid down by the Earl of Halsbury L.C., in *London County Council v. Attorney-General:*[202]

> . . . but the initiation of the litigation, and the determination of the question whether it is a proper case for the Attorney-General to proceed in, is a matter entirely beyond the jurisdiction of this or any other Court. It is a question which the law of this country has made to reside exclusively in the Attorney-General.

Inroads against this general position have been fashioned in recent years by attacks launched, in England, by ordinary citizens against public officers to enforce statutory duties. Two of these cases (involving an individual by the name of Blackburn)[203] were directed at the police commissioner (an individual whose discretion was thought to be unreviewable) in an effort to obtain enforcement of laws relating to gaming and pornography. While the remedy sought in those cases was refused, it was refused not because the exercise of the discretion was unreviewable but because the granting of the prerogative remedy was inappropriate given the facts of each case.

The position of the Attorney-General and his exercises of discretion was at issue in the subsequent case of *Attorney-General (on the relation of McWhirter) v. Independent Broadcasting Authority.*[204] Once again the prerogative remedy sought was denied. The case involved the projected broadcast, on several commercial television channels, of a filmed programme on the life and works of Andy Warhol, the

---

201. *R. v. Smythe* (1970) 12 C.R.N.S. 48 at p. 49 (Ont.).
202. [1902] A.C. 165 at p. 169.
203. *R. v. Metro. Police Commr.; Ex parte Blackburn* [1968] 1 All E.R. 763 (C.A.), and *R. v. Metro. Police Commr.; Ex parte Blackburn (No. 3)* [1973] 1 All E.R. 324 (C.A.).
204. [1973] 1 All E.R. 689 (C.A.).

controversial American artist, film-maker, and producer. Mr. Mc-Whirter had unsuccessfully sought to have the Attorney General move to restrain and enjoin the British Broadcasting Authority (a regulatory body) from breaking its duty to prohibit the broadcast of programmes offensive to good taste and public decency. The judgments rendered contain strong obiter comments that in a proper case the Court would be prepared to oversee the exercise of the Attorney General's discretion. Lord Denning M.R. struck the strongest position in this respect:

> In the light of all this I am of opinion that, in the last resort, if the Attorney General refuses leave in a proper case, or improperly or unreasonably delays in giving leave, or his machinery works too slowly, then a member of the public, who has a sufficient interest, can himself apply to the court itself. He can apply for a declaration and, in a proper case, for an injunction, joining the Attorney-General if need be, as defendant.[205]

Lawton L.J. expressed general agreement with these sentiments:

> I agree with Lord Denning M.R. that if at any time in the future (and in my judgment it is not in the foreseeable future) there was reason to think that an Attorney-General was refusing improperly to exercise his powers, the courts might have to intervene to ensure that the law was obeyed.[206]

It is still a matter of speculation as to whether the obiter remarks in *McWhirter* will be seen "as justifying a new assimilation of judicial attitudes towards statutory and prerogative powers".[207] In Canada the courts have been hesitant to express opinions that the powers of the Attorney General might be other than absolute save in the vaguest of terms (*e.g.* "it is limited by . . . the spirit which has governed the development of our criminal law").[208] It appears realistic to expect that, if there is to be judicial innovation in this sphere, such movement will be extremely slow and cautious. It also seems likely that Lawton L.J.'s observation is correct that such developments are not likely to take place "in the foreseeable future".

With the decision of the Supreme Court of Canada in 1970 in the case of *R. v. Drybones*[209] a great deal of excitement and hope was generated. The feeling among more than a few of the commentators was that our highest Court was at last shedding the shackles of its positivist tradition and was prepared to embark upon the uncertain waters of judicial review. This prophecy has gone unfulfilled.

(e) The Bill of Rights

The *Drybones* case appeared to decide two things: It decided firstly

---

205. *Ibid.* at p. 698.
206. *Ibid.* at p. 705.
207. S. A. DeSmith *supra* footnote 198 at p. 529.
208. See *R. v. Viau* (1961) 37 C.R. 41 (Que.).
209. (1970) 10 C.R.N.S. 334 (Can.).

that the *Canadian Bill of Rights* was more than a mere interpretation statute whose terms would yield to a contrary intention. The case decided that the *Bill of Rights* had a paramount force when a federal enactment conflicted with its terms, and in the event of such conflict it was the incompatible Federal enactment which had to give way. The second principle established by the *Drybones* case was that the accused (in that case an Indian under the *Indian Act*) would be deemed to be denied equality before the law, under s. 1(*b*) of the *Canadian Bill of Rights,* when it was made a punishable offence for him, on account of his race, to do something which his fellow Canadians were free to do without being liable to punishment for that offence.

This wider application of the *Bill of Rights* in *Drybones* has obvious ramifications for all manner of subjects to be found under the general heading of prosecutorial discretion. Since the *Bill* was directed towards not only the actual "content" of legislation but also toward its "construction" and "application" some measure of control over prosecutorial activity was, in theory, at least, possible.[210]

As has been indicated, much of the hope held out by the *Drybones* decision has proved to be illusory. In a series of successive cases, *Lowry v. R.,*[211] *Smythe v. R.,*[212] *Curr v. R.,*[213] and *Duke v. R.*[214] the *Bill of Rights* was not given an invalidating effect over prior legislation, although that clearly was the import of the *Drybones* case. Two more recent decisions, *A.G. Can. v. Lavell; Isaac v. Bedard,*[215] and *Hogan v. R.*[216] appear to have recanted on most of what was accomplished in *Drybones* and *Brownridge v. R.*[217]

In consequence, at present it is manifest that the *Bill of Rights* offers little promise of being the effective weapon, or tool, that is necessary in order to structure, confine and check exercises of prosecutorial discretion.

The decision in *Hogan v. R.* entailed a consideration of the provi-

---

210. See *e.g. R. v. Littlejohn* [1972] 3 W.W.R. 475 (Man.) for an example of utilization of the Bill of Rights by the Courts to compel disclosure of informatoin at the pre-trial (preliminary hearing) stage over the objections of the proseuctor.
211. [1972] 19 C.R.N.S. 315 (Can).
212. *Supra* footnote 200.
213. [1972] S.C.R. 889.
214. [1972] S.C.R. 917.
215. (1973) 23 C.R.N.S. 197 (Can.).
216. (1974) 26 C.R.N.S. 207 (Can.).
217. (1972) 18 C.R.N.S. 308 (Can.). The *Brownridge* decision was another more liberal application of the Bill of Rights. The right to retain and instruct counsel without delay was affirmed and accordingly Brownridge could not be convicted of refusing to submit a sample of breath contrary to s. 235(2) of the *Criminal Code* where his rights were denied. But see *Hogan supra* for the results which ensued where a breath sample was obtained after a denial of the right to counsel.

sion of the *Bill of Rights* (s. 1(*a*)) guaranteeing "the right of the individual to life, liberty, security of the person and enjoyment of property, and the right not to be deprived thereof *except by due process of law*". It was there held that the phrase "due process" merely meant "according to those legal processes recognized by Parliament and the Courts in Canada". In general terms the case stands for the proposition that the contravention or infringement of a right accorded under the *Bill of Rights* is insufficient to render inadmissible otherwise receivable evidence. Relevant to our consideration of prosecutorial discretion, the case offers little encouragement that the "due process" clause of the *Bill* will provide a safeguard against prosecutorial abuses.

(f) Abuse of process

The exact relationship between due process (as expressed in the *Bill of Rights*) and the doctrine of "abuse of process" (involving a consideration of the inherent jurisdiction in Superior Courts to control and supervise the regularity of their processes) is unclear. It would seem logical to assert that where an abuse of process is found to exist there can be no due process of law. For the present, at least, our Courts have tended to isolate the two concepts, from each other.

"Abuse of Process" in Canada appears to be evolving as a doctrine in response to some of the extreme liberties which prosecutors have taken in the discretionary discharge of their duties. *R. v. Beaudry (No. 2)*[218] is only the most extreme of these examples. A good example of how the doctrine is employed in practice is to be found in *R. v. LeClair*.[219] McKay J.A. delivering the judgment of the Court condemned a private prosecutor's conduct in these terms:

> It is a reasonable assumption that the complainant, by threatening prosecution, endeavoured to obtain payment of the debt. There is no doubt that this amounted to an abuse of the process of the Court. The criminal law was not enacted for the assistance of persons seeking to collect civil debts. It seems to be clear that a Court of competent jurisdiction has inherent power to prevent the abuse of its process by staying or dismissing the action. This jurisdiction ought to be exercised very sparingly and only in very exceptional cases.

A number of lower courts in Canada have purported to employ the doctrine in recent years in order to stay proceedings instituted by the Crown which were considered to be vexatious and oppressive. In other instances, although the courts declined to find the necessary element of oppression, the existence of the validity of the doctrine was affirmed.[220] The activity in the purported use of the doctrine is especially

---

218. (1966) 50 C.R. 1 (B.C. C.A.).

219. (1956) 23 C.R. 216 at p. 221 (Ont. C.A.).

220. See P. S. Barton, "Abuse of Process as a Plea in Bar of Trial" (1972-73) 15 Cr.L.Q. 437. Barton cites the following decisions which are of rele-

interesting in light of the fact that the Supreme Court of Canada had occasion to consider the application of the doctrine by the Ontario Court of Appeal in *R. v. Osborn.*[221] Although the judgment of the Ontario Court of Appeal was reversed, the result of the decision as far as the ultimate validity and application of the doctrine were concerned was completely inconclusive.[222]

The Supreme Court of Canada's composition has been considerably altered since 1970. It is possible that in a future case the position of Pigeon J. will prevail ("I can see no legal basis for holding that criminal remedies are subject to the rule that they are to be refused whenever in its discretion, a Court considers the prosecution oppressive") and the "doctrine", such as it is, will be swept away. On the other hand possible acknowledgement of the validity and controlling force of the doctrine by our highest authority would have profound consequences for the entire administration of criminal justice in Canada.

A definitive statement on "abuse of process" by the Supreme Court of Canada could take one further form. It could enter an unsatisfactory half-way house wherein the existence of the doctrine might be confirmed but the scope of its operation might be so severely restricted as to render it for all useful intents and purposes a dead letter. Such a result was achieved (in an analogous situation) by the Supreme Court in *R. v. Wray,*[223] a decision which so narrowly restricted the ability of Superior Courts to exclude illegally or unfairly obtained evidence that "this discretion is very rarely acted upon".[224]

In the light of the foregoing analysis, optimism over our future ability to control the prosecutor appears to be an unwarranted luxury. The discretions of the prosecutor, vast in scope as they are, seemingly are immune to effective challenge. Legislative initiatives when they do appear (such as in the enactment in 1969 of s. 507(3) of the *Criminal Code* with reference to the preferred indictment) appear to do little more than to underline the authority of the Attorney General. Customary checks on this authority are by and large ineffectual. There

---

vance: *R. v. Atwood* [1972] 4 W.W.R. 399, reversed [1972] 5 W.W.R. (N.W.T.); *A. G. Sask. v. McDougall* [1972] 2 W.W.R. 66 (Sask.); *R. v. Kowerchuk* (1971) 3 C.C.C. (2d) 291 reversed [1972] 5 W.W.R. 255 (Alta. C.A.); *R. v. K.* (1971) 5 C.C.C. (2d) 46, *sub nom. R. v. Koski* (B.C.); *Re R. and Carpenter* (1971) 5 C.C.C. (2d) 28 (Ont.) granting a mandamus. *R. v. Thorpe* (1973) 11 C.C.C. (2d) 502 (Ont.); *R. v. Kennedy* (1972) 6 C.C.C. (2d) 564 (Ont. C.A.); See also K. Chasse, "Abuse of process as a control of prosecutorial discretion" (1970) 10 C.R.N.S. 392. Also note the case of *Connelly v. D.P.P.* [1964] A.C. 1254.

221. (1969) 5 C.R.N.S. 183, reversed 12 C.R.N.S. 1 (Can.).

222. See P. C. Stenning, "Observations on the Supreme Court of Canada's Decision in R. v. Osborn" (1970-71) 13 Cr.L.Q. 164. See also B. Haines, "Judicial ombudsmanship — A problem in policy" (1970) 12 C.R.N.S. 11.

223. (1972) 11 C.R.N.S. 235 (Can.).

224. *Per* Laskin J. in *R. v. Hogan supra* footnote 216 at p. 223.

are, to be sure, small enclaves of gathered power or potential power (as with the *Bill of Rights* and the doctrine of abuse of process) but their ultimate worth lies decidedly in the hands of a judiciary that is reluctant to interfere.

Much of our present difficulty surfaces in expressions of fealty and shows of deference to an office much divorced from its historical role. Impartiality, the hallmark of the prosecutor's office, may have always been only the highest form, not the general characteristic of the prosecutor's role. Even the legendary Coke, once Attorney General Coke, was all too human when clothed in prosecutor's garb:

> "I will prove you the notoriest Traitor that ever came to the bar"; "thou art a monster; thou hast an English face, but a Spanish heart"; "You are the absolutist Traitor that ever was"; "thou Viper; for I thou thee, thou Traiter."[225]

Impartiality is not an empty virtue. It is not something to be discarded. Neither is it something to be "assumed". "Settled judicial tradition" has entrenched the prosecutor's position. It would be timely for our courts to re-appraise the basis for this settled tradition.

> Yes, the court is surely right that judicial intrusion into the prosecuting function is contrary to the settled judicial tradition. But why is it? . . . Is it because the tradition became settled before the courts made the twentieth-century discovery that the courts can interfere with executive action to protect against abuses but at the same time can avoid taking over the executive function? Is it because the tradition become settled before the modern system of *limited* judicial review became fully recognized?
>
> On the basis of what the courts know today about leaving administration to administrators but at the same time providing an effective check to protect against abuses, should the courts not take a fresh look at the tradition that prevents them from reviewing the prosecuting function? Throughout the governmental system, courts have found that other administrative or executive functions are in need of a judicial check, with a limited scope of review. *The reasons for a judicial check of prosecutor's discretion are stronger than for such a check of other administrative discretion that is now traditionally reviewable.* Important interests are at stake. Abuses are common. The questions involved are appropriate for judicial determination. And much injustice could be corrected.[226]

---

225. Coke's references cited here are to Sir Walter Raleigh. Extract is from *Howell's State Trials* (2nd ed. 1730) and is quoted in K. Turner, "The Role of Crown Counsel in Canadian Prosecutions" (1962) 40 Can.Bar.Rev. 439 at p. 442.
226. K. C. Davis, *Discretionary Justice* (1969) at pp. 211-212.

4

CONTROLLING THE TRIAL PROCESS: JUDICIAL DECISION - MAKING

1. JUDICIAL DISCRETION — DOES IT EXIST?

Thus far our survey of the criminal justice system has explored the procedural and administrative powers and discretions exercised by two important officials — the policeman and the prosecutor. The concern has been largely with the nature and the breadth of the grants of power wielded by these officials.

The operative definition of "discretion" which has guided the analysis to this point has been this one propounded by K. C. Davis:

> A public officer has discretion whenever the effective limits on his power leave him free to make a choice among possible courses of action or inaction.[1]

Our interest has been to discern and scrutinize the existing framework for confining, structuring and checking these exercises of discretion.

Administrative discretion, as Davis points out is "much dominated by discretion which is unguided by rules or even by standards". As to why this should be the case Davis provides three answers:

(1) Much discretionary justice not now governed by or guided by rules should be
(2) Much discretionary justice is without rules because no one knows how to formulate rules
(3) Much discretionary justice is without rules because discretion is preferred to any rules that might be formulated; individualized justice is often better or thought to be better than the results produced by precise rules.[2]

"Discretion as exercised by the police and the prosecutor differs from judicial decision-making. Police and prosecutorial discretion is largely carried out within the following general confines:

> Not many questions for discretionary justice ever reach the stage of adjudication, whether formal or informal. Discretionary justice includes initiating, investigating, prosecuting, negotiating, settling, contracting, dealing, advising, threatening, publicizing, concealing, planning, recommending, supervising. Often the most important discretionary decisions are the negative ones, such as not to initiate, not to investigate, not to prosecute, not to deal, and the negative decision usually

---

1. K. C. Davis, *Discretionary Justice* (1969) p. 4.
2. *Ibid.* at p. 15.

means a final disposition without ever reaching the stage of either formal or informal adjudication.[3]

"Judicial decision-making" is probably a preferable term to "judicial discretion". Since both judges and scholars have been generally imprecise in their use of language in this regard a good deal of confusion has been introduced into discussions relating to the process of judicial adjudication — a process which (we shall argue) differs markedly from the decision-making process affecting the police and the prosecutor. Professor A. W. Mewett has identified much of the reigning confusion on the subject of discretion in a 1970 editorial:

> I do not know what the word discretion means but it is quite obvious that it is used in a variety of meanings throughout the criminal process. We talk about the discretion of the police — to arrest or issue a summons, to charge or not; about the prosecutor's discretion — as to which charge to lay, whether to withdraw a charge; about judicial discretion — in bail applications, in evidentiary matters; and administrative discretion — of the Parole Board or of the Cabinet. At the same time we are told that there are certain rules or "guidelines" within which the discretion must be exercised.
>
> One may ask, when does discretion cease to be discretion and when does it become a process of decision-making susceptible of an appeal to a higher authority. The narrower the guidelines the smaller the area of discretion. . . .[4]

Although Professor Mewett does not conclude that it is inappropriate to designate judicial decision-making as exercises in judicial discretion (he supposes instead, that "there really are degrees of discretion") the implication of his remarks is that where the process of decision-making becomes structured by rules and principles, and where arbitrariness is checked and confined by an appeal to a higher authority, then the process can no longer truly be described as discretionary in nature.

The denial of the existence of judicial discretion is anathema to the positivists; especially to the modern positivists whose prime spokesman has been H. L. A. Hart.[5] Judicial discretion is indeed, central, to the positivist conception of law. At the risk of over-simplification a skeleton of that philosophy ought to be sketched since much of the ensuing discussion is referable to it. Professor Dworkin of Yale University offers this distillation:[6]

> (a) The law of a community is a set of special rules used by the community directly or indirectly for the purpose of determining

---

3. *Ibid.* at p. 22.
4. (1969-70) 12 Cr.L.Q. 109.
5. See H. L. A. Hart, *The Concept of Law* (1961).
6. R. M. Dworkin, "The Model of Rules" (1967-68) 35 U. Chi. L. Rev. 14 (emphasis added).

which behaviour will be punished or coerced by the public power. These special rules can be identified and distinguished by specific criteria, by tests having to do not with their content but with their *pedigree* or the manner in which they were adopted or developed. These tests of pedigree can be used to distinguish valid legal rules from spurious legal rules (rules which lawyers and litigants wrongly argue are rules of law) and also from other sorts of social rules (generally lumped together as "moral rules") that the community follows but does not enforce through public power.

(b) The set of these valid legal rules is exhaustive of "the law" so that if someone's case is not clearly covered by such a rule (because there is none that seems appropriate, or those that seem appropriate are vague, or for some other reason) then that case cannot be decided by "applying the law". *It must be decided by some official like a judge, "exercising his discretion", which means reaching beyond the law for some other sort of standard to guide him in manufacturing a fresh legal rule or supplementing an old one.*

(c) To say that some has a "legal obligation" is to say that his case falls under a valid legal rule that requires him to do or to forbear from doing something. (To say he has a legal right, or has a legal power to some sort, or a legal privilege or immunity, is to assert, in a shorthand way, that others have actual or hypothetical legal obligations to act in certain ways touching him.) In the absence of such a valid legal rule there is no legal obligation; it follows that when the judge decides an issue by exercising his discretion, he is not enforcing a legal obligation as to that issue.[7]

Dworkin reminds us that "this is only the skeleton of positivism. The flesh is arranged differently by different positivists, and some even tinker with the bones. Different versions differ chiefly in their description of the fundamental test of pedigree a rule must meet to count as a rule of law".[8] Of primary import to modern positivist thinkers has been the refinements and adaptations which Hart has added to the theories of John Austin.

Under Hart's thesis Austin's version of law viewed as a series of commands has yielded to Hart's theory of obligation.[9] Also Hart's version of positivism proves more complex than Austin's in that Hart

---

7. *Ibid.* at pp. 17-18.
8. *Ibid.* at p. 18.
9. "Hart distinguishes between what he calls being *obliged* to obey the law — i.e. the idea of being forced to obey the law that is connoted in the command/sanction theory of law — and what he calls having an *obligation* to obey the law. Hart finds this idea of acceptance, or of felt obligation, in the notion of rules. Rules not only prescribe what people are supposed to do, but, to those who accept the validity of a particular rule or system of rules they provide a reason for acting in accordance with a particular rule over the unpleasant consequences that might result from a failure to observe or obey the rule" (from G. Christie, "The Model of Principles" (1968) Duke L.J. 649 at pp. 650-651).

recognizes "as Austin did not, that rules are of different logical kinds. (Hart distinguishes two kinds, which he calls "primary" and "secondary" rules).

Primary rules, we are told, are those that grant rights or impose obligations, or, put another way, these rules prescribe what citizens should or should not do. Examples of such rules are those which forbid us to rob, murder or drive too fast.[10]

Secondary rules, prescribe who can make law or amend it, and designate who can adjudicate disputes arising under a legal system. Put another way, they are those rules "that stipulate how and by whom, such primary rules may be formed, recognized, modified or extinguished".[11]

Among these secondary rules one is more fundamental than the rest:

> The fundamental secondary rule in a society Hart calls a rule of recognition. It prescribes who is the ultimate law maker (or law making body) and the conditions under which he (or it) can make law. The authority of all subordinate law makers must be traced back to the rule of recognition. Similarly, the validity of all other rules in the legal system must be traced back to this same rule of recognition in the sense that (1) they must be made by someone whose authority can be traced back to the ultimate law maker described in the rule of recognition and (2) their content must not contravene some prohibition contained in the rule of recognition that limits the content of the valid rules of the legal system. The validity of the rule of recognition course, cannot be determined by reference to any other higher rule. Rather its validity must depend in the last analysis, upon its acceptance by the people living in the particular society under the legal system generated by the rule of recognition."[12]

These concepts become important to this discussion when one considers the relationship of legal rules to the adjudicative process. *How does a judge find and apply the law?* According to the positivists the law may be found and applied by recourse to the rules (which, it will be remembered are "exhaustive of the law"). Thus, in the adjudication of a dispute the judge must apply the relevant rule(s), and his decision will flow accordingly.

The task, the positivists caution, should not be minimized. There is no such process as "mechanical jurisprudence". The meaning of many rules is well settled (at least within the "central core"), but others are "open-textured". The further removed a controversy is from a factual situation which might be "subsumed under the core meaning of the rule, the more debatable is the conclusion that the judge can decide the dispute before him merely by applying any pre-existing

---

10. See H. Hart, *supra* footnote 5 at pp. 89-96; Dworkin, *supra* footnote 6 at pp. 19-22; Christie, *supra* footnote 9 at pp. 650-653.
11. Dworkin, *supra* footnote 6 at p. 19.
12. G. Christie, *supra* footnote 9 at pp. 651-652.

rule".[13] Here Hart, like Austin, "recognizes that legal rules have furry edges . . . and, again like Austin, he accounts for troublesome cases by saying that Judges have and exercise *discretion* to decide these cases by fresh legislation".[14]

This conception of a "judicial discretion" is objectionable and deficient in as much as it does not adequately come to grips with, or accurately describe, the precise nature of judicial decision-making. Professor Dworkin's analysis provides a cogent basis for an attack upon Hart's positivist perspective on "judicial discretion".

> Positivism, on its own thesis, stops short of just those puzzling, hard cases that sends us to look for theories of law. When we reach these cases, the positivist remits us to a doctrine of discretion that leads nowhere and tells nothing. His picture of law as a system of rules has exercised a tenacious hold on our imagination, perhaps through its very simplicity. If we shake ourselves loose from this model of rules, we may be able to build a model truer to the complexity and sophistication of our practices.[15]

According to Professor Dworkin (and many of his views are here endorsed) to say that a judge in hard, or troublesome, cases has "discretion" is plainly erroneous (unless one uses the term "discretion" in a trivial, or "weak" sense — in which case its usefulness as an analytical aid is simply destroyed). Two of the "weak" senses in which the term discretion is commonly used are these:

(1) Discretion simply means that for some reason the standards an official must apply cannot be applied mechanically but demand the use of judgment. We use this weak sense of discretion when the context does not already make that clear when the background our audience assumes does not contain that piece of information *e.g.* "the official's orders left him a great deal of information".

(2) Discretion in another simple sense means that some official has final authority to make a decision and cannot be reviewed and reversed by any other official.[16]

---

13. *Ibid.* at p. 653.
14. Dworkin, *supra* footnote 6 at p. 22 (emphasis added). Christie says that "the judge in these circumstances is said to have the discretion to decide the case as he wishes or, perhaps more correctly, to have the discretion *within limits* to decide the case as he wishes" (*supra* footnote 9 at p. 653).
15. Dworkin, *supra* footnote 6 at p. 46. The articles by Dworkin and Christie cited *supra* (footnotes 6 and 9) are in essence a debate. More accurately put, Dworkin's critique of Hart is critically examined by Christie in his article. In this regard see also, Hughes, "Rules, Policy and Decision-Making" (1968) 77 Yale L.J. 411. Further, for an interesting analysis of Hart and Dworkin see, J. M. Steiner "Judicial Discretion and the Concept of Law" (1976) 35 Camb.L.J. 135.
16. Dworkin, *supra* footnote 6 at p. 32. See also S. A. DeSmith, *Judicial Review of Administrative Action* (3rd ed. 1973); although the emphasis is naturally with the field of administrative law a useful discussion of this point occurs under the title "Are There Unreviewable Discretionary Powers?" at pp. 253 *et seq.*

202 JUDICIAL DECISION-MAKING

From the standpoint of the positivists a judge has *no* discretion when a clear and established rule is available. This philosophical perspective flounders in situations where either no discoverable rule is applicable to the case at hand, or, where the judge, confronted by a rule which is applicable (and thus binding) is dissatisfied with it and wishes to overrule it. At this point there is a need for a "discretion" of a stronger type.

Discretion in this stronger sense is not really discretion at all — it is principled decision-making. An official must not only use judgment in applying the standards (rules) set him by authority, for beyond this there will be occasions where he will consider himself not bound by the standards set by the authority in question. The fact that his decision may or may not be reviewable is not particularly relevant to *how* the judge reaches his decision. Judicial decision-making, reviewable or not, is not tantamount to license and does not exclude criticism.[17] The positivist reliance upon the exhaustive nature of rules, and in default, to nebulous "discretion", is the achilles heel of that philosophy.

A judge may not extinguish or amend the law on a whim. Neither may he be wholly arbitrary where no rule exists to compel his decision.[18] The decision as to when a rule is applicable is a difficult one, and formulating a complete statement of the exceptions to a rule is also problematic.[19] But those processes are essential to the positivist conception. In reality the process of judicial decision-making involves a search for applicable standards; standards which are ascertainable and capable of application with a high degree of consistency. In this way the process retains a measure of predictability and litigants are able to entertain confidence in its ability to do justice. Pure reliance upon rules only takes us part of the way down the road in search of this objective. The infusion of a positivist notion of discretion will not carry us the remaining distance.

The answer, Dworkin suggests, is in the role played by principles (as distinct from legal rules) in the judicial decision-making process. Principles differ from rules in these important respects:[20]

(1) Both are sets of standards pointing to particular decisions about legal obligation in particular circumstances, but they differ in the character of the direction they give.

---

17. See Dworkin *supra* footnote 6 at p. 33.
18. "Rules are applicable in an all-or-nothing fashion. If the facts a rule stipulates are given, then either the rule is valid, in which case the answer it supplies must be accepted, or it is not, in which case it contributes nothing to the decision" (Dworkin at p. 25).
19. Christie contends that an exhaustive statement of any rule and its exceptions is an impossibility. See *supra* footnote 9 at pp. 656-659.
20. Dworkin, *supra* footnote 6 at pp. 25-27.

(2) Rules are applicable in an all-or-nothing fashion. If the facts a rule stipulates are given then either the rule is valid, in which case the answer it supplies must be accepted, or it is not, in which case it contributes nothing to the decision.

(3) An accurate statement of any rule takes its exceptions into account. Principles on the other hand are not, even in theory, subject to enumeration.

(4) Principles (unlike rules) do not set out legal consequences that follow automatically when the conditions provided are met.

(5) Principles may conflict with one another yet both may be applicable to a given factual situation. When principles intersect the one who must resolve the conflict has to take into account the relative weight of each.[21]

(6) Principles have a dimension that rules do not — the dimension of weight or importance.

Principles are possessed of a character that is *potentially* binding or obligatory. "It is always a question, of course, whether any particular principle is *in fact* binding upon some legal official. But there is nothing in the logical character of a principle which renders it incapable of binding him".[22] Not unlike a rule, a judge should follow it if it applies and if he does not (and it is of sufficient weight and import) on that account he will have made a mistake.

> it is certainly true that principles do not determine results, but that is only another way of saying that principles are not rules. Only rules dictate results come what may. When a contrary result has been reached the rule has been abandoned or changed. Principles do not work that way; they incline a decision one way, though not conclusively, and they survive intact when they do not prevail. This seems no reason for concluding that judges who must reckon with principles have discretion because a set of principles *can* dictate a result.[23]

Ascertaining the weight and import of a principle is no simple task. The conclusion reached by one judge may not accord with the view of another. These are matters of judgment; matters upon which reasonable men may differ. Mr. Justice Cardozo in his famous lectures on

---

21. "Rules do not have this dimension. We can speak of rules as being *functionally* important or unimportant . . . In this sense, one legal rule may be more important than another because it has a greater or more important role in regulating behaviour. But we cannot say that one rule is more important than another within the system of rules, so that when two rules conflict one supersedes the other by virtue of its greater weight. If two rules conflict, one of them cannot be a valid rule. The decision as to which is valid, and which must be abandoned or recast, must be made by appealing to considerations beyond the rules themselves" (Dworkin at p. 27).

22. *Supra* footnote 6 at p. 35.

23. *Supra* footnote 6 at p. 36.

The Nature of the Judicial Process[24] commented upon the difficulties inherent in such determinations:

> We see that to determine to be loyal to precedents and to the principles back of precedents does not carry us far upon the road. Principles are complex bundles. It is well enough to say that we shall be consistent, but consistent with what? Shall it be consistency with the origins of the rule, the course and tendency of development? Shall it be consistency with logic or philosophy or the fundamental conceptions of jurisprudence as disclosed by analysis of our own and foreign systems. All these loyalties are possible. All have sometimes prevailed. How are we to choose between them? Putting that question aside, how do we choose between them?[25]

These difficulties must be squarely faced by legal theorists. As Dworkin notes "since principles seem to play a role in arguments about legal obligation . . . a model that provides for that role has some initial advantage over one that excludes it. . . ."[26] Since courts not infrequently reject or radically alter established rules, and since these departures from rules may not be arbitarary if the judicial process is to remain credible, the role and the guiding assistance of principles to this process must be acknowledged.[27] It is simply unaccepable to enshroud this part of the process under an impenetrable blanket entitled "discretion".

There is no denying the widespread use of the term "discretion" throughout the legal literature. Discretion has been described as "a science or understanding to discern between falsity and truth, between right and wrong, between shadows and substance, between equity and colourable glosses and pretences, *and not according to their wills and private affections*".[28] Thus defined the term "discretion" becomes a misnomer, the definition implying instead the process of principled judicial decision-making.

Modern statutes abound with expressions which are said to confer a "discretion" upon the sitting judge. Some of these are "if the Judge or Court shall deem it proper", "if the Judge should see fit", "shall not without leave of the court", "the Judge may, where it is in the interests of justice to do so, make an order", "as it thinks just and reasonable", etc. At the same time however, we are reminded that the "Judge's discretion must be exercised judicially according to rules of procedure and evidence",[29] or, putting matters slightly differently, where a judge

---

24. B. Cardozo, *The Nature of the Judicial Process* (1921).
25. *Ibid.* at pp. 64-65.
26. Dworkin, *supra* footnote 6 at p. 37.
27. See Dworkin, *supra* footnote 6 at pp. 38-40.
28. *Rooke's Case* (1598) 5 Co. Rep. 99b, 100a (Assessment by Commissioners of Sewers); reproduced in J. A. DeSmith, *Judicial Review of Administrative Action* (3rd ed. 1973) at p. 248.
29. E. Gabbay, *Discretion in Criminal Justice* (1973) at p. 1.

purports to exercise a "discretion" he is nevertheless required to act "according to the rules of reason and justice, not according to private opinion . . . according to law and not humor", and this discretion was to be "not arbitrary, vague, and fanciful, but legal and regular".[30] In short, a Judge's exercise of "discretion" will not be interfered with *provided he does not derogate from principle.* Judicial decision-making, whatever its form, must be principled decision-making, and, of course, rational decision-making.

Paul Weiler, a respected Canadian commentator has argued for the validity of this thesis:[31]

> At the basis of the adjudicative model [of rational judicial decision-making] then, is the thesis that the legal order is made up of more than simple authoritative *rules.* Equally as important are those policies and social purposes which are refracted into the settled *principles* of the system. Rather than mechanically prescribing a result (which even legal rules cannot do, because of the necessity for the exercise of judgment in their application), these principles link ends (values) and means (legal techniques) in a way which supports a particular decison. Such principles are in fact part of an adequately conceived legal system, and not simply a facet of the non-legal background.[32]

In his examination of judicial decision-making Weiler closely examines what he considers to be the proper confines of the area which so many others have abandoned to the arena of "discretion":

> while social justice must be a prime factor in the judicial resolution of disputes, judges must not exercise a discretion to make fundamental choices for society. The pursuit of substantive values must be limited by adherence to legal values, such as the need for objectivity, communicability and impersonality of judicial decisions. The maintenance of a viable legal order and the task of retrospective adjudication of disputes should shape and control both the occasions for and the extent of judicial creativity. These independent, institutional values are served by limiting judicial advances by an environment or fabric of established *principles.* Self-imposed respect for this legal framework imprints a distinctive quality of judicial decision-making such that the latter is not appropriately characterized as legislative policy-making. Judges are not, and should not be, political actors.[33]

The foregoing analysis should not be regarded as resurrecting the old myth of the completeness of law. As Dworkin has noted principles are not, even in theory, subject to enumeration, it being impossible to conceive of "the numberless imaginary cases in which we know in

---

30. *Sharp v. Wakefield* [1891] A.C. 173 *per* Lord Halsbury L.C. reproduced in DeSmith *supra* footnote 28 at p. 248.

31. P. Weiler, "Two Models of Judicial Decision-Making" (1968) 46 Can.Bar. Rev. 406.

32. *Ibid.* at pp. 432-433.

33. *Ibid.* at pp. 429-430.

advance that the principle [will] not hold".[34] Despite the impossibility of such completeness predictability remains both a highly desirable and realisable objective.

Predictability, in terms of the foregoing analysis, is enhanced primarily through the inclusion of rules, principles, and *values* in the adjudicative process. (The latter may be said to supply the necessary moral content to the process — Weiler is of the belief that a judge must hold a "self-consciously teleological view of his role".)

Of our system it has been said that "the litigants have the right to expect the *correct* result".[35] Professor Weiler responds to this claim thusly:

> That this is the ideal demand put on adjudication does not mean that it is uniformly achievable to a high degree. That reckonability, and communicability, and impersonality of decision is the necessary concomitant of the judicial process does not mean that, in principle, its attainment will be self-evident and indisputable, or that, in fact, it is a human, *institutional* possibility. There is almost always an element of fiat within the narrow interstices left by the reasoning process and the social background and environment of the judge may substanially distort his processes of reasoning. What is demanded by a viable institution of adjudication is that the pursuit of reasoned decisions be the *ideal* towards which the institution tends and that judges accept the demand that their subjective idiosyncratic preferences be overcome. On such a perceived quality to the process rests the "legitimacy" of its results.[36]

Professor Weiler has been classified as a legal realist, although by no means a traditional one.[37] The values of the analytical perspective which he provides in "Two Models of Judicial Decision-Making" have been described as these:

> Weiler expressly recognizes that the process perspective requires value articulation, so that by requiring judges to find the policy reasons which motivate their innovative decisions in the body of principle which is already a part of the legal order he acknowledges the appropriateness of the pragmatic, relativistic ethics of the sociological school. In suggesting the primary of principle he is able to create a standard by which the individual decisions of judges may be evaluated: the "ought" in adjudication is no longer reduced to an empirical probability calculated on the basis of prior statistical data, [as some realists had suggested] but is a normative "ought" determined by the institutional values already present in the legal system. Thus by acknowledging the usefulness of the sociological perspective for the realist view of law, Weiler was able to maintain a basic procedural emphasis while nevertheless

---

34. Dworkin, *supra* footnote 6 at p. 26.
35. R. Dworkin, "Judicial Discretion" (1963) 6 J. of Phil. 624.
36. Weiler, *supra* footnote 31 at pp. 431-432.
37. R. A. MacDonald, "Prolegomena to a Theory of Legal Relevance" (1975) unpublished Master's Thesis (U. of Toronto) at p. 148.

meeting the critiques of its more glaring defects; as a result he was able to articulate a theory of law which was both procedural and functional.[38]

Clearly "law" as viewed by Weiler is a "purposive endeavour" and the authority of law springs not so much from the coercive power of the sanctions it provides but from its integrity. In this sense Weiler's perspective does not differ greatly from the quasi-natural law theories propounded by Lon Fuller,[39] (although a detailed examination of the intricacies of those theories is clearly beyond the scope of this exercise).

It is important, Weiler argues, that jurisprudence "shed the fallacy that simply because the legal rules do not decide the case with objective, impersonal, logically necessary and self-evident certainty . . ." and because reasonable men may find different solutions logically compelled by the same issue, "then there is no *reasoned* way of *justifying* one solution as more *probable* than another." Yielding in such instances to a notion of discretion does not hold the answer. The acknowledgement that judges "operate within a 'law-conditioned matrix' of rules, doctrines, principles, techniques and operative ideals" indicates that there are "leeways" of appropriate and proper judicial behaviour. The answer produced by a given judge cannot be shown to be demonstrably *the* right answer. Yet the *sense of responsibility* of judges operating within this matrix controls the possibilities of decisional deviance, and thus judges may forge new solutions "in accordance with the mutually accepted 'forcefields' or 'grain' of the established legal order". This they do much in the way that a scientist operates and works within the leeways and perimeters of the system regulating his discipline.[40]

In conclusion, if "judicial discretion" may be said to mean anything at all, it means "the responsible exercise, in good faith, of the

---

38. *Ibid.* at p. 162.
39. See L. Fuller, *The Morality of Law* (1964). See also R. A. MacDonald *supra* footnote 37 at pp. 178 *et seq.* It is doubtful that Fuller would have much argument with Weiler's thesis that "the court has the independent role of engaging in a reasoned colloquy with society, of collaborative articulation of what are the enduring shares, moral standards and purposes of the society", or with Weiler's view that the judge may err, the "dialogue can miscarry" for "[T]his does not mean that the judge cannot approach his goal of obtaining adherence to his authoritative decision and choice of values from 'the universal audience', that is, the audience composed of all men both rational and competent" (Weiler, p. 435).
40. See Weiler, *supra* footnote 31 at pp. 435-436. Note also these observations at pp. 433-434: "Principles which are part of a legal system can be both substantive and jurisprudential. The latter would include the conventional techniques for interpreting statutes or assessing precedents. There is no doubt that real problems exist in determining when any legal principle becomes established or eroded, what it means for any particular case, and what is the relative weight which it properly has. This, along with the fact

discretion to pursue justice through law"[41] — which is to say quite a lot, but not nearly so much as most positivists would claim for the term.

2. THE JUDICIAL DECISION TO EXCLUDE RELEVANT EVIDENCE

In a working paper submitted to the Ontario Law Reform Commission's Law of Evidence Project in 1970, the authors argued for the proposition that judicial decisions "depend for their community acceptance and moral force upon a balance of efficiency and fairness in the application of acceptable substantive norms".[42] The authors of the paper in this context define *efficiency* to mean "speed, accuracy, low cost, simplicity, authority and finality".[43] *Fairness,* they use to mean "adaptability, simplicity, informality, the avoidance of surprise, rationality, an impartial decision-maker, the limitation of abuses, the opportunity to exercise rights and a reasonable opportunity to present one's own case and confront one's opponent's case".[44]

It would appear that the law of evidence has evolved and has been formulated in large measure with a view towards striking a balance between the demands of these two criteria. The law of *criminal* evidence (it may be plausibly argued) has not attempted to balance these competing values, but rather has attempted to lay stress upon the aspect of fairness. As Lord Devlin noted in *Connelly v. D.P.P.*[45] "nearly the whole of the English criminal law of procedure and evidence has been made by the exercise of the judges of their power to see that what was fair and just was done between prosecutors and the accused."

Despite this emphasis in the law of criminal evidence it is undeniable that due to aspects of breadth, and generality, the concern for justice and fairness has been relegated to the confines of judicial "choice-making". (This decision-making process we have already

---

that there are usually competing but established premises, sometimes leads writers to say the judge has, and must have, a right to choose on the basis of his own preferences or attitudes. This conclusion simply does not follow if it is true that litigants have a right to the most supportable decision in the circumstances, and this is the ideal towards which courts must tend. Just because any one answer is no more than a probability, and selection between two competing probabilities demands judgment, this does not mean that there is no rational way for exercising a judgment about which is more probable. Moreover, the fact that the exercise of this judgment may be unreviewable does not mean that a court is delegated the discretion to choose in the light of its subjective preferences".

41. Weiler, *supra footnote* 31 at p. 436.
42. Ontario Law Reform Commission: "Law of Evidence Project: Working Paper" October, 1970 (unpublished) at p. 43.
43. *Ibid.*
44. *Ibid.*
45. [1964] 2 All E.R. 401 at p. 438 (H.L.).

argued should be in accord with established principles. Therefore, while admitting of flexibility the process should not be arbitrary, or lacking in consistency.)

In *R. v. Sims*[46] Goddard L.C.J. stated what is regarded as the positive rule respecting the admissibility of evidence: all evidence which is logically probative is admissible unless excluded by established rules. This "positive approach to admissibility" presently appears to hold sway in Canada by virtue of the approach taken by the majority of the Supreme Court of Canada in *R. v. Wray*.[47] As McWilliams notes in his text on *Canadian Criminal Evidence* the positive rule stands in contrast with the so-called "safe rule" stated by Martin C.J.B.C. in *R. v. Picken*,[48] "that everything should be vigorously excluded unless it can be clearly said to have relevance to the case".

If one assumes that the law of criminal evidence has indeed been formulated in order to insure that what is fair and just is done between prosecutors and accused persons then one is left to speculate as to how the notion of fairness squares with the basic rule of admissibility (which, summed up in a single word, is "relevancy"). Must "relevancy" defer to the notion of "fairness"? And, if in theory, we arrive at the conclusion that it must, what is the actual result in practice?

A threshold question might well be "what do we mean by 'fairness'?"[49] The Ontario Commission's Working Paper, as we have noted, has afforded us with a partial answer to this question. In the context of the criminal trial (and more particularly with regard to the evidentiary rules controlling those trials), however, greater particularity is required.

"Fairness" may be said to be involved in the adjudication on the admissibility of evidence in a criminal trial whenever the evidence sought to be introduced in a criminal trial (a) is possessed of preju-

---

46. (1946) 31 Cr.App.R. 158 at p. 164.
47. [1970] 4 C.C.C. 1 (Can.).
48. (1937) 69 C.C.C. 61 (B.C. C.A.) cited in P.K. McWilliams, *Canadian Criminal Evidence* (1974) at p. 19.
49. Lest the objection be raised that "fairness" is a term which is too vague and imprecise to be justiciable in the sense argued for in the analysis *supra* of principled decision-making the following comments (although based upon a different concept of "judicial discretion") make the case well for the ascertainment of workable and manageable judicial standards of fairness: "Though the concept of 'fairness' may seem too vague and uncertain to constitute a judicial standard without more, it is very seldom that any court is asked to apply a criterion of this type in bare form. Subsidiary principles will usually emerge as to what factors ought to be evaluated in deciding whether 'fairness' has been achieved. There comes a point where sufficiently precise subsidiary factors emerge to warrant describing the process of applying principle as a 'judicial' one" (M.S. Weinberg, "The Judicial Discretion to Exclude Relevant Evidence" (1975) 21 McGill L.J. 1 at p. 8).

dicial effect;[50] (b) is illegally obtained; (c) is unreliable for any reason; or, (d) is obtained by the abusive manipulation of orderly, and ordinarily legal, processes.

A consideration of "fairness" and "relevancy" as considerations in issues of admissibility of evidentiary material effected by the four categories enumerated above, follows:

(1) Evidence possessed of prejudicial effect

As Spence J. observed in *Draper v. Jacklyn*[51] allegedly prejudicial evidence will often be the subject of an attempted tender in jury trials:

> The occasions are frequent upon which a judge trying a case with the assistance of a jury is called upon to determine whether or not a piece of evidence technically admissible may be so prejudicial to the opposite side that any probative value is overcome by the possible prejudice and that therefore he should exclude production of the particular piece of evidence.

The right to exclude relevant evidence on the basis of its unfairly prejudicial effect is said to stem from these remarks made by Lord DuParcq in *Noor Mohamed v. R.*:[52]

> It is right to add, however, that in all such cases the judge ought to consider whether the evidence which it is proposed to adduce is sufficiently substantial, having regard to the purpose to which it is professedly directed, to make it desirable in the interest of justice that it should be admitted. If, so far as that purpose is concerned, it can in the circumstances of the case have only trifling weight, the judge will be right to exclude it. To say this is not to confuse weight with admissibility. The distinction is plain, but cases must occur in which it would be unjust to admit evidence of a character gravely prejudicial to the accused even though there may be some tenuous ground for holding it technically admissible. The decision then must be left to the discretion and sense of fairness of the judge.

When one speaks in terms of "prejudicial effect" and the balancing of that effect against the "probative value" of tendered evidence the concern in actuality that is being voiced is that the trier of fact, due to the prejudicial nature of the evidence, may not be able to direct his mind to the issues properly within his province in a fair and impartial manner. The fear is, that in allowing the introduction of evidence possessed of substantial prejudicial effect, there arises a risk (even a probability) that extraneous and legally unjustified considerations will effect the decision-making process, and that an improper inference may be drawn from such evidence, leading ultimately to a

---

50. One writer who disapproves of developments in the law excluding prejudicial evidence is B. Livesey. See his article on "Judicial Discretion to Exclude Prejudicial Evidence in Criminal Cases" (1968) Camb. L.J. 291.
51. [1970] S.C.R. 92 at pp. 96-97.
52. [1949] A.C. 182 at p. 192.

wrong conclusion.

> There are cases where the logical relevance of . . . an exhibit will unquestionably be overwhelmed by its inherently prejudicial qualities which will impair the defendant's right to a fair and impartial trial. When undoubtedly the minute peg of relevancy will be entirely obscured by the quantity of dirty linen hung upon it, fair play directs the exclusion of the exhibit.[53]

(a) *Photographs*

An example of evidence which might be said to be earmarked by "inherently prejudicial qualities" is the physical presentation or depiction of cruel or horrible injuries. Such evidence may be presented directly (*e.g.* a victim revealing a terrible personal injury by removing clothing in court) or indirectly (through the use of vivid photographs.) Such evidence occasionally is said to possess an "inflammatory effect" or it is contended that it "tends to inflame the minds of the jury". The result (it is argued) in such circumstances is that the evidence tends to "prejudice the jury against the accused" in that it "leads the jury to associate the accused with the crime" irrespective of whether the other probative evidence offered in proof of the allegation supports that deduction.[54] (In anecdotal terms countless defence counsel are heard to relate experiences of trials "gone awry" when such evidence was presented to the jury; the usual image depicted being one of the eyes of the jurymen darting back and forth from the photographs before them over to the accused seated in the prisoner's dock.)

The law is presently unsettled in Canada as to the legal consequences of the acceptance of a photograph into evidence. The debate settles around whether photographs may only be used to illustrate and clarify oral testimony, or whether they fall into the general class of "demonstrative evidence" and as such are proof of the matters which

---

53. *Per* Wachenfield J. in *The State v. Bucanis* (1958) 138 Att. (2d) 739; quoted in A. Maloney, "Annotation: The Admissibility of Photographs in Criminal Cases and Resultant Prejudice to an Accused's Fair Trial" (1967) 1 C.R.N.S. 167 at p. 173.

54. In *R. v. O'Donnell* (1936) 65 C.C.C. 299 (Ont. C.A.) Masten J.A. disputed this objection: "With respect to the admissibility of photographs on the ground that they tended to inflame the minds of the jury, I think that the ground put forward is *nihil ad rem*. The only question to be considered is were they admissible under the rules of evidence. If they are, the effect which they may have on the jury cannot interfere with their admission.
As B. MacFarlane indicates in his study of "Photographic Evidence: Its Probative Value at Trial and the Judicial Discretion to Exclude It From Evidence" (1973-74) 16 Cr.L.Q. 149 at pp. 166-167, "This would seem to be the most inflexible view taken in any Canadian decision". Certainly it is not compatible with Supreme Court of Canada's decision in *Draper v. Jacklyn, supra* footnote 51, or even with the decision of that Court in *R. v. Wray* [1970] 4 C.C.C. 1. See also, A. Maloney *supra* footnote 53; and "Case and Comment" (1940) 18 Can.Bar.Rev. 813 at p. 814.

they depict independent of any oral testimony. One commentator, B. A. MacFarlane speculates that Canadian courts will, in all probability, begin to view photographs as "demonstrative evidence" which "once accepted into evidence after having been properly verified, . . . is not restricted in its use merely to illustrate oral testimony, but may also provide direct, substantive and independent proof of a fact in issue".[55] Whether this speculative forecast will come to pass is by no means certain. Nor is it necessarily the desirable development which Mr. MacFarlane depicts it to be.

By "verification", it is assumed that Mr. MacFarlane means "establishing a proper foundation as to the accuracy and authenticity of the photograph".[56] But the word "accuracy" begs the question of "accuracy from what perspective?", and inclines the debate once again to a reliance upon oral testimony. An example of how the requirement of accuracy (in order to insure the fair depiction of the event) affects admissibility is to be found in the case of *R. v. Gallant*.[57] The case stands for the proposition that where there is doubt as to the accuracy of photographs, as to their ability to fairly represent "what actually took place when the photograph was taken", then the accused should be protected from any resultant prejudice by excluding the photographs. Campbell C.J. in ordering the exclusion of photographs of the murder victim's body addressed the issue in this manner:

> In the present case, there does not seem to be any particular necessity or advantage to be served by the admission of the photographs. They do not evidence the steps whereby the witnesses arrived at their opinions; nor do they supply relevant *minutiae* in the appearance of the objects which have been described in the verbal evidence; nor do they seem necessarily to corroborate the evidence of any of the oral witnesses. On the other hand there are some of the pictures, at least, which might tend to over-emphasize certain features which they portray and might therefore create impressions in the mind of the jury which would not be borne out by the oral testimony and by the objects which have been produced in evidence. Though some of the pictures are undoubtedly not open to this objection, I am inclined to deal with all these pictures as a group and to give the accused the benefit of any doubt which may arise by rejecting this group of pictures from evidence, especially in view of the fact that their necessity as explanation or corroboration has not been sufficiently established.[58]

Campbell C.J. in speaking of "no particular necessity or advantage to be served by the admission of the photographs" must be seen to be addressing the aspect of the "trifling probative value" of the evidence. By referring to the tendency of the photographs to "over-emphasize

---

55. *Ibid.* 16 Cr.L.Q. at p. 161.
56. This definition is culled from the author's examination of *People v. Doggett* (1948), 188 P. (2d) 792 (Calif. Dist. Ct. of App.) *ibid.* at p. 153.
57. (1965) 47 C.R. 309 (P.E.I.).
58. *Ibid.* at p. 310.

certain features" and "create [unjustified] impressions" he emphasizes the prejudicial character of the evidence. Thus viewed, the approach taken in Gallant's murder trial is entirely consistent with the
views expressed by the Supreme Court of Canada in *Draper v. Jacklyn.*
Ritchie J. struck the point in this fashion:

> My brother Spence has also referred to a number of criminal cases in
> which photographs were tendered depicting the condition of a victim
> after murder or bodily assault. In some of these cases the trial judge
> exercised his discretion to exclude the evidence on the ground that it
> was of trifling weight and was prejudicial to the accused. In criminal
> cases where the sole issue is the guilt or innocence of the accused, it is
> understandable that such photographs should be excluded unless they
> can be shown to contain some evidence directly connecting the accused
> with the commission of the crime with which he is charged.[59]

It is not simply sufficient that it be shown (1) that the photographs
accurately and truly represent the facts; (2) that they are fair and unaccompanied by any intention to mislead; and (3) that they are verified
on oath by a person capable to do so, as was contended in *R. v.
Creemer.*[60] Such views "are too inflexible [in] that they fail to reflect
the balancing of the probative value as against the prejudicial effect."[61]

(b) *Previous convictions*

Section 12 of the *Canada Evidence Act*[62] allows a Crown Attorney
in Canada to cross-examine an accused who has chosen to testify on
his own behalf as to his previous record of criminal convictions. The
relevant portion of that statute reads as follows:

> 12(1) A witness may be questioned as to whether he has been
> convicted of any offence, and upon being so questioned, if he
> either denies the fact or refuses to answer, the opposite party may
> prove such conviction.

Canadian commentators have found this law to be unsatisfactory
and prejudicial, a positive hindrance to the conduct of a fair and
impartial trial.[63] As Dean Friedland observed "the main objection to

---

59. *Supra* footnote 51 at p. 107.
60. (1967) 1 C.R.N.S. 146 (N.S. C.A.)
61. *Per* Spence J. in *Draper v. Jacklyn, supra* footnote 9 at p. 101, disapproving
    of *R. v. Creemer.* See also *Dilabbio v. R.* (1965) 46 C.R. 131 where a new
    trial was ordered because it was thought on the facts of that case "that the
    exhibition of these articles [blood stained garments of the deceased] and
    photographs [of the body of the deceased] to the jury could only serve to
    inflame their minds and were of little, if any probative value" (p. 133).
62. R.S.C. 1970, Chap. E-10.
63. See *e.g.* M. L. Friedland, "Comments" (1969) Can. Bar. Rev. 656; E. L.
    Teed, "The Effect of s. 12 of the Canada Evidence Act Upon an Accused"
    (1970-71) 13 Cr.L.Q. 70; M. Cadsby, "Cross-Examination of Accused Per-
    sons As to Previous Convictions" (1961-62) 4 Cr.L.Q. 265. On the section
    generally see K. C. MacKenzie, "A Study of the Use of Previous Convic-
    tions" (1967-68) 3 U.B.C.L.R. 300.

the Canadian position is that either it keeps the accused out of the witness box with the result that the court cannot hear his side of the story or it *prejudices him unfairly* if he does testify. Either result is unfortunate".[64]

The section was enacted originally in order to allow for the testing of the credibility of *witnesses*. It was not originally referable to the *accused* since at the time of the initial passage of the legislation a defendant could not testify in his own behalf. Once the accused was afforded this opportunity (by statutory grant in 1893) it was argued that he like all other witnesses was included within the ambit of the section and accordingly he too might be examined as to credit through the use of his record of previous convictions. This view was affirmed in *R. v. D'Aoust*[65] and has held sway down to the present day.

The difficulty which is implicit in the view adopted in *D'Aoust* is that an accused person standing trial approaches court on a different footing from an ordinary witness (who is unencumbered by personal jeopardy). Clearly, an accused person would be seriously prejudiced by the proof of a previous conviction while an ordinary witness is not so prejudiced. Eric Teed graphically illustrates the type of prejudice visited upon an accused in his analysis of "The Effect of s. 12 of the Canada Evidence Act Upon an Accused":[66]

> When an accused is asked if he was convicted of a crime and he truthfully answers "yes", the result is not the view "he's honest by admitting his fault" rather it is "he's a scoundrel, being a criminal and therefore is not to be believed.

As Teed also indicates, the alleged offence which is revealed in such an examination may have no relation or bearing on the criminal allegation before the court but it does have a "material effect" upon the jury.[67]

The importance of these considerations has largely shaped the law in England in this respect. Viscount Sankey L.C. forcefully phrased the argument in *Maxwell v. D.P.P.*:[68]

> It was clear that if you allowed a prisoner to go into the witness box, it was impossible to allow him to be treated as an ordinary witness. Had that been permitted, a prisoner who went in to the box to give evidence on oath could have been asked about any previous conviction,

---

64. M. L. Friedland, *ibid.* at p. 657 (emphasis added).
65. (1902) 5 C.C.C. 407 (Ont. C.A.). See also, *R. v. Mulvihill* (1914) 22 C.C.C. 354 (B.C. C.A) and *R. v. Dalton* (1935) 64 C.C.C. 140 (N.S. C.A.).
66. E. Teed, *supra* footnote 63 at p. 76.
67. *Ibid.* See also *Koufis v. R.* [1941] S.C.R. 481: "The likely effect, if not the only effect upon the jurymen of this line of cross-examination [as to previous convictions] . . . would be that the accused was a person who was very apt to commit the crime with which he was charged".
68. (1934) 24 Cr.App.R. 152 at p. 169.

with the result that an old offender would seldom, if ever, have been acquitted. This would have offended against one of the most deeply rooted and jealously guarded principles of our criminal law . . .

The "jealously guarded principle" referred to in *Maxwell* is of course the basic protection against attacks upon the character of the accused. An accused taking the witness box obviously then puts his credibility in issue, but he does not necessarily also put his character in issue. The difficulty inherent in allowing the accused to be examined as to his previous convictions is that an attack upon character will usually indirectly be allowed under the guise of an attack upon credibility.[69]

> Therefore, we find the Canadian law in the position of not allowing the accused who is a witness to be attacked directly on character, but allowing the accused witness to be attacked indirectly on character, by being questioned on previous convictions under the pretence that such questions relate solely to credibility and not character.[70]

It hardly bears repeating that guilt must only be decided on the factual evidence offered in support of the *particular* charge before the court. It is simply not competent for the prosecution (save in exceptional circumstances) to adduce evidence of other criminal acts committed by the accused in order to compel the drawing of a conclusion that the accused, on the basis of his criminal conduct or character, committed the particular offence on which he presently stands indicted.[71]

Given the demonstrably prejudicial effect of such evidence[72] the question arises as to what steps have been taken by Canadian courts in order to ameliorate that effect. Is there a judicial power to disallow such cross-examination? Do other safeguards exist in order that the courts, within this limiting circumstance, might "insure that what is just and fair be done between the prosecutor and the accused"?

The argument in favour of construing s. 12 to confer a "permissive" jurisdiction upon the judge (others might describe such jurisdiction as "discretionary") stems from the use of the word "may" in subs. (1) of the section (" a witness *may* be questioned as to whether he has

---

69. See C. A. Wright, "Credibility of Witness — Cross-Examination as to Previous Conviction (1940) 18 CanBar.Rev. 808.

70. E. Teed *supra* footnote 63 at p. 75. See also G. A. Martin, "Character Evidence" 1955 L.S.U.C. Special Lectures 313; and E. P. Hartt, "Character Evidence" in Salhany and Carter, *Studies in Canadian Criminal Evidence* (1972) 259 at p. 276.

71. See *Makin v. A. G. New South Wales* [1894] A.C. 57 especially at p. 65 *per* Lord Herschell.

72. "Prejudicial effect" here, as in the case of inflammatory photographs (discussed *supra*), may be determined in terms of the capacity of the evidence to distract the jury from its duty to carefully weigh and consider the *facta probanda* in a fair and impartial manner.

been convicted of any offence . . ." as opposed to wording such as "it is the *right* of the prosecutor to question a witness etc. . . .").[73]

In England the existence of such a permissive jurisdiction was authoritatively asserted by Viscount Sankey L.C. in *Maxwell v. D.P.P.* The late Dean C. A. Wright writing in 1940 expressed the opinion that similar treatment for the accused witness was available in Canada:[74]

> The writer believes that courts approaching the problem of admissibility of previous convictions in cross-examinaton of accused persons from the point of view expressed in the *Maxwell* case have it within their power to prevent an unfair use of previous convictions to create either a prejudice against the accused or to show a propensity to commit a particular act.

On the other hand, P. K. McWilliams in his text on *Canadian Criminal Evidence* opines that "in Canada there is no special discretion as in England, but there is a discretion regarding cross-examining witnesses generally as to credit which applies".[75] In support of this submission McWilliams cites *R. v. Titchener*[76] a 1961 decision of the Ontario Court of Appeal. In *Titchener* Morden J.A. said:

> It may be that a trial Judge has a discretion to disallow questions about previous convictions which would not in fact assist the jury in assessing the credibility of an accused or another witness. This was not argued before us but in this connection I quote what Lord Simon L.C. said in *Stirland v. D.P.P.* [1944] A.C. 315 at p. 324:
>
> > "It must not be forgotten that a judge presiding at a criminal trial has a discretion . . . to disallow questions addressed to the accused in cross-examination if he considers that such questions, having regard to the issues before the jury and to the risk of the jury being misled as to what those issues really are, would be unfair, and the judge's disallowance cannot be challenged on appeal."[77]

The majority judgment delivered by Spence J. in *Colpitts v. R.*[78]

---

73. See M. Cadsby, *supra* footnote 63 at pp. 268-269.

74. C. A. Wright, *supra* footnote 69 at p. 809. Some support for this assertion is to be drawn from *R. v. Leforte* (1961) 29 D.L.R. (2d) 459 (B.C. C.A.) where Norris J.A. asserted the existence of such a "discretion". This decision was reversed by the Supreme Court of Canada (1962) 31 D.L.R. (2d) 1 which restored the conviction on the basis of the reasons offered by Sheppard J.A. in his dissent (Sheppard J.A. recognized the availability of such a discretion but would not have exercised it on the facts of the case). However, Kerwin C.J.C. rejected the notion and noted that the English cases rested on provisions different from s. 12 of the *Canada Evidence Act.*

75. P. K. McWilliams, *Canadian Criminal Evidence* (1974) at p. 503.

76. (1961) 131 C.C.C. 64 (Ont. C.A.).

77. *Ibid.* at p. 71. See also, M. Cadsby *supra* footnote 63 at pp. 270-272 in support of the proposition that s. 12 confers a permissive jurisdiction under which the trial judge should "set the essentials of justice above the technical rule and give the word "may" contained in s. 12 its true meaning". (Cadsby cites *Titchener* and *Leforte* in support of his views.)

78. [1965] S.C.R. 739.

appears to support McWilliams' view of the nature of the "discretion" available to control cross-examination as to previous convictions.[79] In that case one of the grounds raised on appeal was framed in this manner:

> [The learned trial judge] erred in allowing the admission, on cross-examination of the accused, of evidence of his previous conduct and criminal offences.

Although the appeal was allowed, on this issue Spence J. felt that there was "no prejudice to the accused".[80] A new trial was ordered on other grounds. The learned Justice did however address himself to the limits of judicial control over this contentious area:

> However, I am of the opinion that permission to cross-examine the accused person as to his character on the issue of the accused person's credibility is within the discretion of the trial judge and the trial judge should exercise that discretion with caution and should exclude evidence, even if it were relevant upon the credibility of the accused, *if its prejudicial effect far outweighs its probative value.*[81]

Insofar as one can rely upon simulated empirical studies in the field of law, there appears to be substantial support for the view that the introduction of previous convictions into trial verdict deliberations *significantly prejudices the accused*. V. P. Hans and A. Doob recently completed a study on "Section 12 of the Canada Evidence Act and the deliberations of Simulated Juries".[82] Their results tend to confirm the worst fears of most of the commentators:

> The present research leaves little doubt that knowledge of a previous conviction biases a case against the defendant. The likelihood that a jury will convict the defendant is significantly higher if the defendant's record is made known to the jury. The fact that the defendant has a

---

79. One wonders why the case is omitted from reference by the author in this regard. It is referred in another related context in a later chapter of the text at p. 641.

80. The comments of Spence J. in a fuller context are as follows: ". . . even if the questions put upon cross-examination by the Crown counsel were inadmissible and prejudicial the answers resulted in the only evidence being that the accused man had never been convicted or charged with a crime in which he carried or wielded a knife, and further, the accused man invited the Crown to prove otherwise, an invitation which the Crown did not deem it advisable to accept. There was, therefore, in the particular case, no prejudice to the accused" (*supra* footnote 78 at p. 749).

81. *Colpitts v. R. supra* footnote 78 at p. 749 (emphasis added). The words employed here by Spence J. are disturbing inasmuch as they purport to apply a different standard for previous convictions (and their prejudicial effect) than that which was formulated in regard to photographs (and their prejudicial effect). In *Colpitts* Spence J. speaks of the need for prejudicial effect to *"far outweigh"* probative value while in *Draper v. Jacklyn, supra* footnote 51 the decision to exclude proceeds on the basis of "the *balancing* of the probative value as against the prejudicial effect".

82. (1976) 18 Cr.L.Q. 235.

record permeates the entire discussion of the case, and appears to affect the juror's perception and interpretation of the evidence in the case.[83]

The courts are not unmindful of the unfairness occasioned by such cross-examination techniques. Consequently in jury trials the rule has grown up that the trial judge is under a duty to clearly indicate to the jury that admissions of the accused's criminal record are admissible only as going to his credit, and where the judge presides alone he must charge himself accordingly as to the limited effect of such evidence.[84]

The failure to caution a jury that evidence of previous convictions cannot be used to indicate a propensity to engage in criminal activity will not *per se* invalidate a conviction. The appeal court will only quash a coinviction and order a new trial where a substantial miscarriage of justice within the meaning of s. 613(1)(*b*)(iii) of the *Criminal Code* is demonstrable.[85]

Since evidence of previous convictions cannot be used to indicate a propensity to engage in criminal activity (save where they qualify as, and are allowed into evidence in order to demonstrate, similar acts) questions may not be put as to the detailed circumstances of the previous convictions.[86] However, it has been held, in *R. v. Boyce*,[87] a recent decision of the Ontario Court of Appeal, that the proper confines of s. 12 of the *Canada Evidence Act* are not exceeded by cross-examination as to penalties imposed following prior convictions.

With great respect to Martin J.A. (the author of this decision) such a view makes nonsense of the court's avowed concern that attacks upon credibility not be allowed to leak over into the area of attacks upon character. An accused who had been leniently dealt with previously conceivably might suffer from a jury's view that he had not been adequately dealt with in the past; while the accused who had served lengthy terms of incarceration would suffer from the not unlikely

---

83. *Ibid.* at p. 251. See also A. N. Doob and H. Kirshenbaum "Some Empirical Evidence on the Effect of s. 12 of the Canada Evidence Act Upon an Accused" (1972-73) 15 Cr.L.Q. 88.

84. See *R. v. Gaich (Gajic)* (1956) 116 C.C.C. 34 (Ont. C.A.); *R. v. Fushtor* (1946) 85 C.C.C. 283 (Sask. C.A.); *R. v. Bodnarchuk* (1949), 94 C.C.C. 279 (Ont. C.A.); *R. v. Dorland* (1948) 92 C.C.C. 274 (Ont. C.A.); *R. v. Williams* [1969] 1 O.R. 139; for the duty on a judge sitting alone see *R. v. Forrest* [1963] 2 C.C.C. 390; *R. v. Titchener supra* footnote 76; and *R. v. Tennant* (1975) 31 C.R.N.S. 1 at p. 25 somewhat dilute this "duty" by saying that proper direction by the judge in this regard is helpful to the jury, but he is not bound in every case to give such directions.

85. See *R. v. Warren* (1970) 11 C.R.N.S. 217 (Ont. C.A.).

86. See *Colpitts v. R. supra* footnote 78, *R. v. Hartridge*, [1967] 1 C.C.C. 346 (Sask. C.A.). As to proper methods of proving previous convictions see "Practice Note" (1951) 11 C.R. 72; A. E. Popple, "Annotation: A Prisoner's Record" (1949) 8 C.R. 472 at p. 473.

87. (1975) 28 C.R.N.S. 336 (Ont. C.A.).

prejudice of being regarded as a hardened criminal who belongs behind bars.[88] It is submitted that these factors are more likely to influence a jury than those to which Martin J.A. had regard:

> In the present case, two of the three convictions proved against the appellant resulted in fines. If the nature of the penalty had not been disclosed, the jury might have assumed that the convictions were more serious than they appear to have been.[89]

Since this inquiry (at least in theory) is directed only to the issue of credibility, the concerns of the jury expressed above are clearly outside of the proper province of its deliberations.

(c) *Similar facts*

The Ontario Law Reform Commission Working Paper on Evidence makes the claim that "the most frequent exercise of the discretion to exclude prejudicial evidence of little weight occurs with respect to similar fact evidence".[90] Whether it can be said *with certainty* that the decision to *actually exclude* the purportedly prejudicial evidence (as opposed to saying that the point of whether to exclude allegedly prejudicial evidence *arises* most often in regard to similar fact evidence) seems open to question.

There is little doubt that the aspect of possible prejudice will arise in almost any circumstance where an attempt to adduce similar fact evidence is made. The prejudice stems from the *very purposes* for which the evidence is sought to be tendered. In general trms that purpose may be said to be to demonstrate that due to the previous conduct or character of the accused it is likely that he committed the particular offence with which he stands charged. As a general *rule,* such evidence is not admissible, however there are circumstances "in which such evidence is so very relevant that to exclude it would be an affront to common sense";[91] and in those circumstances such evidence will be allowed.

The general rule was laid down by Lord Herschell in the Privy Council case of *Makin v. A.G. New South Wales:*[92]

> It is undoubtedly not competent for the prosecution to adduce evidence tending to show that the accused has been guilty of criminal acts other than those covered by the indictment, for the purpose of leading to the conclusion that the accused is a person likely from his criminal conduct or character to have committed the offence for which he is being tried. On the other hand, the mere fact that the evidence adduced tends to

---

88. For an illuminating contrast to Martin J.A.'s approach in *Boyce* see his special lecture delivered in (1955) L.S.U.C. Special Lectures 313 on the subject of "Character Evidence" especially at p. 322.
89. *R. v. Boyce, supra* footnote 87 at p. 358.
90. *Supra* footnote 42 at p. 18.
91. *R. v. Boardman* [1974] 3 All E.R. 887 at p. 908 *per* Lord Cross.
92. *Supra* footnote 71 at p. 65.

show the commission of other crimes does not render it inadmissible if it be relevant to an issue before the jury, and it may be so relevant if it bears on the question whether the acts alleged to constitute the crime charged in the indictment were designed or accidental, or to rebut a defence which would otherwise be open to the accused.[93]

As Lord Herschell went on to note "the statement of these general principles is easy, but it is obvious that it may often be very difficult to draw the line and to decide whether a particular piece of evidence is on one side or the other". Subsequent cases in expounding upon the general rule established that it was competent for the prosecution to give such evidence in order to show "intent, guilty knowledge, design, system or to rebut the defence of accident, mistake, or reasonable or honest motive. Or where several transactions are so connected as to form one transaction, the others may be proved in order to shew the character of the transaction impeached".[94] It has also been admitted in order to prove identity,[95] and some commentators even hold to the view that similar fact evidence may be admissible in order to prove the criminal act itself.[96]

93. Examples of Canadian cases in which the general rule set out in *Makin* has been approved of and applied are: *Koufis v. R. supra* footnote   ; *R. v. Miller* (1940) 74 C.C.C. 270 (B.C. C.A.); *R. v. Wied* (1949) 95 C.C.C. 108 (B.C. C.A.); *R. v Tilley* (1953) 106 C.C.C. 42 (Ont. C.A.); *R. v. Marshall* [1966] 4 C.C.C. 206 (B.C. C.A.); *R. v. Hartridge,* [1967] 1 C.C.C. 346 (Sask. C.A.); *R. v. Bain* [1970] 2 C.C.C. 49 (N.S. C.A.); *R. v. Pelletier* (1972) 6 C.C.C. (2d) 158 (Ont. C.A.); *R. v. Tripp* (1971) 5 C.C.C. (2d) 297 (N.B. C.A.); (all cited in McWilliams, *Canadian Criminal Evidence* (1974) at p. 181). See also *Lizotte v. R.* (1950) 99 C.C.C. 113 (Can.) at p. 125; *Paradis v. R.* (1933) 61 C.C.C. 184 (Can.); *Holmes v. R.* (1949) 7 C.R. 323 (Que. C.A.); *R. v. Cline* (1956) 115 C.C.C. 18 (Ont. C.A.); *R. v. Christakos* (1947) 87 C.C.C. 40 (Man. C.A.); *R. v. Welford* (1918) 30 C.C.C. 156 (Ont.).

94. *R. v. Ball* [1911] A.C. 47 at pp. 56-57 *per* Darling J. The case has recently been criticized because of a "gross error" by Darling J. contained in his assertion that such evidence is only admissible in order to prove *mens rea.* (See R. Cross, "Fourth Time Lucky — Similar Fact Evidence in the House of Lords" [1975] Crim.L.R. 62). See also *R. v. Bond* [1906] 2 K.B. 389; *R. v. Fisher* (1909) 3 Cr.App.R. 176; and *R. v. Boyle & Merchant* (1914) 10 Cr.App.R. 180.

95. See *Thompson v. R.* [1918] A.C. 221; *R. v. Hall* (1951) 35 Cr.App.R. 167; and *R. v. Sims* (1946) 31 Cr.App.R. 158. Note that certain Canadian authorities oppose the admission of similar fact evidence to prove identity: *Brunet v. R.* (1928) 50 C.C.C. 1 (Can.); *R. v. Campbell* (1946) 86 C.C.C. 410 (B.C. C.A.); *R. v. Hrechuk* (1950) 98 C.C.C. 44 (Man. C.A.); But see *contra R. v. Glynn* (1972) 5 C.C.C. (2d) 364 (Ont. C.A.); *R. v. Naum* (1973) 22 C.R.N.S. 193 (Ont.) and *R. v. Bird* (1970) 9 C.R.N.S. 1 (B.C. C.A.).

96. See Glanville Williams, *Proof of Guilt* (2nd ed.) at pp. 229-230; and P. K. McWilliams, *Canadian Criminal Evidence* (1974) at pp. 203-205. For the opposite view see C. C. Savage, "Corroboration and Similar Facts" (1963-64) 6 Cr.L.Q. 431 at pp. 452-454. And see also *R. v. Arato* (1973) 9 C.C.C. (2d) 243 (Ont. C.A.); and dissent of Rivard J.A. in *Leblanc v. R.* (1972) 19 C.R.N.S. 54 (Que. C.A.).

Lord Herschell's statement in *Makin,* that evidence of similar acts is admissible "to rebut a defence otherwise open to an accused" was qualified by Lord Sumner in *Thompson v. R.*:

> Before an issue can be said to be raised, which would permit the introduction of such evidence so obviously prejudicial to the accused, it must have been raised in substance if not in so many words, and the issue so raised must be one to which the prejudicial evidence is relevant. *The mere theory that a plea of not guilty puts everything in issue is not enough for this purpose. The prosecution cannot credit the accused with fancy defences in order to rebut them at the outset with some damning piece of prejudice.*[97]

This statement in its turn was subjected to qualification (or at least, to greater clarification) by Viscount Simon in *Harris v. D.P.P.*:[98]

> What Lord Sumner meant in *Thompson v. R.* when he denied the right of the prosecution "to credit the accused with fancy defences" was that evidence of similar facts involving the accused ought not to be drafted into his prejudice without reasonable cause.

Earlier Viscount Simon had made reference to Lord DuParcq's judgment in *Noor Mohamed v. R.* [99] in order to clarify when such evidence is properly adducible:

> "An accused need set up no defence other than a general denial of the crime alleged. The plea of Not Guilty, may be equivalent to saying: 'Let the prosecution prove its case if it can, and having said so much, the accused may take refuge in silence. In such a case it may appear (for instance) that the facts and circumstances of the particular offence charged are consistent with innocent intention, whereas further evidence, which incidentally shows that the accused has committed one or more other offences, may tend to prove that they are consistent only with a guilty intent. The prosecution could not be said, in their Lordships' opinion, to be 'crediting the ascused with a fancy defence' if they sought to adduce such evidence."[100]

In essence, the judgment in *Harris* stands for the proposition that the prosecution may adduce all proper evidence which tends to prove the charge. In addition, the prosecution need not, in all circumstances, withhold evidence of similar facts until after the accused has set up a specific defence which calls for a rebuttal.[101] Importantly, behind the rules laid down in *Makin, Thompson* and *Harris* is the *"rule of judicial practice* followed by a judge who is trying a charge of crime

---

97. *Supra* footnote 95 at p. 232 (emphasis added).
98. [1952] 1 All E.R. 1044 at p. 1048.
99. *Supra* footnote 52.
100. *Harris v. D.P.P. supra* footnote 98 at p. 1047.
101. *Ibid.* at pp. 1047-1048. See also *R. v. Thompson* [1954] O.W.N. 156 and *R. v. Campbell* (1946) 2 C.R. 351 (B.C. C.A.) for Canadian cases dealing with when such evidence may be adduced in chief and when it should be saved for rebuttal.

when he thinks that the application of the practice is called for";[102] *i.e.* the rule referred to by Lord DuParcq in *Noor Mohamed*:

> in all such cases the judge ought to consider whether the evidence which it is proposed to adduce is sufficiently substantial, having regard to the purpose to which it is professedly directed, to make it desirable in the interest of justice that it should be admitted. If, so far as that purpose is concerned, it can in the circumstances have only trifling weight, the judge will be right to exclude it. To say this is not to confuse weight with admissibility. The distinction is plain, but cases must occur in which it would be unjust to admit evidence of a character gravely prejudicial to the accused even though there may be some tenuous ground for holding it technically admissible. The decision must then be left to the discretion and sense of fairness of the judge.[103]

The troubling feature of the rule respecting similar fact evidence is that although it is expressed as an exclusionary rule ("it is undoubtedly not competent for the prosecution to adduce evidence tending to show . . ") the number of circumstances in which it may be called in aid are in reality quite vast (*e.g.* to prove intent, to show system, to show design or malice, to rebut defences of innocent or lawful purpose, or accident or mistake, to prove identify, and possibly, to prove the *actus reus* itself). Where such evidence is admissible the risk of real prejudice to the accused is not denied but rather it is deemed to be of less importance than the relevance and probative value which it possesses.[104]

Professor J. C. Smith commenting on the case of *R. v. Hurren*[105] discussed the complexity of the judicial consideration of whether such evidence ought to be excluded:

> Whether evidence of similar facts is admissible or not depends upon its cogency. Evidence that the accused has committed crimes of the same general type before has some probative value, but it will generally

---

102. *Supra* footnote 98 at p. 1048 (emphasis added).
103. *Supra* footnote 52 at p. 192.
104. "The cases do not go so far as to say that one "starts with the general proposition [even in similar fact situations] that all evidence which is logically probative is admissible unless excluded". This view was described as "plainly sensible" by Lord Goddard (L.C.J.) in *R. v. Sims supra* footnote 46, for "then evidence of this kind does not have to seek a justification but is admissible irrespective of the issues raised by the defence . . .". This view was not approved of by the Privy Council in *Noor Mohamed supra* footnote 52 and Lord Goddard in *R. v. Hall* [1952] 1 All E.R. 66 acceded to the view held in *Noor Mohamed*. However Cowen and Carter in "Similar Facts: A Re-Examination" (contained in their text *Essays on the Law of Evidence* (1956) p. 106 at p. 158) claim that the matter was not resolved by Lord Goddard's recanting in *R. v. Hall* since in *Harris v. D.P.P.* Lord Simon once again appears to express the positive rule when he suggests that "the substance of the matter appears to me to be that the prosecution may adduce all proper evidence which tends to prove the charge". Query: what is "proper" evidence? *Cf. R. v. Wray* [1970] 4 C.C.C. 1 (Can.).
105. [1962] Crim. L.R. 770.

be inadmissible because its slight relevance is greatly outweighed by its prejudicial effect. The probative value of the evidence may, however, be greatly increased if it can be proved that there is a degree of similarity in circumstances and proximity in time and place, etc.[106] Obviously there are a great many factors which can contribute to the probative value of evidence, and it would be wrong to have a rigid rule as to the interval which must have elapsed between the alleged similar facts and the crime charged. This is only one among many factors which contribute to the weight of the evidence.

It should be noted that judges commonly distinguish facts as going to weight rather than admissibility (see *e.g. R. v. Wyatt*); but it is submitted that, as regards similar fact evidence, no sharp line can be drawn and that admissibility depends on weight.[107]

The reason for the rule excluding similar fact evidence is not that the law regards such evidence as inherently irrelevant, but because it is believed that if it were generally admitted jurors would in many cases think it to be more relevant than it truly was. In such cases its prejudicial effect would clearly outweigh its probative value.[108] "Circumstances, however, may arise in which such evidence is so very relevant that to exclude it would be an affront to common sense".[109]

In those instances in which the evidence is deemed to be admissible great care must be exercised by the trial judge in instructing a jury as to the legal effect of such evidence. In a recent decision of the Ontario Court of Appeal, Gale C.J.O. cited the following charge as one exemplifying the great care in explanation which is necessary in such circumstances in order that the jury might properly appreciate the limited use to which such evidence might be put:

> For very good reasons of justice and fairness a man should not be charged with a particular offence and be called upon to answer to allegations of previous misconduct. However, there are some exceptions to the general rule excluding that type of evidence in its entirety, and the exceptions — there is only one with which we are concerned here — but it does not mean that in this case you can use any such evidence for concluding that he was a bad man or likely to commit such an offence — that general rule stands — but it is admitted as

---

106. See, *R. v. Benwell* (1973) 9 C.C.C. (2d) 158 (Ont. C.A.) at p. 168 where evidence of similar facts in relation to an off-track betting operation was allowed because it was "quite clear that the required nexus of time, circumstances and similarity or relation to the offences charged fully emerged" *per* Aylesworth J.A. See also *R. v. Kozak* (1975) 30 C.R.N.S. 7 at p. 14 where the necessary nexus between an earlier break-in attempt and a charge of possession of burglar tools was not established and evidence wrongly received at trial resulted in the ordering of new trial and the quashing of convictions by the Ontario Court of Appeal. And see, *R. v. Bain* (1965-69) 8 C.R.N.S. 99 (N.S. C.A.).
107. J. C. Smith, reproduced in C. C. Savage "Corroboration and Similar Facts", *supra* footnote 96 at pp. 432-433.
108. *D.P.P. v. Kilbourne* [1973] A.C. 729 at p. 756 *per* Lord Simon.
109. *R. v. Boardman, supra* footnote 91 *per* Lord Cross.

evidence which tends to show that he has what would be regarded as an abnormal propensity in a certain direction and for the assistance that that may give in determining the identity of the party — of the person — who did the killing in this action.[110]

If one can approach these words with fresh eyes and open ears (as one hopes a juror would) it is submitted that the "great care" taken in expression is more confusing than helpful and that such a charge can hardly be expected to dispel the prejudice visited by similar fact evidence of previous homosexual practices (as was the case in *Glynn*).

This analysis, of course, is not very useful in situations where it would be an "affront to common sense" to exclude the similar fact evidence. Other guidelines seem necessary in addition to the vague search for "prejudice". These guidelines do exist but the bulk of thinking on the subject has not been particularly systematic or coherent. As C. C. Savage points out in what is perhaps the best Canadian discussion of the subject "there does indeed appear to be confusion of thought on the subject".[111] One realizes that such concepts as "relevancy", "cogency", "nexus", "prejudice", "probative value" all have some contribution to make to a general understanding of the problem but these formulations fall short of logical and systematic analysis. Part of the problem appears to be the dearth of compelling Canadian precedents in this area. By and large our courts have been content to pay lip service to the English rules propounded in *Makin, Thompson, Noor Mohamed* and *Harris* without contributing substantially to the scholarship on the subject.

Without making any extravagant claims for what follows it is submitted that the following formulation (which is synthetic and not original) corresponds to accepted norms of fundamental fairness (along the lines suggested in *Noor Mohamed*) without doing violence to the contributions of *Makin, Thompson* and *Harris*:

(1) *Prima Facie* all similar fact evidence is inadmissible;

(2) If the evidence of similar facts sought to be tendered is relevant to an issue before the jury it *may be* admissible;

(3) If the evidence of similar facts is necessary to rebut a defence patently open to the accused or raised by the accused it *may be* admissible;

(4) Whether the similar fact evidence is *in fact* admissible will depend *in part* upon factors such as degree of similarity of circumstances, proximity in time and place, etc.

(5) Regardless of the factors mentioned in number 4 *supra,* similar

---

110. *R. v. Glynn, supra* footnote 95 at p. 365. For other cases indicating the need for care in the direction to the jury, on similar fact evidence see *R. v. Arato, supra* footnote 96 and *R. v. Kozak, supra* footnote 106.

111. *Supra* footnote 96 at p. 431.

fact evidence will not be admissible if the issue on which the evidence is purportedly offered is not a *real* issue in the case;

(6) Similar fact evidence will not be admissible where it may be shown to be unnecessary due to the existence of alternative non-prejudicial evidence on the particular issue;

(7) Similar fact evidence even where relevant will not be admissible where the prejudicial effect of the evidence outweighs the probative value of the evidence on the particular issue.[112]

This formulation of course treats the issue as one based upon a broad rule of exclusion with a limited number of exceptions. As such it proceeds upon the assumption that Lord Goddard's second proposition in *Sims* was in error (he accepted that it was erroneous in *Hall*) and seeks a modern Canadian affirmation of this view.[113] It also ignores the approach of some writers and judges who have attempted to break down problems involving similar fact evidence into categories of admissible relevance.[114] While useful for descriptive purposes to indicate the realm of *occasions* when such evidence might be tendered, the scheme does not really add anything of value in terms of rationalizing the decision-making process. As Julius Stone has indicated:

> The English courts had no difficulty [with the exclusionary rules as to similar fact evidence] in the first half of the nineteenth century. Their more recent difficulties have been because judges and writers have attempted to make categories of admissible relevance, and have tested evidence of similar facts by seeking to determine whether they fitted into some one of the categories.[115]

Stone's observations on the dangers of similar fact evidence in criminal cases merit quotation at some length, and they provide an appropriate note on which to close off this consideration of the problem:

> to admit what has been called a "piece of damning prejudice merely because it is relevant to some subsidiary issue which happens to require

---

112. Numbers 5, 6 and 7 are a formulation suggested by F. St. M. B. Newark, "The Judicial Discretion to Exclude Similar Fact Evidence" (1967) 6 West. L.R. 1 at p. 5.

113. See the discussion of this proposition *supra* at footnote 94. See also E. Williams, "Evidence of Other Offences" (1923) 39 L.Q.R. 212 and "Evidence to Show Intent" (1907) 23 L.Q.R. 28.

114. McWilliams adopts such a system in his chapter on "Similar Fact Evidence" (#11) in *Canadian Criminal Evidence* (1974) at p. 180. See subheading "C" of his outline: "Purposes for which Evidence Admissible" where he lists seven such categories.

115. J. Stone, "The Rule of Exclusion of Similar Fact Evidence: England" (1932-1933) 46 Harv.L.R. 954 at p. 976. Note that, writing in 1932 (before *Sims, Noor Mohamed,* and *Hall*) Stone summed up the rule of exclusion as it existed in England at that time in this fashion: "Evidence which is relevant merely as showing that a person has a propensity to do acts of a certain kind is not admissible to prove that he did any such acts."

proof in the facts of the particular case, is to play into the hands of over-zealous and under-scrupulous prosecuting officers. Defendants must be protected against conviction upon inadequate testimony, but at the same time the jury must not be deprived of testimony which is both necessary and sufficient to establish the guilt of the accused.

There is a human paradox here which logical formulation cannot resolve. In a trial for an unpleasant crime, evidence must be excluded which indicates that the prisoner is more likely than most men to have committed it, but evidence must be admitted which tends to show that no man but the prisoner, who is known to have done these things before, could have committed it. There is a point in the ascending scale of probability when it is so near to certainty that it is absurd to shy at the admission of the prejudicial evidence.

Where that point must be fixed cannot be stated in general terms. It varies with the nature of each class of offense, with the crimes within each class, and with the peculiar facts of each case — the strength of the independent evidence, the specific weakness which the similar fact evidence is admitted to remedy, the strength of the similar fact evidence itself. This wide divergence explains the failure of all attempts to create categories of admissibility. Mitigation of the evil must be sought in other directions.[116]

(2) Evidence obtained by illegal means[117]

Speaking of evidence illegally obtained Martland J. (on behalf of the majority in *R. v. Wray*) observed that "the allowance of admissible evidence relevant to the issue before the Court and of substantial probative value may operate *unfortunately* for the accused, but not *unfairly*".[118] To this extent his judgment does reveal the historical judicial concern that "all that is just and fair be done between the prosecutor and the accused". The learned Justice concludes his remarks in this regard with the narrow statement of what is now regarded as the Canadian rule on illegally obtained evidence:

> It is only the admission of evidence gravely prejudicial to the accused, the admissibility of which is tenuous, and whose probative force in relation to the main issue before the Court is trifling, which can be said to operate unfairly.[119]

"Unfairness" to the accused may take more than one form, and *Wray* rests upon a distinction between "unfairness" in the method of obtaining evidence and "unfairness" in the actual trial of the accused by reason of its admission.[120] Exclusion of evidence purely on the basis of "unfairness" in the method of obtaining it "has nothing whatever to do with the duty of a trial Judge to secure a fair trial

---

116. *Ibid.* at pp. 983-984.
117. In this regard see also the discussion *supra* Part 3 Chapter 2.
118. *R. v. Wray* [1970] 4 C.C.C. 1 at p. 17 (emphasis added).
119. *Ibid.* at p. 1.
120. *Ibid.* at p. 18.

for the accused".[121] Martland J. is, of course, quite correct in this assertion.

However, a rule of law need not be framed from quite so blinkered a perspective. A court of law has other interests to protect—social interests, such as respect for the administration of justice. The protection of society does not rest soley on the platform of efficient law enforcement. Equally important is public trust in public officials, not the least of whom are our law enforcement officials. Official lawlessness must be combatted and deterred just as lawlessness among the general public must be. It is therefore not unrealistic to expect the common law to "seek to balance the competing interests by weighing the social interest in the particular case against the gravity or character of the invasion, leaving it to the discretion of the trial judge whether the balance should be struck in favour of reception or exclusion of particular evidence".[122]

Nevertheless, at least for the present we must live with the rule in *Wray* and thus, before evidence illegally obtained may be excluded it must be shown to be:

(1) gravely prejudicial;
(2) of tenuous admissibility; and
(3) of trifling probative force.

Given the enunciation of the rule in *Wray* it is important to ascertain the limits of its application. In other words, must the rule hold sway over the entire field of evidence? The answer to this question is not entirely without controversy. At least this much may be said without fear of contradiction: different standards from the one laid down in *Wray* have been applied to admissibility considerations of other kinds of evidence.

It will be seen to be useful to contrast some of the various formulations which have been devised by our highest Court.

In *Wray* (illegally obtained evidence) Martland J. pronounced this rule:

> It is only the allowance of evidence gravely prejudicial to the accused, the admissibility of which is tenuous, and whose probative force in relation to the main issue before the Court is trifling, which can be said to operate unfairly.[123]

---

121. *Ibid.* at p. 19.
122. *R. v. Hogan* (1974) 18 C.C.C. (2d) 65 (Can.) *per* Laskin J. See also, Law Reform Commission of Canada "Evidence: 10. The Exclusion of Illegally Obtained Evidence" (Study Paper, 1974) especially at p. 29, and Law Reform Commission of Canada *Report on Evidence* (1976) at p. 22 s. 15(1) and (2). One commentator who seems quite content with the rule in *Wray* is M. S. Weinberg, "The Judicial Discretion to Exclude Relevant Evidence" (1975) 21 McGill L.J. 1 at p. 41.
123. *Supra* footnote 118 at p. 17. It is perhaps a trifle misleading to say that *Wray* was a case dealing with illegally obtained evidence. In reality the case focussed on two issues: (1) when a confession has been found to be invol-

In *Colpitts* (previous convictions and character) Spence J. employed a test both similar to, but *different from, Wray*:

> I am of the opinion that permission to cross-examine the accused person as to his character on the issue of the accused person's credibility is within the discretion of the trial judge and the trial judge should exercise that discretion with caution and should exclude evidence even if it were relevant upon the credibility of the accused, if its prejudicial effect far outweighs its probative value.[124]

In *Draper v. Jacklyn*[125] (inflammatory photographs) Spence J. (again for the majority) propounded this rule:

> The occasions are frequent upon which a judge trying a case with the assistance of a jury is called upon to determine whether or not a piece of evidence technically admissible may be so prejudicial to the opposite side that any probative value is overcome by the possible prejudice and that therefore he should exclude the production of the particular piece of evidence . . . The matter is always one which is difficult for the trial judge and in itself essentially a decision in which the trial judge must exercise his own carefully considered personal discretion.[126]

Using Martland J.'s threefold test (1) grave prejudice (2) tenuous admissibility and (3) trifling probative force it can readily be seen that the test in *Colpitts* is purely directed to prejudice with the quantitative measure being that prejudicial effect must *far* outweigh probative force. In *Draper* the standard is once again purely prejudice, but rather than requiring prejudicial effect to far outweigh probative force the standard employed seeks to reflect "the *balancing* of the probative value as against the prejudicial effect".

It is difficult to delineate exactly how these three tests relate to one another, but it is certain that the Supreme Court will have to address itself to the problems which they import in some future case. It is inevitable that the overlap in principles will indeed surface in a

---

untary and therefore inadmissible, can such of the confession as is found to be true by the subsequent discovery of real evidence be admitted?; and (2) can a judge refuse to admit evidence of substantial weight and relevance solely on the ground that the admission would be unfair or unjust to the accused or calculated to bring the administration of justice into disrepute? For commentary on the decision see B. McDonald, "Comments on *R. v. Wray* (1971) 29 U.T.F.L.R. 99; D. W. Roberts, "The Legacy of *Regina v. Wray*" (1972) 50 Can.Bar.Rev. 19; and A. F. Sheppard, "Restricting the Discretion to Exclude Admissible Evidence: An Examination of *Regina v. Wray*" (1971-72) 14 Cr. L.Q. 334.

124. *Supra* footnote 78 at p. 749.

125. *Supra* footnote 51 at pp. 96-97.

126. *N.B.* that Spence J. indicates that this test essentially reflects "the balancing of the probative value as against the prejudicial effect", *ibid.* at p. 101. See also Sopinka and Lederman, *The Law of Evidence in Civil Cases* (1974) at pp. 351-354; for a discussion of *Draper v. Jacklyn* and *R. v. Wray*; also A. F. Sheppard, *supra* footnote 123 at pp. 342-344.

situation where relevant evidence of highly prejudicial character[127] has been illegally and unfairly obtained.

It has been contended that *R. v. Wray* is, and will remain, an authoritative pronouncement on the Canadian law of "exclusionary discretions" because of its fidelity to precedent and its emphasis upon the "singular importance of the truth inquiry to the exclusion of policy considerations" and that therefore the "decision is a classic example of *stare decisis.*[128] If the claim for authority of the case does indeed stem from the contention that its result flowed inexorably from a close reading of, and adherence to, previously decided cases it is then submitted that its claim for such authority is insubstantial, and that therefore it is vulnerable to attack; and if only for this reason it is susceptible (in theory) to a future reconsideration by the Supreme Court.

The decisions of the Supreme Court in *Draper, Colpitts* and other related cases[129] were not considered and/or distinguished by either Martland J. or Judson J. in their majority judgments in *Wray*. To that extent, as an example of fidelity to the principle of *stare decisis,* the case is deficient. It is in fact a curious exercise inasmuch as the labours of the majority Justices are aimed at distinguishing and revealing errors in reasoning in the leading English decisions without directing similar attention to the highest *related* Canadian authorities.

Before proceeding further it would be useful to outline in some detail the substance of Martland J.'s judgment in *R. v. Wray*. In the course of delivering judgment in the case the following observations were made:

(1) There is no judicial authority in Canada or England to support the proposition that a trial judge has a discretion to exclude admissible evidence which, he believes, would by its admission bring the administration of justice into disrepute.

---

127. "Prejudicial character" is here used to mean something more than "prejudice, because the evidence is indicative of guilt".

128. See R. C. Gibson, "Illegally Obtained Evidence" (1973) 31 U.T.F.L.R. 23 at p. 34.

129. See *e.g. Finestone v. R.* [1953] 2 S.C.R. 107 at p. 109 where Rand J. spoke of a general exclusionary discretion (one not requiring prejudicial effect): ". . . . since the court retains a discretion in admitting the document, any special circumstances tending to qualify the dependability of the entry would be subjected to judicial scrutiny" [A. F. Sheppard, *supra* footnote 123 at p. 339 argues that this dictum is consistent with *Wray*]. A. F. Sheppard also notes at p. 341 that the *Wray* case casts doubt upon a leading case on confessions *Boudreau v. R.* (1949) 94 C.C.C. 1 (Can.) for Rand, Kellock and Locke JJ., in the two leading majority judgments "premised their reasons on the existence of a judicial discretion to exclude the statements of an accused person who had been improperly cautioned". *Boudreau* and *Finestone* are concerned with other admissibility situations in which the trial judge is said to have a discretion. The operative factor in these two cases would appear to be "unreliability" — a factor which operates so as to undercut probative value.

(2) The test of admissibility of evidence is as stated by Lord Goddard C.J. in *Kuruma v. R.* [1955] A.C. 197 at p. 203:

the test to be applied in determining whether evidence is admissible is whether it is relevant to the matters in issue. If it is, it is admissible and the court is not concerned with how the evidence was obtained.

(Lord Goddard then spoke of a discretion to disallow evidence if the strict rules of admissibility would operate unfairly against an accused.)

(3) The discretion to which Lord Goddard refers is supported by reference to the Privy Council decision in *Noor Mohamed v. R.* [1949] A.C. 182, and the House of Lords decision *Harris v. D.P.P.* [1952] A.C. 694. (Lord DuParcq's famous dictum in *Noor Mohamed* in turn stems from the judgment of Lord Sumner in *Thompson v. R.* [1918] A.C. 221.)

(4) The discretion in *Noor Mohamed* spoke in terms of evidence "sufficiently substantial" having regard to the "purpose to which it is directed". If that "purpose" has only "trifling weight" the judge is right to exclude it, for it is unjust to admit evidence of "gravely prejudicial character" though there may be some "tenuous ground" for holding it "technically admissible". The *Harris* decision underscored the need to "set the essentials of justice above the technical rule" if the rule operates unfairly against the accused". Viscount Simon in *Harris* spoke of the well established "judicial practice" of the trial judge (in his discretion) intimating to the prosecutor not to press evidence upon the court where its "probable effect would be out of proportion to its true evidential character".

(5) Some significance is attached to the fact that the words "operate unfairly against the accused" are employed both by Lord Simon in *Harris* (in reference to similar fact evidence) and by Lord Goddard in *Kuruma* (vis-à-vis illegally obtained evidence).

(6) *Callis v. Gunn* [1964] 1 Q.B. 495, *R. v. Court* [1962] Crim. L.R. 697, and *R. v. Payne* [1963] 1 W.L.R. 637 are three cases where Lord Parker C.J. expounded upon the phrase "operate unfairly against the accused". In *Callis v. Gunn* he said at p. 501:

in considering whether admissibility would operate unfairly against a defendant one would certainly consider whether it had been obtained in an oppressive manner by force or against the wishes of an accused person. That is the general principle."

R. v. Murphy [1965] N.I. 138, and *King v. R.* [1968] 2 All E.R. 610 are two cases where the exclusionary discretion was recognized by not being acted upon.

(7) In *Rumping v. D.P.P.* 46 Cr.App.R. 398 at p. 403, Ashworth J. stated his proposition:

There is of course ample authority for the proposition that a judge has an over-riding discretion to exclude evidence even if such evidence is in law admissible."

(8) The *ratio decidendi* of *Wray* is this:

    (i) The dictum of Lord Goddard in *Kuruma* appears to be founded exclusively on *Noor Mohamed*

    (ii) This dictum is in fact a narrow one which has been unduly extended in subsequent cases

    (iii) The discretion recognized provides for disallowing evidence if the strict rules of admissibility would operate unfairly against the accused

    (iv) Even if one accepts the validity of (iii) the discretion in question only arises if the admission of evidence would operate unfairly against the accused

    (v) The allowance of admissible evidence relevant to the issue before the Court and of substantial probative value may operate unfortunately for the accused but not unfairly

    (vi) It is only the admission of evidence gravely prejudicial to the accused, the admissibility of which is tenuous, and whose probative force in relation to the main issue before the Court is trifling which can be said to operate unfairly.

(9) Lord Goddard intended that the exclusionary discretion rule be thus limited. His actions in *Kuruma* in not exercising the discretion are only understandable from this perspective.

(10) Subsequent cases such as *Court* and *Payne* demonstrate a confusion between "unfairness" in the method of obtaining evidence, and "unfairness" in the actual trial of the accused by reason of its admission.

(11) The recognition of a discretion to exclude admissible evidence, beyond the limited scope recognized in the *Noor Mohamed* case, is not warranted by authority, and would be undesirable. The standard of "fairness" required would be difficult, if not impossible, to ascertain and apply if the broader view were adopted.

The judgment in *Wray* is subject to criticism initially because it fails to properly comprehend the nature of the development of the common law on this subject. The exclusionary "discretion" attributed to Lord DuParcq in *Noor Mohamed* did not simply present itself in full flower in 1949. It is impossible to read the House of Lords and Privy Council decisions in the area without an awareness of the importance of the cross-pollinating effects of the rules laid down in cases from Scotland and Ireland. Indeed such cases as *Rattray v. Rattray*,[130] *Lawrie v. Muir*,[131] *Fairley v. Fishmongers of London*,[132] and *R. v.*

---

130. (1897) 25 R. (Ct. of Sess.) 315, 35 Sc.L.R. 294.
131. 1950 S.C. (J.) 19.
132. 1951 S.C. (J.) 14.

Murphy[133] are cited and discussed in such cases as *Kuruma* and *King v. R,* cases which figured prominently in the judgment of Martland J.

> This matter has been discussed in a number of Scottish cases which were reviewed in the *Kuruma* case. It should be prefaced that, in the Scottish cases to which reference will be made, the court is directing its mind to the admissibility of evidence, and in this connexion to a discretion to be exercised whether or not to admit evidence in cases where it could be said to be unfair to the accused to do so.
>
> In the English cases, the evidence under consideration is admissible in law (whether illegally obtained or not) and the exercise of discretion is called for in order to decide whether, even though admissible, it should be excluded in fairness to the accused. *The same end is reached in both jurisdictions though by a slightly different route.*[134]

It is clearly erroneous to trace the development of the exclusionary discretion to 1949 and *Noor Mohamed.* The *Rattray* case occurred considerably before *Noor Mohamed,* prior even, to the turn of the century. Also, it would be incorrect to represent the development of such a "discretion" as occurring exclusively within the iconoclastic outer reaches (Scotland and Ireland) of the English jurisdiction. To do so would be to ignore the important pronouncements contained in *D.P.P. v. Christie;*[135] a decision to which the *Harris* case is referable.[136] The judgment of Lord Moulton delivered in 1914 offers a partial description of the evolution of the "discretion" from a custom to a judicial practice, and (almost) to a rule of procedure:

> The law is so much on its guard against the accused being prejudiced by evidence which, though admissible, would probably have a prejudicial influence on the minds of the jury, which would be out of proportion to its true evidential value, that there has grown up a practice of a very salutary nature, under which the judge intimates to the counsel for the prosecution that he should not press for the admission of evidence which would be open to this objection; and such an intimation from the tribunal trying the case is usually sufficient to prevent the evidence being pressed in all cases where the scruples of the tribunal in this respect are reasonable. Under the influence of *this practice, which is based on an anxiety to secure for everyone a fair trial,* there has grown up a custom of not admitting certain kinds of evidence which is so constantly followed that it almost amounts to a rule of procedure.[137]

From these remarks Viscount Simon in *Harris* derives the "duty of the judge when trying a charge of crime to set the essentials of justice

---

133. [1965] N.I. 138.
134. *King v. R.* [1968] 2 All E.R. 610 at p. 614 *per* Lord Hodson (emphasis added).
135. (1914) 10 Cr.App.R. 141.
136. See *Harris v. D.P.P.* (1952) 36 Cr.App.R. 39 at p. 55.
137. *D.P.P. v. Christie, supra* footnote 135 at p. 160 (emphasis added).

above the technical rule if the strict application of the latter would operate unfairly against the accused".[138]

In summary, the English cases of recent vintage (*Noor Mohamed* and *Harris*) to which the *expression* of discretion is traced by Martland J. in *Wray*, are cases correctly perceived as involving similar fact evidence. However, undoubtedly the origin of the principle (discretion) is more ancient, not arising *ex improvisu* in *Noor Mohamed;* but rather the expression of the rule in *Noor Mohamed* and *Harris* involves a recognition of a long established "judicial practice" (one presumably acquiesced in by prosecutors responding to the court's discretionary promptings). At the root the matter may be seen to arise (as does nearly the whole of English criminal law and procedure) from the inherent jurisdiction of the court to see that what is right and just is done between prosecutors and the accused.

Set against this backdrop the jump is not extreme from a rule adequately accommodating similar fact evidence to one also encompassing illegally obtained evidence. The development of the English law in this respect may accurately be described as incremental. Throughout, the sum and substance of the rule has remained the same, with the linking feature validating its extension being a fidelity to the underlying philosophy which gave rise in the first place to the custom, and latterly to the development of the rule. Thus it was appropriate for Lord Parker to begin with Lord Goddard's words in *Kuruma v. The Queen* and achieve the result which he did in *Callis v. Gunn:*

> I take the general law to be as stated by Lord Goddard C.J. in *Kuruma v. The Queen* . . . [where] giving the opinion of the Board [he] said: "In their Lordships' opinion the test to be applied in considering whether evidence is admissible is whether it is relevant to the matters in issue. If it is, it is admissible and the court is not concerned with how the evidence was obtained. While this proposition may not have been stated in so many words in any English case there are decisions which support it and, in their Lordship's opinion it is plainly right in principle." That is dealing with admissibility in law, and as Lord Goddard C.J. points out, and indeed as is well known, in every criminal case a judge has a discretion to disallow evidence even if in law relevant and therefore admissible, if admissibility would operate unfairly against a defendant. I would add that in considering whether admissibility would operate unfairly against a defendant one would certainly consider whether it had been obtained in an oppressive manner by force or against the wishes of an accused person. That is the general principle.[139]

What is reflected in these comments then, is *not* (as Martland J. contends in *Wray*) a "confusion" between "unfairness" in the method of obtaining evidence, and "unfairness" in the actual trial of the ac-

---

138. *Harris v. D.P.P., supra* footnote 136 at pp. 54-55.
139. *Callis v. Gunn* [1964] 1 Q.B. 495 at pp. 500-501.

cused by reason of its admission, but rather a coherent, unified approach reflecting a concern for the integrity of the entire process.

It is true that the existence of a "broad discretion" in this regard gives rise to difficulties in "achieving any sort of uniformity in the application of the law".[140] However, in these difficult areas of law it is wrong to seek out rules which mechanically prescribe results. More important in these instances are the policies and social purposes which are refracted into the settled principles of the system. Flexibility and proper individualization must not be sacrificed at the altar of complete predictability. As Lord MacDermott said in *R. v. Murphy*:

> Unfairness in this context cannot be closely defined. But it must be judged in the light of all the material facts and findings and all the surrounding circumstances. The position of the accused, the nature of the investigation, and the gravity or otherwise of the suspected offence, may all be relevant. That is not to say that the standard of fairness must bear some sort of inverse proportion to the extent to which the public interest may be involved, but different offences may pose different problems for the police and justify different methods.[141]

Or, as Laskin J. phrased a similar sentiment in *R. v. Hogan*:

> Short of legislative direction, it might have been expected that the common law would seek to balance the competing interests by weighing the social interest in the particular case against the gravity or character of the invasion, leaving it to the discretion of the trial Judge whether the balance should be struck in favour of the reception or exclusion of particular evidence.[142]

The decision in *R. v. Wray* may be criticized for its lack of a unified vision. In the process of attacking the "undue extension" of English exclusionary practices the rules previously formulated in this country to deal with similar fact, character, and prejudicial photographic evidence, were ignored. In the result the Canadian picture is distorted and uncertain—the very opposite result from the one sought: namely, the statement of a narrow rule of general application. Inasmuch as previously existing rules of equal authority in related areas were ignored the claim for general application of the rule in *Wray* cannot be sustained.

Since different standards appear to exist with regard to different types of evidence the claim that the rule in *Wray* holds sway at least over all illegally obtained evidence must also be regarded with some doubt. (Query: what is the test to be applied to illegally obtained inflammatory photographic evidence?)

The claim that there is no judicial authority in England to support the proposition that a trial judge has a discretion to exclude admissible

140. *Per* Martland J. in *R. v. Wray supra* footnote 118 at p. 19.
141. *Supra* footnote 133 at p. 149.
142. (1974) 18 C.C.C. (2d) 65 at p. 80 (Can.).

evidence because its admission would be calculated to bring the administration of justice into disrepute is in error.[143] The claim that there is no similar authority in *this* country does not square the Canadian practice and utilisation of the legacy of the common law with the provisions of s. 7 of the Criminal Code, and with the repeated assertion by Superior Courts of the concept of "inherent jurisdiction"—which jurisdiction allows these courts to safeguard their processes against abuse, and the administration of justice against the spectre of a possible fall into disrepute.[144]

From the point of view of desirable public policy it is submitted that Canadian Courts in re-fashioning a consistent and coherent approach to the problem of illegally obtained evidence should employ the perspective suggested by Lord Cooper in *Lawrie v. Muir* as a suitable jumping off point:[145]

> From the standpoint of principle it seems to me that the law must strive to reconcile two highly important interests which are liable to come in conflict — (a) the interest of the citizen to be protected from illegal or irregular invasions of his liberties by the authorities, and (b) the interest of the State to secure that evidence bearing upon the commission of crime and necessary to enable justice to be done shall not be withheld from courts often on any merely formal or technical ground. *Neither of these objects can be insisted upon to the uttermost.* The protection of the citizen is primarily protection for the innocent citizen against unwarranted, wrongful and perhaps high handed interference, and the common sanction is an action of damages. The protection is not intended as a protection for the guilty citizen against the efforts of the public prosecutor to vindicate the law. On the other hand, the interest of the State cannot be magnified to the point of causing all the safeguards for the protection of the citizen to vanish, and of offering a positive inducement to the authorities to proceed by irregular methods.

(3) Unreliable evidence

The proposition that an individual accused of crime should be convicted only on the basis of evidence possessed of a high degree of trustworthiness, invites no quarrel. Such a pronouncement is consistent with the basic demand which we place upon our criminal justice sys-

---

143. See *Ibrahim v. R.* [1914] A.C. 599 at p. 611 where Lord Sumner discourses on the rationale behind the exclusion of involuntary or induced statements: "It is not that the law presumes such statements to be untrue, but from the danger of receiving such evidence judges have thought it better to reject it *for the due administration of justice*" (emphasis added).
See also S. Freedman, (Freedman C.J.M. of the Manitoba Court of Appeal) "Admissions and Confessions" in Salhany and Carter, *Studies in Canadian Criminal Evidence* (1972) 95 at pp. 105-107 under the internal title "3. The Due Administration of Justice".
144. See the discussion of "The inherent jurisdiction of the Court" *infra* in the Chapter entitled "Abuse of Process".
145. *Supra* footnote 131 at pp. 26-27 (emphasis added).

tem: only those individuals whose complicity in crime may be demonstrated with reference to a standard of proof beyond all reasonable doubt may be adjudged to be guilty as charged.

Although a criminal trial is largely a search for truth, it is not entirely so. An eminent Canadian jurist explains:

> The objective of a criminal trial is justice. Is the quest of justice synonymous with the search for truth? In most cases, yes. Truth and justice will emerge in a happy coincidence. But not always. Nor should it be thought that the judicial process has necessarily failed if justice and truth do not end up in perfect harmony. Such a result may follow from law's deliberate policy. The law says, for example, that a wife's evidence shall not be used against her husband. If truth and nothing more were the goal, there would be no place for such a rule. For in many cases the wife's testimony would add to the quota of truth. But the law has regard to other values also. The sanctity of the marriage relationship counts for something. It is shocking to our moral sense that a wife be required to testify against her husband. So, rather than this should happen, the law makes its choice between competing values and declares that it is better to close the case without all the available evidence being put on the record. We place a ceiling price on truth. It is glorious to possess, but not at an unlimited cost. "Truth, like all other good things, may be loved unwisely — maybe pursued too keenly — may cost too much.[146]

Thus Wigmore's claim that the *sole* basis for the exclusion of induced confessions is that they are "testimonially untrustworthy"[147] has been criticized for failing to account for other factors which have motivated judges to exclude such evidence.[148] The search for truth is but one factor. As Lord Sumner pointed out in *Ibrahim v. R.*,[149] "it is not that the law presumes such statements to be untrue, but from the danger of receiving such evidence judges have thought it better to reject it for the due administration of justice". In reality the rules of evidence (which have evolved in order to control the manner in which our courts elicit truth as to guilt) are "rules of prudence and discretion, and have become so integral a part of the administration of justice as almost to have acquired the full force of law".[150]

Since the criminal trial is in essence an inquiry into human affairs —and since that inquiry depends (for the most part) upon the recollections, narratives, recitations, observations and subjective impressions of individuals with varying capacities for recollection, differing powers

---

146. S. Freedman, *supra* footnote 143 at p. 99.
147. *Wigmore on Evidence* (3rd ed. 1940) s. 822, p. 246. See also Freedman, *supra* footnote 143 at p. 98.
148. See S. Bushnell, "The Confession Rule: Its Rationale (A Survey)" (1973) 12 West.L.R. 47 at pp. 53-65.
149. *Supra* footnote 143 at p. 611. (See also, the discussion on this subject contained in the Chapter on "The Police" under the heading "Interrogation").
150. *D.P.P. v. Christie, supra* footnote 135 at p. 164 *per* Lord Reading.

of articulation, or unequal degrees of intelligence—reality and truth do not characteristically present themselves in neat and precise bundles. Almost *any evidence* presented to the tribunal of adjudication will carry with it at least the shadow of unreliability. Consequently, all admissible evidence is ultimately referable to a requisite standard of proof.

That much may be said of *admissible* evidence. However the need for reliable evidence is manifested in at least three ways:

(1) The evidence is admitted subject to its being accorded due weight in proportion to its perceived reliability.

(2) The evidence is admitted subject to a suspicion which will not usually be alleviated in the absence of other independent corroborative evidence tending to support the reliability of the evidence.

(3) The evidence may be excluded where the dangers inherent in its reception outweigh any possible probative force which the evidence may possess.

The tendency of the modern law is to favour a broad basis of admissibility and consequently most relevant evidence finds its way into the first category enumerated above. As Cockburn C.J. observed in *R. v. Birmingham Overseers*,[151] "People were formerly frightened out of their wits about admitting evidence lest juries should go wrong. In modern times we admit the evidence and discuss its weight."

Category (2) *supra* indicates that although the search for the truth will often militate for the reception of evidence in certain instances (because of the nature, type, or character of the offence itself, or because of the character or nature of a witness) extreme caution earmarks its utilization. In such instances the law either *requires* corroboration before the evidence may be given effect, or the law acknowledges that the absence of corroborative evidence creates a situation in which it is *dangerous* (although possible) to enter a conviction. In such circumstances a judge sitting with a jury must properly instruct the jury as to the dangers inherent in accepting and attaching weight to such uncorroborated evidence. Where he tries the case alone the judge is under a duty to properly instruct himself on this issue.[152]

---

151. (1861) 1 B. & S. 763 at p. 767.
152. On the subject of corroboration generally, see A. Maloney, "Corroboration" (1955) L.S.U.C. Special Lectures 245; A. Maloney, "Corroboration Revisited" in Can. Bar Assn., *Studies in Criminal Law Procedure* (1973) at p. 133; A. E. Branca, "Corroboration" in Salhany and Carter *Studies in Canadian Criminal Evidence* (1972) at p. 133; C. C. Savage, "Corroboration" (1963-64) 6 Cr.L.Q. 159. Also, note that where a judge tries a case alone it no longer is assumed that he has properly instructed himself with respect to corroboration. He must in his reasons for judgment use words sufficient to indicate that he has acted properly: See *Kolnberger v. R.* [1969] 3 C.C.C. 241; *R. v. McMillan* (1967) 57 W.W.R. 677; *Chiu Nang Hong v. Public Prosecutor* [1964] 1 W.L.R. 1279 all cited in A. Maloney, "Corroboration Re-visited" *supra* at pp. 151-152. The matter is developed somewhat more fully by A. E. Branca *supra* at pp. 207-214.

Determining whether or not evidence is capable of furnishing corroboration is not always, or even often, a simple matter. The general definition of what constitutes corroborative evidence was enunciated by Lord Reading C.J. in *R. v. Baskerville*:[153]

> We hold that evidence in corroboration must be independent testimony which affects the accused by connecting or tending to connect him with the crime. In other words, it must be evidence which implicates him, that is, which confirms in some material particular not only the evidence that the crime has been committed, but also that the prisoner committed it. The test applicable to determine the nature and extent of the corroboration is thus the same whether the case falls within the rule of practice at common law or within that class of offences for which corroboration is required by statute. The language of the statute implicates the accused, compendiously incorporates the test applicable at common law in the rule of practice. The nature of corroboration will necessarily vary according to the particular circumstances of the offence charged. It would be in high degree dangerous to attempt to formulate the kind of evidence which would be regarded as corroboration except to say that corroboration evidence is evidence which shows or tends to show that the story of the accomplice that the accused committed the crime is true, not merely that the crime has been committed, but that it was committed by the accused.
>
> The corroboration need not be direct evidence that the accused committed the crime; it is sufficient if it is merely circumstantial evidence of his connection with the crime.[154]

Corroboration becomes a requirement in law in order to insure (within human limits) the reliability of certain kinds of evidence. Arthur Maloney indicates "it [corroboration] must surely be for the purpose of preventing the Court—the Judge or the Jury, as the case may be—from being beguiled into believing seemingly credible evidence. The experience of the centuries in our courts shown that in the case of certain classes of witnesses or cases involving certain classes of crime there is a danger present of a miscarriage of justice that is not so clearly present in cases that involve ordinary witnesses and ordinary crimes."[155]

One category of witness whose testimony is "scrutinized with utmost care" is that of an accomplice. The testimony of an accomplice may be accepted without corroboration but it is regarded as dangerous to do so. The reasons behind this approach were stated in *Lopatinsky v. R.*:[156]

---

153. [1916] 2 K.B. 658 at p. 667.
154. The *Baskerville* case has been accepted in Canada on numerous occasions. The Supreme Court of Canada approved Lord Reading's dictum in *Hubin v. R.* (1927), 48 C.C.C. 172 (Can.); *MacDonald v. R.* (1946) 87 C.C.C. 257 (Can.); and *Thomas v. R.* (1952) 103 C.C.C. 193 (Can.).
155. A. Maloney, "Corroboration Re-visited", *supra* footnote 152 at p. 135.
156. [1948] S.C.R. 220.

The accomplice is a competent witness, but his implication in the crime and the possible motives that may influence him in giving his evidence are such that it is dangerous to found a conviction thereon unless it can be corroborated.

To put matters another way, the danger is that "when a man is fixed, and knows that his own guilt is detected, he purchases impunity by falsely accusing others."[157]

The question of who is an accomplice, in law, is not without controversy. The leading English decision on the subject is that of *Davies v. D.P.P.*[158] Lord Simonds delivered, in the absence of any "formal definition of the term", the following carefully worded definition:

> On any view, persons who are *participes criminis* in respect of the actual crime charged, whether as principals or accessories before or after the fact (in felonies) or persons committing, procuring or aiding and abetting (in the case of misdemeanours). This is surely the natural and primary meaning of the term "accomplice.[159]

The views of Lord Simonds in *Davies* were endorsed by the Supreme Court of Canada in *Horsburgh v. R.*[160] The definition however, does not transfer into the Canadian context without the necessary addition of some refinements, as P. K. McWilliams points out:

> In applying [*Davies v. D.P.P.*] to Canadian law it should be kept in mind that accessories before the fact are parties to an offence under s. 21 of the Criminal Code. It is submitted that in Canada the natural and primary meaning of the term "accomplice includes parties to an offence (s. 21) and persons counselling an offence (s. 22). But an accessory after the fact is not in Canada a party to an offence and has been held not to be an accomplice: *R. v. Grafton* (1971), 5 C.C.C. (2d) 150 (N.B.C.A.), on the ground that his guilt is dependent on that of the principal offender and that by testifying he is giving evidence against his own interest. It is submitted that this overlooks the fact that

---

157. *R. v. Farler* (1837) 8 C. & P. 106 at 108 *per* Lord Abinger C.B.

158. [1954] A.C. 378. On the subject generally, of accomplices see C. C. Savage, "Who is an Accomplice?" (1960-61) 3 Cr.L.Q. 198.

159. *Ibid.* at p. 400. Lord Simon goes on to deal with two additional cases of persons falling outside the strict ambit of his definition which nevertheless have on occasion been held to be accomplices for the purposes of the rule regulating the duties of a judge instructing a jury in instances where such evidence has been tendered: (a) receivers — who have been held to be accomplices of the thieves from whom they receive goods; and (b) in situations involving similar fact evidence proving system and intent or negativing accident evidence or other parties to these previous offences should not be left to the jury without a warning that it is dangerous to accept it without corroboration. (See pp. 399-402).

160. [1968] 2 C.C.C. 288 (Can.). A. E. Branca *supra* footnote 152 at p. 186, is of the opinion that Martland J. in *Horsburgh* offers his own definition of "accomplice". However, the passage which he quotes in support of this contention does not bear him out.

he may be compellable and also that he may still be protected by an offer of immunity.[161]

The definition of an accomplice is a question of law and therefore is within the province of the trial judge presiding over a jury trial. Also, the determination of "all the elements that are necessary in order to constitute corroboration" is similarly the preserve of the trial judge.[162] The function of the trial judge in charging a jury with reference to accomplice evidence and the need for corroboration was delineated by Anglin C.J.C. in *Vigeant v. R.*[163] A. E. Branca (Branca J.A. of the British Columbia Court of Appeal) summarized the judicial duties outlined in *Vigeant*. In commenting upon the decision in that case he asserted that in Canada the trial judge must charge a jury as follows:[164]

(a) What, in law, constitutes a witness called by the Crown an accomplice.

(b) What facts given in evidence may be considered by the jury in affixing that character to a witness in the charge being investigated and which indicates his complicity in the offence charged, leaving it to the jury to say whether upon such directions the witness is in fact an accomplice.

(c) Direct the jury that if a witness is found to be an accomplice that it is dangerous to convict an accused of the crime charged upon the evidence of an accomplice or accomplices standing alone and uncorroborated, but that notwithstanding they are free to do so if they accept the evidence of the accomplices as credible.

(d) There must be an adequate definition of corroboration, a review of the evidence which may bear corroborative characteristics with a direction to the jury that it is for them to decide whether or not the evidence outlined is in fact corroborative and confirms the evidence given by the accomplice.

The duty of the trial judge to perform in the manner indicated is not obviated simply because it is clear that there has been evidence adduced which is capable of being corroboration. The warning must nevertheless still be given to the jury.[165] On the other hand, if there is no evidence capable of furnishing corroboration for an accomplice's testimony the trial judge must so advise the jury.[166]

---

161. P. K. McWilliams, *Canadian Criminal Evidence* (1974) at p. 433.

162. *MacDonald v. R. supra* footnote 154 at p. 261.

163. (1930) 54 C.C.C. 301 (Can.).

164. A. E. Branca *supra* footnote 152 at p. 189.

165. *R. v. Nowell* (1938) 70 C.C.C. 329 (B.C. C.A.). Note that where there is evidence capable of amounting to corroboration the trial judge should direct the jury's minds to such evidence: *R. v. Plantus* (1957) 118 C.C.C. 260 (Ont. C.A.); *R. v. Kelso* (1953) 105 C.C.C. 305 (Ont. C.A.).

166. *R. v. Dutrisac* (1971) 4 C.C.C. (2d) 13 (Ont. C.A.); *R. v. Smith and Gilson* (1956) 115 C.C.C. 38 (Ont. C.A.).

A trial judge will be justified in refraining to instruct the jury on accomplice evidence (and will be relieved also of the need to warn them accordingly) where there is no evidence to support the contention that a given witness could be regarded by the jury as an accomplice.[167]

The example of the accomplice has been offered here in order to demonstrate one of the ways in which our courts have attempted to insure the reliability of evidence offered in proof of a criminal allegation through the requirement of corroboration. Certainly the subject has not been exhausted within the confines of these few short paragraphs. There are numerous "special cases"[168] in which the evidence may fall subject to the accomplice rules. These special cases have not been developed here.

A more stringent method of insuring reliability through the corroboration requirement exists with respect to those situations in which corroboration may not be dispensed or done away with. Of those situations, the example of the evidence of child witnesses has been selected for amplification.[169]

---

167. *Seguin v. R.* (1954) 107 C.C.C. 359 (Can.).
168. P. K. McWilliams in *Canadian Criminal Evidence* (1974) identifies and discusses nine of these "special cases": (1) Receivers, (2) Parties to similar offences committed by accused, (3) Child accomplices, (4) Prostitutes as to whom the accused is charged with living off the avails, (5) Child victims of sexual offences, (6) Females upon whom an illegal operation has been performed, (7) Purchasers of drugs, (8) Police spies and agents provocateurs, (9) Victim of offence (see pp. 434-437). See also C. C. Savage, "Who is an Accomplice?" *supra* footnote 158 at pp. 198-207.
169. A. E. Branca, *supra* footnote 152 at p. 179 offers this synopsis of other situations falling within this general category:
   "The Criminal Code specifies certain offences where no conviction may be entered upon the evidence of only one witness unless the evidence of the witness is corroborated. They include forgery (s. 310), perjury (s. 115), treason (s. 47(2)) and communicating a venereal disease (s. 239). In addition, s. 131 of the Criminal Code provides that no accused shall be convicted of certain offences set out in that section on the evidence of only one witness unless the evidence of that witness is corroborated.

   .   .   .

   "It is also provided under s. 134 of the Criminal Code that where an accused is charged with rape, attempted rape, sexual intercourse with a female under 14, or sexual intercourse with a female between 14 and 16, and indecent assault, the judge must, if the only sworn witness is the complainant and her evidence is not corroborated, warn the jury of the dangers of convicting in the absence of corroboration."
   (Note: s. 134 (now s. 142) was re-enacted by 1974-75-76, c. 93, s. 8. The amendment abolished the requirement of a warning as to corroboration in the case where an accused is charged with rape or another sexual offence referred to in s. 142 involving a female. Further, this amendment excludes questions concerning the sexual conduct of the complainant with persons other than the accused in cases where the offence charged is rape, attempted rape, sexual intercourse with a female under fourteen, or indecent assault on a female save in limited and rigidly controlled circumstances.)

Section 16 of the *Canada Evidence Act*[170] provides:

> 16(1) In any legal proceeding where a child of tender years is offered as a witness, and such child does not, in the opinion of the judge, justice or other presiding officer, understand the nature of an oath, the evidence of such child may be received though not given upon oath, if, in the opinion of the judge, justice or other presiding officer, as the case may be, the child is possessed of sufficient intelligence to justify the reception of the evidence, and understands the duty of speaking the truth.
>
> (2) *No case shall be decided upon such evidence alone, and it must be corroborated by some other material evidence.*

Thus by statutory prescription a distinction is drawn between evidence attested to by children of tender years who are sworn, and those who are not. Only in the case of the latter is corroboration an absolute requirement. With reference to the sworn evidence of child witnesses the common law rule of practice applies: the trial judge must warn the jury of the frailties inherent in such evidence and of the danger in founding a conviction upon such evidence in the absence of other corroborative evidence.[171] The basis for the rule of practice was explained by Judson J. (on behalf of the unanimous Court) in *R. v. Kendall*:[172]

> The basis for the rule of practice which requires the Judge to warn the jury of the danger of convicting on the evidence of a child, even when sworn as a witness, is the mental immaturity of the child. The difficulty is fourfold: 1. His capacity of observation. 2. His capacity of recollection. 3. His capacity to understand questions put and frame intelligent answers. 4. His moral responsibility. (*Wigmore on Evidence*, 3rd ed., para. 506).

Inasmuch as the sworn evidence of a child of tender years may be received without corroboration and acted upon, while unsworn evi-

---

170. R.S.C. 1970 Chap. E-16 s. 16 (emphasis added).

171. Lord Goddard in two English cases in the 1950's established the proposition that even where sworn, the evidence of the child of tender years should be treated carefully:
   "The sworn evidence of a child need not, as a matter of law be corroborated, but a jury should be warned . . . that there is a risk in acting on the uncorroborated evidence of young boys and girls, . . . and this evidence should also be given where a young boy or girl is called to corroborate the evidence either of another child, sworn or unsworn, or of an adult. The evidence of an unsworn child can amount to corroboration of sworn evidence though a particularly careful warning should be given in that case" (*R. v. Campbell* (1956) 40 Cr.App.R. 95 at p. 102).
   See also *R. v. Mitchell* (1952) 36 Cr.App.R. 79. To determine whether or not a child's evidence should be received sworn or unsworn is not always free of complication. See S. T. Bigelow, "Witnesses of Tender Years" (1966-67) 9 Cr.L.Q. 298; Also, generally see J. A. Andrews, "The Evidence of Children" [1964] Cr.L.R. 769.

172. (1962) 132 C.C.C. 216 at p. 220 (Can.).

dence of the same character requires corroboration the judicial decision as to whether to swear the child or not looms as an important one.

The correct practice is for a preliminary examination of the child to be conducted by the trial judge (not by counsel).[173] Leading questions have been regarded as proper.[174] However, it is submitted that since the inquiry is devoted to discovering whether "the child is possessed of sufficient intelligence to justify the reception of evidence, and understand the duty of speaking the truth" *in addition to understanding the nature of an oath* an inquiry conducted entirely through the use of leading questions would be grossly deficient. (The answers thus elicited might merely suggest that the child is highly manipulable and open to suggestion.) It seems clear that although the examination is conducted by the trial judge questions may also properly be put by either defence or crown counsel.[175]

Assuming that a child of tender years is permitted to give unsworn evidence at the trial of an issue certain difficulties may arise in determining whether the necessary corroboration for the child's evidence has been tendered. Can the unsworn testimony of one child corroborate that of another unsworn child? It is clear that the sworn evidence of one child can corroborate the unsworn evidence of another.[176] *D.P.P. v. Hester*[177] a recent decision of the House of Lords holds that one unsworn child cannot corroborate another. This has long been the position in Canada.[178]

Can the unsworn evidence of a child constitute corroborative evidence in any sense? Since corroboration must be "independent" evidence "which affects the accused by connecting or tending to connect him with the crime" *(R. v. Baskerville)* is it possible for a child's unsworn evidence to possess this quality? Estey J. in *Paige v. R.* denied this possibility:

> Such independent evidence must possess probative value, which is the very quality s. 16 denies to the unsworn and uncorroborative evidence of a child of tender years. Such is the effect of the specific

173. See *R. v. Bannerman* (1966) 48 C.R. 110 (Man. C.A.), aff'd. (1967) 50 C.R. 76 (Can.); See also two cases discussed in *Bannerman*: *Sankey v. R.* (1927) 48 C.C.C. 97 (Can.), and *R. v. Antrobus* (1946) 87 C.C.C. 118 (B.C. C.A.).
174. See, the Reasons of Dickson J. in *Bannerman ibid.* at p. 137. S. T. Bigelow in his article on "Witnesses of Tender Years" *supra* footnote 171, commends the form of interrogation conducted in *Bannerman* and suggests that "trial judges and magistrates may well adopt it as a model inquiry of a witness of tender years to ascertain if he understands the nature of an oath" (pp. 311-313).
175. Both defence and crown addressed questions to the witness in *Bannerman*.
176. See *R. v. Campbell, supra* footnote 176 at p. 102.
177. (1973) 57 Cr.App.R. 212 (H.L.).
178. See *Paige v. R.* (1948) 92 C.C.C. 32 (Can.) and the list of authorities cited at p. 37 of the judgment of Estey J.

provision that "such evidence must be corroborated". It follows that if it is not corroborated it does not possess probative value and should be ignored.[179]

D.P.P. v. Hester takes the opposite point of view. It has yet to receive sanction in Canada although at least one respected Canadian commentator claims that it is the proper view,[180] and proposes (somewhat less convincingly) that it is presently the law in Canada.[181] A portion of the headnote of the case reads as follows:

> though the unsworn evidence of one child cannot be corroborated by the unsworn evidence of another child, the unsworn evidence of J could be regarded as capable of corroborating the sworn evidence of V, and the evidence of V could be regarded as corroborating the evidence of J, provided that the jury were satisfied, after suitable guidance and warning, that each child was a truthful and satisfactory witness; but that on the facts of the case, it was unsafe and unsatisfactory to allow the conviction to stand.[182]

It is here submitted that *Paige v. R.* remains the leading authority on this subject in Canada, and that its reasoning is to be preferred to that of the House of Lords in *D.P.P. v. Hester*. The dangers inherent in accepting the sworn testimony of a child of tender years are acknowledged and accepted in this country, and to this extent the search for truth is facilitated, although we move cautiously with such evidence. Where it has been deemed to be unsafe to swear a child, if we can ascertain that the child is possessed of sufficient intelligence and understands the duty of speaking the truth, then we nevertheless feel justified in receiving the evidence. Again, this effort is aimed at facilitating the search for truth. However, it would be to "throw caution to winds" to allow corroborative inferences to be drawn from the unsworn evidence of child witness (evidence which, by itself, is said to require corroboration before it may be given effect). Therefore, while it is sensible to allow sworn testimony (which, by statute requires no corroboration) to corroborate unsworn testimony — irrespective of whether that sworn testimony is that of a child — the reverse proposition does not hold true.

---

179. *Ibid.* at p. 38.
180. P. K. McWilliams in *Canadian Criminal Evidence* (1974) at pp. 440-441.
181. McWilliams bases his opinion, in part, upon the cases *R. v. Hamlin* (1929) 52 C.C.C. 149 (Alta. C.A.) and *R. v. Cowpersmith* [1946] 2 D.L.R. 725 (B.C. C.A.) two cases which were expressly disapproved of in *Paige v. R.* (See Rand J. at pp. 34-35; and Estey J. at p. 38.) *R. v. Campbell* is also cited in support, but as Lord Morris points out in *D.P.P. v. Hester supra*, footnote 177 at p. 228 (also cited in support by McWilliams) "the discussion in *Campbell's Case* does not fully cover the point under consideration". Thus, the fact that *Campbell* was followed in *R. v. Taylor* (1970) 1 C.C.C. (2d) 321 (Man. C.A.), another authority cited by McWilliams, is of little weight in this context.
182. *Supra* footnote 177 at p. 213.

The positions at law of the accomplice and of the child witness (sworn and unsworn) who offer testimony during a trial have been explored here in order to demonstrate examples of instances where evidence is admitted subject to a suspicion (or cautionary perspective) which will not usually be alleviated in the absence of other independent corroborative evidence tending to support the reliability of the evidence.

As has been noted there are, in addition, instances where evidence may be excluded because the "dangers" inherent in its reception outweigh any possible probative force which the evidence may possess. An example of such an instance occurs where a confession has been deemed to be involuntary or induced.[183]

It is important to note that whether one states that a confession is to be excluded because it is untrustworthy, or because it is thought "better to reject it for the due administration of justice", in either event "logically these objections all go to the weight and not to the admissibility of the evidence".[184]

> What a person having knowledge about the matter in issue says of it is itself relevant to the issue as evidence against him. That he made the statement under circumstances of hope, fear, interest or otherwise strictly goes only to its weight. In an action of tort evidence of this kind could not be excluded when tendered against a tort feasor, though a jury might well be told as prudent men to think little of it. *Even the rule which excludes evidence of statements made by a prisoner, when they are induced by hope held out, or fear inspired, by a person in authority, is a rule of policy.* "A confession forced from the mind by the flattery of hope or by the torture of fear comes in so questionable a shape, when it is to be considered as evidence of guilt that no credit ought to be given to it": *Rex v. Warickshall.*[185]

The frank admission by Lord Sumner [in the italicized portion of the quotation *supra*] that the exclusionary rule governing the reception of confession is, in essence, "a rule of policy" is particularly important in the present context. The law of evidence is not so settled that *all* evidentiary matters are firmly ensconced in appropriate cate-

---

183. It will be remembered that the authorities are divided on exactly what those "dangers" are in the case of confessions. Whether the danger be purely that of "untrustworthiness" as Wigmore contends, or involve other considerations such as these suggested by S. I. Bushnell, *supra* footnote 148 at p. 64 remains unresolved: "As the sole basis for applying the voluntary rule I would reject truthfulness. That it is a factor to consider I would not disagree, but as the rationale for the rule, it appears unsupportable. I suggest that the basic rationale is the maxim *nemo tenetur seipsum accusare* with an element of maintaining the "due administration of justice", but the maxim is not unlimited in application."
See also E. Ratushny, "Unravelling Confessions" (1970-71) 13 Cr.L.Q. 453 at pp. 475-479.
184. *Per* Lord Sumner in *Ibrahim v. R., supra* footnote 143 at p. 610.
185. *Ibid.* at pp. 610-611 (emphasis added).

gories of (a) relevant matters which, as a matter of policy, will be excluded when certain preliminary conditions are not met, and (b) relevant matters which, as a matter of policy, are admitted subject only to a reservation as to the weight to be accorded such evidence.

One area of the law which presently exists in a state of ambiguity is that of "continuity over seized items"; otherwise known as "chain of possession or custody", or "authentication of evidence". Scholarship on the subject is almost non-existent in Canada. Where it is considered, the subject ordinarily is broached under the more general heading of the judicial determination of "preliminary facts".

Often before many rules of evidence may be called into operation certain necessary pre-conditions must exist. The determination of whether these factual conditions exist characteristically is carried out within the procedural arena of the "voir dire" (or as it is sometimes referred to, the "trial within the trial"). The most widely known form of voir dire is the one that is held in order to determine the admissibility of a confession taken from an accused person. The voir dire, however, is capable of much wider use than is commonly acknowledged. It is in essence the classic format for the presentation of a requisite degree of proof necessary in order to discharge the obligation of establishing a proper foundation for the admission of evidence.

In Canada it is incumbent upon the Trial Judge to decide all preliminary questions which affect the admissibility of evidence.[186] The

---

186. See *R. v. Dixon* (1897) 29 N.S.R. 462; *R. v. Sunfield* (1907) 13 C.C.C. 1 (Ont. C.A.); *F. v. F.* (1920) 52 D.L.R. 440; *De Blaquiere v. Becker* (1859) 8 U.C.C.P. 167 (C.A.). Ordinarily, issues of fact are left to the jury. However in these instances the courts have found good reason for not doing so. White J. in *F. v. F. supra* at p. 455 said: "It is, I think, established beyond question that when evidence is tendered and objected to it is for the trial judge to decide whether the evidence is 'properly admissible'. When the question of admissibility depends upon 'facts' which are not in dispute, it is entirely a 'question of law' which the judge has to determine; but it not infrequently happens that the 'fact, or facts,' upon which depends the admissibility of the evidence is or are in dispute; and in such case it is necessary to decide the fact or facts in dispute in order to determine whether the evidence objected to is properly admissible. Under our system of trial by jury it would tend to confusion, and indeed be almost impracticable, to require that whenever the admissibility of evidence tendered depends upon questions of fact, these facts should be determined by the jury before the evidence tendered is received. It has, therefore, been held, and is well settled, that it is for the Judge to decide as to whether or not the circumstances are such as to justify the admission of the evidence tendered. His decision in no way affects the right and duty of the jury to give such 'weight' to the evidence thus admitted as, under all the circumsances, they may decide it is entitled to (emphasis added)."

See also C. T. McCormick, *Handbook of the Law of Evidence* (1964) at pp. 122-123; and J. M. Maguire, *Evidence: Common Sense and Common Law* (1947) Chapter IX. And see *R. v. Sproule* (1975) 30 C.R.N.S. 56 (Ont. C.A.) for determining when a voir dire should *not* be held.

necessity for laying a proper foundation for the introduction of evidence affects a great variety of evidential matters; confessions, photographs, tape recordings, the competency of a witness to be sworn or to give evidence, etc. The nature of the evidence sought to be tendered will, of necessity, affect the evidential concerns of a given inquiry. (*E.g.* The concern governing the intended testimony of a child witness is that the witness understands the nature of an oath, understands the duty of speaking the truth, and is possessed of sufficient intelligence to justify the reception of the evidence.[187] Regarding confessions, the judge conducting the voir dire must be concerned with the voluntariness of the statement in the sense that it has not been obtained either by fear of prejudice or hope of advantage exercised or held out by a person in authority.[188])

It is important to realize that these factual determinations are performed quite apart from ordinary considerations of "relevancy".[189] A. E. Popple explains:

> Evidence to be "admissible" must be "relevant". *R. v. Barbour* [1938] S.C.R. 465. *There is a vast difference between "relevancy" and "admissibility".* It should be noted that "relevancy" is a question of "fact" for the trial judge to decide while "admissibility" is a question of compliance with a "Rule of Evidence" founded on "law". Evidence may be "admissible" for one purpose and in one case, and the same evidence be "inadmissible" in another case or for another purpose. The "admissibility", therefore, depends upon the various conditions under which the matter is received in evidence, particularly the "time" when, and the "circumstances" under which, it is put forward for admisison . . . Now it is well settled that the admission of properly "rejectable" evidence; and the rejection of legally "admissible" evidence are both grounds of appeal and where they amount to a "miscarriage of justice" the conviction will be quashed.[190]

On occasion a condition of "relevancy" may be the very preliminary fact upon which the trial Judge is asked to adjudicate. As S. Schiff indicates in his coursebook on *Evidence in the Litigation Process*[191] "while the orthodox doctrine [of preliminary fact determination] is usually stated in words wide enough to encompass all preliminary facts, the justifying reasons are less strong when the particular preliminary fact conditions only the relevancy of offered evidence". If one considers the example of a rape trial in which the accused has denied any form of relationship with the complainant and

---

187. The Canada Evidence Act R.S.C. 1970 Chap. E-10 s. 16.
188. *Ibrahim v. R. supra* footnote 143 at p. 609.
189. The voir dires themselves however are regulated by the admission only of evidence "relevant" to the particular issue towards which the voir dire is directed.
190. A. E. Popple, *Criminal Procedure Manual* (2nd ed. 1956) at p. 170 (emphasis added).
191. Unpublished (4th ed. 1975) at p. 79.

the Crown seeks to offer a torn, blood and semen-smeared undergarment as evidence of intercourse and lack of consent, the operation of the relevancy objection becomes apparent.[192] Must the trial judge hold a voir dire in order to determine whether the precondition of relevancy has been met? Professor Schiff provides this answer:[193]

> since only relevancy is involved, the various policies underlying exclusionary rules of evidence unrelated to relevancy cannot be harmed if the judge admits the evidence subject to the jury's later rejection. Moreover, if the jury later determines that the evidence is simply irrelevant they can easily disregard it. Thus, when enough evidence had been introduced to justify a finding that the preliminary fact existed, judges have usually (particularly in identification cases) admitted the disputed evidence without holding a trial within the trial and have left determination of the preliminary fact to the jury with the instruction that, if the jury found against its existence, they should ignore the evidence.

Leaving aside for the moment matters of pure relevancy, there are innumerable instances in which the preliminary question affecting admissibility will be one involving the authentication of tangible evidence. Falling within this category are issues that are concerned with the integrity of photographic and tape recorded evidence, or laboratory specimens of human bodily fluids (blood, urine, etc.) which (upon analysis) are intended for use as evidence. The preservation of seized evidence (*e.g.* narcotics, weapons, etc.) also falls within this general classification. The primary considerations which earmark the voir dires which are held in order to determine whether such evidence ought to be delivered into evidence are: a concern that the evidence be properly identified; that it in fact be what it purports to be; and that it has been adequately safeguarded and preserved since the date of its initial seizure or delivery into official custody. Consider the example of the use as evidence of results of chemical tests:

> Before the results of any chemical test can be admitted into evidence in a criminal prosecution the party seeking to introduce such evidence must lay a proper foundation for its admission. An important part of this foundation is proof of a complete chain of evidence establishing the identity of the sample. Who took the sample? What did he do with it? Who labelled it? Where was it kept? How was it transported? How was it delivered? Was its location unknown at any time? Is there a possibility that it was confused or mixed up with other samples?[194]

One common form of chemical test which often becomes the subject of this type of scrutiny is the analysis of blood sample. The results

---

192. The example is Schiff's and may be found at p. 80 *ibid.*
193. *Ibid.* at p. 80. See also *R. v. Ashley* (1944) 82 C.C.C. 259 (P.E.I.), and *R. v. Campbell* (1919) 33 C.C.C. 364 (Alta. C.A.).
194. R. E. Erwin, *Defence of Drunk Driving Cases* vol. 2 (3rd ed. 1975) Chap. 27, p. 27-1.

of such tests, where admitted, can be of crucial importance to the proof of an issue of impairment or intoxication. Whether as an aspect affecting intention (as in conjunction with a charge of murder) or as proof of the elements of an offence itself (such as driving an automobile with a blood/alcohol reading higher than .08) the importance of such chemical tests can scarcely be underestimated. Consequently, the courts must employ extreme caution in determining the admissibility of such evidence. In *Rutherford v. Richardson* Viscount Birkenhead, then Lord Chancellor of England said:

> The issues pronounced upon by Courts in criminal, and, indeed, in civil matters, are attended with such decisive consequences that the adoption in matters of evidence of a standard of admissibility which is so cautious as to be meticulous may not only be defended, but is, in fact, essential.[195]

The case of *Rapchalk v. Atlas Assur. Co.*[196] is particularly instructive in the present context as it deals with an allegation (of impaired driving) dependent upon proof of the analysis of a blood sample. In that case the Plaintiff Rapchalk brought his action against the Defendant to recover a sum of money under a policy of insurance. The Defendant refused payment of the monies payable under the policy on the ground that the Plaintiff was in violation of the statutory conditions of the policy which stipulated that the Insured should not drive or operate his automobile while under the influence of intoxicating liquor. A blood sample had been secured from the plaintiff shortly after the accident which gave rise to the action. In *Rapchalk* it was held that the chain of continuity linking the sample of blood taken from the plaintiff with the blood sample analysed (and on which the expert gave evidence) having been broken, the admission of the evidence could not be justified. Sirois J. rejected the evidence and excluded it from admission.

> There is no question but that the reading of the blood sample of the plaintiff was relevant in this instance. But the question remains: Was it properly admissible, on the evidence tendered before the court? Normally, it would be, but how can any one say in the present instance that it was probably the blood sample of the plaintiff that was tested by S/Sgt. Tweed? No one testified as to who handled the blood sample, or as to what, if anything, was done to it from the time it left Yorkton until the envelope with the broken seal came into the possession of S./Sgt. Tweed, some three or four days later. *Had the envelope still been sealed and intact at the time it was handed to the analyst different considerations would have arisen.*
>
> In my opinion, *there is only one proper manner in which facts of this nature may be offered as evidence in any contested matter. This was not done in this case, even though the law enforcement officials*

---

195. [1923] A.C. 1 at p. 5.
196. (1967) 60 W.W.R. 747 (Sask.).

are well aware of the long established practice of proving continuity. Here the chain was broken and I find the evidence of the blood sample reading is not admissible.[197]

The fact that the chain of continuity of possession has been broken does not of itself render an article of evidence inadmissible. This is the import of the remarks by Sirois J. that "had the envelope still been sealed and intact at the time it was handed to the analyst different considerations would have arisen". Where there is evidence that reasonably leads only to the conclusion that a sample was in the same condition when it reached an analyst as it was when dispatched for analysis, and there is no evidence to suggest that it has been tampered with in the interval, such sample, and the results of the analysis, are admissible in evidence.[198]

Similar considerations to those guiding an inquiry into the admissibility of chemical tests govern the voir dire as to the admissibility of tape recorded evidence.[199] Once again there is a clearly acknowledged need for the courts to carefully scrutinize such evidence lest a substantial miscarriage of justice be occasioned. The Ouimet Report on Canadian corrections acknowledged that "there is impressive evidence that tapes can be edited in such a way as to completely distort the meaning of the statements originally recorded. The editings once transferred to new tapes cannot be detected.[200]

The first reported instance of a Canadian criminal case which considered the admissibility of tape recorded evidence on a voir dire was *R. v. Foll,*[201] a case decided in 1956 in Manitoba. Freedman J. (as he then was) felt it best, "because of the potential dangers inherent in this type of evidence".[202] that the objection to the reception of the evidence be considered in a voir dire conducted in the absence of the jury. In that voir dire the accused was accorded an opportunity to test:

(1) whether the tape recording was in fact an accurate reproduction of what is claimed to have been spoken,

(2) whether the tape recording was in any way altered or tampered with.

---

197. *Ibid.* at pp. 751-752 (emphasis added).
198. See *R. v. Kolkiczka* [1933] 1 W.W.R. 299 (Man.). See also, *R. v. Kilgore* (1969) 6 C.R.N.S. 264 (Sask.) which like *Rapchalk* deals with a blood sample analysis in an impaired driving situation. (In both these cases the samples in question were admitted into evidence.)
199. For interesting, but somewhat dated observations on this subject see G. E. Parker, "Tape Recordings as Evidence" (1963-64) 6 Cr.L.Q. 314; and T. B. Radley, "Recording as Testimony to Truth" [1954] Crim. L.R. 96.
200. Canada, *Report of the Canadian Committee on Corrections* (1969) at p. 86 (Ouimet Report). See also, the discussion on electronic surveillance and wiretapping contained in the chapter on "The Police" *supra.*
201. (1956) 25 C.R. 69 (Man.), affirmed 26 C.R. 68 (C.A.).
202. *Ibid.* at p. 70 (Man.).

These criteria on their face are not particularly objectionable. The case however may be criticized for failing to outline with greater precision and particularity what facts must be established in order that a proper foundation for the admission of the evidence be laid. An American decision decided at approximately the same time suggested this formulation:[203] ,

(1) the recording device must be shown to be capable of taking the conversation offered into evidence
(2) The operator of the device must be shown to be competent to operate the device
(3) the recording must be demonstrably authentic and correct
(4) it must be shown that no changes, additions or deletions have been made in the recording
(5) the manner of preservation of the recording must be shown to the court
(6) the speakers must be identified.

These may well be exactly the concerns that guided the court in the *Foll* case. However, if they were the actual concerns of the court the reasons for judgment reflect them only in general terms.

It is not unrealistic to expect that the parties seeking to use tape recordings as evidence at trial be prepared and able to demonstrate due diligence and care in the use, control and safeguarding of electronic equipment and tape recordings. From a *technical point of view* the precautions taken and the use of electronic surveillance techniques employed in the recent case of *R. v. Demeter*[204] are exemplary. The Orwellian aspects of the case aside, *Demeter* appears to signal the arrival of the age of electronics.

Three types of electronic surveillance techniques were employed in *Demeter* all of which produced tape recorded logs. (Grant J. designated the three methods as (1) telephone interception; (2) telephone recording; and (3) body packs.)[205] What follows is a paraphrased description of the precautions taken in order to insure the integrity of the evidence gathered as a result of one of these methods — telephone interception:

(1) By means of a test call, it was verified that the correct line had been tapped;
(2) Only new tapes delivered in sealed containers were used;
(3) The tape recorder used was of a type that would automatically erase any pre-existing recording on the tape;
(4) The receiving and recording apparatus was kept in a locked container to which only specified officers had access;

---

203. *U.S. v. McKeever* (1958) 169 F. Supp. 426.
204. (1975) 19 C.C.C. (2d) 321 (Ont.).
205. *Ibid.* see pp. 323-325.

(5) On each occasion tapes were changed the officer in charge checked the locks on the container and noted the times when each tape was put on and taken off;

(6) The machine was checked periodically to insure that it was working;

(7) The officer in whose house the receiving apparatus was installed testified that to his knowledge the apparatus was never tampered with, the power was always on, and the plug was always in;

(8) After the tapes were removed they were kept in a locked steel cabinet belonging to a given officer;

(9) Where tapes were taken to be tested or processed they were under the supervision of the officer in charge or his delegate.

The tape recorded evidence gathered as a result of the three surveilance techniques previously mentioned was admitted by Grant J. at the conclusion of a thorough voir dire on the subject. The learned trial Judge in admitting the evidence pronounced that he was "satisfied *beyond a reasonable doubt* that the tapes were not edited or tampered with in any way".[206] At page 334 of the judgment he goes on to say:

> In deciding admissibility the Court should, subject to the above dictums, on a *voir dire*, satisfy itself that there is evidence upon which a jury might reasonably be satisfied beyond a reasonable doubt that the tapes are an accurate and authentic reproduction of what they purport to reproduce. The Court should also satisfy itself that the contents and quality of the tapes are such that the tapes will not only mislead and not confuse a jury but will be of assistance to the jury in providing evidence relevant to the issues in the case.

The "above dictums" to which Grant J. makes reference are these: (1) the submission that tapes must be perfectly accurate in order to be admissible is not tenable; and (2) if a conflict of evidence exists as to the accuracy of or possible tampering with the tapes such would not affect admissibility but would be a matter of weight for the jury to determine.

These dicta on the facts of the case, and in view of the standard of proof employed by the trial Judge on the voir dire (beyond a reasonable doubt) are not essential to the decision in the case. It is submitted that at least the second dictum *supra* is seriously in error.

What is important to the determination on the voir dire is the standard of proof which is applicable. If the requisite standard of proof is met by the proponent of the evidence then the evidence should be admitted. If, however, the proof furnished falls below the *requisite degree,* either as to accuracy, or as to the possibility of tampering, then the evidence must be rejected. To deny this general approach would be to render the holding of a voir dire meaningless and absurd. If dis-

---

206. *Ibid.* at p. 332.

crepancies as to accuracy and/or tampering go only to weight, and not to admissibility, the holding of a voir dire becomes incomprehensible.

On the other hand, there may be some evidence that the tapes are in some measure inaccurate (or, as in this case, partially unintelligible), or some evidence may exist that the possibility of tampering cannot be completely discounted. However, where such evidence is insufficient to counterbalance the other evidence verifying the accuracy or integrity of the evidence *to a requisite degree* then the evidence must be admitted for the jury's due weighting and consideration.

What is proof to a requisite degree? What is the burden and standard of proof at a trial within a trial? The present law is sadly undeveloped on this subject in both Canada and England. In *Demeter,* although there appears to be contradictory dicta, it appears that Grant J. applied a standard on the voir dire of "proof beyond a reasonable doubt".[207] It is submitted that in criminal cases this is the appropriate standard to be applied. *Cross on Evidence* (4th ed.) advances the same proposition:

> Where the issue is one which must be decided once and for all to hold that, in civil cases, the preliminary fact must be proved to the satisfaction of the judge on a preponderance of probability and that, in criminal cases, when the evidence is tendered by the prosecution, such fact must be proved beyond reasonable doubt.[208]

Only since 1960 has it emerged that "proof beyond a reasonable doubt" was the appropriate standard to be applied in voir dires concerning the admissibility of confessions.[209] (The English authorities appear also to hold to the view that the reasonable doubt standard applies with regard to dying declarations as well.[210] The rationale offered for the high standard applicable on preliminary fact determinations concerning confessions applies equally well to many other forms of contested evidence. This becomes clear if one substitutes the example of a blood alcohol reading to prove impairment for the example of confessions in the ensuing quotation:

---

207. *Ibid.* at p. 332.
208. R. Cross, *Evidence* (4th ed. 1974) at pp. 64-65.
209. See *R. v. Cave* [1963] Crim. L.R. 371; *R. v. M.* [1961] Crim. L.R. 824; *R. v. Sartori* [1961] Crim. L.R. 397 (Q.B.); *R. v. McLintock* [1962] Crim. L.R. 549 (C.A.); *R. v. Albrecht* (1965) 49 C.R. 314 (N.B. C.A.); *R. v. Demers* (1970) 13 C.R.N.S. 338 (Que.). For an article disagreeing with the view that the "beyond a reasonable doubt" standard should govern see R. S. O'Regan, "Admissibility of Confessions — The Standard of Proof" [1964] Crim. L.R. 287.
210. See *R. v. Jenkins* (1869) L.R. 1 C.C.R. 187; but see also *R. v. Booker* (1924) 88 J.P. 75 where the Court of Criminal Appeal said that a dying declaration might be admitted if the conditions precedent were proved "to the satisfaction of the judge" without specifying what standard of proof he might apply. Similar vague language accounted for the lengthy period of uncertainty as to the standard of proof applicable vis-à-vis confessions in Canada.

The English view at least has the merit of ensuring that the utmost care is taken before a confession is placed before the jury, and this is particularly important because, in many cases, to admit a confession is virtually to ensure the conviction of the accused. [211]

The rejection of the "reasonable doubt" standard does not inevitably lead to the acceptance of a standard of proof on a "balance of probabilities". A competing basis of evaluation could conceivably be a *prima facie* standard. This, of course, is the weakest or loosest standard of all.

Where the judge merely has to be satisfied that there is *prima facie* evidence, for example that a confession was made, or a tape recording was the original, he need theoretically, only hear evidence from the party tendering the confession or recording and it may always be sufficient if such evidence satisfies him on the balance of probabilities. [212]

As has been noted in many instances the entire issue of the guilt or innocence of the accused may hang upon the hinge of preliminary determination of admissibility. To apply a standard of proof less than that of reasonable doubt to determinations of these crucial admissibility issues would be tantamount to holding that in a criminal trial guilt could be established by resort to a standard less than that of reasonable doubt.

In all criminal cases the burden of proof lies upon the Crown. Every ingredient necessary to constitute the offence alleged must be proven. The accused is entitled to the benefit of any reasonable doubt, not only on the whole of the case, *but on each and every issue.* This is trite law, and these matters are the subject of detailed explanation to the jury in each and every trial in which a jury is involved. It is true that the burden of proof may be shifted by legislative interference, and that certain exceptions to the general rule have been recognized by the common law. [213] But generally speaking these exceptions are not relevant in the present context. The duty of the prosecution remains to prove the guilt of the accused beyond all reasonable doubt. Lord Sankey's famous "one golden thread" is still always to be seen as

---

211. Cross, *Evidence supra* footnote 208 at p. 65.
212. *Ibid.* at p. 69. This appears to be at the base of the reasoning of the New Brunswick Court of Appeal in *R. v. Donald* (1958) 121 C.C.C. 304. Bridges J.A. at p. 306 states (re: stolen fire extinguishers), "It is my opinion that an article, which has been taken from the possession of an accused may be received in evidence if it is relevant to the issue, and some witness is able to give some apparently sound reason for believing it to be the article seized. No one can seriously doubt that the fire extinguishers the police found in the truck were those on which Scott placed his initials. Positive identification is not required. The fact an article has been admitted in evidence does not, of course, establish that it is the article involved. After its reception it is a question of fact to be determined by the Judge or jury as to whether or not it is, in fact such article."
213. See *R. v. Appleby* (1972) 16 C.R.N.S. 35 (Can.).

dominating Canadian criminal law.[214] Short of express statutory provision displacing the ordinary burden, a standard of "proof beyond a
reasonable doubt" accords with established notions of the need for
cautious, meticulous standards of admissibility where the issues pronounced upon by the courts are attended with such decisive consequences.[215]

(4) Abuse of process[216]

The judicial decision to exclude relevant evidence on the basis that
its reception will involve an abuse of process is in rather a protean
state. There is some doubt as to whether it exists at all, or even, whether the doctrine of abuse of process will evolve in this direction at all.

The "traditional approach" to the doctrine of abuse of process (if
one can employ the term "traditional" in this context) has been to
suggest that the doctrine may be employed in order to block the commencement of proceedings, or to stay proceedings once commenced,[217]
but it has not often been suggested that the doctrine may properly be
employed in order to regulate the admissibility of evidence.

Laskin J.A. in *R. v. Ormerod,*[218] a case involving the prosecution
of an undercover police agent for narcotics trafficking, flirted with the
question of the scope of the operation of the doctrine. He suggests that
it is arguable that the doctrine may be invoked in order to control not
only procedural manipulation of the criminal process, but also the
methods by which an offence is to be proved. Ultimately, he does not
answer the questions which he poses but he does leave the suggestion
that the doctrine results in the quashing of the entire proceeding, not
merely in the exclusion of evidence thus obtained.

> I do not, of course, say that these would be the findings if the evi-
> dence was evaluated against the background of a principle of an over-
> riding judicial discretion to stay a prosecution because of police
> complicity in the events which led to it. Nor do I say that such a
> principle must be recognized. It may, however, be arguable that it
> should be, but I leave consideration thereof to an occasion when it is
> squarely raised.[219]

When the discussion begins to centre around the methods resorted
to in order to gather evidence (or prove the offence) amounting to an
abuse of process a certain blurring of distinctions takes place. The distinction in question is that which exists between illegally obtained

214. *Woolmington v. D.P.P.* [1935] A.C. 462 at p. 481.
215. *Rutherford v. Richardson, supra* footnote 195.
216. An extensive examination of the doctrine of abuse of process is contained in
Chapter 6, *infra.*
217. See *Connelly v.D.P.P* [1964] 2 All E.R. 401 (H.L.); see also, *R. v. Osborn*
[1969] 4 C.C.C. 185 (Ont. C.A.), reversed (1970) 1 C.C.C. (2d) 482
(Can.). The case points up the inconclusive status of the doctrine in Canada.
218. [1969] 4 C.C.C. 3.
219. *Ibid.* at p. 20.

evidence and abuse of process.[220] An aggrieved prosecutor argued that the two phenomena ran afoul of each other in *R. v. Smith*,[221] and further contended that the doctrine of abuse of process could not be utilized since the rule propounded in *R. v. Wray* held sway in such a circumstance.

In *Smith* the accused had, in return for offers of immunity, cooperated with the authorities. The Crown reneged on its pledge and sought to prosecute the accused. The doctrine of abuse of process was invoked as a bar, and in an action for an order of prohibition Berger J. acceded to the request and the proceedings were barred. Despite the fact that the Crown had utilized a trick or fraudulent representation in order to secure the damning evidence which was expected to form the basis of the charge Berger J. reconciled the rule in *Wray* with the doctrine of abuse of process in this fashion:

> This is not a case relating to the reception of evidence; if it were, the judgment of the Supreme Court of Canada in *Regina v. Wray*, [1971] S.C.R. 272, 11 C.R.N.S. 235, [1970] 4 C.C.C. 1, 11 D.L.R. (3d) 673, might well apply. But what we have here is a case having to do with the bringing of proceedings. Nothing in *Regina v. Wray* can be said to diminish this Court's power to prevent an abuse of process in such a case.[222]

It is submitted that the two concepts do conflict; that by quashing proceedings rather than merely controlling admissibility the courts have thus far been able to side-step a direct confrontation. The matters in issue are essentially those of policy. Since the rule in *Wray* urgently requires relitigating and the doctrine of abuse of process requires the stamp of approval (or, regrettably, possibly even rejection) from our highest court it is not altogether unlikely that greater illumination and definition will be cast upon these areas before this decade is out.

3. JUDICIAL DECISIONS INSURING FAIR TREATMENT OF THE ACCUSED

The assertion that "justice and liberty depend not so much upon the definition of the crime as on the nature of the process, administrative as well as judicial, designed to bring the alleged offender to justice"[223] is not mere rhetoric. Frankfurter J. of the American Supreme Court observed that "the history of liberty has largely been the history of the observance of procedural safeguards.[224] If the criminal law process is unequal to the task of insuring justice through proced-

---

220. The matter becomes even more exacerbated when one asks whether entrapment involves either of these concepts. See the discussion of entrapment *infra* in the Chapter on "Abuse of Process'.
221. [1975] 3 W.W.R. 454 (B.C.).
222. *Ibid.* at p. 458.
223. J. A. Coutts (ed.) *The Accused* (1966).
224. *McNabb v. U.S.* (1942) 318 U.S. 332 at p. 347.

ural rigor then "law" as an institution invariably falls victim to the vaguaries of caprice, whim and arbitrariness. Where these features become endemic tyranny prevails.

In Canada we insist that not only must the law be ascertainable, consistent, and evenly applied, it must also be perceived to be "fair". Accordingly, the judge in controlling the trial process is also charged with the duty of preventing surprise; of insuring that the accused may make his answer and defence armed with adequate information as to the precise nature of the allegations which have been made; and of regulating external conditions in such a manner that the accused will not be prejudiced by either the locale of his trial or the self-serving accusations of others standing in similar jeopardy. As part of this mandate the judicial power exists to (1) order disclosure of information by the proscutor to the accused; (2) order adjournments where the accused is taken by surprise; (3) order a severance of the trial of accused persons who have been jointly charged; and (4) order a change of venue for the trial of the accused where the interests of justice so require.

(1) Disclosure

By and large in our jurisprudence it is only the words contained in the past decisions of Judges which are lionized and venerated, or, which (occasionally) are resurrected for argument's sake as embarrassing mis-statements of law. On occasion the words of respected legal authorities are quoted or incorporated into final reasons for judgment. On even rarer occasions the words of counsel may be quoted either to his personal benefit, or to his unending regret. It is not known whether Mr. W. B. Common Q.C. was pleased or haunted by the subsequent attention which was given to his remarks made before the Joint Committee of the Senate and House of Commons on Capital and Corporal Punishment. Mr. Common's observations (rendered in his capacity as the then Director of Public Prosecutions for Ontario) have found their way into articles, addresses and case law. The wide audience and dissemination of those remarks was undoubtedly in large measure due to their partial incorporation into an address delivered by G. Arthur Martin to the Law Society of Upper Canada in 1955 on the subject of "Preliminary Hearings".[225] A fuller explication of Common's text may be found in Martin's lecture but the crux of those notorious remarks centre around the assertion that in every criminal case "there are no 'fast ones' pulled by the Crown", and "that in all of the cases not only in capital cases, but usually in all criminal cases there is complete disclosure by the prosecution of its case to the defence".[226] A recent survey conducted by the Law Reform Commission of Canada on prosecu-

---

225. (1955) L.S.U.C. Special Lectures 1.
226. *Ibid.* at p. 3 *per* W. B. Common Q.C.

torial disclosure practices demonstrates that if Mr. Common's bold assertions were ever correct, they are certainly not so today.[227]

It has been said that discovery (or disclosure) is "essential to the rational and effective operation of the adversary system".[228] Why this is the case is explained in the following passage:

> In regard to the purpose of the criminal process, defined . . . as pursuing the truth of allegations of criminal conduct while respecting human dignity and privacy and attempting to minimize the risk of convicting innocent persons, it may be argued that in an adversary setting of dispute resolution it is unlikely that this purpose will be achieved on any consistent basis without discovery. The police and the prosecution investigate, gather information, commence criminal prosecutions, and seek to establish the guilt of accused persons beyond a reasonable doubt. They do so in a setting which allows them almost total control over the evidence that will be introduced to establish guilt and conversely, the evidence that will be ignored, either by not being followed up by further investigation or by not being offered at trial. This is not to suggest that in performing these roles the police and prosecution will consciously withhold valuable information from the defence. But it does mean that without pre-trial disclosure of witnesses and their evidence and without tangible evidence, for the vast majority of cases in which the defence does not have its own investigative resources or cannot afford them, or even in cases where such resources are available but the prosecution evidence will not be revealed by an independent investigation, the defence will be less able to examine and challenge the prosecution evidence and expose that which may be suspect. It also means that without disclosure to the defence of evidence which the prosecution does not intend to call at trial because it may seem irrelevant or unimportant, the defence is deprived of evidence which from a different perspective may indeed be relevant or lead to the finding of relevant evidence. It means, therefore, that the absence of discovery to the accused places a serious limitation on the realization of the criminal process.[229]

Full discovery, it has been contended, increases the likelihood of obtaining "truer" verdicts.[230] Full discovery, were it to be given effect, would include access to at least the following information and material:[231]

---

227. See Law Reform Commission of Canada, "Working Paper 4" *Criminal Procedure: Discovery* (1974) pp. 19-23.
228. *Ibid.* at p. 14.
229. *Ibid.* at pp. 13-14.
230. A. Hooper, "Discovery in Criminal Cases" (1972) 50 Can.Bar.Rev. 445 at p. 450.
231. *Ibid.* pp. 471-472. Also, P. Galligan in "Advising an Arrested Client" (1963) L.S.U.C. Special Lectures 35 at pp. 47-51, lists these items as matters which the accused has an *actual right* to receive from the Crown: (1) criminal record of crown witnesses; (2) names of witnesses able to give material evidence whom the Crown does not intend to call; (3) statement of accomplice; (4) evidence in support of defence of insanity; (5) descriptions given

(1) any evidence favourable to the accused;
(2) the names and addresses of witnesses who will be called by the Crown if there is a trial and of other witnesses who have evidence relevant to the accused's guilt or innocence, and any statements made by them;
(3) any statement made by an accused or an accomplice;
(4) any evidence given at the preliminary inquiry;
(5) the testimony before the grand jury of any witness who will be called by the Crown if there is a trial;
(6) any reports by experts and the results of any tests;
(7) any documents, objects, and so on, which were seized from the accused or which will be used if there is a trial;
(8) the criminal record of any witness who will be called by the Crown if there is a trial.

The notion of full discovery does not presently exist, and has not ever existed, in Canada. The practice of *some* pretrial disclosure of information between prosecutors and defence counsel does exist but standards are far from uniform — variances occurring not only from province to province but often also from prosecutor to prosecutor. Additionally, the whole matter of pre-trial disclosure, save for very few exceptions, is generally regarded as one of unfettered prosecutorial discretion.[232] Over the years this process has been regarded as unobjectionable with the prevailing wisdom suggesting that the guarantee of fairness to the accused lay in the fact that the prosecutor was regarded as being more than a mere advocate. Certainly he was to be viewed as other than a pure adversary, and, more properly, he was to be described (and consequently he was expected to deport himself) as a "minister of justice" — an individual at least once removed from partisanship or the devilry of adversarial intrigue. This perspective has quite properly been characterized as a "conceptual error . . . allowing the moral role of the prosecution to substitute for positive rules of law".[233]

The *Canadian Bill of Rights* asserts that every accused person has an unqualified right to a fair hearing in accordance with the principles of fundamental justice for the determination of his rights and obligations.[234] The *Criminal Code* enshrines the right in the accused to make his full answer and defence to the prosecution's case.[235] Neither of these rights can be meaningful without substantial, if not complete, disclosure. Nevertheless actual statutory provisions compelling dis-

---

by eye-witnesses and other previous statements made by Crown witnesses; (6) statements of accused.
232. For an examination of the phenomenon of "prosecutorial discretion" see Chapter 3 *supra*.
233. Law Reform Commission of Canada, *supra* footnote 227 at p. 19.
234. R.S.C. 1970, Appendix III, s. 2(*e*).
235. R.S.C. 1970, Chap. C-34, ss. 737(1), 577(3).

closure by the prosecution are few and insubstantial. Basically, the *statutory* rights of disclosure possessed by the accused are these:

(1) The accused has a right to be informed promptly of the reason for his arrest and detention (*Bill of Rights* s. 2(*c*) (i)).

(2) The accused has a right to a particularized charge; one containing sufficient detail of the circumstances of the alleged offence to give the accused reasonable information with respect to the act or omission to be proved against him and to identify the transaction referred to (*Criminal Code* ss. 510, 516).

(3) After he has been committed for trial or at his trial the accused has a right to inspect, or, upon payment of a fee, to receive a copy of, the indictment, the evidence (taken at the preliminary hearing or trial), his own statement. He is also entitled to inspect the exhibits (*Criminal Code* s. 531.).

(4) On summary application, provided the judge so orders, the accused may have any exhibit released for scientific or other testing and examination (*Criminal Code* s. 533).

(5) After an indictment has been found and at least ten days before arraignment on a charge of treason an accused is entitled to (a) a copy of the indictment, (b) a list of the witnesses to be proved on the trial to prove the indictment, and (c) a copy of the panel of jurors who are to try him returned by the sheriff (*Criminal Code* s. 532).

(6) Before any book or document may be received in evidence the accused must be given reasonable notice of the proposed tender (*Canada Evidence Act* s. 28[236]).

(7) Provided the offence is not a summary conviction offence, or an indictable offence in the absolute jurisdiction of the magistrate, and provided that the accused does not elect summary trial, or the prosecutor does not proceed by direct indictment, (or, where possible, elect to proceed summarily), the accused has a right to a preliminary hearing (*Criminal Code* ss. 427, 483).

Other matters than those set out above which the Crown deigns to divulge *before trial* are largely a matter of presently uncontrolled prosecutorial discretion. It is fair to say that in existing Canadian criminal law there is very little discovery provided to the accused as a matter of right.[237] This is at odds with the generally held belief that a great deal of general discovery is available to the accused as a result of the existence of the preliminary inquiry.

> Now while the preliminary inquiry is still said to serve this latter purpose, [of reviewing the evidence of a charge to determine whether it was sufficient to warrant the accused standing trial] *it is more com-*

---

236. R.S.C. 1970, Chap. E-10.
237. Law Reform Commission of Canada, *supra* footnote 227 at p. 17 (emphasis added).

monly seen as a general discovery vehicle. But this function of the procedure flies in the face of the facts. In reality the preliminary inquiry is only available in a small minority of criminal cases. According to the 1969 information of Statistics Canada only 5 per cent of all criminal cases were tried by either judge alone . . . or judge and jury — being those cases in which a preliminary inquiry is available. As well, even for those cases in which the preliminary inquiry is available, our courts have ruled that its purpose is strictly to determine whether or not an accused should stand trial; it is not if clearly stated then clearly applied, to provide discovery to the accused. Thus, if the prosecution should adduce sufficient evidence at the preliminary inquiry to justify the accused standing trial, the purpose of the preliminary will have been satisfied despite the fact that the prosecution may not have called all of its witnesses or presented all of its evidence.[238]

For some time it was unsettled in our jurisprudence as to whether it was incumbent upon the Crown prosecutor conducting a preliminary inquiry to bring forward *all* the evidence, favourable as well as unfavourable to the accused, at the preliminary hearing stage and not merely sufficient evidence to establish a case of probable guilt (and hence to warrant the committal for trial of the accused). G. Arthur Martin (now Martin J.A. of the Ontario Court of Appeal) was of the opinion that where it was apparent that the prosecutor had merely put in a "skeleton case" at the preliminary hearing that the trial judge "should postpone the trial and direct the Crown to inform the defence counsel of any further evidence that is proposed to be adduced and give counsel sufficient time to prepare to meet it."[239] He based these views in part upon certain pronouncements found in Kenny, *Outlines of Criminal Law* (16th ed., p. 501, footnote 3):

Modern practice concedes to every accused person the right to know, before his trial, what evidence will be given against him. Hence if anyone who was not produced before the committing justice is to be called as a witness, full informaton should be furnished to the accused both as to his name and as to the evidence he will give. If this has not been done, his evidence should not be pressed at the trial if the accused objects (*per* Hawkins J. in *R. v. Harris* (1882), C.C.C. Sess. Pap. xcv, 525). The same principle applies to letters or other documents.[240]

The views expressed *supra* have not prevailed in Canada. In fact

<hr/>

238. *Ibid.* at pp. 17-18 (emphasis added).
239. G. A. Martin, *supra* footnote 225 at p. 4. *N.B.* Martin does not go so far as to say that there is a duty spelled out in the case law suggesting that the prosecution present all its evidence at the preliminary hearing: "But notwithstanding the pronouncements of courts from time to time as to the duty of Crown counsel to adduce at the trial all evidence in his possession, favourable as well as unfavourable to the accused, there has been no case so far as I know that directly says it is the duty of Crown counsel to disclose or adduce all his evidence at the preliminary hearing" (at p. 2).
240. Quoted in G. A. Martin, *supra* footnote 225 at p. 4.

the most recent pronouncement on the subject by the Supreme Court of Canada holds that the "*sole purpose* of the preliminary inquiry is to satisfy the magistrate that there is sufficient evidence to put the accused on trial, and that therefore, the Crown has the discretion to present only that evidence which makes out a prima facie case".[241]

While the decided cases do indeed indicate a discretion in the prosecutor as to which witnesses to call in order to discharge the burden cast upon the Crown at a preliminary hearing they do *not* go so far as to indicate that the *sole* function of the preliminary inquiry is to satisfy the magistrate that the Crown has sufficient evidence to put the accused on his trial. Neither *Patterson v. R.* nor *R. v. Epping; Ex parte Massaro* makes such a claim and those are the two cases upon which the Supreme Court's contentions in *Caccamo v. R.* are premised.

Discovery is certainly *in law,* as well as in practice, one of the purposes of the preliminary inquiry. The decision in *Caccamo* insofar as it is based upon the authority of earlier precedents is in error. *R. v. Epping* denied that the preliminary inquiry was "a rehearsal so that the defence may try out their cross-examination on the witnesses for the prosecution with a view to using the results to their advantage in the Crown court at a later stage."[242] In Canada such a conclusion is unjustified in view of the express provisions of s. 11 of the *Canada Evidence Act* which clearly anticipates cross-examination on such previous oral statements. Also, even accepting the views put forward by the Lord Chief Justice in that case, they clearly do not extend so far as to deny the discovery function of the preliminary inquiry. *Patterson v. R.* as viewed by majority of the Supreme Court of Canada was confined to the "very narrow issues"[243] raised by the case and the ratio of that decision was that the appellant failed to establish or show any jurisdictional defect which would permit a review by certiorari. The decision cannot fairly be read in such a way as to deny the existence of a discovery function for the preliminary inquiry.

There can be no doubt that an accused is entitled to make his full answer and defence at a preliminary inquiry.[244] The *Criminal Code* makes express provision under s. 468(1)(a) for the justice holding a preliminary inquiry to "allow the accused or his counsel" to "cross-examine proscution witnesses. As LeBel J. pointed out in *R. v. Churchman*[245] "at a preliminary hearing an accused person is always entitled to cross-examine for the purpose of demolishing the Crown's case then

---

241. *Caccamo v. R.* (1975) 29 C.R.N.S. 78 at p. 97 (Can.) *per* de Grandpré J. (emphasis added) citing *Patterson v. R.* (1970) 10 C.R.N.S. 55 (Can.), and *R. v. Epping; Ex parte Massaro* (1972) 57 Cr. App. R. 499.
242. 57 Cr.App.R. 499 at p. 500.
243. (1970) 10 C.R.N.S. 55 at pp. 56-57.
244. *R. v. Pearson* (1957) 117 C.C.C. 249 at p. 257 (Alta. C.A.)
245. [1955] O.W.N. 90 at p. 93.

and there if he can, or, as more frequently happens, for the purpose of demolishing it later at the trial".

Usually, in these matters it is not the discovery function itself which is questioned in relation to preliminary hearings, but rather the extent to which the accused may discover the prosecution case above and beyond the confines of the evidence actually tendered by the Crown at that first instance. The two most predominant questions are: (a) is the accused entitled to cross-examine witnesses not produced by the crown at the preliminary?; and (b) can the accused compel production for the purpose of cross-examination of a previous statement of a witness at the preliminary hearing (which it is suspected is at odds with the sworn testimony of the witness) when the Crown has not in examination in chief produced or utilized the statement? (The former question was involved in *R. v. Epping,* while the latter was at issue in the *Patterson* case.)

(a) *Examining witness not called by the crown*

Section 469 of the *Code* affords the accused an opportunity of calling such witnesses to give testimony at the preliminary inquiry as he deems advisable, and as are capable of giving testimony relevant to the inquiry. The section is a much ignored tool; one which potentially is of great use and advantage to the accused as a discovery vehicle.

Where the preliminary hearing has been carefully and meticulously handled by defence counsel the names and identities of important witnesses (most of which information one expects to have been within the knowledge of the prosecuting forces) will often surface during the course of testimony. The testimony of such witnesses may often go unsolicited by the prosecution and yet may well be of vital import from the point of view of the accused. Such evidence might serve to demolish what would otherwise be a sufficient case for committal of the accused.[246]

A good example of such a situation occurred in the case of *R. v. Mishko.*[247] The accused Mishko had been charged with the armed robbery of a bank. Two witnesses were called by the Crown in order to identify the accused as the individual in the bank. Additional witnesses, also in the bank, whose names and addresses had been elicited during cross-examination, were proposed to be called as defence witnesses on the inquiry when the Crown elected not to produce them in proof of its case. After two adjournments Martin P.M. acceded to a Crown motion denying to the defence the opportunity of calling the witnesses. An

---

246. *R. v. Solloway & Mills* (1930) 53 C.C.C. 180 (Alta. C.A.) stands for the proposition that the defence ought to be given a fair chance by cross-examination of Crown witnesses or production of evidence, to show, if it can, that what might otherwise appear to be a *prima facie* case of guilt might have an innocent construction placed upon it.

247. (1945) 85 C.C.C. 410 (Ont.).

application for a writ of habeas corpus with certiorari in aid was brought by counsel for the accused. Hogg J. agreed with the contentions of counsel for Mishko that the committal for trial of the accused should be quashed and ordered that a new preliminary inquiry be held.

> In the majority of cases no witnesses for the defence are called at the preliminary hearing. If the case established at the close of the evidence for the prosecution is such that any proof to be adduced on the part of the accused would only amount at most to a conflict of evidence, the evidence given for the defence would not serve any useful purpose, it being no part of the duty of the Magistrate to determine as to the guilt or innocence of the accused, under such circumstances. But there are cases of *prima facie* guilt which an accused may, by calling witnesses, be able to explain so as to clear up the imputation of guilt against him. See Crankshaw, *op. cit.*, p. 938.

> Although the examination of witnesses for the defence on the preliminary investigation may, as Mr. Common contends, disclose the Crown's case, and might be analogous in certain circumstances to an examination for discovery, I am of the opinion that the authorities hold that the language of s. 686 of the *Cr. Code* is to be taken in its literal sense, and that an accused must be permitted to call witnesses and they are to be heard on "any fact relevant to the case", on the preliminary inquiry.[248]

One of Canada's leading defence counsel, Mr. Harry Walsh Q.C., has expressed the view that where Crown Counsel has not called all of the available witnesses at the preliminary inquiry and seeks to give notice to defence counsel that these other witnesses may be called at the trial counsel for the accused should not accept such notice even if it comes in the form of a copy of the statement of the witness or the gist of his expected testimony. "Defence counsel" he urges, "should insist on the witnesses being called at the preliminary inquiry, and if the Crown refuses he should call the witnesses himself".[249]

There is of course quite a difference between defence counsel calling the witness as its own, and having the Crown produce the witness and tender his evidence as part of its case. Only in the latter situation does defence counsel have the benefit of cross-examination (as opposed to examination in chief). Thus, it is infinitely more desirable

---

248. *Ibid.* at p. 415 *per* Hogg J. See also *R. v. Churchman supra* footnote 245 where the right of counsel to ascertain the identity and addresses of all material witnesses at the preliminary hearing was affirmed. (The denial of counsel's right to seek and ascertain such information led to the ordering of a new preliminary hearing in the case.) Also, *R. v. Clarke* (1930) 22 Cr.App.Rep. 58. And see *R. v. Grigoreshenko* (1945) 85 C.C.C. 129 (Sask. C.A.) which case holds that the preliminary inquiry is the time when all questions should be asked with the object of achieving as full a discovery as possible in the circumstances.

249. H. Walsh, "Discovery in the Criminal Process" in C.B.A., *Studies in Criminal Law and Procedure* (1973).

from the defence viewpoint to have the Crown produce such witnesses as part of its case. How realistic it is to expect such co-operation from the Crown is another matter. (It should be remembered that it was the same W. B. Common Q.C. who spoke of "full disclosure" who objected to allowing the defence to call the "Crown witnesses" who had not been produced in *Mishko*.) But because the Crown does not produce or call the witness in question does not *necessarily* preclude the defence from cross-examination. The Court, if it is so disposed may assist the accused in his efforts at discovery. As McWilliams points out in his text on *Canadian Criminal Evidence* "generally the *judge* has the right to call a witness not called by either the prosecution or the defence without the consent of either, if in his opinion that course is necessary."[250]

It is submitted that in instances where (a) the identity of a given witness could not have been known to the accused prior to the inquiry; (b) it is reasonably expected that the witness can supply material and relevant testimony; and (c) the Crown refuses to produce the witness if only for the purpose of allowing the defence the opportunity to cross-examine such witness; then the court should on the application of counsel call the witness as its own in order that the witness might be cross-examined. Such a procedure is consistent with both the fair hearing requirements of the *Bill of Rights* and the *Criminal Code* provision ensuring the accused an opportunity to make full answer and defence. Also, an active role insuring fair treatment of the accused at this stage might serve to obviate the need for disclosure (and the resultant legal conflict where it is not forthcoming) as was hinted at (in *obiter*) by Judson J. in *Patterson v. R.*:

> We are not concerned here with the power of a trial judge to compel production during the trial *nor with the extent to which the prosecution, in fairness to an accused person, ought to make production after the preliminary hearing and before trial.* This is a subject which received some comment in the British Columbia Court of Appeal in *Regina v. Lantos*, 45 W.W.R. 409, [1964] 2 C.C.C. 52, and Archbold, Criminal Pleading Evidence and Practice, 37th ed., para. 1393.[251]

(b) *Cross-examination on previous inconsistent statements*[252]

By s. 10(1) of the *Canada Evidence Act* a judge "at any time dur-

---

250. P. K. McWilliams, *Canadian Criminal Evidence* (1974) at p. 464 citing in support *R. v. Liddle* (1928) 21 Cr.App.Rep. 3; *R. v. Seigley* (1911) 6 Cr.App.Rep. 106; *R. v. Bull* (1839) 9 C. & P. 22; *R. v. Holden* (1838) 8 C. & P. 606; *R. v. Simmonds* (1823) 1 C. & P. 84. See also P. C. Stenning "Annotation: One Blind Man to See Fair Play: The Judge's Right to Call Witnesses" (1974) 24 C.R.N.S. 49.

251. *Supra* footnote 243 at pp. 57-58 *per* Judson J. (emphasis added).

252. This is a problem which arises at trial as well as on the preliminary inquiry. The emphasis here is on the latter stage. Also, see generally G. G. Brodsky, "Adverse Witnesses: Use of Previous Inconsistent Statements" (1965-66) 8 Cr.L.Q. 383.

ing the trial", may require the production of a statement in writing given by a witness. If the judge is satisfied that the statement is contradictory and at odds with the evidence given under oath by the witness he may allow the statement to be employed for the purpose of cross-examining the witness.[253] According to Judson J. (on behalf of the majority) in Patterson:

> This power is given explicitly to a judge "at any time during the trial". It is not given to a magistrate during the conduct of a preliminary hearing. There is a real distinction here. The purpose of a preliminary inquiry is clearly defined by the Criminal Code — to determine whether there is sufficient evidence to put the accused on trial. It is not a trial and should not be allowed to become a trial.[254]

Normally, such pronouncements emanating as they do from our highest Court would have to be regarded as the final word on the subject. In practice, the issue remains very much a live one — for these reasons:

(1) The remarks of Judson J. must be regarded as obiter since the learned Justice chose to resolve the matters before the Court on very "narrow" grounds; namely, the failure to show jurisdictional defect in order to permit a review by certiorari.

(2) The decision did not consider the effect of s. 2(e) (fair hearing) of the *Canadian Bill of Rights* on the issue.

(3) The decision did not decide whether there was power to order production of the statement apart from the requirements of s. 10(1) of the *Canada Evidence Act*.

Lower court decisions (decided since *Patterson*) have been handed down supporting the view that production of previous inconsistent statements may be compelled at the preliminary hearing. These decisions have been based upon reasons number (2)[255] and (3)[256] *supra.*

---

253. At least one court has held that the judge may *only* be satisfied after the defence has displaced a heavy onus which falls upon it in these situations. The defence must establish that production of the statement is in the interest of justice as distinct from the interest of the accused: *R. v. Lalonde* (1971) 15 C.R.N.S. 1 (Ont.). This is an especially onerous requirement in view of the fact that counsel for the defence ordinarily has not seen the statement and in consequence can hardly be expected to know whether divulging the contents of same would be in the interests of justice.

254. *Supra,* footnote 243 at p. 57.

255. *R. v. Littlejohn* (1972) 21 C.R.N.S. 349 (Man.).

256. *R. v. Harbison* (1972) 20 C.R.N.S. 336 (B.C.) Denroche Prov. J. citing in support *R. v. Lantos* [1964] 2 C.C.C. 52 (B.C. C.A.); *R. v. Imbery* (1961) 35 W.W.R. 192 (Alta.); *R. v. Silvester* (1959) 125 C.C.C. 190 (B.C.).

Further, as to the common law power of judges to compel production of prior written statements "where the interests of justice require" see, *Mahadeo v. R.* [1936] 2 All E.R. 813; *R. v. Finland* (1959) 125 C.C.C. 186 (B.C.); *R. v. Weigelt* (1960) 128 C.C.C. 217 (Alta. C.A.) (although these Canadian cases seem to restrict "production" to "production at trial".) See also *R. v. Torrens* [1963] 1 C.C.C. 383 (Sask.) and *R. v. McNeil* (1960) 127 C.C.C. 343 (Sask.).

On this issue one further point should be noted. Since it is contended that the remarks of Judson J. to the effect that the preliminary hearing "is not a trial, and should not be allowed to become a trial" were merely *obiter* (albeit strong *obiter* in view of the source) it is submitted that the question of whether the preliminary may be regarded in some senses as a 'trial" or a "form of trial" remains open. In this regard these remarks of Maybank J. in *Re Spence* are worthy of consideration:

> The preliminary hearing is, indeed, a trial; not a trial in which an accused may be found guilty or innocent; but certainly a trial of an issue — the issue of whether or not an accused person should be called upon to stand trial in a Superior Court.[257]

Cross-examination of a witness as to a previous inconsistent statement of course is a problem which arises not only at the preliminary inquiry but also (and probably, more often) at trial following committal. Where the Crown has refused to disclose the statement, and the magistrate conducting the inquiry has denied counsel access to the statement an obvious problem arises. The conundrum which counsel is expected to solve is this one: Without knowing the contents of the statement(s) how can counsel demonstrate that it is inconsistent and contradictory? Moreover, without knowing the contents how can counsel determine that it is tactically advantageous to cross-examine upon the statement? Finally, without knowledge of the contents of the statement how can counsel address the court on the issue of production being "required in the interests of justice"?

Quite simply, it is impossible for counsel to resolve any of the aspects of this puzzle without some assistance along the way.

The existing Canadian authorities seem to indicate that although counsel may, in the "discretion" of the court, be entitled to see the previous statements of a sworn witness he is not entitled to them prior to trial.[258] (This should be read subject to what has been said *supra* as to the presently evolving state of the "previous statement" rule on preliminary inquiries.) Since, it is the "duty of the Court to see that all rights of the accused are safeguarded"[259] it is submitted that *as of right* on application by counsel for the accused *at trial* previous (undisclosed) statements should be produced for inspection, and where appropriate, cross-examination thereon ought to be allowed. Only at this latter stage (determining whether cross-examination ought to be allowed) should a judicial determination ("discretion") be requisite. In this way at least at the moment of trial counsel would not be left to guess as to whether key information, vital to his client's defence, is

---

257. (1961) 132 C.C.C. 368 at p. 371 (Man. Q.B.).
258. See *R. v. Silvester supra* footnote 256; *R. v. Finland supra* footnote 256; *R. v. Weigelt supra* footnote 256; *R. v. Lalonde supra* footnote 253.
259. *Per* Tysoe J.A. in *R. v. Lantos supra* footnote 256 at p. 54.

being secreted away in the form of a witness' prior inconsistent statement. At present the law does not go so far. At best it holds that production before trial is in the discretion of the Crown,[260] while production at trial is a discretion in the trial judge,[261] and not a right in the accused.

It has been held that where the *Crown* seeks to impeach its own witness with a prior inconsistent statement that the defence is entitled to inspection of the statement before the court determines whether the Crown may be allowed to cross-examine.[262] The arguments are equally compelling for disclosure or inspection by the defence where the Crown possesses a previous statement (also *potentially* at variance with its own witness' sworn testimony) but chooses not to use the statement for impeachment purposes.

The accused in Canada is far from having attained effective rights of discovery.[263] In England, the situation at present differs markedly. "Although English courts were traditionally hostile to discovery, they have changed their approach in this century".[264] "Discovery" includes far more than merely the identity of witnesses and access to their written statements (these matters have been selected because they are illustrative of the general problems embraced by the area). Discovery ideally (as we have earlier noted) entails the revelation of any relevant evidence, favourable or unfavourable, which can be of assistance in proving or disproving the charge. For discovery to be effective disclosure should, for the most part, take place prior to trial. The preliminary hearing provides a unique opportunity for full, probing

---

260. *R. v. Bohozuk* (1947) 87 C.C.C. 125 (Ont.).
261. *R. v. Lalonde,* supra footnote 253.
262. *R. v. Sinclair* (1974) 19 C.C.C. (2d) 123 (Man.).
263. See H. Walsh *supra* footnote 249 at p. 194.
264. A. Hooper, *supra* footnote 230 at p. 476. This summary provided by Hooper accurately reflects the English position today: "The prosecution has a duty to disclose the existence of any evidence favourable to the accused, such as the fact that a Crown witness has a known bad character or has earlier given a statement which conflicts with his testimony or the fact that there is a person who can give material evidence but whom it is not intended to call. . . . Whether in all circumstances there is a duty to disclose prior statements of prosecution witnesses is not clear . . . The most effective method of obtaining discovery in England is through the preliminary inquiry. The prosecution is obliged to present, not only all the witnesses whom it is intended to call at trial, but also the evidence that those witnesses will be giving — where additional evidence comes to light after the preliminary inquiry "a notice setting out in the form of a statement by the witness the additional evidence he proposes to call" must be served on the defence prior to the trial."

See in this regard *Dallison v. Caffery* [1965] 1 Q.B. 348; *R. v. Casey* (1947) 32 Cr.App.R. 91; *R. v. Clarke, supra* footnote 248; *R. v. Bryant* (1946) 31 Cr.App.R. 146; *Mahadeo v. R., supra* footnote 256; *R. v. Harris* (1882) C.C.C. Sess. Pap xcv 525, all cited by Hooper in support of the above statement.

discovery. Of course new evidence surfacing between the preliminary and the trial should be disclosed prior to trial. By and large the English jurisprudence facilitates the aim of effective discovery.

In Canada, while it is said that a prosecutor must present all witnesses essential to the unfolding of the narrative at trial, it is also said that the decision as to which witnesses best suit this purpose resides with the prosecutor. "Of course, the Crown must not hold back evidence because it would assist an accused".[265] These words spoken by Kerwin J. in *Lemay v. R.* standing alone reffect a degree of fairness. They also reflect an appreciation of the normal imbalance which prevails when the information gathering resources of the state are compared to those of the individual under charge. However, the cumulative picture which presents; of the prosecuting forces needing only to present a skeletal case at the preliminary inquiry; of the Crown being under no obligation to divulge either the prior inconsistent statements of the witnesses it proposes to call, or the names and addresses of those witnesses capable of furnishing relevant and material evidence which it does *not* propose to call (save as an aspect of discretion controllable only where an "oblique motive" is demonstrable) is a disturbing one. This picture is difficult in fact to reconcile with these words of Rand J. in *Boucher v. R.*:[266]

> the purpose of a criminal prosecution is not to obtain a conviction, it is to lay before a jury what the Crown considers to be credible evidence relevant to what is alleged to be a crime. Counsel have a duty to see that all available legal proof of the facts is presented . . . The role of prosecutor excludes any notion of winning or losing.

It is a distortion of the reality of the application of our law in practice to insist that "under our criminal procedure the accused has every advantage."[267] While it is true that in strict terms it is the interests of justice and not the interests of the accused with which the court should be concerned, it must also be remembered that the cause of justice can only be advanced by insuring that all the rights of the accused are safeguarded.[268] The interests of justice may on occasion require the denial of the opportunity of discovery as in the circumstance where the anonymity and safety of informers is involved. In such instances the "clash between the interests of pre-trial discovery and the need for effective crime detection" may well impel a certain amelioration of

---

265. *Lemay v. R.* (1952) 14 C.R. 89 at p. 95 (Can.), *per* Kerwin J. See also *Seneviratne v. R.* [1936] 3 All E.R. 36.
266. [1955] S.C.R. 16 at pp. 23-24.
267. The quotation is that of Learned Hand J. and is found in *U.S. v. Garsson* 291 F. 646 at p. 649. It is cited with approval and set out at greater length by Haines J. in *R. v. Lalonde supra* footnote 253 at p. 13. *Cf.* A. Hooper *supra* footnote 230 at pp. 472-476 where the subject of "Arguments Against Discovery" is dealt with.
268. *R. v. Bohozuk supra* footnote 260 at p. 126 *per* McKay J.

basic procedural safeguards.[269] However, less sustainable is the contention that a prime factor to be kept in the judicial mind is the fear "that many people would be unwilling to talk to the police if they felt that their statements would be given to defence counsel before trial, so that they may be picked apart at leisure in preparation for their embarrassment in the witness stand or accosted by private investigators to recant."[270]

Any witness of necessity, is put to some discomfiture when called upon to give testimony. Cross-examination or even the mere act of testifying can for certain individuals be an embarrassing or nerve-wracking experience. It is however a compellable legal duty in a state under law. It is a moral duty as well. In a certain sense this duty can be regarded as part of the price of citizenship. The witness cannot impose terms upon the manner in which his testimony is to be received. Within limits the court will protect him — from irrelevant probing, from hectoring and abuse — but it cannot shield him from the fog of hazy recollection, from inaccuracy, exaggeration, guesswork or plain lying and prevarication; for on his testimony may hang the future freedom, or possible incarceration, of another individual. If "fear of retaliation" is a very real fear in an "aggressive community"[271] the criminal law provides against extortion, obstruction and resort to force, and the police are charged with the duty of safeguarding the vulnerable, and of deterring those who would seek to tamper with the process. Too great a zeal for the discovery of truth can on occasion serve to mask it.[272]

(2) Ordering adjournments where surprise evidence tendered

This subject flows naturally out of the previous consideration of disclosure. Non-disclosure may result in surprise to the accused at trial. Depending upon the nature of the evidence tendered prejudice may result. The fairness of the trial may be compromised.

In the course of giving judgment in *Caccamo v. R.,* de Grandpré J. observed:[273]

> It is within the framework of our adversary system under which our criminal law is administered, that the accused must be guaranteed a fair trial.
>
> In that light, if the introduction of new evidence at the trial takes the accused by surprise, obviously he is entitled to a postponement.

In most instances an adjournment of reasonable length will suffice

---

269. *Per* Haines J. in *Lalonde supra* footnote 253 at p. 8.
270. *Ibid.* at p. 8.
271. *Ibid.* at p. 13.
272. See H. Molot, "Non-Disclosure of Evidence, Adverse Inferences and the Court's Search for Truth" (1971) 10 Alta.L.R. 45.
273. *Supra* footnote 241 at p. 98.

to remove any aspect of prejudice which might have accrued to the defence due to the introduction of surprise evidence. The question remains as to what response may the court adopt where an adjournment is not able to undo the resultant prejudice. The answer proposed by de Grandpré J. in *Caccamo* is quite categorical

> over the years, the sole effect of the introduction of new evidence at trial has been to allow the accused to obtain a postponement of the trial.[274]

It is, however, softened somewhat by these remarks:

> Of course, I do not deny that there could be cases where the option made could be set aside if in fact there had been a miscarriage of justice. Such was not the case here.[275]

In fact the court receiving the evidence does have these "options":

(1) it can receive the evidence and where appropriate grant a sufficient adjournment;

(2) it can refuse to admit the evidence where its prejudicial effect outweighs its probative value[276]

(3) if the prejudicial effect is grave and the evidence is already before the court it can declare a mistrial.

For the most part the prejudice occasioned in these instances occurs due to the element of surprise and consequent ill-preparation, and usually an adjournment will suffice. As the *Caccamo* case points out on occasion the inability to "discover" the evidence on the preliminary inquiry may, in retrospect, have affected the entire manner in which counsel conducted the inquiry; the line of examination pursued may well have differed had counsel been aware of the evidence.[277] Given the fact, however, that at present the Crown is under no obligation to present its entire case at the preliminary inquiry (according to De Grandpré J. the Crown has a discretion to present only that evidence which makes out a *prima facie* case)[278] the choice of procedure adopted in *Caccamo* and other cases can only (to paraphrase Martland J. in *Wray*) operate unfortunately for the accused, but not unfairly.

On the other hand, it should be borne in mind that the Crown is under a duty to inform the defence of any witnesses who are to be

---

274. *Supra* footnote 241 at p. 99.
275. *Supra* footnote 241 at p. 99. In *Caccamo* the accused had sought and been granted a lengthy adjournment when the Crown had produced surprise evidence in the form of handwritten notes in Italian (which allegedly were a type of constitution used by a Mafia-related secret criminal organization), and supporting expert evidence for verification purposes.
276. See the discussion *supra*, "Evidence Possessed of Prejudicial Effect" in Part 2 of this Chapter.
277. Counsel in *Caccamo* also argued (somewhat unconvincingly) that the existence of the evidence, had it been known, would have effected the election of mode of trial made in the case.
278. See *Caccamo v. R. supra* footnote 241 at p. 97.

called at trial and were not called at the preliminary hearing. This duty is said to extend so far as to require disclosure of the general nature of the expected evidence. Where these conditions are not met and the defence is taken by surprise the cases hold that the trial judge should order an adjournment in order that the defence might be afforded an opportunity to examine the evidence and adequately prepare to meet it.[279]

As to adjournments generally, the law is clear that a refusal of an adjournment although discretionary and within the jurisdiction of a court, may, in particular circumstances, amount to a denial of the accused's right to make full answer and defence.[280] The decision of granting, or refusing to grant, an adjournment is normally not subject to review unless the Court of Appeal is satisfied that the discretion was not exercised properly.[281]

Thus, while statute and case law entrusts the trial judge with power to adjourn the trial from time to time as is seen fit, or to postpone its commencement,[282] the decision, for the most part, is an unreviewable one.

> While it is possible to conceive of cases in which it would be clear that *there had not been any exercise of judicial discretion* in granting or refusing postponement of trial, and in such cases there might be error of law which would be properly reviewable, where, in what was clearly an exercise of his discretion the trial Judge has refused postponement because he was "of the opinion" that further time should not be allowed, . . . I am satisfied that the propriety of that exercise of discretion is not reviewable by an Appellate Court and is not properly the subject of a reserved case under section 1014.[283]

It may accurately be said that *no exercise of discretion at all* has taken place where the accused is denied an opportunity to demonstrate that the existence of requisite conditions justifying the application for an adjournment do in fact exist.[284] Moreover, in view of the remarks

---

279. See *Richard v. R.* (1957) 126 C.C.C. 255 (N.B. C.A.); *Childs v. R.* (1958) 122 C.C.C. 126 (N.B. C.A.); *R. v. Cunningham* (1952) 30 M.P.R. 34 N.B. C.A.). See also *R. v. McClain* (1915) 23 C.C.C. 488 (Alta. C.A.) and *R. v. Flannagan* 15 Cox C.C. 403.

280. *R. v. Dow* (1972) 19 C.R.N.S. 148 (B.C.) where Aikins J. cites the following cases in support: *R. v. Picariello* (1922) 37 C.C.C. 284 (Alta. C.A.); *Rex v. Hallchuk (Elchuk)* (1928) 51 C.C.C. 18 (Man.); *R. v. Dick* [1968] 2 O.R. 351 (Ont.); *R. v. Pickett* (1972) 5 C.C.C. (2d) 371 (Ont. C.A.).

281. See *e.g. Mulvihill v. R.* (1914) 23 C.C.C. 194 (Can.), *Darville v. R.* (1956) 116 C.C.C. 113 (Can.) and see *R. v. Warren* (1973) 24 C.R.N.S. 349 (N.S. C.A.).

282. For statutory provisions in the *Criminal Code* granting rights of adjournment see ss. 501, 529(5), 574, 576(4)(*b*), 556 (2), 732(6), 738, 756, 474, 465(1)(*b*).

283. *Per* Rand J. in *Mulvihill v. R. supra* footnote 281 at p. 198 (emphasis added). See also *R. v. Lahosky* (1972) 7 C.C.C. (2d) 407 (Man. C.A.)

284. See the reasons for judgment of Cartwright J. (as he then was) in *Darville v. R. supra* footnote 281 at p. 117.

of de Grandpré J. in *Caccamo v. R.* to the effect that "the option made could be set aside if in fact there had been a miscarriage of justice"[285] it appears that the right of appellate review is not quite as restricted as was earlier imagined.

(3) Severance of trials of co-accused

Where two or more persons are jointly indicted the Crown has the option of trying them separately or together. There is however, power in the court to order separate trials if such a procedure is justifiable in the interests of justice.[286] An accused person does not *prima facie* have a right to a separate trial. Quite the contrary: Where two or more individuals are jointly implicated in the commission of an offence, and in consequence are jointly indicted, it is settled law that *prima facie* they should be tried together.[287]

With the sole exception of s. 522 of the *Criminal Code* (dealing with offences under s. 312 — possession of property obtained by crime; and s. 314(1)(*b*) — possession of stolen goods) the *Criminal Code* is silent on the issue of joinder, or severance, of trial of jointly indicted persons.[288]

Although the procedure for an application for severance is not laid down by statute the proper time and place for the bringing of such application is at the beginning of the trial, and should be brought before the trial judge. It is not proper to seek an order from another judge sitting in chambers.[289] There is authority to suggest that severance might even be ordered by the trial judge after the commencement of the trial.[290]

---

285 *Caccamo v. R. supra* footnote 241 at p. 99. Query: What is the effect of such decisions as *Mulvihill v. R.* (*supra* footnote 281) and *R. v. Lahosky* (*supra* footnote 283) in the light of de Grandpré J.'s remarks in Caccamo? Both cases involved the denial of requested traversals. *Lahosky* is reconcilable if one limits the judgment to a consideration of the propriety of an interlocutory (in the sense of "before trial") appeal of the decision denying the postponement. *Mulvihill* on the other hand was decided after the trial had proceeded and terminated. (The provisions of the *Criminal Code* in 1914 required the procedure to be handled in this fashion. S. 1014 of that *Code* provided the appeal should be by case reserved. Furthermore the provision of the present *Code* allowing the accused to appeal "on any ground where there was a miscarriage of justice" (s. 613(1)(*a*)(iii)) did not exist in the 1914 *Code*.)

286. *R. v. Prosko* (1921) 40 C.C.C. 109 (Que.).

287. See A. O. Klein, "Trial of Accused Persons Together" (1959) L.S.U.C. Special Lectures 15.

288. Where the accused are separately indicted they cannot be tried together (even with the consent of both counsel); *R. v. Gray* [1947] O.W.N. 971 (C.A.); *Ex parte Peters* [1965] 2 C.C.C. 199 (Ont.); *R. v. Sargent* (1943) 79 C.C.C. 384 (Man. C.A.), *R. v. Dennis; R. v. Parker* [1924] 1 K.B. 867; *Crane v. D.P.P.* [1921] 2 A.C. 299; *R. v. Deur* (1945) 82 C.C.C. 289 (Can.).

289. *R. v. Auld* (1957) 26 C.R. 266 (B.C. C.A.).

290. *R. v. Cassidy* [1963] 2 C.C.C. 219 (Alta. C.A.); and see also *R. v. Grondkowski; R. v. Malinowski* (1946) 31 Cr.App.Rep. 116 at p. 118; and *R. v. Miller* (1952) 36 Cr.App.Rep. 169.

The usual grounds justifying an order for the severance of the trials of co-accused are these:[291]

(1) That the defendants have antagonistic defences;
(2) That important evidence in favour of one of the defendants which would be admissible on a separate trial would not be allowed on a joint trial;
(3) That evidence which is incompetent against one defendant is to be introduced against another, and that it would work prejudicially to the former with the jury;
(4) That a confession made by one of the defendants if introduced and proved would be calculated to prejudice the jury against the other defendants.
(5) That one of the defendants could give evidence for the whole or some of the other defendants and would become a competent and compellable witness on the separate trials of such other defendants.

These grounds may be said to be the guiding principles governing the judicial determination of an issue involving severance. The decisional act is described in the literature as a "discretionary" one. It is clear that the discretion in question must be exercised judicially.[292] It may not be exercised in a "desultory manner but must be guided and regulated by judicial principles and fixed rules".[293] One commentator, J. L. K. Vamplew, suggests the principles set out *supra* are "merely a guideline" and cautions that "one must always bear in mind that the overriding principle, rule or discretionary power is governed by whether or not an imbalance or injustice may be caused towards one or more of the accused".[294]

While Mr. Vamplew is most assuredly correct in his assertions it remains difficult to see how an "imbalance or injustice" will *not* in some sense be occasioned (or, at least, the substantial risk that it will be occasioned must be seen to arise) whenever it can credibly and *bona fide* be argued that one, or several, of the guiding principles would seriously come into play if the trial were allowed to proceed as a joint trial.

The trend, both in England and in Canada is to favour joint trials

---

291. *R. v. Weir* (1899) 3 C.C.C. 351 (Que.); see also *R. v. Tonnancourt* (1956) 115 C.C.C. 154 (Man. C.A.).
292. See A. O. Klein *supra* footnote 287 at p. 15, citing 10 *Halsbury's Laws of England* (3rd ed. 1945) at p. 415.
293. J. K. L. Vamplew, "Joint Trials?" (1969-70) 12 Cr.L.Q. 30, citing *R. v. Weir supra* footnote 291.
294. *Ibid.* at p. 36.
    In support of the view that the factors in *Weir* are not mandatory rules of law but rather are merely guiding principles see *R. v. Quiring* (1974) 27 C.R.N.S. 367 (Sask. C.A.); and *R. v. Lane* (1969) 6 C.R.N.S. 273 (Ont.).

more than separate trials. Some observers are of the opinion that a joint trial is more likely to result in a true conclusion, and that in many cases of common enterprise the guilty person or persons might easily escape justice entirely if they were tried separately.[295] This view reveals the paradox which continually arises to confront judges on applications of this type. On the one hand, where the trial is held jointly amid an atmosphere of mutual recrimination amongst the co-accused (aggravated usually by the admissibility difficulties pointed out earlier) the jury, knowing that one (or several) of the co-accused is guilty but not knowing which one(s), may simply resolve its confusion by convicting everyone charged. (A curious inversion of the reasonable doubt doctrine.) On the other hand, an accused tried separately blaming others not present to contradict him might escape justice as easily as has been suggested.

Thus it can readily be seen that the judicial determination of a severance application is not an easy one. In considering the matter a judge would be remiss if he failed to accord due weight to the fact that in joint trials guilt by mere association can arise; that joint trials may result in increased complexity and length, which in turn may occasion confusion in the jury box; and that almost invariably the task of the trial judge in summing up a joint case to the jury will require an instruction that the jury disregard some damning piece of evidence which it has heard because it is only evidence against one of the accused and not against others — a warning that has been described as "probably . . . of little avail".[296]

Some of the matters raised are *inherently* prejudicial features of *any* joint trial from the point of view of the accused. As such they are not in this sense matters which can determine an application for severance since the interests of justice do not necessarily coincide with those of the accused.

In certain instances where the accused is tried alone he might be in a position at the close of the case for the Crown to apply for a directed verdict of acquittal. However, where he is jointly charged and tried with others "the case is not concluded until all the evidence is in. All the testimony heard throughout the trial is evidence for or against each accused."[297] This view, in a sense "adverse" to the interests of

---

295. A. O. Klein, *supra* footnote 287 at p. 22. And see *R. v. Lane supra* which suggests that where the essence of the case is that the accused were engaged in a common enterprise they should, as a general rule be jointly indicted and tried. Also see *R. v. Emkeit* (1971) 14 C.R.N.S. 290 (Alta. C.A.) to the same effect; affirmed without comment on this point (1972) 17 C.R.N.S. 180 (Can.).

296. *R. v. Chamandy* (1934) 61 C.C.C. 224 (Ont. C.A.) *per* Riddell J.A.; see also *R. v. Morgan* (1947) 90 C.C.C. 1 (Ont. C.A.).

297. *Vander-Beek v. R.* (1970) 12 C.R.N.S. 168 at p. 171 (Can.) *per* Hall J.

an accused, "goes to the very considerations that make a joint trial proper."[298]

The decision of the trial judge on the issue of severance will not, as a general rule, be interfered with unless it can be demonstrated that some manifest prejudice and injustice has resulted from the fact that the trials were jointly conducted.[299]

As matters presently stand it is extremely difficult for an accused jointly indicted with others to win a severance of his trial. This is the case even where antagonistic defences are demonstrable and admissibility problems are patent.[300] The "common enterprise" basis for the general rule requiring joint indictment trial is so broad as to be meaningless. (Almost any joint charge is capable of being categorized as a "common enterprise".) More precision in the definition of the term "common enterprise" for this purpose is desirable. (Query: whether an enterprise can be described as "common" where the two alleged parties have made statements saying that the other committed the act and denying any personal involvement? Or, where both accused are found in suspicious circumstances and one implicates his co-accused while the other stands mute?)

(4) Change of venue

At common law, offences are triable in the county or district in which the offence is committed. The theory that local offences be tried locally has been traced to the fact that early juries tried cases largely on the basis of the personal knowledge of the facts possessed by the jurors. Even after this procedure was phased out of the law the rule of trial in the local venue persisted.[301] The rule was not formed solely out of consideration for the accused but primarily derived from the view that each locality should bear its proportionate share of the task of enforcing the criminal law.[302] At common law there was no right to change the venue of the trial. Statutory enactments have altered this state of affairs.

At present in Canada s. 527 of the *Criminal Code* governs applications for change of venue. By that section either the prosecutor or the

---

298. *Ibid.* at p. 172 *per* Laskin J. (as he then was).
299. See *R. v. Grondkowski; R. v. Malinowski, supra* footnote 290; *Schmidt v. R.* [1945] S.C.R. 438; *R. v. Cassidy supra* footnote 290; *R. v. Quiring* (1974) 27 C.R.N.S. 367 (Sask. C.A.).
300. See *e.g. R. v. Quiring, supra;* and *R. v. Lane supra* footnote 294.
301. See R. Salhany, *Canadian Criminal Procedure* (2nd ed., 1972) at p. 20. For a more detailed history of the law of venue see, Stephen, *History of the Criminal Law of England* vol. I at pp. 276 *et seq.* On procedural aspects of changing venue in Canada see A. E. Popple, "Annotation: Applications for Change of Venue" (1946-7) 2 C.R. 6.
302. See *R. v. O'Gorman* (1909) 18 O.L.R. 427 at p. 430 (Ont. C.A.); and *R. v. Adams* (1946) 2 C.R. 56 (Ont.). For an example of how the accused may be prejudiced by employing a venue other than one where the offence was committed see *R. v. Ittoshat* (1970) 10 C.R.N.S. 385 (Que.).

accused may apply to have the trial of the charge held in a territorial division (in the same province)[303] other than that in which the offence would otherwise normally be tried. Such an application may be made either to (a) a court before which an accused is or may be indicted (at any term or sittings thereof); or, (b) a judge who may hold or sit in that court (at any time before or after an indictment is found).

Although the order for a change of venue may be made any time where it appears expedient to the ends of justice,[304] in practice the courts are reluctant to do so save in the clearest of cases and only upon strong grounds.[305] The power has been described as "discretionary" and only to be used with "great caution".[306] Aside from the phrase "appears expedient to the ends of justice", the *Code* provides no guidelines along which to direct the exercise of this discretion. Standards have evolved to regulate the process under the case law.

Prima facie the accused should be tried in the jurisdiction where the offence was alleged to have been committed.[307] However, where there is a fair and reasonable probability of partiality or prejudice against the accused a change of venue will be ordered.[308] The burden for demonstrating that a fair and impartial trial cannot be held nevertheless rests with the accused, and where the only prejudice which is demonstrable arises merely out of the intrinsic nature of the offence the application will be refused.[309] A mere possibility of prejudice is an insufficient basis for granting a change of venue.[310]

For the most part change of venue applications have arisen in circumstances where adverse publicity has substantially affected the possibilities of the accused's receiving a fair trial in the original locale. Such publicity may take the form of sensational articles (often accompanied

---

303. Note that there is no provision in the *Code* permitting the trial to take place in the territorial jurisdiction of *another province* pursuant to a change of venue order. It is possible, however, where the prosecution consents, and the charge is not enumerated in s. 427, to have charges waived to another province for disposition on a guilty plea (*Code*, s. 434(3)).
304. *The Criminal Code of Canada*, s. 527(1)(a).
305. See *R. v. Adams supra* footnote 302 and *R. v. Martin* [1964] 2 C.C.C. 391 (Sask.); *R. v. O'Gorman, supra* footnote 302 and *R. v. De Bruge* (1927) 60 O.L.R. 277 (Ont.).
306. *R. v. De Bruge ibid.* at p. 278 *per* Kelly J.
307. *R. v. Kellar* (1973) 24 C.R.N.S. 71 (Ont.); *R. v. Stauffer* (1911) 19 C.C.C. 205 (Sask.). The fact that the accused has a right to be tried in the district in which the offence is alleged to have been committed is sometimes the basis for ordering a change of the place of trial: *R. v. Desautels* [1954] R.L. 292.
308. *R. v. Beaudry* [1966] 3 C.C.C. 51 (B.C.). Beyond this the accused should be able to show that peremptory challenges and challenges for cause offer insufficient protection against the alleged prejudice: *R. v. Adams supra* footnote 302 and *R. v. De Bruge, supra* footnote 305.
309. *R. v. Turvey* (1970) 1 C.C.C. (2d) 90 (N.S.).
310. *R. v. Graves* (1912) 19 C.C.C. 402 (N.S.). See also *Re Trusz and R.* (1975) 20 C.C.C. (2d) 239 (Ont.).

by photographs of the accused in custody);[311] publication of some alleged statement of a highly prejudicial character made by the accused or law enforcement officials;[312] reference to a confession by the accused or the premature publication of the contents of same;[313] or even the premature publication of the jury list in the local press before trial.[314] Also, the fact that the accused recently stood trial in the same locale on similar charges (the actual result of the trial — acquittal or conviction — is immaterial in this regard) may also motivate the bringing of a change of venue application[315] for the publicity attendant on the earlier event may well affect the later one.

It is not to be lightly assumed that jurors will refrain from putting aside any prejudice which they might harbor against the accused which has arisen from the nature of the crime when they are instructed to do so by the trial judge, "where the prospective jurymen have been informed that the accused sought to have the trial taken out of the locality. For reason of his mistrust of their fairness, this added knowledge, together with their existing prejudice, makes it improbable that the accused will have a fair trial in that locality and a change of venue ought then to be ordered".[316] Accordingly, it is suggested as good practice for the judge hearing any venue application to impose a ban on publication of all matters relating to that application in order to safeguard the ultimate fairness of the ensuing trial of the accused.[317]

The presence of hostility in the proposed or intended trial locale in the shape of mob demonstrations or other forms of intimidation may be a circumstance rendering it "expedient to the ends of justice" to order a change of venue. In *R. v. Ponton*[318] hostile demonstrations directed against the trial judge who presided over an abortive first trial

---

311. See *R. v. Dick* (1942) 78 C.C.C. 363 (Alta.); *R. v. Martin supra* footnote 305; *R. v. Bochner* (1944) 82 C.C.C. 83 (Ont.); *R. v. Boucher* (1955) 113 C.C.C. 221 (Que.); *R. v. Adams supra* footnote 302; *R. v. Kully* (1973) 15 C.C.C. (2d) 488 (Ont.); *R. v. Fosbraey* (1950) 98 C.C.C. 275 (Ont.).

312. *R. v. Upton* (1922) 37 C.C.C. 15 (Ont.); *R. v. Adams supra* footnote 302.

313. *R. v. Upton ibid.* and *R. v. Adams supra* footnote 302.

314. *R. v. Graves supra* footnote 310.

315. See, *R. v. Dick supra* footnote 311; and *R. v. Beaudry, supra* footnote 308.

316. *R. v. Fosbraey, supra* footnote 311 *per* headnote. The case is also authority for the proposition that second or subsequent applications for a change of venue may be made on this point. See also *R. v. Roy* (1909) 14 C.C.C. 368 (Que.); *R. v. Lynn* (1910) 17 C.C.C. 354 (Sask.); and *R. v. Kellar* (1973) 24 C.R.N.S. 71 (Ont.). Where the subsequent application is to move the trial back to the original venue the grounds in support of the application need not be as weighty or cogent as those in the initial application provided it can be demonstrated that the possibility of prejudice has been or can be eradicated. Such a situation prevailed in *R. v. Kellar.*

317. See *R. v. Kully supra* footnote 311 at p. 493 for a modified example of this suggested practice.

318. (1899) 2 C.C.C. 417 (Ont.).

(the jury failed to agree upon a verdict) resulted in the ordering of a change of venue for the second trial.

Adverse publicity, while a usual consideration, is hardly the only consideration giving rise to change of venue proceedings. The fact that a jury has not been summoned and that the accused would have to wait a long time in custody for the next sitting of the Court has been the basis of an application.[319] Intense political feeling in the locale of such a nature as to be likely to affect the accused's fair trial has also been advanced as a ground for ordering a change of venue.[320] The necessity for the court to view the scene of the crime located in another county has also been put forward as a basis upon which to found an order.[321]

As numerous as are the bases which have been propounded the reality of the situation remains that an order changing the venue of a trial is an extremely difficult one to attain. This remains the reality even in supposedly "strong" cases.

For example, in *R. v. Beaudry*[322] the accused on a non-capital murder charge was denied a change of venue notwithstanding the fact that within the preceding six months he had been acquitted of another charge of non-capital murder; been involved in an inquest; and had been convicted of vagrancy.

In *R. v. Adams*[323] the accused had, before his trial, appeared before a Royal Commission. The report of the Commissioners in effect found the accused guilty of the offence for which he was to be tried, and that the report was published in local and other newspapers. In addition, portions of the preliminary hearing proceedings, including certain allegedly hearsay evidence heard in that hearing, were given wide pre-trial publicity. Nevertheless Adams' application for a change of venue was rejected by McRuer C.J.H.C.

The determination of a change of venue application is a judicial determination which must accord with principle. The most important principle in these considerations is the concept of "expediency to the ends of justice" and however large the orbit of judicial reluctance to grant a change of venue a significant number of cases exist to demonstrate the efficacy of a standard framed even in terms as wide as these.

In *R. v. Kully*[324] circumstances not far different from those in *Beaudry* resulted in a change in venue. *R. v. De Bruge,*[325] like the

---

319. *R. v. Demers* unreported, see *Crankshaw's Criminal Code of Canada* (A. E. Popple ed. 1959) at p. 723.
320. *R. v. Bronfman* (1930) 53 C.C.C. 32 (Sask.).
321. *Clerk v. R.* (1861) 9 H.L. Cas. 184.
322. *Supra* footnote 308. For a similar case see *R. v. Dick supra* footnote 311.
323. *Supra* footnote 302.
324. *Supra* footnote 311.
325. *Supra* footnote 305.

Adams case involved the publication of alleged hearsay evidence heard on a preliminary inquiry, and a change of venue resulted.

Whether these are instances of judicial decisions being made according to subjective preferences or attitudes, or as a result of reasoned distinctions based upon a devotion to principle and precedent is at present difficult to assess. A higher evolution of existing principles and standards seems desirable. Litigants in the criminal process still "have a right to the most supportable decision in the circumstances and this is the ideal towards which the courts must tend."[326]

> Just because any one answer is no more than a probability, and selection between two competing probabilities demands judgment, this does not mean that there is no rational way for exercising a judgment about which is more probable. Moreover, the fact that the exercise of this judgment may be unreviewable does not mean that a court is delegated the discretion to choose in the light of its subjective preferences.[327]

---

326. P. Weiler, "Two Models of Judicial Decision-Making" (1968) 46 Can.Bar.. Rev. 406 at pp. 433-434.

327. *Ibid*. at p. 434; *N.B.* The change of venue decision is in fact an unreviewable decision: *R. v. Sankey* (1927) 49 C.C.C. 195 (C.A.). There is however no bar to subsequent applications although the applicant would be ill-advised to attempt same without some fresh material to present to the court. See the citations *supra o*n this point at footnote 316.

5

CONTROLLING THE TRIAL PROCESS: THE JUDGE AND THE CONDUCT OF TRIAL

1. INTRODUCTION

The role of the judge in the conduct of a criminal trial is one calling for great sensitivity. It often requires the delicate balancing of important societal values. The actual manner in which a judge conducts a criminal trial will either enhance respect for the administration of justice, or it will detract from it.

The purpose of this portion of this study is to place in high relief the nature and complexity of many of the vexing questions which must be confronted and adequately answered by our judiciary if the judicial system is to retain its credibility with the Canadian people.

The adversary system — the basic procedural structure of the criminal trial — merits and receives consideration in the pages which follow. The role and the response of the trial judge to counsel, and to the accused, is analysed — both in terms of ideal types, and of present shortcomings. In this regard, attention is focused upon the various forms of judicial intervention into the trial process which are presently manifest, and an attempt is made to discern the limitations upon such conduct.

Obviously the analysis offered *infra* cannot aspire to the final resolution of such highly complex and contentious issues. Nevertheless, the just resolution of them is absolutely crucial to the criminal justice system, and to the administration of justice generally.

2. PASSIVE AND ACTIVE MODELS OF JUDICIAL DEMEANOUR IN THE CONDUCT OF TRIAL

(1) The adversary process and the search for truth

> Truth, like all other good things, may be loved unwisely — may be pursued too keenly — may cost too much.[1]

An eminent commentator and jurist reflecting on our legal system poses this question:[2] "Is the quest for justice synonymous with the search for truth?" His answer is qualified: "In most cases, yes. Truth

---

1. *Pearse v. Pearse* (1846) 1 De G. & Sm. 12 at p. 28, *per* Knight-Bruce V.C.
2. S. Freedman (Freedman C.J.M. of the Manitoba Court of Appeal) in an essay on "Admissions and Confessions" in Salhany and Carter, *Studies in Canadian Criminal Evidence* (1974) p. 95 at p. 99.

and justice will emerge in a happy coincidence. But not always. Nor should it be thought that the judicial process has necessarily failed if justice and truth do not end up in perfect harmony. Such a result may follow from the law's deliberate policy."[3]

It cannot be denied that the criminal trial process is intimately concerned with the discovery of truth. But, over and above this, its concern is to do justice between man and man. Prejudice, innuendo, opinion and speculation are viewed as poor handmaidens in the cause of justice. Hence the criminal trial is not held "at large" and not "every piece of damning prejudice" will there be received into evidence. The truth is one thing. The law has regard for other values as well, as Freedman C.J.M. (the commentator above referred to) has advised us. A whole network of procedural and evidentiary rules exist to regulate and modulate Canadian trials, and thus secure the end of fundamental justice.

The criminal trial process is therefore best regarded as a *qualified* search for truth.

This well-tempered inquiry is pursued in an unusual setting. The citizen and the state confront each other as opponents, or adversaries, and conduct a battle or "fight" according to age-hardened and time-tested rules and procedures.

The criminal trial is the paradigm of this adversary process. It has its detractors as well as its proponents. There are many who proclaim that it is well-suited to the task of discovering truth:

> Many lawyers maintain that the "fight" theory and the "truth" theory coincide. They think that the best way for a court to discover the facts in a suit is to have each side strive as hard as it can, in a keenly partisan spirit, to bring to the court's attention the evidence favorable to that side. Macaulay said that we obtain the fairest decision "when two men argue, as unfairly as possible, on opposite sides", for "them it is certain that no important consideration will altogether escape notice".[4]

In the adversarial setting of the criminal trial this partisan battle involves a clash between the public interest in the suppression of crime and the protection of the public, and the countervailing public interest in the protection of individual rights and liberties.[5]

Because the state is possessed of enormous manpower and economic resources to aid in the process of fact-finding and research, and because the individual does not have similar resources at his disposal, an attempt is made, through the formulation of evidentiary procedural rules, to "right the balance". This is done in order that the battle of

---

3. *Ibid.*
4. J. Frank, *Courts on Trial* (1949) at p. 80.
5. See J. A. Coutts (ed.), *The Accused* (1966) particularly the introductory essay by the editor on "The Public Interest and the Interests of the Accused in the Criminal Process" at p. 1.

adversaries (which follows the laying of criminal charges) be perceived by the citizenry of the state as an essentially "fair" contest.

As mentioned, in purely objective terms this attempt to strike a balance between the competing claims of the individual and the state must on occasion work in such a way as to actually suppress some of the truth. For example, a wife's evidence is not available in order to condemn her husband, the accused person is generally not obliged to criminate herself, and where the accused does not testify evidence of his prior misdeeds is generally not available to the prosecution in its efforts to prove its case.

The adversary process as carried on in the criminal courts has (in complimentary terms) been described as an attempt to secure "justice between man and man".[6] Truth is pursued, but not over-zealously, and always with an eye toward relevancy and the avoidance of undue prejudice.

To continental lawyers the notion of fabled British justice is something of a puzzle:

> The continental courts claim to have only one aim — the discovery of the truth. The English adversary system claims to settle an issue between the prosecution and the defendant and it is a commonplace remark that this emphasises the sporting element in an English trial. This sporting element is a psychological factor of the greatest importance, for it is out of it that there arises the notion of "fair play" for the accused. It has recently been argued that with the steady growth of professionalism in crime and the increase (as alleged) in the number of acquittals of those guilty of crime, this notion of a sporting element should be abandoned.[7]

Abandoning the "sporting element" of Anglo-Canadian justice is an extreme suggestion. Freeman C.J.M. indicates that our law "makes its choice between competing values and declares that it is better to close the case without all the available evidence being put on the record. We place a ceiling price on truth."[8]

Nevertheless, there are many who feel that we have fixed the price badly; that there has been "too much tenderness toward prisoners"[9] and that in pursuing justice too avidly we have weakened the social fabric.

Jerome Frank is undoubtedly correct when he states that "fre-

---

6. *Per* Sankey L.C. in *Mechanical and Gen. Inventions Co. v. Austin et al.* [1935] A.C. 346.
7. *Supra* footnote 5 at pp. 14-15. Coutts goes on to point out that strong criticism is also levelled at the continental trial system. One commentator, he notes, claims "that a continental trial is not for the purpose of determining guilt or innocence, for the result is pre-determined; the trial itself is simply a 'demonstration trial'. To the common lawyer the phrase is a contradiction in terms."
8. *Supra* footnote 2 at p. 99.
9. *R. v. William Baldry* (1852) 2 Den. 430 *per* Parke B.

quently the partisanship of the opposing lawyers blocks the uncovering of vital evidence or leads to a presentation of vital testimony in a way that distorts it."[10] At the same time however, it must be remembered that "in the system of trial which we have evolved in this country the judge sits to hear and determine the issues raised by the parties, *not to conduct an investigation or examination on behalf of society at large* . . . ".[11] Consequently the criminal trial, as we have noted, is not held "at large". Its terms of reference are circumscribed by many restraints. The requirement of "relevance" is as much an efficiency device designed to avoid needless tangential forays as it is a construct aimed at insuring fundamental fairness in the conduct of the inquiry.

But is there "too much tenderness towards prisoners in these matters"? Is "truth" being sacrificed at the mantle of "justice"? Jerome Frank, himself once a Judge of the United States Court of Appeals for the Second Circuit, found many deficiencies to exist in the adversary trial; deficiencies which not only worked to deny truthful facts to the court, but which also worked to frustrate the cause of justice. Judge Frank felt that certain elements inherent in the nature of an adversarial contest operated so as to frustrate even the *qualified* search for truth which our courts presently conduct. He asserted that:

(1) the whole atmosphere of the courtroom bewilders witnesses;
(2) lawyers, before trial, "coach the witnesses who will appear for their clients, not only with regard to the story they will tell, but also the demeanour they should assume in testifying so as to give the most favorable personal impression;
(3) dishonest lawyers use this accepted practice to encourage perjury;
(4) lawyers attempt to discredit witnesses through exercise of the art of cross-examination, regardless of the truth of what these witnesses may be saying;
(5) lawyers refuse to concede facts harmful to their clients if they think the adversary cannot prove them, and they will not help to correct inaccurate statements of witnesses favorable to their clients;
(6) lawyers rely, wherever possible, upon surprise as a tactic to keep the adversary from preparing to rebut particular testimony favorable to their clients; and
(7) the adversary process is deficient because a party may not have the funds to pay for an investigation, before trial, to assemble evidence on his behalf and rebut evidence on which the other party may rely.[12]

---

10. *Supra* footnote 4 at p. 81.
11. *Per* Denning L.J. in *Jones v. Nat. Coal Bd.* [1957] 2 Q.B. 55 at p. 63 [emphasis added].
12. J. Frank, *supra* footnote 4 at pp. 81-85 and 94-96. This summary is found in L. K. Garrison, *The Legal Process* (1961) at p. 196. As Garrison notes, "Frank did not blame the lawyers for using the techniques mentioned, but the system of litigation which makes it their prime duty to try to win the case rather than aid the court in a mutual search for truth".

In fairness to Judge Frank much of the above commentary is directed at the adversary system in the context of a civil, rather than a criminal, trial.[13] But the remarks have much relevance to criminal trials as well.

Those criticisms of the adversary system are not insubstantial. Basically they imply that one of two serious options ought to be implemented:

(1) The adversary system ought to be drastically altered in terms of its evidentiary and procedural structure. Irrationality ought to be weeded out and imbalances should be rectified.

(2) The adversary system ought to be done away with altogether and should be replaced by an inquisitorial system.

Option (1) *supra,* is already in a protean state of existence. The drift of law reform in Canada is towards a whittling away of the historic rights and privileges which have been accorded to accused persons. The process has been slow, but it is inexorable. Trial by jury is not a commonplace of our criminal justice system; it is a rarity. Indications are that it will become rarer still. Our rules of evidence, their absurdities notwithstanding, are more honored in the breach than in practice.[14] Suggestions for criminal law reform emanating from the Law Reform Commission of Canada include the removal of the accused's right to silence.[15] The present Canadian position with respect to the use of illegally obtained evidence[16] renders much of our rhetoric about "fundamental fairness" a sham and an "embarrassment".[17] Notwithstanding the protestations of some that "the criminal is living in a Golden Age",[18] the record does not support the charge.

Despite the benefit of reasonable doubt which is accorded to an accused; despite the burden of proof under which the prosecution must labor; and despite the prisoner's right to silence—despite all of these

---

13. Judge Frank makes other related observations on the American criminal jury trial, *e.g.,* Frank feels that many of the rules governing the conduct of criminal jury trials (such as the rule excluding hearsay evidence) have "been perpetuated primarily because of the incompetence of jurors" (p. 123). "So, too, of many other exclusionary rules. They limit, absurdly, the courtroom quest for the truth. The result, often, is a gravely false picture of the actual facts. Thus trial by jury seriously interferes with correct — and, therefore, just — decisions."

14. See N. Brooks, book reviews of McWilliams *Canadian Criminal Evidence* and Sopinka and Lederman, *"The Law of Evidence in Civil Cases"* (1976) 54 Can. Bar Rev. 179 at p. 182.

15. See Canada Law Reform Commission, Working Paper 4: Discovery (1974) where *some* pre-trial discovery of the defence case is contemplated (at pp. 29-31).

16. See *R. v. Wray* [1971] S.C.R. 272.

17. See L. Taman, "The Adversary Process on Trial: The Right to Make Full Answer and Defence" (1975) 13 O.H.L.J. 251 at p. 275.

18. See E. Haines, "Future of the Law of Evidence — The Right to Remain Silent — View I" in Salhany and Carter *supra* footnote 2, p. 321 at p. 327.

"heavily-weighted advantages"—"the scales of criminal justice are not balanced".[19]

As mentioned, serious resource imbalances exist as between prosecution and accused. In many cases[20] (and here the field is ever-expanding) the onus of proof has been shifted by legislation to the accused.

Against this backdrop our two adversaries are asked to join arms in regulated battle. While indeed, we still have two adversaries left to fight this battle, the ground under foot is continually shifting. Many hands are "tinkering with the works". Coherency of vision, and unity of purpose, is absent from most of this process.

Its defects notwithstanding, it appears unlikely that there is substantial support in the Canadian legal community for the proposition that the adversary system ought to be *completely* dismantled. Proponents of such change favor the adoption of an inquisitorial system based upon the experience of continental Europe.

The adversary system possesses these "justifications" which (its proponents argue) cannot be compensated for by an inquisitorial process:

(1) truth is more likely to emerge if the parties themselves, motivated by their own self-interest, have control of investigating and presenting the facts to the tribunal; and

(2) the tribunal's decision will be morally acceptable to the parties since it was made by one not involved in the presentation of evidence and therefore by one not committed to the particular cause of any single party.[21]

Proponents of the inquisitorial system are more likely to take issue with the first of these propositions, rather than the second. In their view the continental-style inquiry is unparalleled as a truth-seeking device.

There is, of course, not simply one inquisitorial system utilized by all judicial systems not founded on the Anglo-Saxon. Great differences of approach are apparent from country to country.[22] If a single distillation of the core elements of *the* inquisitorial system is possible, this

---

19. A. Maloney and P. V. Tomlinson, "The Right to Remain Silent — View II" in Salhany and Carter *supra* footnote 2, p. 335 at p. 344.

20. *E.g.* in narcotics prosecutions, liquor offences, Income Tax Act and Shipping Act offences, some motor vehicle offences, etc.

21. J. Sopinka and S. Lederman, *The Law of Evidence in Civil Cases* (1974) at p. 5.

22. This is the whole purpose of the study undertaken by Coutts, in *The Accused supra* footnote 5: to demonstrate markedly different approaches which various countries adopt in dealing with crime, and specifically with accused persons.

admiring portrait offered by Edson Haines (Haines J. of the Ontario Supreme Court) would represent its best qualities as well as any:[23]

> [T]he task of the judge in most foreign systems of law is akin to that of the scientist in the laboratory, to ascertain the real truth by all proper means. Essentially the inquiry into the circumstances devolves upon the court and the investigating judge or officer may take considerable time in developing the evidence both for and in favor of the accused. Frequently those injured in the incident giving rise to the charge are also represented, and it is not unusual for the verdict to deal not only with guilt or innocence but also with civil responsibility, so that all matters may be concluded in the one proceeding. Complicated rules of evidence are unknown. The tendency is to admit all testimony on the theory that the court gives to all evidence the weight it deserves. The accused is questioned as the facts are developed during the investigation and his explanations are checked out by the court which also searches out and examines witnesses for the accused. Serious trials often commence with the examination of the accused which has the advantage at the outset of discovering those areas in dispute and those about which there is no controversy. They really try the man as well as the facts. Consequently the record of the accused, good or bad, is before the court. A feature emphasized in many jurisdictions is that the acquittal of the guilty is a threat to the security of society.

A discourse on the superiority of one system, or another, in this context is not a particularly useful or fruitful exercise. Our history, societal values, and political institutions have quite naturally enclosed us in a cocoon of biases and predilections.[24] However, certain features of the utopian paradigm sketched by Haines J. do invite obvious responses from the common lawyer.

First among these is the grave risk of prejudice which is assumed in the portrait *supra*. Innuendo, speculation, opinion and irrelevancies can present a damning trap for any accused person. To assert that judges will offset this danger by weighing evidence in relation to its perceived reliability is to saddle ordinary humans with a very unordinary burden.

"Judging the man as well as the facts" certainly carries with it the risk of convicting *the man* in absence of truly probative facts.

It may well be true that "the acquittal of the guilty is a threat to the security of society" to to the common law lawyer the graver risk to the *viability* of society is posed by the conviction of the innocent.

---

23. *Supra* footnote 18 at pp. 325-326. See also E. Haines, "The Medical Profession and The Adversary Process" (1973) 11 O.H.L.J. 41.
24. It is for this reason that the adversary process is felt to be "of a piece" with the whole concept of participatory democracy. In fact "one principal justification of participatory democracy assumes [that] . . . conflict will be more fairly and successfully resolved if the adversaries participate in the decision making." (G. Adams, "Towards a Mobilization of the Adversary Process" (1974) 12 O.H.L.J. 569 at p. 594.)

Not mentioned in the summary provided by Haines J. is the standard to be utilized for the assessment of guilt. What contrast is there to the common law's presumption of innocence and the necessity for unanimity among our jurymen? In a French Assize Court, for example, there are three professional magistrates (a president and two assessors) and nine jurymen (selected from twenty-five drawn by lot for each assize). The whole tribunal deals with both law and fact. If the accused is unable to secure a majority in the vote as to his guilt he will be convicted—a far cry from our jury trials where one man's conscience may ultimately hold sway over a jury's deliberations.

The inquisitorial system has been attacked on the basis that its paternalistic character "unavoidably raises suspicions of bias and tastes of despotism."[25] The sufficiency of the inquiry conducted in terms of its fact-gathering mechanism, the ability of the party to bring his views and questions to the attention of the inquisition at the investigative phase, and the inability of the tribunal to contemplate all of the positions which a defendant might wish to advance are pointed to as serious, general defects of such a system.[26]

(2) The role of the trial judge in the adversary process

The greater part of this analysis will be devoted to exploring the specific limitations under which trial judges labor in handling various aspects of the trial process. How far a judge can, or should proceed to enter into the trial arena is to a certain extent governed by the nature of the problem with which he is presented.

Obviously the role of the trial judge in dealing with an accused who is unrepresented by counsel will be far different from the considerations guiding his conduct when both parties are represented.

The proper response of the court to incompetency in counsel also may prompt the trial judge to deviate from otherwise normal standards of judicial conduct.

Other matters, such as the judicial examination or cross-examination of witnesses, or, judicial determinations to call witnesses to assist the court in its fact-finding enterprise, or expressions of personal opinion by the trial judge are not generally situation-inspired, but rather are usually expressions of a particular conception of the role of the trial judge in the entire trial process.

Is the trial judge to be an *active* force in the adversarial contest which he characteristically oversees and regulates? Or is his role more properly conceived as a *passive* one, with his interventions for the most part confined to clarifying obscurities, and keeping the course of the trial within the orderly channels provided for by rules of evidence and

25. G. Adams *ibid.* at p. 580.
26. *Ibid.* Further comparative analysis of the two systems may be found in D. O'Connor, "The Place of Innocence in the Criminal Trial" [1969] Crim. L.R. 587.

procedure? Is the role of the trial judge essentially an active or a passive one? Does he play the role of pilot, participant, or umpire?[27]

In traditional terms, the role of the trial judge conducting a criminal trial has unquestionably been viewed as a passive one.

Lord Denning in *Jones v. Nat. Coal Bd.*[28] details the passive conception of the judicial role as well as it can be sketched:

> . . . it is for the advocates, each in his turn, to examine the witnesses, and not for the judge to take it on himself lest by so doing he appear to favour one side or the other . . . The judge's part in all this is to hearken to the evidence, only himself asking questions of witnesses when it is necessary to clear up any point that has been overlooked or left obscure; to see that the advocates behave themselves seemly and keep to the rules laid down by law; to exclude irrelevancies and discourage repetition; to make sure by wise intervention that he follows the points that the advocates are making and can assess their worth; and at the end to make up his mind where the truth lies. If he goes beyond this, he drops the matter of a judge and assumes the role of an advocate; and the change does not become him well.

Sir Edmond Fry on the occasion of being named a Lord Justice of Appeal in England summarized his view of the duty of a judge in *any* Court:

> Give a benign and receptive listening to each side, so as to feel the full force of the argument on each side, and then judge between them.[29]

It has been said that if a trial judge opts for a more active role; if he, so to speak, "descends into the arena", he then is "liable to have his vision clouded by the dust of the conflict".[30] To this it may be added that it then becomes difficult for him to avoid the appearance of bias or prejudice.

> Whatever the variations, a central core of agreed standards defines the trial judge as the neutral, impartial, calm, non-contentious umpire standing between the adversary parties seeing that they observe the rules of the adversary game. The bedrock premise is that the adversary contest is the ideal way to achieve truth and a just result rested upon the truth.[31]

The author of the statement *supra* acknowledges that even in the passive conception of the judicial role, the idea of the judge solely, or

---

27. See H. Silverman, "The Trial Judge Pilot, Participant or Umpire?" (1973) 11 Alta.L.R. 40.
28. [1957] 2 Q.B. 55 at p. 64.
29. Contained in the judgment of Schultz J.A. in *Delaney & Co. v. Berry* (1964) 49 D.L.R. (2d) 171 at p. 176 (Man. C.A.).
30. *Per* Greene M.R. in *Yuill v. Yuill* [1945] 1 All E.R. 183 at p. 189 (C.A.).
31. M. E. Frankel "The Adversary Judge" (1976) 54 Tex. L. Rev. 465 at p. 468.

even primarily as "umpire" is not universally accepted.[32] Lord Denning to whom we have previously referred, also says as much:

> Even in England, however, a judge is not a mere umpire to answer the question "How's that?" His object, above all, is to find out the truth, and to do justice according to law . . .[33]

An American jurist commenting on the conception of the trial judge as purely playing an "umpireal" role claims that this view suffers from an inadequate appreciation of the true relationship between judges and lawyers in the trial process:

> Unfortunately, true understanding of the judicial process is not shared by all lawyers or judges. Instead of regarding themselves as occupying a reciprocal relationship in a common purpose, they are apt to think of themselves as representing opposite poles and exercising divergent functions. The lawyer is active, the judge passive. The lawyer partisan, the judge neutral. The lawyer imaginative, the judge reflective.[34]

There is a grain of truth in this critique. The qualities of activism and imagination, and to a degree even partisanship (where abuse and obstruction of the court process is involved) are not foreign to the judicial demeanour—even within the parameters of the so-called "passive" conception of the judicial role. The fact is that our system does provide considerable latitude for effective or just intervention by the trial judge in the adversary fight about the facts.[35] (These latitudes are explored more fully in the body of this work.)

However, a major limiting factor circumscribing both the role and aspirations of *any* trial judge is the fact that the trial judge is quintessentially (in criminal matters) unprepared in terms of both advance exposure to, and investigation of, the facts. (In civil cases he will at least have the benefit of the pleadings, affidavits and other supporting material, including on occasion extensive factual admissions.) Unlike his counterpart in civil law countries he does not have the dossier of the investigating magistrate before him.

> Without an investigative file, the . . . trial judge is a blind and blundering intruder, acting in spasms as sudden flashes of seeming light may lead or mislead him at odd times.[36]

---

32. *Ibid.*
33. *Jones v. Nat. Coal Bd., supra* footnote 28 at p. 63.
34. D. Peck, "The Complement of Court and Counsel" (1954) (13th Annual Benjamin N. Cardozo Lecture) at p. 9; reproduced in M. E. Frankel, "The Search for Truth: an Umpireal View" (1975) 123 U. Pa. L. Rev. 1031 at p. 1035.
35. M. E. Frankel disagrees. See his article on the "Umpireal View" of the search for truth *ibid.* at p. 1042: "The judge views the case from a peak of Olympian ignorance. His intrusions will in too many cases result from partial or skewed insights . . . He runs a good chance of pursuing inspirations that better informed counsel have considered, explored and abandoned after fuller study."
36. M. Frankel, *ibid.* at p. 1042.

Its banality notwithstanding, what goes without saying in discussions centering on the nature of the judicial role is the sentiment that "the essence of the judicial role, active or passive, is impartiality and detachment, both felt and exhibited."[37]

There is an activist conception of the judicial role, different in *kind* from the passive one. The activist ideal (if it can be so described) seeks to eschew the vision of a trial judge powerless to enter the fray in instances where he perceives an overt and patent thwarting of the pursuit of justice through the artful, but unfair (not illegal) manipiulation of rules and procedures. To such a trial judge the triumph of "justice" may appear as a different thing from the advocate's notion of victory.

The activist trial judge must basically, and most truthfully, be seen to be at odds with the adversary process. In order to be effective in his role he must constantly be straining and testing the very limits of the role which he has been asked to play. His efforts undoubtedly will on occasion meet with rebuke in the higher courts. But, ultimately the disagreements between these two judicial levels must be perceived to be disagreements over basic philosophy.

The activist judge is a foe of the adversary system. He is most accurately described as an "adversary judge". Since his aim generally is to reform the system, in ideal terms he should do open battle with it. Characteristically such a judge is both "outspoken" and "creative", although his more traditional critics might employ less enthusiastic adjectives in describing his activity.

Jerome Frank and Marvin Frankel are two American jurists who admirably live up to this portrait. In Canada, Edson Haines (Haines J. of the Ontario Supreme Court) has played a similar role.[38] By their learned commentary, their irrascible and uncompromising courtroom demeanour, they vividly present without artifice or deceit—the alternative, full-blown. Basically, these and other "activist" judges do not favour the outright abolition of the adversary process, but rather they operate under "the hypothesis that the tensions and contradictions in the trial judge's role may reflect remediable imperfections in the system he administers."[39]

---

37. M. Frankel, *supra* footnote 31 at p. 468.
38. See E. Haines, *supra* footnote 18; E. Haines, "The Jury, the Judge, the Case, and You" (1959) L.S.U.C. Spec. Lect. 175; E. Haines, "The Right to Remain Silent" (1970) 18 Ch. L.J. 109; E. Haines, "Criminal and Civil Jury Charges" (1968) 46 Can. Bar. Rev. 48.
    See also *Phillips v. Ford Motor Co.* (1971) 18 D.L.R. (3d) 641 (Ont. C.A.); and *R. v. Hawke* (1975) 22 C.C.C. (2d) 19 (Ont. C.A.), as examples of clashes in philosophy over the nature of the trial as a truth-seeking device, and over the nature of the limitations under which a trial judge labors. In both cases there is great divergence between the approach adopted by Haines J. and the approach which the Ontario Court of Appeal felt should have been taken.
39. M. Frankel, *supra* footnote 31 at p. 484.

For the present, the activist model of judicial demeanour is out of the mainstream of normative judicial behavior. However, as we have noted, many hands are at work tinkering with the mechanisms of the adversary process. As these mechanisms are altered the role of the trial judge will, in degree, be affected. If pre-trial discovery (even, partial discovery) of the accused becomes a reality and this information becomes available to the court, the adequacy of the pre-trial preparation of the trial judge will be greatly enhanced. If pre-trial conferences between counsel for all parties and the trial judge become a commonplace of the system this also will alter the role of the trial judge. If the right to silence of the accused is forfeit the adversary system will be immeasurably affected.

Not all, or indeed any, of these changes should be viewed as salutary. As suggestions for reform however, they have been kicked about for a long time. And, as we enter into yet another era of "law and order" (or, as we choose to call it in Canada—"peace and security") there is no predicting the mood of our legislators.

Yesterday's (or today's) judicial iconoclast may well become tomorrow's achetype. For the moment however, this picture (which is really a description of the ideal-passive type) is the one which prevails:

> An overly active judge may give the appearance of a meddler; but equally, a passive and quiescent trial judge may give the appearance of indifference. The public may have a legitimate complaint about the appearance and doing of justice — not just against counsel — but against a Bench which renders judgments based on technical evidentiary deficiencies or errors. . . . A trial judge who endeavours to assist counsel, parties, and witnesses in the proper, complete and logical developments of all aspects of a case within the confines of the rules of evidence and the adversary system, neither favoring one side or the other, nor expressing any bias, but still remaining dispassionate and neutral (but not disinterested or indifferent) will gain the respect of all concerned with the administration of a viable system of justice.[40]

3. JUDICIAL INTERFERENCE IN THE EXAMINATION OF WITNESSES

(1) The aims of, and restrictions on, examination-in-chief and cross-examination

Examination-in-chief, when properly conducted has been said to possess at least the following characteristics:[41]

(1) proof of all the elements of each issue necessary to secure a favourable decision;

---

40. H. Silverman, *supra* footnote 27 at p. 62. See also C. E. Wyzanski, "A Trial Judge's Freedom and Responsibility" (1951-52) 65 Harv. L. Rev. 1281.
41. S. N. Lederman, *A Coursebook of Exercises and Materials in Canadian Trial Practice,* Vol. 1 (1972-73) at p. 195.

(2) the presentation of witnesses and their testimony in a manner likely to prove advantageous to a proponent's case;

(3) the presentation of one's case by proper questioning in accordance with the rules of evidence;

(4) the presentation of all documentary evidence necessary to prove or corroborate all material contentions.

Stylistically, and also from the point of view of building up the confidence of the witness, it is desirable that the testimony of the witness be allowed to unfold naturally, with a minimum of interruption, and with a high degree of orderly, chronological development. A good counsel invariably attempts to control his witnesses within these logical parameters.

To the extent that a witness is channelled through a well-modulated and technically correct examination-in-chief his natural nervousness and apprehension should dissipate. To the extent that preliminary anxiety is relieved, and the witness acclimatizes himself to the unfamiliar environs of the courtroom and witness box, the better prepared, emotionally and mentally, he will be for the subsequent rigors of cross-examination.

From this it may be gleaned that counsel has an extremely important role to play in the presentation of evidence in examination-in-chief. His function goes far beyond merely ascertaining the existence of a witness and presenting him in court. The necessity for adequate pre-trial preparation of the witness, for plotting the course of the trial, ascertaining the proper place for inserting the witness, and for keeping a keen eye on the rigors of evidentiary rules cannot be over-valued.[42] As H. H. Spellman indicates in his work on the *Direct Examination of Witnesses,* "the basic aim of all examination techniques, particularly those involved in the direct examination of witnesses, is to grasp and hold the attention of the trier of the facts and to avoid any actions which would disturb the fact-finder's concentration."[43] Obviously, the witness cast into the fray without adequate direction or guidance cannot possibly serve to further this basic aim.

But the trial judge conducting the criminal trial has an equally vital role to play. If it may be said that counsel producing evidence in chief should not be a principal actor but rather an unobtrusive presence "in the wings directing the way the evidence is unfolding so that it will achieve its maximum effect"[44] then certainly it may also be asserted that the trial judge, while he occupies the position of a benign and objective listener, also exerts at times an even greater directorial

---

42. See generally W. B. Williston, "Preparation for Examination-in-Chief" (1955) L.S.U.C. Spec. Lect. 187.

43. H. H. Spellman, *The Direct Examination of Witnesses* (1968) at p. 77.

44. G. A. Martin, "Examination of Witnesses", Ontario Bar Admission Course Lecture, Quoted in Lederman, *supra* footnote 41 at p. 193.

control than does counsel over the flow and pace of judicial proceedings. The powers to sustain or over-rule evidentiary objections, to interrogate witnesses *proprio motu,* or, to apply to, or to withhold the stamp of veracity, from, a witness's testimony are enormous.

These observations apply with at least equal force to the role of the trial judge with regard to cross-examination.

Keeton, in his text on *Trial Practice and Methods*[45] set out four major aims of cross-examination:

(1) Discrediting the testimony of the witness being examined.

(2) Using the testimony of the witness to discredit the unfavourable testimony of other witnesses.

(3) Using the testimony of those witnesses to corroborate the favorable testimony of other witnesses.

(4) Using the testimony of the witness to contribute independently to the favorable development of your own case.

As a tool, cross-examination has a wider scope and operates under fewer restrictions than does examination-in-chief. The primary burden borne during examination-in-chief is that the examiner is constrained from resorting to the use of leading questions in order to elicit desired responses from his witness. This is a general rule to which there are numerous exceptions.[46]

The editor of *Kenny,* in discussing "General Rules of Evidence" notes that "a question 'leads' if, though it admits of several answers, it suggests that a particular answer is desired by the questioner."[47] The main objections to leading questions are these two (also set forth in *Kenny*):[48]

(1) To a false witness they suggest what particular lie would be desirable; and

---

45. R. E. Keeton, *Trial Practice and Procedure,* (2nd ed. 1973) at p. 94.

46. Rupert Cross in his text *On Evidence* (3rd ed. 1967) lists these instances in which leading questions may be allowed: (a) with respect to introductory matters, which are undisputed, such as the introduction of a witness or the focusing of his or her attention upon a particular subject; (b) where the attention of the witness is directly pointed to persons or things for the purpose of identifying them; (c) where it is desired to have one witness contradict another as to remarks alleged to have been made, he may be directly asked whether or not the remarks were made; (d) where a witness is unable to answer questions put in the usual way because of the complicated nature of the matter upon which it is being questioned; (e) where a witness is a child or ill or has difficulty with the English language; (f) where a witness's memory is so defective that he is simply unable to answer. (Reproduced in E. Ratushny "Basic Problems in Examination and Cross-Examination" (1974) 52 Can.Bar.Rev. 209 at p. 212).

As to leading questions generally, see Denroche, "Leading Questions" (1963-64) 6 Cr.L.Q. 21.

47. J. W. C. Turner (ed.), *Kenny's Outlines of Criminal Law* (18th ed. 1964) at p. 466.

48. *Ibid.*

(2) Even an honest witness is prone to given an assenting answer from mere mental laziness.

Beck J. in *Maves v. G.T.P. Ry.*[49] outlines one other important objection:

> I think a third reason may be added, namely, that a witness, though intending to be entirely fair and honest may, owing, for example, to lack of education, of exactness of knowledge of the precise meaning of words or of appreciation at the moment of their precise meaning, or of alertness to see that what is implied in the question requires modification, honestly assent to a leading question which fails to express his real meaning, which he would probably have completely expressed if allowed to do so in his own words.[50]

Thus, the qualified prohibition against the use of leading questions in the conduct of an examination-in-chief must be viewed as an essential safeguard to the integrity of the trial process.

In contrast to the situation of the in-chief examination of witnesses, leading questions are generally permitted in the conduct of cross-examination. The use of the leading question is an entirely natural cross-examination vehicle. The leading question suggests its own answer. The assertion of controverted facts by way of leading questions in cross-examination focuses attention on the areas of dispute or controversy and serve to underline those matters about which there is no argument or divergence of opinion. As such the leading question is well-suited to the task of accomplishing many of the basic aims of cross-examination.

The permissible resort to the use of leading questions as an examination device points up the fact that cross-examination is broader as to scope and latitude than examination-in-chief.

Although the scope of cross-examination is extremely broad, meaningful restrictions do in fact exist.

The rules of admissibility govern the conduct of cross-examination, and apply as rigorously there as they do in examination-in-chief. Consequently, *relevance* is encountered as a primary parameter on the conduct of cross-examination. The examiner must limit himself, or be limited, to matters relevant to a fact in issue, or to the credibility of the witness. Anglin J. in the well-known case of *Brownell v. Brownell*[51] succinctly states the law on this point:

> No doubt the limits of relevancy must be less tightly drawn upon cross-examination than upon direct examination. The introduction upon cross-examination of the issue of the witness's credibility necessarily enlarges the field. But it does not follow that all barriers are therefore

---

49. (1913) 14 D.L.R. 70 at p. 74 (C.A.).
50. *Ibid.* at p. 74.
51. (1909) 42 S.C.R. 368. See also J. Sedgwick, "Cross-Examination" (1955) L.S.U.C. Spec. Lect.

thrown down. That which is clearly irrelevant to this issue or to the issues raised in the pleadings is no more admissible in cross-examination than in examination in chief.

Although *leading* questions may be employed in cross-examination the assertions of fact contained in those questions must be accurate and correct and counsel must not mis-state facts in the hope of mis-leading the witness.[52] This is not to go so far as to say that counsel may not cross-examine on matters that he is not in a position to prove directly or that an obligation rests on the cross-examiner to prove directly any fact which is asserted at first instance in cross-examination. The law in Canada appears still to follow these pronouncements by Lord Radcliffe in *Fox v. Gen. Medical Council.*[53]

> An advocate is entitled to use his discretion as to whether to put questions in the course of cross-examination which are based on material which he is not in a position to prove directly. The penalty is that, if he gets a denial or some answer that does not suit him, the answer stands against him for what it is worth.

In Canada, cross-examining counsel is expected to conduct his inquiries amid an atmosphere of politeness and courtesy. Two of Wrottesly's[54] "Golden Rules" of cross-examination make the point well:

> Be mild with the mild — shrewd with the crafty — confiding with the honest — merciful to the young, the frail or the fearful — rough to the ruffian and a thunderbolt to the liar —
> But in all this never be unmindful of your own dignity.

and

> Be respectful to the court and to the jury — kind to your colleague — civil to your antagonist — but never sacrifice the slightest principle of duty to an over-weening deference toward either.

In practice these entreaties to civility translate into a prohibition against the vexatious and abusive conduct of cross-examination. Once again the observations of Anglin J. in *Brownell* are germane to this subject. After observing that it must be conceded that "a trial judge

---

52. ". . . those [questions] which suggest the existence of unproved facts might well be disallowed, even in cross-examination, and in *R. v. McDonell,* [(1909) 2 Cr.App.R. 322], it was said that questions put to a prisoner in cross-examination ought to be put in an interrogative form; they should commence 'did you?' and not 'you did'. The judge has a wide discretion in these matters and it is difficult to say more than that leading questions will usually be disallowed in-chief, or in re-examination, although they will generally be permitted in cross-examination" in Cross, *supra* footnote 46 at p. 189 and discussed in Ratushny, *supra* footnote 46 at p. 235.

53. [1960] 1 W.L.R. 1017 at p. 1023; cited recently with approval in *R. v. Bencardino* (1973) 24 C.R.N.S. 173 at p. 179 (Ont. C.A.).

54. Wrottesly, *The Examination of Witnesses* at pp. 103-104.

has *some* discretion to protect a witness against questions which are purely vexatious"[55] the learned justice goes on to state:

> "The character of this discretion, however, is such that its precise limits are not easily defined and in practice its exercise, though undoubtedly reviewable, must be left largely to the sound judgment and wisdom of the presiding judge who, from his observation of the demeanour of the witness and also of the manner of and the conduct of the case by counsel, has means and opportunities of forming a correct opinion as to the importance and real purpose of questions propounded which are not open to an appellate court."[56]

Lord Sankey in *Mechanical and Gen. Inventions v. Austin*[57] a case of high authority, opines that "cross-examination becomes indefensible when it is conducted . . . without the courtesy and consideration which a witness is entitled to expect in a Court of law". At this point, presumably, the Court has a role to play in the restriction of such examination.

This much then, may be accurately stated with regard to the limitations or restrictions upon cross-examination: counsel must ever be constrained by the ordinary rules of admissibility of evidence; of these, the matter of legal relevancy looms pre-eminent (although it is softened somewhat by the open texture of "relevant" inquiries as to the credibility of a witness); while leading questions may be employed as a tool in effective cross-examination, counsel is enjoined from mis-stating facts, and thus, misleading a witness; and, finally, decorum and courtesy shall earmark the conduct of a cross-examination, and where cross-examination descends to the level of hectoring and abuse, or of trivial quibbling, the Court will be justified in intervening.

In all of this the trial judge is not obliged to spectate, or sit idly by, until opposing counsel triggers the restricting process by voicing some valid objection. Quite the opposite. It remains the duty of the trial judge to ensure that only properly admissible evidence is admitted, and the failure of counsel to object to inadmissible evidence (or to the improper examination of witnesses) does not relieve the judge of this obligation.[58] An active role for our judiciary in this regard is con-

---

55. *Brownell v. Brownell supra* footnote 51 at p. 372 *(emphasis added)*.
56. *Ibid.* p. 373. See also *R. v. Rewniak* (1949) 7 C.R. 127 (Man. C.A.): the right of the trial judge to check counsel when cross-examination becomes irrelevant or prolix, or insulting.
57. [1935] A.C. 346 at p. 359.
58. *Schwartzenhauer v. R.* (1935) 64 C.C.C. 1 (Can.); *R. v. Scory* [1945] 1 W.W.R. 15 (Sask. C.A.); *R. v. Stirland* (1944) 30 Cr.App.R. 40; on disallowing unfair or prejudicial questions see *R. v. Jenkins* (1945) 31 Cr.App.R. 1. See also *R. v. MacDonald* (1939) 72 C.C.C. 182 (Ont. C.A.); *R. v. Brooks* (1906) 11 C.C.C. 188 (Ont. C.A.): counsel's failure does not relieve the trial judge of his obligation to scrutinize admissibility. The rule in this area stands in contrast to the practice in civil cases. See Popple, *Canadian Criminal Evidence* (2nd ed. 1954) at pp. 534-535, and McWilliams, *Canadian Criminal Evidence* (1974) at pp. 21-22.

templated.

Where counsel is devious and misleading, or simply inept, incompetent, rude, or insulting, the regulatory features of the role of the trial judge becomes markedly emphasized. But the path of such judicial conduct is marked by degrees, and beyond a certain point regulation merges with overt interference and (at times) even proceeds on into patent partisanship. Here too, there must exist rational restrictions and limitations, in order that process be adjudged as fair. Judicial excesses, not unlike the excesses of counsel, must be curbed.

(2) The parameters of judicial intervention in the trial process

In dealing with the subject of judicial intervention into the trial process two major areas of concern present themselves. The first of these revolves around the judicial examination of witnesses—*i.e.,* the proper role of the trial judge in questioning witnesses, the manner in which such examination ought to be conducted, and the place of the perjury threat as a truth seeking device. The second area of concern is that of judicial interruption and interference into the conduct of either counsel's examination-in-chief or cross-examination. Involved here is a consideration of what constitutes "excessive" interference; and, of the court's ability to place time restrictions upon counsel's conduct of his examination. Also, necessarily bound up in this discussion is a consideration of the proper response of counsel to the interfering trial judge.

(a) *The judicial examination of witnesses*

The formal dress of our trial judges, the shows of deference accorded to them (bowing), the appellations employed (My Lord, Your Honour), and the physical positioning of judges during a criminal trial (up front, and on high), are structures and trappings of the criminal trial process which have evolved and presumably have been designed in order to instill a sense of majesty and awe in the minds and hearts of those who have been summoned to appear.

The positive benefits of such posturing are that they serve to underscore the gravity and solemnity of the occasion. They also serve to chasten and remonstrate the weak, glib, puckish, or wilful witness to adhere to a standard of higher responsibility in the giving of testimony. Thus, in theory the search for truth is facilitated.

A negative feature arising out of the same phenomenon is that the process works in such a way as to promote fright and nervousness in a witness. Thus impaired, the ability of a witness to fairly and accurately recount his or her version of the facts may be seriously affected. In this manner the search for truth is frustrated.

The witness must bear this burden silently while being examined and cross-examined by counsel. In a sense this burden is a "condition of existence" in the courts. As such, its gravity is diminished by the fact that every witness labors under substantially the same hardships.[59] Matters however do not remain in such happy equilibrium once the trial judge enters into the arena as a participant/examiner rather than remaining in his arbitral/adjudicative role.

If one accepts the proposition that the physical setting of the criminal trial does in fact inspire a sense of awe, and even trepidation, then one must accept also that the presiding trial judge personifies and symbolizes many of those same awe-inspiring qualities. Initially his role is perceived by participants as neutral, and to a degree, protective. The examining judge therefore possesses a massive psychological advantage (one not possessed by examining counsel) when he chooses to enter the fray. Improperly utilized, this advantage may lead to a distortion of the trial process's fact-gathering mechanism.

Undoubtedly it is competent for the trial judge to address questions to any witness called to give testimony.[60] But when, and in what manner should such interrogation be conducted? If no standards apply to the conduct of judicial interrogation then undoubtedly the abuse which one respected author perceives, of a frightened or awe-struck witness agreeing to anything the trial judge says, will be perpetuated.[61]

Standards of judicial conduct do in fact exist.

The whole matter proceeds from a framework of insuring that the trial process achieves the end of fashioning justice between man and man. As Lord Chief Justice Hewart observed, and every lawyer knows, "it is not merely of some importance, but of fundamental importance, that justice should not only be done, but be manifestly and undoubtedly seen to be done."[62]

Thus, while the trial judge may interrogate, he must be vigilant not to drop the veil of impartiality. A portion of the headnote in *R. v. Darlyn*,[63] a decision of the British Columbia Court of Appeal, accurately conveys the law on this subject:

> It is proper for a trial judge to participate in the examination of witnesses in order to bring out or explain relevant matters, but where the examination is such that the jury may infer therefrom that the Judge is convinced of the guilt of the accused it is improper and a ground for ordering a new trial.

Bird J.A. in *Darlyn* conceived it to be the function of the trial judge

---

59. This is perhaps an over-simplification. Certain witnesses are entirely familiar with the court environment (*e.g.* police officers) and hence do not suffer from the same malaise as do most ordinary witnesses.

60. See *Yuill v. Yuill* [1945] 1 All E.R. 183.

61. See McWilliams *supra* footnote 58 at p. 589.

62. *R. v. Sussex J.J., Ex parte McCarthy* (1923) 93 L.J.K.B. 129 at p. 131.

63. (1946) 88 C.C.C. 269 (B.C. C.A.).

"to keep the scales of justice in even balance between the Crown and the accused".[64]

Having established that the trial judge may participate in the examination of witnesses so long as his impartiality remains unimpeachable, when and for what purpose may he do so? Lord Green in *Yuill v. Yuill*[65] provides this answer:

> It is, of course, always proper for a judge — and it is his duty — to put questions with a view to elucidating an obscure answer or when he thinks that the witness has misunderstood a question put to him by counsel. If there are matters which the judge considers have not been sufficiently cleared up or questions which he himself thinks ought to have been put, he can, of course, take steps to see that the deficiency is made good. It is, I think, generally more convenient to do this when counsel has finished his questions or is passing to a new subject.

This judicial right extends even to the point of allowing the trial judge to rectify, through judicial interrogation, the failure of the prosecution to prove an essential ingredient of the offence charged.[66]

It appears settled that the trial judge may not only examine the witness, he may also cross-examine. For the most part resort to cross-examination techniques is viewed as undesirable. Where manifest injustice flows from such an exercise of judicial discretion, the discretion is reviewable.[67]

Since the trial judge may cross-examine, leading questions with all the dangers which they implicitly carry may be utilized. The practice has been labelled as "objectionable", but nevertheless permissible, by the Ontario Court of Appeal.[68] So long as the examination conducted is devoid of any "tendency to take sides or to press a witness in any

---

64. *Ibid.* at p. 277.
65. *Supra* footnote 60 at p. 185.
66. See *R. v. Remnant* (1807) 168 E.R. 724; *R. v. Watson* (1835) 172 E.R. 1405. Alternatively, where the Crown has through inadvertence failed to prove an essential element the Court has a discretion to permit the re-opening of the case in order that the requisite facts might be brought before the Court: *R. v. Perreault* (1941) 78 C.C.C. 236 (Que.). See also *R. v. Torbiak* (1974) 26 C.R.N.S. 108 (Ont. C.A.); *Re Cachia* (1974) 26 C.R.N.S. 302 (Ont.).
67. See *R. v. Crippen* [1911] 1 K.B. 149 at p. 157; *R. v. Starkie* (1921) 16 Cr.App.R. 61 at p. 66.
68. *R. v. West* (1925) 44 C.C.C. 109 at p. 111 (Ont. C.A.) *per* Ferguson J.A. See also *Connor v. Brant* (1914) 31 O.L.R. 274 at p. 280 (C.A.) where Meredith C.J.O. claims to know of "no rule which forbids in such a case the putting of leading questions to the witness" but "in considering the weight to be given to this testimony, regard must be had to the form in which the questions were put and the considerations which were urged by counsel."

way which could be considered undesirable"[69] an appeal Court reviewing the matter would be loath to interfere.

Not only does the trial judge present a figure of might and majesty in the trial process, he in fact is well armed to protect his processes from abuse. In his arsenal of weaponry are the contempt power and the power to recommend to the prosecutor *post facto* that a perjury prosecution should be initiated against a particular witness. Neither of these instruments should be used other than to insure orderly process and respect for the administration of justice. They should not (particularly the perjury threat) be used as intimidation devices. If they are so employed a mistrial may result.[70]

In *R. v. Bateman*[71] Humphreys J. had occasion to remark on the proper manner of judicial deportment where the Court encounters a difficult witness:

> It must not be forgotten by those who preside at criminal trials that witnesses, whether called for the prosecution or the defence, are entitled to be treated with courtesy and politeness unless and until they show some symptom of refusing to assist the Court by giving evidence promptly and properly. With all due respect to the Commissioner, it is not the duty of any presiding Judge as soon as the witness says: "I cannot tell you with accuracy what time something happened", to say: "Oh yes, you can, you be careful", *or anything designed to force the witness to say something which she really cannot say.*

On the other hand, Humphreys J. goes on to add that where the trial judge has formed the opinion that the witness is "not trying to help the court", then the judge "may do what counsel cannot do": The judge may instruct the witness to behave himself and tell the truth.[72] Such a power is truly extraordinary, and must be employed only with the greatest of caution. As a general rule "witnesses, whether they are for the prosecution or for the defence, should be allowed to tell their stories; and . . . it should then be left to the jury, subject, of course, to the comments of the presiding judge, to say whom they believe".[73] There is a point beyond which a trial judge must not proceed in expressing his incredulity as to the veracity and credibility of a witness. The matter is one of degree. Excesses have been met with rebuke in appeal courts and new trials have been ordered.

---

69. *Yuill v. Yuill, supra* footnote 60 at p. 185 *per* Greene M.R. and see also *R. v. Torbiak, supra* footnote 66 where the role of the trial judge in that trial was found to be proper, impartial and fair.
70. See *Provencher v. R.* (1955) 114 C.C.C. 100 (Can.) where the perjury threat was contained in the cross-examination of the Crown. See also *R. v. Lockerby* (1933) 49 B.C.R. 247 (C.A.) where a mistrial due to judicial misconduct resulted.
71. (1946) 31 Cr.App.R. 106 at p. 111 [emphasis added].
72. *Ibid.* at p. 111.
73. *Ibid.* at p. 113. See also *R. v. Gilson* (1944) 29 Cr.App.R. 174, and *R. v. Cain* (1936) 25 Cr.App.R. 204 both commented on by Humphreys J. in *Bateman supra*, footnote 71 at p. 111-112.

One such case was *R. v. Augello*.[74] In that case the sole ground of appeal was that the learned trial judge excessively intervened in the conduct of the trial by prolonged cross-examination of the accused, Augello, and that during the course of the evidence of the accused Augello the learned trial judge made numerous comments reflecting on the credibility of the witness and interrupted the witness's answers in such a manner as to indicate his disbelief in the witness's veracity. Although the trial judge gave a lawful and correct charge to the jury as to its position as the sole judge of the facts and credibility of witnesses, the appeal was allowed and a new trial was ordered. Porter C.J.O. in giving judgment on behalf of the court remarked:

> . . . We do not think it to be in the interests of a fair trial for the trial Judge to make statements during a witnesses's testimony which indicate his disbelief in the testimony being given. Nor should questions put by the Judge be so framed as to be open to the criticism of unfairness.[75]

(b) *Judicial interruption and interference*

As a generality it may be stated that our courts have opted for the principle that the least amount of judicial intervention into the examining arena yields the optimum result for the fair administration of justice. Excessive interruption into either the examination of a witness-in-chief, or into his cross-examination, is frowned upon and may yield a mistrial.

The trial judge has no right to take the case into his own hands.[76] Counsel should be allowed to conduct their examinations and cross-examinations without unwarranted interference by the trial judge.[77]

Interruption or interference may take many forms. It may be the breaking up of an examination-in-chief with prolonged bouts of cross-examination from the bench.[78] It may mean the injection of commentary and questions at tactically crucial points of examination, thus tending to destroy the intended effect of counsel's examination.[79] It

---

74. [1963] 3 C.C.C. 191 (Ont. C.A.). See also *R. v. Bevacqua* (1970) 11 C.R.N.S. 76 (Ont. C.A.), and the annotation *post*: M. Teplitsky "The Right to an Impartial Tribunal" at p. 80.

75. *Ibid.* at p.192. See also *R. v. Hircock* [1970] 1 Q.B. 67 for an example of similar judicial misconduct although this time the misconduct occurred during the course of a jury address by Counsel.

76. *Boran v. Wenger* [1942] 2 D.L.R. 528 (Ont. C.A.).

77. *R. v. Anderson* (1938) 70 C.C.C. 275 (Man. C.A.).

78. See *R. v. Cain, supra* footnote 73, where the comment is made that "it is undesirable that during an examination-in-chief the Judge should appear to be not so much assisting the defence as throwing his weight on the side of the prosecution by cross-examinating a prisoner". The judge ought not, in effect, take over the cross-examination of the witness: *R. v. Ignat* (1965) 53 W.W.R. 248 (Man. C.A.).

79. ". . . experienced counsel will see just as clearly as the judge that, for example a particular question will be a crucial one. But it is for counsel to decide at what stage he will put the question, and the whole strength

may take the form of remonstrations to counsel about wasting the court's time,[80] or in the imposition of time limits for the completion of questioning. In each of these the issue is one marked by degrees. Some judicial involvement is proper, and at times is even a duty. It is only *excessive* intervention which is proscribed.

Instances of such excess however, are not isolated. Commenting upon the situation in England (and the situation there is not far different from that which prevails in Canada) Dr. Shimon Shetreet in his recent work *Judges on Trial* documents the fact that trial judges are frequently criticised by the Court of Appeal for excessive interruption of the judicial process, and often their judgments are reversed and the convictions are quashed.[81]

R. v. Perks,[82] an interesting 1973 case cited by Dr. Shetreet, makes the important point that in determining the effect of a trial judge's intervention "the matter should not be decided simply by reference to the number of questions [for] what mattered was the quality of the interruptions".

Delaney & Co. v. Berry[83] was one case where the "quality of the interruptions" was held not to exceed the limits of propriety. Schultz J.A. of the Manitoba Court of Appeal does however conduct an excellent survey of authorities on the subject of undue judicial intervention. The following summary of the case is offered in the *Canadian Abridgment* (Second Edition):[84]

> Under our adversary system for the conduct of trials the responsibility of examining and cross-examining witnesses falls almost entirely on the advocates. The responsibility and the rights it confers and the duty it imposes must always be recognized by the Court. Although the Judge has full control of the proceedings and had the right and sometimes the duty to ask questions it is a right to be exercised with scrupulous care for the rights of the advocates. Excessive judicial interruption may put counsel under a grave disadvantage and certainly will weaken the effectiveness of his examination of witnesses. It also severely handicaps the Judge in retaining his proper role of an objective observer

---

of the cross-examination may be destroyed if the judge, in his desire to get to what seems to him to be the crucial point, himself intervenes and prematurely puts the question himself" (*per* Lord Greene M.R. in *Yuill v. Yuill, supra* footnote 60 at p. 185).

80. See *R. v. West, supra* footnote 68 at p. 111.
81. S. Shetreet, *Judges on Trial* (1976) at p. 210. In support of his contention Dr. Shetreet cites *Yuill v. Yuill, supra* footnote 60; *R. v. Gilson, supra* footnote 73; *R. v. Perks* [1973] Crim.L.R. 388 (C.A.); *R. v. Cain, supra* footnote 73; *Jones v. Nat. Coal Bd.* [1957] 2 Q.B. 55; *R. v. Clewer* (1953) 37 Cr.App.R. 37; and *Bunting v. Thorne Rural Dist. Council* (1957) The Times, 26 Mar. 1957. In discussing these cases interesting figures are offered as to the *number* of interventions of the trial judge.
82. [1973] Crim.L.R. 388.
83. *Supra* footnote 29.
84. P. 2, Can. Abr. (2nd) at p. 405.

of the witness. In general a Judge should "give a benign and receptive listening to each side so as to feel the full force of the argument of each side, and then judge between them.

If one were to choose the greater evil it would be extremely difficult to assess whether excessive interruption in examination (or cross-examination) differs markedly in effect from the actual curtailment of the right to examine. Both are disastrous from the advocate's point of view.

From the vantage point of the trial judge, exasperation and frustration can reach new heights where counsel through ineptitude, or through lack of insight concerning the effect of his examination, tarries and dallies, and saddles the court with repetitious and redundant inquiries. Where the interrogation is also of trivial or of questionable relevance the situation becomes that much more exacerbated. Sarcasm from the Bench can easily become the order of the day: "Why don't you ask the witness what he had for breakfast today, Mr. So-and-So?"

On the other hand, counsel, who may not see things in exactly the same light as the trial judge, may be wondering whether what the *judge* had for breakfast that day was responsible for the bile and cynicism that is being wafted in his direction.

The power of the trial judge to control counsel with respect to the repetition of questions (especially where they are of marginal relevance) is undoubted.[85] However, counsel, whether for the defence or for the Crown, has a right to complete the examination of witnesses even though the relevancy of a particular line of questioning is not immediately apparent to the trial judge.[86]

The line between proper restriction and improper curtailment is vague and often difficult to ascertain. Although at times it may require the patience of Job, the trial judge is well advised to err on the side of caution. One is inclined to feel some sympathy for the trial judge in a case such as *R. v. Anderson,*[87] but ultimately prejudice accrued and the fair trial of the accused was jeopardized:

> Time and again the learned trial Judge appealed to the counsel to keep to the issues. These issues were seven specific charges of theft of securities in 1936, with alternatives as to the proceeds. Yet the case went on into the history of the company from its incorporation in 1927, the mechanism of its business, its financial vicissitudes and the

---

85. *Dickinson v. Harvey* (1913) 24 W.L.R. 777 (B.C.C.A.); *R. v. West supra* footnote 68; *R. v. Treacy* (1944) 30 Cr.App.R. 93.

86. See *R. v. Viger* (1958) 122 C.C.C. 159 (Ont. C.A.) where Crown counsel was curtailed in the examination of his own witness and forced to withdraw. A new trial before a different trial judge was ordered. See also *R. v. Simmons* [1923] 3 W.W.R. 749 (B.C.C.A.) where defence counsel was curtailed in the examination of the star witness of the prosecution. A new trial was ordered.

87. *Supra* footnote 77; see also *Pilon v. R.* (1973) 23 C.R.N.S. 392 (Que. C.A.); *R. v. Marcotte* [1964] Que. Q.B. 155 (C.A.).

personnel of the staff including many trivialities. The learned Judge protested that he was not conducting a Royal Commission. He for a long time gave counsel much scope; but one thing led to another, and he had to do something to stem the flood. I think the rulings complained of were inadvertent and made when the termination of the case was long past due. But nevertheless that happened to be the critical time in the case.[88]

The overt and unjustified curtailment of examination or interrogation is statutorily restricted by the full answer and defence provisions of the *Criminal Code*,[89] as well as by the fair hearing provisions of the *Canadian Bill of Rights*.[90] Nevertheless, it should not be assumed that the Court is powerless to control the misconduct of counsel. Everyday experience in our courts of law well demonstrate that our trial judges are more than equal to this task. It is not only the witness who stands in awe of the court. Most counsel are similarly affected, although experience and polish brings an outward calm.

Furthermore, the latitude for judicial intervention short of overt curtailment remains extremely wide:

We do not doubt that objectionable as it may be, the trial Judge has a right to ask leading questions, also to endeavour to speed the trial, and even to tell counsel that he is wasting time, and that he also has the right to suggest, as he did in this trial, that counsel waive their rights to address the jury. These, we think, are matters of discretion and good judgment, not entitling us to interfere unless we are of opinion that they resulted in a manifest injustice being done to the accused.[91]

(3) The response of counsel to judicial interference

Counsel appearing in a court of law, while an advocate for his client's cause, nevertheless has twin loyalties.

There is no doubt that counsel owes a duty to his client, but also has an obligation to conduct himself properly before any Court in Canada.[92]

Improper conduct (characterized by over-zealousness in carrying out the duty owed one's client to the exclusion of the duty of proper presentation and deportment in court) may result in a citation for contempt of Court.[93] Therefore, although on occasion the temptation may be great to give free rein to his emotions in a particularly frus-

---

88. *Ibid.* at p. 292 *per* Robson J.A.
89. R.S.C. 1970, Chap. C-34, ss. 577(3) and 737.
90. R.S.C. 1970, Appendix III, s. 2(e).
91. *R. v. West, supra* footnote 68 at pp. 111-112 *per* Ferguson J.A. But see *R. v. Bradbury* (1973) 23 C.R.N.S. 293 (Ont. C.A.) as to the impropriety of the trial judge attempting to set a time limit on cross-examination. Such a procedure was held to be "not allowable".
92. *Re Duncan* (1958) 11 D.L.R. (2d) 616 (Can.) *per* Kerwin C.J.C.
93. See *Re Duncan ibid.*, and *R. v. Shumiatcher* [1967] 3 C.C.C. 197, varied [1969] 1 C.C.C. 272 (Sask. C.A.).

trating trial, counsel must be wary to hold them in check. While he may, indeed he should, object to improper judicial intervention, he should at the same time be measured and scrupulous in his commentary.

But, as Lord Atkin observed, "Justice is not a cloistered virtue: she must be allowed to suffer the scrutiny and respectful, even though outspoken comments of ordinary men."[94]

Counsel therefore is left to walk a firm but respectful line in his attempts to secure a fair hearing for his client.

American trial justice, especially as conveyed through high-visibility, media-attracting cases, is regarded somewhat scornfully in Canadian legal circles. The thought has been expressed that a trial such as that of the Chicago Seven (or Eight) in the late 1960's would not have developed into "political theatre" were it conducted in this country.[95] The rough, chaotic and flamboyant elements of American trials are certainly highly muted in Anglo-Canadian trial courts, if they are not absent altogether. Nevertheless, there is much to learn from American trial advocacy, and Canadian law and legal practices have not been entirely resistant to American influences.

Bailey and Rothblatt in their comprehensive text on *Fundamentals of Criminal Advocacy*[96] suggest the following advice (which is here endorsed) on "How to handle an interfering judge":

> The best way to try to stop this interference is to say to the Judge (in a respectful manner): "Your Honor, I intend to cover those points. Will Your Honor permit me to develop them in my own way?" This should politely put the Judge in his place. However, if he continues to interfere, persist in advising him that you intend to cover all of the points he is making, and you respectfully would prefer that he permit you to conduct your cross- examination in your own way.
>
> Be emphatic. Assert your rights firmly — though tactfully — at the very beginning and you should gain the respect of the court. But cower before the court, and this type of judge will ride roughshod over you.

In *R. v. Shumiatcher*[97] a portion of the exchange which took place between counsel and the trial judge (which ultimately resulted in counsel's being cited for contempt) was ostensibly aimed at protecting a witness from abuse by the trial judge:

> The Court: — I am asking you if you ever recommended that she be put in a mental institution, not what somebody else did.
>
> Witness: — Yes, My Lord.

---

94. *Ambard v. A.G. for Trinidad and Tobago* [1936] A.C. 322 at p. 335, approved by McRuer C.J.H.C. in *R. v. Glanzer* [1963] 1 C.C.C. 364 at p. 369.
95. See P. Meyers, "Disruption in the Courtroom" (1972-73) 5 Man. L.J. 229.
96. F. L. Bailey and H. B. Rothblatt, *Fundamentals of Criminal Advocacy* (1974) at p. 323.
97. *Supra* footnote 93 (Q.B.) at pp 205-206.

The Court: — July 13, 1965, she was admitted to the Yorkton Psychiatric Centre.

. . .

The Court: — What is that? Is that a mental institution?
That is just a centre for treatment —

Mr. Shumiatcher: — Well perhaps the doctor can explain this. He is here.

The Court: — Well, I have just asked him that. Now —

Mr. Shumiatcher: — You are not asking him, you're telling him.

The Court: — Don't be rude now.

Mr. Shumiatcher: — Well, I don't think you should try and push this witness around, My Lord, let him answer. I think it is only proper that he should be able to answer.

The Court: — Reporter, would you please note those remarks, I will have that transcribed.

Mr. Shumiatcher: — I think that this witness should not be badgered.

In *Shumiatcher,* counsel's contentions that the trial judge was pushing about and badgering the witness were not supported by the transcript. In the extract of the trial transcript set out *supra* one leading question does appear ("That is just a centre for the treatment —"), but the response of counsel (on the basis of a reading of the reasons for judgment of Davis J.) was clearly intemperate and excessive.

An advocate's major difficulty in fashioning his response to a trial judge who has "descended into the arena" lies in the fact that he must address his objection to the very person called upon to adjudicate the merits of that objection. In most instances a judge is restrained from being the arbiter of his own cause. Practical necessity dictates otherwise in these circumstances.

Appellate review is the only meaningful safeguard against judicial misconduct which the system provides.[98] As we have noted, judicial intervention into the examining process is contemplated as an aspect of judicial discretion; and, this discretion will not be interfered with on appeal unless injustice is manifest. Hence, a certain amount of risk is assumed by the counsel who chooses to stand idly by each time the trial judge sallies forth into the examining arena.

Counsel has a duty to object where he feels an objection is properly taken. Even where he knows that the response to his objection will be negative, and is a foregone conclusion, his obligation is to press his objection firmly within acceptable limits in order that it be noted for the record.

---

98. See S. Shetreet *supra* footnote 81, Chapter X on "The Appellate Court: 1. Methods and Effectiveness in Checking Judges".

(4) The judicial power, to refuse to hear counsel's arguments, or his witnesses; or to determine the order in which witnesses are to be called

(a) *Determining the order of defence witnesses*

In England in 1968 the Court of Appeal endorsed this proposition concerning the calling of witnesses by defence counsel in a criminal case:[99]

> In all cases I consider it most important for the prisoner to be called before any of his witnesses. He ought to give his evidence before he has heard the evidence and cross-examination of any witness he is going to call.[100]

As one commentator has pointed out, "there exists a whole range of intermediate positions in which counsel might wish, if permitted, to postpone the decision whether to call his client."[101] The effect of *Smith* in England appears to leave counsel in the unhappy position of calling his client at the outset of defence evidence or not at all. While the prosecution is free to determine the order of its evidence, the defence, at least in one respect, cannot.[102]

Fortunately, the rule governing Canadian practice in this area has not been fashioned in quite such a rigid manner. In fact, the leading Canadian case on the subject, *R. v. Smuk,*[103] specifically disapproves of the rule enunciated by the English courts in *Smith*.

Branca J.A. in *Smuk* makes these comments which appear to be of general application:

> The accused, or counsel for the accused, is totally and completely free to decide whether or not the accused will or will not testify, and if he does, in what order or sequence he will be called to testify either before or after the witnesses who are called for and on his behalf. The Court cannot *under any circumstances* insist that an accused should testify first no more than the Court can order the accused to testify.[104]

The Ontario Court of Appeal in a decision[105] subsequent to *Smuk* has held that there is *at least one circumstance* where the trial judge has the right to order the defence to present the accused's testimony first — in the instance where counsel, by way of opening address, has indicated that the accused would be called to give alibi evidence. In

---

99. *R. v. Smith* [1968] 2 All E.R. 115 (C.A.).
100. This passage is cited with approval by Cusack J. in *Smith ibid.,* and the words are those of Alverstone C.J. in *R. v. Morrison* (1911) 6 Cr.App.R. 159 at p. 165.
101. E. Griew "The Order of Defence Evidence" [1969] Crim.L.R. 347 at p. 352.
102. *Ibid.* p. 354.
103. (1971) 3 C.C.C. (2d) 457 (B.C.C.A.).
104. *Ibid.* at p. 462 (emphasis added).
105. *R. v. Archer* (1974) 26 C.R.N.S. 225 (Ont. C.A.); see also the annotation *ibid.* at p. 227, A.G. Campbell "The Order of Defence Witnesses".

his extremely brief judgment in *Archer,* Gale C.J.O. fails to offer any cogent reasons for creating this exception to the general rule set out in *Smuk,* other than to say that "having regard to the only defence presented, it was for the appellant's benefit . . ." that the ruling of the trial judge was made.

While it is true that for the defence of alibi to have much chance of success it should be set up at the earliest possible opportunity,[106] it is not true that the alibi need be the first piece of defence evidence offered at the trial (at least, such was not the case in any reported Canadian decision prior to *Archer.*)[107]

Surely the only convincing consideration governing whether an accused ought to testify first or at some other point in the trial is this one outlined by McFarlane J.A. in the *Smuk* case:

> When a witness whether an accused or not, sits in Court and hears the testimony of another witness or witnesses on a subject-matter as to which he later testifies, his evidence is open to the suggestion that it may have been made deliberately to conform. This it seems to me is a plain matter of commonsense. It is a factor to be considered by the tribunal of fact and so relates to the weight of the evidence.[108]

(b) *Refusing to hear submissions of counsel*

A refusal by a trial judge to hear argument by accused's counsel before convicting is a failure to permit full answer and defense. Such a refusal amounts to a denial of natural justice sufficient to result in the quashing of the conviction on certiorari.[109]

However, where the trial judge offers to hear submissions from counsel after prematurely announcing his decision and then retracting it, counsel should take the opportunity. In *R. v. Kovacevic,*[110] counsel declined such an invitation and sought to overturn his client's conviction by way of motion to quash. In dismissing the motion Ferguson J.

---

106. "Alibis which are set up at the last minutes and have never been indicated before are always open to gravest suspicion" (*per* Goddard C.J. in *R. v. Flynn* (1957) 42 Cr.App.R. 15 at p. 16).

107. It is doubtful whether any such case could be found in an American jurisdiction either in view of the decision of the United States Supreme Court in *Brooks v. Tennessee* (1972) 406 U.S. 605. ("Pressuring the defendant to take the stand by foreclosing later testimony if he refuses, is not a constitutionally permissible means of ensuring his honesty." *Ibid.* at p. 611.)

108. *Supra* footnote 103 at p. 458. This raises the question of whether the accused could be excluded from the court during the testimony of other defence witnesses: See Griew *supra* footnote 101 at p. 355. This suggestion, were it possible, is impractical in those situations where counsel has no intention of calling his client but is left with no other alternative when the case for the defence is demolished in cross-examination.

109. See *R. v. Bartlett* (1950) 10 C.R. 220 (Ont. H.C.) and *R. v. Wandsworth JJ. Ex parte Read* [1942] 1 K.B. 281. See also *Felker v. Felker* [1946] O.W.N. 368 (C.A.), a civil action dealing with the dissolution of a marriage.

110. (1951) 11 C.R. 333 (Ont.).

asserted that the court is not to be held ransom to "all of the whims of petulant counsel":

> One must assume, I think, when the magistrate or judge withdraws his judgment, however inadvertently rendered, offering to hear argument, that he will keep an open mind and will be prepared to change his previously expressed opinion if the argument put forward by counsel convinces him that he should do so.[111]

These remarks are attended by logic and plain common sense. One difficulty which is not embraced however, by either these remarks or the cases discussed thus far is that which occurs when the omission, or refusal, to hear counsel does not work a short term harm (as where his client is acquitted) but creates long term prejudice (where a conviction is substituted on appeal). One commentator goes so far as to suggest that *"in no circumstances . . . should a trial judge make a finding either on a factual or legal issue which is adverse to a party's interest, without affording that party an opportunity to make submissions."*[112]

This would make for a rather impractical rule of practice. It should be remembered that for the most part the Court of Appeal is concerned with the adequacy and propriety of the reasons for judgment of the trial judge. If those reasons are deficient in that they fail to reflect consideration of an issue which might become relevant on appeal counsel certainly may ask the court for clarification or amplification of the reasons behind the Court's decision. In so doing counsel might even informally make his submission on the point in question and the subsequent remarks of the Court would thus complete the record. Such occurrences are commonplace. Nor is the matter solely one which is undertaken by the successful counsel. Often one hears the remark, "Am I given to understand then that Your Honour . . .", and the responses which follow may well lay the groundwork for a successful appeal.

The responsibility is one which must by its very nature reside with counsel.[113] Counsel may very well in such instances prefer silence, as the likelihood of appeal may be remote, or, the basis upon which the trial judge has decided the matter may appear sufficient.

(c) *Refusing to hear a witness*

The refusal to hear evidence like the refusal to hear the submissions of counsel is a failure to permit full answer and defence, and constitutes denial of natural justice.

In cases of clear wilfulness and partiality no difficulty arises, but in

---

111. *Ibid.* at p. 337.
112. M. Teplitsky, "Annotation: The right to make submissions as part of full answer and defence" (1970) 12 C.R.N.S. 149.
113. M. Teplitsky takes the view that the responsibility should reside with the trial judge: *ibid.* at p. 150.

those rare cases of judicial inadvertence it appears that there is a divergence between the law respecting submissions (where the judge may withdraw his premature pronouncements and ask counsel to address him as was done in *Kovacevic, supra*) and the law respecting the calling of witnesses.

Hughes J. in *R. v. Bourque*[114] (a case where the magistrate at the conclusion of a motion for no evidence proceeded to adjudicate without calling on the accused for his defence) stated his view of the law in this fashion:

> In the case at bar the magistrate convicted the accused and sentenced him without giving him an opportunity to put in his defence. I think it would be unfair to an accused to hold that a magistrate who even by a slip has delivered judgment in favour of the prosecution can strike out that judgment and take evidence for the defence and then deliver a further judgment. I think that would not be fair to the accused: *Rex v. Graham* (1922), 17 Cr. App. R. 40; *Rex v. Villars* (1927), 20 Cr. App. R. 150. [115]

While the distinctions between *Kovacevic* and *Bourque* may not appear sufficient to justify their very different results it is submitted that the more stringent rule adopted in *Bourque* is entirely appropriate to the circumstances of that case, and would be inappropriate to circumstances of *Kovacevic*.

In *Kovacevic* all of the evidence for both sides had been presented. All that remained were the submissions of counsel. This is a far cry from the situation in *Bourque* where only *half* of the potential evidence had been presented when the court announced its pre-disposition. The different time frame places the two matters in entirely different perspectives. These remarks of Chief Justice Sloan given in the course of his dissenting judgment in *R. v. Northey*[116] indicate the nature of this important distinction, and argue well for the propriety of the rule adopted in Bourque:

> "The function of this Court is not to retry the accused and to decide upon his guilt or innocence. This Court is a court of review, and the issue before us, in this case, is not the guilt or innocence of the accused *but whether or not the accused has had a fair trial on proper evidence.*"[117]

Certainly the appearance of justice is badly damaged where, before a case is half over, the trial judge announces that he has found the accused guilty as charged. In a case such as this rectification can only be had through the holding of a new trial.[118]

---

114. (1947) 4 C.R. 300 (N.B. C.A.).
115. *Ibid.* at p. 304.
116. [1947] 4 D.L.R. 774. The position of Sloan C.J.B.C. and the other dissentients was upheld on appeal [1948] S.C.R. 135.
117. *Ibid.* at p. 777 (emphasis added).
118. See *Harper v. Griffiths* (1929) 64 O.L.R. 668 (C.A.), where a refusal to

4. THE JUDICIAL POWER TO CALL WITNESSES, RAISE ISSUES AND CIRCUMVENT INCOMPETENCY

(1) Calling witnesses

In trying criminal cases the judge has undoubted power to call a witness, or witnesses,[119] but the power to do so has long been felt to be one which *normally* ought not to be exercised. Where such a course has been embarked upon it was only after a full and cautious inquiry as to the necessity of the action. But if the interests of justice would be advanced by the calling of the witness, the trial judge was felt to be justified in calling the witness, and his actions were not predicated on first obtaining the consent of counsel.[120]

This subject is not one which has attracted much judicial commentary, although scholarly writing on the subject has begun to appear in recent years.[121]

A survey of the case law which does exist on the subject (and of the related writings) indicates that there are in essence three distinct heads which exist to justify judicial intervention into the adversary process by calling of witnesses: (a) instances where the "Exigencies of Justice" require the witness to be called; (b) instances where a matter arises *ex improviso* and (c) instances where prosecutorial discretion in the calling of witnesses is being improperly exercised.

(a) *The "exigencies of justice"*

The cases . . . establish the proposition that the presiding judge at a criminal trial has the right to call a witness not called by either the prosecution or the defence . . . if in his opinion this course is necessary in the interests of justice.[122]

---

hear witnesses called in a civil trial was felt to be a denial of justice and a new trial was ordered. See also *R. v. Nunn* (1884) 10 P.R. 395; *R. v. Dom. Drug Stores Ltd.* (1919) 30 C.C.C. 318, affirmed 14 Alta. L.R. 384 (C.A.).

119. English cases of the first half nineteenth century establish the proposition firmly: *R. v. Bull* (1839) 173 E.R. 723; *R. v. Chapman* (1838) 173 E.R. 617; *R. v. Holden* (1838) 173 E.R. 638; *R. v. Edwards* (1848) 3 Cox C.C. 89n; *R. v. Simmonds* (1823) 171 E.R. 1111; *R. v. Frost* (1839) 4 State Tr. (N.S.) 85, 386. See also *R. v. Harris* [1927] 2 K.B. 587.

120. See *R. v. Harris* and *R. v. Holden supra.*

121. See M. Newark and A. Samuels, "Let the Judge Call the Witness" [1969] Crim.L.R. 399; H. Silverman, "The Trial Judge: Pilot, Participant, or Umpire?" (1973) 11 Alta.L.R. 40; P. C. Stenning "Annotation: One Blind Man to See Fair Play: The Judge's Right to Call Witnesses" (1974) 24 C.R.N.S. 49 (The most extensive Canadian work on the subject). See also P. K. McWilliams, *Canadian Criminal Evidence* (1974) at pp. 464-465. And see S. Lederman and J. Sopinka, *The Law of Evidence in Civil Cases* (1974) at pp. 476-477, for the contrasting rules governing civil cases. For the American position in 1957 see "The Trial Judge's Use of His Power to Call Witnesses — An Aid to Adversary Presentation" (1957) 51 Nev.U.L. Rev. 761.

122. *Per* Avory J. in *R. v. Harris supra* footnote 119 at p. 594.

(A basic limitation upon this right of the trial judge is the *ex improviso* constraint which is dealt with *infra*).[123]

Determining whether the interests of justice will be advanced by the court's calling witnesses *proprio motu* (or by allowing the Crown to reopen its case and call the witness) is a process subsumed under the generally impenetrable shroud of "judicial discretion". An appeal court generally will not interfere in these discretionary exercises except where there has been a clear derogation from principle. Discovering relevant legal principles in this area is an often difficult, if not impossible, task. For example, the courts have been reluctant to interfere with the discretion of a trial judge to call witnesses in instances where the witnesses were necessary in order to "avoid acceding to a defence submission of no case based on a technicality arising from the failure of the witness to prove a vital link in the prosecution case."[124]

However, it should be remembered that at the time of the "no-evidence" submission the accused has not yet embarked upon his defence (if he intends to call one) and it is consequently difficult for him to demonstrate prejudice or injustice to his cause. Where evidence is called or allowed at the conclusion of the case for the defence the matter may well be markedly different.

Further, it should be noted that at the stage of the no evidence motion the Court has two procedures open to it: (1) it can call the witness itself; or (2) it can permit the case for the prosecution to be re-opened in order that the prosecution be allowed to call the witness.[125]

These procedures for re-opening a case and calling witnesses do not amount to a judicial *carte blanche*. For the most part, the cases permitting re-opening in circumstances where there has been a failure on the part of the prosecution to prove some essential ingredient of the crime charged have been restricted to matters where the situation arose through a "mere slip" or "inadvertence", and the allowing of additional evidence could not reasonably be said to occasion prejudice or injustice to the accused. Also, where the conduct of defence counsel contributes in some degree to the failure by the Crown to call certain essential evidence, the trial judge has been held to be justified in allowing the Crown to re-open its case.[126] A good example of such conduct is to be found in *R. v. Champagne*.[127]

---

123. This constraint was first laid down as a "rule of practice" by Tindal C.J. in *R. v. Frost supra* footnote 119 at p. 386.

124. Newark and Samuels *supra* footnote 121 at p. 402 citing *R. v. McKenna* (1956) 40 Cr.App.R. 65 in support.

125. See *R. v. Gregoire* (1927) 47 C.C.C. 288 (Ont. C.A.); *R. v. Huluszkiw* (1962) 133 C.C.C. 244 (Ont. C.A.) — re-opening permissible even during the case for the defence; *R. v. Champagne* [1970] 2 C.C.C. 273 (B.C. C.A.); *R. v. Kishen Singh* (1941) 76 C.C.C. 248 (B.C. C.A.).

126. See *R. v. Huluszkiw* and *R. v. Champagne ibid.*

127. *Ibid.*

In *Champagne,* defence counsel agreed to the introduction of two expert certificates, and reserved his right to argue their meaning. He did so in such a way as to lead Crown Counsel to believe that the certificates had become proper evidence, when in fact they had not. The British Columbia Court of Appeal held that in such circumstances the trial judge may properly allow the Crown to re-open its case after the defence had elected to call no evidence.

Where there is no inadvertence and no contributory misconduct by the defence it would be an error in principle (and hence, it is submitted, a reversible error) to allow the Crown to re-open its case in order to correct deficiencies in its case once closed. The Ontario Court of Appeal in *R. v. Ash-Temple Co.*[128] says as much:

> It was not by reason of any change of position on the part of the defence, nor of the discovery of fresh evidence by the Crown, that the decision was made [by Crown counsel] to apply for leave to call more evidence. Neither was there any accidental omission by prosecuting counsel to call evidence. The constant objections by counsel for the accused to the admission of documents in evidence without further proof, had been a prominent feature of the trial. *It would have been a considerable indulgence to counsel for the Crown to re-open his case to permit evidence to be called to supply deficencies in the proof of the case to which attention had been called by opposing counsel since early in the trial.*[129]

To summarize, in assessing whether it would be in the interests of justice to permit the re-opening of a case and the calling of witnesses, the trial judge in the exercise of his discretion should consider (a) whether there would be prejudice to the accused; (b) whether it was by inadvertence that the Crown's case was closed without calling the evidence now sought to be called; and (c) whether counsel for the accused contributed to the situation by some artifice.

The decision of whether or not to permit re-opening, although never an easy one, becomes more complicated as the trial progresses. Thus far, our analysis has largely been restricted to considerations arising on the *completion of the case for the Crown,* or, at the coincident time, of a no case submission. The problem which next arises is whether the court should permit re-opening (to call its own witnesses, or to

---

128. (1949) 93 C.C.C. 267 (Ont. C.A.) at pp. 278-279 *per* Robertson C.J.O. (emphasis added).

129. It should be noted that the Ontario Court of Appeal was not *interfering* in the exercise of a discretion in *Ash-Temple Co.,* they were *sustaining* the discretion of a trial judge who refused to allow the Crown to re-open its case. It is submitted however, that the case stands as authority for the proposition that allowing the Crown to re-open in similar circumstances would be regarded as a reversible error. See *R. v. Dunn* (1969) 9 C.R.N.S. 274 (B.C.) where the discretion of a Magistrate allowing the re-opening of case to correct a similar error was interfered with on appeal. (The Crown in leading its witnesses had incorrectly and carelessly mis-stated the date).

allow them to be called) *during the case for the defence, upon its completion, or even after the matter has been remitted to the jury.* In essence, how far into the chronology of the criminal trial does this aspect of the "interests of justice" extend?

Sloan J.A. in *R. v. Kishen Singh*[130] had occasion to remark on some of these matters:

> "it is clear that a trial judge has the discretionary power to permit Crown counsel to call further evidence after he has closed the case for the prosecution. That discretion when exercised before the accused has entered upon his defence is subject to the limitation that its exercise must be in the interests of justice and the accused be not prejudiced thereby. When at a later stage of the case, that is to say, after the defence has given its evidence . . . the discretion ought not to be exercised except in a case where some matter arises *ex improviso* which no human ingenuity could have foreseen.

The *ex improviso* constraint (the detailed discussion of which follows *infra*) then, must be regarded as a general fetter on the bald assertion that a trial judge is free to call, re-call, or permit the calling or re-calling of witnesses whenever he is of the opinion that the "exigencies of justice" require such action.

(b) *Matters arising ex improviso*

Where an issue or matter arises spontaneously *(ex improviso)* during the course of a trial, and it is of such a nature that no human ingenuity could reasonably have foretold its occurrence, then the trial judge is justified in calling or re-calling such witness or witnesses as are necessary.[131] If this condition of "spontaneity" is met then it matters not whether the case for the defence has been closed, so long as the matter has not been remitted to the jury.[132]

The difficulty which the general proposition set forth *supra* entails is that the trial judge may be seen to be assuming the role of an extra prosecutor. That would certainly be the case if, without limits, he were allowed to call witnesses in order to rebut any defence raised by the accused. While the power in the trial judge to call witnesses is wide, it does not appear to extend quite that far.

---

130. *Supra* footnote 125 at pp. 250-251.
131. See *R. v. Seigley* (1911) 6 Cr.App.R. 106; *R. v. Liddle* (1928) 21 Cr.App.R. 3; *R. v. McMahon* (1933) 24 Cr.App.R. 95; *R. v. Harris supra* footnote 119; *R. v. Cleghorn* (1967) 51 Cr.App.R. 291; *R. v. Bouchard* (1973) 24 C.R.N.S. 31 (N.S.). This last case is strongly criticized by P. C. Stenning, *supra* footnote 121); *R. v. Marsh* [1941] 1 D.L.R. 431 (B.C. C.A.); *R. v. Day* [1940] 1 All E.R. 402; *R. v. Owen* [1952] 2 Q.B. 362; *R. v. Sornsen* [1965] 2. C.C.C. 242 (B.C.); *R. v. Gilbert* (1950) 9 C.R. 372 (Alta. C.A.).
132. See *R. v. Browne* (1943) 29 Cr.App.R. 106; *R. v. Wilson* (1957) 41 Cr.App.R. 226; *R. v. Gearing* (1968) 50 Cr.App.R. 18; *R. v. Brown* [1967] 3 C.C.C. 210 (Que. C.A.); *R. v. Manconi* (1912) 20 C.C.C. 81 (Que. C.A.). When the matter "has been remitted to the jury" in point of fact

Lord Hewart C.J. in *R. v. McMahon*[133] sets forth the general approach adopted in these matters:

> As was said by this Court in *Liddle* (1928) 21 Cr. App. R. 3 at p. 10: "A judge at a criminal trial has the right to call a witness not called by either the prosecution or the defence, without the consent of either prosecution or the defence, if in his opinion that course is necessary in the interests of justice, but in order that injustice should not be done to an accused person, a judge should not call a witness in a criminal trial after the case for the defence is closed except in a case where a matter arises *ex improviso,* which no human ingenuity can foresee, on the part of the prisoner, otherwise injustice would ensue."

To this is added a necessary clarification provided by the case of *R. v. Tregear.*[134] In *Tregear,* the defence had been insisting on the calling of two witnesses whose evidence was not tendered by the Crown. The Court initially declined to make such an order. Consequently the defence elected to call one of the two witnesses as its own. At the conclusion of the case for the defence the trial judge decided "in the interests of justice" to call the remaining witness. Defence counsel at the time of trial did not object to the court's unusual procedure. When the matter was argued before Court of Appeal (Criminal Division) no fault was found with the conduct of the trial judge. (It was suggested that counsel might have objected in this matter: "I have called Chown, but I do not think you ought to call Jarman.")[135] The rationale offered in the Appeal Court decision was that the motivation of the trial judge was all-important, and that in *Tregear* the course adopted was appropriate since the witness was called *"not in order to supplement the evidence for the prosecution,* but to ascertain the truth and put all the evidence before the jury. . . ."[136]

While the clarification provided by the *Tregear* case is that the witness(es) called by a trial judge should not be called purely as an aid to the prosecution of the case, it is difficult to reconcile this refinement of the law with the decision reached in that case.

Both Jarman and Chown were viewed as "very unsatisfactory witnesses". The prosecution, in its discretion, could properly choose *not* to call such witnesses as part of its case. One cannot quarrel with the refusal of the trial judge to accede to the request of defence counsel

---

extends almost up until the eleventh hour: *e.g.,* in *R. v. Sullivan* (1922) 16 Cr.App.R. 121, evidence was called by trial judge after the defence had closed its case, and again after both counsel had addressed the jury. The discretion of the trial judge was not disturbed on appeal. The law appears to be firm however, that once the case has been left in the hands of the jury no new evidence may be presented; this even though the jury specifically requests it: *R. v. Owen ibid.*

133. *R. v. McMahon supra* footnote 131.
134. (1967) 51 Cr.App.R. 280.
135. *Ibid.* at p. 286.
136. *Ibid.* at p. 289 (emphasis added).

that the witnesses be called as prosecution witnesses. Their truthfulness was suspect, and their demeanour once called tended to bear out these suspicions. There is little issue to take with the procedure up to this point.

After this, however, defence counsel was left in the rather unenviable position of having to advance his client's case through apparently unsavoury evidence. Procedurally, counsel had already lost these tactical advantages: (1) he had lost the right to examine the witness last; (2) he had lost the right to cross-examine the witness, while the prosecution had gained that advantage; and (3) he had to forfeit his right to address the jury last.

Counsel in such circumstances did the natural thing — he chose to minimize his losses by selecting only one (presumably the most reputable or favorable one) of the witnesses to testify.

The intervention of the trial judge into the process *at this point* by calling a witness known to the Crown (and hence, whose evidence could hardly be characterized as arising *ex improviso*) directly, and adversely, altered the nature of this adversary contest. (Allowing both Crown and defence to cross-examine the witness can hardly be said to right this imbalance.)[137]

The Court of Appeal's proposition that the evidence was allowable in order to "ascertain the truth" is perplexing inasmuch as it was felt that the evidence was properly not included in the Crown's case at first instance since its truthfulness was in doubt. The desire to "put all the evidence before the jury" does not square with the evidentiary and procedural practices which regulate criminal trials and secure the end result of only placing *some* of the evidence (presumably, that which is most reliable) before the jury for its consideration.

The trial judge who embarks on a course such as was charted in *Tregear* does so at his peril. The same trial judge who presided over *Tregear* entered the arena in the susbequent case of *R. v. Cleghorn*.[138] This foray resulted in the discharge on appeal of the prisoner, and the consequent quashing of the conviction found below.

In *Cleghorn* the trial judge called a witness (one not called by the prosecution) who had been in close proximity to the occasion of an alleged rape. The evidence of the witness, if believed, materially strengthened the case for the prosecution. The trial, after the calling of the witness, "assumed a completely different aspect". Cleghorn had

---

137. Defence counsel was saddled in the result with a "friend" he could live without. "In the event cross-examination by counsel for the defence was more in the nature of re-examination, since this witness was wholly favorable to the defence." *Ibid.* p. 289.
138. (1967) 51 Cr.App.R. 291. See also *R. v. McMahon supra* footnote 131 where the trial judge's procedure in calling six additional witnesses to testify as to a defence not raised by the accused met with disfavour in the Court of Appeal.

to be re-called in order to give evidence, and the calling of two further defence witnesses also was necessitated. The general rule of "practice" of limiting the trial judge's ability to call witnesses to cases where unforeseen matters arise *ex improviso* is re-affirmed in *Cleghorn;* and *Tregear,* although not overruled, is distinguished and is treated basically as an aberration.

The *Cleghorn* case indicates the kind of fine balance on which an entire case may rest when the trial judge decides to call witnesses. Rebuttal evidence which may not have been necessary at the close of the case for the defence may indeed be essential where the judge calls witnesses. Adjournments might be necessary in order to secure such evidence. Further, both adjournments[139] and rebuttal evidence[140] are not matters of right, but rather are privileges handed out as acts of largesse under the mantle of judicial discretion. The denial of either of these requests may in the circumstances of a given case amount to reversible error, whereas acceding to them may allow the trial to take on a "completely different aspect" — also, a potentially fatal circumstance.

(c) *Improper prosecutorial discretion in the calling of witnesses*

An often quoted passage governing a situation where a prosecutor is improperly exercising his discretion as to which witnesses to call as part of the case for the Crown is this one extracted from the case of *R. v. Oliva*[141]:

> The prosecution do not, of course, put forward every witness as a witness of truth, but where the witness' evidence is capable of belief, then it is their duty, well recognised, that he should be called, even though the evidence that he is going to give is inconsistent with the case sought to be proved. Their discretion must be exercised in a manner which is calculated to further the interests of justice, and at the same time be fair to the defence. *If the prosecutions appear to be exercising that discretion improperly, it is open to the trial judge to interfere and in his discretion in turn to invite the prosecution to call a particular witness, and, if they refuse, there is the ultimate sanction in the judge himself calling that witness.*

At one point it was thought that all "witnesses essential to the unfolding of the narrative on which the prosecution is based must . . . be called by the prosecution, whether in the result the effect of their testimony is for or against the case for the prosecution."[142] These

---

139. See *R. v. Crippen* [1911] 1 K.B. 149.
140. See *R. v. McKenna supra* footnote 124; *R. v. Sullivan supra* footnote 132.
141. (1965) 49 Cr.App.R. 298 *per Parker* C.J. (emphasis added).
142. *R. v. Seneviratne* [1936] 3 W.W.R. 360 at p. 378 *per Roche.* See also A. E. Popple "Annotation: Calling witnesses at a criminal trial" (1951) 12 C.R. 76-77 where the author notes that although this is the general principle "it is obvious from a perusal of the *Seneviratne* case and many others that this is merely one phase of a much larger and more comprehensive body of law . . ." and "it is clear even from the *Seneviratne* case

words for a time were accepted at face value but any misconceptions which they may have caused were eradicated by the Supreme Court of Canada's decision in *Lemay v. R.*[143]

In *Lemay* this overlooked passage (attributable to Lord Thankerton in *Adel Muhammed El Dabbah v. A. G. for Palestine*)[144] was said to accurately state the law:

> "While their Lordships agree that there was no obligation on the prosecution to tender these witnesses, and, therefore, this contention of the present appellant fails, their Lordships doubt whether the rule of practice as expressed by the Court of Criminal Appeal sufficiently recognizes that the prosecutor has a discretion as to what witnesses should be called for the prosecution, and the court will not interfere with the exercise of that discretion, unless, perhaps, it can be shown that the prosecutor has been influenced by some oblique motive." [145]

How does *LeMay* square with *Oliva?* Obviously, where the prosecutor is "influenced by some oblique motive" then the prosecution will "appear to be exercising [their] discretion improperly", but *Oliva* by its terminology seems to permit a wider scope for judicial intervention into the process than does *LeMay*. Dean Silverman asserts that in consequence of the decision in *LeMay* a trial judge "cannot interfere with the Crown's right to determine which material witness to call, even where his name appears on the back of an indictment, especially where the Crown decides not to call such witness deeming him to be unreliable".[146]

LeMay establishes the proposition that "the Crown must not hold back evidence because it would assist an accused".[147] Subsequent cases

---

(a) that there is no general obligation on the part the Crown to call *every* available witness; (b) that the Privy Council has refused to lay down any rule to fetter discretion on such a matter as this which is so dependent on the particular circumstances of the case; (c) . . . the Privy Council could not approve of an idea that the prosecution must call witnesses irrespective of considerations of number and of reliability . . ."

143. [1952] 1 S.C.R. 232.

144. [1944] A.C. 156 at p. 168.

145. *Supra* footnote 143 at p. 250 quoted by Locke J. See also the judgments of Kerwin J. at pp. 239-241.

146. H. Silverman, "The Trial Judge: Pilot, Participant or Umpire?" *supra* footnote 121 at p. 54. Dean Silverman cites the following authorities in support of his contention: *R. v. Schneider* [1927] 1 D.L.R. 999 (Sask. C.A.); *R. v. McClain* (1915) 7 W.W.R. 1134 (Alta. C.A.); *R. v. Byrne* (1953) 16 C.R. 133 at p. 136 (B.C. C.A.).

147. *Supra* footnote 143 at p. 241 *per* Kerwin J. This is especially true with regard to eye-witnesses. Recent cases suggest that where the Crown does not make such witnesses part of their case the eye-witness should nevertheless be presented and made available for cross-examination by the defence: *R. v. Taylor* (1970) 1 C.C.C. (2d) 321 (Man. C.A.). See also *Wu (Wu Chuck) v. R.* (1934) 62 C.C.C. 90 (Can.). It is to be doubted that the rule is absolute. Rather it is suggested as a desirable practice. See Newark

support the view that at the very least the trial judge should insure the proper conduct of the Crown at least to the extent of ascertaining that the accused is informed of the witnesses who are to be called against him, and of the nature of the evidence which they are expected to provide.[148]

It is submitted that while LeMay is explicit in stating that the appeal court will not interfere with the discretion of the prosecutor in deciding which witnesses to call for the prosecution, the ruling does not extend so far as to *prohibit* a trial judge from performing his duties and overseeing the conduct of a criminal trial in the manner proposed in *Oliva*. While the prosecutor has one type of discretion to exercise within the bounds of propriety, the trial judge has another. Thus, while the trial judge clearly may not *order* the prosecutor to call a particular witness, he may *suggest* that Crown counsel do so. Just as clearly, a prosecutor may decline such a suggestion, and by way of rejoinder the trial judge may properly choose to call the witness as the Courts' own (subject of course, to what has been said previously as to the "exigencies of justice"). *Both forms of discretion — prosecutorial and judicial — will generally not be disturbed on appeal.*

There is no real inconsistency between these two functions. A prosecutor for a variety of reasons may deem a witness to be unreliable and choose not to call him. One of the considerations in this determination may be that the witness should be subjected to prosecutorial cross-examination but no immediate sufficient basis can be discerned for having the witness declared adverse. If the trial judge chooses to call the witness then procedurally *both* the defence and the prosecution are given the opportunity to cross-examine the witness.[149] In this

---

& Samuels *supra* footnote 121 at p. 400, and note in *Taylor supra* at pp. 330-331 *per* Dickson J.A. that:

"There was no obligation on the Crown to call every person who was present when the offences were committed . . ."

"It might, perhaps, have been preferable for Crown counsel to produce and make available for cross-examination [these] witnesses . . . Failure to do so, however, is not reversible error. If defence counsel had wished any such witness produced for cross-examination a motion to this effect could have been made to the Judge."

148. See *R. v. McClain supra* footnote 146; R. v. Cunningham (1952) 15 C.R. 167 (N.B. C.A.) cited in Silverman *supra* footnote 121 at p. 54, note 116. See also *R. v. Gallant* (No. 1) (1943) 83 C.C.C. 48 (P.E.I.); *R. v. Grigoreshenko* (1945) 85 C.C.C. 129 (Sask. C.A.); and *Agostino v. R.* (1952) 102 C.C.C. 112 (Can.).

149. This was the procedure adopted in *R. v. Tregear supra* footnote 134. Newark and Samuels *supra* footnote 121 at p. 403 assert that "neither side has any *right* to cross-examine, but manifestly it would be unthinkable for the judge not to allow the prosecution and defence, in that order, to cross-examine the witness, and in particular where the evidence was unfavorable to one of the parties." The authors cite *Coulson v. Disborough* [1894] 2 Q.B. 316; *R. v. Cliburn* (1898) 62 J.P. 232; and *R. v. Watson* (1834) 6 C. & P. 653 in support.

manner presumably both defence and prosecution may be assisted, although, as noted, similar attempts aimed (ostensibly) at securing the ends of justice have misfired and resultant verdicts have been overturned.[150]

Since "the law prohibits the judge from participating in the examination of witnesses where such participation is likely to indicate to the jury a pre-disposition in the judge's mind toward one side or another",[151] it is thought, as a corollary to this general rule, that it is unwise for a judge to exercise his discretion to call a witness if the defence would not suffer prejudice by calling the witness itself.[152] This is to say no more than that the defence should assume the ordinary tactical burden under which it labors in any criminal trial — namely, counsel for the accused must decide whether or not to call defence evidence.

(2) Raising issues

Our discussion at this point turns to an examination of the aspect of judicial interposition into the adversary process through the raising of issues not desired or contemplated by counsel for either party. These matters are closely allied, both in nature and substance, to the subjects previously canvassed under the heading "Calling witnesses".

The trial judge possesses the power to raise issues through both informal and formal channels. At a pre-trial conference[153] — one attended by both counsel — (or one held during the trial proper) the trial judge may suggest that a matter be covered by one, or both, counsel. Such "suggestions" are in the nature of advice and have no legally binding character. Psychologically, however, counsel may feel some pressure to comply.

One question which could conceivably arise during the pre-trial conference (if one is held) is "what is the theory of the defence?".[154] Counsel for the accused is not obliged to make any disclosure whatsoever at this time, but where he does divulge at least the general na-

---

150. See *R. v. Cleghorn supra* footnote 138.
151. *R. v. Denis* [1967] 1 C.C.C. 196 (Que. C.A.) at p. 202 *per* Rivard J.
152. *R. v. Ridley* Hampshire Assizes, The Times, 21 March 1969. Tactically such a development will always occasion *some* prejudice in the form of forfeiture of the right of cross-examination and, possibly, of the right to address the jury last. See the discussion of *Ridley* in Newark and Samuels *supra* footnote 121 at pp. 400-401. Undoubtedly, the authors are correct in stating that "the defence cannot hope to use the judge to call their witness to give him a great appearance of objectivity".
153. The desirability and usefulness of the pre-trial conference is canvassed by E. Haines in "Criminal and Civil Jury Charges" (1968) 46 Can.Bar.Rev. 48; and A. Rivard, "The Functions of Judge, Jury and Counsel-Corporation in Search for the Truth" in Salhany and Carter. *Studies in Canadian Criminal Evidence* (1974) at p. 359.
154. See Haines *ibid.* at p. 56.

ture of his defence the door is then open to the trial judge to offer "suggestions".

A good example of this may be found where the defence intends to rely on the defence of automatism and discloses that fact during the pre-trial interview. This may or may not be the first inkling which the Crown has of this intention.

Inasmuch as automatism and insanity are often, if not usually, linked, the trial judge may well suggest that the prosecutor present such evidence of insanity as he possesses as part of his case.

The prosecutor may not wish to raise insanity or deal with it for a variety of reasons: (1) he may feel that the automatism defence is outlandish and unfounded, and could not possibly succeed; (2) he may feel that raising insanity might merely cloud the case for conviction and facilitate the efforts of the defence to lay a proper foundation for automatism; (3) he may have previously concluded that automatism was going to be raised, but his intention was to counter that defence by adducing evidence of insanity in rebuttal. For all of these reasons, and more, the prosecutor may feel resistant to the overtures of the trial judge. Nevertheless, the prosecutor may feel constrained to reconsider his approach in view of the fact that the trial judge could circumvent the tactical scheme of the Crown through the judicial cross-examination of witnesses, or, through a denial of the prosecution request to adduce evidence in rebuttal.[155]

Defence counsel also may not feel particularly enthused with the suggestion of the trial judge. Unless he proposes to raise insanity as an alternative defence to automatism, counsel for the accused may feel that the "last refuge" of his client is about to be jeopardized, if not completely destroyed, by the advice dispensed by the trial judge.

Defence counsel may feel that the Crown has vastly underestimated the value of his defence. The zeal of the prosecutor in attempting to secure a complete conviction, rather than the modified result implicit in the "not guilty by reason of insanity" verdict, may be the trump card of the accused. Defence counsel usually feel constrained in a situation such as has been sketched to avoid the insanity issue altogether (at least to the extent that the prosecution makes this possible).

Both counsel may thus conceivably be dissatisfied with the course suggested by the trial judge. But the trial judge operates entirely within the realm of his authority, and even of his *duty* in so acting.

The automatism hypothetical is well-chosen for it entails a variety

---

155. The matter of whether to allow rebuttal evidence is one of judicial discretion. See *R. v. McKenna supra* footnote 124; *R. v. Sullivan supra* footnote 132; *R. v. Levy* (1966) 50 Cr.App.R. 198; *R. v. Pollard* (1909) 19 O.L.R. 96 (C.A.); *Brunet v. R.* (1918) 30 C.C.C. 16 (Can.); *R. v. Shewfelt* (1972) 6 C.C.C. (2d) 304 (B.C. C.A.); *R. v. Rafael* (1972) 7 C.C.C. (2d) 325 (Ont. C.A.); *R. v. Gross* (1972) 9 C.C.C. (2d) 122 (Ont. C.A.).

of considerations which bear on the right of the trial judge to raise issues.

At the pre-trial stage, during a conference with counsel, we have seen that the trial judge may informally raise issues through the use of suggestions. During trial, his power to question witnesses, and even to call witnesses of his own motion often has the effect of raising issues. Often these issues may not be issues which counsel wishes to raise.

The automatism/insanity issue is one which has occurred with sufficient frequency that standards *in relation to that issue* are ascertainable.

These statements found in *R. v. Hartridge,*[156] a decision of the Saskatchewan Court of Appeal, accurately express the present law of Canada on this subject:

> the judgments in *Bratty v. Atty.-Gen. of Northern Ireland* [[1963] A.C. 386,] *Reg. v. Charlson* [[1955] 1 All E.R. 850], and *Watmore v. Jenkins* [[1962] 2 Q.B. 572, [1962] 3 W.L.R. 463], make it abundantly clear that [whether to put the defence of automatism or insanity to the jury] is a question of law for determination by the trial judge as to the nature of the defence upon which the jury should be instructed. In *Reg. v. Kemp* [[1957] 1 Q.B. 399], which, in part, received the approval of the House of Lords in the *Bratty* case, the principle is laid down that if, in the opinion of the judge, the evidence establishes that the defect of reason, including a state of automatism arises from a disease of the mind, the judge must instruct the jury in respect to the defence of insanity, *notwithstanding that such defence has not been raised.*

It is perfectly conceivable that by select and subtle intervention into the examining process the trial judge may influence the evidence such that it will "establish" a requisite mental state in the accused sufficient to raise an issue and thus justify its being put to the jury. It is to be doubted however, whether the court has power to embark upon a patently unilateral inquiry into an issue which neither counsel wishes raised if that inquiry is facilitated through the resort by the court to its power to call witnesses.[157]

The most notorious recent example of a unilateral inquiry con-

---

156. (1966) 56 W.W.R. 385 at p. 406 (Sask. C.A.) *per* Culliton C.J.S. (emphasis added). See also in addition to the authorities cited in *Hartridge,* the case of *R. v. K.* (1971) 3 C.C.C. (2d) 84 (Ont.) where La Courciere J. left insanity to the jury notwithstanding that the issue was not raised by the defence.

157. Trial judges have chosen to call witnesses in circumstances where evidence which, taken alone fails to establish a defence raised, but which would be sufficient to establish that defence is supplemented by confirmatory evidence. See *e.g. R. v. Bouchard supra* footnote 131, where O'Hearn Co.Ct. J. called a medical witness to supplement evidence of automatism. Here, of course, defence counsel had raised the issue, and in consequence the court's activity could not be characterized as a unilateral inquiry.

ducted by a trial judge occurred in the context of a civil trial.[158] In civil trials the calling of witnesses is thought to be a function of the parties and not the court.[159] Although the rules governing criminal proceedings differ, there is little reason to believe that these remarks of Evans J.A. given on behalf of the majority in *Phillips v. Ford Motor Co.* (the "notorious" case referred to *supra*) would be markedly different in the context of a criminal trial. The relevant passage is worth quoting at length:

> Our mode of trial procedure is based upon the adversary system in which the contestants seek to establish through relevant supporting evidence, before an impartial trier of facts, those events or happenings which form the bases of their allegations. This procedure assumes that the litigants, assisted by their counsel, will fully and diligently present all the material facts which have evidentiary value in support of their respective positions and that those disputed facts will receive from a trial Judge a dispassionate and impartial consideration in order to arrive at the truth of the matters in controversy. A trial is not intended to be a scientific exploration with the presiding Judge assuming the role of a research director; it is a forum established for the purpose of providing justice for the litigants. *Undoubtedly a Court must be concerned with truth, in the sense that it accepts as true certain sworn evidence and rejects other testimony as unworthy of belief, but it cannot embark upon a quest for the "scientific" or "technological" truth when such an adventure does violence to the primary function of the Court, which has always been to do justice, according to law.* While I recognize that the adversary system has been subjected to criticism on the ground that its procedures may on occasions inhibit the search for ultimate truth, I believe it to be a workable system which has proved satisfactory over a long period, and I am not prepared to abandon it in favour of the presumed, but undemonstrable, advantages of a clinical, scientific approach to the adjudication of legal disputes.[160]

Numerous occasions may arise in a criminal trial where the trial judge may feel sorely tempted to convene a unilateral inquiry.[161] For the most part he is wise to desist. Witnesses of the Court often carry, for better or for worse, the judicial "imprimatur" in the eyes of the jury, and mistrials may result where such evidence is attributed undue

---

158. See *Phillips v. Ford Motor Co.* (1971) 18 D.L.R. (3d) 641 (Ont. C.A.).

159. *Re Enoch and Zaretzky Bock and Co.* [1910] 1 K.B. 327; *Kessowji Issur v. Great Indian Peninsula Ry. Co.* (1907) 96 L.T. 859; *Re Fraser; Fraser v. Robertson; McCormick v. Fraser* (1912) 8 D.L.R. 955 (Ont. C.A.); *Coulson v. Disborough* [1894] 2 Q.B. 316. Where the parties consent the rule may be relaxed.

160. *Phillips v. Ford Motor Co. supra* footnote 158 at p. 661 *per* Evans J.A. (emphasis added).

161. Examples of such instances would be where an issue of causation in homicide has been overlooked or downgraded by counsel; or, where the adducing of scientific evidence (readily available) has been dispensed with by the Crown, etc.

weight. Where counsel for either side more properly should bear the burden of adducing the evidence, the trial judge should restrict his impulse to intervene to the making of suggestions (and even then, such suggestions should be made only in appropriate circumstances).

Rivard J. in *R. v. Denis*[162] made the following with respect to the trial judge's usurpation of the role of the Crown, but his observations apply equally well to usurping the role of either counsel:

> It is unlawful for the judge, during the conduct of a trial, to usurp the function of counsel for the Crown. In many cases, the intervention of the judge wishing to make an answer clear and intelligible, or to move the trial further in the direction of an area which he considers important, is desirable, but it must be remembered that all such interventions are subject to the over-riding principle that none of the parties must have reason to believe that they have not had a fair and impartial trial.

Naturally, where the trial judge has a lawful duty to conduct such an inquiry (even unilaterally), these strictures do not operate as a bar. For example, it is arguable (at least for the present) that the trial judge is under a duty to hold a voir-dire in order to determine the admissibility of an accused's statement made to a person in authority irrespective of whether counsel wishes to contest the issue of its voluntariness.[163] More generally, the trial judge has an independent duty to scrutinize the admissibility of evidence; again, even in the absence of an objection from counsel as to its admissibility.[164]

However, these matters are a far cry from the type of unilateral inquiry conducted in the *Phillips* case. Much of the consternation expressed by the Ontario Court of Appeal in that case centred around the calling and utilization of a court-appointed expert. (Haines J. attempted his unusual procedures by invoking Rule 267 of the Rules of Practice and Procedure of the Supreme Court of Ontario[165] which permits the Court to obtain the assistance of experts in such a way

---

162. [1967] 1 C.C.C. 196 at p. 203 (Que. C.A.).

163. This issue is presently before the Supreme Court of Canada: *Park v. The Queen* (leave to appeal granted May 5, 1976). See also *Powell v. R.* (1976) 33 C.R.N.S. 323 (Can.) (9:0) where silence of counsel will not amount to a waiver of the issue.

164. See *Schwartzenhauer v. R.* (1935) 64 C.C.C. 1 (Can); *R. v. Scory* [1945] 1 W.W.R. 15 (Sask. C.A.); and *R. v. Stirland* (1944) 30 Cr.App.R. 40. See generally McWilliams, *Canadian Criminal Evidence* (1974) at p. 21: "Judicial Duty to Scrutinize Admissibility". A related duty, although not in essence a "unilateral inquiry" is the duty of the trial judge to draw to the attention of the jury such questions appearing from the evidence as may raise a defence for the accused even though counsel for the accused has not raised the point himself: *Kwaku Mensah v. R.* [1946] A.C. 83; *Mancini v. D.P.P.* [1942] A.C. 1; *R. v. Hladiy* (1952) 15 C.R. 255 (Ont. C.A.); *Rustad v. R.* [1965] 1 C.C.C. 323 (B.C. C.A.), reversed [1965] S.C.R. 555.

165. R.R.O. 1970, Reg. 545 as amended.

as it thinks fit.) In *Phillips* the court-appointed expert at trial was permitted to play a quite extraordinary role:

> In the instant case Mr. McCaffrey examined and cross-examined freely, challenged the evidence of experts called by the defendants and stated as fact conclusions which he derived from his interpretation of the Lincoln manual, although they were in direct conflict with the sworn evidence. On one occasion the trial Judge and Mr. McCaffrey, after the completion of the examination of the expert, Way, conducted an examination which accounts for 15 pages in the transcript into matters not raised by counsel for the plaintiffs . . . and upon which the trial Judge relied, at least to some extent, in his judgment.[166]

These procedures, it need scarcely be said, met with a sharp rebuke in the Court of Appeal. The observations of Evans J.A., both as to the excessive conduct of the expert, McAffrey, and, as to the proper role of any expert witness,[167] bear repeating and have at least equal applicability in the context of a criminal trial:

> The expert is not a judicial officer charged with the responsibility of determining the matters in issue, nor is he a Court-appointed investigator empowered to advance possible theories and state, as conclusions of fact, opinions based on matters not advanced in evidence. . . . In my opinion Mr. McCaffrey totally misconceived his position and became, with the approval of the presiding Judge, a partisan advocate.[168]
>
> · · ·
>
> An expert who is appointed has the limited role of explaining to the Judge that evidence adduced by the parties which is within his particular area of competence to the end that the Court may be better informed in the spheres of knowledge requisite for the proper determination of those complex questions of fact presented to it.[169]

Whether the witness to be called by the trial judge in a criminal trial is an expert, or a non-expert, the same general rule applies—the witness may be called, without the consent of either the prosecution or the defence, provided that the trial judge is of the opinion that the course of action is necessary in the interests of justice. As noted previously, where the trial judge chooses to call a witness late in the proceedings his power to do so should ordinarily be limited to cases where a matter has arisen *ex improviso,* and is of such a nature that "no

---

166. *Supra* footnote 158 at p. 665 *per* Evans J.A.

167. On expert witnesses in the context of a criminal trial generally, see A. Maloney and P. V. Tomlinson, "Opinion Evidence" in Salhany and Carter, *Studies in Canadian Criminal Evidence* (1972) 219 at p. 231 *et seq.*

168. *Phillips v. Ford Motor Co. supra* footnote 158 at p. 665 *per* Evans J.A.

169. *Ibid.* at p. 666 *per* Evans J.A. *N.B.* The case does not do away with the right of a trial judge to rely on the assistance of experts. See *Featherstone v. Grunsven* [1972] 1 O.R. 490 (C.A.), and see also E. Haines, "The Medical Profession and the Adversary Process" (1973) 11 O.H.L.J. 41 at pp. 50-51.

human ingenuity" could have foreseen the necessity for calling the witness earlier, or at all.[170]

(3) Circumventing incompetency

> Apart from failure to bring out evidence, the mistakes of a man's lawyer may cause him to lose his case — a proper result under strict legal laissez-faire theory. But is it fair that a litigant should be punished because he retained an incompetent lawyer?[171]

In its *Code of Professional Conduct* The Canadian Bar Association partially answers the question posed *supra* by Judge Frank by asserting that a lawyer "owes a duty to his client to be competent to perform the legal services which the lawyer undertakes on his behalf". Further, the *Code* intones that the lawyer "should serve his client in a conscientious, diligent, and efficient manner", adhering to a standard "which lawyers generally would expect of a competent lawyer in a like situation".[172]

It is not surprising that The Canadian Bar Association does not endorse incompetency within its ranks.

The difficulty in this area resides in the translation of a pious sentiment into affirmative action through the effective policing of a professional "brotherhood". Where such controls are absent, or are deficient, the trial judge is left with the unhappy prospect of overseeing a rather shoddy spectacle.

How should the trial judge measure his response when confronted with clearly incompetent counsel? Where is the line to be drawn between clear "incompetence" and "imperfection"? (The C.B.A. Rule, it should be noted, does not provide a standard of perfection.) What should be done where otherwise competent counsel is terribly inexperienced and an adversarial mismatch results? Must the trial judge always be strait-jacketed by the bonds of judicial decorum and the necessity for an appearance of neutrality and impartiality?

These are serious matters which have not altogether escaped thoughtful, scholarly examination.[173]

---

170. See the analysis *supra* in this Chapter on "The Exigencies of Justice" and "Matters Arising *Ex Improviso*".
171. J. Frank, *Courts on Trial* (1949) at pp. 93-94. The concept of "legal laissez-faire" is explained by the author at p. 92.
172. The Can. Bar Assn., *Code of Professional Conduct* (1974) Chap. 11, Rule (a) and (b) at p. 4. See also the nine points of commentary and citation of authority which follows at pp. 4-7.
173. In Canada the best writing to date on the subject has come from a member of the Israel bar: Asher D. Grunis "Incompetence of Defence Counsel in Criminal Cases". See also G. A. Martin, "The Role and Responsibility of the Defence Advocate" (1970) Cr.L.Q. 376; T. G. Bastedo, "A Note on Lawyers' Malpractice: Legal Boundaries and Judicial Regulation" (1969) 7 O.H.L.J. 311; S. Arthurs, "Discipline in The Legal Profession in Ontario" (1969) 7 O.H.L.J. 235. American articles on the quality of defence representation are more profuse. See Grunis *supra* at p. 288 (his footnote #1) for a partial bibliography.

It has been asserted that in Canada the matter of incompetent representation has been only indirectly confronted; that judicial responses to curbing incompetence have been "rather formalistic"; and that the root of the problem lies in the reluctance of those involved in the criminal process to expose the ineffective performance of counsel.[174] Also contributing to the complexity of the issue is the diverse ways in which incompetence may be manifested.

The following is a list of illustrations of trial practice incompetence which reveals a tracing of the general contours of this problem. Depending upon the circumstances these may or may not be examples of incompetency:

(1) fatal factual admissions;
(2) missed time limitations;
(3) ill-preparation, slipshod behavior;
(4) over and under questioning witnesses;
(5) representing clients with conflicting interests;
(6) physical or mental disability of such a nature as to affect the quality of legal service;
(7) self-induced disability from intoxicants or drugs;
(8) plea bargaining against the interests of one's client;
(9) failing to obtain the advise and assistance of experts where necessary;
(10) excessive or undue delay;
(11) inexperience (in conjunction with any of the above).

This list is far from exhaustive.

It should be observed that, where incompetence proceeds unchecked during the trial, appeal remedies may be the only direct solution open to a client in order to redress the harm occasioned. But that route by no means is certain to compensate. In most instances, the decision of the trial court will be affirmed unless there has been a clear and *substantial* miscarriage of justice.[175] That is, the Court of Appeal may afford relief to an individual appellant where irregularities during the course of his trial were not only prejudicial, but were of such a kind as to amount to a miscarriage of justice.[176]

For the most part the Appeal Court is concerned with the conduct of the trial as mirrored in the performance of the trial judge. The conduct of counsel, whether competent or otherwise, is generally not

---

174. A Grunis *ibid.* at p. 306.
175. See *The Criminal Code* R.S.C. 1970, Chap. C-34, s. 613 (1)(a) and (b). A substantial wrong may be done to the accused by irregularities in the course of his trial: *Maxwell v. D.P.P.* [1935] A.C. 309; *Allen v. R.* (1911) 18 C.C.C. 1 (Can.); *F. v. Barrs* (1946) 1 C.R. 301 (Alta.) C.A.); *Northey v. R.* [1948] S.C.R. 135.
176. See *R. v. Allan* (1949) 93 C.C.C. 191 (Ont. C.A.); *R. v. Pascal* (1949) 95 C.C.C. 288 (B.C. C.A.); *R. v. Howell* (1955) 22 C.R. 263 (Ont. C.A.); *R. v. McCormick* (1961) 130 C.C.C. 196 (B.C. C.A.).

the subject of appellate review unless the injustice is manifest, and the result achieved in the trial can be said to bear some causal relationship to the incompetent performance of counsel.[177] The court has a discretion to disregard minor errors or omissions which are so trivial or unimportant that it may be safely assumed that a jury was uninfluenced by them.[178] In cases involving these considerations, although the onus is on the Crown to satisfy the Appeal Court that the verdict would necessarily have been the same had the errors not been committed,[179] the appellant must first satisfy the court that an injustice has actually occurred or, at the very least, that in fact there has been the *appearance* of injustice at trial.[180]

Appeal Courts have relieved, and will continue to lend relief against specific abuses.

An inflammatory address delivered by Crown counsel, whether delivered through incompetence or by design, will not be tolerated.[181]

Pleas entered as a result of incompetent or improper legal advice (as in the situation where on the basis of the factual admissions the accused could not have been convicted of the crime charged, or where the accused has not understood the nature of the charge to which he pled or did not intend to admit his guilt) have been successfully withdrawn on appeal.[182]

Incompetency, in the form of missing a time limitation in order that an appeal might be launched, may be corrected if the Appeal Court in its discretion chooses to extend the time.[183] However, some of the cases assert that an oversight or ignorance on the part of counsel

---

177. See *Grunis supra* footnote 173 at p. 301.
178. See *R. v. Bourgeois* (1937) 69 C.C.C. 120 (Sask. C.A.): But see *White v. R.* (1947) 3 C.R. 232 at pp. 237-239 as to the effect of this decision, and as to the proper rule where substantial errors in conduct of trial are manifest. *R. v. MacDonald* (1939) 72 C.C.C. 182 (Ont. C.A.); *R. v. De Tonnancourt* (1956) 115 C.C.C. 154 (Man. C.A.); *Ruest v. R.* (1952) 104 C.C.C. 1 (Can.); *Chibok v. R.* (1956) 116 C.C.C. 241 (Can.); *R. v. Coffin* [1956] S.C.R. 191.
179. See *Colpitts v. R.* [1966] 1 C.C.C. 146 (Can.); *Lizotte v. R.* (1950) 99 C.C.C. 113 (Can.); *Gouin v. R.* (1926) 46 C.C.C. 1 (Can.); *Schmidt v. R.* (1945) 83 C.C.C. 207 (Can.); *Parent v. R.* (1947) 4 C.R. 127 (Que. C.A.).
180. See *R. v. Darlyn* (1946) 88 C.C.C. 269 (B.C. C.A.); *Vescio v. R.* [1949] S.C.R. 139; *R. v. Bodmin J.J., Ex parte McEwen* [1947] K.B. 321.
181. See *Boucher v. R.* (1954) 110 C.C.C. 263 (Can.); *Pursey v. R.* (1956) 116 C.C.C. 82 (Que. C.A.); *Provencher v. R.* (1955) 114 C.C.C. 100 (Can.); *R. v. McDonald* (1958) 120 C.C.C. 209 (Ont. C.A.). See also *R. v. House* (1921) 16 Cr.App.R. 49 and *R. v. Nerlich* (1915) 34 O.L.R. 298 (C.A.).
182. See *Ex parte Richard* (1916) 26 C.C.C. 166 (Que.); *Re Eustace* (1956) 116 C.C.C. 196 (B.C.); *R. v. Forde* (1923) 17 Cr.App.R. 99; *R. v. Gordon* (1947) 88 C.C.C. 413 (B.C. C.A.); *R. v. Taylor* (1950) 34 Cr.App.R. 138; *R. v. Griffiths,* (1932) 23 Cr.App.R. 153.
183. See *The Criminal Code* s. 607(2) [am. 1974-75-76, c. 105, s. 16]. For a discussion of some of the applicable principles see *R. v. Antoine* (1972) 6 C.C.C. (2d) 162 (Man. C.A.).

for the accused does not constitute a sufficient excuse for the making of such an order.[184]

In a previous section the power of the Court of Appeal to review a trial judge's discretion to permit the re-opening of a case was canvassed. It was there noted that where the error leading to a failure to prove some essential ingredient of the charge was inadvertent, and the matter was one which ordinarily could be readily proved, trial courts have generally permitted rectification (or, on appeal they have been advised that they should have allowed re-opening). However, the matter remains one of judicial discretion, and, short of an obvious derogation from principle, Appellate Divisions generally choose not to intercede.[185] In this regard it is useful to remember that in the *Dunn* case "careless conduct" [read: "incompetent conduct"], in contrast to "inadvertent conduct", was held to be an improper basis upon which to found an order permitting re-opening.[186]

Historically, incompetency has not been accorded a very sympathetic reception in the Courts. The prevailing theory was that all criminal proceedings—proceedings *in poenam*—were thought to be *strictissimi juris.*[187]

> In a criminal proceeding the question is not alone whether substantial justice has been done but whether justice has been according to law.[188]

Modern authorities tend to refute the older sentiment:

> For at least 30 years I have listened to learned Law Lords, including Lord Buckmaster, Lord Devlin, and Lord Justice Denning, and others, as well as to practically every successive President of the Canadian Bar Association, proclaiming the fact that the law is a living and growing organism, adapting itself to ever-changing conditions and seeking always for substantial justice. I think it is fair to state that the modern

---

184. See *Lamson v. Dist. Ct. J.* (1921) 36 C.C.C. 326 (Sask. C.A.); *R. v. Skelly* (1938) 73 C.C.C. 230 (Que.). The over-riding consideration however is whether it is in the interests of justice to grant an extension: *R. v. Alexander* (1957) 22 W.W.R. (B.C. C.A.) 522. And see *Collyer v. Dring* [1952] 2 All E.R. 1004.

185. See the discussion of this subject in this chapter *supra* under the titles "Calling Witnesses" and "Raising Issues". Note especially *R. v. Ash Temple Co. supra* footnote 128; *R. v. Kishen Singh supra* footnote 125; and *R. v. Dunn supra* footnote 129 three cases involving a refusal to permit re-opening.

186. *R. v. Dunn, ibid.*

187. "All proceedings in poenam are, it need scarcely be observed, strictissimi juris; nor should it be forgotten that the formalities of law, though here and there they may lead to the escape of an offender, are intended on the whole to insure the safe administration of justice and the protection of innocence, and must be observed". *Per* Cockburn C.J. in *Martin v. Mackonochie* (1878) 3 Q.B.D. 730 at p. 775, reversed on other grounds (1879) 4 Q.B.D. 697 (C.A.).

188. *Ibid.*

concept of the administration of justice demands freedom from the bonds of technical objections.[189]

The modern criminal trial is not nearly so rigid and formal a structure as its earlier predecessors. The disappearance of the death penalty, the modernization of at least some correctional facilities, and more relaxed parole procedures, are all factors which have contributed to this development. The net effect is that although the post-trial correctional phase of the criminal justice system exhibits more "tenderness" towards prisoners, during the criminal trial proper the prisoner is receiving considerably less consideration than was the case previously. For example, technical arguments over the interpretation of penal statutes receive considerably shorter shrift than in days gone by. The common law rule requiring that penal statutes be strictly construed has yielded to the direction of the *Interpretation Act*[190] that all federal statutes be accorded "such fair large and liberal interpretation as best ensures the attainment of its objects."[191] The result of this has been to shade the emphasis of the law away from, resolving any ambiguity arising from the construction or interpretation of a penal statute in favor of the accused, and towards, an interpretation favoring the attainment of the object(s) of the legislation. (The cases do not put the matter in quite so bold a fashion but if one examines the history of the cases interpreting Canada's breathalyzer legislation for example, the emphasis and pattern described is quite evident.)[192]

This digression concerning the drift and tendencies of the modern era of the criminal law is offered in order to indicate the nature of an on-going process which has been taking place. The unarticulated policy basis for most of these developments has been a concern with burgeoning crime rates, increased urban violence, and, the need to more effectively bring offenders to justice. In certain quarters this concern manifests itself in a distaste for the "practice of criminal law as a confidence game";[193] in a disgust with the "sporting element" of the Anglo-Canadian system of justice; or in a call for modifying the adversary system in order that it might better serve the end of discovering the truth.

These matters are related to the problem of incompetency, it is submitted, by a tacit or unarticulated willingness to accept incompetency in the practise of criminal law if it secures the long range goal of bringing more alleged offenders to justice. In consequence, the prob-

---

189. *R. v. Regal Drugs (1958) Ltd.* (1969) 4 D.L.R. (3d) at p. 503 (Man. C.A.) *per* Guy J.A.
190. R.S.C. 1970 Chap. I-23, s. 11.
191. See *R. v. Robinson (or Robertson)* (1951) 12 C.R. 101 (Can.), especially the judgment of Locke J. at p. 108 *et seq.*
192. A useful reference on the subject of "Impaired Driving and Breathalyzer Cases" is that of M. Angene and appears in (1976) 32 C.R.N.S. 249.
193. See Blumberg, "The Practice of Law as a Confidence Game" (1967) 1 Law and Society Rev. 15.

lem of incompetency in the criminal law field remains in low visibility. Asher Grunis even goes so far as to suggest that "the real problem seems to be the reluctance of those involved in the criminal process to expose the ineffective performance of counsel."[194]

Consequently, appellate scrutiny, for the most part, consists in an examination of the conduct of the trial judge rather than an inquiry into the shortcomings of counsel (even in situations where such an inquiry appears to be justified). There are instances however, where the appellate court will direct itself to the misconduct of counsel in order to set right an imbalance.

Counsel's ill-preparation or lack of diligence in *McMartin v. R.*[195] prompted the Supreme Court of Canada to assert that if evidence exists of sufficient strength that it might reasonably have affected the jury's verdict then it should be admitted as fresh evidence on appeal notwithstanding an earlier failure to exercise reasonable diligence to present it at trial.

(Already canvassed as examples of Appellate relief against specific forms of incompetency abuses were inflammatory addresses of counsel, ill-advised plea bargains, missed time limitations, and failures to prove readily-provable ingredients of the charge.)

But, for many, by the time matters have progressed to the Appeal Court level the damage will have been irreparable. Certainly, the greatest safeguard which the system provides against incompetency is the trial judge.[196] If there is a truly activist conception of his role, surely it must surface in this area. It is not only through the resort of the trial judge to the use of the contempt power that he protects the due administration of justice, and fosters respect for it. He is able to protect the process from abuse by weeding out incompetency.

---

194. A. *Grunis supra* footnote 173 at p. 306.
195. [1965] 1 C.C.C. 142 (Can.). See also the *Criminal Code* s. 610(1).
196. This is not to say that the legal system does not have an over-riding obligation to insure the competency of those servicing it. Better legal education, continuing legal education, periodic qualification of practising members, accredited specialization, strong and responsive disciplinary procedures are all measures which are essential to this task. See The Report on The Arden House Conference: *Continuing Legal Education for Professional Competence and Responsibility* (1959); Q. Johnstone and D. Hopson, *Lawyers and Their Work* (1967) J. Frank, *Courts on Trial* (1949) at p. 225; "Specialization in Legal Practice" (1971) B.C. Branch Lectures 65; Giffen, "Social Control and Professional Self-Government: A Study of the Legal Profession in Canada" in Clark (ed.) *Urbanism and the Changing Society* (1961); H. W. Arthurs, "Authority, Accountability, and Democracy in the Government of the Ontario Legal Profession" (1971) 49 Can.Bar.Rev. 1; S. L. Robins "Our Profession and The Winds of Change" (1972) 6 L.S.U.C. Gaz. 137; Lochridge, "Legal Specialization" (1975) 38 Tex.B.J. 309; Wolkin, "A Better Way to Keep Lawyers Competent" (1975) 61 A.B.A.J. 574; V. Countryman, T. Finman, *The Lawyer in Modern Society* (1966).

The proposition that *the spectacle of incompetency should not be allowed to proceed unimpeded* does not admit of doubt.

Where counsel through ignorance or incompetence attempts to inflame the jury by appealing to prejudice or base instinct the trial judge is justified in interfering.[197] If counsel through inexperience or inadvertence "misses the obvious" the trial judge should draw attention to it. If a plea is entered on agreed facts which do not support guilt the plea should not be accepted. These matters, and others already mentioned, should not be allowed to "hang fire" until an appeal is processed. The rot should be excised before it poisons the entire body politic of the trial.

The general proposition—the spectacle should not proceed unimpeded—carries with it certain self-evident corollaries:

(1) The incompetent practitioner should not be allowed to blunder blindly on. Rectification of the situation (where possible) must be attempted.

(2) Cases of serious or gross incompetency should invariably meet with discipline and an affirmation of the principle of deterrence.

Naturally, one cannot assume that the implementation of these proposals would eradicate the problem in its entirety. Undoubtedly we will have to continue to live with costly blunders and errors occasioned through incompetence—and many clients will suffer in the result. But, there is no denying that there is an urgent need for reform.

What is meant by the statement "rectification (where possible) must be attempted"? Is this merely a meaningless, or trivial, banality?

This statement implies that the trial judge must actively attempt to right the balance. Adjournments should be ordered (even in the absence of a request for same) in order to prepare the unprepared, counsel the untutored, and even, discharge the incompetent. The trial judge has a wide discretion in the ordering of, and in the granting of requests for, adjournments.

While it does not appear that a trial judge can actually bar a lawyer from court because of his incompetence there does not appear to be any compelling reason why in a proper case the trial judge could not report a lawyer to the Law Society in cases involving gross incompetency. It would then be possible for the lawyer to be suspended or otherwise disciplined.[198]

As with all other areas of his official duties, the trial judge must be cautious and circumspect when choosing to enter the fray.

---

197. See *R. v. House* and *R. v. Nerlich supra* footnote 181.

198. See *Re Legal Professions Act, Baron v. "F"*. [1945] 4 D.L.R. 525 at 528 *per* Farris C.J.S.C. where it is stated that the Benchers would be justified in suspending a member "who has been guilty of a series of acts of gross negligence, which, taken together, would amount to a course of conduct sufficient to bring the legal profession into disrepute."

When attempting to alleviate a condition of incompetency he must be doubly so.

> The trial Judge is in a predicament: he does not have all the information available to defence counsel. He might therefore view the actions of counsel as stemming from counsel's better knowledge of his client's case, or he may interpret the moves taken by counsel as motivated by defence strategy. If the judge intervenes to offset the inadequate representation and to expose the lawyer's blunder, and it seems he has a duty to do so, [*McKenna v. Ellis* 280 F. 2d 592, 600 (5th C.R. 1960] he might later be blamed for improper handling of the case. Thus his action, which was originally designed to help the accused, may be termed later a hindrance to the defence.[199]

The trial judge is in a position of influence and power not only with respect to the litigants, but with respect to counsel as well. He should effectively utilize this influence where appropriate. In-trial conferences with counsel for both sides present can easily be convened, and the issue of incompetence can there be bluntly, or subtly, confronted. Recommendations could be put that counsel should seek counsel and advice from others more experienced or more expert in the field.[200] The suggestion might even be put that counsel should withdraw from a matter. It should be indicated that a sufficient adjournment would be ordered.

The Court does not possess the power to discharge incompetent counsel even in cases where the incompetence is flagrant or possibly even unethical. However, the contempt power should not be overlooked in extreme situations. Recent cases have surfaced where the non-attendance of counsel at a duly set hearing date has resulted in a citation for contempt of Court.[201] The power it seems could be applied equally well in other circumstances.[202] This would secure the end, in extreme cases, of barring incompetent counsel from court and thus would indirectly effect a discharge of counsel by the Court.[203]

The corollarly "rectification (where possible) must be attempted" imports the notion of the trial judge's attempting to offset incompetence through the calling of witnesses and by judicial interventions into the examining process. The earlier examination of these topics

---

199. A. Grunis *supra* footnote 173 at pp. 291-292.
200. Query: whether the court could compel the taking of advice by appointing counsel for counsel (a novel form of *amicus curae*)?
201. See *R. v. Hill* (1974) 18 C.C.C. (2d) 458 (B.C.) affirmed (1975) 22 C.C.C. (2d) 64 (C.A.); *McKeown v. R.* [1971] S.C.R. 446.
202. *E.g.,* where counsel accepts the advice of the trial judge and undertakes to obtain assistance and advice, and then wilfully and without apparent excuse fails to do so.
203. This raises the subsidiary procedural and practical problem of insuring that the accused is represented by the counsel of his choice, but it is submitted that the over-riding principle is the due administration of justice. See M. Teplitsky, "The legality of barring counsel from a court until he purges his contempt" (1971) 15 C.R.N.S. 384.

makes it abundantly clear that there is a delicate balancing act to be performed by any trial judge who chooses to descend into the arena by either of these avenues. Nevertheless, in compelling circumstances involving patent, serious incompetency; where the trial is well into its later stages and adjournments and advice in all likelihood will not alleviate, the trial judge should attempt a moderate intervention. He must be mindful at this point, not to appear to throw his weight in favor of one party or the other. Possibly such an impression cannot be avoided, but a shaded performance, done in the light of blatant, incompetent behavior, is to be preferred over prejudicial reticence.

It should be borne in mind that incompetency is far from being a readily identifiable phenomenon. A variety of activities may present as "incompetence" and yet in essence, and upon closer analysis, prove to be something else. Errors in judgment are made in the course of any trial, and may even form the basis of successful appeals, and yet are not characterized as "incompetence". Ethical failings and short-comings cannot receive sanction in our courts (and in fact, do not) but these are separate phenomena from incompetency.[204]

One rough definition of competence defines the term as "an adequate standard of service, skill and knowledge".[205] Utilizing this definition as a basis for attempting to promulgate a standard of judicial conduct to govern situations where incompetency surfaces during a criminal trial leads to this formulation:

> Where the apparent lack of an adequate standard of service, skill or knowledge in counsel has the effect of impairing the fairness of a criminal trial, the trial judge is justified in adjourning the matter, in advising counsel to seek counsel or better prepare himself, and in otherwise intervening into the trial process if the interests of justice so require his intervention.

Does the trial judge have a role to play with respect to the second of the previously enumerated corollaries? Should he be concerned with the discipline and deterrence of incompetent counsel?

Most emphatically, he does have a role to play, and should be concerned with discipline and deterrence.

A part of the jurisdiction exercised by the trial judge does not derive from statute, but rather is properly described as "inherent". This inherent jurisdiction possesses qualities which some writers characterize as "almost metaphysical" in nature.[206] Under this mantle accrues the power of the Court to regulate its proceedings, to safe-

---

204. E.g., The Can.Bar.Assn. *Code of Professional Conduct* has special provision dealing with "Impartiality and Conflict of Interest", Chapter V at p. 16.

205. This definition is employed in the *Report of the Special Joint Committee on Competency Appointed by the Law Society of British Columbia and the B.C. Branch of the Canadian Bar Association* (1973) at p. 3.

206. See I. H. Jacob, "The Inherent Jurisdiction of the Court" (1970) 23 Current Legal Problems 23 at p. 27. See also (1947) 57 Yale L.J. 85.

guard its processes from abuse, and to maintain and foster respect for the due administration of justice.

A portion of the Commentary on the C.B.A. *Code of Professional Conduct* emphasizes that "the lawyer who is incompetent does his client a disservice, brings discredit on his profession and may bring the administration of justice into disrepute."[207] While the incompetence of counsel usually will not amount to a contempt of court, it may be of a type meriting disciplinary action by the Law Society.

For various reasons opposing counsel, or a client may be hesitant to expose the incompetency of a practitioner.[208] The trial judge should not be similarly encumbered. In a great many instances in the name of "duty" we ask for very unordinary service from our judges—often we ask the trial judge to wear two hats (judge and jury), or to exclude from his mind things which ordinarily we would not expect a human being to disregard. An exemplary standard of personal conduct is required in the daily lives of our judges. It is not inconsistent with his other requirements that trial judges be asked to "watchdog" the profession.

Naturally, there is no place in any of this for personal vendettas. The very qualities which the trial judge is daily asked to display in his work—neutrality, impartiality and detachment—are also the hallmarks of this endeavour.

The rules governing most Law Societies are broad enough to make incompetency (or, at least, gross incompetency) a disciplinary offence.[209] If they are not, they should be made so. Justifications for this position are not difficult to find:

> The obligation to maintain high standards of competence and ethical conduct is not discharged once an applicant has been admitted to practice. There is the continuing obligation to see that practising members of the body provide proper service to the public. The service provided will only be valuable so long as it is a combination of a high

---

207. *Supra* footnote 172, no. 9 at p. 6.
208. See A. Grunis, *supra* footnote 173 at pp. 290-296 for a discussion of factors promoting the low visibility of incompetence. Grunis' observations are directed largely at examining the factors inhibiting the exposure of incompetency during the trial but many of the same factors affect the decision to seek disciplinary action against the lawyer at a later stage.
209. See *Re Legal Professions Act, Baron v. "F."* *supra* footnote 198 at p. 528. A contrasting approach has been taken elsewhere: This comment appears in the B.C. Special Joint Committee's *Report on Competency* (1973), *supra* footnote 204 at p. 1: "The Committee considers that the term "professional misconduct" in section 45 [of the Legal Professions Act] implies culpable conduct. The Committee believes that professional competence is an issue apart from professional misconduct. The Committee is convinced, therefore, that the Act and Rules should be amended . . . to allow the profession to deal in a timely and effective way with the issue of continuing professional competence in situations other than those that involve alleged professional misconduct."

degree of technical competence and a vigilant observance of the ethical requirements of practice.[210]

It is submitted therefore, that the trial judge should not hesitate to launch a complaint to the Discipline Committee of the Law Society in cases involving serious incompetency on the part of counsel. The public deserves and requires such protection. The profession itself should welcome initiatives of this type since it has an interest in the maintenance of high standards of professional conduct.

The proposal advanced can hardly be regarded as extreme. Disbarment can result from disciplinary proceedings, but incompetency, in contrast to other forms of misconduct tends to receive more moderate responses.[211] (This itself may reflect a larger problem in need of resolution.) For the present, at least, a more active role played by the trial judge would generally serve to deter incompetent behavior. Certainly, on objective facts, a more active role should not be regarded as seeking to bring "economic death" to any meaningful segment of the legal profession.

5. EXPRESSIONS OF PERSONAL OPINION BY THE TRIAL JUDGE IN A JURY TRIAL

Despite the protestations found in the reported decisions that judicial conduct should appear neutral, impartial and non-partisan, the jury trial offers large temptations to partisanship and the history of appellate review in this area reveals that many trial judges succumb to those temptations.

A charge to the jury can easily be transformed into a soapbox for "third man" advocacy.

The cases dealing with the adequacy of a judge's charge to the jury in a criminal trial are legion.[212] Also, the principles which establish the basic framework for the charge to the jury are well-known.[213]

---

210. Ontario, *Royal Commission Inquiry into Civil Rights* (McRuer Report) Report No. 1, Vol. 3 at p. 1181.
211. See S. Arthurs, "Discipline in The Legal Profession in Ontario", *supra* footnote 173 at p. 238 and p. 240. In this study "poor practice" usually yields a reprimand, while "negligence" resulted in disbarment in only 8% of the cases studied.
212. See A. E. Popple, *Criminal Procedure Manual* (1956) at pp. 266-267, 374; A. E. Popple, *Canadian Criminal Evidence* (2nd ed., 1954) at pp. 152-155, 497-502; *Crankshaw's Criminal Code of Canada* (7th ed. A. E. Popple ed.) at pp. 951-963, 990-995; *Tremeear's Annotated Criminal Code* (6th ed. E. J. Ryan ed.) at pp. 987-1030; (See also the supplements to *Crankshaw* and *Tremeear*).
213. See J. J. Robinette, "Charge to the Jury" (1959) L.S.U.C. Spec. Lect. 147, A. E. Popple, "Annotation; Judge's summing-up to be considered as a whole (1952-53) 15 C.R. 82; A. E. Popple, "Annotation: Summing-up the evidence in a criminal case" (1952-53) 15 C.R. 190; A. E. Popple "Annotation: Correlating the evidence to the issues for the benefit of the jury" (1952-53) 15 C.R. 262; A. E. Popple, "Annotation: Directions to the

Broadly speaking, in charging the jury at the conclusion of a criminal case the trial judge should:

(1) outline the applicable law;
(2) outline the salient features of the evidence;
(3) define the issues;
(4) refer to the facts in evidence in order to enable the jury to fairly consider the issues;
(5) instruct the jury on the verdicts open to them (this is done by defining the crime charged and explaining the difference between it and any other offence open to the jury on which to convict);
(6) save in rare cases where it is needless to do so, review the "substantial" parts of the evidence and give the jury the theory of the defence so that they may appreciate the value and effect of the evidence and how the law is to be applied to the facts as they find them.

How far a trial judge should go in discussing the law and the facts must depend in each case upon the nature and character of the evidence in relation to the charge (*i.e.,* the crime), the issues raised, and the conduct of the trial, but where certain specific matters arise there should be a special direction on applicable law.[214]

No appeal court is going to examine a judge's charge microscopically in a search for *either* errors in law *or* partisanship. It is the charge "taken as a whole" which must be considered.[215] Rand J. in *Ruest v. R.*[216] explains:

> Taken in isolation, passages may be capable of interpretations of an objectionable nature, but as it has been time and again emphasized, the charge is to be considered as a whole and a too meticulous regard to the refinements of possible meanings of individual detached passages avoided. Jurors are not acute and subtle masters of legalistic vocabulary or expressions straining to catch significant variations of meaning, and the less we have of stereotyped or stilted phrases of direction the better for the realistic conduct of trials.

Nevertheless, remarks or instructions by the trial judge to a jury which are unfair and are calculated to discredit the accused may motivate an Appeal Court to reverse a conviction on the basis that there has been a miscarriage of justice.[217]

---

jury on counsel's submissions" (1953-54) 17 C.R. 110; A. E. Popple "Annotation: Judge's opinion as to the facts in evidence" (1948) 5 C.R. 349; R. J. Carter, "Annotation: Instructions by the trial Judge to the jury respecting the defence" (1968-69) 5 C.R.N.S. 236.

214. A. E. Popple in *Canadian Criminal Evidence* (2nd ed. 1954) lists 65 specific matters requiring special direction when they arise during trial, at pp. 497-498.

215. See A. E. Popple *supra* footnote 213 ("Judge's summing-up to be considered 'as a whole'").

216. (1952) 15 C.R. 63 (Can.) at p. 70.

217. See *R. v. McCormick* (1961) 130 C.C.C. 196 (B.C. C.A.); *R. v. Augello* [1963] 3 C.C.C. 191 (Ont. C.A.).

In a trial by jury there is a clearly defined point of demarcation between the province of the judge and that of the jury in regard to the evidence. The trial judge determines all questions relating to the admissibility of evidence. He also is obliged to instruct the jury on all "questions of law" including the "Rules of Law" by which admissible evidence is to be weighed and assessed. "Weighting the evidence" as well as all other "issues of fact" are matters upon which the jury has the sole right of decision.[218]

Notwithstanding this clear division of jurisdictional authority, present Anglo-Canadian jury practice allows a considerable degree of "trenching" by the trial judge on matters which (theoretically) only the jury should consider. Our law permits the trial judge to express his personal opinion to the jury as to the facts in issue, provided that he clearly advise them that the *ultimate* decision as to all factual determinations is for them. Basically this is a twentieth century development in the law regulating jury trials, and although the practice is uniform in Canada and Britain it is not accepted throughout the entire common law world.[219] Mr. Justice McCardie was of the opinion that the "right" was an important feature of the English judicial system:

> A further point is this — that a judge when sitting with a jury is more than a mere recorder of evidence or a mere pronouncer on points of technical law. He is far more than that. He is entitled — yes, fully entitled — to express his personal opinion on the facts for the consideration of the jury, provided he leaves the issues of fact to them. Herein the state judges of the United States of America differ from the English judge. The right of my colleagues and myself on the matter was clearly formulated by the Court of Criminal Appeal in *Rex v. O'Donnell* (1917), 12 Cr. App. Cas., 221, in these words: "It is sufficient to say, as this court has said on many occasions, that a judge when directing a jury is clearly entitled to express his opinion on the facts of the case, provided that he leaves the issues of fact to the jury to determine." That right of the English judge is, I venture to think, essential to the strength and independence of the English Bench.[220]

Not all jurists in Canada or in England regard the rule quite so benignly. O'Halloran J.A. in *R. v. Pavlukoff* was outspoken in his criticism of it:

---

218. See *Gouin v. R.* (1926) 41 Que. K.B. 157, reversed on other grounds [1926] S.C.R. 539; *R. v. Kirk* (1934) 62 C.C.C. 19 (Ont. C.A.); *R. v. Dowsey* (1865) 6 N.S.R. 93 (C.A.); *R. v. Hill* (1944) 82 C.C.C. 213 (Ont. C.A.); *R. v. Stephen* (1944) 81 C.C.C. 283 (Ont. C.A.); *R. v. Koscuikiewicz* (1948) 33 Cr.App.R. 41; *Azoulay v. R.* [1952] 2 S.C.R. 495.

219. "The extensive power of the English trial Judge to express views on the jury's ultimate questions is well-known *and distinctly not emulated among us*.": M. E. Frankel "The Search for Truth: An Umpireal View" (1974-75) 123 U.Pa.L. Rev. 1031 at p. 1043, n. 23.

220. McCardie, *The Law, The Advocate, and the Judge* (1927) at pp. 25-26. See also P. Devlin *Trial by Jury* (1956) at pp. 118-120.

It seems an absurdity for a judge, after telling the jury the facts are for them and not for him, then to volunteer his opinion of facts followed then or later by another caution to the jury that his own opinion cannot govern them and ought not to influence them. If his opinion ought not to govern or influence the jury, then why give his opinion to the jury? To a person who is not a lawyer, but has some training in the science of correct thinking and some knowledge of the workings of the human mind, a judge who expresses his own opinions to the jury is in effect unconsciously perhaps but nevertheless subtly and positively undermining the plain instruction he has given the jury that 'the facts are for them and not for him;' in reality he is in true effect attempting to persuade the jury not to exercise their own minds freely (as in law he has told them they must do) but instead to be guided by the factual conclusions he volunteers to them.[221]

The logic of O'Halloran J.A.'s observations notwithstanding, an objection to a trial judge expressing his own opinion as to facts will generally not be treated as well-founded in law.[222] The subject usually is left to the sense of propriety and fair play of the trial judge, although there are upper limits which have been established in order to rein in excessive conduct. De Brisay C.J.B.C. in ordering a new trial in the case of *R. v. Casagrande*[223] remarked as follows:

"We all think there must be a new trial in this case. It was not enough for the learned judge to say over and over again that the facts are for the jury if he has so dealt with them beforehand as to belittle their significance for the defence, and leave them heavily in favour of the Crown."

Thus, presently it may be stated that provided the trial judge is judicious and cautious in his commentary, his charge to the jury will be unimpeachable. This entails reminding the jurymen that they are not bound to accept his opinions on the facts (indeed, they have a duty to reject his views if they are in disagreement with them); and a clear assertion that the decision on all factual matters is solely a matter for them as jurors to determine.

Voicing "an opinion on the facts" comprehends a number of situations to which the general rule (that a judge, legally, may venture an opinion) for the most part has equal application. Charges to juries have been sustained in instances where trial judges have offered opinions on (a) the credibility of witnesses;[224] (b) the sufficiency of proof

---

221. (1953-54) 10 W.W.R. (N.S.) 26 at pp. 41-42 (B.C. C.A.).
222. See *R. v. O'Donnell* (1917) 12 Cr.App.R. 219; *R. v. Newell* [1942] 1 D.L.R. 747 (Ont. C.A.); *R. v. Moke* (1917) 38 D.L.R. 441 (Alta. C.A.); *R. v. Deacon* (1948) 5 C.R. 356 (Man. C.A.).
223. (1958) 30 C.R. 76 (B.C. C.A.).
224. See *R. v. Stelmasczuk* (1948) 8 C.R. 430 (N.S. C.A.); *R. v. Newell supra* footnote 222; *R. v. Malanik* (No. 2) (1951) 13 C.R. 160 (Man. C.A.) affirmed [1952] 2 S.C.R. 335; *R. v. Dorland* [1948] O.R. 913 (Ont. C.A.).

of material facts;[225] (c) the theory of the defence;[226] (d) the ultimate issue.[227]

Rivard J. in *R. v. Denis*[228] makes the statement that "It is irregular, unjust and . . . unlawful for a Judge in the trial of a case to lead the jury to believe that he is convinced of the guilt of the accused". The decisions in *Casagrande* and *Pavlukoff* discussed *supra* similarly espouse a standard and set limits on judicial commentary. Without a discernible perimeter of this type, the law regulating jury trials would lack rationality and the process would come to be one mutilated by judicial fiat. There are those who contend that even now the standard is set rather too loosely.

It is submitted that the present state of the law regarding the right of a trial judge to express his opinion as to the facts of a given case is deficient, and is therefore subject to manipulation and abuse. The, "But you are the Judges of the Facts" qualification is not a meaningful constraint.

It is not suggested by this that trial judges ought to be forbidden absolutely from commenting upon the evidence. To make such a proposal would be to stumble much in the same manner as that described by Lord Devlin in his short work on *Trial by Jury*:

> "Those who originated the practice [in the United States of restricting such judicial commentary] were misled by the form of trial by jury and missed the reality of it. They fell victims to the deceptive brocard that the facts were for the jury and the law for the judge, into supposing that there could be no proper reason why the judge should meddle with the facts. Of the principle which they introduced Professor Thayer has written: "Trial by jury, in such a form as that, is not trial by jury in any historic sense of the words." "[229]

There can be no doubt the jury requires the assistance of the trial judge in order that they be able to identify, assess and adequately marshall the relevant "facts" for the purpose of coming to a proper conclusion. Without such assistance "trial by jury" would be a chaotic shambles.

What a jury can live without in most instances is "editorial commentary" by the trial judge followed by the confusing *non sequitur*: "but this is a matter for you to decide". On the other hand, there should be no objection to the informal transmission of opinion which

---

225. See *R. v. Malanik ibid.; R. v. Newell, R. v. O'Donnell* and *R. v. Moke supra* footnote 222.
226. See *R. v. Stelmasczuk supra* footnote 224; *Rivet v. R.* (1915) 25 C.C.C. 235 (Que. C.A.); *R. v. Carlin* (1903) 12 Que. K.B. 483 (Que. C.A.).
227. See *Stelmasczuk, Rivet* and *Carlin, ibid.*
228. [1967] 1 C.C.C. 196 at p. 202 (Que. C.A.).
229. *Supra* footnote 220 at pp. 119-120.

necessarily will arise from a recitation of the facts as a trial judge understands them.

It would be naïve to suggest that the proposal offered *supra* does not import difficulties of its own. A too rigid formulation, for instance, would have the effect of forcing trial judges to conduct jury trials under something of a "gag rule"; while one structured too loosely would almost certainly begin to approximate our present situation. These difficulties however, are not far different from the ordinary yet complex, interpretative tasks which confront our courts regularly. Certainly, since the formulation of a workable and realistic standard would serve to clarify the nature of the judicial role, and would promote respect for the administration of justice, there is reason to believe optimistically that our courts would be equal to the challenge.

6

PROTECTING THE PROCESS FROM ABUSE: THE DOCTRINE OF ABUSE OF PROCESS

1. THE DOCTRINE OF ABUSE OF PROCESS AND THE INHERENT JURISDICTION OF THE COURT

The doctrine of abuse of process is a much misunderstood facet of Canadian law; particularly Canadian criminal law.

Some of the commentators tend to view the doctrine as a relatively recent development in the criminal law. It has been argued that if there is a historical basis to the concept it lies, in the criminal law field, by analogy to civil cases and civil rules of practice which allow for the termination of proceedings which are found to be "frivolous, vexatious, and an abuse of the process of the court". By these arguments although the doctrine is said to form part of the "inherent" jurisdiction of our courts it has only recently been gathered into that jurisdiction.

These, by and large, are misconceptions about the true nature of the doctrine. It is true that "abuse of process" has experienced a recent surge of popularity in the field of criminal law. However, while this popularity is recent, the concept is not. Also, the doctrine, applied in a criminal law context, does not spring from civil law origins.

To understand properly the nature of abuse of process, it is first necessary to comprehend what is entailed in the concept of the *"inherent* jurisdiction of the court". (Virtually all of the commentators, judges, lawyers and legal scholars alike, recognize that it is an *inherent* right incident to the jurisdiction of every superior court[1] to enquire into and judge of the regularity or abuse of its process).[2]

Initially it should be noted that it is almost contradictory to argue on the one hand that the basis for the use of the doctrine is a valid exercise of "inherent" jurisdiction, and on the other hand to assert that the validity of the doctrine is established by analogy to civil cases. If the basis for its use is "inherent" then other explanations are superfluous.

The real difficulty resides in establishing the meaning to be ascribed to the phrase "the inherent jurisdiction of the court". This issue is one of some complexity and ambiguity. Nevertheless if we are to free our-

---

1. It will be argued *infra* that the right is exercisable by inferior courts as well.
2. See *Re Sproule* (1886) 12 S.C.R. 140.

selves from this spiral of tautologies and circular arguments a clearer understanding of "inherent jurisdiction" is essential.

> The inherent jurisdiction of the court may be invoked in an apparently inexhaustible variety of circumstances and may be exercised in different ways. This peculiar concept is indeed so amorphous and ubiquitous and so pervasive in its operation that it seems to defy the challenge to determine its quality and to establish its limits. Yet there are insistent questions about inherent jurisdiction which demand and deserve an answer, such as, what is its nature, its juridical basis, its limits, its capacity to diversify, and its claim to viability.[3]

(1) Inherent jurisdiction distinguished from general and statutory jurisdictions

Precise meanings are important to a consideration of this issue. The "inherent jurisdiction" of the court should not be confused with its "general jurisdiction", or for that matter, with its "statutory jurisdiction".

I. H. Jacob, who in 1970 was Master of the Sureme Court in England and had occasion in that year to consider the question of "the inherent jurisdiction of the court" was able to provide the kind of succinct distinctions and clear thinking that is required in this area.[4] Noting that the inherent jurisdiction of the court was only a part or an aspect of its general jurisdiction he drew the following distinctions between general, statutory and inherent jurisdictions which are of import:

(a) *General jurisdiction of the court*

Broadly speaking, this is unrestricted and unlimited in all matters of substantive law both civil and criminal, except in so far as that has been taken away in unequivocal terms by statutory enactment. According to this definition the superior court of record is not subject to supervisory control by any other court except by due process of appeal, and it exercises the full plenitude of judicial power in all matters concerning the general administration of justice within its area. (General jurisdiction thus includes the exercise of inherent jurisdiction).

(b) *Statutory jurisdiction of the court*

The source of this jurisdiction is the statute itself, which will define the limits within which such jurisdiction is to be exercised.

(c) *Inherent jurisdiction of the court*

This is not a concept used in contradistinction to the jurisdiction conferred on the court by statute. The court may exercise its inherent jurisdiction even in respect of matters which are regulated by statute

---

3. I. H. Jacob, "The Inherent Jurisdiction of the Court" (1970) 23 Current Legal Problems 23.
4. *Ibid.*

or by rule of court, so long as it can do so without contravening any statutory provision. The true nature of the inherent jurisdiction of the court is found in a complex of features which Jacob summarises as follows:

(1) the inherent jurisdiction of the court is exercisable as part of the process of the administration of justice. It is part of procedural law, both civil and criminal, and not of substantive law; it is invoked in relation to the process of litigation.

(2) the distinctive and basic feature of the inherent jurisdiction of the court is that it is exercisable by summary process, *i.e.* without a plenary trial conducted in the normal or ordinary way, and generally without waiting for trial or for the outcome of any pending or other proceeding.

(3) because it is part of the machinery of justice, the inherent jurisdiction of the court may be invoked not only in relation to the litigant parties in pending proceedings, but in relation also to anyone, whether a party or not, and in respect of matters which are not raised as issues in the litigation between the parties.

(4) the inherent jurisdiction of the court may be exercised in any given case, notwithstanding that there are Rules of Court governing the circumstances of such case. The powers conferred by Rules of the Court are, generally speaking, additional to, and not in substitution of, powers arising out of the inherent jurisdiction of the court. They are generally cumulative, not mutually exclusive. Thus in any given case the court is able to proceed under either or both heads of jurisdiction.

Further Jacob points out that the inherent jurisdiction of the court must be distinguished from judicial discretion which it resembles. Often the two appear to overlap, but there is a vital juridical distinction between jurisdiction and discretion, which must always be observed.[5]

(2) Major features of inherent jurisdiction

Jacob traces the historical origins and development of the court's inherent jurisdiction along two paths, "namely, by way of punishment for contempt of court and of its process, and by way of regulating the practice of the court and preventing the abuse of its process". Both of these powers existed from earliest times.[6]

But the historical paths which Jacob follows all flow from a common root. The question must still be posed: what was the basis for the court's jurisdiction to punish for contempt and oversee the regularity of its practice?

---

5. *Ibid.* at pp. 25-26.
6. See *R. v. Almon* (1765) Wilm. 243; and *R. v. Lefroy* (1873) 8 Q.B. 134 at p. 137; also see 4 Bl. Com. 286 re contempt and see *Metro. Bank v. Pooley* (1885) 10 A.C. 210 at pp. 220-221 re practice regulation, all cited in Jacob *supra* footnote 3 at p. 26.

The answer is, that the jurisdiction to exercise these powers was derived, not from any statute or rule of law, but from the very nature of the court as a superior court of law, and for this reason such jurisdiction has been called "inherent".[7]

Such an explanation is anathema to the positivists, and has been criticized as being "metaphysical".[8] Far from being a criticism, however, the description points up to the "essential", the "fundamental", nature and quality of this jurisdiction. "Metaphysical" indeed; the inherent jurisdiction of the court exists along that melting edge where ideas transpose into realities. Jacob resurrects Spinoza in this regard: "The endeavour where with each thing endeavours to persist in its own being is nothing more than the actual essence of the thing itself."[9] (or, as Jacob goes on to translate: "The jurisdiction which is inherent in a superior court of law is that which enables it to fulfill itself as a court of law.").[10]

Thus, the inherent jurisdiction of the court may be viewed as the means by which the court ensures its dominion, or at least, safeguards its existence. As such, inherent jurisdiction is an attribute which is "intrinsic", and of essential character. For inherent jurisdiction to be invoked there must first be a challenge to the very fibre of the institution of the court — a direct threat which, if unanswered, would serve to diminish or atrophy the power of the court to conduct its own business.

> There can be no doubt that a court which is endowed with a particular jurisdiction has powers which are necessary to enable it to act effectively within such jurisdiction. I would regard them as powers which are inherent in its jurisdiction. A court must enjoy such powers in order to enforce its rules of practice and to suppress any abuses of its process and to defeat any attempted thwarting of its process.[11]

Since the inherent jurisdiction of the court is the means by which the court protects itself as an institution, it must of necessity employ an arsenal of powers in order to assert its hegemony. These powers are coercive and regulatory in nature.

(3) Rule-making power of the court

The regulation of court process and proceedings finds expression under inherent jurisdiction in a great variety of circumstances, and by different methods. Rules of law, customs and long usage acquiring

---

7. Jacob, *supra* footnote 3 at p. 27.
8. See [1947] 57 Yale L.J. 83 at p. 85: "For the power to punish contempt of court was metaphysically conceived as 'inherent', a conception which served not only to remove contempt from the protection of general criminal statutes but also to induce the emasculation of specific contempt legislation".
9. Spinoza, *Ethics* Pt. III, Proposition VII.
10. Jacob, *supra* footnote 3 at p. 27.
11. *Connelly v. D.P.P.* [1964] A.C. 1254 at p. 1301 *per* Lord Morris.

the force of law,[12] and rules of practice[13] are all to be found within this lexicon.

The power of the court to make rules of court from earliest times was viewed as an original and inherent jurisdiction. Where no relevant rule of practice was to be found then it was held to be for the particular court of competent jurisdiction to make a rule consonant with reason and justice in order that the administration of justice might not be hindered or delayed.[14]

Rules of practice, or of court, provide only one example of the means by which the regulation of court process and proceedings is accomplished through the assertion of inherent jurisdiction. I. H. Jacob catalogues others as well: the right or power of the court to conduct *in camera* proceedings, or prohibit publication of part of court proceedings where the interests of justice so require; the jurisdiction of the court at any stage of the proceedings, to vary, modify or extend its own order so as to express correctly its intention and meaning and thereby ensure that the purposes of justice are not defeated; the power in the court to decline to proceed further so soon as it discovers that the proceedings are not properly constituted, *e.g.,* that a party is dead or non-existent, or that proceedings are hypothetical or relate to a dead issue or to a future event or are fictitious.[15]

All of these examples of court regulation of its process and proceedings point up the correctness of Jacob's perspective on inherent jurisdiction. All serve to bring into focus the attribute of self-preservation, the quality which "enables (the court) to fulfill itself as a court of law." The "interests of justice", "fairness", the "purposes" or "ends" of justice are all co-relatives of the inherent jurisdiction. Matters

---

12. See *e.g. B.C. Packers Ltd. v. Burrard Iron Works Ltd.* (1955) 17 W.W.R. 409 (B.C. C.A.) which held that a long established practice should not be disturbed except on irresistable grounds.

13. In Ontario the Rules of Practice are accorded the force of statute, and by virtue of s. 114 (11) (previously s. 108(1)) of the *Judicature Act,* R.S.O. 1970 c. 228, "The superior powers vested in the rule-making authority overrule statutory provisions respecting practice and procedure . . ." *per* Masten J.A. in *Bendjy v. Munton* [1932] O.R. 123 at p. 129 (C.A.).

14. See *Re Patterson and Nanaimo Dry Cleaning etc. Union* [1947] 4 D.L.R. 159 (B.C. C.A.). See also *Bell v. Wood* [1927] 2 D.L.R. 827 (B.C.); *Prevedoros v. Bilousa* (1951) 3 W.W.R. 700 (B.C.) and *Bell v. Milner* (1956) 17 W.W.R. 432 (B.C. C.A.).

15. See Jacob, *Supra* footnote 3 at pp. 38-39. Note also that Jacob finds under this regulatory control examination the right of the court to dismiss an action for want of prosecution "not only by analogy with the limitation statutes where the action has been allowed to lie dormant for a period exceeding the relevant limitation period, but also where it is satisfied that by reason of prolonged or inordinate delay, which is also inexcusable, the defendant has suffered or is likely to suffer prejudice or that it is no longer possible to have a fair trial between the parties". This will become relevant to the consideration of the recent Canadian practice respecting abuse of process of court and delay.

which work to defeat the ends, purposes or interests of justice; which supplant fairness, and promote prejudice, constitute a threat to the viability of the institution of the court as they serve to undermine the rule of law and undercut respect for law and legal institutions. Without inherent jurisdiction to repel these challenges "the court would have form but would lack substance".[16]

(4) Coercive powers and inherent jurisdiction: contempt of court and abuse of process

Jacob in his analysis contrasts the regulation of process — one form of power of the court exercisable under inherent jurisdiction — with two other main powers incident to inherent jurisdiction, which are both "coercive" in nature:

(1) in the case of contempt of court, to punish the offender.

(2) in the case of abuse of process to stay or dismiss the action or to give judgment or impose terms as it thinks fit.[17]

Insofar as non-compliance with regulation implies a penalty the coercive/non-coercive distinction is unsustainable as coercion is seen to exist at both levels. Nevertheless, there is a distinction to be drawn between these two heads of power of the court which are exercisable under its inherent jurisdiction:

"Regulation" of the court process is an "anticipatory" exercise of inherent jurisdiction — *i.e.*, it moves in advance of any challenge to the existence of the institution and thus precludes destruction through the operation of anarchic or chaotic forces.

Punishment for contempt, the staying or dismissing of actions etc. are powers which are exercisable after the fact of a challenge. These powers operate *ex post facto;* and as such they represent a "retrospective" exercise of inherent jurisdiction.

In the case of the "retrospective" powers of the court (Jacob's "coercive" powers) the important point is struck that the powers are cumulative. Thus in a proper case the court "may not only strike out a frivolous or vexatious claim or defence but also punish for contempt of court".[18] Hence, taken to their furthest limit, the powers of the court to compel observance of its process, and obedience to, and compliance with, its orders, are massive indeed. The inherent jurisdiction of the court, representing as it does the last line of defence of society under law, is suitably equipped for its task.

Under its inherent jurisdiction the court has two available responses

---

16. *Ibid.* at p. 27.

17. *Ibid.* at p. 28.

18. *Ibid.* at p. 28. Such cumulative application is rare indeed and is almost un-thinkable in abuse of process actions where the affected party is the agent of the Crown. In this regard see *R. v. Weisz; Ex parte Hector MacDonald* [1951] 2 K.B. 611.

to deal with neglect, refusal, or disobedience to obey or comply with its orders or process: it can punish the offender under its contempt power, or it may summarily terminate proceedings against the offending party.

Although the power to punish for contempt need not proceed by summary process, it often does.[19] Thus both modes described above may operate by summary process in order to vindicate the authority of the court.

> There is one crucial feature about summary process which clearly distinguishes it from the ordinary trial process. Because the process is summary, "brevi manu" as it is called, and replaces the ordinary method of trial, the party affected may thereby be deprived of his right to a trial. In other words, the resort to the summary process under the inherent jurisdiction of the court involves a serious and severe curtailment of the right of a party to have his case on the merits heard by a court of law in the ordinary way at a trial held for the purpose. For these reasons the court will exercise its coercive powers by summary process to punish for contempt or to terminate proceedings without a trial only with the greatest care and circumspection and only in the clearest cases. In contempt cases, the court will act only where the case is clear and beyond reasonable doubt or argument, and in cases involving abuse of process, the court will exercise its inherent jurisdiction very sparingly and only in very exceptional circumstances, or in what are called plain and obvious cases.[20]

Oswald in his classic work on *Contempt of Court* makes the following comments which are germane to inherent jurisdiction generally:

> A Court of Justice without power to vindicate its own dignity, to enforce obedience to its mandates, to protect its officers, or to shield those who are entrusted to its care, would be an anomaly which could not be permitted to exist in any civilized community.[21]

2. HISTORICAL USE OF THE DOCTRINE UP TO CONNELLY V. D.P.P.

The decision in the case of *R. v. Osborn*[22] (which will be discussed at some length *infra*) must be regarded, somewhat curiously, as a turning point in the development of the doctrine of abuse of process in Canada. This turn of events has been "curious" inasmuch as the Supreme Court of Canada's decision in *Osborn* seen in its best light was inconclusive, although in its result the decision reversed a rather strong affirmation of the doctrine in the Ontario Court of Appeal.

---

19. The contrasting procedure is to proceed upon indictment to a trial and verdict or judgment. See J. C. McRuer, "Criminal Contempt of Court Procedure: A Protection of the Rights of the Individual" (1952) 30 Can.Bar.Rev. 225 at pp. 236-237. See also H. Fischer, "Civil and Criminal Aspects of Contempt of Court" (1956) 34 Can.Bar.Rev. 121.
20. Jacob, *supra* footnote 3 at pp. 30-31.
21. 3rd. ed. (1911) at p. 9.
22. (1971) 12 C.R.N.S. 1 (Can.), reversing (1969) 5 C.R.N.S. 183 (Ont. C.A.)

Although the decision rendered by the highest court in the land marks the turning point in the doctrine's use in Canada it was certainly not a "watershed" decision. Prior to the decision rendered in *Osborn* there had been repeated affirmations of the existence and viability of the doctrine of abuse of process in a criminal law context. Nevertheless it has been said that there does not appear to be any Canadian case before *Osborn* where a Court actually acted to stay a prosecution on the ground that it was an abuse of the Court's process, although several of the cases, in *obiter* comments, have recognized the power to do so.[23] Pigeon J. in *R. v. Osborn* remarked upon the situation as follows:

> In this Court as in the Court of Appeal, counsel have been unable to cite any case in Canada where such a discretionary rule has been recognized or acted upon other than the obiter dictum of MacKay J.A. in *R. v. Leclair* [1956] O.W.N. 336, 23 C.R. 216, 115 C.C.C. 297 at 302.[24]

One can only lament the paucity of the research skills exemplified by these remarks. Note that Pigeon J. speaks of instances where the discretionary rule (I prefer to call it a "doctrine") has been either "recognized" or "acted upon". Nor does he stop there — even obiter comments would merit consideration.

Counsel's failings aside, one surely has a right to expect more from the highest court in the land. The law was there to find and consider. Even the assumption that the consideration of the issue offered by MacKay J.A. in *R. v. Leclair* was *obiter* is open to question. The passage in question reads

> It is a reasonable assumption that the complainant, by threatening prosecution, endeavoured to obtain payment of the debt. There is no doubt that this amounted to an abuse of the process of the Court. The criminal law was not enacted for the assistance of persons seeking to collect civil debts. It seems to be clear that a Court of competent jurisdiction has inherent power to prevent the abuse of its process by staying or dismissing the action. This jurisdiction ought to be exercised very sparingly and only in exceptional cases . . .[25]

P. C. Stenning in his article "Observations on the Supreme Court of Canada's Decision in R. v. Osborn"[26] there expresses the opinion that it is "a matter of doubt, however, as to whether the observations of MacKay J.A. in that case [*R. v. Leclair*] can properly be regarded as *obiter*". He notes that in *Leclair* one of the two grounds of appeal posed for the consideration of the appeal court was that "the court below had failed properly to exercise its discretion to stay the prose-

---

23. See D. W. Roberts "The Doctrine of Abuse of Process in Canadian Criminal Law" (1972) Report of the First Annual Conference of the British Columbia Provincial Judges Association, p. 39 at p. 42.
24. *R. v. Osborn supra* footnote 22 at p. 8.
25. *R. v. Leclair* (1956), 115 C.C.C. 297 at pp. 302-303 (Ont. C.A.).
26. (1970-71) 13 Cr.L.Q. 164 at p. 173.

cution which was an abuse of the court's process since the prosecution had been brought solely for the purpose of enforcing a civil debt".[27] As is evident in the passage of the judgment set out *supra*, MacKay J.A. did indeed find that the prosecution had been launched with this improper motive in mind. Also, MacKay J.A. observed that the Court "has inherent power to prevent the abuse of its process by staying or dismissing the action", but "(t)his jurisdiction ought to be exercised very sparingly and only in very exceptional cases". MacKay J.A. went on to conclude (and Stenning stresses the import of these remarks):

> "This was, however, a matter for the learned Magistrate and in all the circumstances we cannot say that he did not exercise his discretion judicially."[28]

These words indicate that MacKay J.A.'s observations on the existence and purported use of the inherent power to prevent abuse of process were "integral and necessary" to the determination of an issue posed for consideration on appeal. Accordingly it is supportable to argue that the remarks were not *obiter* but rather were part of the *ratio* of the case.[29]

There was, of course, in *Osborn* lengthy amplification and demonstration of the historical validity of the doctrine of abuse of process since the English House of Lords had considered the matter so exhaustively four years previously in *Connelly v. D.P.P.*[30] All five of the sitting justices in *Connelly* affirmed the existence of an inherent power in superior courts to control abuses of the court's practice and procedures (although two of the Law Lords, Lord Morris and Lord Hodson qualified it severely). Both of the major judgments rendered in *Osborn* (those of Ritchie and Pigeon JJ.) contain a consideration of the analyses offered in *Connelly v. D.P.P.*

Lord Devlin (who was joined in his opinion by Lords Pearce and Reid) ventured to claim "that nearly the whole of the English criminal law of procedure and evidence has been made by the exercise of the judges of their power to see that what was fair and just was done between prosecutors and accused". Historically, he argued, in order to combat prosecutorial abuse "the court from its inherent power evolved the pleas of autrefois acquit and convict". Moreover, according to Lord Devlin, "the process is still continuing, and it is easy to think of recent examples".[31] The argument that the power of the court to

---

27. *Ibid.*
28. *R. v. Leclair supra* footnote 25 at p. 303.
29. See Stenning *supra* footnote 26 at pp. 173-174. See also *R. v. Brown* (1963) 7 Cr.L.Q. 238 (Ont.) where Latchford C.C.J. adopts and applies a similar approach, at pp. 241-242. And see *R. v. Lee* (1956) 114 C.C.C. 371 (Alta. C.A.).
30. [1964] 2 All E.R. 401. This decision will also be the subject of detailed analysis *infra*.
31. See *ibid.* at p. 438 *per* Lord Devlin and p. 447 *per* Lord Pearce.

prevent abuses was more limited in a criminal law context than in civil cases was dismissed as untenable — the power to prevent abuse of process being "as applicable to criminal as to civil proceedings".[32]

(1) The doctrine not confined to civil cases

The direct application of the concept of "abuse of process" has quite naturally proved easier to document in the context of the civil cases. Rules of Practice have even incorporated the very words "abuse of process" into their phraseology. That situation continues today.[33] In the civil context "abuse of process" was often used interchangeably, or at least, in conjunction with, the phrase "frivolous or vexatious". This conceivably led to the mistaken belief that the concept was inapplicable to the criminal process; at least in those instances where the state was bringing the prosecution. (Presumably the office of the Attorney General was regarded as being above "frivolous exercise".). A proceeding was said, in the early cases, to be "frivolous" when a party was trifling with the court,[34] or when the bringing of it constituted a waste of the Court's time,[35] or was incapable of supporting reasoned argument.[36]

The concept of a "frivolous" action does however have applicability in the criminal law domain. For example, s. 612 of the *Criminal Code* provides for the summary determination of a frivolous appeal (or a vexatious one) by a simple reference of the matter by registrar to the court of appeal. If no substantial ground of appeal is evident the appeal court may dispose of the matter without full hearing and without calling for the representations or presence of one or both of the parties. It is erroneous to think that "frivolous and vexatious" are concepts reserved purely for civil cases while the analogy in criminal cases (if there is one) is the concept of "oppression". Frivolous and

---

32. *Supra* footnote 30 at p. 443 *per* Lord Devlin.
33. *E.g.* see Ontario Rules of Practice, R.R.O. 1970 Reg. 545, R. 126.
34. See *e.g. Chaffers v. Goldsmid* [1894] 1 Q.B. 186.
35. *Per* Mellor J. in *Dawkins v. Prince Edward of Saxe Weimar* (1876) 1 Q.B.D. 499.
36. *Per* Devlin J. in *Addis v. Crocker* unreported. Cases in footnotes 34, 35 and 36 are cited in I. H. Jacob, "The Inherent Jurisdiction of the Court" (1970) 23 Current Legal Problems 23 at p. 41. Note also, in terms of the more general justification for the use of abuse of process in criminal proceedings Lord Devlin in *Connelly v. D.P.P. supra* footnote 30 draws several examples from the English civil practice, most notably *Metro. Bank Ltd. v. Pooley* [1881-85] All E.R. 949 (augmented by *Castro v. R.* [1881-85] All E.R. 429 at p. 436) *MacDougall v. Knight* [1886-90] All E.R. 762; *Greenhalgh v. Mallard* [1947] 2 All E.R. 255; and *Wright v. Bennett* [1948] 1 All E.R. 227. These authorities, and others, are marshalled in *Connelly not* for the purpose of showing that the doctrine in a criminal law context originates by analogy to the civil cases, but rather because the courts even in these civil cases *always* recognized that the inherent power in the court extended to control over the criminal process as well.

vexatious proceedings may well be oppressive proceedings. Indeed, the concept of trifling with the court has often found expression in the maxim *de minimus non curat lex* — the law does not concern itself with trifles — a maxim which has been held to have applicability in the criminal law as well as in the civil.[37]

In all of this the central point remains that from earliest times the court exercised a power under its inherent jurisdiction by summary process to terminate proceedings which were frivolous or vexatious and/or which were an abuse of process. It did so either by actually using the words "abuse of process'; or, by applying Latin maxims such as *de minimis non curat lex;* or, by evolving special pleas such as *autrefois acquit* or *autrefois convict;* or, through evidentiary and procedural innovation.

Leaving aside, for the moment, the impressively documented verification of abuse of process based upon the English authorities (as discussed in *Connelly v. D.P.P.*) it remains an error to believe that the depth of Canadian authority on the subject prior to *Osborn* begins and ends with the comments of MacKay J.A. in *R. v. Leclair* (although this is the thrust of the remarks of Pigeon J. in *Osborn*).

P. S. Barton notes that in most jurisdictions in Canada rules of court give superior court judges the power to dismiss proceedings by striking out statements of claims for failure to disclose a cause of action, or to strike out scandalous, embarrassing, frivolous or vexatious pleadings.[38] These powers, expressed as Rules of Court, are said additionally to derive from the court's inherent jurisdiction.[39] Barton dislikes the notion that the civil cases are in some way supportive of a criminal law power to prevent abuses of process. Referring to such cases as *Hollinger* and *Tolfree*[40] he strikes the point that

> In none of the above cases was a litigant with a valid cause of action with status to sue, who had followed the then requisite procedural steps, prevented from continuing. This, however, is the power that criminal trial judges are alleged to have and to require by analogy to these cases and others.[41]

Barton realizes that the general point which he seeks to establish is not completely sustainable, and he is forced to concede (by way of footnote) that "admittedly, in the *Vexatious Proceedings Act,* R.S.O.

---

37. For a rejection of the application of the maxim to narcotics prosecutions see B. A. MacFarlane, "Narcotic Prosecutions and the Defence of De Minimis Non Curat Lex" (1973-74) 17 Cr.L.Q. 98.
38. "Abuse of Process as a Plea in Bar of Trial" (1972-73) 15 Cr.L.Q. 437 at p. 448.
39. See *Hollinger Bus Lines v. Lab. Rel. Bd.* (Ont.) [1952] O.R. 366 (C.A.) and *R. v. Clark* [1943] O.R. 319 affirmed at 501 (C.A.) Also see *Sovereign Securities & Holdings Co. v. Hunter* [1964] 1 O.R. 7 (C.A.)
40. Both cited *ibid.*
41. Barton *supra* footnote 38 at p. 450.

1970, c. 481 a discretion does exist to prevent litigants with a good cause of action from continuing if the proceedings would be an abuse".[42] Further, Barton's analysis is limited by the fact that he has strained the cases he cites beyond the limits which they truly are capable of bearing. While it is true that the Courts are interested in seeing that meritorious well-grounded actions are allowed to be litigated, the Rules of Practice nevertheless do confer *discretion* on the court to strike pleadings in clear and exceptional cases (not unlike the jurisdiction of which MacKay J.A. speaks in *Leclair*: "This jurisdiction ought to be exercised very sparingly and only in very exceptional cases.").

Barton emerges in his article as an advocate who would deny our superior courts (in the exercise of their criminal law jurisdiction) the power to prevent abuse of their own process save in the severely limited manner proposed by Lord Morris and Pigeon J. His analysis hinges on the belief that there is no validity to the doctrine of abuse of process *vis-à-vis* criminal proceedings except insofar as a case may be made out for the doctrine's existence by way of analogy to civil procedure. Such an analogy, he contends, is inappropriate and inapt.

The defect in the above reasoning resides in a fundamental misapprehension of the position of Lord Devlin. The latter sought to demonstrate the existence and viability of the doctrine by several means:

(1) by demonstrating that the whole of the development of English Criminal Procedure and Evidence had been achieved out of the exercise of this power

(2) by demonstrating that recent innovations such as the Judges Rules also stemmed from this power

(3) by demonstrating that even in the early civil cases the courts recognized that the power which they were exercising was incident to their position as superior courts and thus extended to the court's activities in the field of criminal law.

Thus it is an error to argue that the *justification* for the use of the doctrine in criminal law *arises by analogy* to the civil cases. There is no analogy. The civil and criminal law powers to prevent abuses are but different expressions of the same general jurisdiction — *i.e.,* the court's inherent jurisdiction.

A close reading of Barton's work reveals that the policy perspective from which he builds his analysis is founded upon a profound distrust in any purported interference with the prerogative power of the Crown.

> in civil proceedings a decision to stay an action does not normally involve an interference with the prerogative power of the Crown. In

---

42. *Ibid.* at p. 450.

criminal cases, a decision by a trial judge to stay a proceeding before plea clearly amounts to this. The judge is really interfering with the prerogative.[43]

At this point, Barton appears to be expressing a preference for the Attorney General's traditionally unreviewable discretion, as opposed to a potentially reviewable exercise of judicial discretion.[44]

The above digression with respect to the Barton article gives a sufficient tracing to the fact that in Canada, as in England, there was a utilization by the courts of inherent powers to control the regularity of their processes in civil cases. To be fair to Barton, he in fact *details* the existence and restricted use of this inherent jurisdiction in civil cases. The Canadian civil cases however bear an intimate connection with such English civil cases as were discussed by Lord Devlin in *Connelly*.[45] Since the English civil and criminal controls both are seen to arise from the same general jurisdiction (*i.e.* the court's "inherent" jurisdiction) it appears strongly to suggest that Canadian abuse of process powers exist in a like manner, be they civil or criminal in nature.

(2) Early Canadian use of the doctrine: the "disgruntled creditor" cases

The Canadian civil cases dealing with abuse of process and *obiter dictum* of MacKay J.A. in *R. v. Leclair* do not collectively constitute the sole Canadian source of authority for the proposition that abuse of process exists as a doctrine to assist courts in controlling abuses of procedure in the criminal law domain. Curiously, both Jessup J.A. and Pigeon J., in observing that counsel were unable to furnish additional authority for the proposition that the trial judge has a discretion to stay an indictment when the laying of it is considered injustice

---

43. *Ibid.* at pp. 451-452.

44. The questions of whether inferior courts have jurisdiction to make findings of abuse of process and to act upon them, and the nature of possible review of judicial decisions concerning abuse of process shall be dealt with *infra*. For a similar perspective to Barton's re: preferring the A. G.'s discretion to that of the judiciary, see K. Chasse, "The re-laid charge and autrefois acquit" (1971) 13 C.R.N.S. 196, and K. Chasse, "Abuse of process as a control of prosecutorial discretion" (1970) 10 C.R.N.S. 392.

45. See also *Haggard v. Pelicier Frères* [1892] A.C. 61 at pp. 67-68 where it was stated *per* Lord Watson:

"Their Lordships hold it to be settled that a Court of competent jurisdiction has inherent power to prevent abuse of its process, by staying or dismissing, without proof, actions which it holds to be vexatious." And see *Lawrance v. Lord Norreys* (1890) 15 A.C. 210 at p. 219 *per* Lord Herschell:

"It cannot be doubted that the Court has an inherent jurisdiction to dismiss an action which is an abuse of the process of the Court. It is a jurisdiction which ought to be very sparingly exercised, and only in very exceptional cases".

amounting to oppression, passed over MacKay J.A.'s citation of *R. v. Leroux*[46] which factually was very similar to the *Leclair* case.

No Canadian court, or commentator, has made reference to what was perhaps the first Canadian implementation of an abuse of process power in a criminal case — the 1886 decision of the Supreme Court of Canada decision, *Re Robert Evan Sproule*.[47] In that case the Supreme Court of Canada found it had inherent jurisdiction, and exercised it, in order to quash a writ of *habeas corpus* which had been improvidently granted" by Henry J. in Chambers. The case involved an allegation of murder against Sproule, who questioned the jurisdiction of the British Columbia courts which had tried, convicted, and detained him. Habeas corpus was subsequently granted by Henry J. in Chambers who acceded to the prisoner's objections to jurisdiction. A portion of the headnote of the case reads as follows:

> Section 51 of the Supreme and Exchequer Court Act . . . does not interfere with the inherent right which the Supreme Court of Canada, in common with every superior court, has incident to its jurisdiction to enquire into and judge of the regularity or abuse of its process[48]

By quashing the writ granted by Henry J. another important feature of the doctrine of abuse of process is highlighted. The decision demonstrates that the doctrine's use is not purely the preserve of the accused, and is not solely directed at prosecutorial excess. It points up that abuse of process in a proper case may also be a weapon in the hands of the state — one useful for reining in *any* conduct which misuses the process of the court.

The *Sproule* case was an unusual case on its facts, and by virtue of its historical circumstance. Nevertheless, in succeeding years there were subsequent invocations of the doctrine in cases with an aspect involving criminal law. In fact, a line of decisions culminating in recent times with the decision in *Leclair* demonstrated the application of the doctrine (if not in direct terms, at least peripherally) in cases involving "disgruntled creditors".[49] These cases involved the initiation of the criminal process by creditors against defaulting debtors. The cases demonstrate that in principle the courts are loathe to allow the criminal process to be employed as an aid to civil debt collection.

The first reported instance of the disgruntled creditor phenomenon occurred in 1907 in *R. v. Michigan Central Railroad Co.*[50] In that

---

46. (1928) 50 C.C.C. 52 (Ont. C.A.) (Jessup J.A. even reproduced the citation in a quotation extracted from *Leclair*.)
47. (1886) 12 S.C.R. 140.
48. *Ibid.* See also at pp. 179-180 *per* Ritchie C.J., and at pp. 208-209 *per* Strong J.
49. The term is employed by John Rook in his case comments in *R. v. Osborn* (1971) 29 U.T.F.L.R. 105 at p. 107 (Can.).
50. (1907) 17 C.C.C. 483 (Ont.).

case the trial judge refused to accede to a resolution of the town council of the town of Essex that he delay the imposition of a fine ($25,000.00) until pending civil claims were settled. The indictment in question involved nuisance and the carrying of dangerous explosives without proper precautions. (The explosives detonated "killing two men on the spot, and more or less seriously injuring about forty others".) Riddell J. considered the somewhat "irregular" suggestion to delay the fine but refused to give effect to it:

> But in any case I could not use the criminal law or allow it to be used as a lever to enforce the payment of civil claims for damages. Any one who puts the criminal law in force for the purpose of bringing about the settlement of a civil claim is guilty, in law and in conscience, of a wrong — and I, administering the law, may not do that which I must, sitting as a Judge, reprobate in others.[51]

In 1926 the British Columbia Court of Appeal quashed the conviction which had been entered against an accused by the name of Thornton.[52] Thornton had been charged with obtaining money by false pretences. The evidence taken at trial revealed (in the opinion of the Court of Appeal) that the complainant had made a thorough investigation before parting with his money. Accordingly, Thornton's conviction was not sustainable. MacDonald C.J.A. writing for the majority of the court (Martin J.A. dissenting) observed:

> This prosecution has the ear marks of an attempt to use the process of the criminal Courts for the collection of a debt, or for the punishment of a defaulting debtor . . . In these circumstances the prosecution should never have been commenced.[53]

Two years after *R. v. Thornton* almost the same situation arose, this time in Ontario, in the case of *R. v. Leroux*.[54] Leroux had been charged under what was then s. 405 (now s. 320) of the *Criminal Code* (obtaining a thing capable of being stolen by false pretences). He was convicted of that charge although the facts did not disclose commission of that offence. They did disclose an offence contrary to the then s. 406 (now s. 321) of the *Code* (obtaining the signature of a person to a valuable security by false pretences). The Ontario Court of Appeal held that Leroux's conviction was wrongly found. It further held that it was improper to substitute a conviction under the proper section of the *Code* for one made under the wrong section. The real policy consideration which guided the court is to be found in these words taken from the judgment of Grant J.A.:

> In effect, the complainant, by threatening prosecution, endeavoured to obtain payment of a debt. What was done in this case amounted to an

---

51. *Ibid.* at p. 495.
52. *R. v. Thornton* (1926) 46 C.C.C. 249 (B.C. C.A.).
53. *Ibid.* at pp. 255-256.
54. *R. v. Leroux supra* footnote 46.

abuse of the process of the Court and should not be tolerated. Assuming that the accused was guilty of a criminal offence, if he had made some settlement with the complainant in consequence of which no charge had been laid, the complainant would have been guilty of compounding a felony. The criminal law was not enacted for the assistance of persons seeking to collect civil debts.[55]

R. v. Bell,[56] a 1929 case involving concealing and disposing of assets with intent to defraud creditors was another disgruntled creditor case to find its way into the British Columbia Court of Appeal. In that case the court asserted that "the criminal Courts are not to be held *in terrorem* over alleged debtors" and when they are used for that purpose the prosecution must be viewed as an unconscionable abuse of the process of the Magistrate's Court which will not be countenanced.[57] Once again the conviction of the accused was set aside.

Lest there be any false impression about these disgruntled creditor decisions it should be underscored that in all the cases discussed thus far (with the possible exception of *Leclair*) the results achieved were accomplished by means other than through the pure application of the doctrine of abuse of process. Consequently it is valid to insist that these references to the doctrine (and, to the Court's views of it) were nothing more than *obiter dicta,* and that therefore they should be viewed as being of little weight.

The modern application of the doctrine cannot be attacked in like manner. The "modern era", which is described *infra* as the "post-Osborn era", has not been reticent to allow the doctrine to stand free as an independent entity. The doctrine in the modern cases has not merely been confined in its operation (in the criminal law field) to the role of an underlying policy-motivator (albeit, a potent one) directing the ultimate result of a given case. These results were usually sustainable on other grounds. In some of the recent decisions the results achieved stemmed solely from an application of the doctrine. In other words the *ratio decidendi* of these cases was that an abuse of process was found to exist and was corrected by application of the court's inherent jurisdiction through the use of the doctrine.

The recent case of *Re State of Nebraska and Morris*[58] is a fine example of this point in action. The case can be properly characterized as a disgruntled creditor action. The State of Nebraska was seeking to extradite a Canadian citizen, one Morris, who was residing in Manitoba. It was alleged that Morris had violated the criminal law of the State of Nebraska by writing cheques based upon accounts having insufficient funds. Wilson J. refused extradition because it was clear that the proceedings were being brought in order to assist in the

---

55. *Supra* footnote 46 at pp. 56-57.
56. (1929) 51 C.C.C. 388 (B.C. C.A.).
57. See *ibid.* at pp. 391-392.
58. (1970) 2 C.C.C. (2d) 282 (Man.).

collection of a civil debt. The learned Judge found support for his reasoning in such early cases as *Michigan Central Railroad, Leroux, Thornton,* and *Bell.* In this regard he said:

> we read that since a crime is regarded as primarily a wrong done to the state, it follows that the criminal Courts are not to be held "in terrorem" over alleged debtors, and anyone who brings a criminal prosecution to compel payment of a civil claim is guilty of an abuse of the process of the Court.[59]

It is submitted that the disgruntled creditor cases cannot be viewed as isolated instances uniquely suited to excessive non-substantive utterances by our courts. Rather a discrete, discernible phenomenon — a thread weaving its way through the jurisprudence — is observable. Not all of the utterances may be dismissed as pure *obiter.* The line of extradition cases discussed by Wilson J. in *Re Nebraska and Morris* appends nicely to the contours of the issue and lends substantive support to it. *Michigan Central Railroad, Leroux, Thornton, Bell, Leclair, Lee, Brown,*[60] and *State of Nebraska and Morris,* represent a living line of acknowledgement by our courts of the vibrancy, viability and virility of the doctrine of abuse of process.

3. CONNELLY v. D.P.P.[61] AND R. v. OSBORN[62]

(1) Connelly v. D.P.P.

> The Solicitor General . . . insists that the Crown has a right to bring forward in its case as many indictments as it chooses and that the court is bound to proceed on each of them, whether or not it considers that the Crown is behaving oppressively. Thus, before the merits of this particular case can be considered there is raised for your lordships' determination a point of criminal procedure of the greatest importance which requires to be dealt with fully.[63]

---

59. *Ibid.* at p. 285. See also *Re McTier* (1910) 17 C.C.C. 80 (Que.) an extradition case cited by Wilson J. in *Re State of Nebraska and Morris* for yet another application of the doctrine to prevent the abuse of the criminal process by disgruntled creditors. And see the following cases (also cited by Wilson J.) as supportive of the proposition that extradition proceedings be not made a pretext for collecting private debts: *Loosberg v. Séquin* (1934) 61 C.C.C. 77 at p. 83 (Que.); *Re Low* (1932) 59 C.C.C. 97, reversed (1933) 59 C.C.C. 346 (Ont. C.A.); *Grin v. Shine* (1902) 187 U.S. Rep. 180 (U.S. S.C.). But see *contra Re Parker* (1890) 19 O.R. 612 at p. 616 and *Washington v. Fletcher* (1926) 46 C.C.C. 226 at p. 229 (Sask.). (Wilson J. distinguishes *Parker* and *Fletcher* at p. 286 of his judgment).

60. *R. v. Lee* and *R. v. Brown* are both cited *supra* in footnote 29. Along with *Leclair* they are of import for their recognition of the fact that while the court has inherent jurisdiction in certain circumstances to stay or dismiss a charge it must nevertheless exercise that power sparingly and only in exceptional circumstances.

61. [1964] 2 All E.R. 401.

62. (1970) 12 C.R.N.S. 1 (Can.), reversing [1969] 4 C.C.C. 185 (Ont. C.A.).

63. *Connelly v. D.P.P. supra* footnote 61 at p. 438 *per* Lord Devlin.

So wrote Lord Devlin. Mr. Connelly claimed that he had been oppressed. And the Crown's retort was that it had an unqualified discretion to behave oppressively (or at least, it was for the Crown to decide whether or not it was behaving oppressively, not the Court).

Connelly's appeal was dismissed. But the position of the Crown was repudiated.

At his original trial Connelly had been convicted of murder in connection with a robbery. His appeal to the Court of Criminal Appeal was successful. The trial judge had misdirected the jury on the issue of alibi. Since there was at that time no provision for the ordering of a re-trial in such circumstances Connelly appeared to have "slipped the noose". But Connelly was then charged, and convicted, of robbery. Once again Connelly appealed to the Court of Criminal Appeal. This time he was unsuccessful. A subsequent appeal was therefore launched to the House of Lords. One of the arguments advanced on his behalf was that the charge of robbery should have been quashed or stayed through the exercise of the trial court's discretionary power to prevent oppression and unfairness.

At issue was a determination of whether there existed in the Court a power, wider and more general than the special pleas of *autrefois acquit* and *convict,* and different from the defence of *res judicata* or issue estoppel. The implications were immense, extending beyond the simple confines of cases of double jeopardy. "For, if such concepts as "unjust", "oppressive" and "abuse of the process of the court" were given sufficiently wide definitions by the courts, the discretion contended for could presumably be exercised to stay an initial prosecution."[64]

Connelly sought to establish oppression by pointing up the multiplicity of proceedings brought against him by the state. This argument, tenable in other circumstances was rejected by the House of Lords in Connelly's case because the initial charge, being one of murder, could not (by virtue of a practice rule in England) be joined in an indictment with any other charge.[65]

Connelly lost his appeal because "it cannot be oppressive for the prosecution to do what the court has told it that it do".[66] But three of the five sitting justices[67] affirmed the existence of an inherent power to control abuses of the court's practice and procedures; with such power being of a breadth of stunning proportions. The remaining two Law Lords, Lord Morris and Lord Hodson, rejected the claim to the specific power argued for. They did however acknowledge that judges

---

64. P.C. Stenning *"Observations on the Supreme Court of Canada's Decision in R. v. Osborn"* (1970-71) 13 Cr.L.Q. 164 at pp. 167-168.
65. See s. 518 of the *Criminal Code* R.S.C. c. C-34 which accomplishes the same result in Canada through statutory enactment.
66. *Connelly v. D.P.P. supra* footnote 61 at p. 438 *per* Lord Devlin.
67. Lord Pearce, Lord Reid and Lord Devlin.

do have a certain inherent jurisdiction but they sought to limit it greatly:

> I accept that the history of the development of our law justifies the contention that all rules of common law which emanate from the breast of the judges may in a sense be said to be discretionary in origin, but I cannot concede that there ought to be given to the judge a discretion, which in my opinion he has not hitherto been allowed, to interfere with anything that he personally thinks is unfair. If one disclaims such a proposal but seeks to substitute a discretion to determine, in accordance with principle, whether or not a prosecution should be stopped, I do not know what principle can be applied. In the case now under consideration different judges will, as the history of the case shows, have different views as to what is unfair and I should find the discretion, if there is one, immensely difficult to exercise at all, nor should I know how to exercise it judicially.[68]

The complexity of the issue is evident in these passages culled from the reasons of Lord Morris:

> There can be no doubt that a court which is endowed with a particular jurisdiction has powers which are necessary to enable it to act effectively within such jurisdiction. I would regard them as powers which are inherent in its jurisdiction. A court must enjoy such powers in order to enforce its rules of practice and to suppress any abuses of its process and to defeat any attempted thwarting of its process . . . While, as I will endeavour to show, there has never been a rule that the same facts may not form the basis of successive charges, there is inherent in our criminal administration a policy and a tradition that even in the case of wrongdoers there must be an avoidance of anything that savours of oppression.[69]

> Indeed, under the English system of law criminal procedure has been conceived of as an action between a plaintiff and a defendant to be tried by a process substantially similar to that employed in any other action . . . It would, in my judgment, be an unfortunate innovation if it were held that the power of a court to prevent any abuse of its process or to ensure compliance with correct procedure enabled a judge to suppress a prosecution merely because he regretted that it was taking place. There is no abuse of process if to a charge which is properly brought before the court and which is framed in an indictment to which no objection can in any way be taken there is no plea such as that of autrefois acquit or convict which can successfully be made.[70]

It was Lord Devlin who argued most forcefully for a broad power to prevent abuses of the court's process. With only small reservations[71]

---

68. *Connelly v. D.P.P. supra* footnote 61 at p. 432 *per* Lord Hodson.
69. *Supra footnote* 61, at p. 409 *per* Lord Morris.
70. *Supra* footnote 61, at p. 411 *per* Lord Morris.
71.   "I agree with the opinion of my noble and learned friend, Lord Devlin, save in so far as I am not in accord with his more general criticism of issue estoppel. I agree with his remarks as to the practice to be followed in future" *per* Lord Pearce at p. 451 in *Connelly supra* footnote 61.

his reasoning was endorsed by Lord Reid and Lord Pearce. He noted (most importantly) "that nearly the whole of the English criminal law of procedure and evidence has been made by the exercise of the judges of their power to see that what was fair and just was done between prosecutors and accused." Further he observed that "the process is still continuing, and it is easy to think of recent examples."[72] The Judges Rules evolved in this way, as did notice requirements for additional witnesses who had not made depositions. The argument of the learned justice was further buttressed by reference to the use of the power in civil law.

Lord Pearce developed some of these arguments in his own judgment in the following fashion:

> "Just as in civil cases the court has constantly had to guard against attempts to relitigate decided matters, so, too, the court's criminal procedure needed a similar protection against the repetition of charges after an acquittal or even after a conviction which was not followed by a punishment severe enough to satisfy the prosecutor. It was, no doubt, to meet those two abuses of criminal procedure that the court from its inherent power evolved the pleas of autrefois acquit and autrefois convict. For obvious convenience these were pleas in bar and, as such, fell to be decided before the evidence in the second case was known. . . . However there is no reason why these two pleas should exhaust the inherent power of the court."[73]

Also, it was Lord Devlin who more strongly swept away the distinction which was being urged on the court; namely, that the position in civil cases was far different from that which prevailed in criminal cases; and hence, while the court in civil cases had wide powers to prevent abusive, vexatious, and harassing proceedings, in the criminal law domain it was not similarly endowed. These dicta of Lord Blackburn in *Castro v. R.*[74] were particularly important to Lord Devlin's analysis:

> I must say at once I totally disagree with what has been repeatedly asserted by both the learned counsel at the Bar — that the pleadings at common law in a criminal case and a civil case were in the slightest degree different. I am speaking, of course, of the time before the Judicature Acts were passed, which swept them all away. Many enactments had from time to time been passed relieving the strictness of pleadings in civil cases which did not relieve them in criminal cases, but the rules of pleading at common law were exactly the same in each case.

Considering Lord Blackburn's later judgment in *Metro. Bank v. Pooley,*[75] Lord Devlin concluded that "there can be no doubt that he

---

72. *Supra* footnote 61 at p. 438.
73. *Supra footnote* 61 at p. 447 *per* Lord Pearce.
74. [1881-5] All E.R. 429 at p. 436; 6 A.C. 229 at p. 243.
75. [1881-5] 10 A.C. 210 at p. 220 *per* Lord Blackburn. "But from early times . . . the Court had inherently in its power the right to see that its process

would have considered his words as applicable to criminal as to civil proceedings."[76]

In the result Lord Devlin was able to conclude that "judges of the High Court have in their inherent jurisdiction, *both in civil and in criminal matters,* power (subject of course to any statutory rules) to make and enforce rules of practice in order to ensure that the court's process is used fairly and conveniently by both sides".[77] As to the Crown's contention that "the danger of abuse is a matter for the Crown; the Crown itself may be trusted not to abuse its powers", this resounding retort, (at odds with the historical unreviewability of the discretionary activity of the Crown)[78] ostensibly signalled a new era:

> Are the Courts to rely on the executive to protect their process from abuse? Have they not themselves an inescapable duty to secure fair treatment for those who come or are brought before them? To questions of this sort there is only one possible answer. *The Courts cannot contemplate for a moment the transference to the executive of the responsibility for seeing that the process of law is not abused.*[79]

(2) R. v. Osborn

Although the decision in *Connelly* was rendered in 1964 Canadian courts did not consider that case until 1968. The first Canadian decision to embark upon such a consideration was *R. v. Osborn,*[80] a case which eventually found its way (via the Ontario Court of Appeal) into the Supreme Court of Canada.

Osborn was originally brought before the Court on an allegation involving s. 327(*b*) (then s. 312(*b*)) of the *Criminal Code of Canada.* He was acquitted. A Crown appeal against the acquittal proved unsuccessful. Notwithstanding these results the Attorney-General's department authorized the laying of a charge against Osborn of conspiracy to commit fraud — essentially the same charge on which Mr. Osborn had already been acquitted. Accordingly at the trial of the "new" charge Osborn pleaded *autrefois acquit* and also raised the defence of *res judicata.* Further, the defence also sought to have the

---

      was not abused by a proceeding without reasonable grounds, so as to be vexatious and harrassing . . ."

76. *Connelly v. D.P.P.* supra footnote 61 at p. 443 *per* Lord Devlin. See also footnote 36 for a portion of the passage referred to by Lord Devlin.

77. *Ibid.* at p. 438 (emphasis added).

78. *See R. v. Allen* (1862), 9 Cox C.C. 120 at p. 122 *per* Cockburn C.J.: "It cannot be contended for one moment that there can have been any abuse exercised by one whose functions are of so highly a responsible character; but if there had been — and I only put it hypothetically — the remedy is not by an application to this court to interfere by the exercise of its undoubted power and prerogative, but to hold him responsible before the High Court of Parliament." See also *Ex parte Newton* (1855) 4 E. & B. 869 at p. 871.

79. *Connelly v. D.P.P. supra* footnote 61 at p. 442 (emphasis added).

80. *Supra* footnote 62.

court exercise its inherent jurisdiction and stay proceedings on the basis that they were unfair and oppressive and an abuse of the process of the court. According to Jessup J.A. considering the matter in the Ontario Court of Appeal, "no express ruling was made by the trial Judge as to whether he considered he had such a discretionary power and after disallowing the plea of *autrefois* he simply directed the trial to proceed."[81] Osborn was convicted.

According to the judgment of the Ontario Court of Appeal, the sole ground[82] for appeal was that "the trial Judge had a discretion to stay or dismiss the indictment on the ground that it was so oppressive and vexatious as to amount to an abuse of the process of the Court and that such discretion should have been exercised in favour of the appellant."[83]

The Ontario Court of Appeal ruled in favor of Osborn, allowed his appeal and acquitted him. The existence of the inherent jurisdiction of the Court to prevent abuses of its own procedure (in criminal as well as in civil matters) was affirmed. Great reliance was placed upon the reasons for judgment of Lord Devlin in *Connelly v. D.P.P.* The judgment of the Ontario Court was delivered by Jessup J.A.[84] and is best summarized in the following passage:

> In my opinion, therefore, the learned trial Judge should have exercised his discretion as to whether or not he should stay the second indictment on the ground that it was so oppressive as to constitute an abuse of the process of the Courts. Since he failed to address himself to that decision this Court must do so. I am not prepared to hold that in the absence of special circumstances the laying of a second indictment upon the same facts is *simpliciter* and in all cases productive of such injustice as to invoke the Court's inherent jurisdiction. Everything depends on all the facts of the case. The discretion is to be exercised in favor of an accused only where a real injustice will otherwise result and such a case should be rare . . . Here . . . I think that the long delay coupled with the Crown's intervening appeal results in unjust oppressiveness from the second indictment. In my view the learned trial Judge would have properly exercised his jurisdiction by staying the proceedings before him.[85]

From this decision the Crown appealed to the Supreme Court of Canada. Only seven of the possible nine Judges sat on the appeal. In the result, the decision of the Court of Appeal was reversed and the conviction on the second indictment was restored. While the result

81. *R. v. Osborn*, [1969] 4 C.C.C. 185 at p. 187 (Ont. C.A.).
82. Phillip Stenning, *supra* footnote 64 at p. 165 indicates that the original Notice of Appeal filed by Osborn contained three grounds of appeal, none of which referred to abuse of process. A subsequent amended notice of appeal raised the issue for the consideration of the Court of Appeal.
83. *Osborn* (C.A.) *supra* footnote 81 at p. 187.
84. Concurred in by Gale C.J.O. and Laskin J.A. (as he then was).
85. *R. v. Osborn* (C.A.) *supra* footnote 81 at p. 191.

was clear in Osborn's case, the future of the doctrine of abuse of process was left mired in a sea of ambiguity.

Fauteux J. (later Chief Justice of Canada) giving judgment on an issue which Lord Devlin characterized as being "a point of criminal procedure of the greatest importance which requires to be dealt with fully" wrote (and this is all that he wrote) "I agree that the appeal should be allowed".[86]

Hall J. (with whom Ritchie and Spence JJ. concurred) felt that Jessup J.A. was "unduly impressed by the aspect of delay", and after reviewing the circumstances of the "long delay" concluded "that such delays as did occur were principally attributable to the respondent and not to the Crown."[87] Rather than decide the issue as to whether or not the doctrine of abuse of process was part of the court's inherent jurisdiction (as essup J.A. asserted in the Ontario Court of Appeal) Hall J. chose to sidestep the issue:[88]

> I do not think that the question of whether or not the Court has juris-diction to intervene to prevent an abuse of its process falls to be decided in the instant case because in my view there was here no evidence to support the conclusion of the learned Justice of Appeal that there was oppression.[89]

Pigeon J. (who was joined in his opinion by Martland and Judson JJ.) does not choose to give the issue such a wide berth. Instead he attempts to finesse the issue by narrowing it and then by rejecting the issue thus narrowed:

> In the instant case it does not appear to me that I need consider whe-ther the trial Judge had jurisdiction to make the order that the Court of Appeal held he should have made. *The real problem, in my view, is whether there exists in our criminal law a rule that in the case of a multiplicity of charges successively made on the same facts, a trial judge has discretion to stay an indictment when, on all the facts of the case, laying it is considered as an injustice amounting to oppression.*[90]

Thus the learned Justice in his formulation of the problem narrowed the general field of abuse of process to oppression caused by a "multi-plicity of charges successively made on the same facts". Proceeding on from this formulation Pigeon J. was then able to distinguish *R. v.*

---

86. *R. v. Osborn* (Can.) *supra* footnote 62 at p. 2.

87. *Ibid.* at pp. 5-6 *per* Hall J.

88. Darrell Roberts' contention in his address on "The Doctrine of Abuse of Process in Canadian Criminal Law" (1972) Report of the First Annual Conference of British Columbia Provincial Judges Association p. 39 at p. 41 that "three judges recognized the doctrine of abuse of process but simply declined to apply it in that case" is wrong. For what was actually decided by those three judges see the quotation taken from the judgment of Hall J. in the following passages.

89. *R. v. Osborn* (Can.) *supra* footnote 62 at p. 5.

90. *Supra* footnote 62 at p. 8 *per* Pigeon J. (emphasis added).

Osborn from *Connelly v. D.P.P.* on the basis that in Canada, unlike England, the practice as laid down in the Criminal Code was that successive multiple proceedings might be had by virtue of the right in Canadian appeal courts to order a new trial when a conviction is overturned.

> Concerning the opinions expressed in *Connelly v. Director of Public Prosecutions* . . . it is essential to observe that the basis of the difficulty in that case was a most important difference between our criminal law and the criminal law of England in force at that time.[91]
>
> .   .   .
>
> In this country Parliament's conception of fairness has always been, on the contrary [to the English practice], that when a conviction is quashed (Criminal Code, s. 592(2)) a new trial can be ordered instead of an acquittal and such is always the order made except in special circumstances.[92]
>
> .   .   .
>
> In our legal system it is not considered unfair or oppressive to have an accused undergo several trials on the same charge when his conviction is quashed, even if this happens repeatedly. In other words, it is not considered desirable that a criminal should escape punishment for a misdeed because an error was committed in his trial that requires his conviction to be quashed.[93]

The above passages represent the *ratio* of Pigeon J.'s judgment. Close inspection reveals that like Hall J. he has allowed the Crown's appeal because he could find no evidence of oppression. (Hall J. could find no oppression in the "long delays" since they were occasioned by Osborn, while Pigeon J. could find no oppression where the accused is acquitted on an incorrect charge and then is "brought to second trial on a fresh indictment for the correct charge.")[94] *Obiter* to the judgment of Pigeon J.[95] are the following observations which have led some commentators to the conclusion that germane to Pigeon J.'s judgment was a dismissal of the viability of the entire doctrine of abuse of process:

> It is basic in our jurisprudence that the duty of the courts is to apply

---

91. *Supra* footnote 62 at p. 8.
92. *Supra* footnote 62 at p. 9.
93. *Supra* footnote 62 at p. 10.
94. *Supra* footnote 62 at p. 10.
95. The concept of *obiter* comments is not lost on the learned Justice who remarked at p. 8 *per* Pigeon J.: "In this Court as in the Court of Appeal, counsel have been unable to cite any case in Canada where such a discretionary rule has been recognized or acted upon other than the obiter dictum of MacKay J.A. in *Regina v. Leclair,* [1956] O.W.N. 336, 23 C.R. 216, 115 C.C.C. 297 at 302." See also B. Haines, Annotation "Judicial ombudsmanship — A problem in policy" (1970) 12 C.R.N.S. 11 at p. 19: "Having found as a fact that Frederick John Osborn was not treated oppressively it may be that the balance of his judgment is obiter".

the law as it exists, not to enforce it or not in their discretion. As a general rule, legal remedies are available in an absolute way ex debito justitiae. Some are discretionary but this does not destroy the general rule. I can see no legal basis for holding that criminal remedies are subject to the rule that they are to be refused whenever, in its discretion, a court considers the prosecution oppressive.[96]

If one rejects the conclusion that the above remarks were *obiter* to the judgment of Pigeon J. then any logical consistency in the judgment is destroyed and one would be forced to conclude, as P.C. Stenning did, that "contradictions and inconsistencies make it almost impossible to find what is the *ratio* behind Pigeon J.'s decision in *Osborn*".[97] Stenning contends the inevitable implication of Pigeon J.'s views is that a multiplicity of successive charges which does not fall under the *autrefois acquit* plea or the *res judicata* defence cannot be considered oppressive by the courts. This quite clearly is what Pigeon J. appears to be saying, and it is consistent with his analysis whereby he distinguishes *Connelly.*

But it denies the very assumption upon which the original limited legal question which he set out to answer was based, namely, that such multiplicity can "on all the facts of the case" be "considered an injustice amounting to oppression". Furthermore . . . if there is truly "no legal basis for holding that criminal remedies are subject to the rule that they are to be refused whenever in its discretion, a court considers the prosecution oppressive", then the question of whether or not any kind of multiplicity of prosecution is oppressive is quite irrelevant. How then can it be said to be one of the reasons for allowing the appeal in this case?

4. THE POST-OSBORN EXPERIENCE — RECENT CANADIAN PRACTICE

(1) Bases on which relief sought

It has been said that an "abuse of legal process" occurs where a party employs the legal process for some unlawful object, not the purpose which it is intended by law to effect.[98] The "disgruntled creditor" cases (discussed *supra*) running through our Canadian criminal law jurisprudence during this century are an example of this phenomenon.

As has also been mentioned, the means by which the Courts protect their processes from abuse springs from the "inherent jurisdiction" of the court. The doctrine of "abuse of process" is convenient terminology for describing the various manifestations whereby the courts wield regulatory and supervisory powers over those who seek to employ the court's process for questionable or unfair advantage. As presently

---

96. *Supra* footnote 62 at p. 10.
97. P. C. Stenning *supra* footnote 64 at p. 173.
98. See *Morphy v. Shipley* 41 A.2d 671 at pp. 673-674.

utilized, the doctrine appears capable of affecting *all* parties concerned with a criminal prosecution: the accused,[99] the prosecutor, and even the police.[100] Without doubt the greatest number of instances where the doctrine has been used since the Supreme Court's decision in *R. v. Osborn* has been in the area of prosecutorial misconduct.

According to P. S. Barton the modern "bases on which the relief seems to have been sought includes the possibility that the administration of justice will be brought into disrepute, estoppel against the Crown by its conduct, harassment by the Crown and oppression of the accused, and delay in bringing the case to trial".[101] Generally speaking, this assessment is correct.

For the purposes of a closer examination and analysis of the use of the doctrine in the post-Osborn era, it is suggested that the following four categories comprehensively encompass the totality of the modern experience:

(1) general fairness and propriety in the conduct of a prosecution (fairness);

(2) dilatory proceedings (or, the aspect of delay in prosecution) (delay);

(3) multiple charges and/or a multiplicity of proceedings as an abuse of process (multiple processes);

(4) the use of the doctrine to establish a defence of entrapment (entrapment).

(2) The prosecutor's previously mythical status

Before entering upon a consideration of each of the four categories set out above, an important point must first be struck. Historically, the courts have always had a special regard for the office of the Attorney General, and for the representatives of that office, the Crown Attorneys. The virtues of the office as propounded in the various judgments from earliest times reached mythic proportions. The following extract from an annotation by Kenneth Chasse[102] accurately conveys the grandeur of these myths:

> Prior to *Osborn* the theory was that charges which were considered abusive would be controlled by the responsibility which the Attorney General owed the Legislature. In theory, other potential abuses would be taken care of by the Crown attorney — that "quasi-judicial officer" (*Regina v. Durocher*, 41 C.R. 350, 42 W.W.R. 396, [1964] 1 C.C.C.

---

99. See *Re Sproule* (1886) 12 S.C.R. 140 (Can.) and the discussion of that case *supra*.

100. In this regard see the discussion of abuse of process and police entrapment *infra*.

101. "Abuse of Process as a Plea in Bar of Trial" (1972-73) 15 Cr.L.Q. 437.

102. "Abuse of Process as a Control of Prosecutorial Discretion" (1970) 10 C.R.N.S. 392.

17), that "thirteenth juryman", that "silver thread in Canadian law" (Boyd McBride J.A. at p. 260 in *Regina v. Pearson* (1957), 25 C.R. 342, 21 W.W.R. 337, 117 C.C.C. 250), whose sense of fair play is as important to the accused as is the "golden thread" of *Woolmington v. Director of Public Prosecutions*, [1935] A.C. 462, 25 Cr. App. R. 72. The Crown attorney is that constant combatant who never wins and never loses (*Boucher v. The Queen,* [1965] S.C.R. 16, 20 C.R. 1, 110 C.C.C. 263) but is constantly effective in representing the interests of the community while being impeccably fair to the accused."[103]

With such high qualities ascribed to the Attorney General, and to the Crown attorney, it quite naturally was extremely difficult even to raise an issue of prosecutorial oppression, harassment, or unfairness. Such a prospect was considered to be almost unthinkable.

It cannot be contended for one moment that there can have been any abuse exercised by one whose functions are of so highly a responsible character; but if there had been — and I only put it hypothetically — the remedy is not by an application to this court to interfere by the exercise of its undoubted power and prerogative, but to hold him responsible before the High Court of Parliament.[104]

It has emerged as a historical fact in Anglo-Canadian jurisprudence that it is the sovereign's constitutional right to prosecute all crimes, and on his behalf the Attorney General institutes all prosecutions.[105] Since the Attorney General's discretion to prosecute emanates "from the Royal Prerogative of the Justice and its enforcement in maintaining the King's Peace"[106] the courts, in the main, have consistently held the bulk of prosecutorial discretionary practices to be immune from judicial supervision and oversight.

However, as Lord Devlin observed in *Connelly v. D.P.P.*[107] "nearly the whole of the English criminal law of procedure and evidence has been made by the exercise of the judges of their (inherent) power to see that what was fair and just was done between prosecutors and accused."[108] Not only did criminal evidence and procedure in *general* evolve in this fashion, said the Law Lords in *Connelly,* but also from its inherent power the court evolved the *special* pleas of *autrefois acquit* and *convict* to meet instances of prosecutorial abuse.[109]

As the decisions rendered in *Connelly* and in *Osborn* indicate, there are circumstances which may occur in which pleas of *autrefois*

103. *Ibid.* at pp. 392-393.
104. *R. v. Allen* (1862) 9 Cox C.C. 120 at p. 122 *per* Cockburn C.J.
105. See *R. v. Smythe* (1971) 3 C.C.C. (2d) 97 (Ont.); affirmed on appeal by the Ontario Court of Appeal and subsequently affirmed by (1971) 3 C.C.C. (2d) 366 (Can.)
106. *R. v. Smythe* (Ont. S.C.) *ibid.* at p. 107 *per* Wells C.J.H.C.
107. [1964] 2 All E.R. 401 (H.L.)
108. *Ibid.* at p. 438.
109. *Ibid.* at p. 447 *per* Lord Pearce.

acquit or *autrefois convict* will be inapplicable, but an abuse of process will nevertheless be manifest. The ordinary rules of evidence and procedure in such circumstances may be powerless to circumvent such an abuse. The doctrine of issue estoppel may be similarly impotent. Is the court then to be left crippled and unable to deal with a clear and open manipulation of its process for what must be regarded as a dubious advantage?

The answer to this last question seems obvious when one examines what the courts have said to be the over-all purpose of a criminal prosecution:

> *It cannot be over-emphasized that the purpose of a criminal prosecution is not to obtain a conviction, it is to lay before a jury what the Crown considers to be credible evidence relevant to what is alleged to be a crime.* Counsel have a duty to see that all available legal proof of the facts is presented; it should be done firmly and pressed to its legitimate strength, *but it must also be done fairly.* The role of the prosecutor excludes any notion of winning or losing; his function is a matter of public duty than which in civil life there can be none charged with greater personal responsibility. It is to be efficiently performed with an ingrained sense of *the dignity, the seriousness and the justness of judicial proceedings.*[110]

Hence the paradox confronting the modern evolution of our law. The prosecutor, a prime actor in the criminal law process, occupies a status, or position, traditionally held to be quasi-judicial in nature, and thus he is largely immune to judicial review of his discretionary activity. The courts, whose process the prosecutor employs, permit a latitude in the use of its process. But some prosecutorial activity, while ostensibly within the letter of the law, so profoundly challenges the role of the courts as the guarantor of the just and fair treatment of accused persons, that the permitting of the activity would serve to cast the administration of justice into disrepute.

Consequently, in the post-*Osborn* era the tendency in our courts has been to assert inherent powers over their jurisdiction, and to block abuses of process, through the termination of proceedings.

What all of this points up is that in a certain sense the evolution of the doctrine of abuse of process must be regarded as standing in opposition to the notion of unbridled prosecutorial discretion. Growth of the doctrine implies a diminution in the hegemony of the prosecutor.[111] This factor should be borne in mind when considering the four categories of cases in which the courts have employed the doctrine in the years since *Osborn*.

---

110. *Boucher v. R.* [1955] S.C.R. 16 at p. 23 *per* Rand J. (emphasis added).
111. For those who think otherwise see the annotations of K. L. Chasse in C.R.N.S. particularly as cited in footnote 102 *supra;* and in "The Re-laid Charge and Autrefois Acquit" (1971) 13 C.R.N.S. 196.

When considering these categories it should be remembered that the terms here employed (fairness, delay, multiple processes and entrapment) are more terms of convenience rather than distinct categories. The concepts often overlap. For instance, "fairness" and its corollary concern "oppression", are relevant considerations to all of the other categories. "Delay" may lead to the use of "multiple processes". And delay coupled with a multiplicity of proceedings may amount to oppression and unfairness. The mere presence of any, or indeed all, of these factors however, may not necessarily, in the eyes of the court, amount to an abuse of process. If there is one classification that is distinct and discrete it is "entrapment" — but it is also the category which is most questionable in validity. The conceptual system proposed here must therefore be viewed in "fluid", rather than "static", terms and cases discussed under one heading may be equally capable of treatment under another.

(3) Fairness

At approximately the same time as the Supreme Court of Canada was reversing the decision of the Ontario Court of Appeal in *Osborn* a Quebec Sessions Judge, Malouf J., was applying the Ontario Court of Appeal decision to a case which had found its way into his bailiwick.[112] The accused, a man by the name of Ittoshat, had been detained and transported from his home, the hamlet of Poste de la Baleine, to Montreal. It was intended that Ittoshat should stand trial (on a charge of causing a disturbance while drunk) in that metropolis. Montreal is one thousand miles distance from Poste de la Baleine.

The headnote of the case is as follows:

It is harsh and unfair treatment and tantamount to a denial of justice to bring an accused a thousand miles from his home to be tried for an offence which he is alleged to have committed. By forcing him to go through a trial in a completely different and unfamiliar environment necessitating the bringing of counsel from his own district or obtaining the benefit of counsel in an area where he does not know anybody and necessitating the transporting of witnesses from the place of the offence to place of trial effectively denies him the right to make full answer and defence. In such circumstances the proceedings should be stayed.[113]

Malouf J. in a thorough judgment did not merely ask whether the court had jurisdiction over the matter (he concluded that it did), he examined additionally the powers of the court to redress a wrong (he found support in *R. v. Osborn* (C.A.), *Haggard v. Pelicier Freres*,[114] *Connelly v. D.P.P.*[115], and *R. v. Shipley*[116]), and most importantly, he

---

112. *R. v. Ittoshat* [1970] 5 C.C.C. 159 (Que.).
113. *Ibid.* at p. 159. See also *R. v. Simons* (1976) 34 C.R.N.S. 273 at 277 (Ont. C.A.) to the same effect.
114. [1892] A.C. 61.
115. [1964] 2 All E.R. 401 (H.L.)
116. [1970] 3 C.C.C. 398 (Ont.).

considered whether the proceedings before him were in fact unjust.

Since the criminal code makes provision for an accused to make full answer and defence, and for an accused to examine and call such witnesses as he thinks fit, Malouf J. thought it "obvious, therefore, that since a defendant or an accused, has these basic rights, he must be given the opportunity to exercise them."

In *R. v. Burns*,[117] a case involving substantial aspects of delay — the accuseds were charged in February *1972* with intending to traffic in narcotics and the indictment was not drawn until April of *1974* — the Crown decided to add a major count to the indictment (importing narcotics) three years after the alleged event.

The Crown was able to satisfy the Court that the delays involved in prosecuting the offence were not oppressive. Delay of itself does not constitute oppression. However, Darling Co.Ct.J. did hold that the preferring of the additional count charging the importing of canabis resin was manifestly unfair and oppressive.

> I find that the Crown, in delaying the bringing of this second count for some 2½ years after the event, thereby not affording the accused the opportunity of giving instructions to counsel thereon prior to the preliminary inquiry, and thereby not giving an opportunity to their counsel to cross-examine Crown witnesses on this issue at the hearing; and the denying to the defence of the ability to consider their position until nearly three years after the event, amounts to behavior so oppressive as to constitute an abuse of the process of this Court if this charge were allowed to continue to trial.[118]

Once again the issue before the court was not merely one of the jurisdiction of the court or of the legality of the process which the Crown sought to employ. By virtue of s. 507 of the *Criminal Code* the Crown had the legal right to add the additional count and the learned county court judge so held. ("Accordingly, I find I cannot give effect to the defence grounds put forth in . . . the notice of motion . . . and I must agree with the position taken by Crown counsel with respect of s. 507 of the Criminal Code.")[119]

Robert Ian Smith was the victim of a broken plea bargain.[120] Smith had been promised immunity from prosecution by the Crown in return for cooperation with the authorities. Smith acting in good faith had yielded up a quantity of marijuana and had voluntarily confessed to complicity in securing the drug. He was thereafter charged with conspiracy to possess narcotics for the purpose of trafficking, and conspiracy to traffic in narcotics.[121] Counsel for Smith moved to prohibit the County Court in British Columbia from trying these two charges.

Berger J. acceded to the representations of Smith's counsel.

---

117. (1975) 30 C.R.N.S. 387 (B.C.).
118. *Ibid.* at pp. 399-400.
119. *Ibid.* at p. 397

I think that in the case at bar it would be an abuse of the process of the Court to allow the Crown to proceed with the trial of the accused Smith on these allegations of conspiracy. I think it would be altogether wrong if the Crown, having made a promise to Smith, were to be allowed to turn around and proceed with charges of conspiracy based on the admissions made by the accused and the evidence turned in by him.[122]

The foregoing cases are not presented in order to leave an impression that whenever an arguable case of unfairness or oppression can be demonstrated the courts will utilize their inherent discretion and stay such proceedings as an abuse of process. The Supreme Court's decision in *Osborn* did leave a legacy of divided opinion within our judiciary.

Thompson J. in *Re R. and Carpenter*[123] confronted with a situation involving one mistrial due to misreceived evidence, a second as a result of a hung jury, and a third stayed by a county court judge as an abuse of process, felt that the "true position is that stated by Pigeon J., in his reasons for judgment in the *Osborn* case . . . concurred in by Martland and Judson, J.J."[124] Accordingly he granted an order of mandamus compelling Carpenter's third trial to continue.

What is unfair or oppressive in such case is not to be determined by the individual or personal views of a presiding Judge of the circumstances, but there must be some legal basis for such a finding.[125]

Carpenter's case might have been resolved as it was without the necessity of disapproving of the doctrine of abuse of process. Not every alleged unfairness amounts to an abuse of process.

Indeed, Thompson J.'s position is decidedly the minority view in British Columbia today. *Burns, Smith,* and *Carpenter* were all decisions of British Columbia courts. Berger J. in fact contends (probably correctly) that since the decision of the British Columbia Court of Appeal in *R. v. Croquet*[126] the law is settled in that province that

---

120. See *R. v. Smith* [1975] 3 W.W.R. 454 (B.C.).
121. Smith had an outstanding charge of possession of marijuana for the purpose of trafficking at the time these events transpired. The preliminary hearing was held and Smith was committed to stand trial. The two additional counts referred to were included in the indictment preferred subsequent to the committal on the initial offence.
122. *R. v. Smith supra* footnote 120 at p. 457.
123. (1972) 5 C.C.C. (2d) 28 (Ont.).
124. *Ibid.* at p. 31.
125. *Ibid.* at p. 31.
126. *R. v. Croquet* (1972) 21 C.R.N.S. 232, affirmed on appeal by 23 C.R.N.S. 374 (B.C. C.A.).
    See also *R. v. Heric* [1975] 4 W.W.R. 422 (B.C.) which involved a charge of "over .08", and, subsequently, after the .08 charge was dismissed, a charge impaired driving. In that case the court held that although proceeding with a matter by way of a new charge where an adjournment has been refused is not *per se* an abuse of the process of the Court, here the defence

abuse of process exists as a viable doctrine and forms part of the inherent jurisdiction of the court.

> Prohibition will lie where there has been a violation of the fundamental principles of justice . . . The superior courts, exercising their inherent power to stop such proceedings, may intervene where the process of an inferior court is being abused. Authority for all of these propositions is to be found in my judgment in *Regina v. Croquet* . . . That case went to the Court of Appeal:
>
> . . . Branca J.A. agreed with my reasons for judgment. Seaton J.A., speaking for MacLean J.A. and himself, did not purport to determine these questions, but indicated that he leaned to the view that the superior courts have the power to restrain proceedings which constitute an abuse of process. That appears to lay to rest in this province any argument as to the jurisdiction of this Court to intervene on such grounds.[127]

The *Croquet* case to which Berger J. refers involved a prosecution under the Income Tax Act. The Crown in that case literally "conceded" the trial when certain exhibits were ruled to be inadmissible and invited the obliging trial judge to dismiss the charge "on the merits". The Crown then sought to appeal by trial *de novo*. Counsel for the accused attempted to block the proceedings by claiming oppression tantamount to an abuse of process. When the county court judge denied these claims an application was made to the British Columbia Supreme Court for certiorari and prohibition. These applications were dismissed as was the subsequent appeal by Croquet to the Court of Appeal. While it is to be regretted that the accused had to linger in jeopardy throughout all this and then to undergo the rigors of a second full trial it is difficult to disagree with the position taken by Berger J. and by Branca J.A.

> The approach now taken by the Crown forces the appellant to face a new trial, new costs and continued anxiety. This is regrettable, but I am unable to say that the conduct constitutes oppression which might be characterized as an abuse of the process of the Court.[128]

An interesting contrast to *R. v. Croquet* is the case of *A.G. Sask. v. McDougall*,[129] a decision of the Saskatchewan District Court. By the addition of one or two extra factors to *essentially* the same fact

---

had requested an adjournment and been refused by the Crown, and then the Crown did not let the defence know it would not be able to proceed. The Court was therefore right to refuse the adjournment and acquit the accused. The procedure then adopted by the Crown — the laying of a new charge — attempted to circumvent the decision of the Court. The actions of the Crown were considered an affront to the Court constituting an abuse of its process.

127. *Per* Berger J. in *R. v. Smith supra* footnote 120 at p. 457.

128. *R. v. Croquet* (1973) 23 C.R.N.S. 374 at p. 379 (B.C. C.A.) *per* Branca J.A.

129. [1972] 2 W.W.R. 66 (Sask.).

situation oppression amounting to an abuse of process was found to exist.

The accused McDougall had been acquitted at an initial trial of a charge laid under the breathalyzer sections of the Criminal Code. As in *Croquet* there had been a failure to adduce certificate evidence. (In *Croquet* it was rejected; in *McDougall* it was simply not tendered due to insufficient preparation by the Crown.) Once again the Crown sought to appeal by trial *de novo*. At this point the Crown indicated its intention to adduce evidence of the breathalyzer test. McDougall through his counsel raised the issue of abuse of process.

This extract taken from the headnote of the case indicates the factual distinctions from *Croquet* and demonstrates how Batten D.C.J. was able to dismiss the Crown appeal as an abuse of the court's process:

> while the process of appeal by way of trial de novo was open to certain abuses by its very nature, these abuses were equally available to an accused as to the Crown; the laying of a second information on the same facts, such as occurred in the case at bar, and the taking of an appeal by way of trial de novo could not, in themselves, be said to be productive of such injustice as to invoke the court's inherent jurisdiction; *but in the case at bar the Crown's first information was withdrawn and another, based on identical facts was laid;* the Crown had ample opportunity in the subsequent trial of adducing all the evidence necessary to support the charge; it did not choose to do so and respondent was acquitted. To permit the Crown now to appeal by way of trial de novo, leading fresh evidence, would, in light of all the circumstances, be a clear case of abuse of the court's process. (emphasis added)[130]

What this summary does not provide (but the judgment reveals) is that the first information was withdrawn at the request of an officer of the R.C.M.P. after numerous adjournments and (impliedly) because the prosecuting forces were simply not prepared to proceed. Obviously, after having the temerity to lay another information the authorities were still in disarray and unable to proceed at the time of the first trial.

Seen in this light it appears that Batten D.C.J. was cognizant of, and operating within the confines of, the dictum that the special jurisdiction carved out by the operation of the doctrine of abuse of process "ought to be exercised very sparingly and only in exceptional cases".

(4) Delay

As Darling Co.Ct.J. pointed out in *R. v. Burns,*[131] delay, in and of itself, does not constitute oppression. Further, he implied that where delay which might otherwise be oppressive can be explained then the situation will not be such as to justify resort to the doctrine of abuse

---

130. *Ibid.* at p. 67.
131. *Supra* footnote 117.

of process. Other cases go on to elaborate that where the delay is in no way due to the conduct of the Crown but is occasioned by the tactics of the defence, or emanates from the Court itself, application of the doctrine cannot be countenanced.

From this it can be learned that even under the doctrine of abuse of process it is possible for an accused to suffer oppression without the opportunity to redress.

In this connection consider the case of *R. v. Atwood*.[132] The accused in that case had been charged with two offences under the Criminal Code. After entering pleas of "not guilty" a date for trial was set. On the date set for trial the Crown requested and was granted an adjournment because an important witness was unavailable for trial on the date originally scheduled. A new trial date was set and marked peremptory. Subsequently the Crown stayed proceedings in order that the accused might be detained and transferred to Alberta for psychiatric examination. Jurisdiction for such procedures exists under the *Mental Health Ordinance, 1971 (2nd Sess.) (N.W.T.), c. 13.* As events transpired two new informations charging the identical offences to those which had been stayed were laid and Atwood was once again brought before a Magistrate. At that time objection was taken to the charges by counsel for Atwood and they were quashed as an abuse of process. Thereupon the Crown applied to the Territorial Court for an order in the nature of certiorari to remove and quash the order of the Court below. This application was granted.

Morrow J. while sympathizing with the plight of the accused noted that the stay of proceedings which were entered with full knowledge of the peremptory trial date were "undoubtedly prompted by the proceedings that had been taken with respect to the accused under the Mental Health Ordinance". The procedure under the Ordinance struck the learned justice as both "reprehensible and dangerous . . . particularly when the same ends could have been achieved under the Criminal Code."[133] Also he expressed sympathy with the plight of the Magistrate who was faced with the entry of a stay "without even the courtesy of the Crown appearing before him, particularly when as here there was a peremptory trial date."[134] The portion of the judgment however, which is most germane is this one:

> But do these two aspects of themselves provide sufficient factual basis for holding that there was an abuse of process. It is to be remembered that defence counsel in his submission made it clear to the learned magistrate that he was making no imputation of bad faith in the motivation of the Crown Attorney. Again, although it may have been inconvenient, none the less, the defence made no attempt to attack what

132. (1972) 7 C.C.C. (2d) 116, reversed (1972) 8 C.C.C. (2d) 147 (N.W.T.).
133. See (1972) 8 C.C.C. (2d) 147 at p. 155.
134. *Ibid.* at pp. 155-156.

was done under the *Mental Health Ordinance* by *habeas corpus* or other proceedings but rather took a submissive role.

While therefore, I have every sympathy with the learned magistrate, and agree that he was completely justified in being upset and disturbed with what went on and in the manner in which his Court was treated, I cannot find evidence that would remove this case from the norm.[135]

Perhaps it would be useful at this point to place a caveat on the analysis thus far. The cases here presented are not offered as evidence of abundant rationality. In many of the abuse of process cases, present and past, civil as well as criminal, there have been questionable applications of the doctrine just as there have been vexing refusals to apply the doctrine. Application of the doctrine while springing from inherent jurisdiction is nevertheless a *discretionary* power. Obviously then there will be instances of its use or non-use upon which reasonable men may differ. What will be regarded as an "exceptional" case calling for the application of the doctrine by one judge may not necessarily be so regarded by another. The division of opinion between Magistrate DeWeerdt and Mr. Justice Morrow in *Atwood* is a case in point.

A good example of a case of delay amounting to such oppression as to justify resort to the use of the doctrine is the case of *R. v. Thorpe,*[136] a decision of an Ontario County Court. In that case the accused Thorpe was charged with indecent assault in June of 1970. Six adjournments (five at the request of the Crown) were had before the preliminary hearing was finally held in March of 1971. It was not until two years later, in March of 1973 that a bill of indictment was presented to the Grand Jury. A "true bill" was returned at that time. No communication had been addressed to the accused or his counsel until April of 1973 when advice was forwarded by the Crown that the trial of the matter was scheduled for April of 1973. A motion made to Shapiro Co.Ct.J. to stay the proceedings as an abuse of the process of the court was granted.

An interesting sidelight to the case resides in this rare but altogether

---

135. *Ibid.* at p. 156.
136. (1973) 11 C.C.C. (2d) 502 (Ont.). See also *Re R. and Rourke* (1974) 16 C.C.C. (2d) 133 (B.C.) where "unconscionable delay" by the Crown in instituting proceedings prejudiced the accused in obtaining witnesses and presenting his defence. Ladner Co. Ct. J. stayed proceedings as an abuse of process, and Rae J. of the B.C. Supreme Court refused the Crown's application for mandamus to compel the proceedings to be continued. This case has subsequently been reversed by the British Columbia Court of Appeal: [1975] 6 W.W.R. 591 and is under appeal to the Supreme Court of Canada. McIntyre J.A. for the Court felt that in order to justify a stay of criminal proceedings the abuse must appear in the proceedings themselves. Inordinate delay in the investigatory stage of proceedings prior to the initiation of proceedings was held not to warrant the exercise of the judicial discretion to grant a stay.

appropriate application of the *Canadian Bill of Rights*[137] *in* "quasi-obiter" fashion:

> Finally, I wish to say something about the *Canadian Bill of Rights,* R.S.C. 1970, App. III. Section 2 refers to the non-infringement of the "right to a fair hearing in accordance with the principles of fundamental justice". If those words are to have any meaning, and indeed if the document itself is to be regarded as something other than a repository for empty platitudes, it must be applicable to a case such as this where there has been a long delay, with its resulting concomitant problems. Even if the *Canadian Bill of Rights* is not applicable . . . at trial but rather on a motion prior thereto, I consider that the matter comes within the purview of this Court to guard against an abuse of its process.[138]

Indictable offences such as were involved in *Atwood* and *Thorpe* are not subject to time limitations in initiation or institution of proceedings stage. The discovery of a dead body many years after the murderous event which caused the death may lead to laying of charges notwithstanding the elapsed time. On the other hand the complainant who wishes to initiate a complaint seven months after the fact of a common assault is statute-barred for the applicable limitation for most summary conviction offences is six months. But what of the situation of the alleged minor transgressor who knowingly, or unknowingly, contravenes a statute and then five months and twenty-six days after the alleged event is charged with committing an offence? Has he been oppressed by the delay? Can there be oppression if the delay is not so great as to contravene a statutory time limitation? Gyles, Chief Magistrate felt that in such circumstances there could be oppression and great unfairness and in *R. v. Muttner; R. v. Acme Produce (1969) Co.*[139] he dismissed two informations laid five months and four days after the commission of alleged offences under the *Weights and Measures Act,* R.S.C., 1952 c. 292. The Manitoba Court of Appeal disagreed with him.

In *Muttner* the unfairness which the accused complained of was that they were engaged in numerous transactions all of a similar nature and without early notification they could not identify the incidents referred to and thus adequately make their full answer and defence. In such circumstances they contended to force them to trial would be to deny them their right to a fair hearing contrary to s. 2(*e*) of the *Canadian Bill of Rights.*

The words "abuse of process" were not employed in either of the judgments. It is to be doubted however, that had they been, that the end result would have been different.

---

137. More detailed consideration of the Canadian Bill of Rights and its connection to the doctrine of abuse of process will be offered *infra.*

138. *R. v. Thorpe supra* footnote 136 at p. 510.

139. [1972] 2 W.W.R. 687, reversed 8 C.C.C. (2d) 114 (Man. C.A.).

In spite of the sympathetic concern one might have for an accused who cannot remember whether he did commit a guilty act or not, Parliament has prescribed what the rights and obligations are between the accused and (in this case) the consumer; and in our view it is not open to this or any other Court to arrogate unto itself the power to amend, alter, or modify the clear and unambiguous words of the enactment. In other words, since Parliament considered six months is a reasonable and fair time in which to prosecute, it is not open to a Judge to substitute his views for those of Parliament.[140]

In the cases discussed thus far for the most part the delays complained of were occasioned by the prosecuting forces (the Crown and the police). As has been mentioned however, there are cases where delay may be occasioned by the Court itself. The accused in these circumstances may suffer oppression and unfairness which is just as real and meaningful as that caused by the Crown. As yet no court has seen fit to take upon itself the responsibility for staying charges as an abuse of process when it itself has been responsible for the abuse.[141]

In *R. v. Myles (No. 2)*[142] the Court admitted responsibility for some adjournments and delay. The accused had earlier been successfully able to argue loss of jurisdiction over his charge due to a procedural defect and the Crown had thereupon validly commenced a second proceeding based upon the same facts against him. This manoeuvre in itself entailed delay. The court declined to find oppression amounting to an abuse of process.

> Can such a procedure be considered an abuse of process? It is my opinion that it cannot. The accused has taken advantage of the judicial

---

140. *R. v. Muttner* (C.A.) *ibid*, at pp. 119-120 *per* Guy J.A.
141. A variant on this point occurred in the unreported decision of *R. v. Martens* [1975] 4 W.W.R. 540 (B.C.). In that case the trial Judge refused to proceed with the hearing of a cause disturbance charge bid against twelve accused because the room furnished for the trial on the date set was deemed to be inadequate for the holding of a proper trial. The Crown requested an adjournment until February 10, at which time the proceedings could only continue for one day and thereafter on Mondays only. In a sense therefore, the delay was occasioned by the original reluctance by the provincial judge to proceed. He felt however that the resulting adjournment and inconvenience would be "unfair to the accused". Therefore he refused the adjournment and dismissed the charges. The Crown appealed by stated case to the Supreme Court and the appeal was dismissed. It was there felt that the failure of the Crown to provide suitable courtroom facilities warranted the provincial judge's refusal to conduct the trial in the small, crowded and inadequate room provided. The exercise of discretion in not allowing the Crown an adjournment was judicial and in keeping with principle in view of the Crown's unreasonableness as to how the trial should subsequently proceed.
142. (1972) 18 C.R.N.S. 84 (N.S.). See also *Re Vroom and Lacey*, 14 C.C.C. (2d) 10 (Ont.) where prohibition did not lie despite repeated delays which were in no way occasioned by the accused. In spite of the delay on the part of the Crown in bringing the accused to trial the facts did not bear out the theory that the proceedings were so oppressive that prohibition should be granted.

process to establish the rule that the Court which held the preliminary inquiry proceeded without jurisdiction and, having done so, he cannot now say that that process was abusive. If anything the contrary is true — it is far from an abuse of process to be able to prevail in one court with that argument which was rejected in another. The accused is again before the court as the result of the relaying of the information; the information was re-laid as the result of the ruling of the County Court which in turn came about as the result of the proper use of the judicial process by the accused. It is my opinion that he cannot now say that there has been an abuse of the judicial process and that he has suffered from it.[143]

The general import of the above comments will be of interest to the ensuing discussion of the aspect of multiple processes and the doctrine of abuse of process.

(5) Multiple processes

It was this aspect of the modern doctrine of abuse of process around which the cases of *Connelly v. D.P.P.* and *R. v. Osborn* revolved. The central or core question embraced by this category is whether a multiplicity of successive charges arising out of the same circumstances (which do not sustain a plea of "autrefois acquit" or a defence of "res judicata") will ever be regarded by a court as being unfair and so oppressive as to justify the termination or quashing of proceedings by operation of the doctrine of abuse of process.

Pigeon J. in *Osborn* appeared to feel that, if the special pleas or defences were not available, then multiple prosecutions could not be viewed as oppressive.

> In our legal system it is not considered unfair or oppressive to have an accused undergo several trials on the same charge . . . even if this happens repeatedly. In other words, it is not considered desirable that a criminal should escape punishment for a misdeed because an error was committed in his trial that requires his conviction to be quashed. I fail to see why a totally different view should be taken if the error consists in not laying the correct charge so that, instead of being irregularly convicted and then ordered to stand a new trial, he is acquitted of the incorrect charge and then brought to second trial on a fresh indictment for the correct charge.[144]

As the previous analysis of the *Osborn* case indicated the judgments

---

143. *R. v. Myles, ibid.* at pp. 87-88.
144. *R. v. Osborn* (1970) 12 C.R.N.S. 1 at p. 10 (Can.) *per* Pigeon J. The quoted passage evidences one of two facets of the "multiple processes" category of abuse of process. The two facets of this phenomenon are: (1) "splitting the case" — where the Crown proceeds at two different times on two separate informations arising out of the same facts; (2) the recommencement of previously terminated proceedings — *e.g.* where the Crown stays proceedings, withdraws charges, presents no evidence etc. and then seeks to recommence or begin proceedings anew.

there rendered "in toto" proved inconclusive and thus have in later years proved to be devoid of authority.

The problem of multiple processes involves more than the issue of re-laying charges. As the *Connelly* case indicated it involves as well the notion of "splitting a case" (breaking one transaction down into several).

Conceptually it (multiple processes) is probably the most complex and confusing of all of the modern manifestations of the doctrine of abuse of process.

During the course of the prosecution of a criminal offence a variety of situations may occur which reasonably give rise to an expectation in the mind of an accused that he has escaped the jeopardy which befell him when he was originally charged. Some of these situations occur when

(1) the Crown enters a stay of proceedings on the charge

(2) the Crown withdraws the charge

(3) the accused makes a motion for want of prosecution and the charges are dismissed

(4) at the conclusion of the preliminary hearing the Crown's motion for committal is rejected and the accused is discharged

(5) at the outset of the proceedings (usually before plea) the accused moves to quash the information for a defect apparent upon its face and the court complies with the request

(6) on the date set for trial the Crown submits no evidence and the accused is acquitted.

Counsel would be remiss in his duty to his client if he did not advise that in any of the above circumstances there remained the possibility of further proceedings. The discretion of whether or not to institute further proceedings belongs to the prosecutor. There have been instances in Canadian legal history where the course of action adopted by a prosecutor has been manifestly unfair, even contemptuous of the court and the jury, and yet fresh proceedings have been allowed. Such a case was *R. v. Beaudry.*[145]

The *Beaudry* case involved a jury trial which had commenced to the stage that the prosecution's entire case had been presented, addresses had been made by counsel, and the trial judge had directed the jury to bring in a verdict of acquittal. Before the jury could return its verdict the prosecutor directed the clerk to enter a stay of proceedings in the matter thus preserving the Crown's right to initiate further proceedings against the accused at a future date. The procedure adopted by the Crown was sustained by the British Columbia Court of Appeal.

It is doubted that *Beaudry* would have been resolved in the fashion

---

145. (1967) 50 C.R. 1 (B.C. C.A.).

that it was, in the Post-Osborn era — particularly in view of the documented use of the doctrine of abuse of process by the British Columbia Courts since 1970.

The plea of "autrefois acquit" has for the most part been ineffective to bar the vexatious and oppressive re-institution of proceedings. The following quotation, (dealing with the *specific* issue of withdrawals) aptly sums up the *general* law on this point.

> The main principle to be gathered from all the many cases, not always consistent or exact, and based in varying circumstances, that we have considered is that, unless it can be said on the facts of the particular case that there has been an adjudication and acquittal upon the merits, the permission of the Court to withdraw a charge is not equivalent to a dismissal which can be pleaded in bar of subsequent proceedings.[146]

The modern usage of the doctrine of abuse of process has dramatically altered this situation. All of which does not sit well with Kenneth Chasse, a Crown Attorney and annotator of the Criminal Reports (New Series).[147] According to Chasse an "adjudication upon the merits" should be the sole determinant as to whether or not the prosecutor may re-institute proceedings against an accused. (It is useful at this point to remember that in *R. v. Beaudry* there had been no adjudication upon the merits.) Characteristics of "unfairness" or "oppression" do not enter into this equation save in so far as they may be factor affecting a Crown Attorney's unfettered discretion.

The following is an unreported judgment of the Manitoba Court of Appeal delivered on September 11, 1970.[148] It as much as any other decision exemplifies the modern practice. Since the judgment is short it is reproduced here in full:

> In our opinion the inherent right of a Court to protect its process from abuse is not limited to civil proceedings but extends to criminal matters as well.
>
> In the present case the charge against the accused had been dismissed

---

146. *R. v. Somers* [1929] 3 D.L.R. 772 at pp. 777-778 (B.C. C.A.) *per* Martin J.A.
147. See the following annotations by K. Chasse: "Abuse of Process as a Control of Prosecutorial Discretion", (1970) 10 C.R.N.S. 392; and "The Re-laid Charge and Autrefois Acquit", (1971) 13 C.R.N.S. 196
148. *R. v. Allison* (unreported, September 11, 1970) (Man. C.A.). But see *R. and Neish, Re* (1975) 24 C.C.C. (2d) 379 (Alta. C.A.) where the Crown failed to appear on the date set for argument on an allegedly duplicitous information. A new charge was subsequently laid and dismissed prior to plea as an abuse of the Court's process. On an application by the Crown for an order of *mandamus, held,* the application should be granted. The action of the Crown did not amount to an abuse of process. The Crown by laying a new charge was merely exercising a right which it would have had in any event had the original charge been dismissed for duplicity. The Crown's "cavalier" disregard for the Court was adequately dealt with by the order of the Court dismissing the original charge.

by the learned Magistrate on February 4, 1969, for want of prosecution. An adjourn — to an unstated date after May 4, 1969, had been asked for but denied by the learned Magistrate. The bar is for the application for an adjournment had been that the complainant was in Nova Scotia and would not return until May 4, 1969.

The second information for the same offence was not laid until September 19, 1969, and no explanation for this long delay is on the record.

In these circusmtances we look upon the second information as vexatious, oppressive and an abuse of the process of the Court. Therefore the motion made by counsel for the accused to dismiss the second information should have been granted.

Accordingly the appeal is allowed and the conviction is quashed.[149]

Clearly not every re-institution of stayed, withdrawn, or dismissed proceedings can amount to an abuse of the process of court. The sections of the criminal code dealing with the re-commencement of stayed proceedings[150] and the preferring of indictments[151] demonstrate a clear power in the prosecutor to renew his efforts in a proper circumstance. But the recent practice most notably in British Columbia has been for the court to oversee these exercises of prosecutorial discretion.

A quartet of recent British Columbia decisions[152] all mirror a judicial concern with prosecutorial attempts to circumvent adverse judicial decisions. This may very well be the legacy of the show of prosecutorial arrogance which took place in *Beaudry*.

None of these cases were "ordinary" on their facts. The circumstances of all (save those in *R. v. McAnish*[153]) were rare and unusual — the clear and exceptional cases of the type demanded by precedent.

The *Koski* case involved an accused who appeared in court at least six times before a peremptory date for trial was set. The Crown was not prepared to proceed subsequently on the fixed peremptory date and the informations were dismissed. The Crown thereupon had new informations sworn and the juvenile accused was brought before Murphy Prov.Ct.J. who held she could not dismiss them as an abuse. Special leave to appeal the denial of the motion to dismiss was sought under s. 37 of the *Juvenile Delinquents Act*.[154] Munroe J. strongly disapproved of the attempts by the Crown to "circumvent the judgment of

---

149. *Ibid. per* Smith C.J.M.
150. See the *Criminal Code,* R.S.C. 1970, c. C-24, s. 508(1) and (2); and s. 732.1(1) and (2).
151. *Criminal Code* s. 505(1) through (4)
152. *R. v. McAnish* (1973) 15 C.C.C. (2d) 494 (B.C.); *R .v. Del Puppo* [1974] 3 W.W.R. 621 (B.C.); *R. v. Kiley* [1971] 2 WW.R. 551 (B.C.); *R. v. Koski* (1972) 5 C.C.C. (2d) 46 (*sub nom. R. v. K.*) (B.C.).
153. This case seems to be little more than an example of poor choice of procedure by the Crown which could merely have recommenced its stayed proceeding rather than lay a new charge. Jones Prov.Ct.J. was moved to observe "Why that particular procedure has not been pursued in this case I do not know".
154. R.S.C. 1970, c. J-3.

the Juvenile Court denying the application for an adjournment". His judgment reveals the oppression and unfairness which was consequent upon the Crown's actions:

> Now, the Crown seeks to begin anew. At least one defence witness is no longer available. More than one year has elapsed since the date of the alleged offence. The appellant has made no less than seven appearances in Court. No part of the delay in proceeding to trial has been attributable to the appellant. He has been subjected during the past 13 months to embarrassment, expense, and a continuing state of anxiety. To permit the Crown now to begin anew would constitute unwarranted harrassment, in my opinion. Proceedings upon the second information should be stayed on the ground that they are so oppressive as to constitute an abuse of the process of the Court and I so hold.[155]

The decision in *R. v. Del Puppo* relied heavily upon the pronouncements of Munroe J. in *Koski*. Once again the familiar pattern of lengthy and numerous adjournments secured at the request of the Crown emerges. Once again an initial information is dismissed (for want of prosecution). And once again the Crown seeks to begin anew; this time perhaps even more insidiously, and more unfairly. This is so because *at the very least* the *appearance* was left that the Crown was using the tactic of adjournment and delay for the purpose of re-arresting and prosecuting *Del Puppo* for his alleged offence *only after* he completed serving a term of imprisonment for a pre-existing charge.

In staying the proceedings as an abuse of process Allan Prov.Ct.J. quoted the remarks of the Chief Justice of Canada which were contained in a previous judgment of Branca J.A.[156] of the British Columbia Court of Appeal:

> It has come to our attention that some law enforcement authorities follow the practice of holding warrants of arrest for inmates of penal institutions, the acknowledged intention being that, after these inmates have served their current sentences, they will be re-arrested and required to face the charges contained in the warrants.
>
> We cannot condemn this practice too emphatically. Where the authorities hold a warrant for the arrest of an inmate serving a sentence of imprisonment for another offence they should direct that appropriate proceedings be taken forthwith to have all known outstanding charges against the prisoner disposed of immediately . . . [157]

Some of the cases are truly curious. The Crown in these particular instances has met with failure at first instance and has had charges dismissed or the accused discharged. Nevertheless there appeared to be left open to the Crown (leaving aside for the moment the aspect of oppression) the possibility of lawfully recommencing proceedings.

---

155. *R. v. Koski, supra* footnote 152 at p. 48.
156. The case in question was *R. v. Parisien* [1971] 4 W.W.R. 81 (B.C. C.A.).
157. *R. v. Del Puppo supra* footnote 152 at p. 630.

In *R. v. McAnish*[158] the Crown sought to lay a new charge rather than validly re-commence its stayed proceedings as is allowed under the *Criminal Code* provisions. This procedure left Jones Prov.Ct.J. somewhat bemused: "Why that particular procedure has not been pursued in this case I do not know".

In *Re Sheehan and R.*[159] the Crown attempted to hold a second preliminary hearing on an almost identical charge to the one on which the accused had previously been discharged. According to Osler J. ". . . the only result of the second inquiry would be to harrass an accused unnecessarily without in any way promoting the interests of justice" and ". . . such a procedure would be an abuse of the process of the Court". The procedure attempted by the Crown was curious in as much as it was open to the Crown after the accused was discharged at the completion of the preliminary hearing to prefer a bill of indictment against the accused merely by securing the consent of a judge of the court or of the Attorney General himself as set out in s. 507(2) of the *Criminal Code*.

(6) Entrapment

It has already been mentioned that the application of the doctrine of abuse of process to situations involving entrapment or the use of entrapping techniques is arguably of questionable validity. This is so because the *defence* of entrapment itself has been considered and re-jected by our courts (save in recent years where resort to the use of the doctrine of abuse of process has been applied successfully in some entrapment cases).

Rather than merely discuss the recent abuse of process/entrapment decisions as purely manifestations of the doctrine of abuse of process a broader approach seems justified. The doctrine of abuse of process will not necessarily rise or fall on the shoulders of the entrapment defence.

Therefore this issue will be approached from a historical and compar-ative perspective with particular emphasis on the American experience with the entrapment defence. The import of the American approach based upon American constitutional provisions for Canadian courts and to the provisions of our much maligned *Canadian Bill of Rights* will merit consideration. Recent Canadian developments in the area can then profitably be set against the backrop of Canadian "due pro-cess" safeguards and the developing doctrine of "abuse of process".

Of course the subject itself (entrapment) has been the recipient of larger, more detailed treatment than what is offered here. Brevity may

---

158. *Supra* footnotes 152 and 153.
159. (1973) 14 C.C.C. (2d) 23 (Ont.). Also, for an example of where multiple processes were employed but in a manner not deemed oppressive see *R. v. Kowerchuk* (1971) 15 C.R.N.S. 95, reversed [1972] 5 W.W.R. 255, affirmed [1972] 5 W.W.R. 255n (Alta. C.A.).

lead to distortion, but hopefully, this has been minimized.

A suitable jumping off point for this discussion seems to be these views expressed by the Canadian Committee on Corrections in 1969:

> Conduct amounting to an offence shall be deemed not to have been instigated where the defendant has a pre-existing intention to commit the offence when the opportunity arose and the conduct which is alleged to have induced the defendant to commit the offence did not go beyond affording him an opportunity to commit it.[160]

The passage cited above does not express the law of Canada at this time. Six years have elapsed since the publication of the Ouimet Report, and while the Canadian jurisprudence on the subject of entrapment has become progressively more muddled no legislative initiatives in this regard have been undertaken.

It is acknowledged in the Report of the Committee on Corrections that the test proposed is derived in large measure from U. S. judicial experience, more precisely, from the case of *Sherman v. U.S.*[161]

(a) *American tests*

The American experience with the problems posed by the activities of informants and 'agents provocateurs' has been far from unified. A multiplicity of judicial tests for entrapment have been proposed. Even the acceptance, in general, of the defence of entrapment itself has met with vigorous dissent despite repeated acknowledgement of its existence by the U.S. Supreme Court.[162]

In consequence no *comprehensive* legal theory of entrapment has emerged in the United States although the existence of the defence itself is well recognized. In Canada in addition to there being no comprehensive legal theory, the existence of the defence itself has yet to receive sanction from our Superior Courts of Criminal Jurisdiction.

Three separate tests have in fact been proposed in the American Courts. Two have gained widespread application. The third has obtained little support in the jurisprudence. J. Shafer and W. Sheridan outline these tests in their essay on *"The Defence of Entrapment"*.[163] In brief these tests may be summarized as follows:

(1) *"creative activity" test* — (also known as the "origin of intent" test) examines the state of mind of the accused at the time of initial approach or instigation to assess whether or not his conduct shall be adjudged blameworthy. If the accused already possessed a general criminal intent or "predisposition" and was merely awaiting an opportunity to implement that intent then the furnish-

---

160. Canada, *Report of the Canadian Committee on Corrections (Ouimet Report)* Ottawa, Queens Printer, 1969, p. 79.
161. (1958) 356 U.S. 369.
162. *Sorrells v. U.S.* (1932) 287 U.S. 435; *Sherman v. U.S., supra* footnote 161; *U.S. v. Russell* (1973) 93 S.Ct. 1637.
163. (1970) 8 O.H.L.J. 277 at pp. 289-292.

ing of it by the police will not afford a defence valid in law. (Note that this "defence" allows a character inquiry to be launched into the accused's previous history and convictions.)

(2) *"police conduct" test* — does not concern itself with subjective elements but examines only the activities of the agent provocateur. The disposition or "pre-disposition" of the accused is not relevant to this determination. If the agent provocateur surpasses standards which are generally accepted as being reasonable in all of the circumstances and thus contravenes basic principles of justice the defence of entrapment is thus established.

(3) *"reasonable cause" test* — has had little or no judicial acceptance in the United States. This approach involves a consideration of the purpose or motivation of the police or their agents in their initial decision to concentrate upon the accused. Relevant to this consideration is the question of whether or not the authorities were acting upon "reasonable suspicion". By this approach if "reasonable suspicion" was involved the defence of entrapment will fail.

As has been mentioned the law in Canada with respect to entrapment has not followed a parallel course to the American experience. While the Ouimet Committee largely based its recommendations upon the reasoning of *Sherman* and its so-called "creative activity test", the decisional law in Canada has thus far been loath to base its reasoning upon cited American case law although at times (thus far, only a very few) the result achieved is much the same. In *R. v. Shipley*[164] a relatively recent decision of the Ontario County Court the court employed the criteria for entrapment enunciated by Warren C.J. in *Sherman*. (In *Sherman* Warren C.J. re-affirmed the "creative activity test" as laid down by Hughes C.J. in *Sorrels.*)

(b) *English practice*

The English position with respect to entrapment most recently was stated in the case of *R. v. Mealey; R. v. Sheridan.*[165] This quotation taken from the headnote of that case is an apt summary:

> *The defence of entrapment is not known to English law.* A defendant cannot entitle himself to an acquittal by showing that he acted in concert with or as a result of the conduct of an agent provocateur, though the matter may be highly relevant on the question of sentence.

To say that the defence is not known to English law is perhaps a trifle misleading. Many early English cases turned on accomplice or corroboration issues. *R. v. Bickley,*[166] *R. v. Mullins*[167] *and R. v. Chand-*

---

164. [1970] 2 O.R. 411, [1970] 3 C.C.C. 398.
165. (1975) 60 Cr.App.R. 59.
166. (1909) 73 J.P. 239.
167. (1848) 3 Cox, C.C. 526.

ler[168] are examples of this to name just a few. In other instances the courts entered acquittals in entrapment situations where the involvement of the agent provocateur was sufficient to negative a constituent element necessary to establish the offence.[169]

Without doubt entrapping techniques violate the British conception of justice and fair play:

> The court recognizes that . . . the police must be able in certain cases to make use of informers, and further . . . that within certain limits such informers should be protected. At the same time, unless the use of informers is kept within strict limits grave injustice may result . . . it is something of which this court thoroughly disapproves, to use an informer to encourage another to commit an offence or indeed an offence of a more serious character, which he would otherwise not commit, still moreso if the police themselves take part in carrying it out.[170]

(c) *Canadian developments*

The English approach to entrapment then stands in stark contrast to the American experience. Canadian developments have not followed either path although there is reason to say the result of past decisions and the projected future development of the Canadian law is more closely related to the American judicial experience. The different paths which Canadian and U.S. Courts have followed is not difficult to understand inasmuch as American developments have occurred "within the context of American constitutional law theory, which has empowered the courts to control the exercise of police power by requiring its adherence to constitutional standards of 'due process' ".[171]

1. *The Canadian Bill of Rights* In recent years, indeed months, the Supreme Court of Canada has wrestled (although not in the context of entrapment) with the meaning and derivation of the "due process" provision of the *Canadian Bill of Rights*[172] which guarantees "the right of the individual to life, liberty, security of the person and enjoyment of property, and the right not to be deprived thereof except by due process of law".

In *Curr. v. R.*[173] there was reason to believe that the court was prepared to reason, in part, by analogy to American constitutional provisions and experience with respect to "due process". Laskin J. (as he

---

168. (1912) 8 Cr.App.R. 82.
169. For a discussion of the "constituent elements" approach to entrapment, see Watt L.J. "Entrapment as a Criminal Defence" (1971) 13 Cr.L.Q. 313 at pp. 330-331.
170. *R. v. Birtles* [1969] 2 All E.R. 1131n.
171. Sneideman, B.M. "A Judicial Test for Entrapment: The Glimmerings of a Canadian Policy on Police Instigated Crime", (1973) 16 Cr.L.Q. 81 at p. 101.
172. 8-9 Eliz. II, c. 44 (Canada) (R.S.C. 1970, Appendix III), s. 1(*a*).
173. (1972) 18 C.R.N.S. 281 (Can.).

then was) ostensibly writing for the majority expressed the position thusly:

> . . . *If there is any analagy at all to be drawn between the Bill of Rights and the American Constitution, it is to be found with respect to the first eight amendments to that Constitution,* which inhibit federal action. . . . As in the first eight amendments (which may be compendiously referred to as the American Bill of Rights) so in the Canadian Bill of Rights, the due process clause does not stand alone, but is part of a scheme which includes among the protected "human rights and fundamental freedoms" (1) the political liberties, (2) the right to counsel, (3) the right to reasonable bail, (4) protection against self-crimination and (5) protection against cruel and unusual punishment.[174]
>
> The very large words of s. 1(a) tempered by a phrase ("except by due process of law") *whose original English meaning has been overlaid by American constitutional imperatives,* signal extreme caution to me when asked to apply them in negation of substantive legislation validly enacted by a Parliament in which the major role is played by elected representatives of the people. Certainly . . . a holding that the enactment . . . has infringed the appellant's right to the security of his person without due process of law must be grounded on more than a substitution of a personal judgment for that of Parliament.[175]

Ritchie J. was content to leave the meaning of "due process" to be determined in a more purely Canadian fashion:

> . . . I prefer to base this conclusion on my understanding that the meaning to be given to the language employed in the Bill of Rights is the meaning which it bore in Canada at the time when the Bill was enacted, and it follows that, in my opinion, *the phrase "due process of law" as used in s. 1(a) is to be construed as meaning "according to the legal processes recognized by Parliament and the courts in Canada".*[176]

The debate on the importance of the American constitutional experience and its import for, and impact upon, the *Canadian Bill of Rights* continued in *A.G. Canada v. Lavell; Isaac v. Bedard.*[177] Ritchie J. and Laskin J. once again staked out opposing positions. The rest of the Court sharply divided. Pigeon J. cast the deciding or "swing" vote in that determination (which involved a consideration of s. 12(1)(b) of the *Indian Act,* discrimination on the basis of sex, and equality before the law) with a rather remarkable departure from the doctrine of "stare decisis". Section 1(a) ("due process") of the *Bill of Rights* was not specifically involved in that determination.

The due process issue did arise again however, in *Hogan v. R.*[178] with Ritchie J.'s position prevailing. The case involved the admissibility

---

174. *Ibid.* at p. 291 (emphasis added).
175. *Ibid.* at pp. 292-3.
176. *Ibid.* at p. 284 (emphasis added).
177. (1973) 23 C.R.N.S. 197 (Can.).
178. (1974) 18 C.C.C. (2d) 65 (Can.).

of breath test evidence — allegedly procured by illegal means or trickery. (Neither Laskin C.J.C. nor Ritchie J. felt that this had occurred in the particular facts of this case). Also involved was a consideration of the effect to be given to a violation of the *Bill of Rights* (Hogan had been denied his right to Counsel) on the admissibility or reception of evidence. Laskin C.J.C. would have excluded such evidence, and drew support in his reasoning from American precedents. Ritchie J.'s view is best summarized in the following passage taken from his judgment:

> Laskin C.J.C., however, characterizes the Canadian Bill of Rights as a "quasi constitutional instrument" by which I take him to mean that its provisions are to be construed and applied as if they were constitutional provisions, and in so doing he would adopt as a matter of policy for Canada, apart from and at variance with the common-law position, the rule of absolute exclusion of all evidence obtained under circumstances where one of the provisions of the Canadian Bill of Rights has been violated. This approach stems from an acceptance of the reasoning of the Supreme Court of the United States in such cases as *Mapp v. Ohio* (1961), 367 U.S. 643, where that rule was accepted in relation to evidence obtained after the violation of a right guaranteed by the American Constitution. These American cases, however, turn on the interpretation of a constitution basically different from our own and particularly on the effect to be given to the "due process of law" provision of the 14th Amendment of that Constitution for which I am unable to find any counterpart in the B.N.A. Act, 1867, which is the source of the legislative authority of the Parliament of Canada and is characterized in the B.N.A. Act (No. 2) 1949 c. 22, as "the Constitution of Canada".[179]

Rather than ending the confusion surrounding the meaning to be ascribed to the term "due process of law" the decision in *Hogan* (confirming Ritchie J.'s view as espoused in *Curr*) has complicated matters. No one knows precisely what is envisioned by the phrase "according to the legal processes recognized by Parliament and the Courts of Canada". When does the process begin? Is it purely procedural? Clearly the decision in *Hogan* has ended one debate only to begin another.

What the *Hogan* decision did accomplish, relevant to the instant problem, was to establish that the contravention or infringement of a right accorded under the *Bill of Rights* is insufficient to render inadmissible otherwise receivable evidence. The sole qualification of this proposition was the affirmation that the Court was prepared to leave untouched the narrow residual discretion of the trial judge to refuse to admit evidence of trifling probative value which was possessed of potentially prejudicial effect as was decided in *R. v. Wray*.[180]

---

179. *Ibid.* at pp. 71-2.
180. [1970] 4 C.C.C. 1, new trial ordered 4 C.C.C. (2d) 378 *sub nom. R. v. Wray* (No. 2) affirmed 10 C.C.C. (2d) 215 (Can.).

The difficulties which the decisions in *Hogan,* and *Wray,* pose for adherents of a Canadian judicial test for entrapment are quite clear. In limiting the court's ability to exclude unfairly obtained evidence to cases in which the evidence thus secured was of trifling relevance and little probative value the door appears to have been effectively closed to situations involving crucially relevant evidence, no matter how unfairly obtained. The fruits of entrapment involve exactly such evidence.

2. *Abuse of process*   At the point in time when Barnett Sneideman wrote his article (1973) on entrapment[181] the *Hogan* case had not yet been considered by the Supreme Court of Canada. Two lower court decisions had been handed down — *R. v. Shipley*[182] and *R. v. Mac-Donald.*[183] In those cases two inferior courts in British Columbia and Ontario had accepted a defence of entrapment basing their remarks, in part, upon the American "creative activity" test enunciated in *Sherman* and, in part, upon the obiter remarks of Laskin J.A. (as he then was) in *R. v. Ormerod.*[184] Of perhaps greater importance was the incorporation of the notion of "abuse of process" into these considerations.

Laskin J.A. was explicit in his judgment in indicating that he was leaving consideration of the issue "to an occasion when it is squarely raised." Nonetheless he did indicate that the defence of entrapment "goes not to the issue of whether the methods employed by the police should be tolerated".

Ormerod was decided prior to the appeal being taken from the decision of the Ontario Court of Appeal to the Supreme Court of Canada in *R. v. Osborn.*[185] Consequently Laskin J.A. was able to base his obiter remarks in part upon the recent implementation of the doctrine of "abuse of process" (the conviction of the accused was quashed because the indictment was found to be oppressive) by the Ontario Court of Appeal.

Subsequent evolution of the case law has revealed that if the defence of entrapment exists in Canada the doctrine of abuse of process must be its legal underpinning.[186] That such a situation has

---

181. B. Sneideman, *supra* footnote 171.
182. *Supra* footnote 164.
183. (1971) 15 C.R.N.S. 122 (B.C.).
184. [1969] 2 O.R. 230 (C.A.); *R. v. Shipley* [1970] 3 C.C.C. 398 (Ont.).
185. [1969] 4 C.C.C. 185 (C.A.) reversed 1 C.C.C. (2d) 482 (Can.).
186. As has been mentioned the viability of a defence of entrapment framed in terms of abuse of process is, at best, uncertain. There is however, one further basis upon which a defence of entrapment may rest. This approach has been characterized as the "constituent elements" argument: ". . . the particular section of the Code violated will be dissected into its *mens rea* and *actus reus* constituents in an attempt to see if one or both are lacking. It is quite conceivable entrapment may negative one of the essential elements as it did in *O'Brien* and *Kotyszyn* for *mens rea* and *Lemieux* for *actus reus*.. . . . "It is submitted that there can be found in the existing Canadian cases a legal basis for a defence of entrapment. If entrapment takes away

prevailed despite the decision of the Supreme Court in *Osborn* (reversing the Ontario Court of Appeal) is an apt testimonial to the confusion and ambivalence in the judgments rendered in that inconclusive case.

The exact relationship between "due process" (as expressed in the *Bill of Rights*) and the doctrine of "abuse of process" (involving a consideration of the inherent jurisdiction in Superior Courts to control and supervise the regularity of their processes) is unclear. It would seem logical to assert that where an abuse of process is found to exist there can be no due process of law. On the other hand the *distinction* between these two concepts may be exactly the kind of nice legal distinction which the courts are presently looking to in order to lend validity to a legal defence which would appear otherwise to have been foreclosed.

It is therefore useful to examine in some detail those few cases which do exist in Canada which have examined entrapment within the context of abuse of process.

Perhaps the most flamboyant of the cases is *R. v. MacDonald*.[187] In that case Selbie Prov.Ct.J. held that the defendant would not have sold a quantity of narcotics "but for the histrionics and persistent opportuning of the accused by the third party informer".

---

one of the elements of the offence be it *mens rea* which is implanted in an erstwhile innocent accused by an *agent provocateur,* or *actus reus* which is made impossible by the activities of the police negativing the criminal attributes of the act, the accused will be *acquitted*. He will be *acquitted* and correctly so because he did not perpetrate the crime as alleged." (J. D. Watt, "The Defence of Entrapment" (1970-71) 13 Cr.L.Q. 313 at pp. 330-331).

The *Lemieux* case (1967) 2 C.R.N.S. 1 (Can.) involved a charge of breaking and entering under what was then section 292(1) of the Code. The Supreme Court held that the actions of the police in providing the key for the commission of the offence (they had been given it, and the authority to deal with it, by the owner) had in effect removed the "actus reus" of the offence. By this view entrapment can negative *actus reus* — this notwithstanding that Judson J. expressed the opinion that the fact that the accused committed an offence at the solicitation of an agent provocateur is irrelevant to the question of the guilt or innocence of the accused.

Kotyszyn (1949) 95 C.C.C. 261 (C.A.) and *O'Brien* (1954) 108 C.C.C. 113 (C.A.) affirmed 110 C.C.C. 1 (Can.) were both cases involving criminal conspiracies. In both cases the important element lacking to prove the offence was common design. (The police participants' designs were aimed at foiling the commission of the offence rather than perpetrating it.)

Each of the cases above mentioned are limited by the nature of the particular charge involved (breaking and entering, conspiracy). The transfer to a charge involving trafficking in narcotics is imperfect at best, and it is submitted, of dubious acceptability. Query whether *Kotyszyn* and *O'Brien* truly involve a failure of *mens rea* as one of the authors suggests. More likely the failing is not "mens rea" but rather "lack of common design".)

187. *Supra* footnote 183.

The evidence allowed, therefore, is that while the police operator was out of the room, I think she was in the bathroom, the undercover operator worked on the accused . . . on the basis that she was sick, in need of drugs and that she had to have them right away as did her friend, that the accused did not wish to sell because he only had enough for himself, but that he did sell when this third party, amongst other things, broke into tears, in her attempt to get the accused to make the sale, and eventually the accused, as a result of this, did so.[188]

Selbie Prov.Ct.J. observed that entrapment had been held to be an abuse of process of court in Canada by virtue of the decision rendered in *R. v. Shipley*,[189] but noted importantly that entrapment is a matter of fact and not of law. "All use of undercover agents and/or informers is, in the very broad sense, entrapment, but it is not always objectionable". Support for that proposition was found in *R. v. Mah Qun Non*,[190] and *R. v. Ormerod*[191] (especially in the "calculated inveigling and persistent importuning of the accused . . . as to go beyond ordinary solicitation" observations of Laskin J.A. in the latter case).

Thus the approach adopted was consistent with modern approach to *all* abuse of process cases where the Court looks for oppressive conduct and manifest unfairness before utilizing its inherent power to quash or stay proceedings.

The *Shipley* case involved an accused who McAndrew Co.Ct.J. described as "a young fellow, naive, lacking in experience, perhaps". The officer, acting undercover and "to the very best of his ability and with perfectly proper intentions", initially developed a relationship with Shipley to discover his suppliers and not for the purpose (which he later pursued) of catching Shipley in the act of trafficking. The learned County Court Judge found as a fact that the accused would not have indulged in the offence without the inducements held out by the officer. Relying on Jessup J.A.'s judgment in *Osborn* (the case had not yet been considered in the Supreme Court of Canada) he further held that "it would be unfair to this accused and an abuse of process of the Court to permit this prosecution to continue". Accordingly the proceedings were stayed.

An important distinction between *Shipley* and *MacDonald* should be observed.

The reasons for judgment advanced in *MacDonald* reveal a diminished concern with the "pre-disposition of the accused to commit the crime". The thrust of the remarks of the learned trial judge are directed towards the unconscionable, unfair and oppressive tactics employed by the agent provocateur in order to secure a conviction. Therefore, the *MacDonald* case, such authority as it is, apparently

---

188. *R. v. MacDonald*, footnote 183 at p. 123.
189. *Supra* footnote 164.
190. (1934) 47 B.C.R. 464 (C.A.).
191. *Supra* footnote 184.

stands for a "police conduct" test for entrapment — a test allied to the doctrine of abuse of process.

The *Shipley* case on the other hand expressly acknowledges the "creative activity test" as laid down by the United States Supreme Court in *Sherman* and *Sorrells*.

An unsuccessful recent attempt to utilize the entrapment/abuse of process "defence" may be witnessed in the Northwest Territories Magistrate's Court decision of *R. v. Pratt.*[192] The case involved breach of a territorial liquor ordinance. The defendant raised three points in his defence:

(1) The defendant acted without mens rea, having been induced to do what he did by a police officer in the course of duty;

(2) The defendant is entitled to enjoy the same de facto immunity from prosecution as the police officer who induced him to do what is charged here as an offence;

(3) Proceedings in the case should be stayed as an abuse of the process of the court in that the alleged offence was instigated by police action.[193]

Magistrate DeWeerdt held that the undercover officer's conduct did not go beyond giving the accused an opportunity to commit the offence charged and did not constitute an entrapment. Consequently there was no abuse of process found.

The case does *not* however disagree with the proposition that in a "proper" case the doctrine of abuse of process may be invoked to terminate and quash oppressive proceedings.

The most recent case to consider the entrapment/abuse of process relationship is *R. v. Bonnar.*[194]

In *Bonnar* the Nova Scotia Court of Appeal arrived at the conclusion that the accused had not *in fact* been entrapped into stealing goods of a value in excess of two hundred dollars. In consequence, Bonnar's acquittal was set aside and a conviction was entered. In the course of delivering judgment however, the Appeal Court affirmed the validity of the abuse of process/entrapment defence.

The Nova Scotia Court in arriving at its conclusion utilized a test of "creative activity" (à la *Russell, Sherman,* and *Sorrells*) as modified by the formulation offered by Laskin J.A. in *Ormerod*. Notwithstanding the scant Canadian authority on the subject the court's opinion was voiced in unequivocal terms:

> I am of the opinion that proceedings should be stayed or the accused discharged if it is clear that the accused did not have a prior intention or predisposition to commit the offence with which he is charged but committed it only because the conduct of the agent provocateur was (as

---

192. (1972) 19 C.R.N.S. 273 (N.W.T.).
193. *Ibid.* at p. 284.
194. (1975) 34 C.R.N.S. 182 (N.S. C.A.).

Laskin J.A. said in *Regina v. Ormerod, supra*) such calculating, inveigling and persistent importuning as went beyond ordinary solicitation.
In such a situation there is an abuse of the process of the Court and
something that is contrary to public policy. Indeed such conduct by an
agent provocateur strikes at the very foundation of the system and
administration of criminal justice in a free and democratic society and
just cannot be permitted or condoned.[195]

5. IS THE ABUSE POWER RESTRICTED TO SUPERIOR COURTS?

It will be recalled that our analysis of the doctrine of abuse of
process began with an inquiry into the notion of the "inherent jurisdiction of the court". Devlin L.J. and Pearce L.J. in *Connelly v.
D.P.P.* led us to an examination of how almost the entire body of
criminal law and procedure sprang from the exercise by the superior
courts of their "inherent power" to see that what was just and what
was fair was done between the prosecutor and the accused.

In Canada "superior courts" are referred to as "courts of original
jurisdiction" or of "original civil and criminal jurisdiction", which
Darrell Roberts construes to mean that "they are possessed of all the
power and authority as by the law of England are incident to a Superior Court of Civil and Criminal jurisdiction".[196] In a sense this
begs the question.

A superior court is most easily understood when contrasted to a
statutory court. The statutory court derives its powers and existence
from statute while the superior court under our law has an essence
which has been described as "almost metaphysical".[197]

Given then that the powers wielded by inferior courts derive from
statute and that the superior courts possess an arsenal of both statutory and inherent powers, can there be any justification for the inferior courts' purported use of an inherent jurisdiction such as has
been done with the "abuse power"?

The problem posed is a most important one to any consideration of
the doctrine of abuse of process — and, it has never been adequately
answered.

In those cases where inferior courts have purported to employ the
doctrine they have merely assumed that they had the power.[198] Su-

---

195. *Ibid.* at p. 192, *per* MacDonald J.A.
196. D. W. Roberts, "The Doctrine of Abuse of Process in Canadian Criminal
     Law" (1972) Report of the First Annual Conference of the British Colum-
     bia Judges Association, 39 at p. 47.
197. *Ibid.* at p. 46.
198. *E.g.* see *Ittoshat* (1970) 10 C.R.N.S. 385 (Que.); *Del Puppo* [1974] 3
     W.W.R. 621 (B.C.), and *McAnish* (1973) 15 C.C.C. (2d) 494 (B.C.).

perior courts considering applications for prerogative writs involving the use or denied use of the doctrine have ventured to pass upon the validity of the doctrine itself, but for the most part[199] have not considered whether or not the power is one which might be employed by the courts below.

Only in one reported lower court decision has a judge who accepted (for the purposes of argument) the validity of the doctrine declined to clothe his court with its jurisdiction. The case originated in the Manitoba Provincial Court. The judge was Sparling Prov.J., and the accused was an individual by the name of Andrest.[200]

In *Andrest* the failure by the Crown to give reasonable notice of its intention to use certificate evidence in a narcotics prosecution resulted in the discharge of the:accused at a preliminary inquiry. A new information was then sworn and counsel for the accused moved to quash it as being an abuse of the Court's process. The application was dismissed by Sparling Prov.J. who in the course of his judgment observed:

> The superior courts have an inherent jurisdiction to redress wrongs but a magistrate or provincial judge has only the powers granted to him by the Criminal Code and they are specific, even more specific on a preliminary inquiry.[201]

The point struck by the learned provincial judge is one of substance. Since the issue is one of jurisdiction, the mere fact that provincial courts assert this jurisdiction and certain superior courts accept their ability to do so will not necessarily insure the ultimate vindication of these exercises. What is important, even crucial, is the legal basis upon

---

199. See *R. v. Barnett* [1974] 5 W.W.R. 673 (B.C.). This case was subsequently considered by the B.C. Court of Appeal: (1975) 24 C.C.C. (2d) 399, which declined to deal with the matter on the merits because it had been rendered academic by the Provincial Court Judge's entering a stay upon considering the matter when directed to do so by the superior court's order of *mandamus*. The Crown was invited to question the subsequent disposition in the Provincial Court by appeal. See also *R. v. Rourke* (1974) 16 C.C.C. (2d) 133 (B.C.) reversed on other grounds [1975] 6 W.W.R. 591 (B.C. C.A.). *R. v. McClevis; Ex parte Wright and Wright* (1970) 1 C.C.C. (2d) 173 (Ont.) stands for the expressed proposition that the inherent jurisdiction to prevent an abuse of process rests in *all* courts of competent jurisdiction (not merely superior courts). Therefore a Provincial Court has jurisdiction to decide whether or not its process is being abused and if so to prevent abuse by staying or dismissing the abusive proceedings. These cases however do not expound upon the *legal basis* for the proposition asserted.

200. *R. v. Andrest* [1974] 4 W.W.R. 417 (Man.)

201. *Ibid.* at p. 421. Note also that the learned Provincial Judge was alive to the niceties of the actual application of the doctrine. At p. 423 he opines "It is an established principle that courts shall only strike out proceedings without a hearing very sparingly and only in the clearest of cases: *R. v. Leclair* . . . *It does not follow that a discharge from an information on a preliminary hearing always warrants a quashing of a further information or indictment"* (emphasis added).

which the jurisdiction of the inferior court is founded. It is not enough to do as Munroe J. did in *R. v. Barnett*[202] and rely upon other judgments (*Croquet* and *Koski*) of other superior courts which merely asserted the existence of jurisdiction without examining the legal rationalia for such assertions. As laudable as the sentiment is, that "it is inconceivable . . . that any court could be without jurisdiction to prevent an abuse of its process in any form"[203] the rule of law requires more.

D. W. Roberts attempted to rationalize the use of the abuse power by inferior courts in a manner which is not wholly satisfactory:

> The approach that might be taken to support this position is to ignore (*with justification*) the fact that the doctrine of abuse of process has its origin in the exercise of inherent jurisdiction by superior courts. *The argument is that once the doctrine has been developed it becomes part of the comman law, by all of the courts — statutory and non-statutory; its origin therefore is unimportant.* Common law principles form an important part of criminal trials and it is expected that all Courts will apply them, not just some of them . . . In fact, should a statutory court refuse to apply such principles, that refusal would give rise to a prerogative writ review by a superior court to oblige it to do so. And I think the same would be true if accepting the existence of the doctrine of abuse of process, a Statutory court in a clear case refused to apply it. Therefore, in my opinion it is sound to conclude that statutory courts have not only an equal claim to the doctrine of abuse of process, but a duty to apply it consistent with the duty on all criminal courts to see that their jurisdiction is not misused and that justice is done.[204]

Professor Roberts' arguments have a certain appeal. But in asking us to ignore the origin of the doctrine he, in essence, is urging upon us a situation involving moral justice, but not law. The very lifeblood

---

202. *Supra* footnote 199. The case is interesting inasmuch as Munroe J. went so far as to remit the issue back to the Provincial Judge in such form as to compel that judge to exercise the "abuse jurisdiction" and rule on the merits of the application. Also not directly on point, but of interest — for the "other side of the coin" see *R. v. Kennedy* (1972) 6 C.C.C., (2d) 564 (Ont. C.A.) where the Ontario Court of Appeal held that it had no jurisdiction to deal with such a non-statutory appeal when Wells, C.J.H.C. refused to stay proceedings before him on an indictment as an abuse of process involving an alleged Crown repudiation of a plea bargain.

203. *R. v. Barnett* footnote 199 at p. 675.

204. *Supra* footnote 196, at p. 47 (emphasis added). For a variant on this approach see P. S. Barton, "Abuse of Process as a Plea in Bar of Trial", (1972-73) 15 Cr.L.Q. 437 at p. 457-459 where Barton develops the notion that even inferior courts have *some* inherent jurisdiction. Barton implies that if there is a place for abuse of process in the inferior courts (Barton's thesis is that the doctrine ought not be available to *any* trial judge in the criminal process) it is possibly to be found in that area.

of the doctrine is its origins in the inherent jurisdiction of superior courts. Sever that link and you kill the doctrine.[205]

This does not mean that inferior courts must be powerless to prevent abuses of their process. Even accepting the weakest conception of the powers of inferior courts, if one does accept the validity of the doctrine for superior courts, then there still remains open to the inferior court a means of preventing abuse. This is the case because the inferior court would remain the forum where the abuse first manifests itself. Applications might still be made to that court to find *as a fact* that the Court's process was being abused — a kind of declaratory function. Also the court of its own motion might find abuse and remark upon it to the accused or his counsel. By providing an adjournment in order for counsel to seek a prerogative remedy, the alleged abuse could thereby be prevented. This was in fact the procedure which was provided in the *Andrest* case:

> Because I feel that I have no jurisdiction to quash the information at this stage, I must refuse the application of the accused. I am prepared, however, to grant the accused an adjournment for such period of time as he requires to make application to a superior court for a writ of prohibition prohibiting me from inquiring into the matter on such grounds as he sees fit to put forward.[206]

Thus the superior court would be the forum where proceedings would be actually stayed or terminated in instances of proven abuse, but the inferior court would nevertheless be playing a role in protecting its process from abuse.

But need we truly have to view the power of inferior courts as thus limited in operation? Is there a legal justification beyond that suggested by Roberts which would allow inferior courts to exercise the abuse power to its full range and extent?

It is submitted that there exists in law a strong basis justifying the present practice of inferior courts to terminate proceedings where their processes have been abused.

It will be recalled that Oswald in writing of contempt (a power also deriving from inherent jurisdiction) made the following observations:

> A Court of Justice without power to vindicate its own dignity, to enforce obedience to its mandates, to protect its officers, or shield those

---

205. Roberts' analysis also fails because it does not recognize an important analogy which exists between abuse of process and the contempt power, both of which derive their existence from the inherent jurisdiction of the court. The inferior court does not exercise a jurisdiction to punish for contempt by virtue of accepting the contempt power as part of the common law whose origins are therefore unimportant. Rather, the inferior court exercises a jurisdiction to punish for contempt by virtue of a statutory grant of that inherent power.

206. *R. v. Andrest supra* footnote 200 at p. 424.

who are entrusted to its care, would be an anomaly which could not be permitted to exist in any civilized community.[207]

The inferior courts presently exercise a power to punish for contempts in the face of the court by virtue of a statutory grant of that "inherent power".[208] Thus, it may be seen that inferior courts are competent to utilize inherent powers so long as there is statutory authority for such use.

It will be remembered that in our discussion of the inherent jurisdiction of the court (Part 1 *supra*) the nexus and points of commonality between the contempt power and the doctrine of abuse of process were explored. In general terms, both concepts evolved in order to insure that the orderly and just process of the court be observed and that the administration of justice be saved from scorn and disrepute. Thus there were even early instances where the two phenomena were employed together for dealing with the same delict — proceedings were terminated, *and* punishment for contempt was meted out.

The intimate relationship between contempt of court and abuse of process should not be overlooked or undervalued, for in this area lies the statutory authority for investing inferior courts with the power to directly prevent abuses of their process.

Section 440 of the *Criminal Code* reads as follows:

> 440. Every judge or magistrate has the same power and authority to preserve order in a court over which he presides as may be exercised by the superior court of criminal jurisdiction of the province during the sittings thereof.

This section has generally been regarded as a part of the statutory framework conferring a contempt jurisdiction upon inferior courts. Such may well be the case, but, if this is so, then the section is redundant for s. 9 of the *Code* is complete, in and of itself.

It is submitted that the section was enacted to insure that inferior courts might possess the same abilities as superior courts to insure the just and orderly administration of justice, and to enable the inferior court to defeat any attempt to subvert its orderly process. To this end broader, more general terms were employed than those to be found in s. 9 of the *Code*. (Section 440 speaks in terms of the "power and authority to preserve order in a court" while s. 9, and s. 8 before it speak of the "power to impose punishment for contempt of court".)

It is therefore submitted that s. 440 of the *Code* embraces the notion of abuse of process as well as that of contempt.

An abuse of process is an oppressive manipulation of the orderly process of the court and thus is a challenge (as much as a contempt is a challenge) to the authority of the court. Since it challenges the authority of the court, an abuse of process poses an impediment to

---

207. Oswald, *On Contempt* (3rd Ed.) (1911) at p. 9.
208. See the *Criminal Code* s. 9.

the ability of the court to preserve order (in the sense of insuring just and orderly process).

Lest there be any argument that the terms of s. 440 should not be construed as broadly as is argued here, let it be remembered that the processes in question — the processes which are sought to be manipulated — are criminal processes, and the oppression thus occasioned involves the liberty of an accused person.

Section 440 of the *Criminal Code* is a federal enactment which must be read in the light of the provisions of the *Interpretation Act*[209] a federal enactment which calls for every federal enactment to be given such "fair, large and liberal construction and interpretation as best ensures the attainment of its objects".[210]

Section 440 of the *Code* appears to be explicit enough in its terms to confer the power to take remedial action against abuses of court process in that every judge or magistrate is given "the same power and authority to preserve order . . . as may be exercised by the superior court of criminal jurisdiction", but, if need be, additional help is offered under section 26(2) of the *Interpretation Act*:

> 26.(2) Where power is given to a person, officer or functionary, to do or enforce the doing of any act or thing, all such powers shall be deemed to be also given as are necessary to enable the person, officer or functionary to do or enforce the doing of the act or thing.

(It should be added (and it will be, but only parenthetically) that further buttressing the case for saying that *any* court of criminal jurisdiction ought to have the power to control and supervise the regularity or abuse of its process are the guarantees of the *Canadian Bill of Rights*[211] which ensure that an accused will be dealt with according to "due process of law",[212] and that if he has a hearing that it will be "a fair hearing in accordance with the principles of fundamental justice".)[213]

In light of the foregoing analysis it is submitted that inferior courts of criminal jurisdiction are fully clothed with requisite statutory authority to utilize and employ the doctrine of abuse of process.

In a recent decision of the Supreme Court of Canada, Ritchie J. contrasted the powers of a superior court judge with those exercised by a magistrate:

> Whatever inherent powers may be possessed by a superior court judge in controlling the process of his own court, it is my opinion that the powers and functions of a magistrate acting under the Criminal Code

---

209. R.S.C. 1970, Chap. I-23, s. 1 (note s. 3(1) which brings the *Criminal Code* under its purview)
210. *Ibid.* s. 11.
211. R.S.C. 1970, Appendix III.
212. *Ibid.* s. 1(*a*).
213. *Ibid.* s. 2(*e*).

are circumscribed by the provisions of that statute and must be found to have been thereby conferred either expressly *or by necessary implication*.[214]

This position does not exclude or otherwise invalidate the views expressed *supra,* as it has there been argued that the power of an inferior court to prevent an abuse of its process arises "by necessary implication" from the words of s. 440 of the *Criminal Code.*

EPILOGUE

A CAUTIONARY NOTE AND SOME REFLECTIONS ON THE DISTEMPER OF THESE TIMES

In addition to the analysis in the previous chapter on "Protecting the Process from Abuse: The Doctrine of Abuse of Process" other consideration has been given to the doctrine at several points throughout this work. At the time of this writing the usefulness and import of the doctrine cannot be underestimated. However, a dark cloud hovers near the horizon in the form of *R. v. Rourke*,[1] a case which, when passed upon by the Supreme Court of Canada, could conceivably render many of the observations *supra* concerning abuse of process, obsolete or ill-founded.

The *Rourke* case involves an allegation of inordinate delay in the bringing of a prosecution. The accused contended that he had been severely prejudiced in the preparation of his defence. (Rourke's affidavit disclosed that witnesses essential to his case died or could not be located due to the passage of time. Consequently, the "unconscionable delay" in bringing of the prosecution — on charges of robbery and kidnapping — was challenged as an abuse of process and proceedings were sought to be stayed.) In the County Court the trial Judge acceded to the request that proceedings be stayed, and mandamus proceedings taken before Rae J. in the British Columbia Supreme Court to compel proceedings proved unsuccessful. An appeal from that decision proved successful in the British Columbia Court of Appeal. The appeal was allowed, and the issuance of a writ of mandamus was directed requiring the County Court Judge to proceed to the trial of the indictment. Rourke subsequently sought leave to appeal to the Supreme Court of Canada and was successful in obtaining same. The crux of the issue which he now raises is bound up in these observations of McIntyre J.A.:

> it is my view that the facts of this case do not warrant the exercise of the judicial discretion to stay proceedings. The delay of approximately two years, the basis of the respondent's complaint, was due, so the County Court Judge found, to the dilatory nature of the investigation carried out by the police. The complaint is made not of the manner in which the prosecution itself has been conducted nor of the form or nature of the indictment but solely of matters which arose in the investigatory stages and before the indictment was preferred. In all the cases cited and in all that I have been able to find the extra ordinary power to intervene and stay proceedings has been exercised only where there has been something oppressive and unjust in the proceedings themselves. The oppression and injustice has arisen either from the nature of the proceedings or in the manner in which they have been conducted in Court. I have not found any case where the matters complained of and considered of sufficient importance to justify judicial

---

1. *R. v. Rourke* [1975] 6 W.W.R. (B.C. C.A.); reversing 16 C.C.C. (2d) 133 (S.C.); leave to appeal granted February, 1976.

interference occurred in the investigatory stages and before any legal proceedings were commenced. There is nothing oppressive on the face of the indictment. It is not suggested that there is any statute of limitations in such matters or that there is any legal impediment to the Crown's proceedings in November 1973. It is simply said when the matter is reduced to essentials that the Crown has taken too long to bring this prosecution because of a dilatory investigation and therefore the Court should not hear the case. To stay these proceedings now upon this ground would be to impose a limitation period for indictable offences by judicial decree where the Criminal Code has not done so and in my view the circumstances of this case do not justify the course taken by the County Court Judge.[2]

The merits of the appeal aside, the Supreme Court of Canada now has the opportunity (should it choose to so regard this situation) to consider the full field of operation of the doctrine of abuse of process — an opportunity which has not presented itself since *R. v. Osborn.*[3]

The possibility that the Court might seize this opportunity to deal a death blow to the entire doctrine should not be discounted. (One should not forget Pigeon J.'s stated views in *Osborn*: "I can see no legal basis for holding that criminal remedies are subject to the rule that they are to be refused whenever in its discretion, a court considers the prosecution oppressive."[4])

On the other hand, a narrower approach to the appeal in *Rourke* is not out of the question. It is open to the Supreme Court of Canada once again to sidestep the larger issues raised with respect to the doctrine, and merely affirm the decision in the Court of Appeal; perhaps, in the following fashion:

Whatever may be the law with respect to the inherent powers of Superior Court Judges to stay criminal proceedings on the ground of oppression the issue does not arise since there has not been oppression shown here.

Such an approach does nothing to clarify and develop the law on a broad subject of major importance. It does allow, however, for the development of theory and principle to proceed (as at present it does with near universal accord) at the appellate level. The authoritative voice of our highest court should be heard, but if it is to be at the expense of a viable and important doctrine, lingering indecision seems preferable.

The third possible approach — that of acceptance of the doctrine coupled with a full explication of guiding principles — appears extremely remote given the present constitution of the Court, and given also the revealed tendencies of its prevailing majority as evidenced by many recent decisions involving fundamental criminal law and/or the *Canadian Bill of Rights.*

---

2. *Ibid* at pp. 602-603 (C.A.).
3. [1969] 1 O.R. 152 (Ont. C.A.), reversed [1971] S.C.R. 184.
4. *R. v. Osborn* [1971] S.C.R. 184 at p. 190.

What must ever be borne in mind in this regard is that the doctrine of abuse of process exists in order to insure and safeguard the integrity of the legal process. Unlike many other matters discussed in this work it does not exist "in order to safeguard the rights of the accused". It exists in order to repulse the manipulations of *any party* who would seek to distort orderly lawful processes and employ them for purposes not contemplated or intended. With some justification it may properly be described as a "Judicial Bill of Rights". The destruction of the doctrine implies impotency in the Courts — a situation which can only foster disrespect for the administration of justice.

The *Rourke* case, possessing as it does the potential to become another *Wray*[5] darkens the horizon, but not nearly so much as the startling appearance of a document known as the *"Christie Memorandum"*.[6]

The proposals contained in the memorandum seek to remove the right of an accused person in what are defined as "high volume" indictable offences to elect his mode of trial. Mr. Christie seeks to replace that election with a grant of prosecutorial discretion which would allow the *prosecutor* to choose between two modes of trial, neither of which allow for the participation of a jury, and neither of which, as formulated, would allow for the holding of a preliminary inquiry. (As to this latter aspect the proposal is made that formalized discovery procedures be implemented with the implication that where the accused obtains discovery his "responses" should also be discoverable.)

A certain amount of pablum is mixed in with the vinegar in Mr. Christie's formula: for example, where the Crown does elect the maximum penalty applicable to the offence would be reduced and the discharge sections of the *Criminal Code* would thus become available (if they were not ordinarily) at the sentencing stage of the proceedings.

Much has been said in this work about the vast and largely unchecked phenomenon of prosecutorial discretion, and the threat which "unbridled discretion" poses to due process of law. The on-going process of atrophication of trial by jury has also been noted. These proposals if they are taken seriously (and in view of the source, they should be) bespeak the emergence of a new and dismal order — one much removed from past historical sentiment if not from the reality itself.

---

5. *R. v. Wray* (1970) 11 C.R.N.S. 235 (Can.)
6. Reproduced in (1976) 35 C.R.N.S. 129 — so named since its author is the Federal Associate Deputy Minister of Justice, Donald H. Christie.

BIBLIOGRAPHY

INTRODUCTION

ABEL, A.—"The American Bill of Rights: What Has it Accomplished?" (1959) 37 Can. B. Rev. 147.

BOWKER, W. F.—"Basic Rights and Freedoms: What Are They?" (1959) 37 Can. B. Rev. 43.

BROCKELBANK, W. J.—"The Role of Due Process in American Constitutional Law" (1954) 39 Cornell L.Q. 561.

BULL, D. A.—"The Breathalyzer and the Canadian Bill of Rights" (1976) 40 Sask. L. Rev. 147.

CAVALUZZO, P.—"Judicial Review and the Bill of Rights: Drybones and its Aftermath" (1971) 9 O.H.L.J. 511.

COHEN, S. A.—"Case Comment: A.-G. Can. v. Lavell; Isaac et al v. Bedard" (1974) 39 Man. B. News 197.

LASKIN, B.—"The Role and Function of Final Appellate Courts: The Supreme Court of Canada" (1975) 53 Can. B. Rev. 469.

LASKIN, B.—"The Judge and Due Process" (1972) 5 Man. L.J. 235.

LERNER, M. J. & ROSS, M. (ed.)—*The Quest for Justice: Myth, Reality, Ideal* (1972).

McILWAIN, C. H.—"Due Process of Law in Magna Carta" (1914) Col. L. Rev. 26.

McINTOSH, J. B.—"Self-Incrimination and the Breathalyzer" (1972) 36 Sask. L. Rev. 22.

MANDEL, M.—"The Presumption of Innocence and the Canadian Bill of Rights: R. v. Appleby" (1972) 10 O.H.L.J. 450.

MARTIN, G. A.—"Self-Incrimination in Canada" (1960-61) 3 Crim. L.Q. 431.

MARTIN, G. A.—"The Privilege Against Self-Incrimination Endangered" (1962) 5 Can. B. J. 6.

MORTON, J. D.—*The Function of the Criminal Law in 1962* (1962).

RAND, I. C.—"Except by Due Process of Law" (1961) Ott. L.J. 171.

RATUSHNY, E.—"Is There a Right Against Self-Incrimination in Canada?" (1973) 19 McGill L.J. 1.

SMITH, G. A.—"Reverse Onus Clauses—Burden of Proof—Bill of Rights s. 2(f)" (1972) 37 Sask. L. Rev. 117.

STENNING, P. C.—"The Breathalyzer Reference" (1970) 12 Crim. L.Q. 408.

TAMAN, L.—"The Adversary Process on Trial: Full Answer and Defence and the Right to Counsel" (1975) 13 O.H.L.J. 251.

TARNOPOLSKY, W.—*The Canadian Bill of Rights* (2nd ed.) (1975).

TARNOPOLSKY, W.—"The Supreme Court and the Canadian Bill of Rights" (1975) 53 Can. B. Rev. 649.

TARNOPOLSKY, W.—"The Supreme Court and Civil Liberties" (1976) 14 Alta. L. Rev. 58.

TARNOPOLSKY, W.—"The Canadian Bill of Rights from Diefenbaker to Drybones" (1971) 17 McGill L.J. 437.

WOOD, V.—*Due Process of Law 1932-1949: The Supreme Court's
Use of a Constitutional Tool* (1951).

POLICE

BARKER, B.—"Police Discretion and the Principle of Legality"
(1965-66) 8 Crim. L.Q. 400.

BORINS, N.—"Police Investigation and the Rights of the Accused"
(1963) L.S.U.C. Special Lectures 59.

BORINS, N.—"Confessions" (1968-69) 11 Crim. L.Q. 140.

BOWES, S.—*The Police and Civil Liberties* Camelot Press, London
(1966).

BRANSON, C. O. D.—"When is a Confession Not a Confession?" 12
Crim. L.Q. 133.

BUSHNELL, S.—"The Confession Rule: Its Rationale (A Survey)"
(1973), 12 West. Ont. L.Rev. 47.

BUSHNELL, S.—"The Legacy of *Regina v. Wray*" (1972 50 Can.
B. Rev. 19.

CANADA—*Report of the Canadian Committee on Corrections*
Queen's Printer, Ottawa (1969).

CANADIAN CIVIL LIBERTIES ASSOCIATION—*Submissions to
the Task Force on Policing in Ontario* (unpublished (1973)).

CHORNEY, N. M.—"Wiretapping and Electronic Eavesdropping"
(1964-65) 7 Crim. L.Q. 434.

COATSWORTH, H.—"Police Efficiency" (1929) 7 Can. B. Rev. 169.

COPLAN—"The Judicial Discretion to Disallow Admissible Evidence"
(1970) 114 Sol. J. 945.

DAVIS, K. C.—*Discretionary Justice: A Preliminary Inquiry* Louisiana State U. Press (1969).

DAVIS, K. C.—"Developments in the Law: Confessions" (1966) 79
Harv. L. Rev. 935.

DELISLE, R. J.—"Evidentiary Implications of Bill C-176" (1973-74)
16 Crim. L.Q. 260.

DEVLIN, P.—*"The Criminal Prosecution in England"* Oxford University Press (1958).

DONNELLY, B.—"Right to Counsel" (1968-69) 11 Crim. L.Q. 18.

DUBIN, C.—"Identification Procedures and Police Line-ups" (1955)
L.S.U.C. Special Lectures 329.

FAULKNER, J.—"Writs of Assistance in Canada" (1971) 9 Alta.
L. Rev. 386.

FOX, W. H.—"Confessions by Juveniles" (1962-63) 5 Crim. L.Q. 459.

GOLDSTEIN, J.—"Police Discretion not to Invoke the Criminal
Process" (1959-60) 69 Yale L.J. 543.

GRABURN, L. K.—"Truth as a Criterion of the Admissibility of Confessions" (1962-63) 5 Crim. L.Q. 415.

GREAT BRITAIN—*Royal Commission on the Police* Her Majesty's Stationery Office London (1962).

GROSMAN, B. A.—*Police Command: Decisions and Discretion* Mac-Millan and Co. Toronto (1975).

GROSMAN, B. A.—"Testing Witness Reliability" (1961-62) 4 Crim. L.Q. 318.

GROSMAN, B. A.—"Right to Counsel in Canada" (1967) 10 Can. B.J. 189.

HEYDON—"Illegally Obtained Evidence (1) and (2)" [1973] Crim. L.R. 603 and 690.

HONSBERGER, J.—"The Power of Arrest and the Duties and Rights of Citizens and Police" (1963) L.S.U.C. Special Lectures, 5.

HORKINS, W. E.—"False Arrest Today" (1973) L.S.U.C. Special Lectures 241.

JOHNSTON, SAVITZ and WOLFGANG (ed.)—*The Sociology of Punishment and Correction* (2nd ed.) John Wiley & Sons Inc. New York (1962).

KADISH, S.—"Legal Norms and Discretion in the Sentencing Process" (1961-62) 75 Harv. L.Rev. 904.

KAUFMAN, F.—*The Admissibility of Confessions in Criminal Matters* (2nd ed.) Carswells Ltd. Toronto (1974).

KETCHUM, P. G. C.—"Writs of Assistance" (1971) Can. B. Ass'n. J. 26.

KILEEN, G.—"Recent Developments in the Law of Evidence" (1975) 18 Crim. L.Q. 103.

LAFAVE, W.—"The Police and Non-Enforcement of the Law (I and II)" (1962) Wisc. L. Rev. 104 and 179.

LINDEN, A. (ed.)—*Studies in Canadian Tort Law* Butterworths Toronto (1968).

McDONALD, B. C.—"Use of Force by Police to Effect Lawful Arrest" (1966-67) 9 Crim. L.Q. 435.

McINNES, H. W.—"Statements to Police by Accused Persons" (1962-63) 5 Crim. L.Q. 14.

MacKAY, R. S.—"Obstructing a Police Officer in the Execution of His Duty" (1962-63) 5 Crim. L.Q. 294.

McWILLIAMS, P. K.—*Canadian Criminal Evidence* Canada Law Book Toronto (1974).

MALONEY, A.—*Report of the Metropolitan Board of Commissioners of Police: The Metropolitan Toronto Review of Citizen-Police Complaint Procedure* (1975).

MARSHALL, J.—"Denial of Counsel at Police Investigation" (1965) 23 U. of T. Fac. L. Rev. 117.

MARTIN, G. A.—"Police Detention and Arrest Privileges in Canada" (1961-62) 4 Crim. L.Q. 54.

MARTIN, G. A.—"The Admissibility of Confessions and Statements" 5 Crim. L.Q. 35.

ONTARIO LAW REFORM COMMISSION—*Report on the Administration of Ontario Courts* (Part II).

ONTARIO ROYAL COMMISSION—*Inquiry into Civil Rights* Report No. Vol. 2 .1969).

OSBOROUGH, N.—"Police Prosecutorial Discretion and the Police Image" (1965-66) 5 Western L. Rev. 62.

PARKER, G. E.—"The Extraordinary Power to Search and Seize and the Writ of Assistance" (1959-63) 1 U.B.C. Law Rev. 688.

POPPLE, A. E.—"Annotation: Conflict Between Two Sets of Witnesses" (1946-47) 2 C.R. 47.

POWELL, C.—*Arrest and Bail in Canada* Butterworths Toronto (1972).

SALHANY and CARTER—*Studies in Canadian Criminal Evidence* Butterworths Toronto (1972).

SAVAGE, C. C.—"Admissions in Criminal Cases" (1962-63) 5 Crim. L.Q. 49.

SKINNER—"Writs of Assistance" (1963) U. of T. Fac. L. Rev. 26.

SMITH, R. A.—"Police Control" (1928) 6 Can. B. Rev. 521.

SMITH, R. A.—"The Legal Status of a Policeman" (1955) 19 J. Crim. Law 264.

TRASEWICK, E. W.—"Search Warrants and Writs of Assistance" (1962-63) 5 Crim. L.Q. 341.

UNITED STATES—*Task Force Report: The Police* U.S. Gov't. Printing Office Washington (1967).

WALDBILLIG—"Symposium on Legal Aid" 30 Sask. B. Rev. 85.

WATT, D.—"Judicial Interim Release" (1973-74) 16 Crim. L.Q. 27.

WEILER, P.—"Who Shall Watch the Watchman? Reflections on Some Recent Literature About the Police" (1968-69) 11 Crim. L.Q. 420.

WILLIAMS, G.—"The Police and Law Enforcement" [1968] Crim. L.R. 351.

WILLIAMS, G.—"Evidence Obtained by Illegal Means" [1955] Crim. L.R. 339.

WRIGHT, C. A.—"Case and Comment" (1940) 18 Can. B. Rev. 808.

PROSECUTOR

BARTON, P. S.—"The Power of the Crown to Proceed by Indictment or Summary Conviction" (1971-72) 14 Crim. L.Q. 86.

BARTON, P. S.—"Abuse of Process as a Plea in Bar of Trial" (1972-73) 15 Crim. L.Q. 437.

BOWEN-COLTHURST, T. G.—"Some Observations on the Duties of a Prosecutor" (1968-69) 11 Crim. L.Q. 377.

BREITEL, A.—"Controls in Criminal Law Enforcement" (1960) U. of Chi. L. Rev. 427.

CANADIAN BAR ASSOCIATION—*Code of Professional Conduct* (1974).

CARTER, R. J.—"The Attorney General's Stay of Proceedings" 50 C.R. 10.

CHASSE, K.—"The Re-laid Charge and Autrefois Acquit" (1971) 13 C.R.N.S. 196.

CHASSE, K.—"Abuse of Process as a Control of Prosecutorial Discretion" (1970) 10 C.R.N.S. 392.

CHASSE, K.—"A New Meaning for Res Judicata and Its Potential Effect Upon Plea Bargaining" (1974) 26 C.R.N.S. 20; Part II, p. 48; Part III, p. 64.

DAVIDSON, A. J.—"Autrefois Acquit—The Same Offence—Adjudication on the Merits" (1958-59) 1 Crim. L.Q. 283.

DAVIS, A.—"Sentences for Sale: A New Look at Plea Bargaining in England and America" [1971] Crim. L.R. 218; Part II, p. 252.

DAVIS, K. C.—*Discretionary Justice: A Preliminary Inquiry* Louisiana State U. Press Baton Rouge (1969).

DeSMITH, S. A.—*Judicial Review of Administrative Action* (3rd ed.) Stevens and Sons London (1973).

EDWARDS, J.—*The Law Officers of the Crown* Sweet and Maxwell Ltd. London (1964).

FERGUSON, G. A., and ROBERTS, D. W.—"Plea Bargaining: Directions for Canadian Reform" (1974) 52 Can. B. Rev. 497.

FRIEDLAND, M. L.—*Double Jeopardy* Clarendon Press Oxford (1969).

GALLIGAN, P.—"Advising an Arrested Client" (1963) L.S.U.C. Special Lectures 35.

GROSMAN, B.—*The Prosecutor: An Inquiry into the Exercise of Discretion* U. of Toronto Press Toronto (1969).

HAINES, B.—"Judicial Ombudsmanship—A Problem in Policy" (1970) 12 C.R.N.S. 11.

HEATHER, D. R. H.—"Crown Bound by Attorney's Undertaking" (1969) 6 C.R.N.S. 149.

HOOPER, A.—"Discovery in Criminal Cases" (1972) 50 Can. B. Rev. 445.

KLEIN, A. D.—"Plea Bargaining" (1971-72) 14 Crim. L.Q. 289.

MARTIN, G. A.—"Preliminary Hearings" (1955) L.S.U.C. Special Lectures 3.

MAXWELL, P. B.—*On the Interpretation of Statutes* (12th ed.) Sweet and Maxwell London (1969); "Nolle Prosequi" [1958] Crim. L. Rev. 573; "Nina Ponomareva" [1956] Crim. L. Rev. 725.

ONTARIO LAW REFORM COMMISSION—*Report on the Administration of Ontario Courts* Part II (1973).

PARKER, G.—"Copping a Plea" (1972) 20 Ch. L.J. 310.

RATUSHNY, E. J.—"Plea Bargaining and the Public" (1972) 20 Ch. L.J. 238.

STENNING, P. C.—"Observations on the Supreme Court of Canada's Decision in R. v. Osborn" (1970-71) 13 Crim. L.Q. 164.

SUN, C.—"The Discretionary Power to Stay Criminal Proceedings" (1973-74) 1 Dal. L.J. 482.

THOMAS, P.—"Plea Bargaining in the Turner Case" [1970] Crim. L.R. 559.

TURNER, K.—"The Role of Crown Counsel in Canadian Prosecutions" (1962) 40 Can. B. Rev. 439.

WHITE, W.—"A Proposal for Reform of the Plea Bargaining Process" (1971) 119 U. of Penn. L. Rev. 439.

JUDICIAL DECISION-MAKING

ANDREWS, J.A.—"Evidence of Children" [1964] Crim. L.R. 769.

BIGELOW, S. T.—"Witnesses of Tender Years" (1966-67) 9 Crim. L.Q. 298.

BRODSKY, G.—"Adverse Witnesses: Use of Previous Inconsistent Statements" (1965-66) 8 Crim. L.Q. 383.

BUSHNELL, S.—"The Confession Rule: Its Rationale (A Survey)" (1973) 12 West. Ont. L. Rev. 47.

CADSBY, M.—"Cross Examination of Accused Persons as to Previous Convictions" (1961-62) 4 Crim. L.Q. 265.

CANADA—Report of the Canadian Committee on Corrections (1969).

CANADIAN BAR ASSOCIATION—Studies in Criminal Law and Procedure (1973).

CARDOZO, B.—The Nature of the Judicial Process (1921).

CHRISTIE, G.—"The Model of Principles" (1968) Duke L.J. 649.

COWEN & CARTER—Essays on the Law of Evidence (1956).

CROSS, R.—Evidence 4th ed. (1974).

CROSS, R.—"Fourth Time Lucky—Similar Fact Evidence in the House of Lords" [1975] Crim. L.R. 62.

DAVIS, K. C.—Discretionary Justice (1969).

De SMITH, S. A.—Judicial Review of Administrative Action 3rd ed. (1973).

DOOB, A. and KIRSHENBAUM, H.—"Some Empirical Evidence on the Effect of s. 12 of the Canada Evidence Act Upon an Accused" (1972-73) 15 Crim. L.Q. 88.

DWORKIN, R. M.—"Judicial Discretion" (1963) Co. J. of Phil. 624.

DWORKIN, R. M.—"The Model of Rules" (1967-68) 35 U. of Chi. L. Rev. 14.

ERWIN, R. S.—Defense of Drunk Driving Cases 3rd ed. (1975).

FRIEDLAND, M.—"Comments—Previous Convictions" (1969) Can. B. Rev. 656.

FULLER, L.—The Morality of Law (1964).

GALLIGAN, P.—"Advising an Arrested Client" (1963) L.S.U.C. Special Lecture 35.

GIBSON, R. C.—"Illegally Obtained Evidence" (1973) 31 U. of T. Fac. L. Rev. 23.

HART, H. L. A.—*The Concept of Law* (1961).

HOOPER, A.—"Discovery in Criminal Cases" (1972) 50 Can. B. Rev. 445.

HUGHES—"Rules, Policy and Decision-Making" (1968) 77 Yale L.J. 411.

KLEIN, A. O.—"Trial of Accused Persons Together" (1959) L.S.U.C. Special Lecture 15.

LAW REFORM COMMISSION OF CANADA—"The Exclusion of Illegally Obtained Evidence" (Study Paper, 1974).

LAW REFORM COMMISSION OF CANADA—*Report on Evidence* (1976).

LAW REFORM COMMISSION OF CANADA—"Criminal Procedure: Discovery" (Working Paper, 1974).

LIVESEY, B.—"The Judicial Discretion to Exclude Prejudicial Evidence in Criminal Cases" (1968) Camb. L.J. 291.

McDONALD, B.—"Comments on R. v. Wray" (1971) 29 U. of T. Fac. L. Rev. 99.

MacFARLANE, B.—"Photographic Evidence: Its Probative Value at Trial and the Judicial Discretion to Exclude it from Evidence" (1973-74) 16 Crim. L.Q. 149.

MacKENZIE, K.—"A Study of the Use of Previous Convictions" (1967-68) 3 U.B.C. L. Rev. 300.

McWILLIAMS, P. K.—*Canadian Criminal Evidence* (1974).

MALONEY, A.—"Corroboration" (1955) L.S.U.C. Special Lect. 245.

MALONEY, A.—"The Admissibility of Photographs in Criminal Cases and Resultant Prejudice to an Accused's Fair Trial" (1967) 1 C.R.N.S. 167.

MARTIN, G. A.—"Preliminary Hearings" (1955) L.S.U.C. Special Lecture 1.

MARTIN, G. A.—"Character Evidence" (19-5) L.S.U.C. Special Lecture 313.

MOLOT, H.—"Non-Disclosure of Evidence, Adverse Inferences and the Court's Search for Truth" (1971) 10 Alta. L. Rev. 45.

NEWARK, F. St. M.—"The Judicial Discretion to Exclude Similar Fact Evidence" (1967) 6 West. Ont. L. Rev. 1.

O'REGAN, R. S.—"Admissibility of Confessions—Standard of Proof" [1964] Crim. L.R. 287.

PARKER, G.—"Tape Recordings as Evidence" (1963-64) 6 Crim. L.Q. 314.

POPPLE, A. E.—"Annotation: A Prisoner's Record" (1949) 8 C.R. 472.

POPPLE, A. E.—*Criminal Procedure Manual* 2nd ed. (1956).

POPPLE, A. E.—"Applications for Change of Venue" (1946-47) 2 C.R. 60.

RADLEY, T. B.—"Recording as Testimony to Truth" [1954] Crim. L.R. 96.

RATUSHNY, E.—"Unravelling Confessions" (1970-71) 13 Crim. L.Q. 453.

ROBERTS, D. W.—"The Legacy of Regina v. Wray" (1972) 50 Can. B. Rev. 19.

SALHANY, R. and CARTER, R.—*Studies in Canadian Criminal Evidence* (1972).

SAVAGE, C. C.—"Who is an Accomplice?" (1960-61) 3 Crim. L.Q. 198.

SAVAGE, C. C.—"Corroboration and Similar Facts" (1963-64) 6 Crim. L.Q. 431.

SHEPPARD, A. F.—"Restricting the Discretion to Exclude Admissible Evidence: An Examination of Regina v. Wray" (1971-72) 14 Crim. L.Q. 334.

SOPINKA and LEDERMAN—*The Law of Evidence in Civil Cases* (1974).

STEINER, J. M.—"Judicial Discretion and the Concept of Law" (1976) 35 Camb. L.J. 135.

STENNING, P.—"One Blind Man to See Fair Play: The Judge's Right to Call Witnesses" (1974) 24 C.R.N.S. 49.

STONE, J.—"The Rule of Exclusion of Similar Fact Evidence: England" (1932-33) 46 Harv. L. Rev. 954.

TEED, E.—"Effect of s. 12 of the Canada Evidence Act Upon Accused" (1970-71) 13 Crim. L.Q. 70.

VAMPLEW, J. L. K.—"Joint Trials?" (1969-70) 12 Crim. L.Q. 30.

WEILER, P.—"Two Models of Judicial Decision-Making" (1968) 46 Can. B. Rev. 406.

WEINBERG, M. S.—"The Judicial Discretion to Exclude Relevant Evidence" (1975) 21 McGill L.J. 1.

WILLIAMS, E.—"Evidence of Other Offences" (1923) 39 L.Q. Rev. 212.

WILLIAMS, E.—"Evidence to Show Intent" (1907) 23 L.Q. Rev. 28.

WRIGHT, C. A.—"Credibility of Witnesses—Cross-Examination to Previous Convictions" (1940) 18 Can. B. Rev. 808.

JUDICIAL CONDUCT OF THE TRIAL

ABEL-SMITH, B. & STEVENS, R.—*In Search of Justice* (1968).

ADAMS, G.—"Towards a Mobilization of the Adversary Process" (1974) 12 O.H.L.J. 569.

ANGENE, M.—"Impaired Driving and Breathalyzer Cases" (1976) 32 C.R.N.S. 249.

ARDEN HOUSE CONFERENCE—*Report on Continuing Legal Education for Professional Competence and Responsibility* (1959).

ARTHURS, H.—"Authority, Accountability, and Democracy in the Government of the Ontario Legal Profession" (1971) 49 Can. B. Rev. 1.

ARTHURS, S.—"Discipline in the Legal Profession in Ontario" (1969) 7 O.H.L.J. 235.

BAILEY, F. L. & ROTHBLATT, H. B.—*Fundamentals of Criminal Advocacy* (1974).

BLUMBERG, A. S.—"The Practice of Law as a Confidence Game" (1967) 1 Law & Soc. Rev. 15.

BRITISH COLUMBIA—*Report of the Special Joint Committee on Competency Appointed by the Law Society of British Columbia and the B.C. Branch of The Canadian Bar Association* (1973).

CAMPBELL, A. G.—"The Order of Defence Witnesses" (1974) 26 C.R.N.S. 227.

CANADIAN BAR ASSOCIATION—*Code of Professional Conduct.*

CARTER, R. J.—"Instructions to the Jury Respecting the Defence" (1968-69) 5 C.R.N.S. 236.

CLARK (ed.)—*Urbanism and the Changing Canadian Society* (1961).

COUNTRYMAN, V. & FINMAN, T.—The Lawyer in Modern Society (1966).

COUTTS, J. A.—*The Accused* (1966).

CROSS, R.—*On Evidence* (3rd ed. 1967).

DENNING, A.—*The Road to Justice* (1955).

DEVLIN, P.—*Trial by Jury* (1966 Rev. ed.).

FRANK, J.—*Courts on Trial* (1949).

FRANKEL, M. E.—"The Search for Truth: An Umpireal View" (1975) 123 U. Pa. L. Rev. 1031; "The Adversary Judge" (1976) 54 Tex. L. Rev. 465.

GRIEW, E.—"The Order of Defence Evidence" [1969] Crim. L.R. 347.

GRUNIS, A. D.—"Incompetence of Defence Counsel in Criminal Cases" (1974) 16 Crim. L.Q. 286.

HAINES, E.—"The Jury, the Judge, the Case and You" (1959) L.S.U.C. Special Lecture 175; "The Right to Remain Silent" (1970) 18 Chitty's L.J. 109; "Criminal & Civil Jury Charges" (1968) 46 Can. B. Rev. 48; "The Medical Profession and the Adversary Process" (1973) 11 O.H.L.J. 41.

JACOB, I. H.—"The Inherent Jurisdiction of the Court" (1970) 23 Current Legal Problems 23.

JOHNSTONE, Q. & HOPSON, D.—*Lawyers and Their Work* (1967).

KEETON, R. E.—*Trial Practice and Procedure* (2nd ed. 1973).

LEDERMAN, S. N.—*A Coursebook of Exercises and Materials in Canadian Trial Practice* (1972-73).

LOCHRIDGE—"Legal Specialization" (1975) 38 Tex. B.J. 309.

McCARDIE—*The Law, the Advocate, and the Judge* (1927).

McWILLIAMS, P. K.—*Canadian Criminal Evidence* (1974).

MARTIN, G. A.—"The Role and the Responsibility of the Defence Advocate" (1970) 12 Crim. L.Q. 376.

MEYERS, P.—"Disruption in the Courtroom" (1972-73) 5 Man. L.R. 229.

MILLEN, A. S.—"Public Confidence in the Judiciary" (1970) 35 Law and Contemp. Prob. 69.

NEWARK, M. & SAMUELS, A.—"Let the Judge Call the Witness" [1969] Crim. L.R. 399.

ONTARIO—*Royal Commission Inquiry into Civil Rights* (1969).

POPPLE, A. E.—*Canadian Criminal Evidence* (2nd ed. 1954); *Criminal Procedure Manual* (2nd ed., 1956); "Calling Witnesses at a Criminal Trial" (1951) 12 C.R. 76; "Judge's Summing-Up to be Considered 'as a Whole'" (1952-53) 15 C.R. 82; "Summing-up Evidence in a Criminal Case" (1952-53) 15 C.R. 190; "Correlating the Evidence to the Issues for the Benefit of the Jury" (1952-53) 15 C.R. 262; "Judges Opinion as to the 'Facts' in Evidence" (1948) 5 C.R. 349.

ROBINETTE, J. J.—"The Charge to the Jury" (1959) L.S.U.C. Special Lecture 147.

ROBINS, S. L.—"Our Profession and the Winds of Change" (1972) 6 L.S.U.C. Gaz. 137.

SALHANY, R.—*Canadian Criminal Procedure* (2nd ed.).

SALHANY, R. & CARTER, R.—*Studies in Canadian Criminal Evidence* (1972).

SEDGWICK, J.—"Cross-Examination" (1955) L.S.U.C. Spec. Lect.

SHETREET, S.—*Judges on Trial* (1976).

SILVERMAN, H.—"The Trial Judge: Pilot, Participant or Umpire?" (1973) 11 Alta. L. Rev. 40.

SOPINKA, J. & LEDERMAN, S.N.—*The Law of Evidence in Civil Cases* (1974).

SPELLMAN, H. H.—*The Direct Examination of Witnesses* (1968).

STENNING, P. C.—"One Blind Man to See Fair Play: The Judge's Right to Call Witnesses" (1974) 24 C.R.N.S. 49.

TAMAN, L.—"The Adversary Process on Trial: The Right to Make Full Answer and Defence" (1975) 13 O.H.L.J. 251.

TEPLITSKY, M.—"The Right to an Impartial Tribunal" (1970) 11 C.R.N.S. 80; "The Right to Make Submissions as Part of Full Answer and Defence" (1970) 12 C.R.N.S. 149; "The Legality of Barring Counsel from a Court until he Purges his Contempt" (1971) 15 C.R.N.S. 384.

TURNER, J. W. C. (ed.)—*Kenny's Outlines of Criminal Law* (18th ed. 1964).

WILLISTON, W. B.—"Preparation for Examination-in-Chief" (1955) L.S.U.C. Special Lecture.

WOLKIN—"A Better Way to Keep Lawyers Competent" (1975) 61 A.B.A.J. 574.

WROTTESLY, F. J.—*The Examination of Witnesses* (1919).
WYZANSKI, C. E.—"A Trial Judge's Freedom & Responsibility" (1951-52) 65 Harv. L. Rev. 1281.

ABUSE OF PROCESS

BARTON, P. S.—"Abuse of Process as a Plea in Bar of Trial" (1972-73) 15 Crim. L.Q. 437.
BIGELOW, T.—"Contempt of Court" (1958-59) 1 Crim. L.Q. 475.
CANADA—*Report of the Canadian Committee on Corrections* (Ouimet) Queen's Printer Ottawa (1969).
CHASSE, K. L.—"Annotation: Abuse of Process as a Control of Prosecutorial Discretion" (1970) 10 C.R.N.S. 392.
CHASSE, K. L.—"Annotation: The Re-laid Charge and Autrefois Acquit" (1971) 13 C.R.N.S. 196.
FISHER, H.—"Civil and Criminal Aspects of Contempt of Court" (1956) Can. B. Rev. 121.
HAINES, B. M.—"Annotation: Judicial Ombudsmanship—a Problem in Policy" (1970) 12 C.R.N.S. 11.
JACOB, I. H.—"The Inherent Jurisdiction of the Court" (1970) 23 Current Legal Problems 23.
McFARLANE, B.—"Narcotics Prosecutions and the Defence of De Minimis Non Curat Lex" (1973-74) 16 Crim. L.Q. 98.
McRUER, J. C.—"Criminal Contempt of Court Procedure: A Protection of the Rights of the Individual" (1952) 30 Can. B. Rev. 225.
ROBERTS, D. W.—"The Doctrine of Abuse of Process in Canadian Criminal Law" (1972) Report of the First Annual Conference of the British Columbia Provincial Judges Association, 39.
ROOK, J.—"Case Comment: R. v. Osborn" (1971) U. of T. Fac. L. Rev. 105.
SHAFER, J. & SHERIDAN, W.—"The Defence of Entrapment" (1970) 8 O.H.L.J. 277.
SNEIDEMAN, B.—"A Judicial Test for Entrapment: The Glimmerings of a Canadian Policy on Police Instigated Crime" (1973) 16 Crim. L.Q. 81.
STENNING, P. C.—"Observations on the Supreme Court of Canada's Decision in R. v. Osborn" (1970-71) 13 Crim. L.Q. 164.
WATT, L. J.—"Entrapment as a Criminal Defence" (1971) 13 Crim. L.Q. 313.

INDEX

419

EXAMINATION; EXAM-
INATION; IDENTIFICA-
TION; ILLEGALLY OB-
TAINED EVIDENCE;
JUDGE; PHOTOGRA-
PHIC EVIDENCE;
PREJUDICE; PROSECU-
TOR; RELEVANCY;
SIMILAR FACTS; VOIR
DIRE; WIRETAPS AND
SURVEILLANCE; WIT-
NESSES

EXAMINATION

aims of examination-in-chief, 292
cross-examination, 294
in-chief, 292
interference in examining process,
292, 298, 302
counsel's response, 305
judge examining witnesses, 263,
298
leading questions, 295
restrictions on examination-in-
chief, 294, 295
see also CROSS-EXAMINA-
TION; DEFENCE COUN-
SEL; EVIDENCE;
JUDGE; LEADING
QUESTIONS; PROSECU-
TOR; RELEVANCY;
WITNESSES

FAIR HEARING

abuse of process and fairness, 371
adjournments necessary for, 270
Bill of Rights, and, 23
extent to which pre-trial occurrences can affect, 28
full answer and defence, 259, 262,
309, 310
Judge's Refusal to Hear Witnesses
or Submissions Affecting, 309,
310
judicial decisions insuring fair
treatment of accused, 256
judicial interference in the examination of witnesses, 292, 298,
302
right to make submissions, 27, 309
severance, 273
venue change to insure, 276
see also ABUSE OF PRO-
CESS; ADJOURNMENTS;
BILL OF RIGHTS; FULL
ANSWER AND DE-

FENCE; JUDGE; PREJU-
DICE; SEVERANCE;
VENUE

FULL ANSWER AND DEFENCE

denial of
by judge refusing to hear submissions, 309
by judge refusing to hear witnesses, 310
judicial Interference in examination affecting, 292, 298, 302
preliminary hearing, at, 259, 262
right to cross-examine on prior
inconsistent statements, 262
see also DISCLOSURE;
FAIR HEARING;
JUDGE; PRELIMINARY
INQUIRY; PROSECU-
TOR

IDENTIFICATION

Canadian practice, 85
consent to be photographed
necessary before charge, 89
eyewitness identification and jury
trials
factors affecting weight, 82
need for citizen to identify self, 80
parades or line-ups
procedure, 83, 84
self-crimination, and, 83
show-up procedure, prejudice, 83,
85
statutory compulsion to submit
to fingerprinting and photographing, 86
use of photographs or mug shots
at trial, 88
before conducting line-up, 88
before trial to identify, 87
see also ARREST; BILL OF
RIGHTS; EVIDENCE;
POLICE OFFICER;
PREJUDICE; SELF-
CRIMINATION

ILLEGALLY OBTAINED
EVIDENCE

American rules
Bill of Rights, and, 19, 20, 390
Canadian rule
does the rule have general application, 234
entrapment, 385
illegality and unfairness, 229